POLICY MAKING AND EXECUTIVE ACTION

McGRAW-HILL SERIES IN MANAGEMENT

KEITH DAVIS, Consulting Editor

Policy Making and Executive Action

Cases on Business Policy

THIRD EDITION

Thomas J. McNichols, Ph.D.

Professor and Chairman
Department of Business Administration
Graduate School of Business, Northwestern University

McGRAW-HILL BOOK COMPANY

New York   St. Louis   San Francisco   Toronto   London   Sydney

POLICY MAKING AND EXECUTIVE ACTION

45687

1 2 3 4 5 6 7 8 9 0 M P 7 4 3 2 1 0 6 9 8 7

PREFACE

Policy Making and Executive Action is designed to provide a basic format and collection of cases for the teaching of business policy in executive development courses, graduate schools of business, and those colleges and universities which offer business policy as an integrating course in the final stages of the undergraduate curriculum. All 43 cases included in this third edition were originally gathered as teaching materials for the Institute for Management of Northwestern University, the business policy course of the undergraduate School of Business, and the advanced business policy course which is part of the curriculum of the Graduate School of Business Administration.

The teaching of business policy no doubt varies to a certain extent from school to school. The particular instructors, the place of the course in the curriculum, and the basic and corollary objectives of the course are factors which determine the teaching emphasis. Despite the varied approaches to this broad subject area, however, there is a common core that is apparent. In practically all instances the major purpose of the course is to develop facility in analyzing business problems and to provide a framework for making decisions, formulating policies, and implementing plans for action.

A somewhat basic approach for developing this conceptual skill was used in selecting and arranging the cases in this book. This arrangement, however, is very flexible. It was not intended as an absolute guide, and changes in the sequence of the cases can readily be made to adapt the material to particular teaching techniques. With the exception of some of the cases in Part Five, practically all the cases have a sufficient variety of policy issues to permit effective use under two or more of the topical headings.

Part One includes introductory cases intended to provide direction and a framework for analysis of business situations. The various functions and levels of the executive group should become apparent to the student in his initial exposure to policy cases, and in this phase of case analysis he should also begin to cultivate a "feel" or "way of thinking" about the management job from the standpoint of top-level administration. The importance of the role of the chief executive in shaping the corporate image and in charting the course of the business operation should become increasingly apparent as the student progresses from the simpler to the more complex cases.

The need for policy making—the "think" aspect of the administrator's job, which leads to the setting of guiding principles for courses of action—should also become apparent to the student at this stage. The case materials indicate that in actual business situations policy making may be a series of either formal or perhaps decidedly informal and unplanned acts or procedures. In some cases it may be quite evident that there is a serious lack of clear-cut policies to guide and direct the company's activities in strategic areas.

The student's ability to recognize the interrelationship of business functions in these early cases should mark the first step in a gradual development of a unique conceptual skill—the ability to see the business enterprise as a whole and the awareness that the various functions of the business organization are interdependent and must be coordinated for successful operation. As he progresses through the sequence of cases, it is not expected that he will perceive any abrupt change in the nature of the cases. His experiences with each distinct business situation are more likely to meld together in easy stages, eventually completing the whole structure of administrative skill.

The cases contained in Parts Two, Three, Four, and Six are integral blocks in the development of the over-all administrative skill. In these sections the student is presented with diverse business situations of increasing complexity, which serve as the raw materials for strengthening his analytical ability and for developing a conceptual and action-oriented approach to the problems of business administration. The cases in this grouping overflow from one topical heading into the next and for the most part can be shifted readily from one section to another. The topical headings are used only to indicate the basic sequential processes of administration which define the executive functions.

This administrative process outlined in the Contents may be described briefly as:

1. Analyzing the situation (Part Two)

2. Determining basic objectives and developing plans for action (Part Three)

3. Organizing to put plans into action and setting up control measures to appraise and interpret management action (Part Four)

4. Reappraising the situation—objectives, plans, and controls—to rechart courses of action (Part Six)

This conceptual framework is described in greater detail in the Introduction under the heading "An Approach to Case Analysis and the Administrative Process."

Although the cases in Part Five represent a logical extension of the framework developed in the preceding sections (particularly Part Four), they are somewhat special in nature. They provide the student with an opportunity to examine more intimately the routine procedural executive functions as well as the important policy-making matters. The cases contain more detailed descriptions of the executive policy-making group and the results of day-to-day decision making.

The significance of the human factor and the interpersonal relationships in executive administration are also more sharply defined in the cases in Part Five. This phase of the administrator's job cannot, of course, be neatly separated from the total business situation and studied in a vacuum. It is constantly present in all business situations and consequently is also clearly evident in all of the business policy cases. The effective utilization of human resources is unquestionably the most important function of the executive. Managerial responsibilities, the role of the board of directors, the delegation of authority, and communication problems within the organization are also highlighted in some of the cases included in this section.

The suggested approach to case analysis and the administrative process described in the Introduction is intended as a sketch or background which might prove helpful to students in their initial encounter with business policy cases. The analytical scheme and the conceptual framework presented are somewhat basic in nature, and the student may find them useful in preparing cases for classroom discussion or in preparing case reports. Students may also find it profitable to supplement the case materials with books and selected articles in journals, magazines, and newspapers in the field of business administration and business policy. Those students who are encountering the case method of instruction for the first time may also be interested in reading some of the current literature describing this method of teaching.

The student will, of course, look to the instructor for guidance and direction in the use of the introductory material of this book and in the use and selection of outside reading materials. The individual instructors are the best judges of the approach the student should take to the course. The utilization and sequence of the case materials and the explanation of the common pitfalls students are likely to encounter in case discussions of business policy can be most effectively determined and explained by those who conduct the course.

ACKNOWLEDGMENTS

This casebook is not an individual work. It represents many years of effort on the part of faculty and staff members of the School of Business of Northwestern University. This collection of cases was made possible by the cooperation of many business executives who provided the opportunity to write business policy cases about their companies and who generously shared their business experiences with case writers of our staff. I am particularly indebted to the Armstrong Cork Company and Mr. Thomas G. Newton of this company for permission to use the Northern Lumber Dealers Supply and the Sooner Distributing Company cases in this volume. The School of Business and the Institute for Management of Northwestern University provided funds for the collection and preparation of many of the cases which make up this volume. I wish to thank Dean John A. Barr, Associate Dean Ralph L. Westfall, and the faculty of the School of Business for permission to use Northwestern cases.

I wish to acknowledge my appreciation to Professor Richard Donham, former dean of the School of Business of Northwestern, to whom this book is dedicated. He developed the original business policy course at Northwestern and initiated the case development program of the School of Business.

The author is deeply grateful to the many faculty members associated with the Department of Business Administration and the Institute for Management who have helped mold and develop the basic concepts of the teaching of business policy at the School of Business of Northwestern University. Their ideas, advice, and counsel have provided the background and basis for the format of this casebook.

Faculty members who have contributed by virtue of valuable suggestions and through ideas advanced as teachers of business policy include Professors Garret L. Bergen, Leon A. Bosch, Richard M. Clewett, Loring C. Farwell, William V. Haney, Richard L. Smith, and Edward T. P. Watson.

Professors at other universities who have used the first two editions of *Policy Making and Executive Action* have very generously reviewed the book and have made significant suggestions which have been incorporated into this third edition. There are a great number to whom I am indebted. I wish to thank each of them for his contribution.

While many of the cases that appear in this book were written by the author, the majority have been prepared by other present and former members of the staff of the School of Business. Present members who have written cases in their original or revised form are Professors Garret L. Bergen, Frank T. Hartzfeld, Edward T. P. Watson, and Research Associate Craig B. Whitehead. Former faculty and staff members who contributed cases include Professors Harper W. Boyd, Jr., Floyd Brandt, Dominic Parisi, and John Watkins, and Research Associates Orville Armstrong, Arne Bennborn, Joseph Connolly, Richard D. Ostrow, John Pixton, and Relonzo Reeves. Special consideration must be accorded Senior Research Associate William L. Dejon for the many cases he has written which appear in this volume.

I wish to express my appreciation to Mrs. Verna Kummer, secretary of the case research department, for her immeasurable aid in the preparation of the cases that went into the three editions of this book, and to Mrs. Joyce Larsen for her assistance in the preparation of this edition. I also wish to thank Mrs. Perle Hill, Mrs. Kathleen King, and Mrs. Carrie Pollack for their secretarial assistance. I am especially indebted to my wife, Willelene McNichols, for her editorial assistance, encouragement, and help.

THOMAS J. McNICHOLS

CONTENTS

PART FOUR   IMPLEMENTATION THROUGH ORGANIZATION AND CONTROL

Attaining Defined Objectives; Plans and Strategies; Structuring and Controlling Programs of Action

PART FIVE   BASIC DAY-TO-DAY ADMINISTRATION

Management Responsibilities; The Human Factor in Administration; Organizational Functions

PART SIX   REAPPRAISING AND RECHARTING COURSES OF ACTION

* Name of company, all individuals, and organizational designations have been disguised.

† International Policy Issues

INTRODUCTION

BACKGROUND AND DEVELOPMENT OF BUSINESS POLICY IN THE ADMINISTRATIVE PROCESS

The teaching of business policy by the case method has gained widespread acceptance in the past decade as a highly effective and practical method of introducing the complexities of the administrative process. The use of cases describing actual business situations from a wide variety of companies has provided a relatively realistic substitute for the practical experience of decision making at the top-management level. Case discussions of business problems in the classroom have also delineated and nurtured important advances in the teaching of business administration. In the broad area of business policy many concepts have been developed for teaching the over-all administrative viewpoint so essential to the executive—whether he be at the top-management level or at one of the subordinate levels of management.

The development of the "integrated" or general-management approach, stressing the companywide viewpoint, has been a direct response to an urgent national need. The prosperity and industrial expansion of the post–World War II period highlighted the need for executives who could bring to their positions a real grasp of the multiple problems that confronted the complex business organization in a changing business society.

The background for this approach can be traced to the early advances made in scientific management, which began over fifty years ago when the writings and ideas of Frederick W. Taylor began to gain notice in the business world. A wave of business training followed the introduction of scientific management principles. Business schools were added to universities and special schools for training in accounting, salesmanship, and other specific areas of business became part of the national scene. Out of this recognition of the need for highly trained personnel in the various functional areas, business developed specialists in production, marketing, accounting, and finance.

Over the years the staff functions of the large business enterprise were expanded, and experts in such essential services as industrial engineering, industrial relations, public relations, law, and other allied areas were added to the commonly recognized staff requirements. Executives with highly specialized training staffed the various departments that formed the corporate whole. New personnel were hired and trained along functional lines in specific departments.

The development of such specialists for each management function caused a business revolution. The changeover from the untrained employee who learned through undirected experience to the expert who received his training through the guided efforts of colleges, specialized schools, or specific in-company training on a departmental basis was not spectacularly apparent; however, the results it produced were manifest.

Specialists could provide basic data in each of the functional areas to pinpoint weaknesses or strong points of the business operation. Charts and graphs became a part of management control. Operational figures that were not even available thirty or forty years ago could now be exhibited for the benefit of management in simple graphic form. Management was thus supplied with facts and figures which gave a picture of the over-all operations of the business.

While the division of business activities created experts that promoted and effected efficiency, it also complicated and increased the problems of developing top managers who could direct the over-all business ventures. The policy makers of the business now had a much more complex organization to deal with. How could they possibly be expert in each functional area? How could they understand the operations of the many departments and staff positions of the large corporate entity? How could each department manager, divisional head, and vice president see even his own position and function in relation to the over-all business operation?

True, top management did look down on the entire operation, but what kind of view did they get? Were they looking at it through the eyes of specialists—each his own specialty? The top-management team were probably all specialists in one line or another. They had received recognition for performing their particular job exceptionally well and thus had earned the right to direct the corporate effort from the higher echelons of their new executive berths. The skills and abilities they brought to their new positions were generally developed along specific lines, but as part of the policy-making team they were required to adapt their special supervisory knowledge to the entire business effort, not to just a segment of its operations. Except in a small number of companies that provided an over-all look at the entire corporate effort through job rotation, the average executive entering the policy-making position brought little or no knowledge of directing, coordinating, and guiding the business as an integrated unit. In many cases the very factor that had catapulted him to his lofty position—his expert knowledge and performance as a director of a specific function—proved to be one of the greatest handicaps to him in adapting to the over-all viewpoint so necessary to the policy maker. The financial executive tended to see many of the corporate problems as essential manifestations of poor financial policy; the marketing expert, now part of the top-management team, was inclined to think that all business situations started and stopped in the sales area; the production-oriented executive attacked his dilemmas initially through the production line; others trained and experienced in different specialties approached the decision-making process through their own familiar channels.

To be sure, the qualified executives, despite their lack of general background, eventually learned through experience that the business entity had to be viewed as a whole, that it was impossible to separate business problems into neat little compartments and proceed to solve them one at a time. A decision to change a basic policy affected all departments to a greater or lesser degree. Certain decisions might also affect the community, might make the company vulnerable to antitrust prosecution, or could foment labor problems or generally disrupt industrial relations.

How long did it take an executive to become a competent policy maker and coordinator of the entire business enterprise? There was no ready answer in terms of time needed to learn this special ability or of the type of person capable of adapting himself to the increased demands of the top executive. Much concern was expressed by business leaders and business educators about the lack of an adequate approach to developing and training executives to fit them for the formidable task of assuming positions as top managers of business and leaders of the business society, with all its consequent responsibilities to the stockholders, employees, and the community.

The war years halted progress in the areas of executive development but at the same time accentuated the need for action in this area. In the immediate postwar period definite steps were taken to provide a better approach to fitting executives for their tasks as business leaders. Corporations stepped up their management development programs, increased job rotation, and outlined specific training programs. They also solicited aid in academic circles, chiefly from schools of business.

Business schools responded to the recognition of a need for developing the "modern executive" by liberalizing their curriculums to include more integrating courses and courses designed to emphasize the social and community responsibilities of the executive. Business policy courses, which had been a part of the curriculum of some university business schools in the prewar period, were rediscovered and accorded new emphasis. This development was also given impetus by the organization of a large number of university-sponsored comprehensive management development programs. In addition, many in-company management programs were added to a growing list of formal courses designed to prepare the executive for policy making and administrative action.

As a result of the emphasis on executive development, we find today that business policy cases are used extensively to meet the requirements of teaching the top-management viewpoint and of providing raw materials for developing skills in problem solving and decision making so necessary to all levels of administrative responsibility.

It is hoped that this collection of cases will contribute to the further advancement of the teaching and study of business policy.

AN APPROACH TO CASE ANALYSIS AND THE ADMINISTRATIVE PROCESS

Analysis of the Situation. The first step in the administrative function involves the fundamental process of examining all the facts and data available in a given business situation. Before any action can be taken or any decision can be made, the administrator must have as full an understanding as possible of the company's position and of the extent

and nature of its problems. The dynamics of business and the changing economic scene make this analytical procedure a never-ending
task. Each situation represents a particular complex of events at a
point in time—subject to change and all the uncertainties and va-
garies of a competitive business society.

The analytical approach designed to accomplish this phase of administration may vary to a great extent among executives. However,
there are in each case basic factors to be considered and common questions to be asked:

What facts, figures, data are available to give as complete a picture
of the company as possible?

What additional information is needed to complete the picture?

What information is available concerning external conditions which
can affect company operations?

Is this information sufficient to analyze the situation? If not, what
additional information is needed and from what sources can it be
gathered?

The gathering, sorting, and assessing of information will lead to
more specific questions, which can be conveniently divided into two
categories:

External or environmental factors considered to be beyond the control
of the company

Internal considerations may include:

How well is the company doing?
Is the company faring better or worse than its competitors?
Is it making or losing money?
Are there information and feedback problems?
What is its financial position?
Are there accounting problems?
What is the situation in marketing and sales?
Are there production problems?
Are there specific problems in allied functional areas?
What is the nature and extent of personnel or labor problems?
Is there evidence of interpersonal relations problems? Between ex-
ecutives and the employee group? Within the employee group?

External factors that may bear scrutiny are:

What is the present state of the economy?

What do forecasts seem to indicate about the immediate and longer-run economic future?

What is the nature of the industry the company is in?

What is the pattern of competition in the industry?

Are there large companies in the industry that hold a great percentage of the market, or many small companies, each with a relatively small share of the market?

How and to what extent does government regulation influence the industry?

What is the political and social environment in which the company operates?

This list of questions which the administrator might logically consider in his analysis of internal and external factors affecting the company by no means exhausts the important and pertinent queries which may be made. They are merely suggestive of a line of reasoning which will direct attention to significant problem areas.

An appraisal of the firm's skills and resources will aid in further defining the analytical process and will tend to integrate the internal and external factors which may affect the company's position. An inventory of the specific assets, both tangible and intangible, which will enable the company to compete favorably and profitably may raise such questions as:

What property, plant, and equipment does the company own or lease?

What is the condition of these assets? Age?

Are there any special or unique features about these assets which give the company competitive advantages?

Is the company's location particularly advantageous? (For raw materials? Distribution? Labor?)

What about the company's product line? Marketing mix? Is it special? Unique? High quality? Diversified?

Is the distribution system of the company good? Exceptional?

What financial resources does the firm have which will enable it to maintain its position or acquire additional needed skills and resources?

Does it have ample working capital? Line of credit?

What prospects does it have for selling securities? Debt financing? Equity financing?

What personnel resources does the company have? An exceptional executive leader? President or chairman of the board? Executive group? Middle-management group? Skilled labor?

Does the company have good labor relations?

What intangible assets does the company possess? Does the public have a good image of the firm?

Does the firm have a good brand name? Trademark? Patent? Copyright?

These questions, and many more which the student will be likely to raise when he appraises the skills and resources of the firm in a particular business situation, will lead to a consideration of the basic processes of administration: What objectives have been set? How are these objectives to be attained? What plans has the company made? And most important, are the firm's objectives compatible with its skills and resources?

Engaging in the analytical process of appraising the functional areas of the business, examining the internal and external factors, and inventorying the skills and resources of the firm will afford an insight into the situation from several angles. While there will be overlapping in the procedures, multiple sightings from different vantage points will aid in putting the problems in perspective and in assessing the information gathered. The process of evaluation of the mass of data obtained, separating of the relevant from the irrelevant, and distinguishing between fact and assumption is a constant one, which must be engaged in throughout the analysis of the business situation. Out of this sifting and refining of the raw data the significant problems of the company will begin to emerge.

Focus on the Administrative Process. The next important step in the administrative process involves the selection of the major problem areas of the firm—the focal point for action. What should be done? Where should we begin? There may be distinct evidence of problems in marketing, production, finance, and other allied areas. These problems represent a collection of matters that need attention; separately they do not provide a clue to the order of needed executive action. The problems cannot be attacked in a piecemeal fashion because of the inter-relationship of the functional areas. Putting out the "fire" in the sales area may only cause a new fire to flare up in production. The major problems of the firm cut across departmental lines, and attempting to treat them as separate self-contained distress areas is much like attempting to cut down the legs of a table with a handsaw.

Functional and departmental problems are really symptoms or manifestations of a more deep-rooted difficulty that lies within the spectrum of the administrative process and in the area of responsibility of top management. The analysis and judgment of the top-management

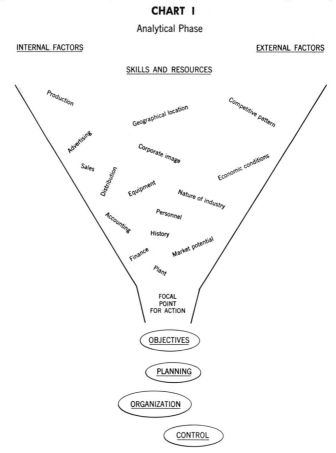

CHART I

Analytical Phase

group, the policy makers of the firm, must therefore transcend functional and departmental lines and conceive of the entity as a single unit directed toward predetermined goals and guided by planned courses of action. They must direct their attention to the underlying problems of the firm and not the surface indications.

The evidence of specific problems can, however, be translated into terms of basic processes of administration. A more generalized diagnostic approach can then be applied to relate the symptoms to possible

failures in one of the four basic areas of the administrative process—
setting basic objectives, planning programs of action, organizing personnel and resources, and controlling efforts toward the attainment of
predetermined goals. In the final analysis, the initial symptoms will
point to one of the major problem areas, where the administrator can

CHART II

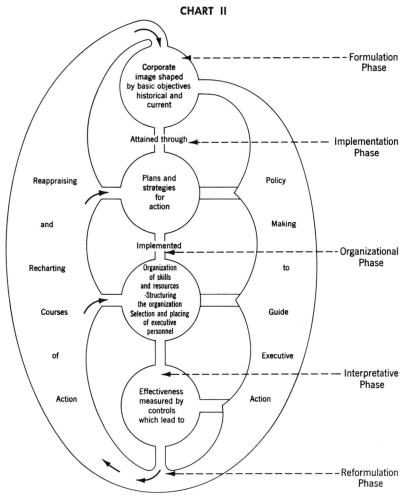

initiate action. Chart I illustrates this phase of the administrator's task.
He considers and analyzes all the facts and data available about the
particular business situation and places them in the "analytical hopper," where they are sifted and refined until the core or the crux of
the administrative problems is released from the bottom of the hopper.

The four basic steps in the administrative process are difficult to isolate in the going concern. They are interdependent and meld together to form an over-all program. However, in most instances it is possible to analyze them separately against the background of the significant problems and difficulties of the firm in each particular business situation. Chart II illustrates this continuous "flow" of the processes of administration and the interdependence of each basic step in decision making and policy formulation.

Formulation Phase. The administrator begins his diagnosis with an appraisal of the corporate basic objectives. Many of the problems and difficulties that are revealed in the analysis of a business situation may be symptomatic of a failure to set well-defined and realistic objectives. The lack of clear-cut goals will lead to uncertainty in planning, in structuring and staffing the organization, and in setting up controls to measure the effectiveness and check the results of administrative action. The objectives of the enterprise serve as the continuing guiding force for all the company's activities, the goal of all its planning, and the base from which the administrative policies of the firm emerge. It is in this phase of the administrative process that management forms the basic or grand strategy of the firm.

In the determination and analysis of the firm's basic objectives, management must constantly keep in mind such questions as:

What place will the firm fill in the social order?
What need or service will it supply to society?
What market niche or industry position does the firm seek to attain?
What specific products or services is the firm going to make and sell?
Does the firm have a single-product line? Multiproduct line?
What decisions have been made about the size of the firm?
What share of the market does it seek?
How will it attempt to integrate? Horizontally? Vertically?
Are the firm's objectives compatible with its skills and resources?
What skills and resources does the firm have, and need, to accomplish its predetermined goals?
What are the strengths and limitations of its skills and resources?
Can it accomplish the stated goals with its financial resources? With its skills and resources in production and marketing? With its organization and personnel?

There are many other factors that are important in shaping the corporate image and guiding the direction of a company. Basic objectives established over time develop a certain character and create an image of the firm in the minds of its customers and competitors.

Some firms are characterized as progressive, the forerunners in the industry, the ones most likely to develop new products. They seek and create new opportunities and assume the consequent risks attached to the innovating process. Others have a reputation for being conservative and steady and are content to make changes and adaptations only when the "groundwork has been laid" and the element of risk in "plowing new ground" has been reasonably reduced by the action of other firms.

The personal objectives of individuals in management may also be a major factor in shaping the image of a company. For example, a desire to maintain ownership control may restrict the size and activities of a business by confining it to its own capital resources. Dominant individuals in management, even in large corporations, may be personally responsible for molding a particular reputation which a firm may enjoy or find a handicap.

The shaping of the corporate image is also inextricably tied in with the firm's relations with external groups. The manner and method it employs to attain its desired place in industry will have a profound effect on its employees, customers, competitors, and the general public. The business entity develops an institutional social philosophy which guides its actions in personnel relations, community relations, and relations with business associates and competitors, the government, and its stockholders.

The basic objectives of a firm are not confined to a single-purpose goal, but comprise a combination of tangible, concrete goals and intangible guides which shapes the business personality and creates an image reflected in all the firm's operations.

Implementation Phase. The second step in the basic processes of administration is the executive function of developing plans and strategies for action. Once the basic objectives have been determined and reviewed, management must chart a course of action to direct the firm toward its predetermined goals through maximum utilization of its skills and resources.

The policies of the company, which constitute the guides for executive action, emerge from the basic objectives of the organization and form the backbone of planning. The plans should consistently reflect these objectives, and their efficacy must be constantly reappraised according to these standards in operation.

The plans of a dynamic business organization at any given time may be difficult to identify and reduce to a list. Most firms have a variety of plans in various stages of completion—long-range plans, short-range plans, single-use plans, or special programs, and so-called standing plans, or basic policies, which have continuing use. In attempting to evaluate company planning it is convenient to think in terms of a master plan supplemented by detailed plans. The master plan should provide the over-all blueprint or coordinating factor for the entire company program of action and should be the directing or guiding force for detailed functional planning.

In any business venture there are no obvious courses of action that will lead the firm to assured success. The master plan, which outlines the principal steps the company will take in attempting to attain its objectives, will in all likelihood be subject to numerous changes because of the uncertainties of the marketplace. Long-range plans which outline action expected to be taken over a period of years, usually considered to be three to five years or longer, are subject to the greatest uncertainties and possibilities of change. Short-range plans, which are usually considered to run from three months to a year or three years, depending upon the nature of the company, are less likely to be changed. All plans, however, must be flexible and should be backed by alternative plans. The ability to keep pace with trends in the market is a necessary element in the planning function. The shifting and adjusting of plans is frequently referred to as strategy, which may be defined as coping with unanticipated moves by competitors or shifts in the economic scene. This ability to meet the demands of particular situations and to provide the necessary flexibility to cope with change is a vital part of day-to-day planning.

Capturing and maintaining market position is one of the most important elements of the planning function. In each particular stage of the company's development and progress toward attaining its objectives, particular functions may need attention. The emphasis may shift from marketing and sales to production or other functional areas that require special consideration at a particular time. The master plan should be designed to balance the company's skills and resources and to utilize them to the best possible advantage. All the functions and departments of the business unit must be coordinated, and conflicts of purpose between them must be resolved. The master plan must outline the comprehensive program and the timing of the principal steps in carrying this program into action.

In reviewing the plans and strategies of the firm the following specific questions may serve as guides in diagnosing problems in this area:

Has a range of alternative plans been considered?

Have well-defined alternative plans been drafted for use if needed?

Which plan best suits the company's skills and resources? Financial resources? Marketing skills and resources? Production skills and resources? Personnel and labor skills?

Have the external factors been considered in the selection of a master plan? Economic conditions? Competitive pattern? Industry factors?

Has the adopted plan been projected to determine extent of skill and resource utilization? Additional skills and resources needed? Possible effects of the plan on competitors? Potential customers and size of market?

Have the long-range and short-range plans been coordinated in the master plan?

Have divisional and departmental plans been coordinated in the over-all program?

Has a time schedule been worked out for each step in the planned program of action?

Has economic forecasting been employed to aid in determining for each product line the market potential? Share of the market expected? Sales goals?

Have a master and detailed budget been prepared?

Have quantitative data been used and evaluated to determine for each product line the costs? Selling prices? Profit margins? Inventory requirements? Cash requirements? Profit goals? Expected return on investments? Break-even point? Pay-out periods for capital investments?

Has an adequate research and development program been set up?

Have specific and detailed programs been developed for each product line in the functional areas and departments to carry out the master plan?

Are the company's plans and policies flexible enough to allow for changes, adaptations, and strategic action to cope with unanticipated changes in the marketplace?

Organizational Phase. The implementation or action phase of the administrative process follows the development of plans and strategies. At this stage the firm organizes its skills and resources to put into operation the plans and programs selected as the most effective measures to attain its objectives. The transition from policy making and operational planning to executive action is accomplished through the essential step of structuring the organization. In the initial steps of organizational planning the firm attempts to develop an "ideal" structure which will provide the best possible grouping of projected activities. This "custom-built" organization structure is designed to cover each phase and function of the firm's operations. It is intended to provide the most effective medium for harnessing and utilizing available skills and resources and for reflecting the firm's objectives and managerial philosophy.

The basic framework for decision making and action must establish the relationships between each level of the management job and clearly define authority links, spans, and limitations to permit executives and subordinates to understand the nature and extent of their responsibilities. In structuring a practical working organization, management will be confronted with many of the following problems:

How should operational activities be divided? By functional departments? By processes of production? By geographical location? Territories? Districts? Divisions?

How should the lines of authority and responsibility be drawn?

Have relationships between units been clearly charted to fix responsibilities and allow for delegation of authority?

What limits should be considered for the span of management control and the length of lines of communication?

To what extent should operations and lines of authority be centralized? Decentralized?

Does the structure allow for the use of specialized functional skills?

How should the relationships between line and staff be defined?

Does the structure provide for balance and flexibility?

While an efficient organization structure will be a major factor in determining successful operations, it still represents only the vehicle or means through which executive action is channeled. The most important and difficult task is the selection and placement of a working management team which will effectively guide the firm along the lines charted in the planning stages. While the organization structure should be initially based on an ideal framework, invariably it must be adapted for the human factor. In the final step of filling out the structure, modifications of the ideal organizational form will be necessary to fit the capabilities and limitations of available executive personnel.

Despite necessary and inevitable deviations from initially drafted ideal structures, organizational planning will provide the firm with a standard which will afford sounder evaluation of personnel, control over organizational changes, and greater flexibility to adapt to environmental changes.

Executive personnel are charged with the responsibility of translating policies and plans into action and developing a smoothly functioning team out of the people within the organization. The personnel of many and varied skills must be properly administered in a great variety of functional activities on a day-to-day basis; their tasks and programs must be arranged and their activities coordinated and directed toward predetermined goals. The type and quality of executives required to perform these managerial functions may vary to a great extent according to the nature, objectives, and policies of the firm. Despite titles, management positions are not standardized. Similarly, management requirements within a firm are not static. Shifts and changes in objectives and plans, and the consequent demand for new and different skills, may require a remolding of the organization structure.

Corporate expansion, in addition to creating a need for increased executive personnel, will also undoubtedly cause shifts in management levels. Problems of line and staff, decentralization, and management training and development will become important factors in organizational planning. Adapting the organization to the dynamics of the business scene demands constant reappraisal of the interrelationship of the multitude of factors affecting the human forces guiding the destiny of the firm.

Interpretative Phase. Once the organization has put into action the plans and strategies designed to attain the firm's objectives, management is confronted with the problem of controlling and appraising day-to-day operations. It must assess the soundness of its plans and measure the performance of subordinates entrusted with the responsibility of putting specific programs into action. The review of the firm's operations requires a continuous flow of pertinent information through organization channels to enable management to make significant judgments regarding such questions as:

How well is the firm doing in relation to its goals and objectives? In relation to competition? In relation to industry trends?

What is the relationship of progress to plan in the over-all program? In the timing and execution of specific programs?

How effectively are subordinates performing specific administrative functions in the execution of the firm's plans and strategies?

The ability of management to answer important questions of this nature depends upon the adequacy of its system of controls. Ideally, control measures are based upon the objectives, plans, and strategies of the firm and are designed to reflect the action, efficiency, and progress the organization has made toward attaining its predetermined goals. It is difficult, however, to examine the control function in isolation because it is so distinctly dependent upon and tied to the other phases of the administrative process. Efficient controls are dependent, first of all, upon good planning, sound administrative policies, and a clearly defined organization structure. The firm's objectives and plans may thus serve as control standards to measure and judge the efficiency of operations. Control measures may indicate that changes or refinements are necessary in these basic objectives, plans, and strategies.

Despite the fact that the control function is so enmeshed with the other processes of administration, it is necessary for management to analyze this function independently to determine whether it meets the requirements of the firm's operations. A well-conceived control system will reflect the organization structure and tie the control standards to individual responsibility. In essence, control always reflects individual performance since specific functions are assigned, and authority and responsibility are delegated to particular persons within the organizational unit. A clearly defined organization structure aids in focusing attention on the individual or individuals responsible for meeting specific goals or standards of performance. The organization thus provides the vehicle not only for directing and coordinating action, but also for maintaining control and appraising individual performance.

The following policy questions will aid in further testing the efficacy of a control system:

Have strategic control points been selected which will most accurately reflect the progress of the firm and the performance of management?

What measures will best reflect the progress toward over-all company objectives? Toward the goals of particular departments?

Can the controls be readily comprehended by the management personnel who will be expected to utilize them in the day-to-day operations?

Are the controls forward-looking so that deviations from the charted course can be detected in sufficient time to apply corrective action?

Are the controls flexible enough to allow for necessary sudden shifts in planning and strategy?

Does the control system, in addition to detecting deviations from plan, provide the means to initiate corrective action?

As indicated in Chart II, all controls lead to a reappraisal of the processes of administration. It is possible that the controls will indicate that the organization is functioning smoothly and according to plan. Almost invariably, however, an organization attempting to execute a complex program of plans and strategies, subject to internal and external forces, will deviate from its charted course. In our dynamic business society corporate objectives and plans can rapidly be rendered obsolete by innovations, technological developments, and sudden changes in the marketplace. When the control system indicates significant weaknesses in the areas of objectives, planning, or organization, the whole cycle of the administrative process is repeated, and new courses of action are charted to conform with shifts in objectives and changes in plans.

PART ONE

top management
in
perspective

BLANE-RADFORD
COMPANY (A)

The Blane-Radford Company was formed in 1942 by Mr. T. L. Blane and Mr. O. J. Radford to manufacture a lathe chucking device. The device was an attachment for converting a standard engine lathe into a production lathe with higher output.[1] Because the machine tool industry lagged behind wartime demand for new equipment, it was thought that the lathe attachment for converting old and little used equipment to production work would find a ready market.

As anticipated, the product was favorably received. A level of operation at the full capacity of one shift was soon reached. Mr. Blane and Mr. Radford, although pleased with the company's early progress, were apprehensive about the peacetime outlook. In time, therefore, a line of products for the automotive trade was developed, with a special lathe for "turning down" worn commutators of automobile generators, as the principal item.

ORGANIZATION

Mr. Blane, President, previously had been in industrial selling and sales promotion work with several large companies. His last position

---

[1] Standard engine lathes are used largely in machine shops for turning out repair parts or parts used in small quantities in the construction of equipment built on a job order basis. Where mass production of a part is required, it is generally more economical to use a production lathe such as a turret lathe or a lathe with other special attachments for stepping up production.

had been sales manager of a well-known manufacturing company with a national sales organization. Mr. Radford, General Manager, supplied the greater part of the initial capital for the business; Mr. Blane contributed most of the ideas and plans. Mr. Radford's previous experience had been largely in the insurance business.

In actual practice, Mr. Blane and Mr. Radford conducted the business as if they were partners at the same administrative level but

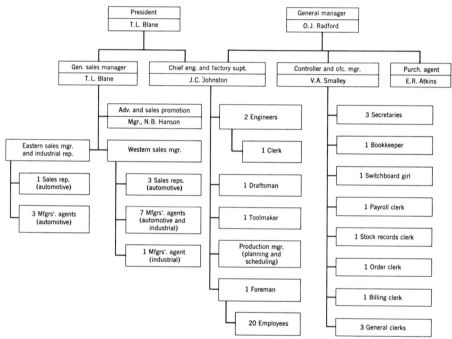

exhibit 1
BLANE-RADFORD COMPANY
Organization Chart, August 31, 1948

with specific functional divisions of executive responsibility. (See Exhibit 1.) Mr. Blane acted as General Sales Manager and supervised product development and engineering activities. Mr. Radford was responsible for manufacturing and financial activities of the company.

Mr. J. C. Johnston, Chief Engineer and Factory Superintendent, reported to Mr. Radford as Production Superintendent, but reported to Mr. Blane as Chief Engineer. Also reporting to Mr. Radford was the Controller and Office Manager, Mr. V A. Smalley.

SALES AND ADVERTISING

When the company was formed, Mr. Blane traveled extensively to accomplish his first objective of building a sales force and distributor organization. By the end of 1942 the sales force consisted of seven manufacturers' agents, who were paid a straight 10% commission on sales, and two sales representatives, who received drawing accounts against commissions. Territory boundaries generally followed state lines and were determined by the areas which were customarily covered by the agents employed, modified by the boundary lines of adjacent territories previously assigned by the company.

An attempt was made to employ men with good personalities who were established in the industrial trade. Agents whose sales performance did not prove to be satisfactory were given one month's notice that the line was being taken away from them.

Sales training activity was confined to occasional sales meetings and to the distribution of product information. An effort was made to avoid applications of Blane-Radford products which would require special engineering and special sales training.

The sales force called on industrial equipment jobbers and mill supply houses who sold the Blane-Radford line on a non-exclusive basis. They occasionally made calls with jobbers' salesmen in following up leads furnished by the company.

A selective distribution policy was followed. Wherever possible, one or two mill supply houses and machinery distributors, including one distributor of moderately priced machine tools, were selected in each principal city. Distributors were supplied liberal amounts of promotional literature and were offered assistance in the preparation of direct mail pieces. Those who carried stocks of the company's products were given a trade discount of 30% of list; non-stocking distributors received 20%.

No effort was made to sell the lathe attachments to original equipment manufacturers for installation on new machine tools. Mr. Blane desired to develop a full line of the product for used equipment before going into the original equipment market for which he believed special engineering would be required.

Sales forecasting was done by Mr. Blane personally. He simply relied upon his judgment to estimate a reasonable sales figure to shoot at for the year ahead. Forecasts for old products were tempered to some extent by past experience. Actual sales usually fell far below the forecasts. On new items forecasts ran about 300% to 400% above actual sales. Once determined, there was no systematic method for adjusting forecasts downward in line with early sales performance.

Territorial sales quotas were established by Mr. N. B. Hanson, Manager of Advertising and Sales Promotion, who reported to Mr. Blane. Mr. Blane's forecast, which was accepted as the national quota, was broken down according to the number of manufacturing plants and the number of manufacturing employees in each territory. For example, if a territory had in it 10% of the manufacturing plants and 8% of the manufacturing employees in the United States, its quota was 9% (average of 8% and 10%) of the national quota. Territorial quotas were usually several times larger than actual sales because of the optimistic forecasts upon which they were based. Mr. Hanson considered the quotas to be of little value in stimulating sales effort but useful as a means of measuring the relative performance of sales representatives and manufacturers' agents.

Annual advertising budgets for each product were submitted by Mr. Hanson and approved by Mr. Blane and Mr. Radford. Advertising appropriations were established as a percentage (approximately 6%) of sales as forecast by Mr. Blane. Because sales rarely reached forecast levels, advertising appropriations were cut back from time to time, requiring complete revision of advertising plans three or four times a year. Advertising expense ran about 6% to 13% of actual sales. Mr. Hanson considered that about 4% of sales would have been a normal advertising appropriation, but believed that the heavy advertising expenditures created a favorable reputation in the trade, giving distributors and customers the impression that the Blane-Radford Company was a "high-powered outfit" much larger than it actually was.

A typical distribution of annual advertising expenditures was as follows:

	Per Cent
Literature (catalogues, etc.)	15
Trade paper advertising	30
Point of sale	15
Direct mail	20
Conventions	15
Dealer helps	5
Total	100

Mr. Hanson favored a reduction, if not complete elimination, of the point of sale advertising, which consisted of display posters for distributors' showrooms. Mr. Blane, however, thought the point of sale advertising to be of definite value and considered the distribution of advertising expense to be quite satisfactory.

The advertising produced many inquiries which were forwarded to distributors. Copies of these "leads" were sent to local agents and representatives of the company who were expected to check with distributors and follow up the leads if orders did not come through promptly.

PRODUCTION

Since neither Mr. Blane nor Mr. Radford was an experienced factory man, they considered themselves fortunate to have Mr. J. C. Johnston as Chief Engineer and Factory Superintendent. He previously had been with several large manufacturing organizations and was experienced in mass production methods. Usual practice in the company was to give Mr. Johnson an overall objective and leave him alone to accomplish it. If the sales forecast of a new product was established as 6,000 units per month, Mr. Johnston would tool up to turn out that number of units. Actually, only 1,000 units might be sold, not justifying the tooling up cost, but Mr. Johnston did not concern himself with the failure of the sales department to meet the established quotas.

Production on the most popular products ran about 1,400 units per month. Usually a minimum lot size of about 50 units would be run on all items except for special design orders. The machine set-ups on the most popular items generally were left in place. For lathe operations and other machine operations on less popular items, the set-ups were frequently changed.

Castings were bought on the outside, as were many small machined parts, such as screw machine parts.

The plant was divided into three departments: (1) Fabricating Department (sheet metal work, welding, and stamping); (2) Machine Shop; (3) Finishing Department (assembly, painting, and shipping). The three factory departments were under the supervision of one foreman assisted by a key employee in each department who acted as "straw boss."

Overall production plans were established in conferences between the General Manager, Factory Superintendent, and Production Manager on the basis of sales forecasts. The details of planning and scheduling were the responsibility of the Production Manager, who adjusted final schedules to correspond with sales orders as they were received.

Two engineers, reporting to Mr. Johnston, devoted most of their time to product design and improvement. They did some work on tool and jig design, but, in most instances, the tool maker was supplied with a print of a new part and he designed the tools and jigs required to make it. An expert machinist, he visualized required operations and turned out tools and jigs to do the job satisfactorily on existing equipment.

Time and motion study was not used, and all production employees were paid on an hourly basis. Mr. Johnston expressed the opinion that it was not practical to employ a time study man and set up a wage incentive system, using piece rates, because of the short runs and variety of work done by the employees.

PURCHASING

The Purchasing Agent, Mr. E. R. Atkins, purchased on his own initiative all standard items which were carried in stock and for which minimum and maximum inventory limits had been approved by Mr. Radford. When the inventory on any standard item reached the established minimum, the stock records clerk would notify the Purchasing Agent. Purchases of major items—such as steel, wire, motors, patterns, tools and dies, and all capital equipment—were made only with the approval of Mr. Radford, who usually talked it over with Mr. Blane. Except for standard inventory items, the Purchasing Agent bought only what Mr. Johnston or Mr. Radford told him to buy. Purchases of materials and parts for the production of new products generally were made on the basis of the sales forecasts made by Mr. Blane. Resulting excessive purchases were cut back in many instances, but even so, heavy and unbalanced inventories resulted.

ACCOUNTING

The Controller, Mr. V. A. Smalley, who previously had been with a large manufacturing company, set up a system of bookkeeping and accounting procedures similar to the one he had used there. More than

200 expense accounts were shown on the books. Numerous reports and schedules were prepared under the supervision of Mr. Smalley for the information of Mr. Blane and Mr. Radford. No cash budget or estimate of short-term cash requirements was prepared.

PRODUCT CHANGES

In 1943 some important design changes were made in the most popular model of the lathe attachment, resulting in increased sales. When the company was formed in 1942 only one model of the lathe attachment was produced, but by the latter part of 1943 the line included seven, consisting of four basic models and three variations.

Most new product ideas came from Mr. Blane or from members of the sales organization. Mr. Blane would first present them to Mr. Johnston, and when there was agreement that a product could and should be produced, Mr. Blane approached Mr. Radford. Mr. Radford usually favored sticking with present products rather than trying something new, but the ideas of Mr. Blane generally prevailed, and when Mr. Radford had been persuaded that a project should be undertaken, it was entered on a project list. By 1944 there were enough projects on the project list to keep the engineering department busy for about two years. Mr. Blane decided which projects should be undertaken.

PRICING

When the design of a new product was completed, Mr. Smalley would prepare a recommended list price for the product. The pricing procedure which he followed can be expressed briefly by the following formula:

$$\text{List price} = \$D \times \frac{1 + S\% + F\% + P\% + T\%}{D\%}$$

$\$D$ = Direct cost of materials and labor in dollars per unit as estimated by the engineering department with assistance of the Purchasing Agent

$D\%$ = Direct costs of materials and labor for the last three months as a percentage of total company sales during that period[2]

$S\%$ = Selling and advertising expense for the last three months as a percentage of total company sales during that period[2]

$F\%$ = Fixed costs including administrative expense and manufacturing overhead for the last three months as a percentage of total company sales during that period[2]

$P\%$ = 20% representing net profit requirement of 20% of sales

$T\%$ = Trade discount on net selling price of 43% (equivalent to 30% of list price) plus cash discount of 1%; total 44%

Hypothetical example of pricing a new product:

$D = Estimated cost of materials $2.10 plus estimated cost of labor $.56
    = $2.66

$D\% = 50.0*$

$S\% = 19.3*$

$F\% = 22.3*$

$P\% = 20.0$

$T\% = 44.0$

$$\text{List price} = \$D \times \frac{1 + S\% + F\% + P\% + T\%}{D\%}$$

$$= \$2.66 \times \frac{1 + 19.3 + 22.3 + 20.0 + 44.0}{50.0}$$

$$= \$2.66 \times (1 + 2.11)$$

$$= \$2.66 \times 3.11 = \$8.27$$

* Assumed values.

Frequently the prices established were competitively high. Whenever Mr. Blane considered a price too far out of line he would reduce it an arbitrary amount, but not enough to equal competitive prices in most instances.

Mr. Hanson thought that Mr. Smalley's procedure for determining the percentage of fixed charges in figuring the price of new products was not practical. Mr. Hanson thought that fixed charges should be spread over the anticipated volume of sales from the new product as well as present products in computing the percentage to apply for fixed charges.[3]

When Mr. Blane had approved a list price, he would direct Mr.

---

[2] Average percentage of sales taken from profit and loss statements.

[3] For example, using 1946 figures from Exhibit 2: Fixed charges = manufacturing overhead 17.8% plus administrative expense 11.7% = 29.5%. Under the method in use this figure would be applied as $F\%$ in computing a price regardless of the anticipated volume of sales of the new product. If, however, it was estimated that the sale of the new product would amount to 20% of the total sales volume, under the method recommended by Mr. Hanson, $F\%$ would be computed as $29.5/120 = 24.6\%$. The difference in method in this instance would amount to 4.9%.

Hanson to prepare an advertising and promotional program for launching the product. Mr. Hanson's occasional suggestions to Mr. Blane to test the product in one or two areas before marketing it nationally were never followed.

NEW PRODUCT LINES

In 1944 Mr. Blane was requested, by two individuals who held the patents, to manufacture a machine for cooling quenching oils. This machine would have had to sell for about $1,000, approximately four times the price of the company's most expensive product at that time. Two leading engineering authorities, retained to study the need for such equipment, submitted very favorable reports. No special market research as such was conducted, but on the basis of the engineering reports, the decision was made to manufacture the product. Two engineers were hired to work in the engineering, production, sales, and servicing of the new product.

Because of the sales engineering required, it was thought that the company's distributors were not the best type for handling the quenching oil cooler, so seven specialty equipment distributors were appointed in different parts of the country. When a distributor or representative got a "hot" prospect, the company was notified, and a sales engineer called on the prospective customer.

Only four of the distributors ever developed a worthwhile volume of sales. A number of reasons were advanced for the lack of success of the quenching oil cooler. Expenses ran much higher than anticipated; therefore, the price was thought to be inadequate. The product was priced as a "package unit,"[4] as were the other products manufactured by the company; but, actually, much special engineering and many expensive trips were required to sell and service it. The sales representatives and manufacturers' agents who were employed by the company did not have the engineering knowledge necessary to work effectively with distributors. The product proved to be practical only for large-volume operations. Moreover, it was subject to mechanical difficulties which required service, but the company had no service organization except the two engineers in the home office. Because it was a new type of product, pioneering sales effort was necessary. Manufacturers in many

[4] This term was applied to a product which could be installed and serviced by the customer without any engineering assistance.

instances were reluctant to give up valuable floor space required for installation. This reluctance was aggravated by the difficulty in determining the exact savings which a potential buyer could expect to get from use of the product.

The company's loss on the product was not known exactly, but was estimated roughly at $20,000. When sales dropped sharply after about three years of steady promotion, the product was discontinued, and the two engineers employed especially for the project were dismissed.

Early in 1946 the sales of the company began to decline. Three new products—a motor flushing device, a motor testing device, and a small battery charger—were introduced in rapid succession to restore sales volume. The first two of these resulted in losses. The small battery charger had a short life of only moderate success.

FINANCIAL PROBLEMS

In June, 1946, depleted working capital prompted a bank loan which was secured by accounts receivable. An interest rate of 7% was charged by the bank. Over a period of several months this loan was increased to a maximum of $25,000, beyond which the bank refused to go.

In November, 1946, arrangements were made to borrow from a finance company against receivables which were not already pledged to the bank. The charges of the finance company amounted to 1% per month on the full invoice amount of receivables pledged.

In February, 1947, the same finance company extended a loan against inventory. To comply with the requirements of the finance company, arrangements were made with a public warehouse company to establish a bonded warehouse in one section of the plant building. The finance company advanced money to the Blane-Radford Company in the amount of 70% of the invoice value of the inventory deposited in the bonded warehouse. The interest rate charged by the finance company was 1% per month on the total invoice value of the average daily balance of inventory stock in the bonded warehouse.

In September, 1947, a chattel mortgage on all machinery and equipment was given to the same finance company to secure a loan of $19,800. Interest charges on this loan amounted to an annual rate of approximately 18%.

In November, 1947, there were 235 accounts payable on the books of the Blane-Radford Company, upon which payments were running behind from 60 to 150 days. Several trade creditors had suits pending against the company. However, credit ratings published by leading credit services at this time did not reflect the true financial condition of the company, and about 75% of the time it was still able to purchase on open account from new suppliers.

In November, 1947, the book value of total assets was $217,629, including current assets of $151,228.

The debts of the company were as follows:

Past due accounts payable	$ 82,500
Chattel mortgage loan on machinery and equipment (payable in 14 equal monthly installments)	15,400
Inventory loan (recurring loan, no urgency to pay off)	11,000
Delinquent taxes with penalties	4,950
Unsecured bank note	11,000
Loan secured by accounts receivable	30,000
Total	$154,850

exhibit 2   **BLANE-RADFORD COMPANY**
Breakdown of comparative profit and loss statements, December 31, 1942–1947

	1942	1943	1944	1945	1946	1947
Sales	$316,021	$460,498	$427,163	$739,976	$598,011	$566,120
Sales	100.0%	99.9%	100.0%	100.0%	100.0%	101.3%
Cost of materials	28.5	29.5	32.0	32.7	34.0	33.5
Cost of labor	9.7	9.4	9.6	7.5	7.5	8.3
Manufacturing overhead	7.6	8.4	15.4	12.8	17.8	24.0
Administrative expense	8.6	11.0	14.3	11.5	11.7	11.5
Selling expense	12.4	11.8	12.6	11.6	16.8	17.3
Advertising	7.2	13.2	11.6	10.1	8.2	5.4
Profit	26.0	16.6	4.5	13.8	4.0	d 1.3
Profit	$ 82,165	$ 76,443	$ 19,222	$102,117	$ 23,920	d $ 7,230

BLANE-RADFORD
COMPANY (B)

In the latter part of November, 1948, the Advertising and Sales Promotion Manager, Mr. Hanson, purchased the controlling interest in the Blane-Radford Company. The Assistant Chief Engineer, Mr. Everett Kruger, purchased a common stock interest of 20%. After disposing of their stock interests, the former President and General Manager left the company.

OPERATIONAL CHANGES UNDER THE
NEW MANAGEMENT

As the new management, Mr. Hanson and Mr. Kruger dismissed all executive personnel and about two-thirds of the office staff, including the following individuals: the Controller, the Chief Engineer and Factory Superintendent, the Purchasing Agent, the Production Manager, two secretaries, the switchboard girl, the stock records clerk, the order clerk, and three other clerks. This reduction in staff was accomplished in a four-month period.

Mr. Hanson assumed the duties of President, General Manager, Controller and Sales Manager, as well as retaining those of the advertising and promotion management. Mr. Kruger took over all engineering duties, factory management, production planning and scheduling, and supervision of purchasing. The actual routine of purchasing was handled by a clerk who previously had worked in the Engineering Department. It was expected that he would assume increased purchasing responsibility, and he was later given the title of Purchasing Agent. After two years, a Production Manager was hired to relieve Mr. Kruger of the production planning and scheduling detail. The organization under the new management is shown in Exhibit 1.

All surplus equipment and supplies were sold, and the proceeds, approximately $2,000, were applied to reduction of the chattel mortgage loan. The company arranged to cancel the lease on all but 20,000 of the

exhibit 1
BLANE-RADFORD COMPANY
Organization Chart, November 30, 1949

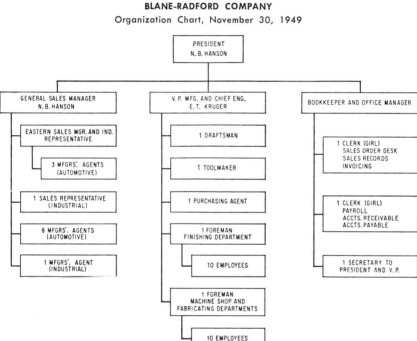

55,000 square feet of manufacturing and office space it had been renting under a leasehold which was to expire in two years. No production employees were dismissed, although several key employees had left just previous to the change in management, expecting that their jobs would run out.

The Assistant Sales Manager resigned and his duties were assumed by Mr. Hanson. Otherwise, no immediate changes were made in the sales organization.

In the first quarter of 1949 sales were averaging about $33,000 per month. Cost reductions put into effect by Mr. Hanson brought the break-even point down from about $37,000 to about $25,000 of sales per month.

One of Mr. Hanson's first acts was to send a carefully drafted letter to all trade creditors, explaining frankly where the company stood— the size of the debt and the problem the new management faced. In this letter he asked for a two-month "breathing spell," during which some plan could be developed for gradual liquidation of the indebtedness.

The creditors cooperated almost unanimously. Mr. Hanson thought they appreciated the frank disclosure of facts, also that they apparently concluded that there was nothing to be gained in forcing bankruptcy. Two months later creditors were promised that debts would be liquidated over a three-year period in monthly installments of increasing amounts. Meanwhile, the company promised to pay within 30 days all new invoices or to pay cash in advance or c.o.d. if desired by creditors on subsequent orders. These proposals were made through letters and personal visits; no formal meeting of creditors was held. Subsequently sales continued to decline, but the proposed payments to creditors were made on schedule.

In March, 1949, the company brought out an inexpensive radiator flusher to be sold about 30% below the popular prices of competitive products. This product was considered to offer some promise of quick profits with little new capital investment. Sales of the product were good, and by June, 1949, total sales of the company reached $50,000 per month. At this point sales of the radiator flusher declined sharply. Brief investigation revealed that 12 additional competitive products had been put on the market at prices from 20% higher to 30% lower than that of the company's product. At the end of September, 1949, production of the radiator flusher was discontinued.

FINANCIAL PROBLEMS OF THE NEW COMPANY

The declining sales ran from $22,000 to $25,000 per month. Several items of overhead were further reduced, bringing the break-even point down to about $23,000 of sales per month.

Scheduled payments on the heavy trade debts coupled with reduced operating profit made the company's cash position hazardous. On three occasions Mr. Hanson obtained bank loans of $5,000, each of which was paid off within four months. In making these loans, the banks accepted

the unsecured notes of the company with the personal endorsements of
Mr. Hanson and Mr. Kruger.

In November, 1948, a small advertising agency had been appointed
by the company. Previously, one of the large agencies in the industrial
field had handled the account. Mr. Hanson believed that the small
agency would concern itself more with holding down expenses, with
more of the company's advertising going into literature and space
rather than into miscellaneous services. In explaining this objective to
the manager of the small agency, he stated that "agencies tend to spend

exhibit 2   **BLANE-RADFORD COMPANY**
Breakdown of comparative profit and loss statements, December 31, 1948–1950

	1948	*1949*	*1950*
Sales	$410,409	$326,131	$335,240
Sales	100.0%	100.0%	100.0%
Cost of materials	39.7	38.0	40.0
Cost of labor	11.9	12.6	10.0
Manufacturing overhead	23.5	13.8	12.8
Administrative expense	16.0	10.0	9.5
Selling expense	18.8	19.5	15.3
Advertising	6.9	3.9	4.0
Profit	d 16.8	2.2	8.4
Profit	d $68,949	$ 7,175	$ 28,160

so much money developing plans that there is no money left to carry
them out." Twice a month Mr. Hanson met with the manager of the
agency to review the advertising schedule and discuss new advertising
plans. The agency prepared most of the literature used, as well as the
published advertising. Its services were considered quite satisfactory.

In August, 1949, creditors were informed by letter that it was neces
sary for the company to discontinue temporarily the regular payments
on past due accounts. Thereafter, about every six weeks a follow-up letter was sent to the creditors, informing them of the current condition of
the company and assuring them that payments would be resumed as
soon as possible. Several creditors started legal action, but about 95%
of them cooperated fully. Mr. Hanson believed that their cooperation

was due largely to the fact that "they had confidence in the management of the company and liked their honesty, frankness and enthusiasm."

Because the security of the business was uncertain and because a good credit rating was desired, the following three methods were considered possible means of eliminating the indebtedness:

1. A long-term capital loan. Several banks and the Reconstruction Finance Corporation were approached unsuccessfully. However, each of them left the door open for the possibility of making such a loan in the future.

2. New capital stock investment. This possibility was discussed with several individuals who were considered prospective investors, but nothing was worked out with any of them.

3. Greatly increased sales.

SALES

In analyzing the situation, it was decided that any substantial sales increase would have to come from (1) new products with a greater market than the present line, or (2) a general expansion of industrial activity which would naturally increase the sales of the present line of products if they were "priced right, designed right, and sold intelligently."

Mr. Hanson believed that increased sales of the present line required several engineering improvements and the addition of several items in order that a well-balanced line of dependable quality could be offered to the trade. With this objective in mind, a large, heavy-duty model of the lathe attachment was developed and added to the line.

Several design and engineering changes were made, which centered around improvement in appearance, reduction of manufacturing costs, and elimination of weaknesses in performance. One type of equipment failure, which had previously been a serious problem, was almost completely eliminated.

Several important cost reductions led to revision of prices of the entire line, with some price reductions of as much as 20%.

In June, 1949, Mr. Hanson had decided to concentrate on increasing sales of the lathe attachment to manufacturers of original equipment. While the lathe attachment had been sold primarily for installation on lathes already in use, Mr. Hanson believed that it would be possible to build a substantial volume of sales to manufacturers of machine tools for installation on new lathes or for sale by the machine tool manufacturers as accessory equipment. In view of the success of the product, he anticipated also that if the company did not go after the original equipment business, it would be captured by competitors or the lathe manufacturers would produce the units themselves.

After conferring with Mr. Kruger and the Production Manager, Mr. Hanson decided to accept orders with special design modifications for any lathe manufacturer with an estimated annual volume of business of 50 units or more. The average list price was about $150 per unit. Discounts to original equipment manufacturers ran from 15% to 30% plus 10% on orders for 500 units or more. When prices were revised in September, 1949, this discount was increased to 30% on small orders for 12 or more units.

By December, 1950, the company had increased the number of original equipment customers from 8 to 35. The volume of business from each ran from about $1,000 to $15,000 per year, with an annual total of approximately $75,000. This progress was considered satisfactory, but by no means the limit.

In January, 1948, the sales organization consisted of four sales representatives and eleven manufacturers' agents. In November, 1949, it consisted of one representative and twelve agents, a shift designed to remove the fixed liability of drawing accounts; sales costs were thereby made much more variable.

Replacements of agents were made where sales performance was unsatisfactory. The new agents employed were brought to the plant at their own expense for two days of intensive training. Agents who employed other salesmen usually brought these men with them or enrolled them in the two-day sales training at a later date.

Traveling and general sales promotion expenses were curtailed from the date Mr. Hanson assumed sales management responsibility. Whenever possible, he handled business matters by letter and occasionally talked to key members of the sales force and leading distributors by phone. Advertising expense was held to 4% of sales. A steady flow of advertising materials, letters, and product information was mailed to sales representatives and manufacturers' agents. New catalogue sheets were prepared to include tabulated engineering information, making it easier for distributors' salesmen to sell directly from the catalogue to meet specific needs of customers.

NEW FINANCING

Between January, 1949, and January, 1951, the critical financial situation was eased by the following sources of working capital:

Sale of surplus equipment	$ 2,000
Long-term loan from an individual (later converted to common stock)	15,000
Preferred stock issued to creditors in payment of accounts receivable	10,000
Three-year non-interest-bearing notes accepted by creditors in payment of accounts receivable	10,000
Profit earned in 1949	7,175*
Profit earned in 1950	28,160*
Total	$72,335

* Because of deficits in prior years it was not necessary to pay income taxes on 1949 and 1950 earnings.

With the company showing a profit the banks became cooperative, and the $30,000 accounts receivable loan, which had been carried by a finance company at a 12% discount rate, was placed with a bank at a 7% discount rate and later at an interest rate of 5%. By January, 1951, the chattel mortgage loan of $11,000, the inventory loan of $11,000, and the delinquent taxes and penalties of $4,950 had been paid off. An agreement had been reached to retire the $11,000 unsecured bank note in a series of seven installments, and the accounts payable had been reduced to the point at which creditors were no longer pressing the company. By February, 1951, a satisfactory credit rating enabled the company to purchase on open account from 90% of its suppliers.

INSTALLATION OF REPORTING SYSTEMS

The following reports and memoranda were prepared for Mr. Hanson's use:

Report on the Status of Purchases. This report was prepared monthly by the Purchasing Agent for a selected list of major materials such as steel, wire, motors, castings, etc. It showed (1) all orders placed and contemplated, and (2) all shipments scheduled to come in.

Report on Major Materials Requirements. The Purchasing Agent prepared this report each month to show (1) requirements for six months based on the sales forecast, (2) requirements to produce present back orders, (3) present inventory. The report covered each item on the selected· list of major materials.

This report was used in comparison with the Report on the Status of Purchases. By use of this formula relationship, given below, Mr. Hanson determined whether the proposed purchases were too high or too low:

Inventory–backlog requirements = unearmarked inventory

Unearmarked inventory ± proposed purchases and materials on order
+ minimum stock requirements should equal forecast sales requirements

Mr. Hanson said he made use of the report (1) to prevent an unbalancing of inventory, (2) to adjust purchasing schedules to monthly corrections in sales forecasts, and (3) to aid in figuring cash requirements for the following six months.

Cash Budget. This report was prepared each month by the bookkeeper and Mr. Hanson working together. It covered anticipated cash receipts and disbursements for the following six months. The forms used for the cash budget were standard forms which were obtained from a local bank. Each month Mr. Hanson compared the figures on the monthly financial statements with those on the cash budget. He explained that the cash budget was useful to him in that it (1) forced him to plan ahead, (2) provided a definite check on expenditures, (3) helped in determining what future action would have to be taken with respect to new financing or operating within financial limitations, and (4) showed trend in the accumulation or depletion of cash.

Proposed Production Schedule. This report, prepared monthly by the Production Manager and submitted through Mr. Kruger to Mr. Hanson, showed quantities of each type and model of product to be produced each week for four or five weeks in advance.

Statement of Delivery Information. Prepared monthly by the Production Manager and submitted through Mr. Kruger to Mr. Hanson, this report gave for each product the approximate number of days between receipt of an order and shipment of that order. This information was forwarded to the sales force as a basis for estimating delivery dates for customers. Mr. Hanson also considered the report to be useful in helping to estimate a schedule of outgoing shipments based on incoming sales.

Monthly Financial Statements. These were ordinary profit and loss statements prepared by the bookkeeper.

Progress Report on New Products and Improvements. Prepared by the Production Manager and submitted through Mr. Kruger to Mr. Hanson, this report described briefly the status of each project previously selected for action. The report was made whenever there was any important change in development but no less frequently than twice a month. There were usually from three to five projects under way at one time. Project selections were decided in conference by Mr. Hanson, Mr. Kruger, and the Production Manager.

Memoranda and Correspondence. Mr. Hanson received memoranda reporting any wage adjustments, changes in personnel, and other miscellaneous information concerning employee relations which were thought by anyone in a managerial position to be of interest to him. Also, copies of all memoranda between departments and copies of all correspondence came to Mr. Hanson's desk.

Sales Report. This report was prepared monthly by the sales record clerk to give the following information: (1) new orders by number of units and dollar volume broken down into product classifications, (2) month's total of dollar sales, (3) total dollar volume of shipments, and (4) order backlog in dollars as of the date of the report.

Sales Commission Reports. These reports, prepared by the payroll clerk, were merely copies of records required in the payroll and accounting procedures. They showed commissions paid to sales representatives and manufacturers' agents, broken down by product classification.

NEW BOARD OF DIRECTORS

Before 1949, the Board of Directors, consisting of three individuals active in the management of the company, served only to satisfy the legal requirements for a corporation. When Mr. Hanson assumed control, he wished to have a "working board." To secure outside perspective, he added three individuals not active in the company management. The new board was composed of the following:

1. Mr. N. B. Hanson, Chairman of the Board, President, and owner of the controlling common stock interest.

2. Mr. Everett Kruger, Vice President, and owner of a 20% common stock interest.

3. Mr. B. L. Edwards, Secretary, a prominent attorney not employed by the company. Mr. Edwards was a specialist in taxes and corporation finance.

4. Mr. C. K. Anderton, an executive in another manufacturing corporation in no way connected with the Blane-Radford Company. Mr. Hanson considered him a very capable manager who had done an outstanding job with his own company.

5. Mr. T. A. Nelson, a small stockholder and one of the company's most successful distributors.

Monthly Board meetings considered an agenda determined by Mr. Hanson and mailed to each member in advance. Sales reports and information on the financial condition of the company were sent to Directors at regular intervals so that time at Board meetings would not be consumed by routine reports.

At the third meeting of the new Board, the following objectives were determined for the company:

1. To double the sales of the company by 1956

2. To design products for new markets and investigate the possibilities of adapting present products to markets with a broader base than those presently served

3. To maintain leadership in the machine tool field for lathe attachments of the type manufactured, establishing the company as a number-one source for that product

4. To increase working capital to enable the company, if necessary, to operate below the break-even point for one year

5. To put the plant and manufacturing facilities in the best possible condition compatible with the type of operation

6. To provide a pleasant place to work, good income, and reasonable security for employees

7. To increase sales of Blane-Radford automotive products to the point at which they would provide a substantial proportion of the income of agents and be considered an important line by distributors

AUTOMOTIVE FIELD

In the third quarter of 1951, 52.7% of the company's sales were in the industrial field and 47.3% in the automotive field. An analysis of costs for the year 1950, as shown in Exhibit 3, revealed a profit of 3.7% on automotive sales as compared to 12.3% on industrial sales.

In order to stay in the automotive field, Mr. Hanson considered it necessary to do at least a minimum amount of advertising and to distribute essential items of promotional literature, regardless of the volume of business done. The company's promotional literature in the automotive field consisted primarily of price sheets and catalogue sheets, with separate catalogue sheets for each automotive product. In the industrial field, only one condensed catalogue was published covering all the company's industrial products. In the industrial field, where the market was relatively limited with respect to the number of prospective customers, advertising expenses, including the cost of promotional literature, was 3.2% of sales.

Credit was slightly more hazardous in the automotive field than in

exhibit 3   BLANE-RADFORD COMPANY
Breakdown of 1950 profit and loss statement by product lines

	Total Business	Industrial	Automotive
Sales	$335,240	$184,576	$150,664
Per cent of total sales	100.0%	52.7%	47.3%
Sales	100.0%	100.0%	100.0%
Cost of materials	40.0	40.0	40.0
Cost of labor	10.0	9.1	11.0
Manufacturing overhead	12.8	12.8	12.8
Administrative expense	9.5	9.5	9.5
Selling expense	15.3	13.1	18.0
Advertising	4.0	3.2	5.0
Profit	8.4	12.3	3.7

the industrial field. The experience of the company showed bad-debt losses to be about $\frac{1}{10}$ of 1% of sales in the industrial field and $\frac{1}{4}$ of 1% in the automotive field.

Terms extended to the industrial trade were 1%–10 days. To the automotive trade, however, it was necessary to extend terms of 2%/10th/proximo. Also, automotive jobbers were always asking for special freight allowances, extended by some manufacturers.

Trade discounts introduced an additional problem. In the industrial field, distributors who carried stocks of the company's products were extended a 30% trade discount, while non-stocking distributors received 20%. Automotive distributors, even though they did not stock the products, usually refused to take on the line unless they got the full 30%

discount. Many of the company's products were sold both to the industrial and automotive trades, and in every locality both automotive
and industrial distributors sold identical products to some of the same
customers.

Difficulty in dealing with automotive jobbers led to the suggestion
that the company sell direct.

IRISH ROPES LIMITED

"I have heard it said," remarked Mr. Michael Rigby-Jones, managing director of Irish Ropes Limited of Newbridge, Ireland, "that when my father moved his plant to this town there wasn't a child in Newbridge who wore shoes; and today, they say, there isn't a child in town who goes barefoot. That is probably a little exaggerated, but there is a lot of truth in it. Twenty years ago there was poverty and decay here, and the stores on our business street were drab and lifeless; today they are brightly painted and are busy and prospering. If someone had prophesied to me at the end of the war that our business would soon double and triple and that we would be selling abroad, I would have thought him daft. But since that time our sales have quadrupled, we have twice the number of employees, sixty per cent of our unit production is sold in a world-wide export market, and we are still growing. But the fight to meet competition, especially abroad, gets tougher all the time, and when I see our profit margin gradually shrinking, I lie awake at night and worry about it."

In 1960, after 27 years of operation, the company was supplying virtually the entire rope and cordage requirements of the Republic of Ireland, and shipping an even larger tonnage of production abroad. In its history of operations the company had experienced only one year when it failed to earn a profit and pay a dividend. The firm's assets expanded from £7,188 ($20,126) in 1934 to £790,541 ($2,213,515) in 1960, and the expansion came almost entirely from retained earnings. Commenting on its progress, the chairman remarked that abroad the company had achieved a reputation for itself—perhaps out of proportion to its size—for the high quality of its sisal products, and that in

Ireland the company had set an example in many fields, particularly in modern management and good labor relations.

IRELAND AND ITS ECONOMY

The Republic of Ireland (previously the Irish Free State) had been an independent and democratic state since the Treaty of 1921. Its territory embraced all of the island of Ireland except six counties known as Northern Ireland, which retained an alliance with the United Kingdom.

The population numbered about 3 million in 1960 and had been declining for many decades. The 1952 census showed an increase of about 5,000, which was the first increase since 1841. At one time the population had been close to 10 million. Emigration was continuing, largely to England and the United States, where employment in industry and in domestic service could be had at higher wages. Of the working population of the Republic, 40% were engaged in agriculture, 25% in industry, 13% in distribution, and 22% in other economic activities.

Although there had been a continuous drive by the government since the formation of the state in 1921 to expand manufacturing industries, agriculture remained the basic industry of Ireland. Two thirds of its land was arable, climate was mild, and the soil was fertile. Most farms were small (between 15 and 100 acres) and the government was attempting to eliminate some 200,000 which were under 15 acres and considered uneconomic. Livestock and dairy produce were the principal farm products, and most of these were exported—mainly to England. The government was encouraging the use of modern farming methods, but primitive farming practices were still widespread.

The expansion of industry was a major aim of the Irish government. Since 1955, the Industrial Development Authority offered new industries outright non-repayable grants up to the full cost of buildings; 50% of the cost of plant and machinery; grants for the training of workers; tax-free profits for a period of ten years; and the guaranteed free transfer, in the investor's currency, of dividends, interest, and profits. Capital, with appreciation, could be repatriated at any time. Ample manpower was available. A typical industrial wage rate was about £8 for men (60¢ an hour, or about $22 a week); £5 for women

(36¢ an hour, or about $14 a week). The Electricity Supply Board, a government agency, had brought adequate power to most sections of the country.

Imports in 1956 were nearly £200,000,000 ($560,000,000) and exceeded exports by £70,800,000 ($198,200,000). This excess was almost offset by net income from capital, £9,900,000 ($27,500,000); tourism, £22,600,000 ($63,300,000); and other receipts, £23,900,000 ($66,-900,000). Of the Republic's imports, £100,000,000 or over 50% came from Britain and Northern Ireland; £12,000,000 or 6% came from the United States; £3,000,000 or 1.5% came from Canada.

Gross national industrial production had increased from £184,000,-000 ($515,000,000) in 1938 to £542,000,000 ($1,518,000,000) in 1956. Ireland had an independent currency backed by sterling and dollar securities and gold reserves. The currency was maintained at absolute parity with sterling.

To maintain a favorable balance of trade and to secure an increase in dollar earnings, the government in 1952 set up the Export Promotion Board. The Board hoped to promote export trade, especially to the dollar area. Irish industrialists were encouraged to aggressively seek export markets, and the Board stimulated their interest by supplying producers with all possible advice and counsel. The increase of exports became a national objective, and the effort to expand abroad came to be considered an act of patriotism.

EARLY HISTORY OF THE COMPANY

Ropemaking had long been a traditional craft in Ireland, but most of it had been limited to the making of agricultural twines. There had been a few makers of heavy ropes for sailing ships in Irish seaports, but, with the coming of steamships, these died out. One of these seaport ropemakers, located in Belfast, Northern Ireland, grew to be one of the largest ropemakers in the world. The partition of Ireland in 1921, however, cut off Belfast from the Free State and left the Irish Free State without any domestic ropemaker of significant size. The bulk of Ireland's rope requirements were imported, mostly from Britain, where British Ropes Limited of England was one of the largest ropemakers in the world.

In 1933, to protect the few remaining rope factories and to encourage the establishment of new ones, the government of the Republic imposed a 33⅓% duty on the importation of ropes, twines, and cables. At the time, Mr. Eric Rigby-Jones (the father of Michael Rigby-Jones) was operating a rope factory in Liverpool, England, where his family had been ropemakers for six generations. This family firm had conducted a small but steady business and had never attempted to grow beyond moderate size. It specialized in ropes and lines which required high quality performance, such as mountain climbers' ropes and lariats. Eric Rigby-Jones also exported common ropes, cords, and twines to Ireland, where his firm had become a factor in supplying that market.

The 1933 import levy forced upon Mr. Eric Rigby-Jones the choice of either abandoning the Irish market, or of establishing a plant in Ireland. He decided to relocate in the Free State. For a location he chose Newbridge, a residential town of about 2,000 located 30 miles below Dublin on the river Liffey. In about 1800, the British had built an extensive cavalry barracks in Newbridge to train troops for the Napoleonic wars, for Newbridge was situated in the Curragh, Ireland's renowned horse-raising bluegrass region. Later the British used the barracks to house a constabulary, which left in 1922. The roomy barrack buildings impressed Eric Rigby-Jones as being ideal for his purposes. He bought a section of the garrison and, with six employees, began production in July of 1933. Equipping and renovating the buildings exhausted most of his family's modest finances, but the firm already had a loyal customer following in Ireland, and the business quickly prospered. Within ten years, it had 300 employees and was supplying the bulk of the Republic's rope and twine requirements.

THE COMPANY'S POSITION IN IRELAND

"In ropes and cordage," said Mr. Michael Rigby-Jones, "we are able to supply all of the requirements of the Irish Republic. We can produce almost any type of rope or twine, and, since we try to keep steady employment, we don't turn down a customer if we can help it. Besides, with tariff protection for our home market, we feel obliged to produce for the national needs of Ireland. Even so, we are trying to be more selective in what we produce, and we are building a stronger sales force. The sales effort is demanding an increasing amount of my own time lately."

In 1960, the company's products which were sold in Ireland fell into two broad categories: cordage, consisting of ropes, cords, and twines; woven products, consisting of Tintawn sisal carpeting and a small amount of fabricated items, such as shopping bags and lined beach bags. At one time it had made fish nets, which proved unprofitable. It had considered making cello-tape under license, to compete with the inroads Scotch tape was making into the parcel twine market, but the market was too small and the idea was dropped. Weaving woolen carpets had been considered, but this would have required buying spun wool from some Irish woolen mill which, Mr. Rigby-Jones said "would have been starting on a weak wicket." Although the company was aggressively looking for new products which held promise, Mr. Rigby-Jones said, "I sometimes feel that our diverse lines of products are getting out of control. Cordage and carpeting use different production processes and sell through different marketing channels, and their only common denominator is the sisal from which both are made." In the Irish market, the company sold a sizeable output of "bogey ropes" which farmers used on their haycarts; sisal rope for driving reins and traces which Irish farmers preferred because they were cheaper than leather; seine fishing ropes which were water-resistant and decomposition-proofed; and a cheap twine, made from sisal waste, which was used for tying down haycocks. (See Exhibit 1.)

exhibit 1   **IRISH ROPES LIMITED**
Product lines

Binder and baler twines	Sisal parcel and packing twines
Colored plastic lines	Sisal floor coverings
Cords of sisal and manila	Sisal webbing
Manila and sisal ropes	Trawl twines
Plaited cords	Tubed sisal cores
Polished parcel twines	Weaving twines
Shopping bags	Yacht ropes

"As to our home market for binder twine," said Mr. J. B. Roche, director of sales, "we feel quite secure. There is not another single binder twine spinner in the Republic, we have intensive coverage, and while we are protected by tariffs, we do not take advantage of this fact; we keep our prices competitive with those of the British. However, the fact that Ireland has a low population and low purchasing power places a limit on the total potential of our home sales."

Irish Ropes sold about a third of its tonnage as harvest twine. Sales of binder twines had been gradually decreasing in recent years due to the growing use of grain combines, but this was offset by the increased demand for baler twines (which were similar but much stronger). Farmers bought the twines at the immediate time when they were needed, which meant, that in rainy summers sales might be delayed. The company almost always sold its total annual production every year, for Ireland seldom suffered a crop failure, and the harvest, although sometimes late, eventually came through. There were years in which the total year's sales were made in two late summer months, but the total sales volume in such a year might be exceptionally high. Prices also tended to advance in a delayed season due to competitive bidding for the available supply. In the mid-summer of 1960, for instance, sales had been slow due to rain, and the company had a large stock on hand. Crop prospects were good, however, and the management decided to hold its stock for the higher prices which would come later in the summer.

For a number of years the company had 2,000 retail accounts. Some of these proved unprofitable because of their limited purchases. Realizing this, some 350 small retailer accounts were dropped, and a minimum requirement of one-half ton per order of cordage, including binder twine, was put into effect. The management believed that the tactic had succeeded, since no appreciable change in total sales volume resulted from the move. Salesmen also urged customers to buy in economic quantities to get the benefit of quantity discounts.

In Ireland, the company had a staff of five salesmen (travelers)— two selling in Dublin (population 522,000), and three covering the remainder of the Irish Republic. All of the salesmen sold all of the company's products. Cordage was sold to any type of retailer who could meet quantity requirements, but Tintawn sales were limited to 70 selected retail outlets, and the company hoped eventually to have one or more salesmen specializing in carpeting. "We favor young men for travelers," said Mr. Roche, "because they are vigorous and aggressive, and we push hard for sales. Our country is small, and we cover it so intensively that we know personally every one of our customers. We aim to oversell our productive capacity, and in recent years we have been successful—we have had a modest backlog of orders for all products."

The company had originally tried to sell its Tintawn carpeting through its general store retailers, because there were only three carpeting wholesalers in Ireland and these were considered ineffective. General store retailers also proved ineffective, for some of them sold only a few yards a year, and few of them were in a position to give their customers proper service. Following the advice of market consultants, the company switched its carpeting distribution to some 70 home furnishing accounts. For these distributors it held promotions three days a year, called Tintawn Days. The Irish Ropes management invited the home furnishing buyers to come to Newbridge for these days, and the company paid their transportation costs. The buyers were given a tour of the plant and were shown how the carpeting was made; they were given cleaning and fitting instructions, and general discussion sessions were held in which mutual problems were discussed.

Although Mr. Michael Rigby-Jones felt that the company's Irish market was reasonably secure, he had some misgivings. "In England, there are five ropeworks," he said, "each larger than we are. Each of them would only have to sell fifty tons in Ireland, which they could do without much effort, and our home market would be gone. Continental twine spinners can also compete with us very favorably. Ireland is a small country, and its rope requirements are limited, but in Tintawn we can generate larger sales demand." Although Irish purchasing power was low, Mr. Rigby-Jones was of the opinion that this might be a point in favor of Tintawn. Householders who had never had any kind of floor coverings might be induced to buy economical sisal carpeting, and in any period of recession users of the more expensive woolen carpetings might switch to sisal mattings.

"We will probably not expand much in the cordage end of our business," said Mr. Rigby-Jones, "and if free trade comes about we will probably lose even a share of the Irish market to larger ropemakers in England and on the Continent. But we will remain in the cordage business and specialize in the spinning of fine twines. I would like to see the firm grow to about a thousand employees, but I would not care to see it grow too large. We will stay in Newbridge, and our growth will be gradual. I hope that the town will keep in step with us."

EXPORT SALES

"The early development of Irish Ropes' export trade," said Mr. Roche, "was a matter of 'necessity being the mother of invention.'

From the start, it was our intention to establish a factory of sufficient size to produce economically, but we quickly reached a stage where we were making more than the home market could consume. Consequently we had to decide whether to remain a relatively small unit operating uneconomically on the home market, or to go courageously ahead and seek foreign outlets for extra production. Ireland needs industry, we have good and willing workers, and while our wage rates are higher than most in Ireland, they still permit us to compete favorably in many other countries. Therefore, there was never any real doubt about the decision we would make." In 1960, 50% of Irish Ropes' money volume of sales and 60% of its tonnage went to foreign markets. Dollar exports in 1959–60 exceeded $400,000 which made the company one of the largest dollar earners for the Irish Republic. (See Exhibit 2.)

Mr. Michael Rigby-Jones agreed. "In general," he said, "our company has no natural advantage in ropemaking. In fact, we are at a disadvantage in that we are burdened by high in-freight charges for raw materials and high out-freight for exported goods. One of our major policies is that we deliberately seek to make products that have a high labor content. This is in the interest of the Irish national economy, but it also enables us to be competitive in the export market." The weekly male wage rate at Irish Ropes averaged £7 to £9 ($19.60 to $25.20) including incentive bonus for a 40 hour week, compared to £9 to £12 ($25.56 to $34.08) for similar labor in England.

In 1959, Irish Ropes sold over £550,000 ($1,540,000) worth of its goods to over fifty countries on five continents. (See Exhibit 2.) While the company had agents representing it in every part of the globe, its principal customers to whom it directed its main sales efforts were Great Britain, the United States, and Canada, where it sold cordage and Tintawn carpeting. The company also sold a sizeable amount of twine in Great Britain, high quality lariat ropes and Tintawn carpeting in the United States, and ropes for lobster fishing in Canada.

While Irish Ropes sold its products on the Continent, it met severe competition there. There were several cordage firms in Portugal which, being nearer to Africa, had lower freight costs for raw sisal. Being closer to the continental market, their out-freight charges were also lower, and it was believed that their freight costs were subsidized by their government in the interest of fostering commercial activity in Portugal. Irish Ropes believed that the costs incurred by the Portuguese cordage producers were considerably lower than their own, and the Portuguese sold their output on a world-wide basis.

In its Tintawn carpeting, Irish Ropes met with competition from Dutch producers of sisal mattings. The Dutch carpetings were lighter in weight and sold for approximately 25% less at retail than Tintawn. However, Tintawn carpeting was considered to be of better quality and more durable. The Dutch had also begun to imitate the colors and designs of Irish Ropes; it was known that they had duplicated Donegal Tweed, one of the most popular designs.

Irish Ropes also met competition from foreign producers of high quality carpeting. There were a number of German firms which produced high quality sisal carpeting and did so at competitive prices. On a trip to England, Mr. Rigby-Jones found that a West German firm was selling a carpeting of superior quality, laid down in London, at prices which were 25% below those of Tintawn.

Although there was a 24% duty on sisal products imported into Holland, and 14% in Germany, Irish Ropes was selling in both countries on the basis of quality, design, and colors. The company shaded its prices to meet competition abroad. The over-all reduction averaged 10%, but Tintawn prices were reduced more than those of cordage. To enable it to sell on the Continent, the company changed the dimensions of some of its production so that customers could be furnished with merchandise measured in meters instead of yards; designs were changed to stripes and bolder patterns; brighter colors were substituted for the mellow shades of Galway Lichen and Donegal Tweed, and these names, which had little appeal on the Continent, were also changed. Even the name Tintawn (in Germany) was changed in spelling to Tintaun.

In its exportation of cordage to other parts of the globe, Irish Ropes met severe price competition from local producers whose basic costs were lower. Mexican producers had a natural advantage in that henequin was a fiber plant which was native to Mexico; also Mexican labor costs were so low that by comparison Irish labor costs were relatively high. Again, in the United States, large binder twine producers such as International Harvester produced twine in such enormous quantities that they were able to use mass production techniques with resulting economies which Irish Ropes could not match.

Shipping facilities from Ireland were inadequate. Most shipments had to go to Liverpool on the west coast of England, to be trans-shipped from there. This added heavily to shipping charges. The freight charge per ton of cordage or carpeting from Dublin to Liverpool was 71 shillings 1 pence ($10.95); the rate from Liverpool to New York for cordage was 182/6 ($25.82) and for carpeting was 212/6 ($29.75). The rate from Dublin direct to any port in the United States was the same as the rate from Liverpool, but direct sailings from Dublin were few. There were now sailings from Dublin direct to the interior of the United States via the Great Lakes Seaway, but only by one line, with sailings about once a month. Most Irish Ropes shipments went via Liverpool. The result was that it cost almost as much to ship to Glasgow, Scotland, 200 miles from Dublin, as to New York, 3,500 miles away.

"Import restrictions, quotas, and tariffs are a chronic problem," said Mr. Roche. "German and Dutch duties drastically limit sales there. United States duties are based upon the American values of the imports, to the disadvantage of Irish Ropes. At times, the Irish Republic, because of dollar shortages, places levies or quotas upon the importation of raw materials and supplies."

Irish Ropes was actively making plans in the event that the Republic would become a member of the Free Trade Area. "The Free Trade Area would offer us great opportunities," said Mr. Cox, chairman of the board, "but like all big opportunities, it would carry with it big risks. We now enjoy protection, and when this goes, our competitors will surely endeavor to sell here. But we believe that we are as efficient as anyone else, and we should be more than able to hold our own. We should be able to swim in the larger sea."

Mr. Roche regretted that the two trade areas had developed—the Free Trade Area and the Common Market. "It is as though in America the North had lost the Civil War," he said, "leaving the United States divided into two competing sections. I firmly believe that eventually the two European trade areas must combine."

Mr. Roche was convinced that personal contacts were necessary to build the company's dealer organization. For that purpose, he traveled to the United States, to Canada, and to the Continent at least once every year, opening new dealerships and making good will calls on others. The Coras Trachtala, the Irish Export Promotion Board, was trying a plan whereby a government representative traveled abroad representing a number of companies which shared his traveling expenses. Irish Ropes had joined five other companies in sending such a representative to the Middle East to visit Cyprus, Egypt, Lebanon, Libya, Malta, and Sudan, but the results had been disappointing. The company was now planning on developing its own sales personnel to travel abroad, and it currently had one young man taking a year-long export sales course from the Irish Export Promotion Board; half of this expense was borne by the government.

"We have exhausted the potential of our home market in Ireland," said Mr. Rigby-Jones. "The only avenue for further expansion open to us lies abroad." Mr. Rigby-Jones constantly strove to impress upon his management staff and his employees the importance of their export trade. Typical of his efforts was this notice which was sent to all of the company's personnel:

> Last week I visited Zurich, Switzerland; Munich, Germany; Amsterdam and Rotterdam, Holland. I went to these countries to try to learn something about sisal carpets in these markets, to obtain experience, visit our agents and endeavor to assist our sales—the while bearing in mind the proposed European Free Trade Area.
>
> It seems that the proposed Free Trade Area will come about in some form, and in my opinion, we have two main alternatives. The first is to carry on much as we are at present and perhaps eventually lose our home and export markets to other more energetic manufacturers with dreadful consequences. The second is to start now to think and prepare for European trade even though a great deal of effort will not necessarily show much result. The latter is the obvious choice, and it is for us to make the effort to safeguard our future.
>
> I believe we must start to think and work "Continentally"—to get used to metric measurements—to foreign languages—different customs and tastes. As we live on an island, we naturally think too much of our own country and not enough of Europe as a whole and its position against Russian domination. Our competitors on the Continent already have more experience than ourselves in trading with other countries, using different languages and different currencies. These markets have a higher standard of living than ourselves, and much of it is derived from hard work at all levels. There is a great variety of goods offered for sale, and competition is considerable so that we shall have to be very good to survive. I believe that we can and will survive if we continue to increase our efforts.
>
> I suggest that our only hope is to try to sell Tintawn as a very high quality floor covering with particular design and colors that are unusual and which other people do not make. We shall not get big business, but the important thing in my opinion is to at least establish our contacts and work in this direction in our own time instead of being forced into

it in ten or fifteen years time. It is a great market and should offer great opportunities to those who work well enough to merit it.

In every country, our prices are higher than our competitors, and the public are not going to buy our goods just because they come from Ireland. They will only buy what gives them the best value, and they have great experience of knowing this."

(signed) *Michael Rigby-Jones*
Managing Director

In his annual Director's Report, Mr. Cox emphasized to the shareholders the importance of the company's export trade. "It is my duty to impress upon you," he said, "how much we depend on exports. Practically any further expansion which we make will have to be made abroad. There are extra risks in export sales, and whilst we realize that we can never expect a high return on them, they do provide employment for over 250 people. The one thing in export trade of which we are certain is—greater competition. We are not pessimistic of our future but realize that it is going to be a hard continuous struggle to maintain our position, apart from improving it. We are proud of what we have been able to achieve."

ROPE PRODUCTION

Ropemaking was an ancient art. By 1960, the relatively few remaining rope firms had standardized the ropemaking process, using machines which were virtually identical. These were textile processing machines which were capable of handling hard, heavy fibers. Almost all of them were made by a single firm—Mackie's of Belfast, Northern Ireland.

Basically, the Irish Ropes process of ropemaking was the same as that of any other ropemaker. The sisal fiber, as it was received in 560-pound bales, varied as to thickness and length of the individual fibers. These were blended into a uniform distribution by passing them through a series of combing and carding machines which straightened the fibers, laid them parallel, and staggered the ends so that there was a continuous overlap. From its initial tangled state in the bale, the fiber came out of these "goods" machines in a continuous ribbon known as a "sliver." The first goods machine produced a sliver as thick as a man's thigh. This was gradually reduced by successive combings through a series of machines culminating in a finished smooth level ribbon less than an inch wide. During the process, the fibers were sprayed with an oil and water emulsion which softened the fibers and made them more pliable, prevented damage to them during the fabricating process, and acted as a preservant in the later life of the rope, giving it water-repellency and making it resistant to rot and mildew.

From the goods machines, the fibers went to the spinning machines. Here the finished sliver was once more attenuated to make it more slender, and by twisting it was converted from a ribbon into a cylindrical form in which the fibers were compressed against each other. This twisted assemblage of fibers, called yarn, was the first basic component part of a rope. The compression of the fibers from the twisting resulted in a friction between the fiber surfaces which held each fiber in place when under tension.

The finished yarns were then twisted together to form a strand. Depending upon the finished rope desired, a strand might require anywhere from two to several hundred yarns. The final operation, known as "laying" a rope, consisted of twisting three or four strands together. Three or four ropes laid together formed a cable. In each twisting operation, the twists were in the opposite direction.

Cordage, the ropes used for such purposes as clotheslines and lariats, was formed by braiding the strands together. Ropes were standardized as to size (measured in diameter or circumference), weight per hundred feet, type of fiber material (sisal, manila, hemp, etc.), and minimum breaking strength.

TINTAWN CARPETING

"Our company has no natural advantages in the production of ropes," said Mr. Rigby-Jones. "In ropemaking, which has become standardized and static, we are subjected to fierce price competition. Tintawn carpeting, however, lends itself to promotion and to merchandising as a quality product. There is a great market potential, and we are developing more. No one, so far, has duplicated the effort of Irish Ropes in producing a sisal matting of high quality and artistic coloring and pattern. Of all Irish Ropes products, Tintawn definitely has the most promise."

The first sisal carpeting which appeared on the market was a low priced floor covering sold in competition with mattings made from coir, the dark brown whiskers of the cocoanut. Mr. Eric Rigby-Jones originally intended to spin fine white sisal yarns to be sold to the carpet weavers. His inability to develop that market persuaded him to weave carpeting. Rather than make cheap matting, he decided to use white, artificially dried fine sisal, which was more expensive but permitted dyeing in lighter colors, making a quality carpeting.

After a number of years of experimenting in weaving and in developing colors, patterns, and styles, production began in earnest in 1952. Tintawn found ready consumer acceptance, and thereafter the company regularly added more looms. In 1960, Tintawn represented 27% of total sales and 50% of export sales, and by then the factory was regularly short of production capacity to keep pace with carpeting sales.

The original carpeting produced by Irish Ropes was a simple cross-threaded flat matting. To improve this, the company tried weaving a pile carpeting, but customers reported that the pile carpeting had a strong tendency to absorb dirt and to hold lint. The company then abandoned pile in favor of looped pile, a weave which presented a top surface of hard, tight-woven loops of fibers. This weave, known as bouclé, although more expensive, lent itself readily to artful designs and colors and sold well. In 1960, the Irish Ropes line of carpeting consisted of the original matting weave, the looped pile bouclé, and an improved bouclé which had a plastic backing.

Management believed that color and design were strong sales points which competitors found difficult to match. To counsel them on these features, the company retained a professional artist—a faculty member of a leading Dublin university. To add romantic appeal, typical Irish names were chosen for each color. The 1960 line included Donegal Tweed, Thatch, Irish Rose, Autumn Bracken, Connemara Red, Galway Lichen, Corregan, and Bog of Allen. In the United States, Donegal Tweed, a neutral tweed mixture of white and fawn, proved to be very popular.

Originally Tintawn had been sold in Ireland by the company's regular traveling salesmen to any customer who would handle it. Following market surveys made by the consultants, the company limited its sales in Ireland to retailers of home furnishings, and in England it organized a subsidiary company, Tintawn Limited, of Slough, London. Elsewhere in the world, Tintawn was generally sold through wholesale agents. In some instances, the company found this to be a decided advantage. In Ireland, the company supported a sales staff and offered customers a cutting and fitting service for as little as five yards; it had no such expense in New York where the distributing agent offered no service and placed orders in large quantities. The company also found that Tintawn could be sold competitively in many parts of the world where its ropes and cordages, because of local competition, were excluded.

PRODUCTION

"The regularity of yarns," said Mr. N. C. Carter, Irish Ropes' works manager, "is a problem to the whole industry, but it is a particular problem to us because of the dyes and emulsions we use. The feeds and speeds of most of our processes are machine controlled, and most of our people are simply machine feeders. By now, we have removed just about all of the slack in efficiency from our production processes. There remains just one variable that we can work on—that is the number of times a yarn breaks in the production process. Thirty per cent of our machine down time is lost by yarn breakages. If we could reduce the frequency of yarn breakages on our looms by just 10%, it would enable us to produce an additional 100 tons of carpeting at no additional cost except the materials. This would increase our net profit substantially."

The problem of breakages stemmed from the fact that dyed and emulsified fibers were used in the weaving of Tintawn carpeting. The dyes and emulsions caused the fibers to form irregular masses in the yarns (called clogs, knots, or slubs) which clogged the machines. Also, thin spots in a yarn resulted in broken yarn. In either case, the entire machine had to be stopped. Mr. Carter estimated that because of "down machine time," the initial stages of processing dyed fibers took twice as long as for natural fibers. Mr. Carter was trying to solve the problem by studying intensively each of the fourteen individual steps involved in the production process.

The dyeing process itself presented difficulties. The dyeing was done in batches, and it was difficult to achieve uniformity of hues and shades. It was estimated that it would cost an investment of £50,000 ($140,000) to convert to a continuous flow process, and the management felt that its present volume of production did not warrant this expenditure.

At the close of World War II, Irish Ropes had retained the Associated Industrial Consultants of England to install the company's first incentive bonus plan and also a standard cost plan. Ten years later the consultants were retained again to work out an improved plant layout for the purpose of obtaining a smoother flow of work. At a later date, the consultants also worked out a merit rating plan for the company's staff personnel. It was believed that these instances were the first occasion on which a firm of management consultants had been used by any firm in the Republic of Ireland.

RAW MATERIALS

All of Irish Ropes' sisal and manila requirements were purchased through a London broker, a leading firm with whom the company had had close connections ever since its early days under the management of the late Eric Rigby-Jones. The broker was in constant contact with many sisal estates in Tanganyika, East Africa, and some of these plantations were owned and operated by the brokerage firm. "Buying from a single source," said Mr. Michael Rigby-Jones in 1960, "means that we have all our eggs in one basket, but we have made very sure that it is a good basket."

Sisal, the principal material used by Irish Ropes, was a fiber obtained from the plant Agave Sisalana, which was grown in British East Africa. On the plantation, the fibers were beaten out of the leaf tissues which contained them—a process known as decortication—and the hanks of fiber were hung in the sun to dry. Some of it was dried artificially by machines. For its rope and cordage requirements, Irish Ropes bought sun-dried sisal from some sixty different estates through a single agent.

A typical sisal yarn was spun by twisting together about fifty fibers, and the yarns in turn were twisted into strands. In the technology of ropemaking, it was recognized that higher tensile strength and regularity could be achieved in the finished cordage if thinner fibers and thinner strands and more of them were used to form the cord. Thus, four thin yarns produced considerably higher performance qualities than two thick ones.

In the interests of securing high quality materials, Mr. Eric Rigby-

Jones, in his day, had visited Tanganyika, and there he recognized the possibilities of spinning fine yarns from sisal. Sisal fibers varied in thickness depending on the age of the plant at the time of cutting, the first cutting of young sisal producing fibers which, although shorter, were much thinner. These fine fibers had previously been blended into the total mix. Mr. Eric Rigby-Jones made arrangements to purchase fine fibers as a separately graded classification. These fine fibers he used to produce light twines of high tensile strength, fine soft webbing, and light sisal cloth, used for buffing and filter cloths.

Sun-dried sisal varied considerably in natural color, in hues that ranged from white to golden buff. In rope production, this was of no concern, but for purposes of color control in the making of Tintawn carpeting the delicate hues and brilliant shades required a natural color that was as uniform and as white as possible. The fineness of the fiber also had a direct effect upon the dyeing. No dye penetrated into the sisal fibers, but only spread itself upon the surface. Since coarse fibers had less total surface to receive the dye, a heavier coating and a deeper shade would result from the application of the same amount of dye. The grade and fineness of fiber, therefore, became a critical matter in color control.

Shipments were received every four or five weeks on ships which sailed directly from Africa into the Port of Dublin. Since the sources of its supplies were so far distant, purchasing requirements were budgeted six months in advance, and a stock of about 1,000 tons of fiber (about a ten week supply) was kept on hand.

RESEARCH AND DEVELOPMENT

"What we need in our company," said Mr. Michael Rigby-Jones, "is more science and engineering rather than to have our operation depend on brute labor." In keeping with this aim, Irish Ropes had on its staff a chemist and a physicist.

Mr. Morrish, the chemist, concerned himself with two principal activities: the dyeing of the fibers which went into Tintawn and the lubrication and rot-proofing of ropes and cordages. In the dyeing of carpeting fibers, Mr. Morrish was attempting to achieve uniform color standards. Since this depended on the type of dye used and on the fineness of the fibers, Mr. Morrish had the routine responsibility for purchasing dyes, for the operation of the dyehouse, and for the inspection of incoming fine grade sisal and the selection of the choicest materials for use in carpeting. Aside from this, Mr. Morrish worked on the development of rot-proofing treatment for ropes, mildew preventives, and rodent repellents. Except on polished twines, however, most cordages and ropes continued to be treated with a refined creosote type of coal tar distillate that was used throughout the rope industry, because rope and twine customers related the pungent coal tar odors to a "treated" rope.

Until 1960, Mr. MacCarvill, the physicist, had been in charge of all quality controls on ropes and cordages. This included routine checks on tensile strengths, the regularity and the twists in yarns, and the turns in ropes. Mr. MacCarvill said that there was actually very little that might be done by way of research on ropes. He had done some work on hardness of ropes and improving their resistance to torsion, and he had succeeded in developing a very light sisal core for wire ropes by using three times as many as the usual nine yarns in a wire rope core. In the summer of 1960, Mr. MacCarvill was relieved of all other duties to permit him to devote his full time to the development of sisal-reinforced plastics.

Fiberglass, the principal material used as a plastics reinforcement, provided tremendous strength, often more than was needed. Sisal did not give as much strength, but cost only $\frac{1}{3}$ as much as fiberglass and had certain mechanical properties that were advantageous.

Sisal reinforcing was either chopped fibers, woven, or a chemically bonded web. Irish Ropes would have preferred to sell fabricators the chopped sisal, but this was a low-cost product, no technical knowledge was needed to produce it, and it was believed that eventually competitors would drive prices down to unprofitable levels. The woven form was attractive, because it had a high labor content, but it presented technical problems. The Irish Ropes management chose to develop the chemically bonded form, a material like felt, which was formed by blowing the fiber on a moving conveyor, saturating it with an adhesive, and drying it out. The firm was currently investing £25,000 ($70,000) in machinery to produce the reinforced plastic, not with the intention of going into the production of fabricated products but to give the company a more practical knowledge of the use of the materials in action.

Sisal-reinforced plastics were used extensively in the United States but not in England. Mr. MacCarvill traveled extensively in the Brit-

ish Isles trying to sell the idea to technical and research people. He
was the only one in the company making this initial sales effort; the
regular salesmen did not handle plastics. "In making this effort," said
Mr. MacCarvill, "we are in the position of little Irish Ropes trying to
arouse the interest of big British industries."

THE INCENTIVE SCHEME

Irish Ropes employed about 400 production workers, most of whom
were classed as unskilled and who did routine machine tending which
could be taught to them in about four weeks. A few, however, who
worked on the weaving of Tintawn carpeting, were rated as highly
skilled and required about six months' training. All permanent employees worked under the incentive "scheme."

In most cases, a machine operator spent about 10% of his time
loading his machine and 90% of his time watching it and tying knots
to mend any breaks in the yarn. This was known as a 10% work load.
The aim of the management was to increase the work load up to about
80%. To achieve this end, the plant layout had been changed several
times to reposition the machines so that a single man could tend more
machines. The result was that men worked in gangs, with three or
four men tending six to ten machines. Every operator could increase
his efficiency by quicker loading and unloading; by anticipating
trouble by watching the material he was using, looking for slubs and
knots; and by developing dexterity in tying knots to mend breaks.
The latter skills were important, because they reduced the "down
time" of his machine.

Efficiency was measured in pounds or tons of product per machine
per hour, which was translated into standard minutes. Bonus payments began at 70% of standard, and the bonus increased up to 110%,
which was the top limit. The average bonus payment for the factory
as a whole was 105%. No one consistently earned under 90%. The
typical man's weekly rate was £6/18/10 ($19.44), and the average
bonus (at 105%) was £1/18/- ($5.32). The typical female weekly rate
was £4/9/6 ($12.53), and the average bonus (at 105%) was 24/-
($3.36). The bonus was paid only for work that measured up to quality
standards, with carpeting inspected 100%, and cordage spot-checked. The
company's annual payroll of about £220,000 ($616,000) included base

rate payments of about £175,000 ($490,000) above which it paid incentive bonuses of £45,000 ($126,000).

The bonus scheme had first been installed by the late Eric Rigby-Jones, who had used consultants to advise him, and the consultants had been re-employed several times to bring the rates up to date. After the initial study, it was estimated that productivity increased between 25% and 50%; after the second study, it increased another 15%. Management attached great importance to the work study department. Two work study officers and two work study assistants spent their full time on production planning, work study, and costing. In reply to the suggestion that in view of the shortage of jobs in Ireland and the prevailing low levels of wages the incentive bonus might be unnecessary, the management of Irish Ropes replied that it believed that the company benefited from the scheme in a number of ways. Less close supervision was needed; Irish Ropes' wages were good, and a job there was attractive; the company obtained high production and at the same time retained the good will of its employees; labor turnover was low and the quality of its employees was high. There was a great amount of interest in the bonus scheme at all levels of the organization.

ORGANIZATION

The Managing Director. Mr. Michael Rigby-Jones, the managing director, was thirty-four years old and had been the chief executive of the company since the age of twenty-five when his father, Eric, had passed away unexpectedly. Michael had learned the rope business under the tutelage of his father. "I think that my training under my father was especially good," said Michael. "He was harder on me than he was on anyone else. In fact, there were times when he was so demanding that I felt he had no confidence in me, and often I was on the verge of leaving, but now I'm grateful for that. I like the idea of family interest. I think it's good, as long as succession is on the basis of merit. I worry some about my own succession. I don't know what the company would do for a successor to me today. I don't know what I'd do if I deliberately set out to arrange for one."

Mr. Michael Rigby-Jones was described by his associates as a man "absolutely dedicated to his work." "He seems unaware of hours," said one of his executives, "and calls on the directors at any hour of the day or night. He not only observes our regular hours of work, but he usually exceeds them, starting early rather than late, taking a short dinner hour, and remaining past quitting time. He makes no demands upon us to do the same, but the spirit is infectious. And he is forever coming in in the morning with thoughts that he had last night about some current problem, or an idea that occurred to him that morning while he was shaving. Sometimes I wonder," mused the executive, "whether it's good for a man to be so dedicated to his work."

The Irish Ropes official Management Manual listed seventeen principal duties to be discharged by the managing director. In addition to drafting major policies, making long and short range plans, meeting with committees, and the general administration of the company's affairs, the list included a number of other functions which Mr. Rigby-Jones dispatched in person. He controlled all capital expenditures of the company; he purchased the company's requirements of sisal and other principal raw materials; he conducted major negotiations with the Trade Unions; he selected, appointed, transferred, and dismissed senior staff personnel; he fixed salaries and office wages; he took over the duties of any of the three functional managing directors when they were absent; his approval was required on selling prices; he examined forecasts, plans, and budgets prepared by each functional controller; he represented the company in public; and he took part in national affairs and in the Irish Management Institute.

"It bothers me," said Mr. Rigby-Jones, "that as we grow I am getting to be too loaded with work to give my attention to many things. I used to walk through the factory every day, but now I am often too busy to take the time. Not long ago, my staff executives hired two staff men—a physicist and an accountant—without my participation while I was away. It's all right, they had my approval . . . I know I ought to delegate more . . . but it gives me the feeling that things are slipping out of my hands."

The executive staff, consisting of the managing director, Mr. Roche, Mr. Shiel, and Mr. Carter, met in Mr. Rigby-Jones' office every Monday, Wednesday, and Friday morning for about forty-five minutes to discuss any matters of major concern. The production committee, consisting of the managing director, the works manager, the production manager, and the works engineer, met in Mr. Rigby-Jones' office every

exhibit 2

Map Showing Areas throughout the World Reached by the Products of Irish Ropes, Ltd.

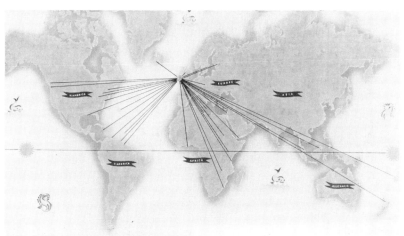

Tuesday morning. On Thursday, Mr. Rigby-Jones met with the general sales manager and the production manager. On Thursday, he also met with the technical staff consisting of the works manager, the chemist, and the physicist. "My father used to have one general meeting every day," said Mr. Rigby-Jones, "but I thought that this was overdone. I once thought that we ought to have a wider crossing of all of our people, and I had as many as twenty lower staff people in on meetings, but this led to too many disputes about who was invited to meetings and who was left out."

Mr. Rigby-Jones believed that his staff executives ought to consider it their official duty to take part in civic, social, and national affairs. "We are a small country," said Mr. Rigby-Jones, "and business leaders are scarce. We ought to help wherever we can." Mr. Rigby-Jones and his staff executives made speeches and took an active part in town affairs, fraternal functions, and made themselves available to the government. They were one of the leading sponsors of the Irish Management Institute and were willing to support any effort to raise the standards of Irish business generally. They were national leaders, for example, in the use of management consultants, but Mr. Rigby-Jones felt that any such advisors had necessarily to take into account the social, political, and economic climate in which an Irish businessman operated. "The American professors," he said, "who come over here

exhibit 3 **IRISH ROPES LIMITED**
Balance sheet as of 31st August, 1959

	1959		1958	
	Authorized	Issued and Fully Paid	Authorized	Issued and Fully Paid
Share capital:				
75,000 5% Cumulative preference shares of £1 each	£ 75,000 ($210,000)	£ 60,000 ($168,000)	£ 75,000 ($210,000)	£ 60,000 ($168,000)
350,000 Ordinary shares, of £1 each	350,000 (980,000)	210,000 (588,000)	350,000 (980,000)	210,000 (588,000)
	£425,000 ($1,190,000)	£270,000 ($756,000)	£425,000 ($1,190,000)	£270,000 ($756,000)
Surplus and reserves:				
Reserve for contingencies		£100,000 ($280,000)		£ 85,000 ($238,000)
Stock reserve		60,000 (168,000)		60,000 (168,000)
Profit and loss appropriation account		31,219 (87,413)		27,613 (77,316)
		£191,219 ($535,413)		£172,613 ($483,316)
Depreciation and replacement reserve:		£388,856 ($1,088,797)		£347,928 ($974,198)
Future taxation:		£ 24,000 ($ 67,200)		£ 21,700 ($ 60,760)
		£874,075 ($2,447,410)		£812,241 ($2,274,274)

Fixed assets at cost price:

	£	$	£	$
Property and buildings	134,172	(375,681)	133,922	(374,982)
Plant, machinery and motor vehicles	325,156	(910,437)	300,648	(841,814)
Total fixed assets	£459,328	($1,286,118)	£434,570	($1,216,796)
Current assets:				
Stock in trade as certified by managing director	£207,622	($581,342)	£234,467	($656,508)
Sundry debtors and debit balances Less: Reserve for bad debts and discounts	152,905	(428,134)	97,910	(274,148)
Investments at cost less reserve	8,246	(23,088)	8,221	(23,019)
Cash at bank and in hand	113,502	(317,806)	88,053	(246,548)
Total current assets	£482,275	($1,350,370)	£428,651	($1,200,223)
Less—current liabilities:				
Sundry creditors, current taxation and accrued charges	£ 55,738	($156,066)	£ 39,794	($111,423)
Proposed dividends (after deduction of income tax):				
On 5% cumulative preference shares	1,028	(2,878)	981	(2,747)
Final on ordinary shares	10,762	(30,134)	10,205	(28,574)
Total current liabilities	£ 67,528	($189,078)	£ 50,980	($142,744)
Net current assets	£414,747	($1,161,292)	£377,671	($1,057,479)
	£874,075	($2,447,410)	£812,241	($2,274,275)

exhibit 4   IRISH ROPES LIMITED

Profit and loss account for the year ended 31st August, 1959 (rounded to nearest dollar)

	1959		1958	
Profit on trading	£67,858	$190,003	£62,796	$175,829
Add: Transfer fees	13	36	10	28
	£67,871	$190,039	£62,806	$175,857
Deduct: Directors' fees	1,000	2,800	1,000	2,800
	£66,871	$187,239	£61,806	$173,057
Deduct: Provision for taxation	28,500	79,800	27,000	75,600
Net profit	£38,371	$107,439	£34,806	$ 97,457
Add: Balance forward from last year	27,613	77,316	31,493	88,180
Amount available for appropriation:	£65,984	$184,755	£66,299	$185,637
Appropriated as follows:				
Reserves:				
Contingencies	£15,000	$ 42,000	£20,000	$ 56,000
Dividends after deduction of income tax:				
5% Cumulative preference shares:				
For half-year ended 28th February, 1959	997	2,792	938	2,626
Proposed for half-year ended 31st August, 1959	1,028	2,878	981	2,747
Ordinary shares:				
Interim of 5%	6,978	19,538	6,562	18,374
Proposed final of 7½%	10,762	30,134	6,803	19,048
Bonus of 2½%	—	—	3,402	9,526
	£19,765	$ 55,342	£18,686	$ 52,321
Balance carried forward as per balance sheet:	31,219	87,413	27,613	77,316
	£65,984	$184,755	£66,299	$185,637

and tell us how to run our business irk me. Their answer to most any problem is to tell us how General Motors does it. For us that is no answer at all. And I often have the feeling that they have never personally come near an actual business in operation."

Management Directors and Staff. "One of my chief concerns," said Mr. Rigby-Jones, "is the excessive turnover we have in our younger

exhibit 5 **IRISH ROPES LIMITED**
Selected financial data (in thousands)

Year	Fixed Assets		Working Capital		Total Invested Capital[1]		Net Profit[2]		% Yield on Total Invested Capital
1948	£127.2	$ 356.4	£108.8	$ 304.8	£183.9	$ 484.9	£ 8.7	$ 24.5	4.1
1949	151.5	424.2	132.5	370.9	220.8	618.2	40.0	112.1	18.1
1950	162.8	455.9	171.3	479.6	237.9	722.1	43.3	121.3	17.0
1951	180.2	504.5	212.1	593.9	301.3	843.6	47.0	131.6	15.6
1952[3]	205.6	575.6	298.3	835.2	396.0	1,108.8	13.0	36.5	3.3
1953	244.8	685.4	309.5	866.7	404.9	1,133.6	41.5	116.1	10.2
1954	258.8	724.8	345.0	966.1	410.8	1,150.2	41.4	115.9	10.0
1955	300.5	841.4	347.8	913.7	409.2	1,145.7	33.5	93.8	8.2
1956	359.2	1,005.7	334.0	935.2	411.2	1,151.3	30.7	86.0	7.4
1957	386.2	1,081.4	353.8	990.6	426.0	1,192.8	42.3	118.4	9.9
1958	434.6	1,216.8	356.0	996.7	442.5	1,231.0	34.8	97.5	8.8
1959	459.3	1,286.1	390.7	1,094.1	461.1	1,291.1	38.4	107.4	8.7

[1] Excluding depreciation reserve.
[2] After taxes and directors' fees.
[3] After new capital issue of 105,000 ordinary shares at £1 per share ($2.80).

exhibit 6   IRISH ROPES LIMITED
Summary of accounts (in thousands)

Year	Sales		Raw Materials		Wages Salaries		Operating Expenses	
1948	£ 473.2	$1,325.0	£314.3	$ 880.0	£ 75.3	$210.8	£ 53.5	$149.8
1949	574.7	1,609.2	354.7	993.2	84.9	237.7	50.9	142.5
1950	715.3	2,002.8	472.4	1,322.7	95.5	267.4	57.3	160.4
1951	1,021.0	2,858.8	734.0	2,055.2	110.0	308.0	75.2	210.6
1952	827.4	2,316.7	600.2	1,680.6	95.3	266.8	81.4	227.9
1953	805.3	2,254.8	475.5	1,331.4	118.4	331.5	104.3	292.0
1954	879.9	2,463.7	506.5	1,418.2	151.1	423.1	115.8	324.2
1955	922.0	2,581.6	520.3	1,456.8	160.3	448.8	139.1	389.5
1956	945.5	2,647.4	517.9	1,450.1	183.6	514.1	146.8	411.0
1957	990.2	2,772.6	504.9	1,413.7	207.7	581.6	169.5	474.6
1958	1,024.7	2,869.2	524.5	1,468.6	229.2	641.8	170.3	476.8
1959	1,084.2	3,035.8	567.8	1,589.8	241.1	675.1	166.7	466.8

staff people. It seems that we have half a dozen changes every year. People are eager to join us because we have a good reputation, but in spite of this we have difficulty getting good staff people, who are very scarce in this small land. People join us, stay for a year or two, and then leave us for something better. I would not like to see my company become a training academy for others, or my staff jobs become something that people take on to enhance personal careers." (See Exhibit 7.)

Lack of trained staff people and specialists was a chronic problem that Mr. Rigby-Jones felt might never be solved. There were no people of staff caliber in Newbridge, only a few in Dublin, and fewer in the rest of Ireland. Soliciting in England was unsatisfactory, because no Englishman would care to emigrate to the poorer living conditions in Ireland, and certainly not to Newbridge, which was barren of social and recreational facilities.

Mr. Rigby-Jones felt that staff people with other companies in Ireland took advantage of their own scarcity. "With our protectionist policy," he said, "they hide behind tariff walls and are free to make shoddy goods and take life easy. It is not uncommon for many Dublin

exhibit 6 (continued)

Depreciation		Dividends		Taxes		Retained	
£11.0	$ 30.8	£ 4.4	$12.3	£10.3	$ 28.8	£ 4.4	$ 12.3
13.1	36.7	6.0	16.8	31.1	87.1	34.1	95.5
14.4	40.3	6.1	17.1	32.4	90.7	37.3	104.4
17.3	48.4	6.1	17.1	37.5	105.0	40.9	114.5
19.4	54.3	8.8	24.6	19.6	54.9	2.7	7.6
22.1	61.9	11.7	32.8	43.5	121.8	29.7	83.2
24.1	67.5	15.0	42.0	41.5	116.2	25.9	72.5
27.4	76.7	15.0	42.0	41.5	116.2	18.5	51.8
32.5	91.0	15.0	42.0	34.0	95.2	15.7	44.0
33.9	94.9	18.3	51.2	32.0	89.6	24.0	67.2
38.9	108.9	18.7	52.4	27.0	75.6	16.1	45.1
41.8	117.0	19.8	55.4	28.5	79.8	18.6	52.1

managers to make their working day from ten to three, to take two hours for lunch, and to go off fishing in mid-day."

Lack of supply of adequate foremen was also a chronic problem. Most of the company's foremen had been brought up from the ranks. Almost every one of them had numerous relatives among the employees, and few of them realized the importance of keeping their distance from their subordinates. The typical foreman spent his evenings as a drinking companion of his workers in one of the town pubs, and this familiarity made discipline difficult to maintain in the factory.

"I think that one of the first serious mistakes I made after my father died," said Mr. Michael Rigby-Jones, "was to choose all young men on my management staff. I was only twenty-five at the time, and I had the idea, perhaps unconsciously, that young men would be easier to control. Now I am wondering whether I would not have done better to choose a few older men of seasoned judgment."

Mr. Bernard Roche, the sales director, had one of the longest records of seniority with the company. He had joined the company in 1936 as director following upon a partial merger with his family busi-

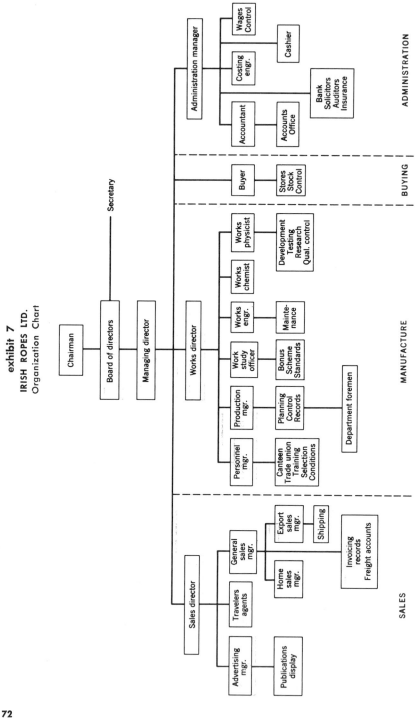

exhibit 7
IRISH ROPES LTD.
Organization Chart

Chairman

Board of directors ——— Secretary

Managing director

Works director

ADMINISTRATION

Administration manager

Wages Control

Costing engr.

Cashier

Accountant

Accounts Office

Bank
Solicitors
Auditors
Insurance

BUYING

Buyer

Stores Stock Control

MANUFACTURE

Works physicist

Works chemist

Development Testing Research Qual. control

Works engr.

Maintenance

Work study officer

Bonus Scheme Standards

Production mgr.

Planning Control Records

Department foremen

Personnel mgr.

Canteen Trade union Training Selection Conditions

SALES

Sales director

General sales mgr.

Export sales mgr.

Shipping

Home sales mgr.

Invoicing records Freight accounts

Travelers agents

Advertising mgr.

Publications display

exhibit 8

(a) Aerial View of Factory at Newbridge

(b) Preparing Sisal Fiber for Spinning   *(c) New 12-foot Loom. This loom is the first of its kind in the world and is capable of weaving sisal carpet of superb quality up to 12 feet in width.*

ness. He had early shown a talent for salesmanship and an aptitude for dealing with people, and soon became the company's sales manager. "I am the general manager of all sales activities," said Mr. Roche, "but more and more over the years my time is being taken up by matters of general administration of the company." Mr. Roche was influential in most major planning and policy decisions, and he acted as managing director in the absence of Mr. Rigby-Jones, who, in turn, acted as sales director when Mr. Roche was away. Mr. Rigby-Jones also assumed the duties of any other of the senior executives, such as the works manager, or the administration manager, when they were absent—a practice made necessary by the fact that there were no "back-ups" in assistants who could temporarily handle these responsibilities.

Mr. Arthur Shiel, an accredited accountant, was secretary of the company and administration manager, and had also been with the company many years, having served as accountant before his election to his present offices. As secretary, Mr. Shiel handled the company's share capital. Over-all finances were handled jointly by him and Mr. Rigby-Jones. As administration manager, he had many responsibilities; he personally managed the headquarters office and set up and supervised clerical procedures. Accounting and credit control, also Mr. Shiel's responsibility, were handled by Mr. Nally, the company's accountant. The company's tax returns were filed by its firm of auditors, working with Mr. Shiel, and the auditors also handled the employees' payroll tax deductions in the same manner. Mr. Shiel supervised inventory records, which were kept by the works manager. He also supervised dividend payments, which were made by the company's registrar. Legal matters were first referred to him for transmission, if necessary, to the company's solicitor. He personally supervised the insurance program, payroll, pension fund, and personnel records.

Most of the other staff personnel, with a few exceptions, were younger men, none of whom had been with the company very long. Mr. Gerard Byrnes coordinated domestic sales, by correspondence, under the direction of Mr. Roche. Mr. Patrick Brady, the buyer, had previously been a stock record clerk, and he still performed the record-keeping function for the fiber buying, the actual buying of fiber being done by Mr. Rigby-Jones. The works manager, Mr. Carter, who had been with the company less than a year, performed the duties of the former works director, but he was not a member of the board of directors. Mr. Patrick Jones, the general sales manager, and Mr. Miles Byrne, the export sales manager, were both new in their positions, and both of them, as well as Mr. Gerard Byrnes, the home sales manager, worked under the direct supervision of Mr. Roche. The work study officers, the works engineer, the chemist, and the physicist all reported to the works manager. All of them were in their late twenties or early thirties; none had been with the company very long.

Because there was a shortage of adequate housing in Newbridge, the company had, years ago, renovated a building which had been the British Army Hospital and used it to house staff personnel. In the company's early years, Mr. Eric Rigby-Jones, Mr. Roche, Mr. Shiel, and other staff members lived there. In 1952, the company built four modern residences on land it owned just outside Newbridge. The group represented an investment of £16,400 ($45,920) on the part of the company. They were tenanted by Mr. Shiel, Mr. Carter, the production manager, and the company physicist, who paid an annual rent of £143 ($300), which was about 60% of the going rate set by the County. In 1957, the company built at a cost of £9,000 ($25,200) a "hostel" for those of its staff members who were bachelors or who had not been able to find accommodation for their families in Newbridge. The men lived there on a self-governing basis, sharing the cost of room and board and the salary of the housekeeper-cook. Since the company made no charge for rent to hostel residents, the resulting rates were nominal. A typical monthly charge for room and meals was about £10 ($28). The hostel was modern and well-appointed, but the residents felt some dissatisfaction at being forced into association with their fellow staff members both during and outside of working hours. Table conversations tended to be dominated by rope and carpet themes. In 1960, the company was building a second group of residences at a net cost to Irish Ropes of £16,150 ($45,240) which were to be rented to staff men at the same rate as the existing houses.

The Board of Directors. Mr. Arthur Cox, chairman of the Board of Directors, was, except for the Rigby-Jones family, the largest stockholder in Irish Ropes. Mr. Cox had been associated with the company ever since it began doing business in Ireland, when Mr. Eric Rigby-Jones had engaged him as solicitor for the company. A man of means, he headed a law firm in Dublin and was reputed to be a brilliant attorney. He was solicitor in Ireland for Sir Winston Churchill, and Bernard Shaw had also been his client. "Mr. Cox never imposes his opinions upon us," said Mr. Michael Rigby-Jones. "This might be a blessing, but at times I find it a trial. It leaves the burden of all of the critical decisions to me."

Mr. Patrick Doyle, a director who was a minority stockholder, was one of the company's traveling men and was now nearing retirement age. Mr. H. E. Guinness was a merchant banker and was on the boards of other leading Irish companies. Capt. T. B. Murphy, an engineer who had formerly been works director, had resigned as works director and as a board member simultaneously and had not been replaced. Mr. Michael Rigby-Jones and Mr. Roche constituted the remaining membership of the board.

NORTHERN LUMBER DEALERS SUPPLY COMPANY

As he drove to the offices of the Northern Lumber Dealers Supply Company, Roy Freemont mentally reviewed the information contained in a folder in his brief case. Since his promotion in July to the position of district sales manager for Arnett-Townson, a large manufacturer of builders' supplies, Freemont had called upon almost all of the wholesalers in his district.

During the first week in September, Freemont had scheduled a meeting for October 3, 1966, with Jerry Perkins, general manager of the Northern Lumber Dealers Supply Company. From the notes left in the file by his predecessor, Freemont recalled that Jerry Perkins shared the management of Northern with his cousin, James Hayward. Perkins worked as office manager, purchasing agent, warehouse manager, and bookkeeper, and his cousin Hayward performed similar duties in addition to acting as sales manager.

During the depression of the 1930's, the fathers of the two cousins started the Northern Supply Company with a very limited amount of capital. In 1939, the ill health of the senior Hayward forced him to leave the business. Both Jim Hayward and Jerry Perkins joined the firm after they got out of the service following World War II. The senior Perkins died in 1949, and that year the two cousins took over complete management of the firm.

Freemont noted that Northern was the only Arnett-Townson wholesaler in that urban area; Capital Supply, the other A-T wholesaler, went bankrupt in 1964. He also noted that during the last five years Northern had experienced a slight decline in sales (see Exhibit 1, 1961 to 1966 income statements). The folder also contained a note explaining that Northern owned its own land and buildings and borrowed sparingly from the bank (see Exhibit 2, 1961 to 1966 balance sheets).

In addition to Perkins and Hayward, the company employed one woman in the office who worked full-time as a bookkeeper, another woman who worked three days each week, a warehouse foreman, one truck driver, a part-time summer warehouseman and one salesman who spent almost all of his time on the road calling on accounts. Hayward divided his time between the office and selling on the road.

After he parked his car, Freemont went into the offices of the Northern Lumber Dealers Supply Company and met Jerry Perkins. After some introductory comments, Freemont asked Perkins if he would tell him a little more about Northern Supply. Perkins agreed, and after he finished taking care of a customer at the counter, they walked to a small private office and began to talk.

COMPETITION

Jerry began by commenting that the best way to characterize Northern Supply management was by their cautious waiting to see what was going to happen to their competitors. "This is about the most competitive town in the country. I don't think there is any such thing as a really intelligent competitor in this town. All they know is price competition, and they have sold that way for so long that they have educated the customer to shop for the best price. The results have been pretty drastic, because so many wholesalers around here have gone bankrupt, including Capital Supply, that there are only three of us left who are in direct competition. To give you an example, Central City is one half as large as this city but it supports 10 wholesalers. In effect, the local wholesalers cut their margins so low and waged such vicious fights over price that they just put themselves out of business."

Jerry went on to explain that both of Northern's competitors, each with sales of approximately $500,000 per year, were operating at a loss. In spite of losses, one continued to deliver almost everything to his customers at carload prices regardless of the quantities ordered. Jerry related a story about one of his competitors who offered to sell his business to an out-of-town buyer for $5,000 provided the buyer would take over receivables and payables. After a brief analysis of the books, the buyer allegedly refused to even consider the offer.

"One change that has occurred during the last few years," Perkins continued, "has been the drop in direct sales or direct billings. A few years ago we were doing almost half a million dollars a year in direct sales and now our direct sales are down to about $80,000 per year." He attributed most of the change to the increasing number of manufacturers who were willing to sell directly to the customer rather than bill the goods through the wholesaler. He indicated that two large cash-and-carry lumber and supply yards had obtained a sizable amount of business, but that most of the lumber yards in the area were either just getting by or actually operating at a loss. "Frankly, we lost a lot of customers who just could not make a profit, so they folded up."

SALES AND PROFITS

Before Jerry could answer Freemont's question about how Northern was performing in its market, he answered several telephone calls and waited on two more customers at the counter. When he returned he said, "We are getting by. Because we are flexible and willing to work hard, we have been able to hold out in this market. We have two trucks, for example, and on any given day or evening you may find me, Jim, or our salesman driving a truck making deliveries. We got into the delivery business in 1963, and this may help some. We are careful not to make unprofitable deliveries—the trucks don't go out of here with one little bundle on the back. By keeping our overhead low, working nights, and everybody working hard, we have been able to stay out of the red."

Jerry explained that because of the shift away from direct sales to more warehouse sales Northern had to increase its inventory and its product-handling activities. The net result was an increased gross profit but a decreased net profit as costs tended to increase. He attributed the 1963 drop in profits to the advent of a delivery service for the company and the 1964 and 1965 experiences to a wave of business failures which produced losses in excess of $10,000 in bad debts for Northern. He estimated, however, that Northern's net profit would probably rise from $8,000 to $10,000 in 1966.

Northern supplied goods to about 165 accounts, mostly lumber yards and building specialty accounts. The largest account purchased about $22,000 worth of goods per year and the next largest about $17,000. The remainder of the accounts were relatively small. He stated that an average month would yield sales divided roughly as follows:

Products	Sales	Approximate gross margins %
Ceiling panels	$ 8,200	11–18
Insulated board	2,700	4–10
Masonite products	21,000	15
Marlite	4,000	20–25
Roofing material	10,000	12
Asbestos	1,300	16–20
Gypsum	1,600	10
Finishes	600	20–25
Floor tile	2,400	20
Metal products	3,300	20
Cedar products	7,100	20
Insulation	4,400	10
Direct sales	6,600	5

Another factor that influenced Northern's profit experience was the institution in 1963 of an insurance and profit-sharing plan, which cost almost $7,000 per year. Jerry commented that the cash value of the insurance was beginning to increase and would begin to improve the appearance of the balance sheet within the next few years.

SOME PROPOSALS

Jerry stated that he and his cousin did not know which way to go. "We don't know whether to get larger or smaller. Right now we are just watching our competitors and waiting to see what happens to them. It looks like they may go out of business, and if they do, we may be able to get a bigger share of the local market, which we estimate to total about $2 million per year."

Jerry explained that Northern would like to increase its profits but that neither he nor his cousin were sure how to do it. He stated that he listened to every salesman who came in, hoping that he could find another good line which would require no more than a $35,000 to $45,000 investment in inventory but would improve sales and profits.

"We do not want to go into hardware, because that is a little out of our line, but we would like to take on some more sheet goods lines, which are what we are best equipped to handle. We have been thinking about taking on a line of plywood, because it is a high-volume, high-turnover item, but its profits are a little unpredictable.

"One thing that we are trying to do," Jerry continued, "is to increase our margins on sales to individuals who are either sent here by a retailer or who just walk in off the street. We have two price lists, a retail and a wholesale price, and any individual who comes in to buy something pays cash and pays the retail price. The dealers were sending customers to us for goods which they did not have. In effect, we were expected to perform all the services and do all the work for the very low markup we realize on most of our products. In July we did about $3,000 worth of retail business, and it is increasing every month. The dealers don't like it, but we almost have to do it to stay alive."

Jerry continued his discussion of direct selling to individuals by stating that both he and his cousin had been looking for a retail outlet of some kind for their products. They envisioned a cash-and-carry type store, but one which provided more services than are normally provided by cash-and-carrys. He predicted that they would probably have to put up their own buildings, because they had not been able to find a structure which exactly suited their idea of what the store should look like.

The conversation between the two men closed with Jerry's mentioning that he had a lot of questions about the wholesale type of business in that particular area and in the country as a whole. He commented that he was not sure that the traditional wholesalers had much of a future unless they were willing to adopt new and somewhat revolutionary means of doing business. He expressed the idea that more and more of the wholesale function was being performed by large retail outlets that served as wholesalers and retailers.

Just before the two men said good-by, Jerry said, "Well, Roy, I have told you quite a bit about our business, since you have a real interest in how well we do because we do buy about 20% of our merchandise from Arnett-Townson. What's your opinion? Do you have any solutions for our problems?"

exhibit 1 NORTHERN LUMBER DEALERS SUPPLY COMPANY

Income statements, 1961–1966 (in thousands)

	(9 months) Sept. 30, 1966 Amount	Per cent	Dec. 31, 1965 Amount	Per cent	Dec. 31, 1964 Amount	Per cent	Dec. 31, 1963 Amount	Per cent	Dec. 31, 1962 Amount	Per cent	Dec. 31, 1961 Amount	Per cent
Sales	$654.9	100	$933.5	100	$1029.1	100	$935.0	100	$1032.4	100	$1055.3	100
Cost of goods	568.4		811.1		901.5		833.1		913.3		937.8	
Gross profit	$ 86.5	13.2	$122.4	13.1	$ 127.6	12.4	$101.9	12.7	$ 119.1	11.8	$ 117.5	11.1
Expenses:												
Executive salaries	$ 30.0	4.6	$ 44.1	4.8	$ 42.8	4.2	$ 41.6	4.3	$ 38.1	3.8	$ 36.3	3.4
Other salaries and wages	14.9	2.2	23.0	2.5	20.7	2.0	17.5	1.9	16.0	1.5	15.0	1.4
Traveling expenses	1.8		2.0		3.3		3.2		4.7		5.0	
Stationery and postage	1.7		1.6		2.1		2.0		1.8		1.6	
Telephone and telegraph									1.6			
Utilities	2.1		3.1		2.8		2.4		2.0		2.1	
Social security and unemployment insurance	1.7		1.8		1.6		1.3		1.3		1.3	
Professional services	1.2		.6		.9		1.9		1.3		1.1	
Real estate and property taxes	2.9		7.3		7.5		5.9		6.5		5.3	
Depreciation	6.5		9.5		11.5		10.7		8.3		7.6	
General insurance	1.6		2.5		2.1		2.1		2.0		1.7	
Hospital insurance	1.2											
Executive insurance	3.5		.6		2.2		1.9		1.3		2.1	
Auto expense	.3		.5		.6		.8		.9		.7	
Provision for bad debts	2.0		5.4		6.0				.5			
Freight	1.1		1.3		1.7		1.9		2.5		2.7	
Pension trust	3.7		4.8		4.9		4.6		4.3			
Lift truck and expenses	2.2		3.2		3.1		2.3					
Miscellaneous	1.6		3.8		3.8		2.8		2.3		2.8	

	$	%	$	%	$	%	$	%	$	%	$	%
Advertising	.1		.6		.7		.5		.5		.7	
Profit-sharing trust	......		.6		.6		1.1		1.2			
Donations	......		.3		.3		.5		.8		.8	
Total expenses	$ 80.1	12.2	$116.6	12.5	$119.2	11.6	$105.0	10.7	$ 96.9	9.7	$ 86.8	8.2
Net operating profit	6.4	1.0	5.8	.6	8.4	.8	14.9	1.6	22.2	2.1	30.7	2.9
Other income (expense)	(2.3)		(2.2)		(3.8)		(3.1)		(3.4)		(3.9)	
Profit before taxes	$ 4.1	.6	$ 3.6	.4	$ 4.6	.4	$ 11.8	1.2	$ 18.8	1.8	$ 26.8	2.8
Estimated income tax	$ 1.4	.4	$ 1.2	.3	$ 2.5	.2	$ 4.5	.8	$ 6.9	1.2	$ 9.8	1.6
Net income	$ 2.7	.4	$ 2.4	.3	$ 2.1	.2	$ 7.3	.8	$ 11.9	1.2	$ 17.0	1.6

exhibit **2**   **NORTHERN LUMBER DEALERS SUPPLY COMPANY**
Balance sheets, 1961–1966 (in thousands)

	Sept. 30, 1966 (9 months)	Dec. 31, 1965	Dec. 31, 1964	Dec. 31, 1963	Dec. 31, 1962	Dec. 31, 1961
Assets						
Current assets:						
Cash	$ 8.7	$ 5.9	$ 11.0	$ 16.0	$ 1.0	$ 4.6
Accounts receivable (less bad debt reserve)	77.5	92.5	98.1	101.9	107.3	114.1
Inventories	108.0	91.0	99.0	128.1	96.8	95.0
Unexpired insurance	5.6	3.2	2.6	3.0	3.6	2.5
Real estate tax deposit					1.3	1.2
Total current assets	$199.8	$192.6	$210.7	$249.0	$210.0	$217.4
Fixed assets:						
Land at cost	22.3	22.3	22.3	22.3	22.3	22.3
Buildings and equipment (less depreciation)	76.5	82.7	83.0	92.1	94.1	90.5
Cash surrender value life insurance	17.9	17.9	12.5	9.3	6.4	3.9
Total assets	$316.5	$315.5	$328.5	$372.7	$332.8	$334.1
Liabilities						
Current:						
Notes payable (bank)	$ 11.0	$ 11.0	$	$ 16.5	$ 16.5	$ 16.5
Stockholders' notes payable		3.3	3.3	7.7	7.7	7.7
Accounts payable	42.3	31.1	57.7	77.4	53.6	63.5
Mortgage payments (1 year)	4.9	3.8	3.5	3.3	3.5	3.1
Accruals	5.4	13.2	9.4	11.5	13.8	15.8
Total current liabilities	63.6	62.4	73.9	116.4	95.1	106.6
Fixed:						
Mortgage loan	29.4	32.4	36.3	38.1	28.8	30.3
Common stock	44.0	44.0	44.0	44.0	44.0	44.0
Preferred stock	114.4	114.4	114.4	114.4	114.4	46.1
Retained earnings	65.1	62.3	59.9	59.8	50.5	107.1
Total liabilities and capital	$316.5	$315.5	$328.5	$372.7	$332.8	$334.1

SOONER DISTRIBUTING COMPANY

Early in July, 1966, Mr. Richard Taylor, president of the Sooner Distributing Company, reviewed the results of his firm's business during the first six months of 1966. Sales for the Gordon Taylor Company, a Sooner Company subsidiary distributing floor products, were about $60,000 below the company's sales during the first six months of 1965. If the sales trend continued during the second half of the year, the consolidated operating statements for both companies would show a small loss during 1966 or, at best, only break even on a sales volume of about $4 million. His initial comment was "Ridiculous!" as he reviewed again both companies' profits for the preceding year. For the three years 1962 to 1965, the two companies earned a profit of less than 1% of sales. It seemed apparent to Dick Taylor that the impending decline in the Taylor Company sales for 1966 would make it almost impossible for the combined companies to show a profit. (See Exhibits 2 to 6 for operating statements. Exhibit 7 contains a study of 28 firms conducted by Western Rubber and Tile Company.)

Taylor's concern about the profits of his companies and the existing levels of sales prompted him once again to review the history, strategy, and effectiveness of his organizations in a search for weaknesses and possible opportunities.

BACKGROUND INFORMATION

In the increasing automobile population of the early 1900's, Gordon Taylor saw an opportunity for a new business in his home town of

85

Tulsa. In 1919 he opened the Sooner Distributing Company, a small wholesaling firm organized to distribute auto parts to the eastern and central Oklahoma territory. After World War I Mr. Taylor added a line of appliances. As appliance sales increased, the auto parts business declined and within a few years was eliminated completely. Except for the Depression years, the company grew steadily through its first 46 years of existence.

In 1939 Mr. Taylor accepted a franchise from the Western Rubber and Tile Company to sell their line of floor tile and linoleum. During World War II the Sooner Company distributed an extensive line of gas and electrical appliances, along with the new line of floor coverings.

Richard ("Dick") Taylor, the only child of Gordon Taylor, graduated from college in 1944. He began with the Sooner Company as a clerk and during the years that followed worked in almost every job in the organization. He became president of the company when his father died in 1955.

In 1946 the Sooner Distributing Company organized the Gordon Taylor Company as a wholly owned subsidiary. The Gordon Taylor Company distributed Western Rubber and Tile flooring products; the Sooner Company continued as an appliance distributor (see the organization chart in Exhibit 1). In 1966 Sooner was distributing TV and hi-fi sets, washing machines, refrigerators, and air conditioners, together with parts for each line.

ADMINISTRATIVE ORGANIZATION

When Dick Taylor took over as president of the Sooner Distributing Company, he owned well over 50% of the stock of the corporation. As president of the Sooner Company, he felt he could do his company the most good as an administrator and consequently directed most of his energy toward the administrative, organizational, personnel, and financial activities of the corporations. He stated that, in the position of top executive of his company, he did not feel he should contact dealers on a regular schedule or travel with the salesmen. He tried, however, to see every dealer who came into the offices. He attended as many dealer meetings as possible, although he stayed in the background. He knew many dealers, especially in the appliance field, on a personal basis and when a large promotion was on offered to have the salesmen bring their major accounts to his office for a conference.

Because of his background in the appliance business, Dick Taylor spent most of his time on matters pertaining to the Sooner Company. In 1964 he began to take a more active role in the Taylor Company as Burl Kavens, the president of the Gordon Taylor Company, approached retirement age. In 1965 Dick received $9,000 in salary from each company plus 10% of the total profits.

Although he was president of the Sooner Distributing Company, Dick Taylor assumed almost all of the financial and administrative responsibilities of the Gordon Taylor Company. The two companies operated with a single manager, controller, and clerical staff under the supervision of Dick Taylor.

In 1966, at the age of 69, Burl Kavens finished his 45th year with the company. He had played a major role in the decision to accept the Western Rubber and Tile line of products in 1939. From 1939 until the Gordon Taylor Company was organized in 1946, he functioned as the sales manager for the floor products. When the Gordon Taylor Company was organized, he was appointed president by Mr. Gordon Taylor. He had innumerable friends throughout the industry in both retailing and manufacturing circles. His relationships with dealers were described as being exceptionally close and cordial. Although he was president of the Gordon Taylor Company, his primary duties were those of sales manager, because most of the other administrative and financial aspects of the company were handled by Dick Taylor. Burl received $13,000 per year and 8% of the combined companies' profits.

In 1957 when the Tulsa branch was opened, Burl Kavens and Dick Taylor selected Neal Nelson to operate the branch and to begin training for the position of sales manager when Burl retired. His official title was that of sales manager; however, he actually functioned as branch manager. In 1965 Neal's salary was increased to $10,000 per year plus 2% of the profits, and he was given the position of vice president.

Only the sales organizations of the two companies were completely separate; salesmen in the Gordon Taylor Company did not sell appliances, or Sooner salesmen flooring products. Selling costs were recorded separately, but all other operating and administrative costs were combined and then divided between the two companies at the end of the year on the basis of sales volume (see Exhibit 5).

SALES AND COMPETITION

The sales organization of the Gordon Taylor Company included Burl Kavens, president of the Gordon Taylor Company; Neal Nelson, vice

president; and seven salesmen divided between the Oklahoma City and
Tulsa offices. The Sooner Distributing Company also employed seven
salesmen in the two offices. The two company presidents, Taylor and
Kavens, had their offices in Tulsa, while the two vice presidents, Neal
Nelson (Gordon Taylor Company) and Carl Harrison (Sooner Com-
pany—appliances), were located in Oklahoma City.

In 1956 the Western Rubber and Tile Company granted permission
to Sooner to open a branch in Oklahoma City. At that time Western
flooring products were being distributed by the Oklahoma City Furniture and Supply Company, an old firm that distributed a large number
of furniture and hardware products. Because floor coverings was only
one of many lines which Oklahoma City Supply handled and thus was
viewed as a minor activity for the company, Western decided to allow
the Taylor Company to open a branch in the same city. The Taylor
Company wished to open a branch not only because they realized the
potential of the area, but because they knew of internal dissension
within the Oklahoma City Furniture Company management and the
possibility of that firm's discontinuing business.

The Sooner Distributing Company and the Taylor Company rented
a warehouse which they stocked with both floor coverings and appliances. The Taylor Company assigned three salesmen to the warehouse
early in 1957 to begin calling on accounts. The annual sales of flooring
materials during the ensuing years were as follows:

Oklahoma City

1957	$260,000	1962	$772,000
1958	380,000	1963	884,000
1959	608,000	1964	890,000
1960	635,000	1965	925,000
1961	678,000	1966	815,000 (estimated)

Each of the salesmen received a monthly payment of $750 out of
which he paid his expenses. In addition, each salesman was eligible
for a bonus which had ranged from $2,000 to $3,000 per year during
the period 1963 to 1965. The drop in sales during the first half of
1966 would probably have the effect of greatly reducing or eliminating
1966 bonuses. The present method of making a monthly payment to
each salesman that included both salary and expense allowances was
introduced in January, 1966. The new compensation program for the
Gordon Taylor salesmen was inaugurated because of the steady increases in the size of salesmen's expense accounts. The program was

already in effect for Sooner's salesmen. Many of the salesmen did not like the new plan, although there was no indication that it would reduce their actual monthly income. Dick Taylor thought that the company might lose one or possibly two salesmen at the end of 1966, particularly if there was no year-end bonus.

The Gordon Taylor Company had 825 to 875 active flooring accounts, which were serviced by seven salesmen. Of the total active accounts, 500 accounts signed a seasonal contract to buy a designated amount of goods from the Taylor Company. The 20 largest dealers were responsible for 60 to 70% of the Taylor Company's sales, and about one-third of the accounts that signed seasonal contracts purchased $2,000 worth or more of flooring materials each year.

The average salesman for the Taylor Company called on slightly more than 100 accounts, plus calls on potential customers. The territories were so structured that it took approximately three weeks for a salesman to call on all of his accounts. Dick Taylor commented that he did not believe that his salesmen were able to spend the time necessary to dig out new accounts because of the size of their territories. In an attempt to motivate salesmen to make more intensive selling efforts and spend extra hours, the company began a campaign to increase the number of orders of $25 or more and the number of salesman calls.

The Taylor Company estimated that an average salesman would have to produce a sales volume of about $300,000 per year in order to meet all costs involved and provide a small profit. The 1965 sales volume for each of Taylor's salesmen was as follows:

1.	$303,000
2.	384,000
3.	457,000
4.	228,000
5.	295,000
6.	274,000
7.	254,000

The combined territories of the Taylor salesmen included almost all the counties in Oklahoma and a few adjacent counties in Kansas, Missouri, Arkansas, and Texas. The population of the counties totaled about 3.1 million, according to the 1960 census. Because the area was primarily agricultural, the population was undergoing some distinct changes. During the last few decades the average size of farms had increased fivefold, thus greatly reducing the number of farm homes in the territory. One county in the state had over 1,000 fewer farms than in 1940. Although there had been a 2 to 3% increase in population during the last decade, the rate of increase was one of the lowest for any state in the United States.

The geographical scattering of the population within the state tended to limit the effectiveness of the salesmen. The company estimated that their average salesman could make only about eight calls per day, because at least one third of his time was spent traveling.

Many of Taylor's customers were mechanics who left their jobs as floor tile layers in order to start a business of their own. For example, eight out of ten specialty floor tile stores within the city limits of Tulsa were owned by former floor tile layers. Although some of the tile layers became good businessmen, many of them were poorly trained and inept. Therefore, it was imperative that the sales force and management spend a certain amount of time in teaching their dealers simple and sound business principles.

Within the state of Oklahoma there were five Western Rubber and Tile distributors, including Taylor's two branches. In addition to the five distributors within the state, there were nine other Western distributors in adjoining states that sold some goods within Taylor's territory, particularly in the border counties.

Dick Taylor observed that competition had become much tougher as his competitors, both within the state and outside the state, had grown and become more aggressive. He attributed some of the increased competitiveness to the acceptance by his competitors of the specialty salesman concept. Most of his major competitors restructured their sales forces about 1960 to 1961 by designating and training their salesmen as specialty salesmen. As he reflected on the competitive situation within the state, Dick stated, "As the enemy deploys more and better-trained troops in the field, we have to meet them with more and better-trained troops." Because of increased competition, Taylor wanted to add an additional salesman but did not believe that either the existing sales level or sales potential would justify the increased costs. Dick was also afraid he would demoralize the sales force if he suggested dividing the area into more sales territories. Although competition was more intense, the Taylor Company had succeeded in holding 50% or more of the Western Rubber and Tile Company sales in Oklahoma (see Exhibit 8).

Both Taylor and Kavens believed that the most frustrated salesmen on the Taylor sales force were those working in and around Oklahoma

City, because of the competition they encountered there. Three years after Taylor opened its branch in Oklahoma City, the Oklahoma City Furniture and Supply Company sold its floor products business to the Rand Company, a carpeting wholesaler. The Rand Company deployed three salesmen in the area to match the three employed by Taylor. Dick Taylor estimated that the Rand Company's sales of hard-surface flooring products were only about half those of Taylor's Oklahoma City branch, yet they employed as many salesmen. He claimed that there were too many salesmen in the area for the amount of business and that the salesmen were actually only playing ring-around-a-rosy with each other as they chased the major accounts.

WAREHOUSING AND INVENTORY CONTROL

The Sooner Distributing Company owned a three-story building in Tulsa which housed the two companies' offices, appliance showrooms, service department, and some appliance warehouse space. The company had about $50,000 invested in the building, which was constructed some time before the turn of the century. The two floors and the basement of the building contained about 10,000 square feet of floor space. The top floor housed the executive and clerical offices, a display room, and some appliance storage area. The main floor housed the parts and repair division and some storage. The basement contained a small parts–storage area.

The company rented 13,000 square feet of space in a building immediately behind and adjoining the Sooner building. Flooring tile was stored in a basement room containing 4,500 square feet. A second-floor area containing 15,000 square feet was used as storage space for large appliances.

A small one-story building containing 10,000 square feet, some 50 feet behind the other rented building, was rented as a storage area for flooring sheet goods. A short railroad spur ran between the two buildings. One section of the sheet goods building was used for a small display room and provided office space for two women who processed orders and purchases.

All of the warehousing activities were performed by the warehouse manager, four full-time warehousemen, and one half-time worker. Three of the men were assigned to flooring materials, one was assigned to appliances, and the part-time worker divided his time between the two companies. The rental on each building averaged about 25¢ per square foot.

When an order for flooring materials was presented by a salesman or issued over the telephone, the warehouse manager or one of the girls in that office accepted the order. A four-copy work order was prepared immediately for use in filling the order. The order was numbered by a stamping machine when the processing of the order began. The original was a work copy; the second copy went to the customer; the third copy was called an office guard copy and was retained in the office for reference until the order had been processed and shipped; and the fourth copy served as a packing slip. The work copies were filed in numerical order, including any voided copies, which provided a check against misplaced orders.

A partial physical inventory of some goods was conducted almost every day. Thus, a complete inventory was conducted every two weeks. The results of the daily checks were compared with the inventory records kept in the main office. The company had no recorded pilferage losses of any significance.

Early in 1966 the Taylor Company began to search for another warehouse building in Oklahoma City. The established warehouse location contained 24,000 square feet of space, which was not adequate to meet the floor space requirements of the branch warehouse.

In July, 1966, the company rented a building which was located a few blocks from the old location. The building consisted of two floors and a basement, a railroad siding, and truck docks on both sides of the building. Like the Tulsa buildings, the Oklahoma City building had a lagre freight elevator. The building contained 47,000 square feet of floor space, enough to allow the companies to handle up to 50% more than their 1963 to 1966 volume of sales. For this additional space the two companies paid $1,000 per year more than the rental on the old location.

Dick Taylor was pleased with the warehouse operations of the two companies; eight full-time warehouse employees and one part-time employee handled a volume of sales exceeding $4 million per year. As well as he could determine, his warehousing costs were about equal to or lower than that of his competition. He favored multifloor warehousing because normally the rent per square foot was much lower than in new, single-floor warehouses. He explained that there would be few, if any, savings in labor cost, because a warehouse required a certain number of workers to take care of orders and to cover for each other during lunch periods and vacations. Since the size of the crew was fixed at some number larger than the number actually required to handle incoming and outgoing goods, they might as well be employed moving goods to upper floors. He speculated that even with the most modern and efficient storage area his companies would still require about the same number of warehouse employees. But the rent on modern warehouses was three to four times the figure he was paying for multistory warehousing facilities.

As Dick Taylor prepared to close his office for the day he wondered what he could do during the remaining months of 1966 to increase sales and profits. What should he do in 1967? He wondered specifically what he could do about the problem of selling costs and the area's limited potential for sales.

exhibit 1
SOONER DISTRIBUTION COMPANY AND GORDON TAYLOR COMPANY
Organization Chart

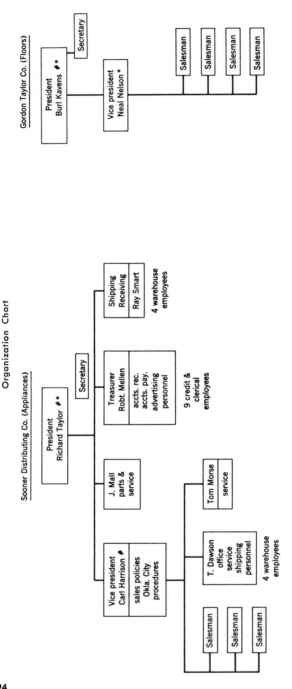

Gordon Taylor Co. (Floors)

President
Burl Kavens #*

Secretary

Vice president
Neal Nelson *

Salesman
Salesman
Salesman
Salesman

Sooner Distributing Co. (Appliances)

President
Richard Taylor #*

Secretary

Treasurer
Robt. Mellen

accts. rec.
accts. pay.
advertising
personnel

9 credit &
clerical
employees

Shipping
Receiving
Ray Smart

4 warehouse
employees

J. Mall
parts &
service

Vice president
Carl Harrison #
sales policies
Okla. City
procedures

T. Dawson
office
service
shipping
personnel

4 warehouse
employees

Tom Morse
service

Salesman
Salesman
Salesman

Director, Sooner Distributing
* Director, Gordon Taylor Co.

Resident Offices

Tulsa	Oklahoma City
Richard Taylor	Carl Harrison
Burl Kavens	Neal Nelson
Robt. Mellen	T. Dawson
Ray Smart	Tom Morse
J. Mall	

exhibit 2 GORDON TAYLOR (FLOORING)
Income statement, 1961–1965 (000's)

	1965 Amount	1965 Per cent	1964 Amount	1964 Per cent	1963 Amount	1963 Per cent	1962 Amount	1962 Per cent	1961 Amount	1961 Per cent
Sales	$2195	100	$2100	100	$2240	100	$2120	100	$1912	100
Cost of sales	1812	82.6	1727	82.2	1879	83.8	1753	82.0	1568	82.0
Gross profit	383	17.4	373	17.8	361	16.2	367	18.0	344	18.0
Selling expense*	124	5.7	128	6.1	128	5.7	124	5.8	122	5.9
Selling profit	$259	11.7	$245	11.7	$233	10.5	$243	12.2	$222	12.1
Operating expenses:										
General and administrative*	40		40		49		55		53	
Personnel expense	2		2		1		1		1	
Intercompany charges for service, buildings, personnel, and internal expenses	171		168		143		131		127	
Total operating expenses	$213	9.6	$210	10.0	$193	8.5	$187	8.8	$181	9.6
Operating income	46		35		40		56		51	
Nonoperating income (expense)					9		(3)		(5)	
Income before contributions to profit sharing or taxes	46		35		49		53		46	
Contributions to profit-sharing trust	6	.3	5	.3	5	.2	6	.3	4	.3
Income before taxes	40		30		44		47		42	
Income taxes	14	.6	9	.4	17	.6	18	.8	16	.8
Net income	$26	1.2	$21	1.0	$27	1.2	$29	1.4	$26	1.4

* Selling and warehouse expenses are presented in detail in Exhibit 4.

exhibit 3 SOONER DISTRIBUTING COMPANY AND GORDON TAYLOR COMPANY

Consolidated income statement, 1961–1965 (000's)

	1961		1962		1963		1964		1965	
	Amount	Per cent	Amount	Per cent	Amount	Per cent	Amount	Per cent	Amount	Per cent
Sales	$3528	100	$3886	100	$4212	100	$4142	100	$4090	100
Cost of sales	2902	82.3	3246	83.6	3564	84.6	3450	83.3	3430	83.8
Gross profit	626	17.7	640	16.4	648	15.4	692	16.7	660	16.2
Selling expenses	241	6.7	244	6.3	242	5.7	259	6.3	234	5.7
Selling profit	385	10.9	406	10.5	406	9.6	433	10.6	426	10.5
Operating expenses:										
Warehouse expense	52	1.5	51	1.3	53	1.3	65	1.6	61	1.6
Service department	13	.4	15	.4	19	.5	21	.5	16	.4
Building expenses	51	1.4	58	1.5	59	1.4	59	1.4	57	1.4
General and administrative expenses	174	4.9	179	4.6	182	4.3	189	4.6	197	4.8
Personnel expenses	12	.3	11	.3	12	.3	14	.3	14	.3
Total operating expenses	$ 302	8.5	$ 314	8.1	$ 325	7.7	$ 348	8.4	$ 345	8.5
Operating income	83	2.3	113	2.9	108	2.6	85	2.2	81	2.0
Other income (expense)	6	.2	(7)	(.2)	(16)	(.4)	(18)	(.4)	(12)	(.3)
Income before contributions to profit sharing and taxes	89	2.5	106	2.7	92	2.2	67	1.8	69	1.7
Contributions to profit-sharing trust*	6	.2	15	.4	15	.4	15	.4	15	.4
Income before taxes	83	2.3	91	2.3	77		52	1.4	54	1.3
Income taxes	25	.6	29	.7	29	.7	15	.4	19	.5
Net income	$ 58	1.5	$ 62	1.1	$ 48	.9	$ 37	.9	$ 35	.9

NOTE: Some variation due to rounding.

* In 1948 Dick Taylor instituted a retirement trust plan; no contributions were made by employees. The original plan called for a specific company contribution only after a fixed percentage of profit arrived at by a government-approved formula was set aside for stockholders. However, because of a decline in operating profits during the early 1950's, no contributions were made. Government regulations regarding company profit-sharing trusts changed; therefore, amendments were made to the original trust providing that the directors of the company could use their discretion in determining the amount of the company's contribution to the employees' profit-sharing trust. Dick Taylor believed the employees should receive some contribution to the profit-sharing trust as long as the company showed some profit. In 1966, through company contributions and investment earnings, the trust's assets totaled approximately $150,000.

exhibit 4   **GORDON TAYLOR COMPANY (FLOORING)**
Balance sheets, 1961–1965 (000's)

	1965	1964	1963	1962	1961
Cash	$ 9.0	$ 13.0	$ 1.5	$ 47.8	$ 55.1
Receivables	248.0	264.1	201.0	167.8	132.2
Less collected loss reserve	(29.4)	(27.2)	(18.4)	(15.9)	(12.3)
Net receivables	219.6	233.9	182.6	151.9	119.9
Inventories—lower of cost or market	295.0	262.1	295.0	285.0	266.0
Total current assets	$523.6	$508.0	$479.1	$484.7	$441.0
Fixed assets—depreciation	3.5	3.9	3.5	5.3	1.0
Total assets	$527.1	$511.9	$482.6	$490.0	$442.0
Notes payable		$ 8.4			
Accounts payable	$ 65.3	$ 80.3	49.4	$ 81.7	$ 23.8
Estimated taxes	14.0	9.3	16.6	18.7	16.3
Accrued liabilities	20.8	19.3	27.0	34.6	18.1
Total liabilities	$100.1	$108.9	$101.4	$135.0	$ 58.2
Preferred stock	$117.0	$117.0	$117.0	$117.0	$117.0
Common stock surplus					
Donated					
Earned	310.0	286.0	264.2	238.0	266.8
Stockholders equity	$427.0	$403.0	$381.2	$355.0	$383.8
Total liabilities and equity	$527.1	$511.9	$482.6	$490.0	$442.0

exhibit 5   **SOONER DISTRIBUTING COMPANY AND GORDON TAYLOR COMPANY**
Sales and warehouse expense detail, 1961–1965 (000's)

	1965				1964			
Direct sales costs	*Gordon Taylor*		*Consolidated*		*Gordon Taylor*		*Consolidated*	
	Amount	*Per cent*	*Amount*	*Per cent*	*Amount*	*Per cent*	*Amount*	*Per cent*
Sales managers:								
Salaries	$ 26	1.2	$ 44	1.0	$ 26	1.1	$ 38	.9
Travel	6	.3	10	.2	6	.3	10	.2
Auto depreciation	....	.0	1	.2	1	.1	2	...
Intercompany admin-								
istration	3	.2	0	...	4	.2	0	...
Services	....	...	....	...	....	...	....	...
Salesmen:								
Salaries and commis-								
sions	54	2.5	99	2.4	52	2.5	108	2.5
Travel	28	1.2	52	1.3	28	1.4	59	1.4
Depreciation—cars	1	.1	2	.5	1	.1	2	...
Total direct selling								
expenses	119	5.4	211	5.1	119	5.6	219	5.0
Advertising	6	.3	12	.3	10	.5	29	.7
Postage	....	...	5	.1	....	...	5	.1
Collection expenses	....	...	6	.1	....	...	6	.1
Total selling ex-								
penses	124	5.7	234	5.7	128	6.4	259	6.0
Warehouse expenses:								
Salaries	....	...	48	...	....	...	45	
Drayage and storage	....	...	9	...	....	...	13	
Shipping supplies	....	...	1	...	....	...	2	...
Parcel post	....	...	2	...	....	...	4	...
Truck repairs and de-								
preciation	....	...	1	...	....	...	1	...
Total warehouse								
expenses	....	...	61	...	....	...	65	...

exhibit 5 (continued)

| 1963 | | | | 1962 | | | | 1961 | | | |
| Gordon Taylor | | Consolidated | | Gordon Taylor | | Consolidated | | Gordon Taylor | | Consolidated | |
Amount	Per cent	Amount	Per cent	Amount	Per cent	Amount	Per cent	Amount	Per cent	Amount	Per cent
$ 25	1.1	$ 47	1.1	$ 23	1.1	$ 42	1.1	$ 21	1.1	$ 40	1.1
4	.2	9	.2	4	.2	8	.2	3	.2	7	.2
1	.1	2	...	1	.1	2	...	....	...	1	
3	.2	0	...	4	.2	0					
54	2.4	105	2.4	51	2.4	95	2.3	51	2.6	108	2.9
31	1.4	57	1.3	33	1.5	64	1.5	29	1.5	59	1.6
2	.1	3	.1	1	.1	4	.1	1	.1	2	.1
120	5.4	222	5.3	118	5.5	215	5.1	104	5.5	218	6.2
8	.4	8	.2	7	.4	19	.5	7	.4	14	.4
....	...	5	.1	....	...	5	.1	....	...	5	.1
....	...	6	.1	....	...	5	.1	....	...	5	.1
128	5.7	242	5.7	124	5.8	244	5.6	112	5.9	241	6.7
....	...	38	...	....	...	37	...	....	...	39	
....	...	8	...	....	...	8	...	....	...	8	
....	...	3	...	....	...	2	...	....	...	2	
....	...	3	...	....	...	3	...	....	...	2	
....	...	1	...	....	...	1	...	....	...	1	
....	...	53	...	....	...	57	...	....	...	52	

exhibit 6   **SOONER DISTRIBUTING COMPANY AND GORDON TAYLOR**
Consolidated balance sheets, 1961–1965 (000's)

	1965	1964	1963	1962	1961
Cash	$ 41.6	$ 71.9	$ 14.2	$ 186.0	$ 184.0
Receivables	508.0	619.4	563.0	470.0	391.0
Less collection loss reserve	66.5	48.5	36.1	40.2	32.0
Net receivables	$ 441.5	$ 570.9	$ 526.9	$ 429.8	$ 359.0
Inventory—lower of cost or market	712.3	768.0	772.0	675.0	576.5
Total current assets	$1195.4	$1410.8	$1313.1	$1290.8	$1119.5
Bonds and insurance (cash value)	2.5	2.6	2.6	2.8	3.1
Fixed assets—depreciation value	24.1	27.6	23.4	29.9	28.2
Total assets	$1222.0	$1441.0	$1339.1	$1323.5	$1150.8
Total notes payable	137.5	269.2	126.4	9.8	11.7
Trade acceptances	. . . .	16.1	72.4	172.5	180.0
Accounts payable	76.5	106.0	83.6	118.8	28.6
Estimated taxes	19.5	17.5	29.8	29.2	25.4
Accrued liabilities	52.4	57.6	71.0	69.2	44.0
Total current liabilities	$ 285.9	$ 466.4	$ 383.2	$ 399.5	$ 289.7
Long-term notes (7%) stockholders	110.3	154.8	154.8	147.9	108.0
Total liabilities	$ 396.2	$ 621.2	$ 538.0	$ 547.4	$ 397.7
Preferred stock	$ 117.0	$ 117.0	$ 117.0	$ 117.0	$ 117.0
Common	77.5	77.5	77.5	77.5	77.5
Surplus					
Donated	77.5	77.5	77.5	77.5	77.5
Earned	575.0	568.0	543.0	518.0	496.0
Total capital stock and surplus	$ 847.0	$ 840.0	$ 815.0	$ 790.0	$ 767.0
Less stock reacquired for treasury	20.2	20.2	13.9	13.9	13.9
Stockholders equity	$ 826.8	$ 819.8	$ 801.1	$ 776.1	$ 753.1
Total liabilities and equity	$1222.0	$1441.0	$1339.1	$1323.5	$1150.8

exhibit 7   COMPARISON OF 28 WHOLESALE FIRMS

	Weighted Averages			
	Eight firms with annual sales of $1,800,000 or more	Seven firms with sales of $1,100,000 to $1,800,000	Eight firms with annual sales up to $1,000,000	All firms
Net sales:	100.00	100.00	100.00	100.00
Cost of goods sold	82.65	82.69	82.62	82.65
Gross margin	17.35	17.31	17.38	17.35
Selling expenses:				
Salesmen's salaries, commissions, and travel expenses	4.45	4.26	4.27	4.32
Showroom rent	.08	.13	.02	.08
Miscellaneous sales expenses	.31	.33	.27	.31
Total	4.84	4.72	4.56	4.71
Warehouse expenses:				
Wages of warehouse labor	1.10	1.43	1.45	1.25
Warehouse rent	.49	.60	.57	.53
Outbound freight, cartage, et cetera	.34	.34	.04	.39
Upkeep depreciation	.26	.10	.22	.21
Warehouse supplies and miscellaneous expenses	.07	.14	.19	.11
Total	2.26	2.61	2.47	2.49
Administrative and general expenses:				
Executive salaries	1.44	1.49	1.83	1.52
Officer salaries and wages	1.67	1.69	1.62	1.67
Utilities	.34	.53	.46	.41
Office rent	.13	.09	.05	.11
Insurance and taxes	.76	.71	.97	.79
Interest on mortgages and borrowed money	.19	.37	.33	.27
Repairs and depreciation of office equipment	.09	.11	.08	.10
Miscellaneous	.59	.46	.77	.59
Total	5.21	5.45	6.11	5.46
Losses from bad departments	.35	.40	.22	.34
Grand total expense	12.72	13.22	13.38	12.97
Other income	.12	.01	.21	.11
Profit before taxes	4.74	4.10	4.19	4.47

exhibit 8   WESTERN RUBBER AND TILE COMPANY AND THE GORDON TAYLOR COM-
PANY, 1963–1966
Oklahoma sales of floor covering

	Spring, 1963			Spring, 1964		
Product	Total Oklahoma Sales*	Taylor Company Sales	% of Business	Total Oklahoma Sales*	Taylor Company Sales	% of Business
Group 1—Linoleum and corlon, sq. yd	$ 417,000	$ 208,000	49.7	$ 392,600	$ 202,100	51.2
Group 2—Felt base and accolon, sq. yd	316,000	147,500	46.5	219,000	94,300	43.1
Group 3—Excelon and asphalt, sq. yd	2,785,000	1,493,000	53.6	3,070,000	1,725,000	58.8
Group 4—Luxury tile, sq. yd	317,000	182,000	46.7	186,500	73,500	45.9
Group 5—Wall covering, sq. ft	29,300	13,600	46.3	30,200	14,800	49.0

exhibit 8 (continued)

Spring, 1965			Fall, 1965			Spring, 1966
Total Oklahoma Sales*	Taylor Company Sales	% of Busi- ness	Total Oklahoma Sales*	Taylor Company Sales	% of Busi- ness	Taylor's Estimated Sales Were About 15% Below 1961
$ 366,500	$ 179,000	48.9	$ 323,000	$ 185,000	54.5	
254,100	126,100	49.5	174,100	112,200	64.3	
3,500,000	2,095,000	60.1	2,710,000	1,790,000	66.0	
214,700	73,600	34.1	133,800	79,700	59.7	
30,650	15,900	51.7	26,600	18,300	68.7	

* Western Rubber and Tile Company sales in Oklahoma and a few counties in neighboring states.

PART TWO

analysis of
the situation

BARTL'S
BREWERY

On January 1, 1965, control of Bartl's Brewery, of Dayton, Ohio, was turned over to Mr. Royce Chandler and his associates. The management of Bartl's had been in turmoil for several years, and during the preceding two years the company had been operated by a court-appointed receiver. Mr. Chandler's acquisition of the company climaxed protracted negotiations which eliminated the old stockholders and management, and a reorganized company emerged. Publicly, Mr. Chandler voiced enthusiasm about the prospects for Bartl's future. "We will see to it," he said, "that this fine old firm, which has weathered many a storm in its hundred-year history, will maintain its rightful place in Dayton industry." Privately, he and his associates in the new management were still trying to settle upon a definite course of action.

HISTORY

Bartl's, the oldest brewery in Ohio, was founded in 1862 by Bernhard Bartl, who learned brewing in Germany and emigrated to America in 1855. After working as a brewer in St. Louis and Milwaukee, he leased the plant of a defunct brewery on the site of the present Bartl's Brewery and began his own business. Success came quickly; when Bernhard Bartl died in 1898, he was reputed to be wealthy, and Bartl's was a thriving concern.

Bernhard Bartl, Jr., nicknamed "Judge" Bartl because he had studied law, followed his father as manager of the brewery. He preferred

107

the brewing business to the practice of law and spent two years in Cincinnati studying "modern and scientific brewing techniques," then joined his father. Judge Bartl's management of the brewery was thrifty, conservative, and prudent. He added a chain of taverns which Bartl's began operating in 1900, introduced a limited line of bottled beer in 1913, switched to near beer during Prohibition, and enlarged the plant to double its capacity when Prohibition was repealed.

In 1935, Judge Bartl was joined by Bartl Koerner, the only son of the Judge's only sister, who had shared equally with the Judge in the inheritance of the brewery. Bartl started as a salesman and subsequently held a number of offices in sales and operations. After five years he was sharing the management of the brewery with his uncle. The Judge supervised production; Bartl Koerner managed everything else. The joint management went smoothly for 11 years. During this period Bartl's was making a profit and continued to expand. Bartl Koerner extended sales into the periphery of the Dayton market, added canned beer, and in a single spectacular crash promotion entered Bartl's in the Indianapolis market, which eventually grew to be as large as Bartl's home market in Dayton.

Before World War II the large national brewers had operated from single central breweries because the lack of a uniform water supply would have caused beers brewed at other points to be "off flavor." Their strategy had been to produce beers which were presumably premium in quality and could command the higher prices which warranted the expense of shipping them to distant points. After the war new technologies solved the water problem, and national breweries proceeded to establish branch plants, brew locally, and sell at local prices. Canned beer became popular, and a myriad of competitive innovations were introduced by the nationals: "pop-tops," "rack-packs," "zip-caps," and "cold-packs." A wide variety of shapes and sizes appeared in cans, bottles, and widemouthed "mug-jugs." The total consumption of beer increased substantially, but the increase was in home consumption, while there was a trend away from tavern drinking (see Exhibits 7 to 9). Throughout its history Bartl's had featured draught beer sold to the bar trade. Company profits declined from $1.7 million net in 1947 to $92,000 in 1951.

In 1952, Judge Bartl, then 81, became chairman of the board, and Bartl Koerner, who had been executive vice president for 11 years, was elected president. Judge Bartl brought in James Randall, a furniture executive, whom he made executive vice president and general man-

ager. Bartl Koerner succeeded in ousting Mr. Randall and voiding his
10 year contract, publicly charging his uncle with senility and saying
that "he never knew anything more than how to make beer—the way it
was made 60 years ago. . . ." Thereupon, the Judge forced Bartl Koerner from the presidency, stating that he had developed megalomania
and believed himself capable of succeeding at anything, even converting
Bartl's into a national brewery. For 15 months—January, 1953, through
March, 1954,—Koerner was in a state of psychic depression, the presidency remained vacant, and the company was managed by the sales
manager. Backed by his mother and his wife, who was independently
wealthy, Bartl Koerner appointed six board members who re-elected
him president. The first thing Bartl Koerner did was to fire the sales
manager. The Judge tried again to oust Bartl, charging him with wasteful and extravagant management. Failing in this attempt, the Judge
resigned from the board in 1956, leaving control of the company to
Bartl Koerner. In 1957 Judge Bartl died.

Sales and profits continued to decline in the period from 1956 to
1962. Local retailers were not sure that Bartl's would survive the effects
of the previous infighting for control. Within a year of Koerner's return
in 1956, sales volume fell 45%. Koerner blamed his uncle, who, he
said, had put all the company's capital into bricks and mortar. He
launched a huge sales drive with little result, and after another five
years of losses—January, 1958, to December, 1962—the company went
into voluntary receivership (Exhibits 1 and 2). The first official act
of the trustee was to dismiss Bartl Koerner

In January, 1965, the reorganized company emerged, the trustee
asserting: "We released many employees, cut salaries and wages, cut
many expenses, and insisted on a general austerity program. Within a
year we were no longer operating on a hand-to-mouth basis. We were
able to make ends meet, were earning a profit, and didn't have to
borrow additional funds from the banks." (Exhibits 1 to 3. See also
Exhibits 11 and 12 for comparable national figures.) On January 1,
1965, the reorganized company was turned over to the group headed
by Royce Chandler.

THE REORGANIZATION

Royce Chandler, who played the leading role in the reorganization,
had been operating a Dayton advertising firm called Chandler and

Associates. Bartl's Brewery was one of his clients. Mr. Chandler was described as "a warm and enthusiastic man, always buoyant and with an ever-hopeful disposition." His agency had a reputation for creativity and had launched numerous successful advertising campaigns which were said to have made Mr. Chandler a millionaire. At the end of 1964, Bartl's owed Mr. Chandler a total of $70,000, an accumulation of approximately two years of fees (Exhibit 2).

Under the Chandler reorganization plan effected January 1, 1965, holders of the old preferred stock received, on a share-for-share basis, new preferred stock in the reorganized company. Holders of the old common stock received nothing. Five hundred thousand dollars in new common stock ($1 par) was subscribed and paid for. All delinquent accounts were paid in full; all other accounts were carried forward to the reorganized company.

Mr. Chandler called his plan the "Chandler–Dayton-Businessmen and Bartl's Brewery Employees' Reorganization Plan." "This is not just an ordinary business reorganization," said Mr. Chandler, "this is the fulfillment of an ideal."

"Raising capita was not our prime objective," said Mr. Chandler, "we were more interested in people than in money. We wanted to make Bartl's Brewery a 'people's brewery' operated by Dayton businessmen, with every employee and every stockholder a part owner of the business. We eliminated the 'beer baron' concept, under which one man dominates a brewery. We have selected carefully the business leaders we have permitted to join us, and we have limited their subscriptions to 20,000 shares each. Thus, no one individual will dominate the board and dictate policy. We are especially proud of the fact that every employee and key executive of Bartl's has become a co-owner of the brewery. I could have bought the brewery myself. Several of my friends offered to buy all of the common stock. We rejected all these offers and have selected instead a plan whereby the investors will work together as a team of coequals."

Upon the request of Chandler, all active employees subscribed to the minimum of 100 shares of the new issue of common stock; some bought more. Mr. Chandler, with undisclosed associates whom he represented, subscribed to 100,000 shares and became president of the brewery at a salary of $2,500 a month. He brought into the company two of his agency associates: Selden Spears, who was made vice president of operations, at $1,500 a month; and Elbert Holbrook, vice president of sales, at $1,300 a month. The brewmaster, treasurer, controller, and purchasing agent were each invited to subscribe 10,000 shares, which they did, and they were continued in their offices (Exhibit 6). "Our group recognizes and commends the loyalty and the willing efforts of the supervisory and management personnel," said Mr. Chandler. "Each of them will be given job security and the opportunity for advancement."

The Dayton businessmen who subscribed were vendors and other creditors of Bartl's. A strong advocate of the plan had been Jacob Pardisi, regional agent for the United Brotherhood of Brewers, which represented the Bartl employees.

THE TAX LIEN

Mr. Chandler's reorganization had been based upon the assumption that Bartl's would be exonerated from a pending Federal claim for taxes. The claim arose from four years under Bartl Koerner's management during which, the revenue bureau claimed, Koerner and his friends had charged lavish Bahama winter vacations to company expense when these trips actually had nothing to do with the brewery. The original claim was for an additional $390,000. In a preliminary decision which ruled out fraudulent intent, the claim was cut to $272,800. From this action Mr. Chandler had assumed that the entire claim would eventually be dropped.

On January 14, 1965, two weeks after the reorganization date, the courts declared $125,600 of the $272,800 government claim valid, payable by the end of 1965. The new Chandler management was shocked at the realization that this would cut into the $500,000 additional capital it had raised. After take-over expenses and the payment of delinquent claims, working capital amounted to about $245,000. However, management was considering borrowing the money from two Dayton banks where Chandler had established lines of credit for Bartl's as part of the reorganization process. The banks had extended the credit on the understanding that they would receive a first mortgage on all of the brewery's real estate, plant, and equipment if the credit were used.

COMPETITION AND PACKAGING

When Mr. Chandler took over, he estimated that only 40% of Bartl's volume was in packaged form (15% canned and 25% bottled) and that the remaining 60% was sold as draught beer. He realized that in 1963 over 80% of national beer consumption was in packaged[1] form (see Exhibit 9).

Bartl's had always produced premium beer and sold it in draught form. It had been slow to get into packaging and when it did tended to favor bottles. Its market was mostly local, confined to Dayton, Indianapolis, and other areas of Ohio and Indiana. In recent years all of its markets had been invaded by the nationals, whose brands were backed by strong national advertising and promotion programs.

Mr. Chandler saw Bartl's competition as (1) Henkel's, a Dayton brewery smaller than Bartl's whose output was 50% draught and 50% packaged; (2) the Superb Brewery of Fort Wayne, larger than Bartl's, which sold mostly packaged beers, marketed in several states and in Chicago, and was a direct competitor in Indianapolis; (3) several national breweries, which sold mostly canned beers. Bartl's was the only one featuring a superior brew.

Bartl's had always been an advocate of draught beer. Beer drinkers of discriminating taste considered draught beer to be superior in flavor to packaged beer, and brewmasters generally agreed with them. August Burg, Bartl's brewmaster, was also strongly of this conviction. "Packaged beers taste as differently from draught beer," he said, "as cabbage tastes from sauerkraut. Can or bottle it and it is no longer the real thing. People don't seem to care about taste anymore, though. They'll even drink bottled beer at a bar that serves the same beer on tap."

Initially Bartl's produced draught beer only; it added bottles in 1913. In 1946, the industry turned to canned beer and found immediate consumer acceptance. Judge Bartl had waited until every competitor was selling canned beer before he reluctantly joined the trend in 1951, and then he permitted only the canning of Bartl's standard-grade, lower-priced brew, Bartl's Bonus Brew (Triple B brand). Later a beer between the standard and premium grades was added which was sold only in cans. The cans were sold in selected non-tavern areas through grocers. Bartl's Premium was sold only in kegs and as recently as 1958 had been delivered in central Dayton on a wagon drawn by a team of elegantly-harnessed Clydesdales. It had been an axiom of Judge Bartl that "the brewery that makes the best brew and has the biggest horses and the fanciest brass ornaments makes the most sales." When Mr. Chandler

[1] Packaged beer is beer sold in cans and bottles. All other beer is draught beer sold in kegs or barrels.

took over, Bartl's was still canning only its two bread-and-butter brands on two canning machines which were over 10 years old and turned out only one third as many cans per minute as modern equipment.

Mr. Holbrook, sales vice president, was in favor of switching all brands to cans and placing heavy promotion behind the move, concentrating on retail grocery outlets and packaged-liquor stores. He had statistics showing that over half of all packaged beer was sold in grocery stores, and that women purchased 50% of this, even though they drank only about 30% of it. "They don't buy for taste," he said. "Even the men don't care about flavor anymore. After the first glassful, they don't care what they're drinking " Mr. Burg, the brewmaster, argued against the idea. He pointed out that this would require the purchase of modern canning machines; that more plant space would have to be built; and that draught beer wholesaled for less, yet brought higher margins to both brewers and distributors.

Bartl's had six draught beer salesmen calling on the local tavern trade to take orders for beer, which was delivered to them once a week. Four draught beer salesmen traveled in the rural areas of Ohio and Indiana. Sales of bottled and canned beer were handled as house accounts. Packaged liquor stores' and grocers' orders were taken by two sales assistants. Draught deliveries were made in Bartl's trucks; package deliveries were farmed out to a cartage company except for Bartl's own taverns (see Exhibit 5 and 9).

Taverns selling Bartl's draught beer were not sold bottled beer. Mr. Chandler proposed to sell them any and all forms. Grocery stores preferred cans to bottles, because cans took less shelf space and eliminated the nuisance of handling return bottles. Canned national brands which were coming into local markets were heavily advertised. Mr. Chandler was not convinced that the quality of any brew was of first importance. "The housewife who buys in a grocery store will choose whatever name first pops into her head," said Mr. Chandler. "If we advertise enough, that name will be Bartl's."

MARKET RESEARCH

In 1957, Bartl Koerner had for the first time used market consultants to make studies of the local markets. Mr. Chandler held that this had been done out of desperation and at exorbitant expense, and he questioned Bartl Koerner's ability to interpret the findings. Mr. Chandler stated that his long experience in advertising gave him ample knowledge of the market and he had no intention of using consultants. He would use only *Brewer's Almanac* data and surveys made by local newspapers (see Exhibit 13).

THE UNIONS AND PROFIT SHARING

In the third week of January, Mr. Chandler met with the employees to discuss a profit-sharing plan which he had devised. He wished to do this before meeting with the union leaders on April 1 to negotiate the annual union contract. Mr. Chandler handled this himself because the company no longer had a personnel manager. "We might hire a personnel director again when we have need for one," said Mr. Chandler. "Now that our employees are co-owners of the brewery we may never again need one." Mr. Chandler emphasized to the employees that he was now talking to them in their new role, in which they were co-owners and co-managers of the brewery. In his profit-sharing plan he proposed that the first 10% of net profit after taxes be reserved as a base return for stockholders. Above that, each worker would receive an additional ½ of 1% of his gross pay for each additional 1% of net profit earned. Above 15% net earnings each employee would receive a 1% bonus for each 1% addition to net profit. Sales, production and financial figures were to be given to each employee monthly. The profit-sharing plan was to take the place of any current increase in wage and salary rates, but only for the present.

The initial employee reaction to the plan was cool, but when 59% of them voted for it, unanimous agreement was obtained. Included in the majority group were office employees, who were not union members. When they learned of the employees' decision, the union leaders objected strongly and had several discussions with the employees and with Mr. Chandler, but the employees held to the plan.

The bonuses were to be paid out after each monthly accounting period. January and February both resulted in losses. In mid-March, at a time when the company was short of working capital, a canning machine was shut down for repairs and 24 employees were laid off for two weeks. March figures again showed a loss.

When Mr. Chandler met with the union for contract negotiations, the union leaders, claiming unanimous employee backing, asked for a cancellation of the profit-sharing plan and a straight 35¢ per hour increase. Negotiations were conducted in an atmosphere which Mr. Chandler described as "belligerent and hostile and altogether unrealistic." At times during the bargaining the union threatened to call a strike. It also threatened to publish advertisements in the Dayton papers challenging Mr. Chandler to make good his boast that Bartl's was now managed by its employees who were co-owners, a threat which Mr. Chandler called blackmail.

The bargaining ended in the dropping of the profit-sharing plan, and the company settled for a wage rate that was no higher than wages generally in Dayton, but that placed Bartl's wages 32¢ above the national brewing industry average. The office employees, who were non-union, retained the profit-sharing plan. "One of these months," said Mr. Chandler, "we will be earning substantial profits and will be sharing them with our office staff. It will be interesting then to see the reaction of the union members."

PRICING

In April, 1965, Mr. Chandler announced his intention of raising Bartl's prices to retailers. "Dayton," said Mr. Chandler, "is the cheapest beer market in the United States. The retail price of beer here is just about the same as the wholesale price in other areas." The new schedule of prices included a 23¢ increase to retailers on a case of twenty-four 12-ounce bottles, raising the price from $2.60 to $2.83 a case. Henkel's, a Dayton competitor, announced that it also intended to raise prices. The Superb Brewery of Fort Wayne, another competitor did not raise prices but publicly stated that increased costs justified a raise in prices.

Bartl-owned taverns, which featured draught beer, did not raise the bottle price. Other taverns in Dayton and Indianapolis raised their prices from 30¢ to 35¢ a bottle. Contrary to expectations, the competitive breweries did not raise their Dayton and Indianapolis prices but did raise their prices in other markets where prices in general were higher. To make the new price more acceptable to customers, Mr. Chandler ran a series of ads in local papers, featuring the theme "the 30¢ bottle of beer, like the 5¢ cigar, is on its way out."

Three weeks later, after suffering a substantial loss in volume, Mr. Chandler rescinded the price increase. "We had assumed," said Mr. Chandler, "that the general level of local prices would go up. It is incredible that our competitors raised prices in other places but not in Dayton and Indianapolis. We hope that most of our old customers will return to Bartl's beer and sell it again for 30¢ a bottle" (see Exhibit 4).

VELVET GOLD

In May, 1965, a faulty canning machine left too much air in the cans, allowing the beer to continue to ferment inside them and resulting in a beer that brewers termed "skunky" because its strong flavor gave the drinker "beer breath." In eliminating the trouble the Bartl brewers did two things: first, they adjustd the vacuum controls, and in doing so they inadvertently overcompensated; second, they removed the light brown crust of foam which appeared as a normal thing on the surface of all fermenting beer in the open fermentation process. To their surprise, they found that they had brewed a beer that was excepitonally light and pale, comparable to the highest quality premium beers. Also, the new brew seemed to leave absolutely no aftertaste.

Mr. Chandler believed that they had chanced upon a revolutionary improvement in the age-old brewing process. In presenting their discovery to the board of directors, Mr. Chandler said, "Elimination of 'beer breath' will put us leagues ahead of anyone in the industry, including the nationals."

Mr. Chandler proposed that Bartl's introduce the new brew as a fourth item in its line. He named it Velvet Gold and planned to market it in golden cans and gold-foil–sheathed bottles. The introduction was to be launched by heavy promotion and advertising on radio and television and in the regional editions of national magazines. His ad theme featured the slogan "Smooth as Velvet, Rich as Gold." Canned and bottled Velvet Gold was to be sold as a super-quality brew at prices which were higher than those of most premium beers.[2] It was to be distributed through all channels, with heavy emphasis on grocery stores.

Mr. Chandler had the brewers condense the crust of foam which they had removed and put it in pill-sized bottles labeled "Slurge." These bottles were mounted on a placard which explained that the nauseous-looking moldy liquid in the little bottle was the dregs which other brewers left in their beers, giving the drinker "beer breath," and that only Bartl's was purified of "slurge." These exhibits were presented to taverns to be placed on bars.

[2] Premium beers are considered lighter, smoother, and in general easier to drink.

DISTRIBUTORSHIPS

Mr. Chandler believed that operating the brewery at full capacity would be the only means of achieving low-cost production; that high volume would help to absorb overhead expenses; and that rising sales would have an immeasurably stimulating effect on Bartl's employees and customers alike and relieve Bartl's of its tarnished public image.

In June, Mr. Chandler and Mr. Holbrook proceeded to expand Bartl's regional territory by taking on additional distributorships in neighboring areas. At first distributors were to cover Ohio and southern Indiana; later southern Michigan, western Pennsylvania, and West Virginia were to be added. A third campaign would take in all of Kentucky, where beer sales were regulated by counties.

Mr. Chandler thought that Bartl's premium quality beer could compete favorably with the nationals and that his personal skill in advertising would enable him to match the national advertising of the national brands. As an initial inducement, prices to new distributors were shaded by as much as 11¢ in the expectation that strong consumer acceptance would later enable prices to be raised. Quick delivery in Bartl's trucks in LCL lots would be at lower cost than the carload shipments of the national brewers.

After two months Mr. Chandler considered the first phase to be successful. Sales volume had increased substantially, but costs had risen disproportionately, resulting in a slight loss on the new business. Some national brands had resorted to a strategy of selling at local prices, which caused Mr. Chandler to delay raising prices in the new territories. He also hesitated to enter Kentucky without further investigation.

BARTL'S TAVERNS

In 1965, Bartl's was still operating nine taverns in Dayton, the remnant of a chain of twenty-eight which Judge Bartl had viewed as a means of selling draught beer. The Judge had called them rathskellers or *Bierstubes;* the public called them saloons.

There was a growing realization in the brewing industry that local barrooms were passing out of the American scene. "The old-fashioned neighborhood tavern," said a brewery executive, "was once a comfortable haven where work-sore husbands and fathers could take refuge and relax . . . but it is now slowly but surely heading for oblivion. Brewers' eyes have to be on the supermarket, on back-yard patios, and on picnic grounds. That's where you sell beer today." Mr. Chandler was undecided about keeping Bartl's nine remaining taverns in operation.

One tavern on the suburban edge of the city was known as "The Garden" because it had attached to it an open-air beer garden so popular that it gave promise of becoming a Dayton tradition. When the weather permitted, the beer garden, where only draught beer was served, was filled to overcapacity. In the barroom, which had the atmosphere of a cocktail lounge, considerably more liquor than beer was served. The Garden did a big business at cocktail hours all year round, and the beer garden did an overflow business weekends and holidays, weather permitting. It served food only in the evenings and offered a limited and unchanging menu of plate suppers: roast beef or pork, a fish item, and steaks. Portions were hearty, the cooking was plain but excellent, and a meal cost from $1.50 to $2.

A second tavern, located in an old industrial section and dubbed "The Gashouse," served cold sandwiches of hearty proportions to local factory workers. Its offerings were limited to ham, salami, swiss cheese, hardboiled eggs, pickled herrings, and kippers, which were served only at lunch hours. The Gashouse served only men and sold mostly beer.

The largest of the Bartl taverns, known simply as "Clark Street," was situated in downtown Dayton between the shopping and office section and the railroad depots. Clark Street was open from 10 A.M. until 2 A.M. It served a fairly wide variety of cold sandwiches, hot sandwiches of beef, pork, corned beef, and baked thüringer, and plates of hot corned beef or roast beef hash. It was the only Bartl tavern that served food at all hours. It was renowned in Dayton for the size of its sandwiches—four slices of ham or almost an inch of swiss cheese was normal—and the price was only 50¢. A very mixed clientele was served, and the sales of beer and liquor were about equal.

A fourth tavern, the University Pub, situated adjacent to a branch of a large university, did a sizable volume that was almost entirely draught beer. The Pub had no cooking facilities but served snack items such as potato chips and pretzels. It was heavily patronized by students, both men and coeds.

Every tavern required union grill men, and some of them required bus boys and dishwashers. The Garden and Clark Street required full-time chefs. Bartenders and food service employees belonged to different unions, and each refused to share the others' work. Headquarters had constant union and personnel problems with the food taverns. The small staffs made any absenteeism a critical problem. Day help was used to fill vacancies, there were frequent jurisdictional disputes, and most of the food-service help remained only a short time.

The Garden regularly incurred sizable losses in its food business which were offset by the profits it made on cocktails and liquors. Clark Street made a regular profit on beer and liquor sales and a modest but steady profit on its large volume of food sales. The Gashouse broke even on food sales, and made a profit on its large draught beer volume.

According to the income statements (Mr. Chandler questioned the accuracy of the accounting data) the whole chain of taverns was operating at a profit, but in some years the final net profit of the chain was less than $1,000. Some taverns were profitable; some were not. The profits and losses, however, had averaged less than $1,000 for the past five years. The controller wanted to close them; the brewmaster, however, was in favor of keeping them and proposed starting a few in Indianapolis. Mr. Chandler felt that he ought to give his attention to regional and national marketing.

There were 178 independently owned taverns in Dayton, and most tavern operators resented the Bartl-owned taverns, believing that Bartl's Brewery subsidized the taverns and operated them at losses for the public-relations benefits involved. Only 48 independently owned taverns handled Bartl's draught beer. No other brewery operated its own taverns. No Bartl-owned tavern sold competing packaged liquors. Virtually every independently owned tavern did.

The taverns were a constant subject of argument among the Bartl management. Some claimed the effort was not worth the small profit. Tavern managers claimed the actual net was larger; that too much headquarters overhead was charged to them although headquarters gave them no service. All the taverns managers claimed the taverns generated business for Bartl's everywhere.

Some believed that the cocktail-lounge atmosphere of the Garden barroom was not in keeping with the Bartl image. Others charged that Clark Street and Gashouse sandwiches were too large and their prices too low. The managers claimed that the outsized sandwiches drew trade from a six-block radius and that changing prices or portions would kill their business. The Gashouse manager insisted that it was the large sandwiches which supported his profitable beer trade. Some criticized the taverns for being just as simple and austere as they had been 40 years ago. There was no entertainment, no dancing, and a minimum of decor. Even the Garden did not use linens for table service.

DIRECT DISTRIBUTION

By September, 1965, sales volume had exceeded expectations and was continuing to rise, but profits had not improved. Mr. Chandler and Mr. Holbrook were discussing the possibility of converting to direct distribution in the new territories. This would mean tripling the sales force and adding a sales supervisor. It would involve inventories, credit, bad-debt losses, smaller trucks, and more frequent deliveries. Canned beer would be featured, saving 1/3 of the shipping space, but more canning machines would be needed. Mr. Chandler hesitated to make the move because of the capital requirements involved—one fully automated line of canning equipment would cost from $275,000 to $400,000.[3] "We prefer to be a self-sustaining operation," he said, "and not get involved with the banks."

VELVET GOLD

Velvet Gold had produced an initial spurt of volume, but by October, 1965, sales were steadily declining. Unexpected developments had occurred. The "slurge" sales theme was resented by all competitors, who used paid advertisements to refute it, saying that there was a normal amount of residue in all brewing processes. The National Brewers' Association deplored the publicity being given to the possible impurity of all beers and censured Bartl's sales tactic as "unorthodox, if not unethical, and certainly not in good taste." It asked Mr. Chandler to desist from using the "slurge" bottles. At the height of the publicity a competing tavern operator derisively nicknamed Velvet Gold "Vicious Gook," a name that caught on and spread through tavern circles and through the trade.

In mid-October, Mr. Chandler offered Velvet Gold in draught form to local tavern operators at regular beer prices. Every one of them turned it down. Thereafter, Mr. Chandler wondered if he should quietly withdraw Velvet Gold from the Bartl line. He was reluctant to do so because sizable expenditures had been incurred in promoting it, and he felt it might catch on in the future.

---

[3] Included in the line would be a canner, a sealer, filling equipment, packers, and required conveyors.

BARTL'S BAVARIAN

Mr. Chandler was still convinced that there was a place in the Bartl line for a super-quality, premium-priced beer. Imported beers such as Dortmund DAB and other pilsner beers were gaining rapidly in popularity and sold at high prices. Recognizing this, some national breweries had undertaken to produce pseudo-foreign beers which they marketed under names that gave the impression that they were actually foreign. Mr. Burg, the brewmaster, thought that this would be a good strategy for Bartl's and assured Mr. Chandler that he would have no difficulty brewing a beer that was genuinely "German import" in character. Mr. Holbrook thought that the idea had merit. In December, 1965, Bartl's Bavarian was introduced in draught form to the tavern trade in Dayton at regular prices, and it met with a good reception. If consumer acceptance proved good enough, it was planned to extend its sales in bottle form, but there was no intention to sell it in cans.

SHIPMENTS CROSS-COUNTRY

The initial response of Bartl's Bavarian was good, but it was followed by a sales slump. Mr. Chandler interpreted this as the normal pattern for a newly introduced product and felt sure that the new brew had good potential. He proposed that it be sold in draught and in bottle form on a national basis, beginning in markets which were far from Bartl's home territory. His thinking, said Mr. Chandler, was in keeping with the Biblical saying that "a prophet is not without honor except in his own country." Mr. Chandler and Mr. Holbrook traveled to Arkansas and Texas to secure distributorships. In mid-January one carload was shipped to Little Rock and another to Dallas, each carload covered with huge decorative signs announcing the arrival of Bartl's Bavarian in the new territory. Mr. Chandler also arranged extensive advertising to launch the newly introduced Bavarian entirely at Bartl's expense. If results in the next two months were satisfactory, he was considering extending sales into Oklahoma and other parts of Texas.

MERGER RUMORS

In January, 1966, Mr. Chandler met with the press to deny rumors that Bartl's was in financial difficulty and was seeking to sell out.[4]

[4] The $125,600 tax lien had not yet been paid.

"Bartl's Brewery is now operating profitably," he said, "and we do not intend to cheapen the value of its properties by putting them on the auction block. I did not become president of this respected and long-prosperous institution to preside over its liquidation. The brewing industry is going through a period of trial. Since repeal over 600 breweries have gone out of business. Of the 200 that remain, less than half will survive the coming decade. Cutthroat competition from national breweries, price cutting, rising wages, and taxes will bankrupt many more small breweries. Only the strong regional or semi-regional breweries will survive. Bartl's Brewery will definitely be one of the survivors."

exhibit 1 **BARTL'S BREWERY**
Statement of consolidated income (years ending December 31)

	1959	1960	1961	1962	1963	1964
Sales	$3,502,108	$3,141,244	$2,782,824	$2,422,401	$2,871,264	$3,500,367
Less federal and state excise taxes	990,941	877,525	771,111	672,526	1,012,159	1,200,814
Net sales	$2,511,167	$2,263,719	$2,011,713	$1,749,875	$1,859,105	$2,299,553
Cost of goods sold	1,767,240	1,572,652	1,383,584	1,180,044	1,270,044	1,672,267
Gross profit	$ 743,927	$ 691,067	$ 628,129	$ 569,831	$ 589,061	$ 627,286
Selling and delivery expenses	572,636	514,574	509,253	478,745	411,991	420,034
Administrative and general expenses	269,447	214,206	209,777	193,427	125,207	137,207
Total	$ 742,083	$ 728,780	$ 719,030	$ 672,172	$ 537,198	$ 557,241
Profit from operations	1,844	(37,713)	(90,901)	(102,341)	51,863	70,045
Other income	14,466	22,583	19,512	16,154		
Gross income	$ 16,310	$ (15,130)	$ (71,389)	$ (86,187)	$ 51,863	$ 70,045
Income charges:						
Interest	10,800	7,528	7,805	16,154	12,837	13,569
Other	21,700	11,291	7,791	12,116	17,116	19,046
Total	$ 32,500	$ 18,819	$ 15,596	$ 28,270	$ 29,953	$ 32,615
Income before provision for taxes	(16,190)	(33,949)	(86,985)	(114,457)	21,910	37,430
Provision for income taxes						
Net income for the year	$ (16,190)	$ (33,949)	$ (86,985)	$ (114,457)	21,910	37,430

exhibit 2 BARTL'S BREWERY
Balance sheet, 1959–1965

Assets	1959	1960	1961	1962	1963	1964	Jan. 30, 1965*
Current assets:							
Cash	$ 74,261	$ 63,763	$ 31,767	$ 28,928	$ 34,071	$ 31,601	$ 365,924
Revenue stamps	18,569	15,569	14,931	10,284	12,412	13,987	30,791
Trade accounts receivable	265,690	302,360	354,326	328,884	339,301	341,044	343,640
Other receivables	31,426	27,512	16,966	14,791	14,439	13,038	13,068
Total	$ 389,946	$ 409,204	$ 417,990	$ 382,887	$ 400,223	$ 399,670	$ 753,423
Less allowance for bad debt	8,714	9,856	12,132	19,577	12,877	13,695	13,781
Total	$ 381,232	$ 399,348	$ 405,858	$ 363,310	$ 387,346	$ 385,975	$ 739,642
Inventories:							
Finished goods	67,134	54,413	49,990	44,794	47,895	64,127	65,533
Materials and supplies	41,420	39,176	41,176	47,432	41,717	42,770	41,111
Total inventories	$ 108,554	$ 93,589	$ 91,166	$ 92,226	$ 89,612	$ 106,897	$ 106,644
Prepaid expenses	8,413	9,169	19,700	8,178	12,717	13,905	13,905
Total current assets	$ 498,199	$ 502,106	$ 516,724	$ 463,714	$ 489,675	$ 506,777	$ 860,191
Miscellaneous investments	8,571	27,512	28,145	26,008	31,359	28,811	28,811
Property—at cost:							
Land	82,850	82,850	82,850	82,850	82,850	82,850	82,850
Buildings, machinery and equipment	1,696,943	1,684,294	1,907,177	1,918,903	1,886,917	2,040,280	2,040,280
Cooperage and bottles	217,123	203,151	181,560	164,107	200,191	248,614	251,739
Total	$1,996,916	$1,970,295	$2,171,587	$2,165,860	$2,169,958	$2,371,744	$2,374,869
Less reserve for depreciation	868,492	959,856	1,075,619	1,162,941	1,184,587	1,275,900	1,283,421
Net of depreciation	$1,128,424	$1,010,439	$1,095,968	$1,002,919	$ 985,371	$1,095,844	$1,091,448
Leasehold improvements (unamortized)	77,136	73,365	67,862	89,171	82,316	20,579	18,364
Total property	$1,205,560	$1,083,804	$1,163,830	$1,092,090	$1,067,687	$1,116,423	$1,109,812
Deferred charges	14,284	6,114	20,359	20,146	7,840	16,363	15,887
Total assets	$1,726,614	$1,619,536	$1,729,058	$1,601,958	$1,506,561	$1,668,374	$2,014,701

exhibit 2 (continued)

Liabilities	1959	1960	1961	1962	1963	1964	Jan. 30, 1965*
Current liabilities:							
Accounts payable and accruals	$ 485,264	$ 535,939	$ 524,346	$ 524,116	$ 499,925	$ 498,654	$ 437,331
Notes payable—due in one year	28,600	27,800	37,300	37,100	35,300	35,300	35,300
Federal taxes payable	14,100						134,873†
Other taxes payable	35,000						7,294
Total current liabilities	$ 562,964	$ 563,739	$ 561,646	$ 561,216	$ 535,225	$ 533,954	$ 614,798
Deposits on containers	34,385	27,931	27,146	37,210	39,191	49,390	46,303
Notes payable: 5% due 1975‡						454,600	454,600
4%	328,500	305,600	536,100	512,200	483,400		
4½% due 1970‡	91,400	91,400	88,200	81,700	75,200	68,700	68,700
3¾%	17,100	12,200	6,700				
Total notes payable	$ 437,000	$ 409,200	$ 631,000	$ 593,900	$ 558,600	$ 523,300	$ 523,300
Consulting fees owed					32,000	70,000	
Capital stock and surplus:							
Preferred stock	377,540	354,540	330,300	330,300	330,300	330,300	330,300
Common stock	119,999	113,943	115,366	118,895	119,743	119,743	500,000
Surplus: paid in	142,310	131,716	132,118	133,412	133,412	133,412	
Surplus: earned	52,416	18,467	(68,518)	(172,975)	(151,910)	(91,725)	
Total capital stock and surplus	$ 692,265	$ 618,666	$ 509,266	$ 409,632	$ 431,545	$ 491,730	$ 830,300
Total liabilities	$1,726,614	$1,619,536	$1,729,058	$1,601,958	$1,596,561	$1,668,374	$2,014,701

* After reorganization.
† Inclues the tax lien of $125,600.
‡ Maturity dates renegotiated at a time of reorganization.

exhibit 3 BARTL'S BREWERY
A six-year comparison

	1959	1960	1961	1962	1963	1964
Barrels sold	106,813	95,930	85,714	74,522	78,081	95,975
Net sales	$2,511,167	$2,263,719	$2,011,713	$1,749,875	$1,859,105	$2,299,553
Earnings before income taxes	....	....	....	....	21,910	37,430
Net earnings	(16,190)	(33,949)	(86,985)	(114,457)	21,910	37,430
Per cent of net earnings to net sales	....	....	....	....	1.2	1.6
Amount earned on common stock	....	....	....	....	21,910	37,430
Earnings per share	....	....	....	....	.004	.075
Plant property and equipment	911,301	807,288	944,890	838,812	785,180	1,080,604
Current assets	481,199	502,106	516,724	463,714	524,675	571,777
Current liabilities	562,964	563,739	561,646	561,216	444,860	533,954
Working capital	(81,765)	(61,633)	(44,922)	(97,502)	79,815	37,823
Long-term debt	437,000	409,200	631,000	593,900	558,600	523,300
Wages, salaries, benefits per barrel	5.46	5.54	5.68	5.75	5.90	5.92
Revenue per barrel after taxes	23.51	23.61	23.47	23.48	23.81	23.96
Retained earnings	....	....	....	....	21,910	37,430
Taxes (excise)	990,941	877,525	771,111	672,526	1,012,159	1,200,814

exhibit 4 BARTL'S BREWERY

Stated approximate retail beer prices, January 1, 1965

Brand	12 Oz. No return		12 Oz. Return		32 Oz. No return		32 Oz. Return		12 Oz. Can		16 Oz. Can	
	Six Pack	Case of 24	Six Pack	Case of 24	1 Bottle	Case of 12	1 Bottle	Case of 12	Six Pack	Case of 24	Six Pack	Case of 24
Bartl's Standard	$.99	$3.85	$.97	$3.79	$.43	$5.00	$.40	$4.70	$1.09	$4.20	$1.29	$4.90
Bartl's Premium	1.25	4.85	1.15	4.50	.52	6.20	.48	5.65	1.15	4.50	1.45	5.65
Brand A	1.29	4.90	1.19	4.60	.53	6.26	.48	5.66	1.19	4.60	1.50	5.80
Brand B	.99	3.86	.99	3.86	.45	5.30	.40	4.70	1.19	4.60	1.50	5.80
Brand C	1.24	4.30	1.19	4.60	.52	6.20	.48	5.65	1.19	4.60	1.50	5.80
Brand D	1.29	4.90	1.19	4.50	.51	6.10	.48	5.65	1.19	4.60	1.50	5.80
Brand E	.99	3.80	.93	3.65	3/1.10	4.35	3/1.00	4.00	1.09	4.20	1.30	5.00
Brand F	1.29	4.90	1.19	4.60	.53	6.26	.48	5.66	1.19	4.60	1.50	5.80
Brand G	1.26	4.85	1.17	4.50	.43	5.00	.39	4.60	1.17	4.50	1.35	5.20
Brand H	1.09	4.20	.99	3.80	.43	5.00	.39	4.60	1.09	4.20	1.29	4.90
Brand I	1.29	4.90	1.19	4.65	.52	6.20	.48	5.65	1.39	5.30		
Brand J	1.24	4.30	1.19	4.60	.53	6.26	.48	5.65	1.19	4.60	1.50	5.80
Brand K	1.09	4.20	.99	3.80	3/1.10	5.00	3/1.00	4.60	.99	3.85	1.29	4.90
Brand L	.99	3.80	.89	3.45	.43	4.30	.39	4.00			.99	3.80
Brand M	.99	3.80	.99	3.80	.42	4.95	.39	4.60	.99	3.80	1.29	4.90
Brand N	1.00	3.90	.90	3.50	3/1.10	4.30	3/1.00	4.00	.92	3.45	1.19	4.60
Brand O	.75	2.85	.65	2.45	.31	3.60	.29	3.35	.75	2.85	.95	3.65

* Obtained locally; does not include special promotions or sales.

Includes prices of Schlitz, Pabst, Budweiser, Millers, Blatz, Old Style, Black Label, Drewry's, Ballantine, Hamm's, Peter Hand, Champagne Velvet, Tavern Pale, Van Merritt, and Canadian Ace.

exhibit 5   **BARTL'S BREWERY**

Shipments by months for Bartl's breweries, 1964

Month	Barrels Shipped	Per cent Change over Previous Year
January	6,478	1.7
February	6,321	7.3
March	8,187	5.7
April	8,345	−5.7
May	9,397	7.7
June	10,904	2.9
July	9,013	−7.5
August	9,201	5.6
September	7,323	−9.6
October	6,750	−6.3
November	6,391	4.6
December	7,665	1.0
Total	95,975	Net 0.3

exhibit 6
BARTL'S BREWERY
Organization Chart, January, 1965

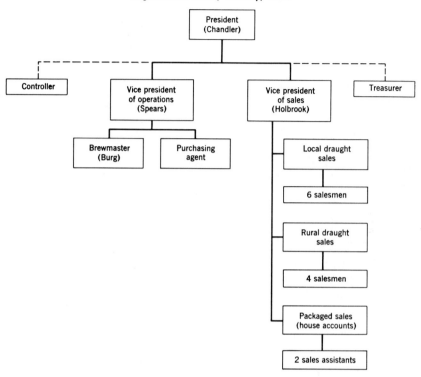

exhibit 7   INDUSTRY WITHDRAWALS AND PER CAPITA
CONSUMPTION OF MALT BEVERAGES
Fiscal years ending June 30, 1934–1963

Year	Estimated or Actual Population	Total Taxpaid Withdrawals (Barrels)	Per Capita Consumption (Gallons)
1934	126,373,773	32,266,039	7.9
1935	126,250,232	42,228,831	10.3
1936	126,053,180	48,759,840	11.8
1937	128,824,829	55,391,960	13.3
1938	129,824,939	53,926,018	12.9
1939	130,979,718	51,816,874	12.3
1940	131,669,275	53,014,230	12.5
1941	133,121,000	52,799,181	12.3
1942	133,920,000	60,856,219	14.1
1943	134,245,000	68,636,434	15.8
1944	132,885,000	76,969,764	18.0
1945	132,481,000	79,590,598	18.6
1946	140,054,000	81,286,821	18.0
1947	143,446,000	82,629,441	17.9
1948	146,093,000	86,992,795	18.5
1949	148,665,000	85,809,068	17.9
1950	150,697,361	83,511,994	17.2
1951	153,383,000	83,246,162	16.8
1952	155,761,000	84,293,646	16.8
1953	158,312,000	84,559,162	16.6
1954	161,190,000	85,747,439	16.5
1955	164,302,000	84,456,627	15.9
1956	167,262,000	85,537,307	15.9
1957	170,295,000	84,321,156	15.3
1958	173,452,000	83,948,536	15.0
1959	177,135,000	85,638,382	15.0
1960	179,323,175	88,928,883	15.4
1961	183,057,000	87,925,801	14.9
1962	185,822,000	90,693,253	15.1
1963	188,531,000	91,493,577	15.0

SOURCE: *Brewer's Almanac*, 1964 (United States Treasury Department, Internal Revenue Service, Alcohol and Tobacco Tax Division, and Bureau of Census), p. 12.

exhibit 8 **TAXPAID PACKAGED WITHDRAWALS OF MALT BEVERAGES BY TYPE OF CONTAINER** (Industry)

Calendar years 1959–1963 (based on a standard 12-ounce bottle or can)

Type of Container	1959		1960		1961		1962		1963	
	Barrels	% of Total	Barrels	% of Total	Barrels	% of Total	Barrels	% of Total	Barrels	% of Total
Metal cans	28,069,945	39.9	26,879,524	37.9	26,494,948	36.9	27,501,674*	37.1	29,622,697	38.8
One-way bottles	4,324,007	6.2	5,884,812	8.3	8,436,364	11.7	10,347,305	14.0	11,681,115	15.3
Returnable bottles	37,914,510	53.9	38,191,259	53.8	36,979,445	51.4	36,279,520*	48.9	35,043,346†	45.9
Total packaged withdrawals	70,308,462	100.0	70,955,595	100.0	71,910,757	100.0	74,128,498	100.0	76,347,158†	100.0

* Revised.

† Last six months unaudited.

SOURCE: *Brewer's Almanac*, 1964 (United States Treasury Department, Internal Revenue Service, Alcohol and Tobacco Tax Division), p. 25.

exhibit 9 **INDUSTRY PRODUCTION, DRAUGHT AND PACKAGED SALES, AND TOTAL TAXPAID WITHDRAWALS OF MALT BEVERAGES**
Calendar years 1933–1963 (quantities in 31-gallon barrels)

Calendar Year	Production	Packaged Sales	% of Total	Draught Sales	% of Total	Total Taxpaid* Withdrawals
1933†	24,501,678	6,467,400	31.6	14,002,241	68.4	20,469,641
1934	43,155,146	10,022,344	25.0	30,012,563	75.0	40,034,907
1935	48,013,218	13,311,837	29.5	31,831,195	70.5	45,143,032
1936	56,134,316	20,218,406	38.1	32,791,610	61.9	53,010,016
1937	58,259,570	24,431,399	43.8	31,300,794	56.2	55,732,193
1938	53,630,463	23,734,562	46.2	27,668,571	53.8	51,403,133
1939	55,222,501	26,043,002	49.3	26,744,031	50.7	52,787,033
1940	53,863,734	26,761,946	51.7	25,049,151	48.3	51,811,097
1941	60,636,547	32,199,010	56.1	25,204,362	43.9	57,403,372
1942	68,271,501	37,917,179	58.7	26,666,939	41.3	64,584,118
1943	75,624,489	44,248,184	60.9	28,444,754	39.1	72,692,938
1944	85,779,934	49,534,252	62.3	29,970,952	37.7	79,514,204
1945	88,205,537	52,664,148	64.3	29,177,247	35.7	81,841,395
1946	83,312,516	53,010,253	66.6	26,530,243	33.4	79,540,496
1947	91,742,212	58,899,447	67.6	28,272,887	32.4	87,172,334
1948	88,125,320	58,699,355	69.0	26,367,959	31.0	85,067,314
1949	88,618,322	59,443,805	70.3	25,113,802	29.7	84,557,607
1950	88,178,356	59,487,521	71.8	23,342,616	28.2	82,830,137
1951	89,742,138	61,706,743	73.6	22,116,893	26.4	83,823,636
1952	90,489,824	63,359,469	74.7	21,477,011	25.3	84,836,480
1953	92,104,063	65,830,505	76.5	20,214,611	23.5	86,045,116
1954	88,940,268	63,927,035	76.7	19,377,986	23.3	83,305,021
1955	90,285,488	66,179,019	77.9	18,798,255	22.1	84,977,274
1956	90,338,445	67,087,002	78.9	17,921,154	21.1	85,008,156
1957	89,465,986	66,982,200	79.4	17,388,825	20.6	84,371,025
1958	90,120,512	67,168,341	79.6	17,256,368	20.4	84,424,709
1959	93,127,427	70,308,462	80.2	17,313,897	19.8	87,622,359
1960	93,415,363	70,955,595	80.7	16,957,244	19.3	87,912,839
1961	95,030,031	71,910,757	80.8	17,117,674	19.2	89,028,431
1962	96,831,989	74,128,498	81.3	17,068,659	18.7	91,197,157
1963‡	100,576,505	76,347,158	81.4	17,446,815	18.6	93,793,973

* Withdrawn from production for selling purpose.
† April through December.
‡ Figures for last six months unaudited.
SOURCE: *Brewer's Almanac*, 1964 (United States Treasury Department, Internal Revenue Service, Alcohol and Tobacco Tax Division), p. 19.

exhibit 10 MALT BEVERAGE INDUSTRY—FEDERAL SPECIAL-TAX PAPERS*
Post-Prohibition—fiscal years ending June 30, 1933–1963

Fiscal Year	Brewers	Wholesale Dealers	Retail Dealers	Retail Dealers at Large†	Temporary Dealers‡
1933	331	14,135	262,639		
1934	756	17,630	230,322		
1935	766	15,300	181,770		
1936	739	14,640	186,282		
1937	754	13,813	177,834	11	13,850
1938	700	12,727	166,615	2,566	19,535
1939	672	11,472	157,985	144	22,834
1940	683	13,068	150,952	161	21,600
1941	587	10,820	145,447	191	20,476
1942	523	10,105	141,327	179	17,864
1943	491	8,885	121,100	158	10,010
1944	480	8,902	113,625	40	7,973
1945	476	9,062	118,815	29	9,146
1946	471	10,145	125,716	40	11,070
1947	485	12,374	140,213	98	11,104
1948	475	13,617	160,970	71	13,533
1949	444	14,038	167,434	56	13,090
1950	407	14,015	177,203	83	13,060
1951	390	13,735	175,448	96	12,812
1952	359	13,226	175,147	63	11,861
1953	333	12,190	183,175	67	11,568
1954	334	12,015	182,080	92	10,856
1955	299	11,792	178,163	90	11,122
1956	274	11,537	172,924	102	9,866
1957	278	11,320	168,394	97	9,603
1958	255	11,088	161,041	169	8,875
1959	260	10,879	158,712	173	8,867
1960	240	8,685	153,541	186	8,783
1961	230	8,174	147,933	182	9,172
1962	224	8,046	145,865	183	9,050
1963	217	7,783	144,116	214	8,078

* These figures show the total number in each category purchasing special-tax stamps at any time during the fiscal year.
† All permanent retail establishments selling beer.
‡ Those dealers which are of a seasonal nature such as concession stands at ball parks and race tracks.
SOURCE: *Brewer's Almanac*, 1964 (United States Treasury Department, Internal Revenue Service, Alcohol and Tobacco Tax Division), p. 92.

exhibit 11 ESTIMATED PERCENTAGE PROFIT AND LOSS STATEMENTS FOR ENTIRE BREWING INDUSTRY
Calendar years 1962–1964

	1962		1963		1964	
	Returns with Net Income	Returns with No Net Income	Returns with Net Income	Returns with No Net Income	Returns with Net Income	Returns with No Net Income
Gross sales*	90.8	99.2	99.4	99.5	99.1	99.2
Interest, rents, royalites, etc.	2.0	.2	.2	.2	.3	.3
Other receipts	6.9	.6	.4	.3	.6	.5
Total receipts	100.0	100.0	100.0	100.0	100.0	100.0
Cost of goods sold †	46.0	37.2	48.3	40.6	44.6	41.9
Compensation of officers	.6	.8	.6	.9	.5	1.0
Rents paid on business property	.2	.4	.3	.3	.3	.2
Repairs	.9	1.2	1.0	1.3	1.1	.6
Bad debts	.1	.2	.1	.2	.1	.4
Interest paid	.3	.4	.3	.5	.3	.0
Contributions or gifts	.1	.0	.2	.0	.1	.0
Depreciation, depletion, and amortization	2.5	3.4	2.8	2.8	2.6	2.4
Advertising	7.0	6.8	6.5	6.8	6.7	7.0
Contributions under pension plans, etc.	1.0	.0	1.0	1.3	1.0	1.4
Loss (net) on sales of other than capital assets	.0	.0	.1	.5	.1	.6
Taxes other than Federal income taxes‡	24.3	31.7	23.1	27.6	25.2	31.0
Other deductions	10.4	21.1	10.3	20.1	11.3	16.4
Total deductions	93.4	103.2	94.6	102.9	93.9	102.9
Net profit (or loss) before Federal income taxes	6.6	(3.2)	5.4	(2.9)	6.1	(2.9)
Federal income taxes	3.3		2.7		3.1	
Net profit (or loss) after taxes	3.3	(3.2)	2.7	(2.9)	3.0	(2.9)

* "Gross sales" consists of amounts received for goods, less returns and allowances, in transactions where inventories are an income-determining factor. Beginning with the year 1958 "Gross sales" and "Gross receipts from operations" have been combined under the term "Business Receipts."
† "Cost of goods sold" and cost of operations exclude indemnifiable amounts of taxes, depreciation, depletion, amortization, advertising, and contributions under pension plans and other employee benefit plans included therein.
‡ This item excludes (1) Federal income and excess profits taxes, (2) estate, inheritance, legacy, succession and gift taxes, (3) income taxes paid to a foreign country or possession of the United States if any portion is claimed as a tax receipt, (4) taxes assessed against local benefits, (5) Federal taxes paid on tax-free covenant bonds, and (6) taxes reported under "Cost of goods sold."

exhibit 12 ESTIMATED PERCENTAGE BALANCE SHEET FOR ENTIRE BREWING INDUSTRY
Calendar years 1962–1964

	1962		*1963*		*1964*	
	Returns with Net Income	*Returns with No Net Income*	*Returns with Net Income*	*Returns with No Net Income*	*Returns with Net Income*	*Returns with No Net Income*
Assets:						
Cash	9.2	7.3	8.3	9.7	8.2	7.6
Notes and accounts						
receivable	11.0	10.5	10.2	10.7	10.0	16.3
Less: reserve for bad						
debts	.3	.6	.3	.6	.3	.9
Inventories	12.8	13.2	14.6	15.1	13.6	10.7
Government securities	5.3	3.3	7.8	3.9	7.8	1.6
Other investments	4.8	3.8	4.0	3.7	5.4	11.6
Gross capital assets						
(except land)	80.3	105.0	81.8	103.3	85.5	96.5
Less: reserves	30.4	49.4	33.6	52.9	37.0	53.1
Land	2.7	3.9	2.7	3.3	2.8	3.9
Other assets	4.6	3.0	4.5	3.8	4.0	5.8
Total assets	100.0	100.0	100.0	100.0	100.0	100.0
Liabilities:						
Accounts payable	6.3	6.4	6.2	6.8	5.5	8.0
Bonds, notes,						
mortgages payable:						
Maturity less than						
1 year	.9	3.8	1.8	2.9	1.7	6.9
Maturity more						
1 year	8.5	11.8	8.4	12.9	.9	17.3
Other liabilities	9.4	4.8	11.0	5.5	9.6	9.1
Capital stock preferred	3.4	2.2	2.2	2.0	1.8	3.4
Capital stock common	15.0	20.9	14.8	16.8	16.0	15.7
Surplus reserves	1.3	2.6	.6	2.3	.7	.6
Surplus and undivided						
profits	55.2*	47.5*	55.0*	50.8*	56.8*	39.0*
Total liabilities	100.0	100.0	100.0	100.0	100.0	100.0

* Deficit. Amounts shown as "Deficit" consist of negative amounts of earned surplus and undivided profits. Note that both groups had negative earned surpluses.

exhibit 13   EXTRACTS FROM SURVEY OF LOCAL NEWSPAPERS

1. Why use fancy-dressed people in beer advertising when beer is not a prestige product?

2. The upper-class man does not drink beer; he drinks hard liquor. The middle-class, everyday man serves beer before, during and after dinner, whereas the upper-class man serves cocktails, wines, and highballs.

3. The consumer couldn't care less if an advertisement shows a member of high society, a celebrity, or a movie star, drinking beer. He feels that the individual wouldn't ever drink the beer and is only being paid for his endorsement.

4. The average consumer does not want to drink in the same establishment as the man from the upper class, as a beer will cost a minimum of 50¢, and it doesn't taste any better than when purchased at the local beer hall.

5. Beer is a drink for sociable people; it allows people to relax. The fact is accepted that beer puts everyone on the same social level. When drinking beer, the president of the company becomes "one of the boys."

6. Beer drinkers are particular about the taste of their beer. The average consumer may not understand the words the beer drinker uses; he applies terms such as "smooth," "light," and "refreshing" to the beers he likes, and to those he dislikes, he applies terms such as "bitter," "biting," "smelly," and "sickening."

7. The average man prefers beer advertising which conveys the impressions of "relaxation," "wholesomeness" and "pleasure." He detests "sexiness" in beer advertising. If the former "attitudes" or "images" can be applied to a brand of beer, the consumer will like and drink the beer.

8. The average consumer cares little about how beer is processed, its place of production or the type of water used. All he is concerned with is taste.

9. Beer is found at ball parks, at picnics, at home, and at other informal gatherings where friendliness and fellowship is sought Beer is a social refreshment along with soft drinks as contrasted to the more formal hard liquors or "mixed drinks."

10. An individual can enjoy the leisurely drinking of beer, through an evening and not "overdo it." No constant counting of intake is needed. The consumer is even able to participate properly in sporting events without his abilities being handicapped.

11. Women, previously considered non-consumers, are becoming more important to the sale of beer though they still drink only when their male companions do, and then usually drink the same brand they do.

ASTRA-LITE
CORPORATION

HISTORICAL DEVELOPMENT

The Astra-Lite Corporation was a medium-sized producer of industrial and commercial lighting fixtures located in Brooklyn, New York. The company was founded by John Cutter in 1920 to manufacture general electrical supplies for the building trade. Through specialization in light shields and light reflectors Astra-Lite gradually developed a relatively wide variety of commercial and industrial lighting fixtures. By 1930 the company had established a reputation as a producer of a quality line that was well accepted in a highly competitive industry. Many of the company's fixtures were of an exclusive design which permitted them to charge a higher price for their products than their competitors.

The building boom of the 1920's provided a ready market for Astra-Lite's products and the company grew from a small-sized operation to one with sales of over one million dollars.[1] The depression severely curtailed the construction of new commercial and industrial buildings and the remodeling of old ones. Astra-Lite suffered serious losses from 1931 to 1936 because of this drop in building activity, and did not recover until 1937 when the company showed a small profit from operations. With the increase in construction activity in the 1937–1941 period, Astra-Lite managed to show a profit each year.

In 1942 the company received a contract for lighting fixtures for military installations. By virtue of such contracts and the subcontracts received for the manufacture of airplane parts, the firm operated at full capacity throughout the war period.

[1] The sales of the company reached an all-time high of $4.5 million in 1952, and in 1956 amounted to $3.9 million. See Exhibit 3.

POSTWAR PROBLEMS

In 1946 Astra-Lite found itself in a postwar boom so great that it could not provide the lighting fixtures to keep pace with the demands of the building contractors. It was during this period, however, that many new manufacturers came into the field to take advantage of the unprecedented demand for lighting fixtures, chiefly of the fluorescent type. Astra-Lite managed to hold its position in the industry, despite the advent of new competition, mainly because of the backlog of new designs the company had held over from the war period. The intensity of the competition after 1950, however, created a serious problem for the company. The number of manufacturers in the field caused an oversupply of fixtures and allowed the building contractors to squeeze the suppliers for lower prices. This practice became very common when the contractors were faced with the rising labor and operating costs of the postwar period. The costs of producing fluorescent lighting fixtures were also constantly increasing in this period, mainly because of the rising raw material cost of steel, aluminum, and ballast. These materials accounted for over 50 per cent of the cost of the fluorescent fixture. Because of the intense competition in the fluorescent lighting field, Astra-Lite could not raise its prices to pass on the added costs of manufacture to the contractors. As a result their profit margin and the margins of producers in the same category were reduced substantially.

Astra-Lite was able to incorporate rising material costs only when it introduced new designs in fluorescent fixtures to the market. But because of the lack of any secure protection on new designs, other companies soon copied the design or introduced a similar one and the same competitive pattern of price competition again prevailed. The company, however, continued its policy of stressing quality and attempting to be an innovator in the lighting field. Despite changes in the management in this period of market difficulties, no thought had been given to lowering the quality or specialty design on which the company had built its reputation.

ORGANIZATION AND PERSONNEL

John Cutter, the founder of the company, had been responsible for the initial success of Astra-Lite. He had personally designed many of the fixtures that had established the company's reputation in the field. It was mainly through his efforts that the company gained a foothold in the fluorescent market. He served as president and general manager of the company from its inception in 1920 until his death in 1945.

Mr. Ronald Johnson became general manager of the company upon the death of Mr. Cutter. In 1946 he was appointed president of Astra-Lite at a special meeting of the stockholders. Mr. Johnson had been the general manager of the company's branch plant in Los Angeles, which served as a shipping point and performed some sub-assembly work. In addition to his duties in this capacity, he acted as the sales manager of the entire west coast area. Mr. Johnson was 52 years old, a graduate of New York University, and had been with the company for 15 years. Prior to joining Astra-Lite, Mr. Johnson had been employed by a public accounting firm and as an auditor for General Electric. During the war period he spent two years as a naval supply officer. He returned from service in 1944 and resumed his duties as general manager of the Los Angeles plant and sales district.

Mr. Robert Caswell was vice-president in charge of sales. He was 59 years old and had been with the company for 20 years. Prior to joining Astra-Lite he had served in various capacities as salesman, district sales manager, and assistant sales manager of a medium-sized electrical supply house. He was generally considered to have been John Cutter's right-hand man and had served as the acting general manager of the company during the frequent illnesses of Mr. Cutter from 1942–1945.

In 1953 the company suffered a loss of $44,000 and a special meeting of the stockholders was called. George Cutter, the brother of the founder of the firm, acting as the executor of the Cutter estate which still represented over 60 per cent of the outstanding stock, conducted the meeting. He accused Mr. Johnson of poor business tactics and failure to keep abreast of the current market situation. George Cutter maintained that Astra-Lite would be at the top of the heap if his brother were alive. Mr. Johnson attempted to explain the problems of selling lighting fixtures in the present changing and shifting market which was overrun with small manufacturers who stole designs and engaged in price cutting, often to their own detriment. He also pointed out that the business had changed considerably since the death of John Cutter, and the intensity of the competition prevented any of the medium-sized companies from showing much, if any, profit. Mr. Cutter was not satisfied with this explanation and demanded Mr. Johnson's resignation. Mr. Johnson agreed to resign but only if the company would honor the remaining year of his contract. A settlement was agreed upon and Mr. Robert Caswell was appointed acting president.

Mr. Cutter called a series of meetings of the Board of Directors, which had served only in a perfunctory capacity up to this time. Prior to the death of Mr. John Cutter a five-man board served the company. It was composed of John Cutter, George Cutter, Robert Caswell, Randolph Worth, a bank president, and Mrs. John Cutter. As a result of George Cutter's insistence, the Board was increased to seven members and Mrs. John Cutter, who never attended meetings, was dropped from the board by mutual agreement. The new directors included George Cutter's son, Frank Cutter, 31 years of age, a partner of a prominent New York law firm; Mr. Thomas Rand, the head of the industrial engineering department of Astra-Lite, who was promoted to vice-president at the time of his appointment; Warren Clifford, the president of a steel warehousing firm and a long-time business associate of the late John Cutter; and Frank Lochley, one of the largest minority stockholders, who had recently retired as an officer of a small Brooklyn bank. Mr. Lochley had personally handled the Astra-Lite account in the early stages of the company's development.

PERSONNEL CHANGES

After serving as acting president for one year, Mr. Caswell requested that he be relieved of his assignment and returned to his position as sales manager. He maintained that the duties of the president were too much of a strain on him, particularly because of his recent illness. Caswell also complained of the interference and lack of cooperation of Mr. Rand, the head of the industrial engineering department. At a special meeting of the Board of Directors in February of 1955, Mr. Frank Cutter was appointed president of the firm, and Mr. Rand was made executive vice-president in charge of industrial engineering.

Six months after Frank Cutter took over as president, drastic personnel changes were made and the firm's organization structure was changed. Mr. Caswell, who had become increasingly dissatisfied with Mr. Rand's operations, retired. His assistant, Andrew Sandage, 35 years of age, was appointed sales manager.

John Nelson, vice-president in charge of manufacturing and plant engineering, was dismissed, mainly on the recommendations of Mr. Rand, who maintained that he had not followed recommended cost-cutting techniques that were so necessary to increase the company's declining margin. Nelson insisted that such cuts would be at the sacrifice of quality and he openly stated that he saw little or no value in the procedures recommended by Rand's department. Nelson had joined the company in 1946 at the time of the postwar expansion. He took over a newly created position and assumed charge of the function previously performed under two departments, manufacturing and engineering. On the recommendation of Mr. Rand the functions of Nelson's department were again divided into two areas, engineering and manufacturing. The manufacturing operations were placed under a newly hired works manager, Mr. Leslie Butler, who formerly worked for Western Electric as an engineer and assistant works manager. Because of the importance of research and development in the lighting industry, Frank Cutter and Mr. Rand were both of the opinion that a top-flight man should be placed in charge of an engineering and product development department. Mr. Dennis Reed, who had twenty years' experience in engineering and development in a radio and television manufacturing firm, was chosen for the position and was given the title of vice-president in charge of engineering and product development. Mr. Reed left his former position to accept the Astra-Lite offer because of difficulties encountered when his firm, a medium-sized producer, was purchased by one of the largest manufacturers of radios, television sets and household appliances. Mr. Reed also assumed the position on the Board of Directors left vacant by Mr. Caswell's retirement.

As a result of Nelson's dismissal, the chief production and tool engineer, Clifford Wall, who had 20 years' experience with the company, resigned and later accepted a similar position with a New Jersey aircraft producer. Elliott Howe, the assistant chief engineer, who had been with the company for fifteen years, took over the position.

Harold Ramsey, the general purchasing agent, left in late 1954 over a salary dispute with Frank Cutter. Robert Sears, who had been the assistant purchasing agent of a competing company, was hired to replace Ramsey.

John Hill, the controller, resigned. He was 63 years of age. In submitting his resignation he stated: "I am not going to spend the last years of my working life being subjected to the whims of a nincompoop efficiency expert and the wild hallucinations of a boy still wet behind the ears." Hill's position was not filled. Frank Cutter stated that the department would be run by Hill's assistant, Raymond Cowden, and he,

Cutter, would personally assume the executive direction until Cowden proved his ability or they hired a competent man.

John Sima, in charge of sales promotion and advertising, left, mainly because he had expected to replace Mr. Caswell upon his retirement. In informing Frank Cutter of his intention to leave, he bluntly stated that the only reason Sandage was assistant sales manager prior to his

exhibit 1
ASTRA-LITE CORPORATION
Organization Chart, 1954

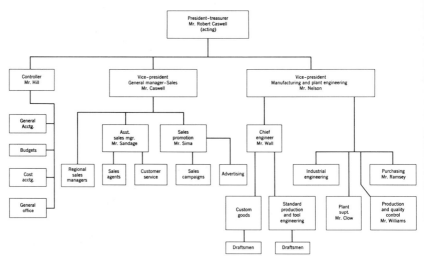

Organization Chart, 1955

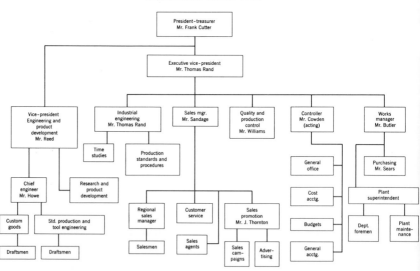

promotion was because he was not capable of handling the important end of the business, pushing sales, and he could be trusted only with the administrative details of handling salesmen's accounts and customer services. Sima was replaced by Sandage's assistant, John Thornton, who had been with the company for three months. Thornton had ten years' experience in advertising and sales.

The changes in the organization of Astra-Lite between 1954 and 1955, when Frank Cutter became president, are indicated in Exhibit 1.

DEPARTMENTAL OPERATIONS

In July of 1955 Mr. Edward Williams, the head of production and quality control, who had joined the company in November 1953, submitted a proposal to control scrap in the manufacturing process. A procedure had been worked out with the accounting department to provide the needed information and reports that would indicate where the scrap was originating. These reports would then be submitted to the proper production departments to originate corrective action. Mr. Rand opposed this method and maintained that his department could eventually work out a more practical method of controlling scrap. The president concurred in this opinion and rejected Williams' plan.

In late 1955 no formal scrap control procedure had been instituted. The quality control department, without the necessary reports to indicate where the scrap was originating, attempted to control scrap through the inspection of the incoming fabricated parts and through sample checking of parts produced in the punch press department.

The industrial engineering department, under Mr. Rand, reported to the vice-president of manufacturing until Rand was appointed executive vice-president. Industrial engineering was responsible for time study, the development of standards and the issuing of standard manufacturing layouts. Because of short-staffing and the overlapping of functions with the production control department, industrial engineering had been an organizational problem since its inception. Because of this situation and the friction between the plant manager and the head of the production control department over the scheduling of orders to be manufactured, six men had held the position of production control manager in the period 1950 to 1955.

Thomas Rand, prior to his appointment as executive vice-president, had served as the firm's industrial engineer for a period of two years. He had been hired upon the recommendation of Mr. Lochley, the largest

minority stockholder. Mr. Rand was 45 years of age, a graduate industrial engineer, with twenty years' experience in his field. When hired by
Astra-Lite he was on the staff of Graybar, a former subsidiary of American Telephone and Telegraph. Several inducements unusual to Astra-
Lite's general executive employment policy were made to acquire the
services of Mr. Rand. His salary at the time he was hired was exceeded
only by that of the president. In addition, he was promised an opportunity to advance to the vice-president level if his work proved satisfactory to the president and Board of Directors.

In the first two years of his employment with Astra-Lite, Rand was
confronted with the problem of establishing an industrial engineering
department, which was formerly a function of general engineering. He
encountered much opposition from the vice-president of engineering,
the chief engineer, and the plant superintendent. Rand became particularly incensed when the engineering department refused to accept a
somewhat revolutionary plan he had devised to speed up the assembly
of fluorescent fixtures. Rand submitted this plan in article form to a
monthly industrial engineering magazine which featured it as a lead article. It attracted much interest in the lighting industry and was incorporated into the assembly lines of several medium-sized producers.

Shortly after being appointed executive vice-president, Rand added
five men to his staff to prepare manufacturing layouts of all standard
fixtures. When possible, standards on new parts and fixtures were to be
determined from similar parts manufactured in the past. On new parts
that could not be compared to those previously manufactured, a pilot
run was to be made to determine initial standards. Rand also received
the president's approval to install his own system for manufacturing
layouts and production orders. Many of the foremen in manufacturing
complained of the newly installed standards and contended that they
were highly inaccurate. In addition, they stated that the manufacturing
layouts contained very little information about how to perform the actual operations.

The layouts prepared prior to Rand's reorganization of the department contained detailed instructions for the most complex operations;
for example, the final assembly and pack on Ex-Lite fixtures required
16 detailed steps, and each of these steps was explained and the standard time for each was outlined. Under the new system the layouts for
Ex-Lite contained only the assembly-pack information and a total of
standard hours required for the whole operation.

Five months after the new system had been in operation, returns and allowances for fixtures improperly wired increased greatly. The works manager contended that if it had not been for the assembly department foreman and the sub-assembly foreman, with twenty and thirty years' experience, respectively, the returns would have been much greater. Because of the low efficiency rating of the assembly department, Mr. Rand transferred the foreman who had the job for the past fifteen years and hired a new man from another company that manufactured lighting fixtures. This foreman resigned within one month, stating that he could not raise production under the present system of layouts and standards. The works manager and the chief engineer concurred in this opinion. In a special report to the president they stated that it was not possible to assemble fixtures in the present allowable standard time and without detailed instructions being furnished the women assemblers.

Mr. Butler, the works manager, stated that he had little chance of solving the problem unless he had the opportunity of sitting down with the president and showing him in black and white just how the new system was working. He felt that there was no opportunity for this since Rand authorized the plan and he was likely to sidetrack any report or effort to get such information to the president.

The controller, chief cost accountant, and the head of the payroll section all complained of the difficulties created by the new system. They contended that the payroll section and cost department were not getting the necessary information from the producing departments to allow them to process the payroll on time and to record cost data for the budget analysis.

Mr. Rand also introduced a cost-saving program in the factory and office. Each department was given a stated quota to save out of their normal budget during the fiscal year. The controller considered this plan in direct competition with the annual budget, which was put into effect at the beginning of each fiscal year.

MARKETING

Astra-Lite sold its products through distributors who in turn sold to the contractor. In addition to distributors, Astra-Lite employed sales agents and salesmen. These men called on distributors to aid them in selling Astra-Lite fixtures. All distributors handled more than one line of lighting fixtures. In addition to calling on distributors, these salesmen contacted contractors and architects in an effort to get them to specify Astra-Lite fixtures in their proposals and specifications for new buildings and remodeling contracts.

The sales promotion was done by a small amount of advertising in trade publications, heavy expenditures for exhibits at building and association shows, and by intensive catalog promotion. Illustrated price catalogs were sent out to a mailing list of distributors, contractors, architects, and electrical consultants. Astra-Lite encouraged cooperative advertising by bearing approximately one-half of the expense of distributors' catalogs.

The company revised its catalog in July 1955 with a new illustrated edition, at an expense of $75,000. It was expected that the new catalog would not need to be replaced for several years. However, between July 1955 and July 1956, the company introduced more new products than during any comparable period in its history. To cover these products a new illustrated price list and catalog would have to be issued, which would cost approximately $40,000 to $50,000.

Prior to 1950 Astra-Lite employed a large number of sales agents who handled other electrical lines and were paid on commission. Since it was difficult to control the agents, the company started a program to replace them with salesmen. The replacement was rapid and the sales organization soon became a centralized function. But in the eyes of management it did not produce satisfactory results. In the spring of 1952 a reorganization of the sales department was instigated and a regional sales management plan was adopted. The salesmen were paid a high monthly salary, expenses were reimbursed, quotas were established for each salesman, and a commission was paid on all sales over the quota. The remaining sales agents, however, were still paid on a straight commission basis.

A regional sales manager was appointed for three geographic sections, the East, the Middle West and the West. This plan, after functioning for two and one-half years, was deemed unsatisfactory by the new president, Frank Cutter. He ordered a complete revamping of the entire sales program. The framework of the regional plan was retained, however, and in late 1955 a new sales plan calling for a scaled commission on all sales, a small salary and no reimbursement of expenses was instituted. This plan met with resistance from the salesmen. A few who had sold over their quota the previous year accepted the new basis of compensation. But the majority of the salesmen resisted and were eventually granted a salary scale that would work them into the new plan over a period of six months. Seven of the sales staff resigned rather than accept the new payment plan.

GENERAL

In July 1956 Frank Cutter told stockholders that, "a plant modernization program, with new facilities, new products, redesign and improvement of existing products, a new catalog and illustrated price list, more aggressive sales promotion, and the addition of key personnel on the managerial level . . . had a serious effect upon current operations. Consequently, the company experienced a net loss of $185,000 for the fiscal year. . . . Astra-Lite's raw material cost increased $40,000. However, the increase in sales volume and the beneficial effect of the mentioned major changes are expected to produce a more favorable profit picture in the current fiscal year."

Frank Cutter also informed the stockholders that the company was three years behind in development of products when he became president. But a concentrated effort was being made to remedy this situation.

He also stated that the company was considering setting up a complete assembly operation in its branch plant on the west coast. This, he stated, was necessary to get business in California where a firm needed a "Made in California" label on its products, and to reduce the high shipping costs of fixtures to that market area.

One month following the stockholders meeting a private consulting firm submitted a report on the feasibility of complete assembly of Astra-Lite products on the west coast. The report, based mainly on the confidential operations of another lighting manufacturer, indicated that it was cheaper to ship complete fixtures to the west coast rather than to assemble them out there. The logical place for an assembly plant on the west coast, according to the report, was in the San Francisco Bay area and not in Los Angeles.

In September 1956 Frank Cutter signed the contract to provide for the assembly of Astra-Lite fixtures in the Los Angeles plant. The vice-president of engineering and product development was of the opinion that the company should spend the money on research and development rather than expand their operations on the west coast.

exhibit 2   ASTRA-LITE CORPORATION
Balance sheet, 1946–1956, fiscal years ending June 30 (rounded to thousands of dollars)

	1956	1955	1954	1953	1952	1951	1950	1949	1948	1947	1946
Current assets											
Cash	$ 160	$ 79	$ 94	$ 225	$ 480	$ 410	$ 490	$ 451	$ 251	$ 240	$ 250
Accounts receivable	361	308	310	350	390	346	380	342	374	360	361
Inventories:											
Finished goods and work in process	342	345	340	360	410	340	361	240	220	180	200
Raw materials	370	352	350	348	377	293	313	280	270	300	180
Prepaid expenses	6	8	9	11	10	6	9	10	4	2	5
Total current assets	$1,239	$1,092	$1,103	$1,294	$1,667	$1,395	$1,553	$1,323	$1,119	$1,082	$ 996
Fixed assets											
Plant, property and equipment, net	1,140*	680	740	770	790	702	740	773	830	780	720
Deferred charges	8	6	8	9	10	8	9	6	7	7	6
Total assets	$2,387	$1,778	$1,851	$2,073	$2,467	$2,105	$2,302	$2,102	$1,956	$1,869	$1,722
Current liabilities											
Accounts payable	$ 167	$ 136	$ 165	$ 175	$ 197	$ 123	$ 182	$ 134	$ 130	$ 122	$ 110
Notes payable	75										10
Employees' withholding tax	18	12	16	14	18	12	14	10	6	8	7
Accrued wages	140	108	110	125	145	115	137	110	82	85	75
Accrued Federal income taxes	—	—	—	—	248	67	189	187	195	235	200
Total current liabilities	$ 400	$ 256	$ 291	$ 314	$ 608	$ 317	$ 522	$ 441	$ 413	$ 450	$ 402
Fixed liabilities and capital accounts											
Long-term debt	650										
Common stock	560	560	560	560	560	560	560	560	560	560	560
Paid-in surplus	100	100	100	100	100	100	100	100	100	100	100
Earnings retained in business	677	862	900	1,099	1,199	1,128	1,120	1,001	883	759	660
Total liabilities and capital	$2,387	$1,778	$1,851	$2,073	$2,467	$2,105	$2,302	$2,102	$1,956	$1,869	$1,722

* Mortgaged for debt of $650,000.

exhibit 3   ASTRA-LITE CORPORATION

Statement of profit and loss, 1946–1956, fiscal years ending June 30   (rounded to thousands of dollars)

	1956	1955	1954	1953	1952	1951	1950	1949	1948	1947	1946
Net sales	$3,900	$3,800	$2,700	$1,500	$4,500	$2,400	$4,100	$3,720	$3,300	$3,100	$3,000
Less cost of goods sold	2,960	2,850	1,970	1,100	3,000	1,590	2,580	2,350	1,980	2,015	1,950
Gross profit	940	950	730	400	1,500	810	1,520	1,370	1,320	1,085	1,050
Less expenses:											
Selling and engineering	970	798	648	300	750	480	820	740	726	465	450
General administrative	195	228	210	120	250	170	307	245	200	170	180
	$1,165	1,026	858	420	1,000	650	1,127	985	926	635	630
Operating profit	$ 225*	$ 76*	$ 128*	$ 20*	$ 500	$ 160	$ 393	$ 385	$ 394	$ 450	$ 420
Add other income	40										
	185*										
Deduct:											
Other expense			43	24	25	30	29	25	19	60	45
Federal income taxes					248	67	189	187	195	235	200
			43	24	273	97	218	212	214	295	245
Net income after taxes	$ 185*	$ 76*	$ 171*	$ 44*	$ 227	$ 63	$ 175	$ 173	$ 180	$ 155	$ 175
Dividends paid			$ 28	$ 56	$ 56	$ 56	$ 56	$ 56	$ 56	$ 56	$ 56
Retained earnings	$(185)	$ (76)	$(199)	$(100)	$ 171	$ 7	$ 119	$ 117	$ 124	$ 99	$ 119

* = loss.

( ) = reduction in retained earnings.

149

LAKELAND
MANUFACTURING
COMPANY

In 1948 the Lakeland Manufacturing Company of Waukegan, Illinois, entered the expanding field of garden tractors and attachments. After a small loss in the first year on a volume of $927,000, the company expanded its sales rapidly to more than $4.4 million in 1952. In 1953 sales declined to $3.7 million although profits exceeded those of the previous record year. With the close of the fiscal year 1953 on August 31, the officers felt that Lakeland had "shaken down" on its new product; and, while recognizing that there were still many problems, they believed the company had earned a permanent place in the industry.

BACKGROUND

The company originated in 1911 as the Roscoe Manufacturing Company. In 1913 the controlling group was bought out and the name changed to the Schultz Manufacturing Company. The principal products at that time were items of harness hardware. The company purchased castings from the Starbuck Manufacturing Company, of which R. A. Powell was vice-president and general manager. In 1914 the Schultz Company was in need of additional capital, and Powell, together with two of his associates, invested in and gained control of the business.

In 1919 Powell bought out the other owners of the Schultz Company, moved it to a new location in Waukegan, and changed the name to the Lakeland Company. In that same year his eldest son, Clair P. Powell, graduated from Cornell University and took charge as vice-president and general manager. Sales then were about $200,000 annually. C. P. Powell had acquired some experience in the business, working on the company books during summers and, for a period after graduating from high school, as a salesman. From 1928 to 1932 he took on the vice-presidency of an investment counseling firm in addition to his duties as manager of the Lakeland Company. During the depression, the company struggled along with the elder Powell managing the factory and his son working as a salesman and gradually taking on additional managerial responsibility. In 1940 the elder Powell retired, and C. P. Powell became president and treasurer, the position which he held in 1953.

In 1928 a younger Powell brother, Robert, left the University of Wisconsin; and, after several years in investment counseling and then as a salesman of paper products, came to Lakeland as purchasing agent in 1935. In 1942, after experience in other phases of the business and a term of office as secretary, he became vice-president in charge of production, as well as secretary.

After 1937 the market for harness hardware began to shrink appreciably. Lakeland added some hand garden tools to its line and also manufactured railroad-car door-hangers. The first garden tractor was assembled in May of 1948, and production expanded from 1,000 units in that year to more than 17,000 in 1952. In that period a large mail-order house took about 90 per cent of Lakeland's production. Lakeland supplied the higher-priced line of garden tractors carried by the mail-order house, the standard line being manufactured by the Simplicity Manufacturing Company of Port Washington, Wisconsin. C. P. Powell regarded Lakeland's "niche" in the market as that of a quality producer, receiving a somewhat higher than average price.

The plant was 60,000 square feet in size. The Powell family controlled the company through ownership of 50.2 per cent of the stock.

THE GARDEN TRACTOR MARKET

The rise of the garden tractor industry to a position of importance occurred after World War II. Annual shipments during the five years before the war averaged about 10,000 units. But after 1945, because of farm mechanization, expansion of suburban living, and the impulse which high food and labor costs gave to home gardens, annual shipments rose rapidly to 197,540 units with a value in excess of $27 million in 1952. Exhibit 1 illustrates this growth and the increasing importance of attachment sales to the industry. Production and shipments for the

exhibit 1　DOMESTIC SHIPMENTS OF GARDEN TRACTORS

Year	*Units*	*Value $1000*	*Attachments Value $1000*
1937	9,752	1,466	
1938	8,970	1,226	
1939	8,952	1,326	
1940	8,816	1,237	
1941	16,118	2,070	
1942	12,493	1,771	
1943	9,124	1,337	
1944	14,889	1,958	
1945	26,401	3,353	1,579
1946	109,179	22,166	3,250
1947	158,984	29,995	8,804
1948	158,865	28,086	10,567
1949	126,331	20,075	7,460
1950	149,704	21,529	8,520
1951	164,323	24,069	10,328
1952	197,540	27,344	11,559

SOURCE: U.S. Department of Commerce, *Facts for Industry,* "Tractors," 1952. These figures include motor tillers. This series is based on reports covering the entire industry.

years 1950 through 1952 are shown in Exhibit 2. A breakdown by type is given in Exhibit 3.

The executives of Lakeland's mail-order-house customer made the following estimates of the garden tractor industry and market: (1) about 30 per cent of garden tractor sales were through mail-order-house outlets, and brand line sales through dealers of five manufacturers accounted for another 43 per cent; (2) garden tractor attachments were about 50 per cent of their total sales of garden tractors and attachments; (3) they anticipated that industry sales would roughly

exhibit 2 TOTAL SHIPMENT OF GARDEN TRACTORS, 1950–1952

Year	Production Units	Shipments	
		Units	Value $1000
1950	151,198	153,827	22,249
1951	177,169	168,352	24,758
1952	199,321	202,492	28,098

SOURCE: U.S. Department of Commerce, *Facts for Industry*, "Tractors," 1951 and 1952. This series is based on reports covering the entire industry.

increase to 300,000 units annually by 1957, and that their requirements from Lakeland would increase to about 20,000 units per year.[1]

In response to written inquiries, individual garden tractor manufacturers made estimates for 1957 industry sales ranging from 175,000 to

exhibit 3 TOTAL SHIPMENT OF GARDEN TRACTORS BY TYPE, 1950–1952

Tractor Type	No. of Mfrs.			Total Units Shipped			Total Value $1000		
	1950	1951	1952	1950	1951	1952	1950	1951	1952
Riding types:	27	29	26	5,152	4,249	5,504	1,985	1,665	1,927
Under 6 hp	12	9	8	2,374	956	1,330	841	358	432
6 hp and over	16	23	23	2,778	3,293	4,174	1,144	1,307	1,495
Walking types:	63	53	50	131,464	138,005	155,490	17,362	19,104	21,082
2 hp and under	42	34	35	75,353	51,279	57,679	8,000	5,866	6,049
Over 2 hp and under 6 hp	48	43	39	55,786	86,338	96,328	9,232	13,066	14,517
6 hp and over	6	6	5	325	388	1,483	130	172	516
Total all types, except motor tillers	77	68	64	136,616	142,254	160,994	19,347	20,769	23,009
Motor tillers	19	15	18	17,211	26,098	41,498	2,902	3,989	5,089
Total				153,827	168,352	202,492	22,249	24,758	28,098

SOURCE: U.S. Department of Commerce, *Facts for Industry*, "Tractors," 1951 and 1952. This series is based on reports covering the entire industry.

[1] References to the views of the mail-order-house executive opinions are drawn from a consultant's report on the Lakeland Manufacturing Company, 1952.

276,000 units. Most of them indicated they did not expect the trend in garden tractor sales to follow the trend of the agricultural implement industry, although some thought it would to some extent.[2]

One trend in the industry was toward tractors of greater power. The proportion of tractors in the 2- to 6-horsepower range increased from 28 per cent in 1948 to 62 per cent in 1952. Motor tillers amounted to 15.6 per cent of the industry shipments in 1951 and nearly 20.4 per cent in 1952. (See Exhibit 3.)

The principal market for garden tractors was the suburban dweller with a sizeable lawn and garden, although the garden tractor had been important on the farm in "replacing the last horse," as Lakeland execu-

exhibit 4   **FARM INCOME AND CAPITAL OUTLAYS ($BILLIONS)**

Year	Cash Receipts	Net Cash Income	Buildings	Vehicles	Machinery and Equipment
1940	9.1	4.5	.6	.4	.4
1945	22.3	12.5	.7	.4	.7
1950	28.6	8.9	2.3	1.5	1.7
1951	33.1	10.8	2.3	1.7	2.0
1952	32.6	9.6	2.2	1.5	1.8
1953	31.0	8.6			
1954	29.5	7.5			

SOURCE: U.S. Department of Commerce, *Historical Statistics*, 1945; Federal Reserve Bank of Chicago, "Business Conditions," January, 1954.

tives explained it. The number of farms with garden tractors increased from 1.2 per cent of the total in 1945 to 5.6 per cent in 1952. The actual scope of this market may be inferred from the regional statistics given in Exhibit 5.

As of January 1954, farm outlays for machinery, equipment, and buildings were expected to decline. After World War II, with new equipment available for the first time since 1941 and with farm income rising, capital outlays averaged about 24 per cent of net farm income. While obsolescence was expected to help sustain this rate, declining farm income and the rapid buildup in capital equipment on farms in prior years was expected to cause new outlays to fluctuate and decrease for several years.[4] (See Exhibit 4.)

[2] Inquiries by mail made by the case writer, January, 1954.

[3] In dollar value; excludes motor tillers.

[4] Federal Reserve Bank of Chicago, "Business Conditions," January, 1954.

exhibit 5   GARDEN TRACTORS ON FARMS

Division	No. of Farms Reporting—1950		No. of Garden Tractors		
	Total Reporting Garden Tractors	Total Reporting Garden Tractors Only	1945 Census	1950 Census	1953* Estimate
New England	9,069	5,624	8,603	9,748	11,850
Middle Atlantic	26,567	11,755	14,852	28,497	39,150
East North Central	69,595	22,252	19,524	71,793	110,900
West North Central	27,625	8,958	5,109	28,802	49,200
South Atlantic	19,217	12,433	6,194	19,970	31,250
East South Central	8,165	5,737	2,116	8,506	13,600
West South Central	12,832	7,507	2,765	13,467	21,350
Mountain	7,302	3,338	1,732	7,741	12,400
Pacific	25,652	14,434	8,850	26,997	42,300
Total	206,024	92,038	69,745	215,521	332,000

N.E.   —Me., N.H., Vt., Mass., R.I., Conn.
M.A.   —N.Y., N.J., Pa.
E.N.C. —Ohio, Ind., Ill., Mich., Wisc.
W.N.C.—Minn., Iowa, Mo., N.Dak., S.Dak., Nebr., Kan.
S.A.   —Del., Md., Va., W.Va., N.C., S.C., Ga., Fla.
E.S.C. —Ky., Tenn., Ala., Miss.
W.S.C. —Ark., La., Okla., Texas
Mt.   —Mont., Wyo., Idaho, Colo., N.Mex., Ariz., Utah, Nev.
Pac.   —Wash., Oreg., Calif.

* Based on figures from *Farm Implement News*, Sept. 10, 1953, p. 84.
SOURCE: 1950 Census Reports of Agriculture, Vol. II., General Report, pp. 193 ff.
    A farm, for statistical purposes, includes all establishments of more than 2 acres raising not less than $150 in products for market.

LAKELAND BRAND LINE SALES

The relationship between Lakeland and their mail-order-house customer had always been a cordial and satisfactory one. It was for reasons of general policy rather than any dissatisfaction with their largest customer that the company in 1949 inaugurated a brand line of their own to be sold through dealers. Banks and insurance companies had upon occasion declined to extend credit because they felt that an 80 to 90 per cent concentration of sales to one customer rendered Lakeland particularly vulnerable to a general business recession or a saturation of the garden tractor market.[5] Although Lakeland executives did not entirely agree with this reasoning, they felt it was desirable to develop a market for their product under their own name.

George Bancroft was hired in 1949 as sales manager of the brand line which was named "Great Lakes." Bancroft's previous experience included fifteen years selling newspaper space and writing advertising copy, and five years as advertising and sales promotion manager for a power equipment manufacturer.

Bancroft's job was to establish distribution channels through independent dealers. Starting with farm implement stores, he soon added various other types of outlets: hardware stores, lawn and garden shops, large service stations, chain stores such as Firestone and Western Auto, and some rural bottled gas distributors. Manufacturers' representatives and jobbers were not used. Robert Powell explained that this was typical of the industry; the problems of servicing, demonstrations, and covering the diverse types of outlets utilized could be handled more effectively by direct factory representatives. Further, he thought Lakeland could, with its own sales force, do the job for less than the 15 per cent markup which jobbers and manufacturers' representatives received.

By November, 1953, Lakeland had 375 active dealers; about 100 dealerships had been canceled for inactivity. Exhibit 6 shows the distribution of dealers by region and by number of tractors sold in 1951. The company's main strength had been in the upper Middle West, but representatives were working in the Mid-Atlantic and New England states. Bancroft aimed at national distribution of the "Great Lakes" line.

Bancroft believed that getting a dealer required a good job of education by Lakeland's sales representatives. Many small retailers are hampered by limited space and capital. Consequently, the retailer had to be convinced of the merit of the equipment and of its salability. To facilitate this job, the company's six salesmen were equipped with Chevrolet metal station wagons and demonstrator units and attachments. These men called on dealers and prospective dealers. They were paid on a 5 per cent commission basis with a monthly drawing account and expenses provided. For every call, a report form was filled out and forwarded to the company. New dealers signed a brief "Request for Franchise" in which Lakeland agreed to use this outlet exclusively in the area and to sup-

[5] The percentages of Lakeland's sales going to the mail-order house were as follows: 1949–96.5%; 1950–97.6%; 1951–93.2%; 1952–92.8%.

ply sales promotion literature and help. The new dealer agreed to maintain and display a "representative" stock of tractors and attachments, actively promote sales, and provide service facilities. Regular discount was 25 per cent off list price with an additional 5 per cent for cash. Quantity discounts were also offered: 2.5 per cent of total sales if twenty or

exhibit 6

State	Number of Dealers	Tractors Sold 1951
Illinois	68	224
Indiana	47	272
Ohio	70	243
Michigan	32	139
Wisconsin	31	58
Missouri	11	60
25 other states	80	144
Total	339	1,140

Number of Tractors Sold	Number of Dealers
0	97
1	78
2	38
3	30
4–5	37
6–9	30
10–24	24
25–49	5
50–up	0

SOURCE: Consultants' report.

more units were sold, and 5 per cent of total if fifty or more were sold. Sales quotas were set up from Robert Powell's operating forecast and allocated to salesmen in three-month forecasts which were periodically revised.

GARDEN TRACTOR DISTRIBUTORS

Interviews with three tractor distributors in suburban areas north of Chicago revealed no uniformity of opinion as to the best type of outlet for garden tractors.[6] One distributor serving an urban suburb sold 35 tractors, 60 power mowers, and 3 roto-tillers in 1953. This outlet was a garden specialty shop which had a sizeable service and repair business. Typical repairs were replacing bad knives and sharpening and adjusting power mowers. On garden tractors, servicing was more significant than repairs; engines rarely required repairs or replacement of parts. Although several lines of tractors were carried, Lakeland's was not among them. The repair man said that the Bolens tractors were very durable and customers were well-satisfied with them.

Another distributor serving a rural suburb in which there were large farms carried a complete line of Ford tractors and accessories, and was a manufacturer of a gang mower used with them. He had carried garden tractors after the war, but sales were slow and he had abandoned them, although lawn rollers, tillers, and power mowers were still carried. He believed that garden tractors were basically a side-line business for hardware stores, gas stations, and other such outlets not dependent solely on them.

A third distributor was a garden specialty and repair shop serving a rapidly growing suburb with farms adjoining it. He carried a large line of power mowers and roto-tillers, and several garden tractor lines, Lakeland's not among them. His sales for 1953 were approximately: power mowers—170; roto-tillers—35; garden tractors—2 (Bolens). He indicated emphatically that garden tractor attachments for tilling and mowing were greatly inferior to implements made for that purpose alone. He also revealed an animosity toward Lakeland because of their policy of accepting any sort of outlet for their product. He believed garden tractors would in the long run be sold most successfully and steadily through garden specialty shops exclusively.

Manufacturers were also divided in their opinions as to the type of outlet for garden tractors.[7] Several thought that the new garden specialty shops and farm implement dealers were the most effective and reliable type of distributors. Others indicated that a variety of outlets was desirable to get coverage of the potential market. All agreed that "a strong dealer" organization was important. One of the older established companies said that newcomers to the industry had a problem in living down a bad reputation resulting from poorly engineered products sold in the period immediately after World War II.

[6] Interviews with case writer, January, 1954.
[7] Inquiry by mail by the case writer, January, 1954.

THE LAKELAND LINE

A garden tractor consisted basically of a framework with handles for guiding the machine and a motor providing power to one or more wheels for traction. Attachments were mounted in front or in back by means of a hitch, and those requiring power were usually coupled so as to receive it directly from the motor. Lakeland manufactured three two-wheel tractor models, the 2½-horsepower "Standard" ($199.50 list price), the 3-horsepower "Special" ($258 list price), and the 5-horse-power "Deluxe" ($310 list price). Each had five forward speeds available by shifting the belt on step-cone pulleys; a reverse gear was standard on the larger horsepower models and optional at extra cost on the "Standard." All three had Lakeland's special quality features: two-wheel drive with an over-running ratchet which permitted short "free-wheeling" turns, an adjustable handle, and adjustable tread width.

Lakeland's attachment line consisted of nineteen devices for farm and suburban estate work. Exhibit 7 compares the price and performance of the principal attachments of leading garden tractors. Exhibit 8 compares the horsepower and price of nine leading garden tractor lines.

FINANCE

In order to finance its entry into the garden tractor industry, Lakeland sold an issue of preferred stock which was underwritten by a Chicago broker. Twenty thousand shares, $10 par value, of 6 per cent cumulative preferred was sold, each share accompanied by a warrant to buy one share of common stock for $3. An additional 10,000 warrants were issued to the investment bankers for their participation in the sale of the issue. The contract called for 25 per cent of earnings after taxes to be applied yearly for the retirement of this stock; the warrants expired May 1, 1953. As of August 31, 1953, all but $73,910 of this issue had been retired; 24,000 of the 30,000 warrants were exercised. The comptroller, who came to Lakeland after this stock issue was arranged, observed that these shares of preferred stock, with the provision for retirements out of earnings, were really debentures, and that the company could have saved some money by so designating them and entering the 6 per cent interest as an operating cost, thus reducing taxable income.

C. P. Powell said the company had never had as much capital as it could use. The problem was accentuated by the desire of the Powell family to retain control of the business, which limited the possibilities

exhibit 7 PERFORMANCE RATING AND PRICE OF PRINCIPAL ATTACHMENTS OF VARIOUS MAKES OF GARDEN TRACTORS

Make and Model	Cultivator	Plow	Sickle Bar	Rotary Mower	Dozer	Hitch
Bolens Power-Ho	$29.00 Very Good	$20.00 Very Good	$68.00 Good	$66.00 Very Good	$41.00 Very Good	Very Good
Sears David Bradley	$16.75 Very Good	$23.25 Very Good	$47.50 Very Good	$66.50 Good	$16.50 Very Good	Fair
Ward Chor-Trac	$25.50 Fair	$26.50 Good	$49.75 Fair	$59.95 Good	$19.50 Very Good	Good
Ward Hoe-Trac	$18.75 Fair	$22.75 Fair	$49.75 Fair	$59.95 Good	$16.75 Very Good	Good
S. L. Allen Co. Planet, Jr.	$32.50 Good	$36.50 Good	$76.50 Fair	$89.50 Very Good	$31.50 Fair	Good
Lodge & Shipley Co. Choremaster C	$22.50 Fair	$9.00 Poor	$91.25 Fair	$41.50 Poor	$18.00 Poor	Fair
Lodge & Shipley Co. Choremaster A	$13.80 Fair	$9.00 Poor	$71.75 Fair	$33.95 Poor	$18.00 Poor	Fair
Bready A	$25.00 Poor	$22.50 Good	$76.50 Poor	$65.00 Poor	$41.50 Good	Poor
Bolens Handi-Ho (one-wheel tractor)	$29.00 Fair	$2.00 Poor	$42.00 Fair	$42.00 Good	$18.00 Fair	Good

SOURCE: Consumer Reports, June, 1950, p. 247.

exhibit 8 COMPARISON OF GARDEN TRACTOR LINES*

Type of Tractor	Bolens Hp	Bolens Price	Sears Hp	Sears Price	Ward Hp	Ward Price	Lakeland Hp	Lakeland Price	Choremaster Hp	Choremaster Price	Bready Hp	Bready Price	Maxim† Hp	Maxim† Price	Gravely Hp	Gravely Price	Planet Hp	Planet Price	Bantam Hp	Bantam Price
One-wheel: Walking Tractor	1.6	$123			2.0	$100														
	2.5	149														$338				
Two-wheel: Walking Tractor	2.0	174	1.75	$176	2.0	160	2.5	$200	1.3	$132							1.5	$170		
	2.5	194	1.75	194													2.5	199		
	2.5	219	2.5	216							2.5	$265					2.5	265		
	3.6	259			3.0	225	3.0	258	3.0	179										
	4.3	332											4.6	$495						
	4.3	336			5.0	293	5.0	310							5.0	358				
	4.3	340			6.0	312														
													7.5	725						
													7.5	850						
Three-wheel	6.0	515																	5	$352
Four-wheel: Riding Tractor	6.0	595																		

* Prices are 1953 list, excluding freight, except for Choremaster, Planet, and Bready, which are 1950 prices from *Consumer Reports*, June, 1950, previously cited. Other data are from dealer price lists.
† The Maxim tractors are designated and delivered as Snow-Throwers, although a group of mowing and rolling attachments are available. As an attachment in the other lines, Snow-Blower prices range from $100 to $200.

of equity financing. The president also observed that he would like to expand into a related line of business such as motor tillers, but limitations of facilities and capital prohibited such a move at that time.

B. K. Lewis had been comptroller of the Lakeland Company since 1948. His previous experience, after a tour of duty in the Navy, included service as comptroller of U.S. Mineral Wool Corporation, in a private accounting firm, and in the accounting department of Allis-Chalmers.

Lakeland's accounting was based on a system of standard costs established for each part manufactured. Overhead or manufacturing expense amounted to approximately four times the cost of direct labor, but was absorbed monthly regardless of the volume of production. In September, 1953, manufacturing expense was 5.0 times direct labor on a volume of $65,000; in October it was 4.6 times direct labor cost on a volume of $172,000. Lewis believed that a complete system of cost accounting should be installed so that the company could know exactly the cost of its various products. He believed this would become more important should Lakeland encounter increasing competition or a shrinking market. In such a situation he believed it would be desirable to increase sales efforts; but to apply the increased effort most effectively, exact costs would have to be known. Exhibits 10 and 11 summarize balance sheets and income statements after the company entered the garden tractor business.

PRODUCTION

Lakeland's plant superintendent was W. H. Burns, who came to the company in 1948 as a foreman. He graduated from the University of Wisconsin as a mechanical engineer, served in the Navy as an engineering officer, then went through a training program at an automotive parts manufacturing concern, after which he became foreman of the connecting rod department. He served as assistant superintendent at Lakeland for six months before becoming superintendent.

Lakeland purchased most screw machine parts, all its motors, wheels and tires, and jobbed out heat-treating and plating. In 1953 raw steel was procured directly from steel mills instead of warehouses as formerly, a change which resulted in better quality, which in turn eliminated some annoying production problems. The company performed ordinary machining operations, sheet metal fabrication, welding, and had presses up to 100 tons in capacity. These presses were too light for some of the stamping operations, which made it necessary to break them down into several steps using several dies instead of one.

Two assembly lines with conveyors were operated; one was for tractors and one for all attachments. The tractor line ran steadily through about half of the year; model change-overs involved only minor changes which posed no particular problem. However, changing the attachment line from one product to another was an awkward problem involving delays while boxes of parts and sub-assemblies were moved to and from storage areas. Burns changed the plant layout adjacent to the attachment assembly line, moving a storeroom in order to provide more space. This enabled him to anticipate changes and cut down the amount of time the line was not in operation; in the new arrangement, boxes of parts for the next attachment scheduled for production were brought in before stopping work on the one currently in production. He had also been pressing for longer runs on attachments to cut down further the proportion of change-over delays.

Burns believed that the company had solved most of its big production problems and could concentrate on details to increase efficiency. Inventory control was a serious problem for a time, but a new purchasing agent, M. A. Hanson, was hired, and an improvement in control and quality of the company's suppliers soon followed. Burns also gradually increased the operations done in the plant; gear hardening and broaching of keyways, for example, which had formerly been jobbed out, were now being done successfully.

Robert Powell managed the plant through a production committee consisting of the plant superintendent, the purchasing agent, the production manager, and himself. It met three times weekly. General management problems were handled in intermittent meetings of the nine top executives. Robert Powell received the following reports: production—orders received, production, and shipments—weekly and cumulative for the fiscal year; labor—monthly employment (broken down thus—salary, indirect labor, direct labor). A four-month operating forecast by product was the basis of production scheduling; it was revised from month to month. Monthly operating statements and estimated profit and loss were also made out.

Labor relations at Lakeland were under the direction of J. F. Henry, personnel manager. Most of the factory employees were on piecework, and this had accounted for many grievances when someone was shifted temporarily to work paid on an hourly basis. Workers insisted that, since they were normally on piecework, they should receive the same pay they ordinarily earned on piecework, which was considerably more than the straight hourly rate. The problem was solved in a new contract negotiated in September, 1953, by applying the difference in the form of a general increase of the minimum pay guaranteed those on piecework, and the union abandoned the claim that pieceworkers should be guaranteed their average piece-rate earnings when assigned to hourly-rate work.

The principal labor problem at Lakeland was occasioned by the seasonal character of garden tractor shipments. In 1952 the summer layoff amounted to 10 per cent; in 1953 to 30 per cent. This fluctuation increased the difficulty of getting good labor, most of whom were in semi-skilled work. Production reached its maximum rate during the spring months. Cash receipts also reached their peak at that time. Borrowing to finance operations in the period of maximum production began in October and was normally repaid by July. Exhibit 12 shows the typical seasonal fluctuation of shipments, production, factory employment, and other factors.

MANAGEMENT CONSULTANTS' REPORT

In 1952 Lakeland retained a management consulting firm to study its operations. The consultants focused their attention on the effect of seasonality on production and inventories and the relationship of these factors to the interests of Lakeland's main customer.

The consultants found that the Lakeland Manufacturing Company was in good standing with the mail-order-house executives. However, the latter criticized Lakeland's inadequate warehousing facilities which made it necessary for them to take off-season shipments and carry reserve inventories amounting to approximately $1.5 million. They estimated that this inventory and the extra handling it involved cost them about 3 per cent. They also thought Lakeland should be more aggressive in developing improvements in design. In one season tardiness in adopting reversing gear-shift mechanisms had resulted in the mail-order house splitting its orders for heavy tractors, normally supplied by Lakeland, between Lakeland and another manufacturer. The consultants concluded: "We believe the company must find a way to meet both these requirements."

Lakeland's practice had been to assemble tractors at a relatively uniform rate. The consultants recommended that instead, parts be manufactured the year round and inventories accumulated for assembly as required by the shipping schedule. Their findings as to space and capital requirements for this arrangement were as follows:

exhibit 9   SPACE AND CAPITAL REQUIREMENTS FOR EXPANSION

	Production Rate Garden Tractors	Total Area Required, Square Feet	Additional Area Required, Square Feet	Peak Inventory Investment
Not stocking finished goods for mail-order house	20,000	60,250	10,450	$ 382,042
	24,000	69,500	19,700	616,829
	30,000	90,700	40,900	1,225,179
Stocking finished goods for mail-order house	20,000	82,600	37,800	1,410,970
	24,000	93,900	44,100	1,727,794
	30,000	115,250	65,450	2,332,730

The production rates selected were based on the mail-order-house executives' estimates that their requirements would increase to 20,000–22,000 units annually and the consultants' assumption that the Great Lakes line should develop a 10,000-unit annual sales volume in order to be worth the effort it entailed. They estimated that Lakeland's equipment would require about $30,000 of additions for a production of 30,-000 units annually. Their estimates took no account of increased stocks of raw materials, work-in-process, and the larger accounts receivable required.

The consultants recommended renting the additional space required for assembling and storing rather than building an additional plant even though it would probably be more costly. Their reasons were the lack of funds and the possible consequences in the event of a business recession. They suggested that the mail-order house might help Lakeland secure additional working capital.

In December of 1953 the vice-president, Robert Powell, said, "We have moved along the lines that the consultants recommended. This past spring we rented a large warehouse and stored considerably more mail-order merchandise than we had previously. Competition may force us to go even further in subsequent years." He also noted that

while scheduling final assembly to coordinate with the shipping schedule accentuated the seasonal demand for labor, this disadvantage was
offset by the *decreased* financial requirement, because the concentration of final assembly into a brief period shortened the time during
which large inventories of engines, tires, and wheels were carried.

"The key problem in holding a permanent place in our industry,"
declared Powell, "is to develop a well-rounded line, not only of garden
tractors, but allied equipment such as power mowers, rotary tillers, and
(*Text continues on page 169.*)

exhibit 10   **THE LAKELAND MANUFACTURING COMPANY**
Comparative balance sheets, 1948–1953, fiscal years ending August 31st (in thousands
of dollars)

	1948*	1949†	1950	1951	1952	1953
Current assets:						
Cash	38	16	141	43	75	106
Receivables (net)	131‡	29	146	191	53	42
Inventory	380	294	320	426	682	672
Investments: life ins.	2	3	3	3	3	4
Prepaid expenses	9	9	8	12	12	15
Total	560	351	618	675	825	839
Current liabilities:						
Notes payable—bank	150			100		
Accounts payable	212	51	86	167	238	40
Accrued expenses	19	26	41	34	55	88
Provision for income taxes		35	132	81	197	239
Total	381	112	259	382	490	367
Working capital	179	239	359	293	335	472
Fixed assets:						
Land	7	7	7	8	14	23
Buildings	120	121	127	176	181	190
Machinery and equipment	149	167	183	238	295	316
Less: depreciation	56	83	93	110	154	205
Net after depreciation	93	84	90	128	141	111
Total	220	212	224	312	336	324
Net assets	399	451	583	605	671	796
Capital stock:						
Preferred stock	200	200	172	133	109	74
Common stock	166	166	166	170	173	222
Capital in excess of par value¶			2	4	5	16
Retained earnings	33	85	243	298	384	484
Total equity	399	451	583	605	671	796

* Year ended June 30th.
† Fourteen months ending August 31st.
‡ Includes claim for refund on Federal tax equal to $57,000.
¶ Net gains from stock sales and retirements.

exhibit 11   THE LAKELAND MANUFACTURING COMPANY

Comparative operating statements, 1948–1953, fiscal years ending August 31st (in $1,000s)

	*1948**	*1949*†	*1950*	*1951*	*1952*	*1953*
Net sales	927	2,494	2,728	3,830	4,415	3,723
Cost of goods sold:						
Material	531	1,569	1,624	2,566	3,048	2,102
Direct labor	88	241	166	254	269	181
Manufacturing expense	300	515	454	667	779	745
Total manufacturing cost	919	2,325	2,244	3,487	4,096	3,028
Inventory variation increase (decrease)	(5)	(54)	11	(34)	(237)	(9)
Total cost of goods sold	914	2,271	2,255	3,453	3,859	3,019
Gross margin	13	223	473	377	556	704
Selling and admin. expense	121	111	161	186	222	309
Operating profit (loss)	(108)	112	312	191	334	395
Other income (expense)	(13)	(19)	(2)	(12)	(9)	(19)
Federal taxes	(56)‡	35	132	87	197	239
Net profit (loss)	(65)	58	178	92	128	137
Retained earnings Sept. 1st	118¶	33	85	243	298	384
	53	91	263	335	426	521
Dividends:						
Preferred	20	6	20	10	8	5
Common				27	34	32
Retained earnings Aug. 31st	33§	85	243	298	384	484

* Year ended June 30th.
† Fourteen months ending August 31st.
‡ Tax refund.
¶ Retained earnings July 1, 1947.
§ Retained earnings June 30, 1948.

Income statements, 1948–1953, fiscal years ending August 31st (percentage analysis)

	*1948**	*1949*†	*1950*	*1951*	*1952*	*1953*
Total manufacturing cost	100	100	100	100	100	100
Materials	57.8	67.5	72.4	73.6	74.4	69.4
Direct labor	9.6	10.4	7.4	7.3	6.6	6.0
Manufacturing expense	32.6	22.1	20.2	19.1	19.0	24.6
Net sales	100	100	100	100	100	100
Total cost of goods sold	98.6	91.1	82.7	90.2	87.4	81.1
Gross margin	1.4	8.9	17.3	9.8	12.6	18.9
Selling and administrative expense	13.1	4.4	5.9	4.8	5.0	8.3
Operating profit (loss)	(11.7)	4.5	11.4	5.0	7.6	10.6

* Year ending June 30th.
† Fourteen months ending August 31st.

exhibit 12 THE LAKELAND COMPANY
Factors reflecting seasonality (items in $1,000s)

Fiscal 1952–1953 End of Mo.	Net Sales	Sales Value of Production	Accounts Receivable	Accounts Payable	Notes Payable	Cash	Inventory (Estimated)	Operating Profit (Loss)	Employment Factory	Office	Total
1951 Sept.	187	—	121	222	100	29	556	(19)	140	66	206
Oct.	255	262	86	292	100	57	629	10	143	66	209
Nov.	314	403	226	522	100	23	767	27	144	68	212
Dec.	433	372	415	470	250	24	698	47	152	65	217
1952 Jan.	462	446	279	395	200	68	692	49	148	68	216
Feb.	454	442	299	303	200	46	622	47	153	68	221
Mar.	512	525	431	258	200	49	506	63	154	69	223
Apr.	469	540	331	230	150	91	528	59	153	69	222
May	578	532	264	130	—	47	440	91	153	67	220
June	471	500	259	136	—	111	411	62	147	69	216
July	206	360	204	178	—	112	495	(12)	147	69	216
Aug.	74	134	56	227	—	75	682	(67)	114	68	182
Sept.	287	90	116	234	—	40	669	6	111	63	174
Oct.	188	209	120	373	—	46	756	(19)	109	60	169
Nov.	184	289	138	305	200	20	790	(28)	127	59	186
Dec.	441	431	306	292	250	39	686	39	130	64	194
1953 Jan.	486	466	257	212	250	119	609	40	118	64	182
Feb.	421	412	189	250	250	76	709	44	119	64	183
Mar.	549	514	242	177	250	87	656	85	119	64	183
Apr.	572	528	255	144	100	128	521	92	128	63	191
May	329	303	169	104	—	145	417	11	129	64	193
June	168	152	109	47	—	173	349	(19)	83	63	146
July	68	88	80	1	—	137	317	(58)	76	63	139
Aug.	30	30	49	30	—	106	672	(58)	71	53	124

snow-throwers." He thought if such a line could be developed, there would be little difficulty in building a strong dealer organization handling Lakeland products exclusively. Only one firm in the industry had succeeded in accomplishing this—Bolens, Division of Food Machinery and Chemical Corporation.

Lakeland's quality type of tractor was about 25 per cent of the total market. Asked about plans for building a cheaper tractor, Robert Powell answered, "Definitely we should build a competitive tractor, but the only question is what position it should take in the sequence of new products. Should it come before or after the riding tractor?" He added, "The riding tractor is still pretty much in the dreaming stage. Even if we carry through our plans to make one, it would be the spring of 1956 before we would have one on the market."

GRANT PHILLIPS MANUFACTURING COMPANY

In 1888 Mr. Grant Phillips started a small plumbing shop in Detroit, Michigan. The business soon was expanded to include a steel foundry and a machine shop. Gradually, from a variety of iron fittings and machine valves, the output of the plant became more and more concentrated in a line of plumbing supplies, primarily small pipe fittings and bathroom fixtures. In 1900 the business was moved to Dearborn, Michigan, and the Phillips Manufacturing Company began the manufacture of pipe by a butt-welding process. The expansion was considered a sound move in that the pipe would complement the plumbing supply line, and could be marketed through the same selling and distributing organizations. Pipe proved to be a profitable item, and sales of pipe climbed rapidly to about 60% of the company's total sales volume.

Mr. Phillips had thought of getting into the steel business for a number of years. Because of the large volume of steel which the company purchased for the manufacture of pipe, he considered a vertical integration into the steel business a logical move. The heavy demand for steel during World War I was another important factor in the decision to begin construction of a steel mill in Detroit in 1915. When the construction was completed in 1917, the capital structure of the company consisted of $5,000,000 in common stock and $4,000,000 in bonds.

Just after the close of World War I, when the steel mill was completed but by no means all paid for, the steel industry—which had been operating near capacity—entered a slump. Operating without an established market against the stiff competition of large, well-entrenched and well-financed steel companies, the company sustained heavy operating losses. Mr. Phillips concluded that there was not much chance of obtaining enough business to operate his plant at a profit for some time and realized that he could not stand his heavy operating losses for many months. In order to get out from under the heavy debt and salvage what he could from the company, he proposed selling the entire business to the Consolidated Steel and Mining Company.

The Consolidated Steel and Mining Company was considered the most logical purchaser. It had been a large supplier of the Phillips Manufacturing Company for many years and relations between the executives of the two companies were excellent. Executives of the Consolidated Steel and Mining Company were especially anxious to acquire steel capacity in the Detroit area and were interested in securing the well-established pipe business of the Phillips Manufacturing Company. An agreement was reached for sale of the entire business, including the name and good-will of the company. The Consolidated Steel and Mining Company continued to operate the pipe and plumbing supply businesses under the name of the Phillips Manufacturing Company. The only immediate personnel changes were the replacement of members of the Phillips family, who had occupied key executive positions.

The Consolidated Steel and Mining Company later shifted production of pipe for the Phillips Manufacturing Company to its integrated pipe mills but continued to use the Dearborn plant for manufacture of plumbing supplies. The plumbing supply business was a very minor operation for the Consolidated Steel and Mining Company, which had not been engaged in that business prior to acquisition of the Phillips Manufacturing Company.

In 1924 Mr. Grant Phillips formed a new company under the name of the Grant Phillips Manufacturing Company, acquired a plant site in Detroit, and started over in the manufacture of plumbing supplies and pipe. By 1930 the business of the Grant Phillips Manufacturing Company had grown to the point at which its sales of both pipe and plumbing supplies were about equal to those of its competitor in nearby Dearborn, the Phillips Manufacturing Company. Competition between the two companies was keen but friendly.

Mr. Grant Phillips owned 85% of the stock and held the position of Chairman of the Board, President, and Treasurer of the Grant Phillips Manufacturing Company. His son-in-law, Mr. Boyle Langford, was Executive Vice-President. A son, Mr. Carl Phillips, held the title of Assistant Treasurer and Plant Manager. An organization chart of the company is shown in Exhibit 1.

The executive offices located in downtown Detroit were headquarters for Mr. Grant Phillips and for the sales and accounting departments of the company. Each morning Mr. Grant Phillips arrived at his office about 9 o'clock. After looking over the mail, he would discuss with

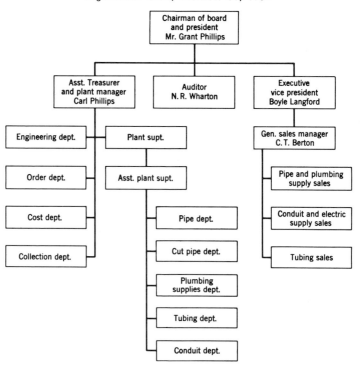

exhibit 1
GRANT PHILLIPS MANUFACTURING COMPANY
Organization Chart, December 31, 1935

Mr. Langford questions regarding sales. Around 10:30 he would drive out to the plant, located about four miles from the downtown office, taking with him the original copies of all new orders received in the morning mail. He usually would spend about an hour with his son, Mr. Carl Phillips, discussing current manufacturing problems and walking around the plant. Although responsibility and authority for running the plant rested in Mr. Carl Phillips, Mr. Grant Phillips kept well informed on the manufacturing activities. He knew personally all of the supervisory personnel and would stop to answer questions or chat with various individuals on his rounds through the plant. His afternoons usually were spent at the downtown office.

Mr. Grant Phillips personally handled all financial management activities of the company. The auditor, who reported directly to him, had supervision over accounting and bookkeeping.

Mr. Langford, Executive Vice-President, was in charge of sales and devoted most of his personal attention to pipe sales. Reporting to him was Mr. C. T. Berton, General Sales Manager, who in 1935 had general supervision over three separate sales organizations. One sold pipe and plumbing supplies; the second, rigid and thin wall conduit; and the third, electric welded tubing.

Because of the keen competition among pipe manufacturers, it was often necessary to employ a salesman to service, and more or less "control," as few as six pipe accounts. In some instances, these same salesmen also sold plumbing supplies and conduit, a portion of their salaries and expenses being charged to these divisions.

In the manufacture of pipe, the company used a butt-welding process. This process consisted of charging high-temperature furnaces with a flat semi-finished steel product, known as skelp, and pulling the heated skelp through a bell at the discharge end of the furnace, thereby making a butt-weld piece of tubing. In order to improve the quality of the weld by this process, the company developed a method of applying oxygen gas to skelp the instant it passed through the bell. The additional heat application at this point made a stronger weld.[1]

[1] Other popular methods of welding pipe and tubing include: (1) Lap welding: This method of welding tubing is generally restricted to sizes two inches in diameter and higher. The skelp is prepared with bevelled edges and then pre-formed and heated before it goes through the welding operation. After it is heated to a welding heat, it is passed over a ball held on a mandrel and drawn through rolls which form a lap weld that can carry higher pressure than pipe or tubing made by the butt-weld process. (2) Forming of seamless tubing: This method of making tubing consists of piercing billets or solid steel rounds, with drawing and annealing to obtain the desired diameters and physical qualities. (3) Gas welding: This method, usually restricted to smaller diameters and lighter gauges (thinner wall), consists of passing hot-rolled or cold-rolled strip steel (without heating) through forming rolls while gas heat is applied to weld a seam when the two edges of the strip are formed into a tube. (4) Arc welding: This method is usually confined to large diameters and heavy gauges of tubing. The strip with bevelled edges is formed into a cylindrical shape and a welding rod is applied to make an arc weld in the "v" groove formed between the two edges which are brought together. (5) Electric welding: This process involves the cold forming of the strip steel into cylindrical form, and passing the edges through electrode welding rolls where electric current is applied to produce heat. Where alternating current is used, the number of welds depends upon the

In the pipe business, the company was in competition with large steel companies whose integrated mills had much lower production costs than those of independent pipe manufacturers producing pipe from purchased skelp. Apparently, steel companies were in a position to lower the price of pipe and maintain a high price on skelp to a point at which independent pipe manufacturers would have difficulty in operating profitably. Because that was exactly what company executives believed was happening in the 1930's, expansion into other lines was undertaken.

As one means of putting the company in a better competitive position with respect to manufacturing costs and selling price, the possibility of installing a continuous pipe mill was considered. It was estimated that a continuous pipe mill would require a fixed investment of about $3,000,000 and that pipe sales[2] of approximately $1,000,000 per year would be required to break even in the operation of such a mill.

In the tubing business, as in the pipe and conduit businesses, the company was in competition with large steel companies. It had the advantage, however, of some improved methods of welding and finishing of tubing. From a competitive point of view, it was considered prudent to concentrate on the smaller sizes of tubing, from one-eighth to two inches in diameter.

The engineering development and tooling-up to get into the tubing business was a slow, expensive process for the company. A separate set of forming rolls was required for each diameter of tubing to be manufactured. Polishing machines were required to obtain proper finish for certain industries. Draw benches to obtain exact sizes and wall thicknesses were necessary. Annealing ovens to obtain specified physical properties in tubing, machines for flanging tubing to specifications, and spinning machines for closing tube ends for various uses (oil lines, etc.) in the automotive industry were among the engineering developments necessary to place the company in a position to sell electric welded tubing to various industries.

---

speed with which the tube passes through the welding rolls—the slower it passes, the closer the welds are placed on the edge of the strip. Where a continuous flow of direct current is applied through electrodes at the seam, a continuous homogeneous weld of the tubing is produced instead of a stitch weld.

[2] Calculated by using gross margin, 25% of sales, fixed operating costs, $750,000, selling and administrative expenses, 10% of sales, and interest on borrowed money, 5%.

In 1932 the company started production of electric welded tubing. It had one tube mill equipped with only four sets of forming rolls to produce four different diameters of tubing, three of which were for thin-wall conduit.

Approximately seven hours were required for a welding crew to change the forming rolls in the tube mill to manufacture a tube of a different diameter. Since this cost made it unprofitable to make runs of less than 50,000 feet on any given size, it was necessary for the company to make long runs and carry stocks to fill orders as they came in. Substantial amounts of working capital were employed in maintaining inventories of different sizes of finished tubing and of different sizes of cold-rolled strip steel. A large portion of the orders for electric welded mechanical tubing had to meet exacting specifications. This required advance placement of orders for steel of specific analysis, gauge, and width.

From the butt-weld furnaces of the company, a structural pipe was produced in round, square, and rectangular shapes for further processing by the fabricating pipe department. This department performed the simple operations of cutting pipe to the required lengths and punching holes in it for sale, principally to playground equipment manufacturers.

Rigid conduit, for the electric supply trade, was produced by a further processing of raw pipe which came from the butt-weld furnaces. Thin-wall conduit was produced from tubing which was made in the company's electric welded tubing mills. The rigid and thin-wall conduit were sold to electrical jobbers. In order to give the sales organization a full line to sell, the company contracted to distribute electrical products of other manufacturers under the Grant Phillips name.

In the latter part of 1933, when prospects for the tubing business were beginning to look good, the Industrial Tube Company, a wholly owned subsidiary of the Eastern Steel Corporation, charged the company with infringement of one of its patents covering a method of producing electric welded tubing. The Industrial Tube Company secretly had in its employ one of the employees of the Grant Phillips Manufacturing Company who kept it informed on developments in the company's method of producing tubing. In addition, the representatives of the Industrial Tube Company informed all potential customers of the company that they too would be held liable for patent

exhibit 2   GRANT PHILLIPS MANUFACTURING COMPANY

Cost breakdown of comparative profit and loss statements, 1936, 1937, and first quarter 1938

	1936										
	P & L Statement	% of Sales		Per Cent of Sales by Product						P & L Statement	% of Sales
Net sales:											
Pipe	$2,111,936	48.44	100%							$2,333,428	47.18
Rigid conduit	715,488	16.48		100%						775,366	15.67
Thin-wall conduit	331,638	7.68			100%					565,918	11.44
Fabricated pipe	533,413	12.28				100%				589,820	11.93
Plumbing supplies	445,003	10.30					100%			423,737	8.56
Electric welded tubing	204,825	4.82						100%		246,875	4.99
Mechanical tubing									100%	10,872	.23
Total	$4,342,303	100%								$4,946,016	100%
Cost of sales:											
Costs exclusive of depreciation	3,843,722	88.52	92.72	98.88	93.24	77.92	72.41	63.86		4,344,921	87.85
Depreciation:											
Buildings	37,148	} 2.68	2.37	2.84	2.84	2.37	3.07	5.02		37,300	} 2.07
Machinery and equipment	79,239									65,237	
	$ 116,387									$ 102,537	
	$3,960,109									$4,447,458	
	$ 382,194									$ 498,558	
Selling expense:											
Sales commissions	51,119	1.18	.26	3.85	3.85	.25		1.91		68,682	1.39
Other	171,509	3.95	3.96	4.00	3.96	3.96	3.96	3.95		158,949	3.21
	$ 222,628									$ 227,631	
	$ 159,566	3.67	.69	9.57*	3.89*	15.50	20.56	25.26		$ 270,927	5.48
Deduct											
Bad debts	$ 43,060	.99								$ 49,460	1.01
General and administrative expenses	149,458	3.44								137,137	2.77
	$ 192,518									$ 186,597	
	$ 32,953*	.76*								$ 84,330	1.70
Other income:											
Purchase discounts	$ 21,983	.51								$ 31,815	.64
Dividends received	21	.00								22	.00
Profit on sale of securities										1,450	.04
Reversal of provisions for bad debts										10,000	.20
Interest received	3,067	.07								2,422	.05
Miscellaneous										100	.00
	$ 25,071									$ 45,809	
	$ 7,882*	.18*								$ 130,139	2.63
Other charges:											
Interest and discount	$ 57,686	1.38								$ 84,836	1.71
Loss on retirement of fixed assets	837	.02								5,833	.11
Legal fees—patent infringement										6,858	.14
Miscellaneous											
	$ 58,523	1.35								$ 97,527	
Net profit or loss for period	$ 66,405*	1.58*								$ 32,612	.67

exhibit 2 (continued)

			1937				P & L Statement	% of Sales			First Quarter 1938			
		Per Cent of Sales by Product									Per Cent of Sales by Product			
100%	100%	100%	100%	100%	100%	100%	$333,512	42.38	100%	100%	100%	100%	100%	100%	100%
							98,826	12.56							
							73,623	9.36							
							93,303	11.86							
							138,051	17.53							
							38,403	4.88							
							11,244	1.43							
							$786,962	100%							
94.70	92.25	81.61	81.76	72.74	63.28	105.98	710,843	90.33	97.96	93.46	90.01	87.30	76.85	73.46	86.92
1.91	1.80	1.80	1.91	2.77	4.36	1.91	7,821 / 11,645 {2.47		2.36	2.53	2.53	2.36	1.94	5.36	2.37
							$ 19,466								
							$730,309								
							$ 56,653								
.12 / 3.21	4.48 / 3.21	4.48 / 3.21	.12 / 3.21	.29 / 3.21	1.47 / 3.21	.12 / 3.22	10,431 / 38,674	1.33 / 4.91	.12 / 4.91	5.25 / 4.91	5.25 / 4.91	.12 / 4.91	.24 / 4.91	1.42 / 4.91	.12 / 4.91
							$ 49,105								
.06	1.74*	8.90	13.00	20.99	27.68	11.23*	$ 7,548	.96	5.35*	6.15*	2.70*	5.31	16.06	14.85	5.68
							$ 7,362	.93							
							26,824	3.41							
							$ 34,186								
							$ 26,638*	3.38*							
							$ 3,888	.49							
							6	.00							
							247	.03							
							85	.01							
							$ 4,226								
							$ 22,412*	2.85*							
							$ 16,870	2.14							
							572	.07							
							2,589	.33							
							$ 20,031								
							$ 42,443*	5.39*							

* Indicates loss.

infringement if electric welded tubing were purchased from the company. This action prevented the company from exploiting its own patented process of producing electric welded tubing. All potential customers, with one exception, refused to purchase the company's product. One large customer purchased the product under the explicit condition that the company guarantee him against liability arising from the alleged infringement.

The company, confident that its electric welding process did not infringe the patent of the Industrial Tube Company, placed firm purchase orders for a second welding unit, consisting of a tube forming mill and electric generator sets, for delivery during the first quarter of 1935.

On April 24, 1934, the Industrial Tube Company filed a bill of complaint against the company in a district court of the United States, which alleged infringement of its patents and prayed for (1) a perpetual injunction restraining the company from making or selling tubing manufactured by its method and (2) a decree that the Industrial Tube Company recover profits realized by the Grant Phillips Manufacturing Company and damages suffered by the Industrial Tube Company because of the alleged infringement. The trial lasted from June 29, 1936, to July 17, 1936. At one point the Industrial Tube Company was so well impressed with the court presentation by the Grant Phillips Manufacturing Company that an offer was made to withdraw the suit. This offer was refused as the company wanted and expected to get a clear-cut court decision in its favor.

In September, 1937, an interlocutary decree was entered by the court holding that the patent of the Industrial Tube Company was valid and had been infringed. In October, 1937, a petition for appeal was filed. As of the end of the first quarter of 1938, the appeal was still pending. The patent of the Industrial Tube Company was due to expire in August, 1938.

In July, 1936, Mr. Grant Phillips died. The offices of Chairman of the Board and President of the company were not filled for some time. Mr. Boyle Langford, Executive Vice-President, continued his general supervision over the sales department and assumed authority over the auditor. Mr. Carl Phillips, Assistant Treasurer and Plant Manager, continued to be in charge of manufacturing. For about a year no one individual held top management responsibility. Mr. Langford and Mr. Phillips ran their respective divisions independently. They did not work on a partnership basis, but each left the other pretty much alone.

On one fundamental company objective, the two men had long been in disagreement. Mr. Langford considered that the company was primarily in the pipe business and he did not want to get involved in the production and sale of a variety of miscellaneous products. He was especially unsympathetic towards the development of the electric welded tubing business. On the other hand, Mr. Carl Phillips thought the pipe business was a losing proposition and believed the greatest hope for future profit was in the development of other lines. In his opinion, electric welded tubing offered the greatest promise.

A liberal dividend policy in the 1920's was followed by a series of operating losses in the early 1930's, which seriously depleted working capital. Because of this depletion of working capital and series of losses, additional unsecured bank loans were not available, so early in 1937, the company sold its accounts receivable, with recourse, to a commercial banking firm. The effective rate of interest paid by the company, based on average advances against accounts receivable, varied between 12% and 14% per annum. The company was in such a poor working capital position that it was frequently necessary to ship out an order of merchandise and immediately borrow against that particular account in order to meet a payroll or to purchase materials.

In February, 1937, the city instituted condemnation proceedings to open a street for an arterial highway which would run through the center of the company's manufacturing property and through two of its principal buildings. Mr. Carl Phillips believed that continued operation of the plant would not be economically feasible with a highway bisecting the plant and plant site. The condemnation payment offered to the company by the city was considered to be entirely inadequate in view of the anticipated loss of operating efficiency.

The will of Mr. Grant Phillips provided that the executor of his estate should be his son, Raymond Phillips, and that the trustees should be his sons, Richard Phillips and Dudley Phillips.

Mr. Raymond Phillips was a member of the Board of Directors of the company and was active in the management, holding the position of Chief Engineer. Mr. Richard Phillips, whose entire career had been in the banking business, was at the time of his father's death a senior executive of a large international bank. Mr. Dudley Phillips had worked for his father as a young man but after the sale of the original Phillips Manufacturing Company had gone into the banking business.

At the time of his father's death, he was president of a successful manufacturing company of his own.

As Mr. Grant Phillips had owned 85% of the common stock of the Grant Phillips Company, voting control of the company was in the hands of the Executor and trustees.

Mr. Dudley Phillips assumed the position of Chairman of the Board in 1937 and undertook the job of analyzing the company's operations in the process of straightening out the estate. He brought to Detroit Mr. J. K. Harvey, an accountant from his own company, to serve as auditor for the estate and for the company. Mr. Wharton, who had held the position of auditor for a number of years, was released.

At the end of the first quarter of 1938, the trustees had made no important changes in the conduct of the business. Exhibit 2 shows operating statements for 1936, 1937, and the first quarter of 1938, with a breakdown of costs by product, considered important as a basis of planning for the future. Exhibit 3 gives comparative balance sheets for December 31, 1935, 1936, and 1937.

In April, 1938, while the appeal was still pending, a settlement of the patent suit was reached: (1) The company gave a promissory note to the Industrial Tube Company in the amount of $101,524. (2) The company entered into an agreement with the parent company of the Industrial Tube Company, the Eastern Steel Corporation, for the purchase of cold-rolled strip steel (used in making electric welded tubing) and skelp (the raw material for merchant butt-weld pipe) in amounts sufficient to amortize the promissory note at the rate of 5% of the net value of raw materials purchased. This arrangement was so devised that eventual settlement of the suit could be made at no net cost to the company, as the 5% amortization of the note given was to be represented by a discount of 5% from the prevailing market prices of raw materials to be purchased from the Eastern Steel Corporation. (3) The company was required to pay royalties on its production of electric welded tubing until August of 1938, when the patent of the Industrial Tube Company expired.

During 1938, the company developed a process of making tubing for the automotive industry which eliminated the heavy costs of straightening and polishing operations prior to chrome plating. As a result, during 1938, sales of tubing to the automobile industry grew to include more than 50% of the company's total tubing sales. Other principal customer groups in the order of importance were the electrical, avia-

exhibit 3   **GRANT PHILLIPS MANUFACTURING COMPANY**
Consolidated comparative balance sheets, December 31, 1935, 1936, 1937

	1935	1936	1937
Assets			
Current assets:			
Cash	$ 3,182	$ 11,326	$ 4,337
Notes and accounts receivable, trade	634,323	821,546	473,133
Less: Res. for bad debts	(18,693)	(57,581)	(98,512)
Inventories	690,261	525,419	594,951
Total current assets	$1,309,073	$1,300,710	$ 973,909
Investments	$ 103,913	$ 83,937	$ 80,436
Prepaid items and deferred charges	$ 26,214	$ 13,547	$ 9,623
Plant, property and equipment—operating	$2,000.418	$2,025,688	$2,083,531
Less: Res. for depreciation	923,643	1,044,026	1,154,169
	$1,076,775	$ 981,662	$ 929,362
Land	462,000	462,000	462,000
	$1,538,775	$1,443,662	$1,391,362
Patents	$ 20,788	$ 116,509	$ 114,761
Sundry receivables, etc., not current	$ 337,249	$ 291,008	$ 339,924
Total assets	$3,336,012	$3,249,373	$2,910,015
Liabilities			
Current liabilities:			
Notes payable due within one year— secured by mortgage of fixed assets and/or pledge of receivables	$ 387,382	$ 426,390	$ 174,533
Accounts payable	504,221	507,686	404,361
Liability for merchandise not shipped	—	—	26,532
Accrued expenses	122,292	147,640	168,822
Total current liabilities	$1,013,895	$1,081,716	$ 774,248
Reserve for repairs and renewals	$ 25,015	$ 24,611	$ 26,755
Employee's stock allotment	96,350	58,331	50,945
Preferred stock	657,610	642,500	639,100
Common stock	1,395,000	1,395,000	1,395,000
Paid-in surplus	193,421	193,421	193,421
Earned surplus (deficit)	(45,279)	(146,206)	(169,454)
Total capital and liabilities	$3,336,012	$3,249,373	$2,910,015
Contingent liability consisting principally of notes, trade acceptances and accounts receivable discounted and/or sold with recourse (does not include unknown liability in respect to patent litigation pending)	$ 390,640	$ 329,258	$ 452,136

tion, washing machine, agricultural, bicycle, and refrigeration industries. More than half of the total tubing sales were to the automobile
industry.

The company's tubing sales were small in comparison to the total
market. In the opinion of the manager of tubing sales, the entire output
could have been sold to one or two large customers. Care was taken to
avoid dependence upon a few customers, who might go into the
manufacture of their own tubing at any time.

With respect to tubing sales, some thought was being given to moving
more toward the manufacture of end products in order to build a
controlled market. By expanding into the fabrication and finishing
of tubing parts for assembly by manufacturers of end products, it was
thought that the company could increase control over the market by
having customers not in the tubing business, except for assembly.

The large steel companies in the tubing business were not engaged
in the fabrication of parts from tubing.

THE MOHAWK
RUBBER
COMPANY

ORIGIN OF THE COMPANY

"When the Mohawk Rubber Company started in Akron forty-eight years ago," said Mr. William T. Ernst, treasurer of the company, "it was at a time when it was as much the fashion to organize an automobile or a tire company as it is today to go into electronics. Since that time over five hundred companies started out to make tires. Today, there are only thirteen left."

In 1913 Mr. Samuel Miller, an executive of the Goodyear Tire and Rubber Company, formed the Mohawk Rubber Company by purchasing the assets of the Stein Double Cushion Tire Company, a producer of solid and pneumatic tires. At that time the major companies (Goodyear, Goodrich, Firestone, and U.S. Rubber—known as "the Big Four") had been in existence for only about a dozen years. Mohawk enjoyed profitable operations until 1930. In the early 1930's, however, sales decreased sharply causing sizable operating losses. In 1934 Mr. Ray E. Bloch, then credit manager of the company, worked out a financial arrangement with the company's banks and creditors who were threatening it with bankruptcy. As part of the deal Mr. Bloch was made president and general manager of the company. He immediately set out to rehabilitate the company. By 1937 the company had earned a modest profit and although sales remained between two and three million dollars per year until World War II, operations were profitable each year.

After World War II sales increased steadily from $8 million to nearly $21 million in 1951. Profits in this period more than quadrupled, amounting to more than $1 million in 1951. Both sales and profits declined precipitously during the next three years and in 1954 the company sustained a loss of more than $600,000 when sales dropped

exhibit 1

THE MOHAWK RUBBER COMPANY

```
                          ┌─────────────────────┐
                          │   R. E. Bloch       │
                          │ Chairman of the board│
                          └─────────────────────┘
        ┌─────────────────┐  ┌─────────────────┐  ┌─────────────────┐
        │ C. E. Sauvain   │  │ H. M. Fawcett   │  │ W. F. Kruspe    │
        │ Vice president  │  │   President     │  │ Asst. to the pres.│
        └─────────────────┘  └─────────────────┘  └─────────────────┘
```

| W. T. Ernst | T. C. Johnson | F. F. Silver |
| Sec. treasurer | Gen. sales mgr. | Dir. of prod. |

| R. B. Payne | T.L. Ackerman | J.R. Brock | J.E. Broadbent | Factory mgr. | R. D. Juve |
| Credit mgr. | Comptroller | Dir. of purch. | Asst. sales mgr. | Akron | Dir. of res. & dev. |

| C. C. Miller | Factory mgr. | W.M. Nonnamaker |
| Asst. comptroller | Helena | Mgr. tire eng. |

Factory mgr.
Stockton

D. W. Gates	W. F. Irvin	J. L. Burnsed	P. E. Nicholson
Mgr.	Adv. mgr.	Mgr.	Mgr. special
sales oper.		TR & RM sales*	accts. sales

8
Regional mgrs.

*TR and RM = Tread rubber and
repair materials

to $8.8 million. The company's loss in 1954 resulted from the termination of government contracts, and also from the writing off of certain fixed assets no longer required. From 1950–1953 government contracts accounted for average annual sales of approximately $9.2 million, representing approximately half of the company's sales during that period.

In 1956 Mr. Bloch became chairman of the Board and Henry Fawcett, then thirty-six years old, became president and executive officer of the company. Sales rose steadily from 1955 to 1961, reaching a peak of $36 million in 1961 with net income of $1.75 million. (See Exhibit 2.)

In 1961 the company was engaged in the manufacture and sale of

exhibit 2 MOHAWK RUBBER COMPANY
Statement of income, years ending December 31st (in thousands of dollars)

	1961	1960	1959	1958	1957	1956	1955	1954	1953	1952	1951	1950	1949
Net sales	$36,379	$32,326	$31,657	$25,513	$20,842	$15,127	$14,330	$8,865	$16,264	$19,190	$20,884	$11,551	$8,360
Cost of products sold	28,739	25,749	25,543	20,526	17,807	13,012	12,709	9,104	14,969	16,347	16,486	9,724	7,284
	7,640	6,577	6,114	4,987	3,035	2,115	1,621	(239)	1,295	2,843	4,398	1,827	1,076
Selling, administrative & general expenses	3,603	3,910	3,406	2,673	1,755	1,287	1,009	830	1,021	1,096	1,047	775	628
	4,037	2,667	2,708	2,314	1,280	828	612	(1,069)	274	1,747	3,351	1,052	448
Other income	49	34	112	95	26	16	54	21	16	30	23	13	39
	4,086	2,701	2,820	2,409	1,305	844	666	(1,048)	290	1,777	3,374	1,065	487
Other deductions	475	430	259	191	136	72	25	293	28	1	19	4	9
Income before taxes	3,611	2,271	2,561	2,218	1,169	772	641	(1,341)	262	1,776	3,355	1,061	478
Federal taxes	1,860	1,203	1,342	1,153	666	402	320	(cr)694	(cr)365	1,092	2,283	465	182
Net income	$1,751	$1,068	$1,219	$1,065	$ 563	$ 370	$ 321	$ (647)	$ 627	$ 684	$1,072	$ 596	$ 296

185

exhibit **3   MOHAWK RUBBER COMPANY**
Balance sheet, years ending December 31st (in thousands of dollars)

	1961	*1960*	*1959*	*1958*	*1957*
Assets					
Cash	$ 833	$ 906	$ 686	$ 835	$ 368
U. S. tax notes	—	—	—	—	—
Less amount applied on taxes					
Receivables (net)	9,900	7,346	6,648	5,378	3,787
Tax refund due	—	—	—	—	—
Inventories	6,564	5,793	5,958	4,469	3,827
Total current assets	17,297	14,045	13,292	10,682	7,982
Other assets	341	149	385	443	102
Plant and equipment	11,369	9,899	8,552	6,023	5,867
Depreciation	3,999	3,329	2,572	2,271	2,219
Net plant and equipment	7,370	6,570	5,980	3,752	3,648
Deferred charges	—	193	259	189	124
Total assets	$25,008	$20,957	$19,916	$15,066	$11,857
Liabilities					
Bank loans	$ —	$ 1,000	$ 750	$ —	$ 550
Accounts payable	5,059	3,743	3,733	$ 4,031	2,816
Current part of term debt	—	128	—	—	323
Accrued expenses	1,723	1,278	1,369	192	188
Advances	—	—	—	—	—
Taxes	1,357	833	812	970	481
Total current liabilities	8,139	6,982	6,664	5,193	4,358
Long term debt	5,500	4,106	4,000	2,500	1,524
Common stock	636	516	492	225	144
Capital surplus	4,544	4,316	3,858	3,075	606
Earned surplus	6,189	5,037	4,902	4,073	5,225
	11,369	9,869	9,252	7,373	5,975
Total liabilities	$25,008	$20,957	$19,916	$15,066	$11,857

rubber and rubber products used in the transportation field. It manufactured passenger and truck tires in the popular sizes for the replacement market which it sold through dealers and distributors, principally in the Middle West and South. Its inner tubes were produced by another manufacturer. Mohawk's sales divided into two major product groups—automobile tires and tubes which accounted for approximately 75% of 1961 sales, and tread rubber and repair materials which constituted 25% of sales. In 1961 Mohawk produced more than 1,400,000 tires, approximating 1.8% of the industry replacement tire

exhibit 3 (continued)

1956	1955	1954	1953	1952	1951	1950	1949
$ 489	$ 564	$ 109	$ 320	$ 400	$1,269	$ 323	$ 609
—	—	—	—	—	—	—	402
							(176)
2,297	1,680	1,222	1,057	1,431	1,919	1,762	923
—	—	701	192	—	—	—	—
3,703	2,580	1,906	2,542	3,595	3,654	2,480	1,451
6,489	4,824	3,938	4,111	5,426	6,842	4,565	3,209
100	100	97	95	93	92	90	88
5,353	3,835	3,765	4,155	3,939	3,261	2,656	2,115
1,964	1,804	1,634	1,538	1,324	1,207	1,062	959
3,389	2,031	2,131	2,617	2,615	2,054	1,594	1,156
75	39	52	68	39	45	32	30
$10,053	$6,994	$6,218	$6,891	$8,173	$9,033	$6,281	$4,483
$ 300	—	$ 350	—	—	—	—	—
1,873	$1,205	749	$ 842	$1,238	$1,292	$1,421	$ 269
249	—	—	—	—	—	—	—
80	88	73	124	74	72	36	15
—	—	—	—	—	—	—	14
347	376	7	89	1,092	2,290	222	0
2,849	1,669	1,179	1,055	2,404	3,654	1,679	288
1,650	—	—	—	—	—	—	—
142	142	142	142	142	142	142	142
557	557	557	557	557	557	557	557
4,855	4,626	4,340	5,137	5,070	4,680	3,903	3,486
5,554	5,325	5,039	5,836	5,769	5,379	4,602	4,185
$10,053	$6,994	$6,218	$6,891	$8,173	$9,033	$6,281	$4,483

volume, and some 40,000,000 pounds of tread rubber and repair materials, which approximated 8% of the industry volume. In tread rubber and repair materials used in recapping and repairing tires, the company had been the country's largest producer for many years.

Manufacturing operations were conducted in the company's own plants in Akron, Ohio, and West Helena, Arkansas, and at a leased plant in Stockton, California. The company had 1,180 employees, most of whom were hourly rated production workers. The Akron plant had a capacity of 2,000 tires per day while the Helena plant had a daily capacity of 7,800 tires. In addition, the two plants each had a capacity of 75,000 pounds of tread rubber and repair materials daily. A small amount of tread rubber was produced in the Stockton plant by its subsidiary, the Mohawk Corporation. Service to the company's 1,500 dealers and distributors was provided from four warehouses in Ohio, Arkansas, Georgia, and California. The company's home office was in Akron.

THE RUBBER INDUSTRY

The rubber industry was dominated by four large producers known as "the Big Four" or the "Majors." Each had annual sales of over a half billion dollars. The industry also included a number of small producers, known as "independents," whose sales were generally between $15 million and $100 million a year. General Tire, which was also classed as an independent, was an exception, and had sales of over $500 million. (See Industry Notes.)

The Majors manufactured synthetic rubber for their own use and for resale to the independents. Their supply of crude natural rubber was obtained partly from plantations they operated themselves and partly by purchase on the open market. The Majors also manufactured materials allied to rubber, such as plastics and chemicals, both for their own use and for resale to others.

The Big Four sold a full line of tires and tubes under their own brand names to the original equipment market and in the replacement field. These large producers considered original equipment tires (called first-line tires) to be good business, even though it yielded a relatively low profit. They believed that this large volume production paid a considerable portion of their overhead expenses; that it enhanced their reputation for prestige; and, probably most important, they believed that the motorists would be inclined to continue to buy the brand of tires which came with the car. Only the Big Four and General Tire and Rubber shared the original equipment market.

In the replacement field the Big Four sold their tires through independent dealers, or through company-owned retail stores. They also produced private brand tires for mail order houses and for the large oil companies. Both the number of private brands and the total volume of this type of business had been showing a sharp rising trend. A recent survey showed Sears Roebuck & Company's Allstate brand to be ranking third, behind Goodyear and Firestone, as national sales leaders. Department stores and chain stores were becoming an increasingly popular outlet for tires. In addition to tires, the Big Four fabricated numerous other rubber products, such as hose, belting, and rubber footwear. The Big Four engaged in extensive research, both pure and applied.

The independents generally sold their tires in the replacement market through independent dealers. This market had considerably more potential, since there were 80 million replacement tires sold annually, while new car production seldom exceeded 25 million tires per year. (See Exhibit 4.) Some independents manufactured private brands for mail order houses and oil companies.

Within each quality grade the raw materials used by the various tire manufacturers were generally the same, and so was the design and the construction of the various types of tires. Manufacturing methods and processes were almost uniform throughout the industry. In fact, most tire makers secured their rubber mixing mills, their tire building equipment, and their molds from the same equipment manufacturers. The result was that the quality of the tires of each of the leading manufacturers was comparable at the same quality grade, and their prices within quality brackets were fairly uniform.

The rubber industry was traditionally affected by new automobile sales. To offset this in the postwar period all of the majors had diversified to the extent that only about half of their production was in tires. (See Exhibit 5.)

SOME SPECIAL ASPECTS OF SELLING TIRES

Historically, the tire business was highly competitive. All members of the industry, including the Big Four and the small producers alike, strove to increase their share of the market by high pressure advertising and price competition. The advertising copy in their newspaper and national magazine advertisements at one point became so filled with wild and exaggerated claims that the industry leaders agreed with the Federal Trade Commission to restrain their excesses in copywriting. The superlatives and boasts continued, however, and companies publicly accused each other of publishing misleading claims for their products.

Although most producers continued to emphasize advertising, it

exhibit 4

(a) Sales of Motor Vehicles and Production of Automobile Tires, 1929–1939; 1947–1960.
(b) Indexes of Shipments of Replacement and Original Equipment Tires, 1929–1939;
1947–1960

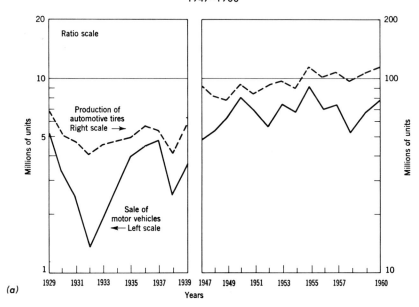

(a)

SOURCE: *Rubber Products Industry—A Statistical Compendium*, N.I.C.B., New York, 1959, and Bureau of the Census, 1960.

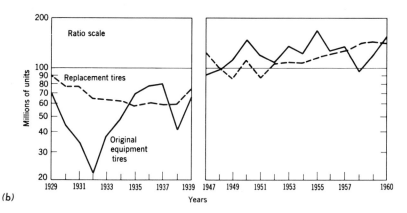

(b)

SOURCE: *Rubber Products Industry—A Statistical Compendium*, N.I.C.B., New York, 1959, and Bureau of the Census, 1960.

exhibit 5

Employment in subindustries of the Rubber Products Industry, 1929–1939; 1947–1960

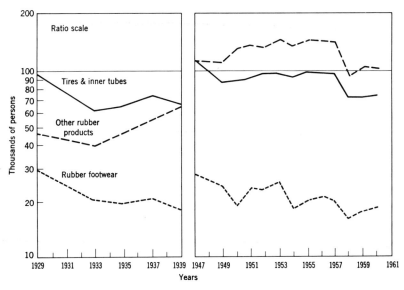

SOURCE: *Rubber Products Industry—A Statistical Compendium, N.I.C.B.*, New York, 1959, and Bureau of the Census, 1960.

was generally recognized that price was the most powerful factor in achieving tire sales. The major producers, by virtue of their predominance in size, took the lead in setting general price levels. No small producer was in a position to set his prices above those of the Big Four; in fact, it was typical of the small producer to shade his prices to a level slightly below that of the Majors.

Selling tires was distinctly different from the selling of most other products in that it was virtually impossible to generate additional demand for tires. "People simply do not want to buy tires," said a sales executive of a competitive company. "They buy tires only when they are forced to do so. There is no impulse factor; there is only the emergency factor." For this reason it was the strategy of the major producers to have a widespread distribution network, intensively covering the country geographically. The major producers were undertaking a program of building their own outlet stores, which handled their tires, and, in addition, many other types of merchandise. The volume of tires sold by large department stores such as Macy's in New York and Wieboldt's in Chicago was rising rapidly; many chain stores of all kinds were adding tires to their lines; variety chains, such as Neisner's; food supermarkets, and even drug chains; and a few enterprising wholesalers were having tires manufactured under their own brand names, which they marketed through any and all of these types of outlets.

The Mohawk management was in general agreement with the industry trend toward more widespread outlets. "To sell tires," said Mr. Fawcett, "you have to knock on doors. In our case, it is the dealer's door."

SALES

"In tread rubber," said Mr. William T. Ernst, "we have been a leader in the industry for many years. In tire sales, however, our largest competitors—Goodyear and Firestone—each do more business every two weeks than we do in a year. But despite the great and almost overwhelming advantages which rightfully belong to the Big Four, 25.3% of the replacement tires bought in 1960 were brands that did not belong to the Big Four, to Sears, Montgomery Ward or Standard Oil. A Look Magazine survey the same year showed that 33.4% of the people asked said they would buy tires not made by the large companies, or that they didn't know what make they would buy. Certainly if one-third of the replacement market is open to all tire manufacturers, there is plenty of room for more Mohawk growth."

In 1961 passenger car tires accounted for about $18,000,000 of Mohawk's sales volume; truck and farm tractor tires about $9,000,000; and tread rubber and repair materials about $9,400,000. Of the $27,000,000 tire sales, the premium grade tubeless Golden Arrow represented nearly 25%; the tubeless Arrow Chief 17%; Arrow Chief, tube, 33%; and Braves, tube, 25%.

When Henry Fawcett became president of the company in 1956, Mr. Charles Sauvain, a veteran of over thirty years' service with Mohawk, was the company's general sales manager. For many years Mr. Sauvain had been in the financial end of the business, principally as credit manager under Mr. Bloch, and when the sales manager left rather suddenly in 1952 Mr. Sauvain, feeling that this would be in the nature of a promotion, asked for the position and received it. One of Mr. Fawcett's first major objectives, when he became head of the company, was to stimulate a more aggressive attitude toward sales. Before the end of 1956 Mr. Sauvain had been promoted to treasurer, and Mr. Fawcett brought into the company Mr. Thomas Johnson to direct the sales function. Mr. Johnson had had considerable experience in the tire business as a tire adjuster, doing general field service work, traveling as a salesman in a territory, and finally as a district sales manager.

Until Mr. Johnson became sales manager, salesmen had been paid on a straight commission basis, drove their own cars, and paid their own expenses. In his first nine months Mr. Johnson dismissed nine of the company's thirteen salesmen, and then he proceeded to build a new sales force. The company sought college men, but accepted high school graduates. Previous tire sales experience was required, and preference was given to those having major rubber company experience. The aim was to hire men in their middle thirties or younger, but exceptions were made. Salesmen were paid a base salary plus a liberal bonus after they reached a certain quota. On this basis the average salesman earned from $8,500 to $11,000 a year.

Each salesman was furnished with a new car every fifteen months and had an expense account which ran around $400 a month. At the end of Mr. Johnson's first year in office, the company had a sales force of 48 men.

With the new sales force, a methodical campaign of developing the dealer organization in one limited territory at a time was undertaken. The first objective was the southeastern states, where the Mohawk management believed buyers were less brand conscious. The Big Four had done extensive national advertising in this region but it was believed that this advertising did not reach the southern rural population effectively, since they were not regular readers of the national magazines. Management also believed that the lower prices of Mohawk tires would have appeal. The first campaign—twelve weeks of television and radio advertising (Grand Ol' Opry)—was aimed at Florida and Alabama, and gave away 50 sets of tires every two weeks to holders of the "lucky license" numbers posted in Mohawk dealers' stores. The company also began to use regional advertising that was available in such magazines as *Life*. The advertising program cost about $50,000 and the give-away tires another $24,000.

In 1956 the company had about 750 dealer accounts. During 1957 fifty new dealer accounts were being opened each month, and by the middle of 1961 the company was adding an average of 100 dealers a month to its distribution system and had approximately 1,500 active dealers and distributors.

The company's next campaign was aimed at developing Georgia and South Carolina and a warehouse was built at Atlanta to service the territory. In addition, serious consideration was being given to the market in the East where the company hoped to establish a new automated plant by 1963.

The company had eight regional sales managers directing forty-eight salesmen. The sales volume in each territory was between $240,000 and $1,000,000. The practice was to have the regional manager in each new territory sign up enough accounts to reach the $240,000 break-even point, whereupon the territory was turned over to a salesman. If a salesman developed over $1,000,000 volume in his territory, the area would be divided to form two sales territories.

Mr. Fawcett believed that the Majors sold their tires principally on a brand preference basis through national advertising, but that Mohawk tires could best be sold on the basis of dealer-customer relationships. Therefore the initial sales effort was aimed at attracting new dealers and building a loyal dealer organization.

To attract new dealers the company offered exclusive territory franchises. The guarantee of a protected territory was a concession which none of the Majors granted, and the Mohawk management considered it their most important sales point. The salesmen emphasized this by pointing out to prospective dealers that the Big Four had opened many of their own retail stores in areas of high potential and that this was a constant threat to independent dealers. Mohawk also offered a price differential which was thought to be approximately 8% to 11% below the Majors for tires of like quality. (See Exhibit 6.)

exhibit 6 PRICE COMPARISON OF MOHAWK
TIRES AND "BIG FOUR" TIRES

	Mohawk	*Big four*
Golden Arrow	$14.75	$16.17
Arrow Chief	13.98	15.32
Brave	9.63 (nylon)	9.63 (rayon)

The company also assured its customers that its tires conformed to industry standards of quality at each grade. Mohawk also offered its retail customers an unconditional road hazard guarantee which no other manufacturer granted. Adjustments on defective tires cost

Mohawk about $\frac{1}{2}\%$ to $\frac{3}{4}\%$ of its sales dollar; the road hazard guarantee raised this expense to about 2%.

Salesmen called on their dealers about every ten days. They took carload orders themselves, and the dealers sent in fill-in orders. The salesmen spent their time seeking new accounts, giving the dealer sales and merchandising help, aiding him in planning advertising, seeing that he was properly identified as a Mohawk dealer, and keeping his relations with Akron smooth.

Any dealer buying over $100,000 per quarter received a 3% quantity weight discount on all carload orders, 2% on truckloads and on fill-in orders. To qualify for the discount he had to take another carload every three months. Distributors, who usually received this discount, operated on a very narrow markup, sometimes as little as 75¢ to $1 a tire. Oil companies usually used a markup of 15%.

The company paid the freight on each shipment of 200 pounds or more to a single destination. It cost 25¢ to ship a tire from Akron to New York City, $1 to ship it from Akron to Texas, and $3 to $4 to ship it to California. Because of the freight expense, a higher price per tire had to be charged at distant points, and promotions on a cut-price basis could not be extended to the West Coast.

To overcome this disadvantage the company established what it called "dealer-warehousemen." Dealer-warehousemen were distributors to whom the company shipped in carload lots to get the benefit of the low freight rate. The dealer-warehouseman acted as the company's warehouseman and local shipper. These distributors were paid 5% over cost on the first $65,000 annual volume, and $3\frac{1}{2}\%$ on any volume over $65,000. When Mr. Fawcett became president of the company he believed that lack of an adequate warehouse system and insufficient stocks of tires in the field had been one of the company's major problems. In 1959 the company had warehouses at Akron, Ohio; Helena, Arkansas; Atlanta, Georgia; and Stockton, California. It planned eventually to have additional warehouses at Minneapolis, Minnesota; Portland, Oregon; Memphis, Tennessee; and Dallas, Texas.

The company did no forecasting, nor did it do any market research. Management assumed that there was enough potential in every territory to warrant its sales effort. In estimating the extent of its overall volume, it considered that replacement tire sales were definitely keyed to new car production; that good new car years were followed two years later by good tire replacement years. Also, in especially poor new car years, the rise in replacement tire sales came the same year, due to buyers switching from new to used car purchases and replacing the tires. Management, however, was beginning to follow car registrations more closely, and breaking them down according to salesmen's territories.

The management considered it important to limit its line to the 72 most popular sizes and types of tires, compared to 120 to 135 sizes offered by other companies. This simplified production and limited inventory, but there was a higher profit margin in the odd sizes and the salesmen were feeling pressure from their dealers to expand the line in this direction.

"The rubber industry," said Mr. Fawcett, "has become a vast complex in the American economy. It involves chemicals, industrial rubber goods, miscellaneous rubber products, as well as the familiar automobile tire. Although we have no genuinely reliable yardstick to measure by, it is probable that seventy-five percent of the rubber industry is still concerned with tires. In the tire field there are three principal categories: tires sold as original equipment on new vehicles; tires sold in the replacement market; and rubber materials sold to recap and repair tires. Barely 1% of our sales are in the original equipment field. This is because the auto manufacturers buy in such substantial quantities that it would take a far greater percentage of our capacity than we can afford to spare. Also, the margin of profit on such business is too small to justify the large percentage of over-all production capacity that would be committed. We believe that it will be in our interest to build solidly for the long-range future by establishing a loyal dealer organization. At present no single Mohawk customer, including the government, accounts for as much as ten percent of our sales."

As a matter of policy, the company did not manufacture tires for new equipment, nor did it accept contracts from mail order or chain stores, considering that this business was too uncertain to permit it to monopolize production facilities. Management thought this type of business might disrupt the normal flow of production destined for the company's retail dealers.

"There are certain advantages in being a small company," said Mr. Bloch, chairman of the Board. "We can turn on a dime. The big companies are too ponderous and slow moving to be able to do that."

Until 1959 Mohawk produced both nylon and rayon cord tires. Management believed that this raised production costs considerably. It meant twice as much cord purchasing, more complex production schedules, shorter production runs, and additional inventories. Management also believed that the rayon manufacturers had been opportunists in their price policies. In the summer of 1959 there had been a price spread of only about 7% between nylon and rayon tires. When Mohawk dropped rayon in 1959 it was the only major tire manufacturer to do so. (See Exhibit 7.)

TREAD RUBBER AND REPAIR MATERIALS

Mohawk had for many years been a leading producer of tread rubber and repair materials used in the recapping of tires. Prior to World War II it had been known in the industry as being principally a producer of "camelback" (the trade name for rubber used in recapping), and the management had treated tires as a secondary product line. In 1961 the company was still a factor in the camelback industry, supplying approximately 8% of the national production, which represented 25% of its total sales. In addition, tire sales, which comprised 75% of Mohawk's sales, accounted for 1.8% of the national production.

The Mohawk management believed that the retread business had a great future potential. Research had produced improved materials and application processes that had largely eliminated most of the former disadvantages of recapping. Recapping had become the accepted practice for trucks, taxis, and commercial fleets. Industry shipments of tread rubber had grown from 95 million pounds in 1947 to more than 500 million pounds in 1961. During that period Mohawk's tread rubber production had increased from 6 million to more than 30 million pounds a year.

In spite of heavy emphasis on the expansion of tire sales, the Mohawk management expressed determination to remain a factor in the tread rubber industry. "We are still the largest producer of camelback and repair material in the country," said Mr. Fawcett, "and the recapping business is growing. Today there are 105 million new tires made a year; but each year 60 million tires are recapped. Recapping has become the accepted standard practice of taxis and trucks. Even the commercial airlines are now experimenting with recapping their tires. The growing popularity of nylon casings will make many more sound casings available which will be suitable for recapping. The day will come when there will be a tire recapped for every new tire made."

Mohawk sold retread rubber to independent recappers and distributors on a technical specification basis, with standards set according to the performance required for usage on either taxis, light or heavy duty trucks, passenger cars, or other vehicles. Mohawk served about 600 of the 10,000 tread rubber dealers in the country. Sales were through 24 tread rubber distributors. It also did special compounding on a "prescription" basis and, through its close connections with major manufacturers, it was able to provide tire recappers with technical advice on compounds and on processing methods. Profit margins were lower on retread materials but overhead and selling expense were also lower. Price competition in tread rubber was keen—½¢ to 1¢ a pound might switch a customer from one product to another. Mohawk's prices were average for the industry, and in its advertising it featured the quality factor. The general theme was usually expressed as follows:

"Why buy cheap retread rubber? Is
your reputation worth 1¢ a pound?"

LABOR AND LABOR RELATIONS

At the Akron plant some 600 hourly and 160 administrative employees turned out nearly 1,500 passenger and truck tires a day. It took about ten days to train an employee for most jobs, and about a month to six weeks for an employee to develop skill on the most exacting job—that of tire building. In keeping with a gentleman's agreement with the other rubber manufacturers of Akron, the Mohawk plant did not hire anyone in the employ of another rubbermaker, even if he voluntarily asked Mohawk for a job. Neither did the Mohawk employment manager advertise in Akron papers, but used the Cleveland and Canton papers instead. The Mohawk personnel director believed that most of his employees had less than average education, came from lower-than-average income families which lived in the poorer residential districts. Rubbermaking, with comparatively high pay, was attractive to them in spite of the fact that much of the work was hot, heavy, and dirty. The personnel director also believed that the work situation created problems; management believed the employees were easily led by their union leaders, and were typically suspicious of anything coming from the company.

Exhibit 7

THE WALL STREET JOURNAL, Monday, September 14, 1959

Mohawk Rubber Drops Rayon Cord Tire Lines For All-Nylon Output

President Says Move Is Caused By 'Rising Public Preference' For Nylon Replacement Tires

By a WALL STREET JOURNAL *Staff Reporter*

AKRON, Ohio—Mohawk Rubber Co. has discontinued using rayon cord in passenger car tire production and converted entirely to nylon.

H. M. Fawcett, president of Mohawk, said, "Our move to nylon reflects our research findings which show nylon cord tires to be superior in all performance characteristics. It also reflects the rising public preference for nylon in the replacement tire market."

Mohawk's move follows by less than a month a general round of price cuts by makers of nylon tire cord, led by Du Pont Co. The reductions, which ran from 8% to 11%, cut sharply the differential between nylon and the best grades of rayon, or rayon-derived, tire cords. Following the reduction, an official of one big tire maker said it made the price difference between the two types of cords "very thin, if any at all."

Mohawk officials, however, did not specify the price cut as a reason for their move. They indicated that the increasing proportion of nylon tire production was the primary reason for their action.

Mohawk's total production goes to the replacement tire market. In 1956, nylon cord tires accounted for 22% of Mohawk's sales. This year, prior to discontinuance of the rayon line, nylon tires accounted for 70% of the company's production, according to Thomas Johnson, sales manager.

Mr. Fawcett gave as an additional reason for the changeover, the simplification of dealer inventory problems. "By offering only nylon cord tires," he said, "Mohawk dealers across the country will be able to simplify and standardize their inventories. This will enable them to offer their customers better service than ever before."

Mr. Fawcett also said the line simplification should eliminate much confusion among buyers about the many types and kinds of tires available.

Nylon cord tires now account for about 40% of the total passenger car replacement market, up from 10% of the market in 1955.

In 1936 Goodyear adopted a modified Bedaux incentive system in connection with a six-hour work day as a share-the-work proposition to spread employment during the depression. Under this system a man was able to produce in six hours as much as he would normally put out in eight, and the two hours saved were added to his wages as a bonus. The original plan allowed no lunch or relief period and called for six hours of continuous production. The employees liked the short work day and later the unions came out strongly in favor of it. The rubber companies were unable to eliminate it so that the six-hour day became industry practice in Akron.

Plants operated around the clock, with shifts changing at noon, 6 p.m., midnight, and 6 a.m. Each shift had an 18-minute rest period and a lunch period which totaled about an hour per shift.

Typical wages were about $2.90 an hour plus fringe benefits of approximately 75¢ per hour. Piece rates were such that the average employee was able to produce his daily quota in 4½ to 5 hours ("capping out," in employee jargon), after which he would remain idle rather than earn an additional bonus. Under a general tacit agreement among themselves, employees would not exceed their quotas.

Because of the six-hour shifts, most of the employees found time to work at another job outside of the plant. Some held a second full-time job, while many operated small service businesses from their homes, such as auto repairs, saw sharpening, gardening, house painting, or farming. The Mohawk personnel management believed that since most employees had a second source of earnings, their annual incomes were relatively high for their station in life. As a result it was difficult to deal with many of the employees because they had achieved some degree of financial independence. Supported by their secondary source of income, employees could take a strike without much suffering. The result was a strong union which constantly and vigorously sparred with management. By 1957, when grievances regarding wage rates, work methods, departmental jurisdiction, and working conditions multiplied to what management considered a "prohibitive degree," the company decided to take a "hard nosed" attitude toward the union. Thereafter they met with the union an average of seven hours each week on grievances, and in a two-year period took 88 of them to arbitration, winning 80% of them. During the same period two other tiremakers took 2 and 7 grievances to arbitration and most of these were compromised.

After experiencing four illegal work stoppages in 1958 management announced that the next wildcat strike would result in an automatic seven-day suspension. Later in that year when a fifth stoppage occurred, management held firm and invoked the rule, closing the plant for seven days. This was the last work stoppage. The Mohawk management, nevertheless, professed that its attitude toward the union was one of respect and cooperation. It believed that the rubber unions were entirely honest and free from scandal, and had never been known to indulge in any double-dealing or "sweethearting." Management stated that it believed the rubber unions were here to stay, and that it was willing to continue to deal with them in spite of the daily sparring.

In June 1961 a new 2-year contract, matching the pattern set by the rubber tire industry, was negotiated with the United Rubber Workers increasing hourly workers' wages 7½¢ an hour the first year and 7¢ an hour the second year. In addition, supplementary unemployment benefits were extended from 26 to 39 weeks and the weekly maximum benefit was raised $5 a week. Other fringe benefits negotiated included an eighth paid holiday, four weeks vacation for employees with 22 years' service (formerly 25 years' service) and three weeks vacation for employees with 10 years' service (formerly 11 years' service).

PRODUCTION PROCESS

The process of tiremaking used by all manufacturers was virtually identical. The crude rubber, both natural and synthetic, was mixed with carbon black, oil, and sulphur in specific proportions to produce a desired grade. Initially mixed in a "Banbury" mill, whose beater blades speedily achieved a uniformly smooth blending of the ingredients, the rubber was then kneaded by "warm-up" roller mills till it reached the desired temperature to give it the plasticity required for forming. The batch was then extruded through dies into the shape and size of the tread to be formed. Concurrently the fabric for the cord which formed the carcass was impregnated with rubber by a "Z" calender train, in which the fabric was coated with rubber as it passed through a highly precise series of cylindrical rollers somewhat like a newsprint roller press. The bead, the rubber-coated wire cable reinforced band which held the tire rim to the wheel, was fabricated separately.

The various components of the tire—the tread and sidewall rubber, the cord material for the plies, the beads, flipper strips and chafing strips—were then brought together to the tirebuilder, who assembled the parts on a tirebuilding machine, an ingenious apparatus whose central cylinder expanded to form the tire and collapsed to permit it to be removed. The crude tire then went to the curing mold where it was inserted in a die of the desired dimensions and tread. Here it was heated by steam, under pressure, for the time required to vulcanize the rubber. After curing, the tire was shaved smooth of mold-marks, painted, powdered, inspected, and wrapped for shipment.

Calender tolerances were as close as plus or minus 1/1,000th of an inch. In a twenty-pound tire, which used twelve pounds of tread rubber, no more variation than 3/10ths of a pound of rubber was permitted. All materials were bought by the pound, while tires were sold on a per-unit basis. The assembly operation performed by the tirebuilder required a high degree of accuracy.

PLANTS AND FACILITIES

Mohawk's Akron plant had been built in 1898 by another manufacturer and it was acquired by Mohawk in 1913. It was situated literally within the shadow of the original and principal plant of Goodyear, whose huge complex of multi-storied buildings, separated from Mohawk only by a railroad track, surrounded and dwarfed the little Mohawk factory. The Akron plant consisted of four units: a compounding plant, where the crude was milled; a tire-building plant, where the tire parts were assembled and cured; a warehouse and service garage; and the executive office building. The compounding building was across the street and separated from the other buildings.

At the time Mr. Fawcett became president in 1955 he believed that lack of local plants and warehouses was one of Mohawk's major problems. In 1956 the company bought a plant in West Helena, Arkansas, which had been built in 1948 by the Chrysler Corporation for the production of wooden frame station wagon bodies. The plant had been idle since Chrysler switched to metal bodies. The facility, which had been built at a cost of over $1 million by Chrysler, was purchased by Mohawk for $300,000. The purchase was financed by an $800,000 bond issue made by the Arkansas Development Corporation, with guarantee by Mohawk. The funds were used to pay for the plant, to buy six new Bag-o-matic presses, and to furnish working capital.

Since there were no rubber workers in the Arkansas labor market, the management undertook to train a work force. For this purpose nine Akron supervisors were chosen, one for each of the principal production operations, such as tread tubing, curing, Banbury milling, tire building, etc. Each man was chosen for having shown exceptional competence in his operation and, in an attempt to avoid carrying over to West Helena the bad work habits and practices which had been built up at Akron, only men who were known to be good "company men" were chosen.

Believing that younger men would better lend themselves to being trained, the management at West Helena gave preference to the hiring of men in their twenties. Almost none of them had had any previous factory experience similar to that at Mohawk; most of them had worked in Arkansas hardwood lumbering mills, or on farms. No requirements as to education or previous experience were set, but employee applications were screened for ability through a series of tests such as a physical test, manual dexterity tests and intelligence tests. Most of the new employees lived within a radius of twenty miles of West Helena, because they had local family connections. Trained and skilled personnel, such as motion and time study men or maintenance mechanics, were recruited from cities as far away as Memphis.

The West Helena plant was single storied, high ceilinged, with a long rectangular floor pattern, and lent itself well, the Mohawk management believed, to the laying out of an efficient production flow. Where the Akron production process was complicated by the multi-storied buildings and by the fact that it was housed in several buildings, necessitating considerable in-plant transportation, the Helena operation was designed to bring in the raw materials at one end of the plant and transport them within the plant automatically by belts, chutes, and conveyors through a production system that flowed from the raw materials at one end of the plant to the finished tires at the other end.

Most of the tire makers, including Mohawk at its Akron plant, still cured their tires on "pot heaters" or "watch-case" molds—split section molds in which the tire had to be inserted and withdrawn by

hand, limiting one man to the servicing of only two molds. In 1949 the
bag-o-matic process was introduced. Under this process an insert, a
heavy rubber inner tube, was inflated inside the uncured tire to mold
it. The bag-o-matics were entirely automated, being served by conveyors which inserted the uncured tires into the mold and carried away
the cured tires. One man attended a battery of 24 machines. West
Helena was the only tire plant in the industry using bag-o-matics
exclusively.

West Helena employees belonged to Local #539 of the United Rubber Workers. Being a newly organized local, management was able, it
believed, to write into the contract the best phases of its Akron experience, and to eliminate the items which had caused its difficulties.
Where the piecework rates at Akron had made substantial allowances
for sub-standard buildings, work methods, and working conditions,
the West Helena rates were considerably tighter; they also allowed less
fringe benefits and contained considerably stricter disciplinary rules.
In its first three years of operation the Helena plant averaged two
grievance meetings a month, each of which lasted about two hours.
No grievance had ever been carried to arbitration. Where the Akron
management had considerable difficulty with certain vices, such as
excessive drinking, the West Helena plant had no such experience.

The West Helena superintendent found, however, that his employees
required close supervision and that he was short of competent supervisors and of employees who were of supervisory caliber; he considered
absenteeism his major employee problem.

The supervisors who had been trained from the employee group
tended to lack initiative and as a result they themselves needed constant direction. It was common for a supervisor to be on close friendly
terms with his employees and often they were blood relatives, a situation which bred familiarity, lack of discipline, and disrespect. Two
attitudes, both extremes, appeared among these foremen—one group
was too easy-going; the other quite autocratic.

The Helena plant, contrary to the industry practice, worked an
eight-hour day, three shifts a day, six days a week. Although wage
levels were below those of Akron and in the rubber industry generally,
they were high compared to other wages in the area. Employees were
generally eager to turn out high production, but only during their
standard eight-hour day. They were so eager, in fact, that the management found it necessary to put a ceiling of 25% over normal on

incentives in order to keep a smooth and undisrupted flow of production. Most employees were unaccustomed to earning much money, a circumstance which caused them to work hard until their weekly earnings reached, say, $100, beyond which the employee would not be interested in higher earnings. It was difficult to get employees to work overtime, almost impossible to get them to work on Sundays, and the rate of absenteeism on Mondays was exceptionally high. The West Helena plant management nevertheless considered their employees' morale to be high, for the employees appeared to be appreciative of their high wages; they made an effort to conform; and most of them were receptive to company problems.

At West Helena the average plantwide wage rate was substantially below the rate paid by Mohawk at Akron. Mohawk's wage rates were about 7¢ higher than those of the Big Four. About 30% of the cost of a finished tire was made up of labor costs. In 1959 the per unit cost of direct labor and overhead at West Helena was running about 75% of that at Akron. The West Helena superintendent believed these savings resulted from lower wage rates, more efficient machinery and plant layout, higher employee morale, and higher per employee production at the lower wage rates.

The Akron plant obtained the bulk of its raw materials from one of the major rubber companies. The Helena plant obtained its raw material requirements independently, and directly from producers. Latex, refined from "wild" rubber, coming from abroad, was purchased from brokers at New Orleans, the port of entry. Synthetic rubber was bought from chemical concerns, whose principal refineries were located at Texas gulf ports. Both sources were only a short distance from West Helena.

The West Helena plant opened in September 1956 with a production of 600 tires a day plus 20,000 pounds of tread rubber; in June 1957, the rate was stepped up to 1,500 tires a day; in September 1958, to 3,000 tires a day; and in June 1959, to 4,200 tires a day. In the fall of 1959 an addition was built which added 50% to the floor area of the plant and a new $750,000 Z-calender train was installed. The original battery of six bag-o-matic presses was increased to 34. By mid-1961 there were 350 hourly workers and 50 staff personnel, and production increased to 5,700 tires a day plus 60,000 pounds of tread rubber.

"In the years following 1961," said Mr. Ernst, "we must rely on the crystal ball. We do know, however, that there will be more cars on the road and more people driving them. The Interstate Highway System will enable people to drive faster at safer speeds. Tires for compact cars might cost less, but it is doubtful whether they will wear any longer than regular tires. They have less weight to carry, but they revolve faster. In our opinion, both the tire market and the recapping industry will expand as they did in the fifties. . . . Mohawk should be able to increase its sales by the mid-sixties to the $40 to $45 million range, and by the late sixties to the $45 to $55 million range . . . earning on a consistent basis $1,700,000 to $2,000,000 annually."

U.S. TIRE INDUSTRY NOTES

Goodyear, the world's largest rubber fabricator, derives approximately 60% of its total sales from tire lines, which is fairly evenly divided between original equipment and replacement. Other products include: synthetic rubbers, plastic resins, plastic films, adhesives, aviation products, film cushioning, and vinyl flooring. Foreign operations, mainly tire lines made outside the U.S., account for over 20% of sales. Defense work averaged ⅛ of the total sales in 1950–54 and has continued important.

Daily tire capacity approximates 130,000 units with Chrysler its main original equipment outlet, and lesser amounts being supplied to Ford, American Motors, and General Motors. Replacement sales are handled through an estimated 70,000 dealers, oil companies, and some 600 company stores.

Firestone Tire & Rubber Co. is the nation's second largest tire producer and obtains nearly ⅔ of its sales from tires. The rest comes from about 770 company stores, natural and synthetic rubber, mechanical rubber goods, foam rubber, plastic and chemical products, metal items, and military items. Approximately 1,000 different sizes and types of pneumatic tires are manufactured, as well as more than 12,000 products in other fields. Daily tire capacity approximates 130,000 units. Original equipment normally accounts for about half of the unit tire volume, with Ford and General Motors the main outlets. In addition, the company also supplies a majority of the original equipment tires used by Studebaker-Packard. Replacement tire business in the U.S. and Canada is handled through approximately 60,000 independent dealers, oil companies, and company stores.

United States Rubber Company is the third largest rubber fabricator and derives about half of its sales from its tire division. The rest comes from the mechanical rubber goods, footwear and general products, textile, and chemical divisions. Military work is relatively small. Foreign business accounts for slightly more than 20% of sales.

Daily tire capacity approximates 113,000 units. Nearly ⅔ of the tire volume is replacement. General Motors is by far the largest customer for the company's original equipment tires with smaller amounts being supplied to Studebaker-Packard. The company owned 11 retail stores in 1959 and by 1961 it had more than 140, reflecting the acquisition of two tire store chains and the opening of additional units.

B. F. Goodrich Co. is the fourth largest rubber company and is the most diversified of the "Big Four," deriving about 55% of its revenue from nontire lines. The balance comes from an extensive line of industrial rubber products, flooring and footwear, chemical and plastic products, foamed and sponge rubber products, aviation and missile components, and textile items.

Daily tire capacity approximates 65,000 units, with General Motors its main equipment outlet, and lesser amounts being supplied to Ford, American Motors, and Chrysler. Replacement sales, which are more important volume-wise than original equipment sales, are handled through several thousand independent dealers, through more than 600 company-owned stores, and through the sale of private brand tires to oil companies and a large mass merchandiser.

Armstrong Rubber Company ranks fifth in the tire industry on the basis of unit volume, having a daily tire capacity of 47,000. Roughly 95% of sales is attributable to tires, solely for the replacement market, with Sears Roebuck taking about 67% of the tires produced (about 70% of Sears' total requirements). Miscellaneous rubber products account for approximately 5% of total sales.

Distribution of tires is made through 1,200 independent distributors who sell to dealers throughout the country. Export sales to 70 foreign countries are handled by 125 foreign distributors.

General Tire & Rubber Company is fifth in size among domestic rubber fabricators. However, less than 50% of its volume and net income in 1961 was derived from tires, plastics, chemicals, and other miscellaneous products. Wholly-owned RKO General accounted for approximately 14% of net income. About 36% of its consolidated net income came from 84%-owned Aero jet-General Corporation (a leader in rockets and propellants and related atomic energy products). Daily tire production approximates 26,000 units, supplied mainly to the replacement and fleet markets.

Lee Rubber & Tire Corporation derives an estimated ⅔ of total sales from tire lines, including replacement passenger car, truck, and bus tires, camelback, and various tire sundries. The other ⅓ comes from more than 1,000 items of mechanical rubber goods, including

FINANCIAL DATA OF THE BIG FOUR AND LEADING INDEPENDENT TIRE MANUFACTURERS*

Income statistics (in millions of dollars)

Goodyear Tire & Rubber

Year Ended Dec. 31	Net Sales	% Oper. Inc. of Sales	Maint. & Repairs	Deprec.	Net Bef. Taxes	Income Taxes	Net Inc.
1961	1,473.4	14.6	....	52.67	154.48	77.14	76.19
1960	1,550.9	12.3	40.1	49.82	138.38	66.52	71.02
1959	1,579.3	12.3	41.2	49.70	141.59	64.68	76.01
1958	1,367.6	13.7	34.7	47.41	135.04	66.49	65.74
1957	1,421.9	12.9	37.0	43.27	135.58	67.73	64.83
1956	1,358.8	12.8	36.6	38.14	130.49	66.30	62.46
1955	1,372.2	12.0	36.7	32.88	126.64	66.97	59.67
1954	1,090.1	11.7	30.4	33.83	91.43	43.37	48.06
1953	1,210.6	12.7	34.0	30.19	117.77	68.45	49.32
1952	1,138.4	12.6	30.6	25.94	108.11	69.10	39.01

Firestone Tire & Rubber

Year Ended Oct. 31	Net Sales	% Op. Inc. of Sales	Oper. Inc.	Maint. & Repairs	Deprec.	Net Bef. Taxes	Net Inc.
1961	1,182.7	14.6	171.7	....	49.1	124.2	63.63
1960	1,207.2	14.1	170.6	40.5	45.7	126.6	65.03
1959	1,187.8	14.4	171.2	34.9	40.7	129.0	64.60
1958	1,061.6	14.3	151.6	33.0	41.4	107.2	53.75
1957	1,158.9	13.9	161.4	37.5	39.0	119.8	61.69
1956	1,115.2	14.2	158.0	35.3	36.9	119.8	60.54
1955	1,114.9	13.3	148.6	23.2	32.0	114.3	55.38
1954	916.0	12.2	111.8	19.9	27.9	81.5	40.51
1953	1,029.4	11.8	121.7	22.1	24.7	94.2	46.75
1952	965.4	12.0	115.8	19.5	20.7	84.0	43.08

packing and conveyor belting, hose for the automotive, mining, steel and petroleum industries, and accessories for the automotive industry. Tire sales are normally confined to the replacement and fleet markets. Distribution is nationwide, through 51 factory branches in principal cities east of the Mississippi, and in Dallas and Fort Worth, Texas, through Phillips Petroleum and Signal Oil. Daily tire capacity approximates 7,500 units.

The company also sells batteries under the Lee name.

FINANCIAL DATA OF THE BIG FOUR AND LEADING INDEPENDENT TIRE MANUFACTURERS (continued) *

Pertinent balance sheet statistics (in millions of dollars)

Goodyear Tire & Rubber (continued)

Gross Prop.	Capital Expend.	Cash Items	Inventories	Receivables	Cur. Assets	Cur. Liabs.	Net Workg. Cap.	Cur. Ratio Assets to Liabs.	Long-term Debt
908.8	82.64	75.7	349.8	262.4	687.9	147.9	540.1	4.7-1	230.98
844.1	74.55	72.4	342.0	234.8	649.2	127.7	521.5	5.1-1	227.14
789.0	55.64	46.8	348.1	236.9	631.8	121.4	510.4	5.2-1	231.02
747.2	53.35	49.1	309.4	225.7	584.2	107.1	477.1	5.5-1	236.35
708.5	82.95	44.3	341.4	198.6	584.3	135.1	499.2	4.3-1	241.09
638.4	88.85	50.6	317.1	196.9	564.6	113.3	451.3	5.0-1	243.03
561.6	70.96	67.3	303.2	177.4	547.9	87.4	460.6	6.3-1	240.21
501.5	33.08	51.1	249.4	168.4	468.9	106.8	362.1	4.4-1	191.44
476.9	50.37	68.0	246.0	149.9	463.9	62.5	401.5	7.4-1	195.44
435.6	52.76	44.8	275.4	160.4	480.7	83.5	397.2	5.8-1	200.00

Firestone Tire & Rubber (continued)

Gross Prop.	Capital Expend.	Cash Items	Inventories	Receivables	Cur. Assets	Cur. Liabs.	Net Workg. Cap.	Cur. Ratio Assets to Liabs.	Long-term Debt
604.0	70.87	45.5	287.7	233.6	566.8	183.1	383.7	3.1-1	76.0
555.9	82.81	43.9	283.6	226.6	554.1	173.5	380.6	3.2-1	76.9
501.5	48.48	69.5	250.1	227.7	547.4	152.9	394.5	3.6-1	91.8
472.5	37.77	45.7	245.3	197.3	488.3	128.3	360.0	3.5-1	96.5
456.2	73.72	45.3	268.6	199.6	513.5	184.4	329.1	3.8-1	101.2
399.2	58.57	45.3	241.7	195.0	482.0	160.7	321.3	3.0-1	105.7
358.9	55.72	53.1	211.5	169.1	433.7	125.5	308.2	3.5-1	110.2
320.7	43.69	65.1	199.7	128.3	393.1	92.4	300.7	4.3-1	114.5
292.9	43.68	67.1	192.2	132.7	392.7	98.6	293.3	4.0-1	118.8
266.1	42.95	74.8	185.3	123.7	383.7	95.5	288.2	4.0-1	121.5

**FINANCIAL DATA OF THE BIG FOUR AND LEADING
INDEPENDENT TIRE MANUFACTURERS (continued) ***

Income statistics (in millions of dollars) (continued)

United States Rubber

Year Ended Dec. 31	Net Sales	% Op. Inc. of Sales	Maint. & Repairs	Depr. & Obsol.	Net Bef. Taxes	Net Inc.	$8 Pfd. Earns.
1961	940.4	8.6	. . . .	25.7	52.79	27.10	41.97
1960	966.8	9.4	31.36	24.2	67.31	30.74	47.21
1959	976.8	10.7	31.27	24.4	78.02	35.58	54.65
1958	870.6	9.2	26.00	24.7	50.15	22.67	34.82
1957	873.6	8.9	26.80	22.7	57.13	29.70	45.61
1956	901.3	9.5	28.70	21.8	61.83	31.87	48.95
1955	926.2	11.3	27.19	19.6	76.91	33.56	51.54
1954	782.5	9.6	23.73	17.6	54.53	27.96	42.94
1953	839.9	10.4	26.57	16.0	72.61	32.73	50.27
1952	851.1	12.4	24.57	14.4	88.56	28.17	43.27

Armstrong Rubber (continued)

Year Ended Sept. 30	Net Sales	% Oper. Inc. of Sales	Maint. & Repairs	Depr., Depl. & Amort.	Net Bef. Taxes	Inc. Taxes	Net Inc.
1961	119.39	13.2	1.88	4.55	9.58	4.73	4.85
1960	116.78	12.8	3.59	4.02	9.72	4.75	4.96
1959	117.16	13.8	. . . .	3.43	11.92	6.02	5.90
1958	81.32	12.4	1.87	2.71	6.44	3.21	3.23
1957	76.14	12.0	1.87	2.47	5.84	2.89	2.95
1956	71.31	11.9	2.25	2.15	5.49	2.69	2.80
1955	68.98	12.0	1.38	1.96	5.32	2.59	2.73
1954	55.38	10.8	1.01	1.69	3.41	1.74	1.67
1953	62.29	9.8	1.11	1.31	4.14	2.42	1.72
1952	55.44	8.9	0.86	0.96	3.76	2.11	1.65

FINANCIAL DATA OF THE BIG FOUR AND LEADING
INDEPENDENT TIRE MANUFACTURERS (continued)*

Pertinent balance sheet statistics (in millions of dollars) (continued)

United States Rubber (continued)

Gross Prop.	Capital Expend.	Cash Items	Inven- tories	Receiv- ables	Cur. Assets	Cur. Liabs.	Net Workg. Cap.	Cur. Ratio Assets to Liabs.	Long- term Debt
556.77	36.09	54.0	240.7	150.8	445.5	134.0	311.5	3.3–1	149.70
529.25	26.51	57.6	243.5	138.3	439.4	121.1	318.3	3.6–1	154.67
526.95	25.00	56.8	252.8	144.8	454.5	142.2	312.3	3.2–1	159.92
507.87	27.58	54.8	226.6	143.4	424.8	129.0	295.8	3.3–1	164.66
461.51	36.11	39.4	234.9	120.0	394.2	112.1	282.1	3.1–1	169.03
449.19	32.51	33.3	252.2	138.3	423.9	138.1	285.8	3.1–1	174.48
417.71	35.28	51.4	225.0	130.3	406.8	147.0	259.8	2.8–1	155.50
389.26	31.69	53.1	189.6	112.4	355.1	122.7	232.4	2.9–1	120.90
365.43	26.03	70.5	192.9	96.2	359.6	128.3	231.3	2.8–1	120.90
346.69	26.26	73.0	193.7	95.1	361.8	155.5	206.3	2.3–1	102.72

Armstrong Rubber

Gross Prop.	Capital Expend.	Cash Items	Inven- tories	Receiv- ables	Cur. Assets	Cur. Liabs.	Net Workg. Cap.	Cur. Ratio Assets to Liabs.	Long- term Debt
62.22	9.55	21.65	31.38	15.68	68.76	21.59	47.17	4.5–1	34.95
53.54	10.09	6.07	40.84	16.75	63.74	31.57	32.17	2.0–1	17.67
44.57	6.92	5.95	35.94	11.65	53.64	24.56	29.08	2.2–1	10.90
29.39	2.32	4.52	23.19	10.55	38.32	17.22	21.10	2.2–1	8.17
27.42	3.40	4.15	22.23	9.91	36.33	19.52	16.81	1.9–1	6.04
24.45	1.97	3.77	21.46	9.77	35.03	19.69	15.34	1.8–1	5.09
23.14	2.71	2.88	17.42	8.50	28.84	14.52	14.32	1.9–1	7.39
21.22	2.56	3.67	12.39	7.62	23.68	9.08	14.60	2.6–1	10.37
19.12	3.32	2.52	14.63	6.00	23.15	15.00	8.15	1.5–1	3.79
16.14	2.31	4.00	13.21	6.89	24.09	14.48	9.61	1.7–1	4.19

FINANCIAL DATA OF THE BIG FOUR AND LEADING
INDEPENDENT TIRE MANUFACTURERS (continued)*

Income statistics (in millions of dollars) (continued)

Lee Rubber & Tire

Year Ended Oct. 31	Net Sales	% Oper. Inc. of Sales	Maint. & Repairs	Depr. & Depl.	Net Bef. Taxes	Inc. Taxes	Net Inc.
1961	44.68	2.2	. . . .	0.83	0.45	0.17	0.28
1960	44.30	2.1	1.18	0.82	0.52	0.19	0.33
1959	52.16	7.9	1.28	0.72	3.37	1.85	1.52
1958	46.56	9.4	0.99	0.63	3.81	2.01	1.80
1957	48.60	8.6	1.05	0.60	3.65	1.88	1.77
1956	46.58	8.5	1.19	0.58	3.40	1.79	1.61
1955	45.91	9.2	1.10	0.54	3.73	1.98	1.75
1954	39.39	8.4	0.77	0.54	2.92	1.52	1.40
1953	46.30	9.2	0.76	0.74	3.63	1.96	1.67
1952	45.34	7.3	0.83	0.47	3.11	1.34	1.77

B. F. Goodrich

Year Ended Dec. 31	Net Sales	% Oper. Inc. of Sales	Maint. & Repairs	Deprec. & Amort.	Net Bef. Taxes	Income Taxes	Net Inc.
1961	757.8	10.7	. . . .	25.10	59.78	28.75	31.03
1960	764.7	10.2	30.18	23.78	57.51	27.49	30.02
1959	771.6	11.5	28.37	21.77	73.38	35.80	37.58
1958	697.3	12.7	26.12	21.34	70.64	35.18	35.46
1957	734.7	12.4	29.93	21.13	75.91	36.54	39.37
1956	724.2	14.1	27.89	19.47	86.85	43.08	43.77
1955	755.0	14.8	20.94	19.68	94.99	48.33	46.66
1954	630.7	14.4	20.30	16.12	75.29	36.47	38.82
1953	674.6	15.1	20.70	13.44	88.09	53.86	34.23
1952	624.1	16.2	17.24	11.27	89.44	57.08	32.36

FINANCIAL DATA OF THE BIG FOUR AND LEADING
INDEPENDENT TIRE MANUFACTURERS (continued) *

Pertinent balance sheet statistics (in millions of dollars) (continued)

Lee Rubber & Tire (continued)

Gross Prop.	Capital Expend.	Cash Items	Inventories	Receivables	Cur. Assets	Cur. Liabs.	Net Workg. Cap.	Cur. Ratio Assets to Liabs.	Long-term Debt
19.80	1.02	3.78	10.06	7.39	21.67	3.39	18.28	6.4–1	Nil
19.05	0.80	3.89	11.92	5.97	22.12	3.11	19.01	7.1–1	Nil
18.44	1.60	4.14	11.72	7.57	23.64	4.01	19.63	5.9–1	Nil
17.05	1.28	4.80	11.29	6.97	23.15	3.57	19.58	6.5–1	Nil
15.97	0.66	6.70	9.84	6.48	23.11	3.72	19.39	6.2–1	Nil
15.50	0.49	5.64	10.93	6.00	22.67	3.79	18.88	6.0–1	Nil
15.25	1.41	5.75	10.68	5.29	21.80	3.68	18.12	5.9–1	Nil
13.95	0.21	8.42	8.90	4.19	21.56	3.67	17.89	5.9–1	Nil
13.79	1.10	6.90	8.46	4.42	20.00	3.12	16.88	6.4–1	Nil
13.09	2.07	6.13	8.89	3.99	19.40	3.23	16.17	6.0–1	Nil

B. F. Goodrich (continued)

Gross Prop.	Capital Expend.	Cash Items	Inventories	Receivables	Cur. Assets	Cur. Liabs.	Net Workg. Cap.	Cur. Ratio Assets to Liabs.	Long-term Debt
419.8	56.17	61.2	169.5	155.7	386.4	95.7	290.7	4.0–1	98.56
378.4	41.38	66.9	160.5	131.2	358.5	78.0	280.5	4.6–1	98.52
357.3	34.28	24.3	177.7	140.6	342.6	90.9	251.7	3.8–1	41.31
347.4	27.62	59.7	154.1	132.6	346.4	94.0	252.4	3.7–1	43.80
331.1	38.87	45.4	168.7	119.2	333.3	89.3	244.0	3.7–1	45.75
302.9	37.01	73.4	147.3	123.0	343.6	98.5	245.1	3.5–1	46.99
277.6	30.29	85.6	147.3	117.7	350.6	109.5	241.1	3.2–1	49.65
264.6	28.03	92.1	121.6	105.3	319.0	93.4	225.6	3.4–1	51.66
227.1	23.42	93.1	128.3	94.5	316.0	105.6	210.4	3.0–1	54.60
210.0	21.92	82.3	131.2	95.2	308.8	111.7	197.1	2.8–1	56.56

**FINANCIAL DATA OF THE BIG FOUR AND LEADING
INDEPENDENT TIRE MANUFACTURERS** (continued)*

Income statistics (in millions of dollars) (continued)

General Tire & Rubber

Year Ended Nov. 30	Net Sales	% Oper. Inc. of Sales	Maint. & Repairs	Deprec. & Amort.	Net. Bef. Taxes	Net Inc.
1961	809.02	8.6	. . . .	17.37	53.93	27.34
1960	753.95	7.3	24.14	14.61	44.81	22.79
1959	676.94	8.6	23.42	13.62	50.32	26.62
1958	469.78	8.0	18.00	11.38	24.69	11.28
1957	421.17	6.8	13.74	10.48	19.68	11.30
1956	390.47	7.3	11.54	7.95	22.09	10.86
1955	295.73	8.6	9.05	5.77	21.63	11.60
1954	216.99	5.3	7.22	4.68	6.92	4.50
1953	205.37	6.0	5.67	3.84	9.74	6.28
1952	185.91	7.4	4.66	3.13	12.08	6.15

FINANCIAL DATA OF THE BIG FOUR AND LEADING
INDEPENDENT TIRE MANUFACTURERS (continued)*

Pertinent balance sheet statistics (in millions of dollars) (continued)

General Tire & Rubber (continued)

Gross Prop.	Capital Expend.	Cash Items	Inven-tories	Receiv-ables	Cur. Assets	Cur. Liabs.	Net Workg. Cap.	Cur. Ratio Assets to Liabs.	Long-term Debt
206.38	. . . .	14.36	78.95	153.47	246.78	122.74	124.04	2.0–1	102.28
179.02	25.91	11.04	73.48	151.81	236.34	129.74	106.60	1.8–1	82.57
157.03	28.63	13.18	72.93	106.86	193.14	80.42	112.72	2.4–1	87.67
134.59	16.12	13.11	60.06	95.04	168.22	92.03	76.19	1.8–1	66.96
121.61	24.70	10.20	62.23	77.05	149.50	70.05	79.45	2.1–1	71.01
98.07	21.85	10.71	59.47	75.01	145.20	77.99	67.21	1.9–1	53.61
79.59	10.84	10.79	48.26	63.75	122.80	70.40	52.40	1.7–1	21.08
70.15	7.17	9.93	43.31	47.16	100.41	55.68	44.73	1.8–1	22.05
52.03	6.26	6.66	39.48	34.38	80.53	35.81	44.72	2.2–1	23.02
44.78	4.57	8.28	33.30	35.40	77.00	38.81	38.19	2.0–1	18.99

* *Standard Listed Stock Reports, 1962.* Standard and Poor's Corporation, Ephrata,
Pa.

the
decision-making
process

WILKINSON
SWORD
LIMITED (A)

Early in 1966 the financial press in London reported:

> Wilkinson Sword is one of the great success stories of British industry in recent years. Within ten years the profits of this family-owned firm have gone up a hundred fold. In 1954 they amounted to £20,451 ($57.3 thousand) before taxes. In 1963, having expanded from earnings alone, profits were £2,048,076 ($5.7 million). The directors estimated that profits for 1964 would be £3,250,000 ($9.1 million); actual profits earned in 1964 were £3,534,520 ($9.7 million); in 1965 the company earned £2.2 million ($6.1 million) before taxes. (See Exhibits 1 through 4.)

The company, which manufactured swords, garden tools, and fire protection devices, had introduced a newly developed razor blade in 1956. In the years which followed, the number of its employees quadrupled, it built numerous new plants in the United Kingdom and other parts of the world, and it entered its products in more than 50 world markets. In 1966 the Randolph and Latham families, which had been in control of the company for almost 100 years, continued to own 70% of the capital stock (see Exhibit 5).

COMPANY HISTORY AND DEVELOPMENT

The Wilkinson Sword Company Limited traces its origins to Henry Nock, a gunsmith who established one of the largest gun and bayonet factories in the city of London in 1772. Nock had an enterprising apprentice named James Wilkinson, who married his daughter and became his partner. When Nock died in 1804 Wilkinson took over and in 1820 added swordmaking for Navy and Army officers to his gunmaking activities. His son Henry, who succeeded him, moved the business to Pall Mall in central London, close to the Admiralty and War offices in Whitehall. James Wilkinson had secured an appointment as gunmaker to King George III, the first of nine royal appointments to British sovereigns which were to follow. Sword production was at its peak during the latter decades of the nineteenth century, when the Wilkinson firm supplied arms for the Crimean and Boer Wars and for the vast British armies throughout the Empire. In addition to making swords, cutlasses, sabers, and boarding pikes, the company also made lances. By the close of the century cavalry-sword production alone was between 30,000 and 60,000 a year, and it was estimated that at any time Queen Victoria's armed forces had in use about half a million Wilkinson weapons.

The reign of Edward VII was peaceful and production dropped sharply. Under George V during World War I, the Wilkinson factory, moved to larger quarters in the Acton area of London, converted to emergency production and turned out 2.5 million bayonets in addition to capacity production of swords. After the war, production virtually ceased, and the company reverted to the making of a hollow-ground straight-edged razor which it had been producing in modest quantities since 1890. At the turn of the century the company had developed a safety razor which could be stropped automatically. In 1920 it began to make pruning shears, and it soon became the leader in the British Isles. During the 1930's it also had fleeting experiences in the making of nail clippers, scissors, table cutlery, and other cutting tools. At one time it manufactured the Wilkinson Touring Autocycle and the Pall Mall Bicycle. The company began, in 1938, the manufacture of fire detection and protection equipment for aircraft, a joint venture with the Graviner Manufacturing Company Limited.

During World War II Wilkinson again converted entirely to war work, producing for the Allied armies millions of bayonets, swords, commando knives, armor-piercing shot, flak suits, and bullet-proof waistcoats. During the war the Graviner Company installed its fire-fighting equipment in a vast fleet of Allied aircraft.

With the cessation of hostilities the Wilkinson plants were again abruptly idled. Safety-razor production was later resumed, but was slowed up by the postwar shortage of brass. There was some activity in Graviner fire protection equipment, which was adopted for use by the commercial airlines, then a fledgling industry. Garden tools became a major product, with the line expanded to include all garden tools with cutting edges, both clippers and cultivating tools. Sword production slowly picked up with the change of the army to its peacetime role.

In 1956 Wilkinson brought out its first stainless steel razor blade. In 1961 it introduced its historic Teflon-coated Wilkinson Sword Blade.

ORGANIZATIONAL STRUCTURE AND POLICY

"Ten years ago," said Mr. Denys Randolph, assistant managing director, "we were a little company with a total employee strength of 750, and we were owner-managed. Direct control of all sides of the business was possible by the chairman and the managing director."

With the rapid expansion of the business in the decade which followed, the management undertook a series of organizational moves to effect more decentralization. As a result the company was divided into six operating divisions: shaving, hand tools, fire protection, swords, research and international (see Exhibit 6, organization 1965).

Until 1964 razor blades and garden tools had been handled on a joint basis throughout the world. Overseas subsidiaries had handled both products, and originally even the United Kingdom sales force had done the same. In 1964 two separate divisions were established and their activities clearly separated.

Wilkinson Sword (West End) Limited controlled the Pall Mall office and showroom. It dealt mainly with sword activities and armored waistcoats, but it also provided a public-relations function for the group as a whole.

Wilkinson Sword (Research) Limited dealt with research on a group basis, with its managing director answering to the parent board.

Wilkinson Sword (International) Limited provided a service to the parent board and the several divisions on financial, legal, planning, and property matters.

The parent board met monthly and controlled over-all policy, but the day-to-day business of the group was managed by the international board, which acted as a management committee. The international board was comprised of H. B. Randolph, chairman; Peter Randolph, deputy chairman; Roy Randolph, managing director; Denys Randolph, assistant managing director; R. Griffiths, assistant managing director; and Bernard Hansom, managing director of the international and research divisions. The international board met every two weeks and made the operating decisions, which the parent board usually approved at its monthly meetings (see Exhibit 7).

The Randolph family held about 65% of the non-public capital stock, and a further 35% was held by the Latham family. Mr. H. B. Randolph, the chairman, was past 70. He officiated at board meetings, acted as titular head of the company, and represented it in public affairs.

Since the majority of the company's turnover (sales) was now from overseas operations, one or the other of the top executives was abroad at almost any time. Therefore it was arranged that the deputy chairman and the managing director share the executive responsibility for operating activities. Except for occasional misunderstandings, the arrangement seemed to work well. Peter, the oldest Randolph son, was clearly conceded to be the top authority. He was the principal planner, coordinated the groups, made the most critical decisions, and delegated to the division heads. It was observed that he was acting more and more in the role of chairman of the group. Roy Randolph, the second son, was considered the company's marketing man. In Peter's absence he acted as chief executive. Denys Randolph, the youngest of the brothers, was seen as the "project" man, because he had exhibited a talent for launching special programs and seeing trying problems to successful conclusions.

For marketing purposes the world was divided into four areas: (1) Europe, including the United Kingdom; (2) the Americas, North and South; (3) the Far East, Australia, and New Zealand; and (4) the Middle East and Africa. The pattern of operations in each of these areas varied according to the nature of the activities involved (see Exhibit 7).

In the course of the reorganization each of the major activities of the group had been incorporated as a separate corporation. Some of these incorporations were said to be for the purpose of providing director status to a man who had formerly exercised extensive authority but was in title only a department manager. Each of the subsidiary companies had its own board. Many of the boards were interlocking, with some individual directors sitting on many boards. All the subsidiary companies were wholly owned except Graviner and Wilkinson Sword G.m.b.H. in which Wilkinson held a 66⅔% interest.

"The reorganization of our company," commented a Wilkinson official, "seemed to follow more along personality lines than along the lines of organizational objectives. We seem to have accommodated the place and the personalities of people now in the management, rather than to structure the organization according to the needs of the various divisions." A case in point was the Graviner organization. Prior to the merger of Graviner and Wilkinson, Mr. N. G. Bennett had directed the activities of the Graviner organization, which handled the sales of Graviner products. In Wilkinson, Mr. D. R. Gatley had been in charge of Graviner technical matters and manufacturing. In the reorganization each of these men was made joint managing director of Graviner (Colnbrook) Limited, with equal authority. Thereafter Bennett handled all sales and promotional activities. He had spent 15 years in Graviner sales activities, was considered an excellent sales director, and had shown a disinclination to become involved in production matters. Gatley, who had been in charge of Wilkinson fire protection activities for eight years, took charge of all Graviner inside activities, including design, engineering, production, finance, and personnel.

PRODUCT DIVISIONS

Shaving Division. Wilkinson Sword dated its entry into the razor business back to 1890. In 1898 the company introduced its first safety razor. Wilkinson became a factor in the razor blade industry in Great Britain; the company was only moderately successful, however, in this venture. Production of razor blades was suspended in World Wars I and II. In the post-World War II period Wilkinson Sword decided to become a major re-entry in the razor blade market. In pursuing this policy it developed a somewhat revolutionary coated stainless steel blade which was introduced in 1961. The new blade proved to be successful almost instantaneously and catapulted the firm into a position of market leadership rivaling the international giant, Gillette of the United States.

Blade production between 1961 and 1965 increased over 500%. Wilkinson Sword's market share in Great Britain increased from 20% in 1962 to 45% in early 1966. In the United States market the company's position increased from a 2 to 3% share to 15% of stainless blades in the same period. In the early part of 1966 Wilkinson was exporting over 60% of its razor blade production and had established itself as a major factor in the industry on an international basis.

Gillette filed a patent-infringement suit against Wilkinson in West Germany in 1963. The suit stated that Gillette had filed a patent application on a Teflon-coated stainless steel blade three months prior to Wilkinson's patent application for the same process. This action resulted in an agreement by Wilkinson to pay Gillette one fifth of a cent on each 15¢ blade sold in the United States and slightly more on each blade sold in other international markets. Despite this handicap, Wilkinson's sales continued to increase, mainly at the expense of Gillette.

Garden Tools. Wilkinson Sword had actively participated in the garden tool market since 1920. In 1948 the company initiated an attempt to develop a complete line of implements and in 1958 and 1962 redesigned the line to keep pace with the British market. The company made 17 varieties of garden tools and was engaged in the manufacture of lawn mowers as a result of the acquisition of the Flexa Lawn Mower Company in 1964. Approximately 30% of the garden tool sales were exports, mainly to the United States, which accounted for one half of the export sales. The remaining half were distributed in Europe, South Africa, Australia and New Zealand.

The sale of garden tools in the United States was initiated in 1960. The promotion and development of distributors for the garden tool line were tied to the introduction of the company's Teflon-coated stainless steel blade introduced in 1961. The popular and somewhat revolutionary razor blades were offered as an incentive to the garden tool dealers, who soon became engrossed in selling the limited supply of razor blades they could obtain and relegated the garden tool line of Wilkinson Sword to a secondary position. The razor blades were withdrawn from the garden shops in 1963 and 1964 and distributed through the conventional channels of drug-stores and supermarkets. In 1964 the garden tool line was separated from the company's other products in both manufacturing and sales.

In the first few years after World War II heavy emphasis was placed on garden tools. This gradually gave way to a heightened interest in Graviner products, which in turn was eclipsed by the booming razor blade business. The garden tools were not deliberately neglected, but the other activities of the company tended to receive priority. Garden tools had always been profitable but at a rate which was unattractively low. In 1965 it was the lowest in profitability of the company's several product lines, accounting for approximately 8% of the total sales. Management expected an increase in sales in future years of about 30% per year. The company's sales in garden tools had shown an increase of approximately 7% per year in the period from 1960 to 1965.

Graviner Division. In 1964 the Graviner Division was made a separate operation with Wilkinson Sword owning two thirds of the stock and Graviner one third. The Graviner operation was considered by manage-

ment to be autonomous except for capital expenditures, personnel matters, and plant location. By company policy Graviner's products were
limited to safety and control equipment, mainly in the area of fire protection and control. The Graviner equipment had gained a world-wide
reputation in the field of highly sophisticated fire protection equipment
used in aircraft, ships, boats, industrial plants, and stationary engine
rooms. Military use accounted for 40% of the division's sales; the remainder was for civilian use. Graviner produced about 19% of the total
sales of Wilkinson Sword and accounted for a substantial portion of
the company's total profit. Prior to the introduction of the new razor
blade and its corresponding increase in sales, Graviner accounted for
approximately 60% of the total company sales.

The manufacturing of Graviner products was mainly on a job-shop
basis. About 400 products were in production at any given time and
only a few orders were for 1,000 pieces or more. The company's reputation and product line were based on engineering skill and the development of highly technical products. The management of the Graviner
Division felt there was great potential for their products throughout
the world and mainly in the highly developed countries of Europe and
the United States.

Sword Division. "In understanding our company position," an executive of Wilkinson Sword remarked, "you must be aware of the important
role the sword has played throughout our development. I think it is
fair to say that the sword image and craftmanship have been key factors
in our marketing policy through the years and explain a good deal about
our company's approach."

In an article describing Wilkinson's activities, a popular news magazine reported:

> Contrasted with its automated razor blade factory and assembly lines,
> Wilkinson's highly skilled swordmakers ply their craft in dingy corners,
> using tongs and hammers as much as five hundred years old to forge,
> grind and polish ribbons of high-tensile steel.
> The company pridefully recalls that its blades were bloodied in the
> Battle of Waterloo; that its heavy curved sabers were used in one of
> history's last cavalry charges, the Sudan Uprising, in which a then young
> officer named Winston Churchill took part. . . .

Commenting on this, Major John Latham, director of the Wilkinson
Sword Division and a member of one of the company's owning families,
explained: "It is the variety of patterns in swords which has prevented
the craft of swordmaking from adopting modern manufacturing tech-

niques. Each and every country has different designs, no two regiments
have exactly identical swords, and most customers require special em-
bossing on the blades of their names and ranks. True, the blade is now
forged from bar steel by pneumatic hammers instead of the smith's
brawny arm, and mechanical stamping and acid etching have largely
done away with hand engraving. But the craft is about the only remaining one in which the basic methods of manufacture have not changed
since the Bronze Age."

Over the thousands of years of sword history there had come to be
an endless variety of swords, and Wilkinson took pride in the claim
that it could make any sword in the world. There were blades with
cutting edges on both sides, single-edged blades, straight blades, curved
blades, and blades purely for thrusting. Hilts varied from simple grip
and cross-guard to complicated basket hilts. The parts might be fine-
plated with gold, silver, nickel, or rhodium, and handles might be set
with jewels. Scabbards were of steel, leather, or wood covered with
leather or velvet. "It was not until 1908," said Major Latham, "that
a British War Office committee, which had sat intermittently since 1884,
produced the 1908 pattern British Cavalry Trooper's Sword, which is
reputed to be the best sword ever designed. It was a great triumph,
but unfortunately it came at a time when the sword, as a weapon of
war, was completely outmoded. It is also a bit of an anomaly," reflected
the major, "that the swords Wilkinson turns out today, thanks to modern
metallurgy and forging techniques, are better fighting weapons than the
swords it made in the days when its swords were actually used as fighting
weapons."

In 1966 the Wilkinson Sword Division had about 50 employees, whose
production amounted to about $\frac{1}{2}$ of 1% of the company's total turnover. Of the 4,000 swords it produced each year, only about 20 were
alike, and its catalogue listed over 1,000 types which had been codified.
Of the 4,000 swords it made in 1965, 25% were "cheap" swords—Ma-
sonic, cadet, lodge, and dancing swords—which were made of quality
materials, but not subjected to the most rigorous tests. These sold for
about $20 to $25. Sixty per cent were regulation swords for armies,
navies and air forces. These sold for $60 to $110. Some 15% were custom-
built. These were literally hand-crafted, and might cost $500 to $10,000,
depending on finishes and jeweling. In this category were the sword of
honor presented to General Eisenhower after V-E Day, the Sword of
Stalingrad presented to Stalin by Winston Churchill, the NATO sword
presented to General Lauris Norstad, and the Traveling Sword of the

Lord Mayor of London. The most costly sword Wilkinson had ever made was one presented by an Indian raja to Edward VII on his coronation. The hilt was embossed with jewels, and the sword was valued at about $30,000.

The heyday of the sword had been in the latter part of the nineteenth century when it served as a fighting weapon, was a regulation part of army and navy dress, and was also a part of a fashionable man's clothing, as the umbrella today is part of the proper attire of a London City man. Although the sword was largely an anachronism in 1966, there was, nevertheless, still a world sword industry, with competing producers in England, Germany, Spain, France, and Japan. The greatest demand was for low-priced cadet, ceremonial, and stage swords, in which Wilkinson found itself unable to compete with the low prices offered by foreign producers, even the high-quality producers in Solingen and Toledo. As a matter of policy Wilkinson declined to lower its quality standards, and so an increasing part of the world sword trade was pre-empted by the Spaniards and the Japanese. The swords which Wilkinson once made for the American cadets at West Point, Annapolis, and Quantico now came mostly from Germany and Japan. Traditionally, the Commonwealth countries had maintained in England buying agents known as crown agents, who had always favored Wilkinson with their sword purchases and continued to order in substantial quantities.

Wilkinson considered itself to be a factor in the world sword business. It regularly received orders from some 60 countries and was looked upon in the industry as the most eminent sword manufacturer in the world. The sword division had no salesmen, did no advertising, took only what business came to it, and in 1966 had a backlog of nine months of orders. "Competitors have an advantage over us," said Major Latham, "in that they can deliver promptly. If our order book ever gets down to a month or two, we will go out and sell swords."

Wilkinson believed that swords would continue to be in demand and that the potential would grow. "As long as there are wars," said Major Latham, "there will be swords . . . even if they are used only for recruiting purposes. Furthermore," he said, "everybody loves a military parade. But modern scientific weaponry and functional combat uniforms are not very thrilling, and all of the glamour would be gone if it were not for swords."

Major Latham said that sword demand had increased almost 50% in recent years, the chief demand coming from the emerging nations in Africa and Asia. "These nations are newly sovereign," said the Major, "and they place a high premium on ceremony. What can be more cere-monious than flourishing a hand-tooled sword? There is a growing de-mand for them from African and Asian government officials who wear them with their ornate ceremonial dress uniforms. Wilkinson had on hand orders from Sudan, the Hashimite Kingdom of Jordan, Kuwait, Israel, Ghana, Canada, Australia, Singapore, Bahrein, and Venezuela.

There was also evident a budding fashion in the use of specially de-signed swords as a corporate status symbol. American industrial com-panies were beginning to use decorative swords to add a touch of Old World color to their corporate board rooms. Lodges, orders, and fraterni-ties were beginning to use them for the same purpose.

For decades Wilkinson had been refurbishing old swords—hereditary swords which had been handed down from fathers to sons who were entering military service. The restoration activities had grown to be a brisk business. Incidental to it Wilkinson had come to operate an antique weapon-trading business in which it bought and sold historic weapons from all over the world. These activities had come into being sponta-neously and had grown to such volume that they interfered with the production of new swords. Wilkinson also operated a museum of weaponry and a showroom on London's prestigious Pall Mall. These were open to the public without charge.

"In the old days," said Major Latham, "our company relied mainly on swords for its bread and butter. Today, even though swords are less than 1% of our company's business, we still do considerably better than breaking even. The Sword Division has always paid its way, and if it were a completely separate unit and relieved of the Pall Mall show-rooms, we would make a very tidy profit. But swords are the traditional product of our company, and as a prestige item they mean much more to us than their profitability. The public-relations aspect of our swords is fantastic, and we look upon our sword business as having far greater value to us than its monetary value. It has given Wilkinson world-wide publicity. Our competitors in any of our lines have nothing like it."

The Wilkinson razor blade was called the Wilkinson Sword Blade, and behind the words were pictured crossed swords. Garden tool adver-tising featured such themes as "Swordsmanship in Shears," and tools were given such names as the Saber Pruner or the Super-Sword Pruner. Some Graviner advertising also carried the theme. One Graviner bro-chure announced: "The Swordsman Fire Extinguisher—Extinguishant: Bromochlorodifluoromethane."

Research Division and Product Policies. "In recent years," said Mr. H. B. Randolph, chairman of Wilkinson, "we have built new factories in England, Canada, America, Germany, and Australia. Our name has been prominent in exhibitions of British industrial design in Malta, Moscow, Tokyo, Sweden, Spain, Belgium, and Holland. We sell our products in more than 50 territories throughout the world. These are vital activities now, but the real future of our company lies in new products and developments. The key to our prosperity 20 years from now is labeled "Research."

Mr. Randolph said that this meant an investment in men as well as in facilities. Wilkinson believed that no less than 10% of its work force should be engaged in some form of research, and it now had over 300 people engaged in research activities. The company provided university scholarships for postgraduate research students, retained senior faculty members of leading universities as consultants, and also used professional consultants.

"As a matter of policy," said Mr. B. S. Hansom, director of research, "we always choose high-priced professional consultants. We try to ensure that we are buying good advice by paying high fees to consultants who have established reputations."

Mr. Hansom pointed out that until a few years ago most of the company's research had been in Graviner activities. Graviner had been steeped in short-term projects, and no one was doing genuine research. For research in depth Graviner had depended upon the government-sponsored Farnborough Aircraft Research.

Mr. Hansom saw the distinction between research and engineering as being threefold. First, the time scale was different, research being directed to the activities of future years rather than to the urgent problems of manufacture today. Second, the emphasis on equipment was different, enabling research to investigate much more radical changes than would be feasible in the engineering departments. Third, some projects involved such depth of scientific investigation that specialist teams had to be recruited and provided with elaborate apparatus. By integrating a number of such teams Wilkinson believed that a proper continuity of interest and utilization of equipment could be maintained, which was especially important in a company with a diversity of products.

In 1959 research was separated from engineering and development and formed into a new division. Five years later, having grown to ten times its original size, it was incorporated as Wilkinson Sword (Research) Limited to give it equal status with other companies in the group and to prevent operating managers from imposing their daily problems upon the research people. The research group was provided with its own new building at Colnbrook, equipped with offices, laboratories, work shops, and a technical library. Project teams were supported by service groups on matters such as information searching, library, patents, analytical laboratories, and statistical surveys. Their findings were available to any section of the company.

"It is surprising," said Mr. Hansom, "how often the knowledge gained in one field can later be applied to quite a different area." Mr. Hansom cited as a dramatic example the Teflon stainless steel razor blade coating. Wilkinson's original stainless blade developed at Solingen was not a remarkable success and posed production problems. The indicated solution seemed to be some kind of coating which would make the blade more honable and stroppable and protect the cutting edge from corrosion. This project was deliberately taken away from the Solingen firm, which had vast experience in cutting edges, and was assigned to the Graviner research group, which knew nothing about razor edges. "This was on the basis," said Mr. Hansom, "of the old joke that runs, 'He didn't know it couldn't be done, so he went ahead and did it.' But we were not joking. The Solingen people would often have looked back to research data of 10 years ago to find that the process they were about to test had already been tested and had been found worthless. But science has moved ahead very rapidly, and during those 10 years changes in technologies might have made that worthless process entirely adequate. Our Graviner people had had experience with Teflon, which they used to coat some of their high-performance components, and they knew it to be an extremely tough coating. They may not have known that it does not do well under the 400° temperature at which carbon steel blades are tempered—which the Solingen people would have known—but stainless blades do not require such tempering. At any rate, the Graviner people successfully developed our present coated stainless steel blade.

"We need to do more scientific investigation in depth," Mr. Hansom said. "We suddenly find ourselves with a large business, and we are compelled to defend it. To find out what a razor actually does, we think we should investigate the whole process of shaving. What is hair? Why is young hair different from old hair, thin, thick, live, dead hair? How is hair cut? What happens when any kind of blade cuts any kind of material? Does the edge go between the molecules? Does the edge go through individual molecules? The tip of a razor blade edge is one millionth of an inch wide. Viewing it requires an electronic microscope, which is laboratory equipment. Engineers can't handle that small a dimension, can only work to thousandths. Wilkinson now has blades that cut very well. If they did not do so tomorrow, would we know why?

"Seven years ago we had no shortage of research problems. We listed them, weighted them roughly for priorities. Now we have a research planning team which formulates research policies and makes recommendations to the board. We now have three research groups—Graviner, shaving and hand tools—and we are thinking of forming a fourth group for developing new product lines which would not necessarily be related in any way to our present ones.

"We may be in danger of overdoing on innovation and neglecting sales aspects. Our Graviner people are aircraft-oriented, accustomed to selling to governments, but not too skillful in selling in the civilian markets. Take Graviner's hand-held fire extinguishers, which are high-quality and expensive. Most people don't have fires, but laws and insurance regulations require some people to keep on hand fire extinguishers. Therefore, if you don't have a fire problem, but you do have a fire insurance problem, then don't buy our expensive extinguishers. This means that Graviner's market is only those people who do have fires. Graviner ought to find that there is a great deal more potential in fire extinguishers."

As to patent protection, the Wilkinson management expressed an attitude of cynicism. "The question of patenting," said Mr. Hansom, "often catches us in a dilemma. Only truly new ideas can be patented. Obvious ideas—like Columbus balancing an egg on its tip by denting the shell—cannot be patented. If an idea is thought by its inventor to be obvious and is not patented, the inventor has no protection at all. But if the obvious idea is patented, it can be contested for infringement."

Wilkinson was deeply involved in patenting in its Graviner operation, which, as a normal routine, carried on extensive research and development programs involving the ultimate in intricate engineering. "Patents play a significant role in our Graviner business," said D. R. Gatley joint managing director. "Graviner holds many good master patents which cover very wide areas, some of which are almost principles. But we do not depend upon patent protection. Competitors are quick to make Chinese copies of our innovations, and patents only serve to delay them. But they do delay them. And by that time we mean to be ahead of them again with something new."

exhibit 1 **WILKINSON SWORD LIMITED AND ITS SUBSIDIARY COMPANIES**
Consolidated balance sheet, 31st December, 1965

	1965, £	1964, £
Issued share capital of Wilkinson Sword Limited	2,000,000	2,000,000
Capital reserve (Note 1)	703,093	723,796
Revenue reserves and retained profit (Note 2)	2,932,144	2,218,706
Total interest of Wilkinson Sword Limited shareholders	5,635,207	4,942,502
Future taxation:		
Income tax 1965–1966		938,715
Taxation equalization reserve (Note 3)	288,000	247,000
	288,000	1,185,715
Interest of outside shareholders in subsidiary companies	274,214	257,109
Current liabilities:		
Creditors and accrued expenses	1,154,390	1,624,609
United Kingdom and Overseas taxation,		
including corporation tax £902,770 (Note 4)	2,165,911	1,317,205
Proposed dividend of Wilkinson Sword Limited	500,000	293,750
	3,820,301	3,235,564
	£10,017,722	£9,620,890

	1965, £	1964, £
Fixed assets (Note 5):		
Land and buildings	1,207,745	879,137
Machinery and equipment	1,658,369	1,324,115
Motor vehicles	128,516	75,954
Capital work in progress	308,941	503,344
	3,303,571	2,782,550
Current assets:		
Stocks and work in progress (Note 7)	2,487,314	1,857,143
Debtors and prepayments	2,282,370	2,617,313
Quoted investments		62,207
Bank deposits	1,150,000	1,500,000
Cash and bank balances	794,467	801,677
	6,714,151	6,838,340

On behalf of the Board

H. B. RANDOLPH ⎱ *Directors*
P. RANDOLPH   ⎰

	1965	1964
	£10,017,722	£9,620,890

exhibit **2**   **WILKINSON SWORD LIMITED**
Balance sheet, 31st December, 1965

	1965, £		*1964, £*
		Issued and	
	Authorized	*fully paid*	
Share capital:			
Ordinary shares of 4/- each, fully paid	500,000	500,000	*500,000*
Non-voting 'A' ordinary shares of 4/- each,			
fully paid	2,000,000	1,500,000	*1,500,000*
	£2,500,000	2,000,000	*2,000,000*
Capital reserve (Note 1)		827,573	*827,573*
Revenue reserves and retained profit (Note 2)		2,156,749	*1,528,785*
Total capital and reserves		4,984,322	*4,356,358*
Future taxation:			
Income tax 1965–1966			*937,615*
Taxation equalization reserve (Note 3)		288,000	*247,000*
		288,000	*1,184,615*
Current liabilities:			
Creditors and accrued expenses		732,433	*1,076,742*
Provision for unrealised profits on stocks of			
subsidiary companies		277,460	*277,460*
United Kingdom taxation, including corporation tax			
£670,000 (Note 4)		1,672,160	*780,047*
Proposed dividend		500,000	*293,750*
		3,182,053	*2,427,999*
		£8,454,375	*£7,968,972*
Fixed assets (Note 5):			
Land and buildings		1,033,907	*829,262*
Machinery and equipment		1,188,752	*917,971*
Motor vehicles		75,060	*47,625*
Capital work in progress		304,640	*412,836*
		2,602,359	*2,207,694*
Shares in, and amounts owing, by subsidiary companies			
(Note 6)		2,187,157	*1,548,057*
Current assets:			
Stocks and work in progress (Note 7)		1,340,329	*935,983*
Debtors and prepayments		908,075	*1,251,156*
Bank deposits		1,150,000	*1,500,000*
Cash and bank balances		266,455	*526,082*
		3,664,859	*4,213,221*

On behalf of the Board

    H. B. RANDOLPH ⎱ *Directors*
    P. RANDOLPH   ⎰

	£8,454,375	*£7,968,972*

exhibit 3   **NOTES ON THE ACCOUNTS**

1. CAPITAL RESERVE

	£
Balance at 31st December including share premium £484,681	827,573
Deduct: Goodwill arising on consolidation	124,480
	£703,093

2. REVENUE RESERVES AND RETAINED PROFIT
Wilkinson Sword Limited

	General Reserve £	Fixed Asset Replacement Reserve £	Retained Profit £	Total £
Balance at 31st December 1964	100,000	240,500	1,188,285	1,528,785
Transfers	(100,000)	(240,500)	340,500	
Transfers from subsidiaries			38,327	38,327
Profit for year retained by Wilkinson Sword Limited			589,637	589,637
			£2,156,749	£2,156,749

The Group

	£
Retained profit of Wilkinson Sword Limited	2,156,749
Add: Profits attributable to Wilkinson Sword Limited retained by subsidiary companies	775,365
	£2,932,114

3. TAXATION EQUALIZATION RESERVE

The taxation equalization reserve represents the taxation benefits arising from accelerated depreciation of fixed assets allowed for taxation purposes in the form of capital allowances.

4. CORPORATION TAX

Corporation tax on 1965 United Kingdom profits has been provided at the rate of 40% and is payable on 1st January, 1967.

exhibit 3 (Continued)

5. FIXED ASSETS

	Wilkinson Sword Limited			The Group		
	Cost or Valuation	Accumulated Depreciation		Cost or Valuation	Accumulated Depreciation	
	£	£	£	£	£	£
Land and buildings	1,080,935	47,028	1,033,907	1,265,677	57,932	1,207,745
Machinery and equipment	1,687,902	499,150	1,188,752	2,422,422	764,053	1,658,369
Motor vehicles	105,223	30,163	75,060	183,100	54,584	128,516
Capital work in progress	304,640		304,640	308,941		308,941
	£3,178,700	£576,341	£2,602,359	£4,180,140	£876,569	£3,303,571
Increase in 1965	£600,954	£206,289	£394,665	£842,903	£321,882	£521,021

Depreciation of fixed assets is calculated at rates sufficient to write off the assets during their expected normal lives.

6. SHARES IN AND AMOUNTS OWING BY SUBSIDIARY COMPANIES

	1965, £	1964, £
Shares held in subsidiary companies at cost	434,337	434,238
Amounts owing by subsidiary companies	1,774,903	1,125,665
	2,209,240	1,559,903
Less: Amounts owing to subsidiary companies	22,083	11,846
	£2,187,157	£1,548,057

7. STOCKS AND WORK IN PROGRESS

Stocks and work in progress have been valued at the lower of cost and net realizable value. The cost of work in progress and finished stocks includes an appropriate proportion of manufacturing overhead costs.

8. CAPITAL COMMITMENTS

Contracts for capital expenditure for which no provision has been made in the accounts are estimated to amount to £136,000 (1964 £360,000).

9. FOREIGN CURRENCY

Assets and liabilities of overseas subsidiary companies have been converted into sterling at rates of exchange ruling at the balance sheet date.

exhibit **4**   **WILKINSON SWORD LIMITED AND ITS SUBSIDIARY COMPANIES**
Consolidated profit and loss account for the year ended 31st December, 1965

	1965, £	*1964, £*
Group trading profit for the year, before taxation, and after deducting and adding the items set out below	2,194,516	*3,534,520*

After deducting:		
Directors' remuneration		
Fees	3,500	*2,600*
Other emoluments	106,091	*92,035*
	109,591	*94,635*
Auditors' remuneration	22,559	*16,508*
Depreciation	337,437	*196,646*
	469,587	*307,789*
And after adding:		
Interest received (gross)	78,338	*68,952*

Taxation on the profit of the year:		
United Kingdom taxation		
Corporation tax (Note 4)	902,770	
Profits tax		*352,000*
Income tax	16,895	*842,309*
Taxation equalization reserve	41,000	*167,000*
	960,665	*1,361,309*
Overseas taxation	99,580	*572,096*
	1,060,245	*1,933,405*
Less:		
Overprovision for taxation	292,444	
(including overseas recoveries of £178,684)		
	767,801	*1,933,405*
Group profit after taxation	1,426,715	*1,601,115*
Outside shareholders' interest after taxation in subsidiary companies	105,357	*118,203*
Group profit after taxation attributable to Wilkinson Sword Limited	£1,321,358	*£1,482,912*

	1965, £	1964, £
Group profit after taxation attributable to Wilkinson Sword Limited	1,321,358	1,482,912
Deduct:		
Profit retained by subsidiary companies	114,221	345,929
	1,207,137	1,136,983
Deduct:		
Interim dividend paid: 10%	200,000	200,000
Final dividend proposed: 25%	500,000	500,000
	700,000	700,000
Less:		
Income tax deducted from dividends and retained	82,500	283,750
	617,500	416,250
Retained profit of Wilkinson Sword Limited:		
Remaining from the year 1965	589,637	720,733
Brought forward from previous years	1,188,285	467,552
Transfers from reserves (Note 2)	378,827	
Retained profit of Wilkinson Sword Limited at 31st December, 1965, carried to balance sheet	£2,156,749	£1,188,285

exhibit 5
DEVELOPMENT OF WILKINSON SWORD LIMITED

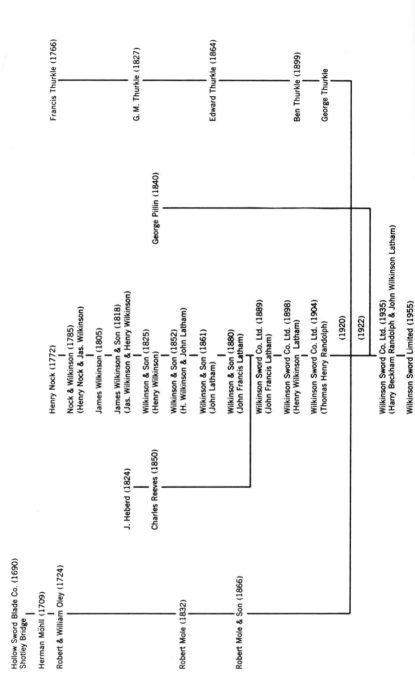

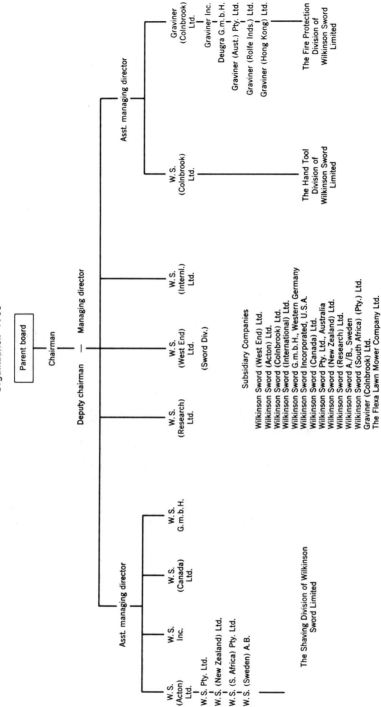

exhibit 6

WILKINSON SWORD LIMITED AND MEMBER COMPANIES

Organization 1965

exhibit 7

WILKINSON SWORD THROUGHOUT THE WORLD

For many years now we have considered the world to be our market and do not think in terms of the Home Market and Exports.

For Management purposes, we are divided into six Operating Divisions: the Shaving Division; the Hand Tool Division; the Graviner Division; the Sword Division; the Research Division; the International Division, which co-ordinates all plans.

For marketing purposes we have divided the world into four areas:

Area 1 Europe, including the United Kingdom.

Area 2 The Americas, North and South.

Area 3 The Far East, Australia and New Zealand.

Area 4 The Middle East and Africa.

Area 1 Europe

Acton (manufacture of swords, razor blades, garden tools, management headquarters).

Colnbrook (manufacture of Graviner fire and hazard protection and detection systems, group research and development).

Brentford (warehouse and distribution; headquarters for U.K. and International marketing).

Slough (plastic moulding, classified projects).

Cramlington (manufacture of razor blades).

Staines (manufacture of industrial fire and explosion detection equipment and marketing).

Solingen (West Germany) (manufacture of razor blades; marketing, distribution and sales promotion of both razor blades and garden tools).

Dusseldorf (part assembly Graviner products and marketing).

Paris (Graviner sales and service).

Area 2 U.S.A. and Canada

Mountainside, New Jersey (part manufacture of razor blades, sales and marketing, including garden tools).

Toronto (part manufacture of razor blades, sales and marketing, including garden tools).

Washington D.C. (Graviner—sales and service).

Area 3 Far East, Australia and New Zealand

Australia (part manufacture of razor blades, sales, exports and Graviner sales and service).

New Zealand (sales and distribution and Graviner sales and service).

Hong Kong (Graviner sales and service).

Area 4 Middle East and Africa

Wilkinson Sword (South Africa) (Pty.) Limited, Marketing Company established in 1964.

Throughout the world, razor blades are now sold in 50 countries and garden tools in 26.

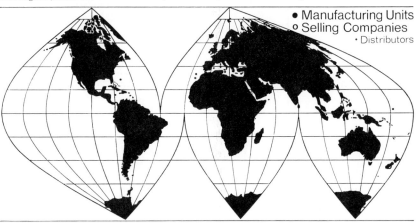

• Manufacturing Units
○ Selling Companies
· Distributors

WILKINSON
SWORD
LIMITED (B)

THE SHAVING DIVISION

Wilkinson's first experience with making cutting implements other than swords came in 1890 when it initiated the manufacture of a straight-edged (cutthroat) razor. The razor gained a reputation for being superior to German razors, which until then were considered the best ones made. In 1898 Wilkinson developed the first safety razor with a hollow-ground, single-edged blade. In 1920 it produced the Empire Safety Stropping Razor, which was so designed that its blade could be stropped automatically while in the razor.

In 1954 Mr. H. B Randolph, Wilkinson's chairman, made the acquaintance of Rud Osberghaus, of Solingen, Germany, which was world-renowned as the center of the high-quality German cutlery industry. Rud Osberghaus made excellent razors, but the firm was chronically short of capital. Mr. Randolph first licensed production from Osberghaus, and eventually Wilkinson bought a majority interest in the business.

At the end of World War II, Wilkinson, which had been fully occupied with war work, decided to return to the razor business, this time as a serious contender. Contrary to later press reports, which indicated that Wilkinson had unwittingly stumbled into the discovery of its dramatically successful stainless steel blade, the venture into stainless steel was the result of deliberate and methodical planning. Wilkinson had decided to re-enter the razor blade business, but not as a marginal producer. Its decision was to withhold its re-entrance until it had developed a strong blade which was clearly exceptional and which would allow the company to achieve a position in the world blade industry.

Stainless steel had long been known to razor blade manufacturers, who had shied away from it because it posed technical and commercial problems. The Wilkinson management was aware of these problems, but it believed that there were possibilities in stainless which the industry had not explored. It started discussions with a company in Solingen which was soon to become Wilkinson's affiliate. After years of development Solingen produced a blade which Wilkinson adopted for production in 1956. Consumer reaction indicated that it was looked upon as a high-quality blade, but it had some features that were questionable. The "first-shave" quality of the blade was not much better than that of high-quality carbon steel blades.

Believing that a friction-free protective coating was the solution, Wilkinson relieved Solingen of further development responsibility and assigned the project to its own U.K. research group, which had extensive experience with highly durable preservative coatings for metals but no experience with razor blades. As a result, after several years of research, Wilkinson, in 1961, introduced its phenomenally keen and long-lasting stainless steel blade, which was clearly an advance over any existing competitive blade.

News of the new blade's remarkable sharpness and durability spread rapidly by word of mouth as one shaver told another of its wonderful qualities. One London barrister commented, in a widely publicized quotation: "It doesn't just shave off your whiskers. It *breathes* them off." As the whispering campaign gained momentum, demand soared far beyond the company's capacity to produce. "We were swamped with orders," said Mr. Peter Randolph, the managing director. "But we were not going to permit ourselves to be stampeded into wild expansion. Increasing production capacity at great speed and maintaining quality do not always go together, and we were determined that in our case they should do so."

The company quickly stopped advertising, but the blades continued to gain publicity from newspapers and periodicals, which carried their remarkable story as news. By the end of 1961 Wilkinson had 6% of the total United Kingdom blade market (previously dominated by Gillette, 75% share), and stores distributing Wilkinson blades were constantly out of stock. Retailers began a self-imposed rationing system, selling the blades singly, or selling them only to favored customers. Many retailers reported that their supply would be exhausted within 15 minutes of its receipt by customers who had been waiting in line to capture a few blades.

Plans were drafted to increase production by 100% in 1962 and 300% in 1963. Production was carried on in portions of the Acton sword and hand tool plant, to which additions were made. The German factory at Solingen was enlarged to meet the demand from the Common Market, and in 1964 a new plant devoted to razor blade production alone was erected at Cramlington in northeast England. In the home market there was a functioning distribution organization and Wilkinson had obtained 20% market share by the end of 1962, and 31% by the end of 1963. In spite of the massive and mounting competition, Wilkinson's United Kingdom market share at the end of 1964 had risen to 36%. During 1964 advertising had been resumed, and in early 1966 Wilkinson had a reported 47% share of the United Kingdom razor blade market. In the United States, during 1964, when major competitors were introducing similar stainless steel blades with extravagant introductory campaigns, Wilkinson switched its blade retailing away from its garden tool dealers to chemists, grocers, newsagents and tobacconists. In early 1966 Wilkinson had 15% of the United States market for stainless blades.[1]

In 1963 the company was already selling abroad to such an extent that Mr. Randolph was saying "The world is our market." Within three years new plants had been built in Germany, the United States, Canada, and Australia. Fifty export markets had been opened and the company was aggressively establishing itself "in every part of the world which shaves the modern way" (there were parts of the world where

[1] There are different ways in which market share can be expressed. For razor blades there are four possible categories in any national market:
    1) All adult males of shaving age;
    2) All wet shaves (double edge and single edge);
    3) All double-edge blade shavers;
    4) All stainless double-edge blade shavers;
In the United Kingdom (4) is 90% of (2). In the United States, (4) is 75% of (3) and 60% of (2).

To add yet another complication, market shares are sometimes expressed in percentages of blade units and here it must be remembered that one stainless unit equals three carbon units in terms of life. Hence, the conflict in claims made by Wilkinson Sword and Gillette where both may correctly claim to be market leaders in a particular area. Wilkinson Sword, being exclusively stainless, is talking of share of users; Gillette, being manufacturers of both stainless and carbon units, can simultaneously claim leadership in share of units.

primitive people shaved with broken glass). In 1966 over 60% of Wilkinson's production was exported.

Early in June, 1964, the press made known to the public that Wilkinson was paying the Gillette Company a royalty of about ⅕ of a cent on every 15¢ blade Wilkinson sold in the United States and slightly more for each blade sold elsewhere in the world. The royalties, explained Mr. Randolph, stemmed from a patent infringement suit which Gillette had brought against Wilkinson in West Germany in 1963. Wilkinson and Gillette had developed the same Teflon razor blade coating concurrently, but the Gillette patent filing had preceded that of Wilkinson by about three months.

At the time of the announcement both firms made statements giving as their reason the wish to avoid protracted litigation. The consent decree came as a surprise, for Gillette attorneys were known to have prepared a vigorous prosecution of their claim. Wilkinson, in turn, had asserted that it had a clear right to the patent and that it intended to carry its defense to the highest court. Observers noted that shortly after the royalty agreement Wilkinson floated a public stock issue. That Wilkinson intended to "go public" had not been known to the Gillette management. When Wilkinson and Gillette first started negotiations for a royalty agreement, Wilkinson had not planned to go public. This was a separate decision taken during the course of the negotiations which lasted about one year. Shortly after the agreement Gillette launched its new Silver Stainless Blade with a tremendous fanfare of advertising. Wilkinson had been long awaiting Gillette's introduction of a competitive product.

While sales continued to increase, profits were declining largely because Wilkinson now needed to advertise. "We made certain forecasts and we geared our output to them," said Mr. Randolph. "But we underestimated the marketing resources of our competitors, our blue friends. Well, it has proved more difficult than we expected. Believe me, though, we don't intend to stand still"

THE RAZOR BLADE MARKET

Until Wilkinson became a major producer, the world razor blade industry had consisted of (1) three large American producers which had international plants and markets; and (2) numerous small producers who manufactured and sold nationally or regionally.

The big three were Gillette, which produced the Blue Blade and the Super Blue Blade (the Randolphs always referred to Gillette as "our blue friends") and later produced the Silver Stainless; the American Safety Razor Company Division of Philip Morris, which made the Gem (carbon) and later the Personna (stainless); and the Schick Safety Razor Company Division of Eversharp, Inc., which made the Pal (carbon) and later the Krona-Plus (stainless). Each of the big three had long experience in the razor blade business.

Wilkinson, like most others in the industry looked upon Gillette as its principal competition. Gillette dominated the world market. Until Wilkinson produced its coated blade, Gillette claimed 70% of the $175 million United States blade market, 75% of the United Kingdom market, and an estimated 50% of the total world market. While Wilkinson sold in 50 world markets, Gillette sold in 100.

Gillette's main plant was a new 10-acre factory in Boston, where all its American razor blade production was concentrated, and it had sizable foreign plants to which it exported its expert technical knowledge. In a typical year Gillette produced 10 million razors and 2½ billion blades in the United States and an additional 4 billion blades abroad.

In 1962, Gillette's peak year, it earned a record profit of $45 million, which represented a margin of 16% on sales volume. In 1960 Gillette had introduced its Super Blue Blade, which was priced 40% higher than its regular Blue Blade. It was estimated that the Super Blue accounted for 25% of Gillette's total sales and returned one third of the company's net profit.[2]

Although Gillette had been paying out 75% of its earnings in dividends, it had accumulated a substantial surplus. Its recent statement showed assets of about $200 million, of which about one third were in cash and marketable securities. Carl Gilbert, Gillette's chairman, spoke of his reserves as "artificial courage." "Companies that have to worry about cash sometimes get pushed," said Mr. Gilbert. "Sometimes they try to do in twelve months what can't be done in twelve months, but could be done in eighteen. With Gillette, if something requires five years, we'll take five years."[3]

RAZOR BLADE PROMOTION

Wilkinson accompanied its introduction of the coated stainless steel blade in 1961 by a modest program of advertising. When the unprece-

[2] Company Annual Reports, 1962–1965.
[3] Walter Guzzardi, Jr., "Gillette Faces the Stainless-Steel Dragon," *Fortune,* July, 1963, p. 160.

dented word-of-mouth campaign quickly created a wave of demand far beyond the company's ability to produce, the company decided to cease all advertising. "We didn't think it was a good idea to advertise something people couldn't readily obtain," said a Wilkinson sales executive. "It leaves a nasty taste."

Wherever possible, advertising contracts were canceled, but there were some instances in which agencies had made commitments to others. Rather than pay out fees and get nothing in return, the Wilkinson management sought to put the time and space to some good use. The management decided to apologize to the public for being unable to furnish them with blades. The result was a fresh wave of demand from people who were now hearing about the blades for the first time.

For three years Wilkinson did virtually no advertising. During the period its share in every market area it entered rose rapidly, the rise generated only by the spoken testimonials of satisfied customers.

In 1964, faced with massive and mounting competition, Wilkinson resumed advertising, now on a national and international scale. "The company's pre-eminence as a craftsman in steel and cutting edges was reflected in our advertising," said Mr. Randolph. "The sword image, which is unique to our company alone, was powerfully exploited. The Wilkinson Sword has become a byword for the best in British craftsmanship and engineering. We believe that quality products supported by quality advertising make an unbeatable combination" (see Exhibit 1).

In 1964 Wilkinson used television for the first time in the United States. Its allocation for the year's advertising approached $3 million. In 1963 Gillette had launched its new Silver Stainless Blade with $4 million worth of television and radio commercials. It was estimated that Gillette had been spending over $30 million per year on world-wide razor blade advertising. In 1965[4] it increased this expenditure significantly (see Exhibit 2).

RAZOR BLADE MANUFACTURE

A razor blade was a highly engineered product, mass produced on automated machinery at the rate of 700 blades a minute, yet precise to tolerances of a millionth of an inch. The ultra-high precision requirements, when combined with high-speed mass production, presented continuing problems in quality control.

A carbon steel blade was made of steel containing 1.2% carbon, a

[4] *Ibid.,* p. 247.

tractable material which was subject to corrosion but which took a good edge. Stainless steel contained 11.5% chrome, was resistant to corrosion, and kept its edge longer. But stainless was tough, hard to grind and hone, and took a poor edge. It required a chemical coating to insure good shaveability. Stainless steel as a raw material cost three times as much as carbon steel. Wilkinson, like all other producers, bought its stainless steel from Uddeholms A/B of Sweden.

In manufacturing there were nine main processes: perforating, hardening, normalizing, polishing, cleaning and drying, etching, grinding and honing, stropping, and coating. There were numerous detailed inspections during production, including the use of microscopes and blue lights. Over 20% of the razor blade work force was engaged in quality control. "If a man happens to get a bad blade," said a production executive, "he remembers it." In its early experiences, Wilkinson had critical manufacturing problems, sometimes scrapping over 20% of production.

Research findings, according to company officers, showed that men's beards differed, as did their standards for a good shave. The age of the shaver made a difference, and hair thickness varied from person to person. The technique of shaving had a decided effect: the heat of the shaving water, the soap used, and the time allowed for the soap to soften the beard were all factors that influenced blade performance. Because of this, Wilkinson was not satisfied that razor blades lent themselves entirely to objective testing. Therefore it subjected its daily production of blades to an actual shaving test. In a test-shaving room at the plant numerous staff members shaved every day, using soaps or creams of their own choice and their own personal techniques of shaving. Their opinions were recorded and the blades checked microscopically after use. Only after these final user-tests was any batch of blades released for sale.

Initially Wilkinson had concentrated its attention on the edge of the blade. In 1966 it was giving attention to the body of the blade and to its packaging.

Wilkinson kept a statistical record of letters of complaint, which, in 1966, were running about four-tenths of a letter per million blades. The management attempted to answer every letter.

FACTORS IN RAZOR BLADE COMPETITION

When Wilkinson made its re-entrance into the razor blade business, it made only its coated stainless steel blade. Gillette had no stainless steel blade in its line but placed heavy emphasis on its highly profitable Super Blue Blade. For three years Wilkinson and others, with their new stainless steel blades, cut deeply into Gillette's market share. Gillette had earned record profits in 1962, but its profits fell 8% in 1963 despite higher sales volume and dropped another 11.5% in 1964. During these years, as one commentator put it, Gillette literally sat back and thought. Factors considered by razor blade manufacturers were: stainless steel cost three times as much as carbon, production costs were higher, but there were no additional expenses. All told, stainless blades did not cost three times as much as carbon blades, while the price of the stainless blade would be about 15¢ versus 6.7¢ for the Super Blue Blade.

How long a stainless steel blade would last was an open question, and both shavers and blade makers indulged in playing the "numbers game" of counting shaves per blade. Wilkinson believed its blades gave ten good shaves, and it advertised at least seven. Analysts reasoned that the industry now had stainless blades which lasted three times as long as the best carbon blades, cost less than three times as much to make, but sold for more than twice the price. But the shaves-per-blade estimates might prove inaccurate, and as technology improved, stainless blades might give three or four times as many shaves as a good carbon blade, which would give stainless blades an overwhelming advantage over competitive carbon blades.

What type of shaver would be drawn to the stainless blades was uncertain. Wilkinson's initial experiences indicated that they attracted the high-price, quality buyers and prudent buyers as well, since they resulted in a lower cost per shave. If this proved true in the long run, it held the prospect of the entire industry becoming largely a one-blade industry, with a cut to one third of its present unit production. Such a cut would have drastic consequences for the big producers of carbon blades and might result in mass dismissals of employees and idle plant capacities.

By the end of 1965, in terms of total blade markets, stainless steel blades had taken over 85% of the United Kingdom market, 40% of the German market, and 25% of the American market.

exhibit 1

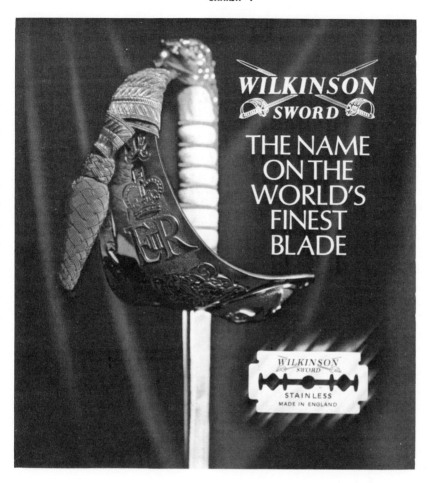

exhibit 2 HOW THE RAZOR-BLADE MANUFACTURERS ALLOCATE THEIR AD DOLLARS (U.S. MARKET)
(Figures are in thousands of dollars and are gross time or space billings)

| | Network TV | | Spot TV | | Magazines (general and farm) | | Newspapers (incl. supplements) | | Radio | |
| | | | | | | | | | Spot | Network |
	1963	1964	1963	1964	1963	1964	1963	1964	1964	1964
Gillette										
Razors and blades	$1,971.2	$ 45.6	$1,000.5	$ 888.1	$......	$......	$ 434.4	$......	$ 137.0	$ 220.0
Razor blades	11.4	......								
Razors, blades and Right Guard	474.2	......					98.9			
Razors, blades and Foamy	2,237.9	1,174.9			......	......				
Razor blades and Sun Up	89.2	181.7			......	......	......	487.2		
Razor blades and Right Guard	1,097.2	......								
Stainless-steel blades and Foamy	424.7	2,896.3								
Stainless-steel blades	873.6	2,136.7								
Men's gift sets	320.4	331.7								
Lady Gillette razors and blades	451.3	......	......	......	18.0	156.9				
Shaving kits	......	942.4								
Total	7,951.1	7,709.3	1,000.5	888.1	18.0	156.9	533.3	487.2	137.0	220.0

Schick										
Razor blades	615.0				553.3	37.0			392.0	1,370.0
Razors and blades		63.4	2,685.6	1,530.7	36.0	11.5	1,379.2			
Razors, blades and shave cream								873.0		
Stainless-steel blades and Hot Lather		147.0								
Stainless-steel blades		493.4						22.5		
Stainless-steel blades and shave cream		441.9								
Injector razor		96.8								
Lady Eversharp					88.9					
Total	615.0	1,242.5	2,685.6	1,530.7	678.2	48.5	1,379.2	895.5	392.0	1,370.0
Pal										
Stainless-steel blades	0.4	25.9								
Stainless-steel razors and blades	35.3	260.8		28.4						
Razors and blades	555.6	84.7			238.8	28.7				
Injector razor and blades	173.2		113.4							
Total	764.5	371.4	113.4	28.4	238.8	28.7				
Personna	1,396.8	3,178.0	531.4	39.6	1.8	162.6				
Wilkinson		74.6		682.7						

SOURCES: Publishers Information Bureau; Bureau of Advertising, ANPA; TvB-Rorabaugh; Leading National Advertisers/Broadcast Advertisers Reports, Radio Advertising Bureau.

Table reproduced from *Printers' Ink*, June 11, 1965, p. 50.

WILKINSON SWORD LIMITED (C)

<hr />

GARDEN TOOLS

"We believe," said Mr. Denys Randolph, managing director of the hand tool division, "that the best way to get into any line is to make the best quality products in the world. There weren't any quality garden tools in England until we introduced our line. Now customers are demanding quality tools. In pruners, shears, and cultivators we have creamed 80 to 90% of the top price market in England. Furthermore, we now have about 25% of the total garden tool market."

Wilkinson had first introduced a line of pruning shears in 1920 to combat the post-World War I depression. Moderately successful, the garden tool activities were virtually discontinued during World War II, only to be revived again in 1948 when Wilkinson concentrated seriously on making a fairly complete line. "The Wilkinson management keeps in mind," said Mr. Denys Randolph, "that garden tools tided the company over after each world war."

In 1958 and again in 1962 the company undertook a complete design alteration of its hand tool line. The redesign was based upon findings from research the company had done covering garden tool users and dealers in the United Kingdom. Price groups were studied, as were their social characteristics, sizes of gardens, the plants grown in them, the tools used, the types of retail shops, their size, the tools they handled, and the variations by areas. As a result the company proceeded to make seventeen varieties of tools, including seven pruners, four cultivators, five shears, and a lawn-edging knife. On every tool specific attention was given to the geometry of cutting edges, styling, strength, lightness, and durability. Floating bearings were made for shearing tools, and a myriad of patterns were tried to perfect a streamline styling in tune with modern taste. The company's first public annual report to stockholders announced that on May 8, 1964, Mr. S. A. Randolph had the privilege of receiving from H.R.H. Prince Philip, the Duke of Edinburgh, a design award for the company's hand shears.

Garden tools were originally manufactured in the Acton plant, where swords and razor blades were also produced, and production was somewhat intermingled. The low volume did not permit mass-production economies. There were numerous hand operations, and many components, such as wooden handles, were bought. Wilkinson considered that its special talents lay in design and in the processing of the cutting edges. Prices were based upon a cost formula and were shaded somewhat to make them competitive. The resulting prices and gross profit were high, but the final net return was low.

Exports of garden tools had increased in the post-World War II period and at the end of 1964 accounted for 30% of garden tool sales. Half of the exports went to the United States, with Europe, South Africa, New Zealand, and Australia making up the remainder. The United States was believed to have a high export potential, followed by Australia. South Africa was believed to have promise because of the high standard of living of a segment of the white population. Europe as a whole was a large market, but there were many competitive producers on the Continent, and Wilkinson had made little headway there.

In 1964 Wilkinson bought the Flexa Lawn Mower Company, Ltd. which manufactured a lawn mower on a new principle, with flexible steel blades and a flexible cutter bar which adjusted to each other. It was a small company which had sold about 1,000 mowers a year. The Wilkinson management bought Flexa with the thought of entering the lawn mower market as a whole, later adding other models. Mr. Randolph pointed out that in the United Kingdom one competitor, Qualcast, had 90% of the mower market; it also had 40% of the German market. "Qualcast might at this time," said Mr. Randolph, "be in just as vulnerable a position as Gillette was. Who knows?"

In 1960 Wilkinson had decided to launch the sale of its garden tools in the United States market, where it believed that there was huge potential for a line of super-high-quality garden implements. Mr. Charles

Coe was engaged as Wilkinson's United States representative, and from an office in Manhattan he set out to invade the New England market.

Wilkinson garden tools were priced to retail at two to three times the price of comparable American tools. Meeting strong price resistance, Mr. Coe resorted to placing his tools with garden shops and hardware stores on a consignment basis, and he tried aggressively to convince his dealers that while Wilkinson tools might provide only 15% of the retailer's sales volume they would provide 30% of his profit. Mr. Coe provided his dealers with attractive placards and display stands. A typical stand displayed Wilkinson's self-developed Swoe (sword-hoe), which was described as the first significant improvement on the common garden hoe in 2,000 years. The stand displayed the three-edged Swoe, an implement which had the appearance of a long-handled golf putter with a twisted shaft. A placard described it as "The wonderful, wonderful Swoe," adding, "To Swoe is a pleasure" (see Exhibit 1).

Mr. Coe was meeting only frustration when, in November, 1961, he received a sample shipment of the new stainless steel razor blades from London. Stories had drifted back to him of their skyrocketing success in England. Mr. Coe made passing reference to the blades in a promotional letter to his garden tool dealers, and he received an immediate and positive reply. He distributed his limited supply, and within days his dealers were begging him for more.

Mr. Coe then hit upon the thought of using the blades to promote the sale of garden tools. Thereafter he supplied the blades to his dealers, rationing his limited supply. Dealers were told that they were to offer the blades as an inducement to each customer to buy a garden tool. Dealers found that their scant supply of blades was quickly exhausted and that their customers returned promptly, not for more garden tools, but for more blades. By the spring of 1962 it was discovered that a black market had developed, with dealers selling them one blade at a time and only to those customers who were willing to pay premium prices.

Mr. Coe then modified his distribution policy. The blades, he announced, would be available only to "authorized dealers." A retailer became an authorized dealer by purchasing from Wilkinson one each of its line of garden tools, which entitled the dealer to also purchase two cartons of razor blades. In return for the order Wilkinson would supply the dealer with a handsome floor display for the garden tools and would mail to 400 of the dealer's customers a free razor blade together with a brochure promoting the tools. Customers tried the new blades and about a third of them immediately wanted more; some dealers reported conversions of over 75%. To get more blades the customers were drawn into the garden shops—the only place where more blades were available. There the customers were to be sold on the garden tools. Since only rarely were drugstores and supermarkets willing to stock expensive imported pruning shears and garden hoes, the policy limited Wilkinson blade distribution to hardware stores, garden shops, and greenhouses. Under pressure because of the limited availability of the blades, Mr. Coe explained: "Actually, we are trying to restrain our dealers from advertising our blades."

The blades moved into distribution, and as word of their qualities spread Mr. Coe's New York office was flooded with orders. Wholesalers of sundries and druggists' supply houses besieged him. Macy's asked for six cartons a week. People traveled in from the suburbs to try to wheedle a few packages from Mr. Coe personally. With supplies grossly inadequate, wild rumors sprang up, all of them unfounded. It was said that Wilkinson's plant in England had been mysteriously burned out; that the company had been bought up by Gillette; that Wilkinson's production machinery had been sabotaged; that desperate competitors had cornered the world supply of stainless steel. "We have three girls here answering phone calls and writing letters explaining that our blades are rationed," said Mr. Coe. One frustrated American wrote an open letter to the *Daily Telegraph* criticizing the British for failing to supply the demand and ending: "Wake up, Britain!" Wilkinson replied that it was awake, but it was having production problems.

In England, where the blade shortage was just as drastic, the company was marketing its blades through chemists and chain stores and it was meeting problems parallel to those in the States. At length, Mr. H. B. Randolph, the chairman, decided to reverse the marketing policy. "The garden-tool side of our activities has now been settled," he announced. "Distributors have been informed that garden tools henceforth will be sold through hardware stores and garden shops, and the blades will be sold through druggists and food stores."

Wilkinson then stepped up its advertising, added more salesmen, and undertook expensive promotions of garden tools (see Exhibits 2 and 3).

While this was occurring, razor blade sales continued to soar, but the blades were constantly in short supply. "Until supply catches up to demand," said Mr. Coe in New York, "if people like our razor blades, we hope that they might try our garden tools. . . ."

In 1964, to revitalize the garden tool activities, Mr. Denys Randolph, who was reputed to be the company's "trouble shooter," was made managing director of the hand tool division. In an early move he separated garden tool activities from other products in manufacture, sales, and distribution. "Wilkinson, as a whole, has smarted under the 'one-product' criticism," said Mr. Randolph. "We mean to correct this image. Recreational spending is growing, but gardening seems to be diminishing because people are tending toward recreation which takes them away from home. Nevertheless, there is today a £50 million English gardening market. We already have the distribution. We should be able to capture more of that market. Our annual growth has been 7%. We mean to aim for a progressive advancement of about 30% per annum." The garden tool line accounted for approximately 8% of the company's turnover and had the lowest profit return in the product line.

exhibit 1

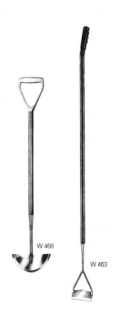

exhibit 1 (continued)

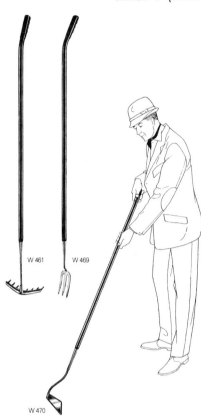

W 461   W 469

W 470

W 470
SWOE 60/-. Combines the principles of the dutch and draw hoe. New stainless steel blade has three cutting edges and is hollow forged to prevent even damp soil sticking and impairing its efficiency. Aerates the soil, creates tilth, hoes fast and safely between plants. Maroon plastic sleeve to aluminium tube handle (58" long). Shock-absorbing, comfort-shaped grip. Design Centre Award Winner.

W 461
Wrake 60/-. Cultivates as it rakes. Rustproof aluminium bronze head, very hard wearing, resists abrasion. Swept back head rakes safely between plants, prevents overspill of soil at sides. Handle (57½" long) as SWOE.

W 463
Standard Hoe 45/-. A conventional hoe of unconventional quality. Sword steel blade chromed for protection against rust, hardened and tempered to withstand heavy and constant use, even in the heaviest soil. Edge retains its sharpness far longer than similar types. Overall length 58¼". Handle as SWOE.

W 469
Long-Handled Fork 45/-. Three-pronged forged carbon steel head, chromed for protection against rust. Light and strong, it gives a long, effortless reach—ideal for wide flower beds. Overall length 56¼". Handle as SWOE.

W 468
New Edging Knife 60/-. Stainless steel blade, slightly pointed to cut effortlessly into hard turf. Permanently sharp, it stands up to the hardest wear, even in stony ground. Maroon plastic sleeve to light, strong aluminium shaft. Aluminium handle, covered in grey nylon. Overall length 39".

exhibit 2

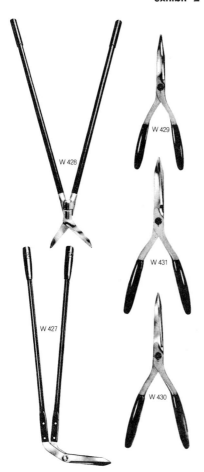

W 431
Notched Shear 70/-. For heavier hedges, such as beech and yew. Unique serrated cutting notch grips thicker branches and slices through cleanly and effortlessly. Floating bearing ensures smooth action, never tightens or slackens. Double cushion stop prevents arms getting tired. $8\frac{1}{2}''$ blades.

W 430
Sword Shear 65/-. For grass and light hedges : perfect for privet. Floating bearing ensures effortless action, never tightens or slackens. Double cushion stop eliminates arm fatigue. Light and beautifully balanced, can be used continuously with great comfort and little effort. $8\frac{1}{2}''$ blades.

W 429
Ladies Shear 60/-. Weighs less than 24 ozs. Though so light it adds great strength to a lady's arm. She will specially appreciate how the floating bearing ensures smooth, effortless action : how the double cushion prevents her arms tiring : how its beautiful balance makes it so comfortable to use. 7″ blades.

All the above shears have won Design Centre Awards.

W 427
Edging Shear 75/-. Tapered, hollow — forged, rust — resisting sword steel blades and long, light, tubular steel handles (with shock-absorbing rubber grips) make light work of trimming edges. Floating bearing maintains correct tension along the entire cutting edges. 8″ blades.

W 428
Lawn Shear 100/-. Designed to cut grass no mower can reach. New, push-button, *detachable handles* in tough aluminium alloy with maroon plastic sleeves. New bolt assembly includes stainless heel plate and unique pivot spring to ensure smooth cutting action. $8\frac{1}{2}''$ blades.

exhibit 3

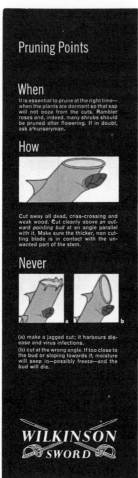

Pruning Points

When

It is essential to prune at the right time—when the plants are dormant so that sap will not ooze from the cuts. Rambler roses and, indeed, many shrubs should be pruned after flowering. If in doubt, ask a nurseryman.

How

Cut away all dead, criss-crossing and weak wood. Cut cleanly above *an outward pointing bud* at an angle parallel with it. Make sure the thicker, non cutting blade is in contact with the unwanted part of the stem.

Never

a

b

(a) make a jagged cut; it harbours disease and virus infections.
(b) cut at the wrong angle. If too close to the bud or sloping towards it, moisture will seep in—possibly freeze—and the bud will die.

WILKINSON SWORD

SWORDSMANSHIP IN PRUNERS

W 43

All Wilkinson Sword Pruners are designed on a tried and proved principle—that of the pruning knife. Thus, the holding blade steadies the stem, while the cutting blade slices through with surgical precision, making a perfectly clean cut without bruising—whether it be the tender sprig of a rose bush or the sturdy branch of a tree. The rust-resisting blades stay sharper far longer. The aluminium alloy handles combine lightness with strength, fit snugly into the hand. The nylon bearings ensure smooth action, less wear, never have to be adjusted or oiled. And the range provides for every pruning need the amateur—or professional—gardener is likely to meet.

WILKINSON
SWORD
LIMITED (D)

GRAVINER DIVISION

Early in the 1930's a retired officer, Captain Salmon, invented an inertia switch which triggered automatically to extinguish crash fires in automobiles. The switch was developed by an engineer named Mathison who later adapted it to aircraft. Mathison's switch proved to be reliable and was in demand, but he lacked sufficient funds and so was embarrassed by sizable orders tendered to him by the British government. Mutual acquaintances introduced him to Mr. H. B. Randolph, and an arrangement was made whereby Mathison's Graviner Company (gravity-inertia) did the selling and Wilkinson did the developing and manufacturing.

Graviner production began in the sword factory at Acton. In 1939, when it became evident that Graviner equipment would become vital in the war effort, a new plant was erected at Colnbrook adjacent to the London International Airport.

Expansion of the Graviner business continued steadily, and Graviner equipment became increasingly complex. In 1958, working in cooperation with the Royal Aeronautical Establishment at Farnborough, Graviner developed an explosion suppression system designed to prevent explosions of the fuel tanks in case of an incendiary strike on bombers. Graviner now supplied protective equipment for most British military aircraft. Its equipment was also fitted to all British civil aircraft, including the Comet, Britannia, Viscount, and Vanguard. The company also developed adaptations of its equipment for other types of fighting vehicles and for railroad equipment and ocean-going ships.

261

Prior to 1964 Graviner and Wilkinson had been separate, privately owned companies, each operating from the site at Colnbrook. The relationship was harmonious, but there were problems of communications between the two companies and occasionally conflict of opinion over product development and investment. In July, 1964, it was decided to eliminate these difficulties by merging the two companies. A new company, Graviner (Colnbrook) Limited was formed, with Wilkinson Sword owning two-thirds of the stock and Graviner one-third. This operation was designated as the Graviner division and was independent in operations except for capital expenditures, personnel policies, legal matters, and building and site locations (see Exhibit 1). It followed very wide policy guidelines laid down by the headquarters management. For example, its products were to be limited to safety and control equipment.

Since the Graviner facilities were geographically separate from the others in the Wilkinson group, most of which were ten miles away at Acton, the Graviner Division tended to be especially autonomous. The Graviner Division made capital equipment, whereas the other Wilkinson divisions made consumer products.

In 1966 Graviner had a world reputation for its special skills and technologies associated with protection of aircraft and missiles, and its equipment was being increasingly adapted to railroad locomotives and cars, armored fighting vehicles, ocean-going freighters, tankers and passenger ships, small boats, hover craft, industrial plants, and stationary engine rooms. It was also producing general-purpose hand-held fire extinguishers. Its product line included (see Exhibits 2, 3 and 4):

Fire protection equipment for military aircraft
Fire protection equipment for commercial aircraft
Explosion suppression equipment for military aircraft
Explosion suppression equipment for industrial purposes
Fire protection for power boats and auxiliary yachts
Gas turbine temperature-monitoring systems
Dual-purpose fire extinguishers
Temperature control switches
Indicating thermistor controllers
Oil mist detectors
Marine diesel scavage-duct fire detectors
Explosion protection systems for industry
Centralized temperature monitoring

In 1965 the approximate split among the total Wilkinson turnover (sales) was shaving 73%, hand tools and swords, 8% and Graviner 19%. The turnover split for 1966 was expected to be the same. Prior to the recent growth of the shaving business, Graviner turnover had represented 60% of the total Wilkinson volume. Graviner produced 19% of the company's total turnover, and it produced a substantial portion of the company's total profit. It had consistently earned more profit than the sword or the hand tool divisions; 40% of its sales were military, 60% were civilian, and 30% of its total sales were exported. The military portion of its business was subjected to costing by governmental bureaus on a labor, materials, and overhead formula which allowed a 5% profit. Civilian sales were priced out according to a formula which resulted in prices that were high but were considered competitive. Of the company's 3,000-plus employees, 850 worked in the Graviner division.

Since there was a growing tendency for the British government and others to buy American airplanes or American air frames in which were installed home-manufactured engines, Graviner had formed a subsidiary company to represent it in Washington, D.C. Since Graviner equipment was being used increasingly in German military equipment, Graviner formed a German company, Deugra Gmbh, to exploit Germany and the Common Market, and it was acquiring a German plant site in expectation of the entrance of England into the Common Market or to be used in the event that England failed to gain entrance. A policy decision was made to manufacture in Australia to circumvent the 30% Australian import duty. Subsidiaries were also formed in New Zealand and Hong Kong, and consideration was being given to establishing a Graviner subsidiary in France. Some of these subsidiaries had been the outgrowth of representatives of the company who for years had been performing after-sale services for Graviner, such as holding spares, undertaking systems overhauls, and doing maintenance and repair work. It was intended that the new companies would continue these services but would henceforth also expand the Graviner markets in their areas.

The Graviner manufacturing processes tended to be job-shop in nature, with some 400 products in production at almost any time, and only a few in batches of 1,000 or more on a single order. There was a great amount of product design and development engineering, which required a high order of engineering skill. Eighty per cent of materials were purchased on a "released" basis, which required strict conformance and certified compliance with mechanical specifications. Graviner equipment included many micro-miniaturized electrical and electronic components, many of which had been in existence for only a few years. Graviner had, for example, been using transistors long before they were popularly used in radios.

Graviner production involved very close controls on manufacturing processes and the ultimate in inspections. The management felt that it had a moral obligation to produce an ultrareliable product, since safety and human lives were at stake, and costs and prices were secondary. Therefore it sought high-grade employees, paid premium wages, and as a matter of policy would permit no wage-incentive scheme of any kind. Wilkinson felt that in an industry in which quality was generally high, its Graviner quality was the highest; that its production efficiency was low compared to that of manufacturers generally, but high compared to that of others in the industry.

The Graviner management felt that there was a great unexploited potential for the future expansion of its business. "Most marine engine-room systems," said Mr. D. R. Gatley, joint managing director of Graviner (Colnbrook) Limited, "are archaic, primitive. During the next three or four years most ships will probably have remote engine-room controls, not only for temperature control, but also for pressure, flow of fuel, level of fuel, and many other parameters. By way of strategy for expanding our business, we are always looking for new products, mostly via the research and development route. The world population of airplanes is not increasing, and it may even diminish, with the trend toward larger airplanes. But there is a vast unexploited market for automated industrial processes and marine engine rooms. We also have a large potential for geographic expansion. The United States market is ripe for geographic expansion, even based upon our now-existing line of Graviner products."

exhibit 1

GRAVINER (COLNBROOK) LIMITED

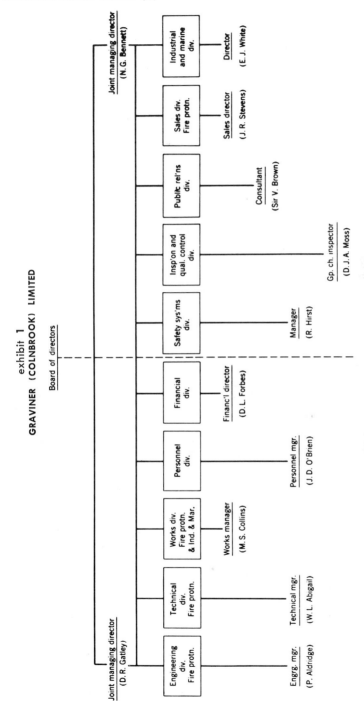

Board of directors

Joint managing director (D. R. Gatley)

Joint managing director (N. G. Bennett)

Engineering div. Fire protn. — Engrg. mgr. (P. Aldridge)

Technical div. Fire protn. — Technical mgr. (W. L. Abigail)

Works div. Fire protn. & Ind. & Mar. — Works manager (M. S. Collins)

Personnel div. — Personnel mgr. (J. D. O'Brien)

Financial div. — Financ'l director (D. L. Forbes)

Safety sys'ms div. — Manager (R. Hirst)

Insp'on and qual. control div. — Gp. ch. inspector (D. J. A. Moss)

Public rel'ns div. — Consultant (Sir V. Brown)

Sales div. Fire protn. — Sales director (J. R. Stevens)

Industrial and marine div. — Director (E. J. White)

exhibit 2

A TYPICAL 1000 GALLON TANK

How does it work?

An EXPLOSION PROTECTION SYSTEM reacts instantly to sense the explosion and render it harmless.

IGNITION COMMENCING
Time: 0 Milliseconds
Pressure: 0·00 p.s.i.

There is a measurable time between the ignition of a combustible mixture and the build-up of pressure to destructive proportions. Although this time may be only a few milliseconds, it allows in fact, plenty of time for the EXPLOSION PROTECTION SYSTEM to operate. These diagrams show pressure time relationships in the suppression of a typical explosion.

DETECTOR OPERATES
Time: 35 Milliseconds
Pressure: 0·20 p.s.i.

A system of such rapidity offered a new safety tool to industry and GRAVINER has developed this for combating DUST AND GASEOUS EXPLOSIONS.

SUPPRESSION COMMENCES
Time: 40 Milliseconds
Pressure: 0·55 p.s.i.

An Explosion Protection System detects an incipient explosion and actuates devices that suppress, vent or initiate other action to prevent the spread and effects of the explosion. The patented system is based on the discovery that an explosion is not an instantaneous occurrence but requires a definite time for the development of destructive pressure.

Time: 45 Milliseconds
Pressure: 0·9 p.s.i.

During this time, it is possible to take whatever protective action the application requires.

Time: 50 Milliseconds
Pressure: 1·30 p.s.i.

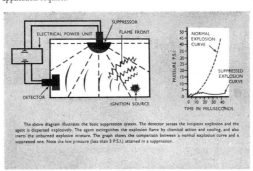

The above diagram illustrates the basic suppression system. The detector senses the incipient explosion and the agent is dispersed explosively. The agent extinguishes the explosion flame by chemical action and cooling, and also inerts the unburned explosive mixture. The graph shows the comparison between a normal explosion curve and a suppressed one. Note the low pressure (less than 3 P.S.I.) attained in a suppression.

Time: 55 Milliseconds
Pressure: 1·65 p.s.i.

SUPPRESSION COMPLETE
Time: 60 Milliseconds
Pressure: 2·00 p.s.i.

exhibit **2** (continued)

Where can an Explosion Protection System be used?

The Factories Act requires steps to be taken that will limit the effects and spread of an explosion should a plant be handling materials which can explode.

It is not possible in a brochure of this size to cover all possible applications, but a study of the typical examples described here will show the flexibility of the system and suggest how it may be adapted to different problems. An experienced engineer can visit you to discuss how these and other techniques can be related to your particular problem.

Whilst these methods were originally developed for the more severe gaseous or fuel/air mixture type of explosion, the majority of applications have so far been in the dust explosion field.

In all the following illustrated applications, the plant is automatically shut down when the explosion occurs.

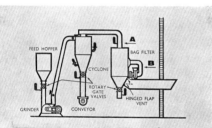

PROTECTION SYSTEM FOR A TYPICAL GRINDING PLANT
Explosion is detected at mill or cyclone. Cyclone suppressed. Filter advance inerted and vented. Inlet and outlet via Rotary Gate Valves inerted. Mill not shown suppressed but can be if necessary.

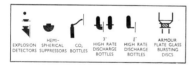

EXPLOSION DETECTORS	HEMI-SPHERICAL SUPPRESSORS	CO₂ BOTTLES	HIGH RATE DISCHARGE BOTTLES	HIGH RATE DISCHARGE BOTTLES	ARMOUR PLATE GLASS BURSTING DISCS

PROTECTION SYSTEM FOR A FLUID ENERGY MILL
Mill itself usually able to withstand the explosion pressure and is allowed to vent itself into filter. Filter is vented. Explosion is detected at micronizer exit and filter inlet. CO_2 injected in micronizer extinguishes following fire, and additional CO_2 Bottles advance inert filter.

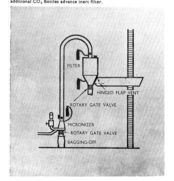

exhibit 4

EXPLOSION PROTECTION

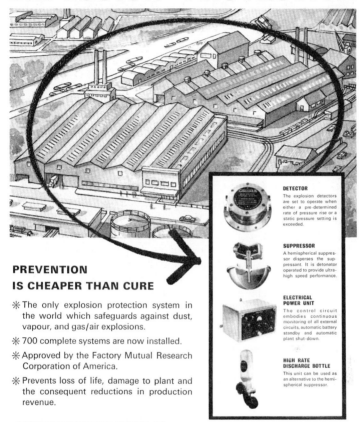

WILKINSON
SWORD
LIMITED (E)

On December 14, 1965, the *Guardian,* Manchester and London, reported:

> Wilkinson Sword's non-voting shares dropped to 17s (shilling = 14¢) 6d (penny = .01¢) at one time yesterday. Earlier this year they stood at 39s. In April, 1964 they had come to the market at 54s. This is, in many respects, a classic case. . . .
>
> Wilkinson Sword, a company first registered in 1889, came in the market after several years of spectacular success. This is nothing unusual. Many private firms succumb to the temptation to cash in when the going is good. Like others, Wilkinson went along to a top City merchant banker and asked for help. The banker—Lazards—made one of its rare mistakes. It marketed the shares at what was widely regarded as much too fanciful a price. The issue, which had initially promised to be one of the most successful ever, was barely subscribed and Wilkinson got off to an unfortunate start.

Mr. Peter Randolph, the company's deputy chairman, told financial reporters that the decision to go public had not been made without a certain amount of regret, but that the board had been forced to decide whether to control the company back to a level rate of progress, which might be as low as 10% yearly, or really go ahead progressively by raising extra capital. Mr. Denys Randolph, assistant managing director of the hand tool division, explained:

> Many people claimed that our issue was a failure, and certainly in retrospect it appears that it should have been handled differently. In

lower sale price may be fixed. . . . All applications below the sale price will be rejected.

2. Preferential consideration will be given, in respect to a total of not more than 10,000 units, to applications from employees of the company . . . at the minimum price of £13 10s per unit. . . .

[The following extracts were taken from a letter from Mr. H. B. Randolph reproduced in the Offer for Sale:]

Working Capital: The company has hitherto found from its own resources substantially the whole of the funds which it has required. The Directors have decided, however, that new capital should now be raised from outside the company to finance the rapid expansion of its business at home and overseas. For this reason the company has agreed to allot to you for cash 500,000 ordinary and 155,775 Non-Voting "A" Ordinary Shares, all of ·4s. each, being part of the shares comprised in your Offer for Sale. The net proceeds of this issue, based on the minimum price at which the units are being offered for sale, will amount to approximately £1,687,000, which with depreciation and retained profits will, in the opinion of the Directors, ensure that the company will have sufficient resources for its present needs. In order to provide sufficient shares to obtain quotation and to establish an adequate market, shareholders of the company have in addition agreed to sell 200,000 ordinary and 894,225 Non-Voting "A" Ordinary Shares which you have agreed to purchase.

Profits Prospects and Dividends: Taking all known factors into account and subject to any unforeseen circumstances, the Directors expect that the combined profits before tax (calculated on the same basis as that used in the Accountants Report) for the year to 31st. December, 1964 will be not less than £3,250,000 as compared with £2,048,076 for 1963; turnover is expected to increase at an even greater rate. On profits of this order the Directors would expect to recommend total dividends for the year on the Ordinary and Non-Voting "A" Ordinary shares of 35%, less income tax, of which 10% would be declared as an interim in about December, 1964, and 25% would be payable as a final dividend in May or June, 1965. The net cost of such dividends (£428,750) would be covered 3.5 times by net profits of £1,503,125, this figure being arrived at by deducting United Kingdom income tax of 7s 9d in the £ and profits tax at 15% from the profits, before tax, of £3,250,000 referred to above. . . . Dividends totaling 35% would show a gross return of nearly 2.6% at the minimum price at which you are proposing the shares for sale. Looking further ahead we expect sales to increase in volume but profit margins on razor blades to be reduced, particularly as the Directors are determined to maintain the lead the company has already achieved which will entail increasing expenditure on advertising and on research and development. . . . In general, therefore, the Directors expect that from 1965 onwards profits should continue to increase although not at the same rate as in the period 1962 to 1964.

Financial commentators were unanimous in the view that the indicated dividend yield of 2.6% had "left little to go for." Opinions were voiced in various financial journals:

> Wilkinson Sword had the unenviable distinction of being one of the few issue flops of 1964. In fairness to the company's financial advisers, they were confronted with formidable problems last April. The public appetite for straightforward issues "with something to go for" threatened to reach South Sea Bubble proportions. The spectacle of offers being subscribed 100, 150 and 175 times over had aroused a storm of criticism.
>
> Wilkinson admitted that it had rejected "well over one thousand attempts to combine with, associate with, or take us over" before it went public last April. . . .

Commenting on the issue in January, 1966, Mr. Randolph said: "The group turnover in 1965 increased by 16.9%, and the profit was 2.2 million against 3.5 million for 1964—still a very large profit for a company our size. To say that things had gone as we had expected would be foolish and false. We underestimated to some extent the competition's marketing resources, which enabled them to exploit the world markets more quickly than we had expected, and their financial resources, which enabled them to pour money into advertising. Despite this, in January to November, 1965, our share of the double-edged users in the United Kingdom has increased from 37 to 43% and our share of the stainless blade market in the USA has increased from 10 to 15%. All other markets have increased, albeit not as fast as we had hoped. Also, there are still large areas of the world which have not been tapped, and it is felt that our forecast for a further 100% increase in turnover could be achieved by opening up in these new markets."

PROSPECTS IN 1966

In 1966 the Labor Government had under consideration a Finance Act which would introduce a corporation tax. The Act was not yet complete, and the rate and terms of the tax were not yet fixed, but the expectation was that full relief for overseas taxation would not be obtained in all cases on overseas profits brought into the United Kingdom.

"It would be premature," said Mr. H. B. Randolph, "before the passing of the Finance Act to prophesy the future, but a company such as ours, which obtains nearly 60% of its turnover and profits from overseas operations, cannot but be concerned about the effect of present thinking on its trading. It has been our policy slowly but surely to place more of our assets in terms of men, money, plants, and buildings over-seas, and almost without fail we have found that, although the road is hard, the journey is worthwhile in terms of ultimate volume of turnover, and in terms of stability of operations, and in terms of local government support, which is so important. We wish to continue this progress and hope that we shall be allowed to do so."

Management weighed the prospects for the future. In 1965 it found itself deeply involved in the razor blade business, which accounted for 73% of sales. Garden tools and swords accounted for 8% of sales, and the company was adding to this line on the basis of attractive prospects. Sword sales were negligible in amount (approximately 1% of sales), but the management was convinced that the sword image was invaluable in advertising and public relations. The Graviner Division accounted for 19% of sales and represented, in the mind of management, a venture into the important and growing area of scientific research and development, coupled with highly developed and complex product lines. It was felt that the divisional shares of turnover would be approximately the same in 1966 as in 1965.

BUCYRUS-ERIE

For the Bucyrus-Erie Company of South Milwaukee, Wisconsin, 1961 was a year of return to profitable operations. Shipments during the year totaled over $75 million, an increase of 18% over the 1960 volume of $63 million, and backlog of orders at the end of the year was $32 million, up 17% from 1960. The year's operations had returned net earnings of $1.12 per share, and further improvements in earnings were expected. Management, nevertheless, in the interests of prudence, decided to forgo any distribution of dividends. They stated that this was for the purpose of strengthening the financial position of the company and providing working capital to finance the increased volume of orders which was expected in the coming years.

The favorable operations of 1961 followed three years of losses which were unprecedented for B-E. Prior to these years, the company had been able to point to an almost unbroken record of profitable operations. During the loss years management drastically contracted its operations, sold plants and facilities, and pared down costs. This retrenchment was a direct reversal of the tactics of the first half of the fifties when management expanded its production capacity to meet the increase which was generally expected in the construction industry, particularly in road building, but which had failed to materialize.

In his letter to the stockholders which accompanied the 1961 Annual Report, Mr. R. G. Allen, who joined the company in 1957 and became chief executive officer in 1958, was cautiously optimistic. "Moderately higher sales of the company's small machines," he said, "should follow the U.S. and Canadian recovery and increased spending on highway and building construction. Large machine business should remain excellent both here and abroad." Then, Mr. Allen added a word of admonition: "It becomes imperatively critical to recognize," he warned, "that future profits and wages can be assured only if our costs and productivity can match those of manufacturers at home and abroad who are becoming increasingly competent, productive, and eager for orders."

EARLY COMPANY HISTORY

The Bucyrus-Erie Company was formed on December 31, 1927, as a consolidation of the Bucyrus Company of South Milwaukee and the Erie Steam Shovel Company of Erie, Pennsylvania, both of which had been founded in the 1880's. The former was the world's largest producer of small power shovels. Although the product lines were somewhat related, there were considerable differences in the two companies. The customer groups, buying habits, channels of distribution, problems of engineering design, manufacturing techniques, and physical location of plants all differed. The consolidated company was organized to fit the centralized pattern of the Bucyrus Company. This meant that there were manufacturing, sales, and engineering departments—each separate and responsible for its function. Within each major department, product divisions were developed. With the exception of one brief experiment in decentralization in a plant at Richmond, Indiana, which the company owned for only a few years in the latter 1950's, the organization structure of the company was always centralized.

Throughout its history B-E had been headed by men who had spent their business careers in the earth-moving industry. Mr. W. W. Coleman, who became head of the combined companies in 1927, had been president of the Bucyrus Company since 1912. Mr. George A. Morrison, the senior vice president, had risen through the ranks from his first job in South Milwaukee as a machinist apprentice. Together they set the company's policies and directed its affairs. When Mr. N. Rulison Knox became president in 1943, Mr. Coleman continued as chairman of the board of directors, and Mr. Morrison became vice chairman of the executive committee. When Mr. William Litle became president in 1952, Mr. Coleman and Mr. Morrison were still active in management. These men, together with a few other senior executives, made the critical decisions.

PLANTS, PRODUCTS, AND COMPANY POSITION

With gross assets of over $77 million and a payroll of four thousand employees, Bucyrus was one of the four largest firms in the construction and mining machinery industry. The company's products enjoyed a reputation for high quality and premium price. About 25% of its production was exported, and export sales had been increasing. About 75% of shipments was original equipment, and the remainder replacement parts. Major products (see Exhibit 5) were classified in the following categories:

Large Excavators (35% of total sales). These were power shovels and draglines, most of which were 2½ to 36 cubic yards capacity, and a few whose capacity was over 100 cubic yards. (See Exhibit 8.) Bucyrus was the leading manufacturer in the large excavator field. Its broad line of power shovels and draglines, which were used for stripping, quarry, and mine excavating, accounted for about 50% of the industry's sales. Bucyrus had only one competitor in the stripping excavator field (Universal Marion), and four competitors who produced quarry and mine excavators. Sales of stripping machinery typically accounted for about 25% of the company's sales, quarry and mining machinery 10% to 15%. The sales of these products were increasing in relation to total company sales. Quarry and mine excavators sold for $200,000 to $500,000 each; walking draglines for $200,000 to $800,000; most stripping excavators sold for about $1 million, with a few very large ones priced over $2 million. In walking draglines Bucyrus had only two competitors and supplied about 30% of the total market demand.

General Purpose Excavators (55% of total sales). These were power shovels, cranes, and draglines of ⅜ to 4 cubic yards capacity. There were over twenty companies in the general excavator field; over forty companies, if cross-competitors manufacturing other types of earthmovers were taken into account. Bucyrus-Erie manufactured the most complete line in the industry, and usually supplied 10% to 15% of the industry demand. Prices ranged from $15,000 to $175,000.

Drills (about 5% of total sales). This category included cable-type water well, oil well, and blast hole drills. Bucyrus-Erie was the world's largest producer of cable-type drills, most of which were water well drills, and supplied over 70% of the market demand. There were less than half a dozen manufacturers of this type of drilling equipment. Bucyrus' production of small size blast hole drills (about 6 inches) was insignificant, but the company was a factor in the production of large size blast hole drills (9 inches and over), supplying well over 50% of the market demand. Prices of most cable-type drills were from $1,000 to $30,000; blast hole drills ranged as high as $175,000.

Special Products (about 5% of total sales). Included in this category was a newly developed tower crane used in the construction of large multi-storied buildings, whose long boom had a reach of over twenty stories in height. Also included were hydro cranes, whose hydraulically powered booms delivered great power with ultimate precision, and flame piercing drills, capable of blast hole drilling into solid rock at tremendous speed.

Plants. In 1962 the company had three plants: South Milwaukee, Wisconsin, where it manufactured strippers, large excavators, walking draglines, quarry and mine shovels, railway cranes and drills; Evansville, Indiana, which produced general purpose excavators, cranes, hydrocranes and drills; and Erie, Pennsylvania, which produced general purpose excavators and cranes.

EARLY PRODUCT LINE POLICIES

Prior to the consolidation, the Bucyrus Company had not actively sought opportunities for product diversification. Although it had added material loaders, gasoline tractors, and trenching machines to its line during World War I, it had not continued their manufacture after the war. For the most part, this policy was carried over to the consolidated Bucyrus-Erie Company. The new company's management and its engineers devoted their efforts to building larger and more efficient power cranes, shovels, and draglines. In those few instances in which the company added other machinery to its line, management purchased the manufacturing rights from smaller companies.

In the depression years of 1931 to 1935, in an effort to sustain its sales volume, B-E acquired three new products which could be manufactured and distributed through the company's existing facilities. These products—walking draglines (a type of large excavator), drills of the cable churn type, and tractor equipment (scrapers, bulldozers) soon developed substantial volume, and by 1939 accounted for 39% of the company's total sales of new equipment, and over 50% of its profits.

THE WAR PERIOD—1941 TO 1946

During the war years Bucyrus-Erie maintained high levels of production but management deliberately chose to undertake only a limited amount of special war work. Over 90% of the company's wartime production was of its regular lines of equipment for highway and construction projects at home and abroad. There were no additions to plant facilities or product lines. Expenditures for maintenance slightly exceeded depreciation allowances, and the company emerged from the war with its equipment in good condition and in strong financial condition. It was equally well prepared for either a boom or a depression.

At the beginning of 1946 management believed that the market potential for its products was excellent, and that it had ample finances to undertake an expansion program. It was reluctant to do so, however, because of its concern over the possible saturation of postwar markets. At the end of the war industry production of excavators was running at three times the normal rate and about 85% of this was in general purpose excavators. B-E management was aware that many of these would be offered for sale secondhand after the war and it feared that this might undermine the sale of new equipment for years to come.

Immediately following the end of the war B-E received a flood of orders. Even though it was generally recognized that this swollen demand was temporary, management felt itself caught upon the horns of a dilemma. Operations were now at capacity level and two years would be required to expand facilities, by which time management felt sure the boom market would decline. At the same time it feared that failure to expand would result in a permanent loss of a substantial share of the market. Those B-E customers who had been obliged to turn to other suppliers for their equipment during the boom would probably continue to look to their new suppliers for service, parts, and additional equipment.

After weighing these factors, the executive committee in August of 1946 approved a modest expansion of the South Milwaukee and Evansville plants. The expansion was to be limited to the estimated supply of available labor and as much work as possible was to be subcontracted, even at above normal cost if necessary. In making this decision the company was aware that the expansion would fall short of allowing it to maintain its "normal" share of demand.

POSTWAR EXPANSION PROGRAMS

Bucyrus-Erie undertook three expansion programs in the ten-year period between 1946 and 1956. By 1956 the company had expected to double its World War II capacity and all of its production facilities were expected to be completely modern and better coordinated than ever before.

The first expansion took place during 1946 and 1947 and involved an expenditure of $3.8 million. This program doubled erecting and plate shop capacity at Evansville and increased erecting and casting capacity at South Milwaukee. Nothing was done at Erie. During these years, however, subcontracting rose from its wartime peak of $3.8 million to $4.8 million in 1946 and $7.2 million in 1947. Shipments in 1946, nevertheless, were only 65% of the wartime peak and in 1947 rose only to 88%. During 1946 and 1947 the company had experienced shortages of steel and electrical equipment and had suffered from strikes, friction in labor relations, and high employee turnover.

The sales department compiled a new ten-year forecast for the period beginning January 1, 1948. This predicted a "normal" annual volume of $48 million, and projected an $8.4 million, four-year program of replacements, improvements, and additions which was to achieve the "normal" volume by 1951 and eliminate the necessity for subcontracting. By 1951 the company's over-all capacity had been increased by 20%. Of the capital expenditures involved, South Milwaukee's heavy shovel plants had received 61%; Evansville's general purpose excavator shops received 34%; and the Erie shops, 5%. Production in 1950 was, however, 20% below that of 1947, backlogs fluctuated from a peak of $75 million in early 1948 to $15 million in late 1949, and substantial subcontracting continued.

During the postwar years significant industry changes took place. Demand for large excavators and blast hole drills declined, while the demand for general purpose excavators, tractor equipment, and other types of drills continued relatively high. Industry capacity expanded and keen competition appeared in some areas. The growing strength of competition was a source of particularly serious concern to the Bucyrus-Erie management. Mr. Coleman, chairman of the board, emphasized to the executive committee in March, 1951, the growing financial strength and productive capacity of the company's competitors, as well as the "continued increase in the demand for the company's products." He then called for a new study of the market and concluded: "No time should be lost in making this study, as it is most essential that the position of our company in the industry be maintained." It was as a result of this request that the company undertook its third long-range forecast of the postwar period. This third forecast resulted in the May, 1951, decision of management to further expand by purchasing existing plant capacity to increase general purpose excavator production.

In this third expansion B-E spent $3.7 million to buy 97½% of the capital stock of the National Erie Corporation of Erie, Pennsylvania, a commercial steel foundry and machine shop. This increased B-E's foundry capacity by 50%, its machining capacity by 25%, and while the added facilities were not modern and efficient, management considered that high-cost production would still not be as costly as subcontracting. Volume, however, was still only at what the management called "normal" and 50% short of anticipated peak requirements. In planning for future sales the company set as a goal a 50% increase in general purpose excavator capacity over the 1952 production facilities. The planning provided for an expenditure of $2.8 million for improvement of the production facilities at Erie Plant No. 1, and $1.1 million to increase by 50% the casting capacity of the National Erie plant. In the expansion program plans were made to make 70% of the floor space at the Evansville plant available for the production of general purpose excavators.

In the aggregate, these expansion programs increased the company's investment in plants and equipment 400% from $4.7 million in 1945 to $18.5 million in 1954. Shipments rose from $32 million in 1945 to $66 million in 1954. Backlog of unfilled orders which had fluctuated during the ten-year period amounted to $3.8 million at December 31, 1953.

Management recognized that any expansion program would be complicated by the company's multiple-product line. It would be necessary to decide upon the priority and the extent of the expansion of each item since the manufacturing facilities varied substantially both in character and in location. Also, large excavators required casting facilities, machine tools, and erecting equipment of such large size that there were few opportunities for subcontracting. On the other hand, general purpose excavators, drills, and tractor equipment lent themselves more readily to subcontracting, a factor affecting the decision for any expansion of facilities.

During this period the senior B-E officials were brought under heavy pressure by mining officials, with whom they dealt directly, to increase their production of large excavators. Although a strong demand existed for general purpose excavators, management felt less pressure here because of the impersonal nature of marketing these machines through distributor channels. Tractor sales were also at peak demand and B-E felt obliged to fulfill its obligation as the chief tractor equipment supplier for International Harvester dealers. The demand for all types of drills was also heavy, and management felt compelled to maintain its leading position in each field of drilling.

BUCYRUS-ERIE AND THE TRACTOR EQUIPMENT BUSINESS

In the early 1950's a number of major machinery manufacturers expanded their lines to include excavating, earth-moving, and road construction equipment. Leading companies such as Caterpillar Tractor, Allis-Chalmers, Westinghouse, and General Motors added tractor-drawn and tractor-mounted earth-moving equipment to their product lines. Some of these companies also diversified into allied lines, adding such construction equipment as ready-mixers, tampers, road graders, road pavers, pile drivers, and cranes.

These moves, in the opinion of industry observers, indicated that intense interest had been aroused in the enormous road-building program that was to take place during the coming decade. The actions of many firms, particularly the tractor manufacturers, reflected their thinking that a broad line of equipment would help them to expand their market share. Of these, Caterpillar, International Harvester, Allis-Chalmers, Oliver, Euclid (General Motors), and LeTourneau (Westinghouse) accounted for almost all of the tractor business, as well as for most of the desirable distributors.

Bucyrus-Erie had added tractor attachments (bulldozers, scrapers, graders, rollers—see Exhibit 6) to its product line in the depression years of the early thirties when the sale of power shovels was at low ebb and the company needed a product line to keep its shops busy, even on a partial basis. At that time, when the development of modern tractor prime earth-movers was still in the pioneering stage, B-E undertook the design and production of a line of tractor-mounted earth-moving accessories designed to fit the track-type heavy duty tractors made by International Harvester Company (IHC). The result was a joint cooperative undertaking in which both companies exchanged every modification in design and planning, and coordinated their sales and production schedules. IHC made the tractors; B-E made the attachments; both were marketed through IHC's established organization of industrial equipment dealers, who presented B-E equipment as the IHC approved attachments for IHC tractors.

From 1936 through 1946 tractor equipment was the fastest growing segment of the company's products, both in respect to sales and profits. From 1946 to 1952 tractor equipment represented 25% of the company's sales volume of new machinery. Forecasts indicated that this volume was not temporary and in the postwar expansion program top priority was given to tractor equipment facilities.

By 1950 many of the major objectives of the tractor equipment program had been achieved. The most significant part of the program that was not realized concerned the amount of manufacturing capacity which B-E provided for the production of tractor equipment. The company had aimed to maintain an 80% parity with IHC's crawler output, but had been unable to do so because postwar demand exceeded B-E's capacity, and lengthy strikes had reduced output. Furthermore, Bucyrus-Erie management had consistently been reluctant to commit additional manufacturing capacity to tractor equipment because of the uncertainty of IHC's plans. IHC had been unwilling from the beginning to commit itself exclusively to Bucyrus-Erie equipment.

International Harvester, determined to compete for Caterpillar's position as leader of the industry, strongly desired to have an integrated tractor and equipment operation. Caterpillar built and had full control over the design, manufacture, and distribution of its tractors and tractor equipment. IHC, in contrast, controlled only its crawler tractor line and its distributors had to deal with some twenty manufacturers who supplied the allied tractor equipment. This put IHC at a twofold disadvantage: coordination of manufacture and distribution was difficult, and IHC's entire marketing expenses had to be absorbed by its tractor line alone.

Since there was no assurance that IHC would continue the co-operative arrangement, B-E was reluctant to commit more production facilities to tractor equipment without an offsetting agreement by IHC. With this in mind, the B-E management, in its various postwar plant expansions, had designed its additions to the tractor equipment plants to permit easy conversion to the production of the company's other products.

In May, 1952, the senior executives of International Harvester invited the B-E management to a top-level meeting of the executives of both companies. The discussion at this meeting was entirely ami-cable with both parties exhibiting an appreciation of the differing implications to each of their mutual problem and with both agreed that some major change in the existing arrangement was imperative. As a result of this meeting the International Harvester management proposed to the B-E management that IHC would, beginning in November, 1953, design, produce, sell, and service its own line of trac-tor equipment. This proposal was acceptable to the Bucyrus-Erie management, which agreed to retire from the tractor equipment field. The transition was to be programmed over a period of three years. The Bucyrus-Erie management stated that it felt its facilities used in the production of tractor attachments could best be utilized in the production of its traditional product lines—cranes and exca-vators.

PLANNING FOR THE FEDERAL HIGHWAY
PROGRAM AND ITS AFTERMATH

In the mid-50's management felt that the outlook for the company as a whole was very promising. Its 1955 Annual Report stated: "For the longer term, forecasts generally indicate that the next decade may be one of unprecedented growth." In its planning, the Bucyrus-Erie management leaned heavily on expectations that the Federal Aid Highway Act of 1956 would set in motion the biggest construction job in history. The Bucyrus-Erie management believed that, of the estimated total of fifty billion dollars to be spent on roads, a con-siderable part would be spent for the earth-moving and materials handling equipment. Accordingly, the company prepared for greatly increased sales volume in the years immediately ahead. It expected sales volume to approach $150 million annually by 1960. Most of the increase they anticipated would come from small and medium-sized commercial cranes and excavators.

At Evansville, Indiana, an expansion and modernization program costing $2 million was completed in 1957. At the same time, the company built a new $12 million plant at Richmond, Indiana, for the manufacture of drilling machines and drill tools. The Richmond plant, completed early in 1958, released facilities at South Milwaukee and Evansville to be used for the expansion of small excavator production. Expenditures for property, plant, and equipment in 1957 amounted to $13.6 million.

The year 1958 was a year of depression for the mining industry. The market for construction equipment also went into a severe decline. The company's entire line of shovels and cranes, from the smallest to the largest, was affected by the recession. There was a sharp reduction of Bucyrus-Erie shipments in 1958. The year ended a decade of expansion during which the company's property account more than quadrupled. (See Exhibit 7.)

exhibit **7**   SELECTED STATISTICS ON BUCYRUS-ERIE SHIPMENTS (IN MILLIONS)

Year	Pounds Shipped	Property Account	Dollar Volume Shipped
1948	175	$ 9.1	$65
1955	135	20.4	75
1957	132	33.3	87
1958	100	37.6	58

Commenting in later years on this performance Mr. Allen said: "If we interpret boom period growth rates as normal, and project these rates progressively into five-year sales forecasts, disaster is bound to follow. It appears from the record that that is precisely what happened in the past." The decline in tonnage, Mr. Allen thought, could be traced to several causes: the liquidation of the tractor equipment division, which had yielded as much as $17 million in sales; the disposal of the dredge division; the growing popularity of front-end loaders for earth-moving, which cut into small excavator sales; the demand for cranes designed specifically for lifting alone was competing with B-E's dual-purpose equipment; and lastly, the sharp recession of 1958. The great expectations of the road program never materialized, and the entire construction industry suffered.

Mr. Allen's first major official act as president was to shut down the Richmond plant to stop the heavy losses from that operation, to offer the plant for sale, and to move the production of drills back to South Milwaukee and Evansville. Concurrently, a program was undertaken to reduce the heavy investment in fixed and working assets in order to reestablish an acceptable profit to capital invested ratio.

Plant capacity was designed to allow for prescheduling to 85%, leaving 15% available for emergency work. Formalized monthly progress reports were instituted showing direct labor a.1d cost variances from budgets. To stress the profit objective the controller had set up seven profit centers: large excavators, commercial crane excavators, blast hole drills, well drills, hydrocranes, subcontracting, and the Canadian operation. Emphasis was placed on the return on investment employed as the most valuable yardstick. According to Mr. Birk, the new controller, there was an increasing awareness within the company of the relationship of turnover to profits.

"I am fully aware," said Mr. Allen, "that there is a limit to shrinking assets, to consolidations and to the mothballing of existing facilities. This can hardly be called a growth policy. Our former strength, however, has been sapped to the point where retrenchment is essential to preserve our corporate health. We are retreating temporarily from an extended front which we could not hold. By so doing, we gather our strength and then we move forward."

DOMESTIC MARKETS IN 1962

"Today, with at least 85 direct competitors bidding for customers' dollars throughout the world," said Mr. Lewis C. Black, vice president, domestic sales, "our company is facing the most highly competitive conditions in its 82-year history." Mr. Black was convinced that a keen awareness of market desires and needs was imperative and that the ability to produce designs rapidly in order to capitalize on changing market trends was more important now than at any time in the history of the earth-moving equipment industry. Mr. Black felt that it would be highly desirable if the company could find some way of diversifying into other areas to avoid its heavy dependence upon the fluctuations of the construction and mining industries.

Bucyrus-Erie marketed machinery and equipment to four major groups of customers. Arranged in the order of their total purchases they were: (1) construction contractors; (2) pit, quarry, and mine operators; (3) oil and gas field drillers; and (4) water well drillers. The principal customers for Bucyrus-Erie's general-purpose excavators were construction contractors. Their business was usually based on subcontracting and was often specialized. Therefore, despite the fact that there were more than 400,000 building contractors in the country, a relatively small number of them accounted for the major portion of Bucyrus-Erie's shipments to the construction market.

It was estimated that over 50% of the construction industry's top executives were engineers, and in selling to them all cost elements were usually reduced to a common denominator, such as cents per cubic yard. Most of the selling to these contractors was done by distributors with the assistance of manufacturers. Typically, distributors stocked, sold, and rented all classes of construction equipment, maintained spare parts inventories, repaired and rebuilt equipment. Usually a contractor could buy or rent from a local distributor all the equipment necessary for any construction job. Distributors also often financed their customers. Generally a distributor carried anywhere from 20 to 150 noncompeting lines of products to meet the varied needs of his customers. His salesmen knew every equipment user in the territory.

Bucyrus-Erie reached the construction contractors' market through approximately 65 construction machinery distributors, and Mr. Black felt that his set of distributors were the best in the country. He considered them to be a vital link in his sales effort because of their intimate knowledge of local conditions and customers and because they were better equipped to handle the intricate trade-in business.

Nearly half of the company's distributors carried a line of tractors and tractor equipment, usually of one of the four major producers—Caterpillar, International Harvester, Allis-Chalmers or Euclid. Some B-E executives considered this to be a subject of major concern, because tractor equipment gave the distributor a higher gross profit (27%) than Bucyrus-Erie shovels (15%), which certain company executives felt would influence the dealer to give priority to his line of tractors in his sales efforts. Caterpillar and IHC both painted their equipment a brilliant yellow, and often a Bucyrus-Erie salesman, returning from a call on a distributor, would make wry jokes about having found "yellow paint all over the place." Mr. Allen felt that this was a matter of major importance that ought to be corrected as soon as possible. "We cannot," he said, "continue to tolerate being in a secondary position with our distributors. We must insist that ours be their first line." Mr. Black agreed. "Of course you must insist on your fair share of your distributor's time," he said, "but it might often happen that the best distributor for us is one who also handles a major tractor line, and the two might go very well hand-in-hand. Some of our best distributors today also represent major tractor manufacturers. These are usually the distributors who have the financial strength, the good organization, and the shop facilities that are important to Bucyrus-Erie."

LARGE EQUIPMENT

"Heavy" or "engineering" construction—such projects as highways, dams, bridges, and industrial construction—was a principal market for Bucyrus-Erie general-purpose equipment.

Large excavating equipment, such as that used in open-pit mining, was usually custom-built to the customer's specifications, and it might take several years to open and develop the mine, and plan and fabricate the excavator. Final decisions regarding the purchase of large equipment were usually made by the top executives of the mining firm upon the advice of the engineering and operating management. Because almost all of these large machines were custom-built, their sales were supervised directly by the general sales manager and they were sold directly from the company's home office.

Mr. Black felt that customers were better informed today than ever before, and that perhaps because of this they had become, as he put it, "very nickel and dime conscious." For many years B-E had been able to maintain its prices at a level 5% to 15% higher than competition, a premium the company attributed to its long-standing reputation for high quality, performance, and service. "More and more," said Mr. Black, "we are finding that our prices must be set to meet competition. Old customers tend to be loyal, but the new ones need to be convinced that they are getting something additional in return for the higher price." Bucyrus-Erie had a long-standing policy of keeping its prices firm, with only minor adjustments in recessions.

"There isn't a single manufacturer in the excavating machinery and drill industry today," said Mr. Black, "who even comes close to matching Bucyrus-Erie in the range of models available. Our salesmen can meet any customer demand with our line of over forty models." In recent years efforts had been made to fill out and broaden the line, and numerous new models had been introduced.

In the post World War II years, Bucyrus-Erie had been reluctant to concede to the growing demand for cranes for building construction. This stemmed from management's thinking that cranes which were designed for lifting only would not produce as much of the profitable parts business as would dual-purpose machines and excavators, and furthermore, these were years in which most of the company's plants had been operating at full capacity. In the late 1950's, however, management deferred to market demands and introduced a tower crane especially designed for high-rise building projects, and also a line of mobile truck-mounted cranes. (See Exhibit 5.)

Mr. Black saw a mixed future for the company's various product lines. "I expect the large stripping machinery business to be good for the next five years," he said, "in fact, it will probably be a growth market. The demand for medium-size excavators will be somewhat static. Larger cranes and excavators will probably also be static or, at best, show modest growth. The market for smaller cranes and excavators will continue to fall off, while sales of hydrocranes might show some upward trend. The picture for water and oil well drills is muddled and we really don't know what to expect."

The market for the larger machines, according to Mr. Black, was showing promise now because the development of the very large stripping machines (100 cubic yards) had made it possible to further exploit played-out coal mines where thin veins of remaining coal had been buried so deep under overburden that mining it had been uneconomical. The market for medium-size pit and quarry shovels was static because the industry was currently well supplied with shovels that had a life expectancy of over twenty years. The small excavator market continued to dwindle because of the inroads made into it by front-end loaders and tractors.

ADVERTISING AND SALES PROMOTION

"There has been a drastic change in our approach to advertising, sales promotion, and public relations over the past few years," said Mr. Frank T. House, manager of public relations and sales promotion. "The new management is convinced of the importance of these tools."

Mr. House mentioned in particular in-plant training schools for sales-men; weekly mailings to 800 distributor salesmen; monthly field re-ports of on-the-job machine performances; sales training films to train distributor salesmen; and a new approach to advertising, featur-ing a large photo, a captive headline, and small copy.

"We have a new concept in our public relations theme," remarked Mr. House, "where we center around three things: (1) we see ourselves as the spokesman for the industry; (2) we are the oldest and most reputable firm in the field; (3) we are a company on the move (new ideas, new products, up to date, aggressive, and progressive)."

The advertising theme for 1962 was "the longest line on earth" stressing the company's ability to fill every need within their field. In institutional films, the company was featuring its production facilities and technical know-how and skills in designing new and larger exca-vators. "I think these films are adding prestige to our company," said Mr. House. "They show something spectacular, the biggest excavators on the earth. Of course, a small buyer is not in the market for these machines, but it gets him to think about Bucyrus-Erie. If we can make the big machines, we can certainly make the small ones."

FOREIGN MARKETS

Export sales had long been an important segment of Bucyrus-Erie's business. The first steps initiating foreign sales were taken by Mr. Coleman as early as 1913. Mr. Coleman devoted much of his time during his long career as president to the development of a global system of distribution. In 1913, 6% of the company's production was exported. By 1927 the export share of sales had risen to about 25% of the company's total volume, and it had remained at about that percentage ever since.

During the period 1913–1927 machines were shipped to nearly one hundred countries, although a few major purchasing areas such as Chile, India, Japan, Manchuria, Mexico, Russia, and Sweden ac-counted for the bulk of sales. Most of the company's exports were of large machines to be used in major expansion programs affecting a nation's transportation system, its mining facilities, or its agricultural resources (irrigation and reclamation). For this reason the company's sales to particular countries fluctuated widely from year to year as major programs were initiated or completed.

Ruston-Bucyrus Ltd., Bucyrus-Erie's English affiliate, was formed in 1930 to take over the entire business of Ruston & Hornsby Ltd., B-E's principal competitor in the world market. B-E management thought this move was necessary to compete on favorable terms in foreign markets. For example, Ruston & Bucyrus had been able to offer its ½-cubic-yard shovel in France for 35% less than the comparable B-E model, with delivery time of five days compared to five weeks for the American machine. As part of the affiliation agreement Bucyrus-Erie and Ruston-Bucyrus arranged to act as distributors of each other's products in the various world markets. Also, Ruston-Bucyrus was given access to Bucyrus-Erie designs and production methods. Ruston-Bucyrus personnel continued to be British, but the company's policies and procedures were to follow patterns prescribed by Bucyrus-Erie.

In 1962 Bucyrus-Erie had an Export Sales Department of 35 people headed by Mr. Jorge A. Rossi, director of the International Division. Under him were two regional sales managers, one responsible for the Bucyrus-Erie sales in Ruston-Bucyrus territory. Figures compiled by the American Power Shovel Association indicated that in 1961 Bucyrus-Erie accounted for about 20% to 30% of the total United States exports of excavators.

"There is a world-wide trend," said Mr. Rossi, "toward the use of more excavators to develop underdeveloped countries. I would estimate the world market potential to be $50 to $60 million a year in addition to the total business now being done. It is in this area that our company has its greatest potential in years to come." The problem, said Mr. Rossi, was not to develop demand, but to find a means of financing the sales. In most of the foreign projects in which Bucyrus equipment might be used, the foreign government was involved in some way in the project. The prospective buyers in most underdeveloped countries were short of dollars, and so were their governments. This presented B-E with two different problems in financing: one to the contractor; the other to the country. Often there was no solution. "If financing were available," said Mr. Rossi, "we could double our export sales volume."

The source of a large part of Bucyrus-Erie's business abroad was the foreign aid program of the United States. Sales were also made possible by the World Bank. In former years Bucyrus-Erie had been able to make use of the Export-Import Bank in Washington which had furnished financing and assumed all of the credit risk. Bucyrus-Erie had also made use of the Export-Import Bank in Washington in financing project sales to foreign governments or sales sponsored by foreign governments. Under such arrangements the Export-Import Bank assumed all of the credit risks. With the decline of project sales and the increase in commercial sales in foreign markets, Bucyrus-Erie found it increasingly difficult to arrange for financing. In addition to the problem of financing, B-E management felt import restrictions presented formidable barriers.

B-E's major competition in the world market came from other American manufacturers. With overcapacity in the American market, the domestic competitors of B-E made every effort to find prospective customers abroad. The Germans also presented some competition, but their capacity was so limited that they were hardly able to supply their own demand and that of Western Europe. Their lower labor rates, however, gave them a strong competitive advantage, and they had an advantageous position within the Common Market. If England joined the Common Market, Bucyrus-Erie felt that through Ruston it would be able to compete in the Common Market area on equal terms.

Bucyrus-Erie, as well as Ruston-Bucyrus, worked through local distributors in all foreign markets. These intermediaries were deemed most important as sales outlets because of their knowledge of the languages, local customers, and governments. They supported Bucyrus-Erie in getting import licenses, helped with financing, and took care of the necessary service. Many of these distributors also represented a major American tractor account which sometimes caused a problem. With a 27% discount on tractors compared to 15% on Bucyrus-Erie products, the distributors tended to put their money and effort behind the higher discount lines. "This is a problem we have to live with," said Mr. Rossi. "We try to overcome it through persuasion, friendship, credit help, and a constant training of their salesmen."

"To sell excavators abroad requires quite a different approach than to sell them in the U.S.," said Mr. Rossi. "The foreigners are less sophisticated in this field. Their lack of knowledge is evident, but as a seller, you have to be careful in not showing them that you feel this way about them. Operating costs which are considered so important in the U.S. mean very little to a foreigner. What he is concerned about is the initial price and the expected lifetime of the equipment." Mr.

Rossi said that Bucyrus-Erie faced a problem in getting qualified salesmen to their export organization. The turnover was high. High salaries could not offset this. A high caliber Bucyrus-Erie man was a family man and he would not like to stay away from home more than 4 to 6 weeks. In addition, after a couple of trips around the world, he had no desire whatsoever to continue traveling.

"The world is becoming more nationalistic," said Mr. Rossi. "In drills, we do very little business abroad today. Selling expenses are too high and local manufacturers have grown up in most countries. Many of them are copying our models. Even in excavators, we have seen in some areas attempts made toward local manufacturing. It is easy to make a cheap shovel, but difficult to make one which will last. Therefore, most of them have failed. But, the nationalistic trend and problem of financing export sales have forced us to seriously consider if we should not open joint production facilities with local people in some of the most promising foreign countries." In such a venture, said Mr. Rossi, Bucyrus-Erie would primarily export its technical know-how and skills and teach the foreigners to make a quality excavator. The higher production costs through smaller volume was expected to be offset by savings in labor costs. The protection given a local industry would give it a good start, and it was felt that it would not take away any of Bucyrus-Erie's present export business because such a venture would primarily capture the market share the company could not get anyway under prevailing conditions.

"One day, we might see Bucyrus-Erie and Ruston-Bucyrus as one big international company with a centralized sales and service organization for the entire world market with production facilities placed at strategic points around the globe," concluded Mr. Rossi.

RESEARCH AND DEVELOPMENT

Bucyrus-Erie had always regarded the continuing improvement of its product lines as being basic to the success of the company. Because of the keen competition in the industry, management felt that no effort should be spared in "the continuing development of excavators that will move more material faster and at lower cost, and drilling equipment that will drill water wells, oil wells, and blast holes even more rapidly and economically."

In 1962, the company had an engineering department of 200 people.

a modern laboratory, and extensive testing grounds. The department was headed by Mr. George Y. Anderson, vice president of engineering, a veteran of many years of service with the company. The engineering department was organized into the following divisions:

1. Commercial cranes and excavators from ⅜ to 5 cubic yards.
2. Large excavators from 5 cubic yards and up
3. Special products (tower cranes; hydrocranes; jet-piercing drills)
4. Drills
5. Dragbuckets and dippers
6. Administration (day-to-day operational procedures, records, assignments, etc.)

Mr. Anderson felt that it was only in rare instances that a man might be found who had both creative design ability and administrative skill, and therefore technical work was separated from routine clerical work. Each chief engineer in the technical product divisions had an administrative assistant assigned to him, and this assistant reported, in a staff relationship, to a man in charge of over-all engineering administration. Dragbuckets and dippers were placed in a separate division because they were stock items of a replacement nature, which were interchangeable on many shovel models. Lumped together in the Special Products Division were those products which were too small in sales volume themselves to support a specialized engineering staff.

Although the engineering department was organized in product divisions to obtain the benefits of specialization, engineers were shifted from one product to another. There were decided differences in the engineering required for the various product lines. The large machines, it was thought, required the most skilled engineers. The engineering of drills was quite different from the engineering of excavators. To design drills required a practical "drill ability" on the part of the designer—an intimate knowledge of how well-drillers operated in the field, and so a typical senior engineer in drills spent half of his time traveling to observe well-drillers in action. There was close daily contact between the sales and engineering departments for all product lines, and product specialists from both the sales and engineering departments often visited distributors and customers.

"We don't put all our brains and effort behind the development of large excavators," said Mr. Anderson, "but there has been a continuous market trend toward larger and larger machines, and especially today, there is a terrific demand for the very large ones." As an example, Mr. Anderson pointed out the development of Model 3850-B for the Peabody Coal Company. This machine would be the world's largest mobile land machine, with a dipper capacity of 115 cubic yards, and priced well above $5 million. This size was required to remove an overburden with a depth of 150 feet before the coal was reached. Through long-term sales contracts of coal, the Peabody Coal Company for the first time had been able to finance such an investment. Financing, and not engineering, had hampered the development of this machine in the past.

"To develop, for example, four new models of large machines over a four-year period," remarked Mr. Anderson, "requires 60,000–70,000 man-hours of engineering. With a fluctuating demand, we can't keep a fulltime staff of such a size that we can take care of the peaks ourselves which might, from time to time, require a 50% increase of capacity. In these situations we have found it very helpful to turn to outside consultants for help. The men brought in temporarily need the guidance of strong internal leadership."

"We are engaged in an active search for new opportunities outside our present product lines comparable to our skills, knowledge, and facilities," he continued, "but, so far, we haven't been able to find anything worthwhile." He felt that the mechanical principles of machines designed for lifting and digging were essentially the same today as always. No new concepts had cropped up. Improvements made over the years had to do more with details than basics. New manufacturing techniques and lighter and stronger materials had made it possible to substantially reduce the weights of the machines. A 1-cubic-yard excavator weighed 75,000 pounds in 1930. Today the same shovel weighs 55,000 pounds. Electrical controls had made the operations of a machine speedier and safer. Auto safeguards were used for acceleration and deceleration. Air controls had shortened cycle times. There were fewer patents in the excavating industry today than ever before. Many details invented by Bucyrus-Erie were now standard. In the small machine area, copying among competitors was very common. "No one in the industry has ever come up with anything really revolutionary," said Mr. Anderson. "The basic concepts of our products have always remained the same, and our research and development have been limited to making refinements. We have never tried to come up with something of a 'Buck Rogers' science-fiction nature— something, say, like a method of disintegrating or vaporizing earth instantly, on the spot."

The most revolutionary earth-moving machine that had ever been introduced into the industry was the recently developed giant wheel excavator. The idea had not been originated by Bucyrus-Erie, but came from Germany where the wheels were used for mining brown coal, an extremely soft, low-grade form of coal. Bucyrus-Erie, which was the only maker of wheel excavators in the United States, had made only a few of them. These had been very large ones, designed to strip overburden from coal deposits. Reaction to these machines within the company was mixed. Some engineers felt that use of these wheels in American mines would be limited because of the large rock deposits encountered. They pointed out that every wheel so far sold had since been transferred by the purchaser to other uses. Others in the company, especially among the sales personnel, were enthusiastic about the prospects of the wheel.

The largest machines were usually designed to be used for specific purposes and under specific operating conditions. These could never be entirely copied for another customer. Although Bucyrus-Erie was willing to accommodate the specific requests of customers for minor design changes, a studied effort was being made to eliminate these small accommodation requests. Toward this end, the company produced the broadest line of machines in the industry, and tried in every way to standardize component parts. The power plants, for example, lent themselves to the design of interchangeable units.

ORGANIZATION

In the early 1950's a program of promoting younger men to positions in middle management was undertaken, but by that time serious gaps had appeared in the middle and top management ranks. It was for this reason that Mr. Allen was brought into the company to become chief executive; both Mr. Litle and the company's bankers were of the opinion that there was no one within the company who had the broad gauge executive talents required to head the company. Mr. Allen recognized this deficiency in management personnel. When he came to the company and sought someone who could be groomed to succeed him on his retirement, he found no one whom he thought young enough and with enough perspective. He brought Mr. Berg into the company as executive vice president. Because it was felt that staff specialists were also lacking at the top level, Mr. Chantry was hired as treasurer and Mr. Birk was invited to join the company as controller.

In 1962 Mr. Allen and Mr. Berg shared the top management responsibilities. Mr. Allen was clearly the head of the company, decided major policy matters, strove to give the company a sense of direction, acted as the general administrator of the business, and personally supervised sales, distribution, finance, banking, and the Bucyrus-Ruston affiliate; Mr. Berg, who worked closely with Mr. Allen, gave his attention to manufacturing, engineering, and certain areas of finance and control.

When the Richmond plant came into operation, Mr. Litle, seeking to revamp the company and make it a decentralized operation, set up a management organization at Richmond. This unit was intended to be autonomous, a pilot-run experiment that was intended to be duplicated at other units of the company. With the sale of the Richmond plant, however, and the retrenchments which followed, the plan was abandoned, and the trend was reversed. To cut overhead expenses staff positions were eliminated wherever possible, and so were some management levels, such as the coordinating office of vice president, finance, which had formerly joined the activities of the treasurer, the controller, and the corporate secretary. General managers at each of the company's three plants were also eliminated—all functions at each plant reported to Mr. Berg.

Mr. Allen intended to concentrate on matters of organization. "Now that we have taken care of most of our crises," he said, "I can turn my attention to getting the company into better shape as an organization." Mr. Allen intended to make divisions more autonomous, and to concentrate on bringing up additional younger people. He was especially interested in seeking out people with administrative ability. "In the past," he said, "the management would promote the brilliant design engineer who had seniority. I think this was a mistake and might waste the talents of a good man. I would prefer to reward the brilliant design engineer in his paycheck, and give the administrative job to the man who has shown that he has management talent."

FUTURE PROSPECTS

"For years our company was like a great old ship riding at its moorings and collecting barnacles," said Mr. Allen. "We were falling behind the competitor parade because our predecessors had their feet too firmly planted in tradition." Mr. Allen characterized the present management as one of progressive conservatism. "Present executives are better informed than the old ones who never traveled in the field to see customers and distributors," he remarked. A product planning committee had been formed consisting of Mr. Berg, Mr. Anderson and Mr. Black. They were working on five-year plans for the company. The aim was to make the plans fairly stable but not rigid. Any program changes had to be signed by either Mr. Allen or Mr. Berg. "We are actively looking for mergers to broaden our product lines," continued Mr. Allen. "Two years ago we hired an outside consultant, a specialist in acquisitions, to look around for us. I must admit, however, that we so far haven't taken any steps in this direction. Our cash position and deflated stock have, up to now, prevented any action."

"Our main objective is a profitable growth," he said, "but I would like to stress that in the light of our past experience no brick will be laid or any money spent on expansion unless an analysis can clearly show us that the additional investment will give us a reasonable return at all times—even in down swings of the economy."

He felt the growth would come primarily from four sources: (1) cranes for lifting, (2) foreign markets, (3) subcontracting, and (4) acquisitions. The company had been late in entering the crane business but had made rapid progress over the past three years. He considered tower cranes and climbing cranes as the most promising of the company's new designs. The expansion abroad would be directed toward joint ventures with local manufacturers in foreign countries. No financial commitments were intended. Bucyrus-Erie would export its technical know-how and skill. "Of course this will not put any smoke up our own chimneys but it will add to our profits," said Mr. Allen. "I think we Americans are living in a fools' paradise. In our striving for higher living standards we let our manufacturing costs grow higher and higher . . . continuously diluting our ability to export our goods. In the excavator business we will see a dynamic growth in underdeveloped countries for years to come. Bucyrus-Erie would very much like to compete for this business but I am afraid we will not be able to do so because of our high costs. The Germans and the Japanese are today still producing for their own domestic markets. When they have the capacity to export, Bucyrus-Erie's foreign markets could very well dry up over night." A policy of the old management had been that a government contract should be avoided. This was reversed under Mr. Allen and the company was now engaged in making heavy components for transportation of missiles. It was felt that government contracting would provide excellent opportunities in the future.

A new staff department to engage in market research and economic planning was to be formed, and it was to report directly to Mr. Allen, who emphasized that he intended to take a close personal interest in its activities. "Too often in the past," said Mr. Allen, "it was discovered, when it was too late, that the thing we had stubbed our toe on was a golden nugget. I want to be very sure that from here on we don't kick aside any more of those golden nuggets." Mr. Allen cited as an example the front end loaders which had drastically cut into Bucyrus-Erie's sales of small excavators. It was ironic, he said, that an engineer at Bucyrus-Erie had first developed this equipment principle, and when he took his design to his superior, he was rudely rebuffed. The engineer quit on the spot, took his designs to a competitor, who hired him, accepted his designs, and went into production. "We missed a golden opportunity there," said Mr. Allen, "and now it's too late. We could still go into production of them now, but we wouldn't be able to find any distribution outlets. They are all tied up by our competitors."

Mr. Allen was concerned that Bucyrus-Erie was in a secondary position to the major tractor manufacturers with the distributors. He felt an objective of the company should be to become a prime account to all of its distributors. How this could be done was not solved yet. "We have to broaden our line," said Mr. Allen. "However, I don't think we are in a position to reenter the manufacturing of tractor equipment. Purchased parts would be too great. We would have to acquire an engine manufacturer. Instead it might be possible for us to work out a marketing combination deal with a major tractor manufacturer to approach the distributors with a package."

"In summary, it is my confident belief that we can build back toward the strong and enviable position which Bucyrus-Erie once held and I think 1961 marked the turning point," he concluded.

exhibit 1 **BUCYRUS-ERIE COMPANY**
Balance sheet trends and ratios 1955–1961 (in thousands of dollars)

	1961	1960	1959	1958	1957	1956	1955
Net assets							
Cash & equiv.	$ 4,065	$ 5,216	$5,387	$ 3,177	$ 2,054	$12,735	$10,353
Receivables, etc.	14,399	15,807	11,183	10,925	8,928	10,876	8,045
Inventories	32,055	35,020	36,318	36,117	41,241	36,276	26,256
Total current assets	50,519	56,043	52,888	50,219	52,223	59,887	44,654
Total current liabilities	19,244	20,840	15,843	13,408	17,559	15,121	13,476
Working capital	31,275	35,203	37,045	36,811	34,664	44,766	31,178
Net fixed assets *	25,058	26,512	35,202	37,620	33,349	22,382	20,430
Other tang. assets	1,873	2,211	2,133	2,201	2,199	2,126	2,279
Total net tang. assets	$58,206	$63,926	$74,380	$76,632	$70,212	$69,274	$53,887
(*Gross fixed assets)	42,549	42,755	52,378	51,745	46,211	33,492	30,709
Debt and equity							
Long term debt[1]	10,200	18,000	18,500	19,000	9,500	10,000	10,000
Pfd.Stock							
Common stock †	9,331	9,331	9,331	9,331	9,331	9,331	7,776
Surplus (less intang.)	38,675	36,595	46,549	48,301	51,381	49,943	36,111
Reserves & approp. surpl.	—	—	—	—	—	—	—
Total capitalization	$58,206	$63,926	$74,380	$76,632	$70,212	$69,274	$53,887
(†Outstanding com. shs.)	1,866	1,866	1,866	1,866	1,866	1,866	1,555
Balance sheet ratios							
Current ratio	2.63	2.68	3.34	3.74	2.97	3.95	3.32
Quick ratio	.21	.25	.34	.24	.11	.84	.77
% L.T. debt to capitalization	17.50	28.20	24.90	24.80	13.51	14.43	18.56

NOTE: Fiscal year ends December 31.   [1] Includes insurance Reserves.

exhibit 1 (continued)

Balance sheet trends and ratios 1947–1954 (in thousands of dollars)

1954	1953	1952	1951	1950	1949	1948	1947
$13,642	$12,119	$12,172	$ 8,167	$ 7,858	$12,978	$ 6,226	$ 7,103
4,253	3,808	6,120	8,735	8,260	5,630	8,198	6,016
22,546	27,734	28,549	25,926	19,301	16,341	21,982	17,535
40,441	43,661	46,841	42,828	35,419	34,949	36,406	30,654
10,019	14,151	17,671	20,102	11,720	11,207	12,699	12,752
30,422	29,510	29,170	22,726	23,699	23,742	23,707	17,902
18,548	18,188	16,560	16,457	13,440	12,270	9,114	7,098
2,342	2,181	2,242	2,349	2,084	1,971	1,985	1,744
$51,312	$49,879	$47,972	$41,532	$39,223	$37,983	$34,806	$26,744
28,366	27,279	24,900	24,092	19,506	18,090	14,681	12,723
10,365	10,365	10,365	339	313	310	347	298
—	—	—	4,445	4,445	4,445	4,445	4,445
7,776	7,776	7,776	7,776	7,776	7,776	7,776	6,176
31,921	30,488	28,581	27,722	25,439	24,202	20,616	15,825
1,250	1,250	1,250	1,250	1,250	1,250	1,622	—
$51,312	$49,879	$47,972	$41,532	$39,223	$37,983	$34,806	$26,744
[a]1,555	[a]1,555	[a]1,555	[a]1,555	[a]1,555	[a]1,555	[a]1,555	[a]1,271
4.04	3.09	2.65	2.13	3.02	3.12	2.87	2.40
1.36	.86	.69	.41	.67	1.16	.49	.56
20.20	20.78	21.61	.82	.80	.82	1.00	1.11

[a] Adjusted common shares.

exhibit **2**   **BUCYRUS-ERIE COMPANY**
Operating trends and ratios 1955–1961 (in thousands of dollars)

	1961	*1960*	*1959*	*1958*	*1957*	*1956*	*1955*
Income statement							
Net sales	$75,166	$63,629	$75,362	$58,272	$87,510	$86,586	$71,737
Cost of sales	70,084	62,743	70,750	58,848	73,435	70,491	57,031
Depreciation	2,702	2,736	2,915	2,500	2,580	2,369	2,137
Operating profit	$ 2,380	$(1,850)	$ 1,697	$(3,076)	$11,495	$13,726	$12,569
Other income,							
chgs. net	990	739	982	798	742	1,185	1,268
Interest chgs.	778	1,150	1,083	830	363	397	375
Income taxes	510	(990)	887	(1,428)	6,703	7,716	6,945
Net income	$ 2,082	$(1,271)	$ 709	$(1,680)	$ 5,171	$ 6,798	$ 6,517
*Special charge		8,684	2,465				
Net income to							
surpl.		($9,955)	($1,756)				
Ratio analysis							
Cost of sales as							
a % of sales	93.2	98.5	94.0	101.0	83.8	81.5	79.6
Oper. profit as							
a % of sales	03.18	(02.9)	02.3	(05.3)	13.1	15.9	17.5
Net income as							
a % of sales	02.78	(02.0)	00.9	(02.9)	05.9	07.8	09.1
Sales as a % of							
net fixed assets	300	240	214	155	263	388	350

* 1960: Losses and expenses in realigning, closing, and disposing of plants and equipment (after $1,230 refundable income taxes) $3,394; adjustment and losses on disposal of obsolete and excess inventories (less $1,717 allocated refundable income taxes) $550; total: $8,684.
1959: Provision for possible losses on future disposal of idle facilities and related deactivation costs ($1,710), less gain from disposal of other facilities sold during the year ($95,000), $1,615; provision for inventory adjustments $850; total: $2,465 (after applicable income taxes $2,898).

exhibit **2** (continued)
Operating trends and ratios 1947–1954 (in thousands of dollars)

1954	*1953*	*1952*	*1951*	*1950*	*1949*	*1948*	*1947*
$65,990	$78,582	$78,554	$78,886	$49,587	$58,055	$69,133	$56,538
54,779	65,029	64,081	61,890	40,822	46,519	58,457	46,872
1,928	1,733	1,670	1,481	1,123	966	940	748
$ 9,283	$11,820	$12,803	$15,515	$ 7,642	$10,570	$ 9,736	$ 8,918
836	718	533	430	527	438	217	269
352	364	132	—	—	—	—	—
5,225	7,157	8,115	9,930	3,510	4,373	4,129	3,732
$ 4,542	$ 5,017	$ 5,089	$ 6,015	$ 4,659	$ 6,635	$ 5,824	$ 5,455
—	—	233	311	311	311	311	311
$ 4,542	$ 5,017	$ 4,856	$ 5,704	$ 4,348	$ 6,324	$ 5,513	$ 5,144
83.0	82.8	81.6	78.5	82.3	80.1	84.6	82.9
14.1	15.0	16.3	19.6	15.4	18.2	14.0	15.8
06.9	06.4	06.5	07.6	09.4	11.4	08.4	10.3
356	432	474	479	369	473	759	79

exhibit 3

BUCYRUS-ERIE COMPANY

Organization Chart, March 1, 1962

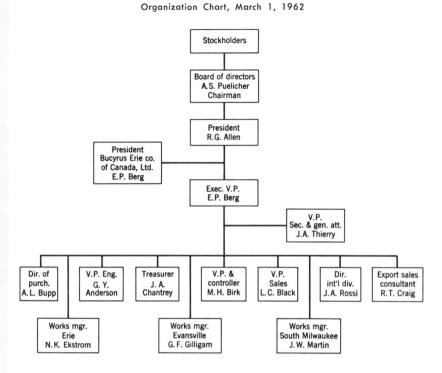

exhibit **4**   **SOME COMPETITORS TO BUCYRUS-ERIE AND THEIR PRODUCT LINES IN 1960**

Thew: Total net sales in 1960—$24.9 million.
> Material handling and excavating machinery including diesel, gas and electric power shovels, light portable cranes, clamshells, draglines, skimmer scoops, back diggers, motor truck cranes, shovels, locomotive cranes and moto-loaders.

Northwest: Total net sales in 1960—$11.1 million.
> Excavating machinery, power shovels, cranes and other excavating and material handling equipment of the crawler type, draglines, clamshells, trench digging machinery.

Koehring: Total net sales in 1960—$57.2 million.
> A varied line of heavy construction equipment for roads, general construction etc., including power shovels, cranes and draglines, pavers, mixers, finishers, trenchers, rollers and compactors, also hydraulic presses.

Caterpillar Tractor: Total net sales in 1960—$716.0 million.
> Crawler tractors, heavy-duty off-highway wheel tractors, motor graders and other earth-moving equipment. Machines are used principally for road building and maintenance, heavy construction, earthmoving, logging, snow removal, oil field work, quarrying, freighting, material handling and agriculture operations.

Clark Equipment: Total net sales in 1960—$196.8 million.
> Transmissions, driving and steering axles, axle housings, tractor drives, lift trucks, towing tractors, Ross carriers, powered hand trucks, excavator cranes, tractor shovels, tractor dozers, tractor scrapers, electric steel castings, gears, hydraulic pumps, forgings and material handling equipment.

Gardner-Denver: Total net sales in 1960—$84.8 million.
> Patented rock drills, equipment and accessories, air tools, air motors, portable drill mountings, steam and electric driven pumps, compressors, electric and air hoists, steam drilling engines and mechanical loaders, air powered drills, screw drivers, nut setters, hoists, grinders and chipping and riveting hammers, seismograph and geophysical drilling equipment for the oil industry, and light oil well drilling rigs and rotary drilling equipment for construction and mining industries.

Ingersoll-Rand: Total net sales in 1960—$185.8 million.
> Air and gas compressors, rock drills, oil and gas engines, pumps, condensers, pneumatic tools, air conditioning and refrigeration machinery, general mining, tunneling and quarrying machinery.

SOURCE: Standard and Poor's, *Industry Surveys*, 1961. Moody's *Manual of Industrials*, 1961.

exhibit 5
Bucyrus-Erie Product Lines

GENERAL PURPOSE EXCAVATORS — ⅜ to 4
cubic yard shovels, cranes, draglines and hoes.

TRUCK CRANES — 10 to 45 ton capacity
truck-mounted crane-excavators.

QUARRY AND MINING MACHINES — 2½ to 18
cubic yard electric shovels and draglines.

PRODUCTS

BUCYRUS-ERIE COMPANY, with its Canadian
subsidiary and British affiliate, is the world's
largest manufacturer of power cranes and excavators. The Company is also a large producer of
drilling machinery.

Other lines manufactured by Bucyrus-Erie are
railway cranes to 250 ton capacity, dragline
buckets from $\frac{3}{8}$ to 34 cubic yards, drilling
tools, and specialty items for use with excavating
and drilling machinery.

HYDROCRANES — 5 and 12 ton
capacity.

DRILLS — Rotary, flame piercing and
cable tool drilling machines for blast
holes. Cable tool and rotary drilling
machines for water wells, oil wells and
seismograph prospecting.

STRIPPING SHOVELS — 2 to 115 cubic
yard capacity.

WALKING DRAGLINES — 4 to 34
cubic yard capacity.

WHEEL EXCAVATORS — 850 to 2500 cubic
yards per hour normal capacity.

BUCYRUS-ERIE COMPANY
OFFICES AND PLANTS

GENERAL OFFICES — SOUTH MILWAUKEE, WIS-
CONSIN

PLANTS
SOUTH MILWAUKEE, WISCONSIN — Excavators; walk-
ing draglines; railway cranes; drills
EVANSVILLE, INDIANA — Excavators; cranes;
Hydrocranes; drills
ERIE, PENNSYLVANIA — Excavators and cranes

REGIONAL OFFICES
NEW YORK, NEW YORK — 30 Rockefeller Plaza*
CHICAGO, ILLINOIS — 105 West Adams Street
ATLANTA, GEORGIA — 32 Peachtree Street, N. E.
SOUTH SAN FRANCISCO, CALIFORNIA — 120 Freeway
Street

*9 Rockefeller Plaza after April 15, 1960.

SUBSIDIARY
BUCYRUS-ERIE COMPANY OF CANADA, LIMITED
GENERAL OFFICE AND PLANT — GUELPH,
ONTARIO
SALES OFFICE — TORONTO, ONTARIO, 2489
Bloor Street West

AFFILIATE
RUSTON-BUCYRUS, LIMITED
GENERAL OFFICES AND PLANT — LINCOLN,
ENGLAND
SALES OFFICES:
LONDON, ENGLAND — Crompton House
GLASGOW, SCOTLAND — 223 St. Vincent Street

Representatives and distributors throughout the United
States and in other principal countries of the world.

exhibit 6
Bucyrus-Erie Tractor-Mounted Equipment

exhibit 8
The Bucyrus-Erie 3850-B Stripping Shovel

The Model 3850-B now being built by Bucyrus-Erie for Peabody Coal Company will be the world's largest stripping shovel.

This earthmoving giant will:

... Tower as high as the deck of the Golden Gate Bridge.

... Stand 56 feet higher than the Statue of Liberty and 45 feet higher than Niagara Falls.

... Have a working reach of 1/12th of a mile.

... Be more than twice the size of any shovel now in operation.

... Consume power equal to the requirements of a city of 12,000 population.

... Require 250 railroad cars for delivery to the erection site.

ONE DAY'S PRODUCTION of the 3850-B, the world's largest earthmoving machine with its 115 cu. yd. dipper, would fill 1,700 railroad cars in a train nearly 15½ miles long.

DIVERSEY
CORPORATION

INTRODUCTION

The 1961 earnings of Diversey Corporation, a small but growing producer of sanitation chemicals, cleaning compounds, processed clays, and other specialty products, reflected a continuation of the company's aggressive foreign expansion program. Net sales for Diversey Corporation and all subsidiaries, but not including affiliates 50% or less owned, came to $18,489,906 as compared with $17,798,290 for 1960. Earnings amounted to $521,542 in 1961 as contrasted with $516,929 in 1960. In the 1961 annual report to the stockholders of the company, Mr. Herbert W. Kochs, chairman of the corporation, commenting on the company's total accomplishments, including affiliates, made the following statement: "Your company, its subsidiaries and affiliates, achieved world-wide sales in 1961 of $20.4 million compared with $19.2 million in 1960, a gain of 6%. Total company earnings amounted to $1.08 per share in 1961 compared with $1.02 per share in 1960, reflecting the two-for-one stock split in 1960 and the issuance of 16,000 additional shares in 1961."

Mr. Kochs also explained that Diversey's interest in the earnings of subsidiaries and affiliates (excluding North American subsidiaries) was $198,000 in 1961 compared with $71,000 in 1960. Of these earnings, dividends of $36,850 were paid to the parent company compared with $28,500 in 1960.

Commenting further on the improved overseas operations, Mr. Kochs went on to say, "In some cases, notably Canada and Brazil, . . . improved results have been partly offset by a decline in the value of their currency against the United States dollar."

In concluding his message to the shareholders, Mr. Kochs emphasized the importance of the contribution of the managers in Diversey's growth and stressed the need for organization and control of these diverse activities.

CORPORATE DEVELOPMENT

1923 to 1935. The Diversey Corporation was organized in Illinois on August 4, 1923, as a subsidiary of the Victor Chemical Works of Chicago. The company was established to develop the sale of chemical compounds for cleaning and disinfecting purposes for the parent company, which supplied most of the raw materials. By 1930 sales reached $600,000, on which a profit of $25,000 was made. When the sales and net profit declined in 1931 and continued to decline in 1932 the incumbent general manager was released and a former chemistry professor, who was in his early 60's, was appointed to the position.

The new general manager, whose remuneration consisted of a salary plus 5% of the net profits of the company, immediately embarked on a policy of expense reduction, disposing of half the clerical force and methodically cutting away at what he called "dead wood in the sales force." His program caused a substantial sales decline for the next two years, but profits soared 140% in 1933 and an additional 43% in 1934.

Messrs. Kochs and Shere, who had been appointed vice president and secretary respectively, opposed most of these moves. They pointed out that if the company were to grow on a national basis it would have to improve its customer service, particularly its delivery service in the more remote locations. Mr. Kochs proposed the establishment of local warehouses and recommended that more salesmen be added to the force, and when the general manager refused to consider these suggestions Mr. Kochs went to the Victor management with the proposals. After reviewing the problems, the Victor management asked the incumbent general manager to reconsider the proposals and suggested that he carry out certain of the expansion moves. When the Victor management realized that the divergence in thinking between the younger management officers and the general manager could not be reconciled, the latter was released on May 1, 1935, and Messrs. Kochs and Shere were appointed president and vice president respectively.

The New Management, 1935. The new management team headed by Mr. Kochs immediately introduced a number of basic policy changes. Instead of direct shipping to customers from the factory in Chicago Heights, decentralized distribution of products was introduced through the establishment of regional and local warehouses in New York, St. Louis, Minneapolis, Cleveland, Atlanta, and San Francisco. In addition, the company established its first subsidiary company, the Diversey Corporation (Canada) Limited, in Toronto, Canada, on May 6, 1937. By the end of the year the combined sales of the growing company approximated $1 million. Further expansion at this time was hampered because of World War II.

Post-world War II Developments. Prior to World War II, Diversey purchased all its products in finished form from Victor Chemical Works, and later, some from Dow Chemical Company.

In 1945, Diversey embarked on an expansion program designed to take it into markets other than the food industries and to place the company in a strategic position of producing all or nearly all of its products in its own plants. "Since I was a director at Victor," remarked Mr. Kochs, "I knew how much Victor was making from our products, so I decided to get producing plants of our own." In 1945, Diversey instituted its own research laboratory on its premises and then established its first manufacturing facility by purchasing the Trojan Products and Manufacturing Company and the Nabs-Oyle Corporation, manufacturers of industrial detergents in Chicago. Two years later the company acquired the Enoz Chemical Company of Chicago, producers of insecticides and household products, and the General Reduction Company of Macon, Georgia, processors of clay products used in insecticidal dusts, for various filtration purposes, and in miscellaneous chemical processes. Less than a year later Diversey expanded its detergent production facilities on the West Coast, leasing a plant for five years at South Gate, California, a suburb of Los Angeles.

As Diversey continued to expand into different fields, the difference in the characteristics of the business between Diversey and Victor became so great that Victor decided to sell its holdings in Diversey. In December, 1950, as a result of a refinancing program, Victor's 75% interest in Diversey was sold to the public at $10 per share. Messrs. Kochs and Shere retained their 25% holdings in the company.

In 1951, Mr. Kochs established the General Reduction Company of Illinois to handle the sales of the Macon, Georgia, clay processing plant, which had been integrated with the manufacturing division of Diversey Corporation.

As the demand for Diversey's products continued, the company established a plant in New Jersey in 1952 and one year later acquired the Selcon Engineering and Chemical Company of Chippewa Falls, Wisconsin, manufacturers of electronic devices sold in connection with Diversey's chemical business. Late in 1957 the Apex Chemical Manufacturing Corporation of Detroit, producers of general line detergents, and the plant of Black Leaf Insecticide Company of Waco, Texas, were purchased to provide manufacturing facilities for Diversey in these areas. A year later the company bought the Lewis Chemical Company of Brigantine, New Jersey, a distributor of industrial cleaning compounds and janitorial supplies in southern New Jersey.

CORPORATE STRUCTURE

Organization. In 1945 Diversey established research laboratories and began its own manufacturing. This action transformed the company from a sales organization to a fully integrated company. As Diversey added plants, either through acquisition or by establishing them, it changed from a small United States company to an international company with 4 United States subsidiaries, 8 manufacturing plants and 12 branch offices located in the United States, 14 foreign subsidiaries and affiliates with 12 factories and 31 branch offices located in 12 foreign countries (see Exhibit 1).

The company had from time to time prepared organization charts, and some divisions of the company had organization charts for their own use. (Exhibit 2 represents the organization as it operated in mid-1960.)

Diversey operated on a geographical division and consumer industry-line basis in the United States and on a geographical basis in all foreign subsidiaries. Mr. Kochs, as chairman of the corporation, was the principal authority in both the United States and the foreign operations.

Board of Directors. Diversey's board of directors in 1960 consisted of seven members. The board was management-dominated, but its outside members, representing high-caliber legal counsel and experience in the fields of chemical manufacturing and construction materials, brought a favorable balance to it.

Mr. Kochs, chairman and chief policy maker, who owned 56,340 shares

exhibit 1

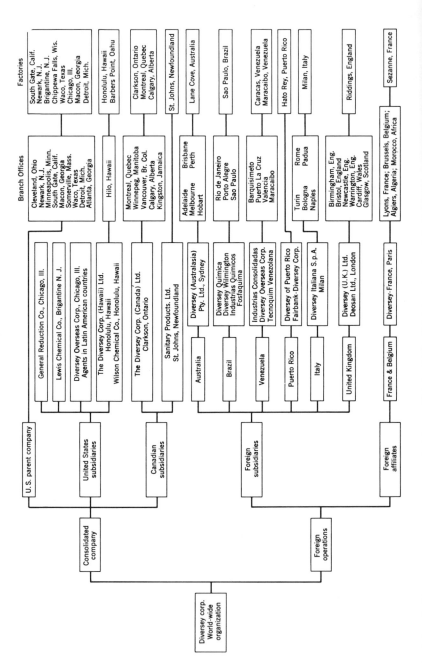

exhibit 2

DIVERSEY CORPORATION

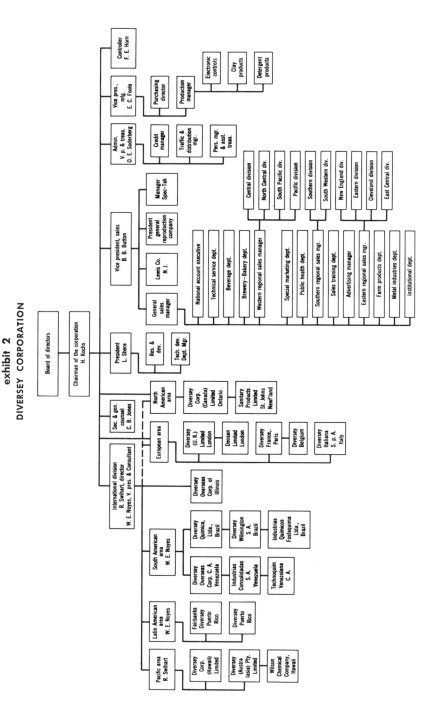

of common stock directly and held the right to vote 78,100 additional shares held in two trusts, planned the agenda for the board meetings and directed company policy. Whenever subjects of more than ordinary importance were brought before the board for consideration, they were discussed informally among the members prior to the meeting or reduced to writing and forwarded to those members who were unable to participate in these informal discussions. Diversey's board was relatively inactive in determining management policies. These policy matters were handled more directly by Mr. Kochs and his immediate subordinates.

Management. All members of Diversey's top management group had been associated with the company for at least 20 years, with the exception of Mr. Foote, vice president of manufacturing, who had 13 years' service, and Mr. Jones, secretary and general counsel, who had served the company for 7 years. All members of the top executive group, including the general managers of most foreign subsidiary companies, reported directly to Mr. Kochs.

Mr. Kochs, age 57, chairman of the corporation and chief policy maker, started to work for Diversey Corporation as an office boy in January, 1924, after attending M.I.T. and Northwestern University. Considered a "human dynamo" by other members of the organization, Mr. Kochs recalled with pride his first assignment, when he was given a large bag filled with twenty 1-pound demonstration samples of Diversey's products with orders to "visit auto service stations and salesrooms and use up the entire bag of samples," which he did, making a sale with each demonstration. After several very successful years as a salesman, he was made technical director and then promoted to sales manager for the eastern half of the United States. A short while later he was made vice president and sales manager, eastern division. In 1935 Mr. Kochs was appointed president, and eight years later, in 1943, he was elected chairman of the corporation It was Mr Kochs' personal interest in foreign affairs that eventually resulted in Diversey's expansion into international markets.

Mr. Shere, age 64, president of Diversey Corporation, started with the company in the research department in 1928. Prior to coming to Diversey, Mr. Shere worked for the state health departments of Minnesota and Illinois and the Chicago Health Department. Although use of chemical disinfectants had been frowned upon by public health authorities, Mr. Shere successfully demonstrated the superiority of the chemical sterilization process and was instrumental in getting the Chicago Health Department to approve Diversey's new disinfectant, Diversol. In 1932 he became sales manager for the western half of the United States and later in the year was appointed secretary of the company. In the 1935 management shakeup, Mr. Shere was appointed vice president, and in 1943 he became president. In 1959 only the research laboratories and technical development remained under Mr. Shere's direct supervision.

Mr. Button, age 46, vice president in charge of sales, joined Diversey in 1939 as a graduate chemist in the technical service department. Somewhat later he helped organize the metal products department. He also worked as a salesman for a few years before becoming manager of the department. In 1953 Mr. Button was promoted to general sales manager. Two years later he succeeded Mr. Noyes as vice president in charge of sales when the latter expressed a desire to become less active in the day-to-day affairs of the company.

Mr. Soderberg, age 53, administrative vice president, treasurer, and director, started with Diversey as a clerk in the accounting office in 1929. Subsequently he was promoted to cashier, credit manager, assistant secretary, and in 1939, secretary. In 1947 he was elected a vice president and three years later was made a director. In 1953 he was appointed administrative vice president and treasurer.

Mr. Horn, age 43, controller and assistant secretary, started with Diversey in September 1936 as a junior accountant. In 1946 he was appointed controller with specific duties to organize the complex tax problems of the company, which involved the handling of over 700 tax returns annually. As controller he reported to Mr. Soderberg until 1953, at which time he was given full responsibility for all accounting functions, reporting directly to Mr. Kochs.

Mr. Swihart, age 43, director of the international division, began working as an analytical chemist for Victor in 1941. When Diversey established its own research facilities in 1947, Mr. Swihart was named supervisor. In 1953 he was promoted to general manager of the newly formed Diversey (Australasia) Pty. Limited to start the operations of the company. In 1955 he was appointed technical advisor of Diversey Corporation (Hawaii) Limited and in the next four years added other foreign operations to his jurisdiction as subsidiary firms were acquired or established. In 1958 Mr. Swihart assumed more direct responsibility in all of the overseas subsidiaries and, in 1960, was elected vice president of international operation.

Mr. Jones, age 53, secretary and general attorney of the corporation, started with Diversey in 1953. He was brought into the company to handle the increasingly complex legal problems arising from foreign and domestic expansion. In addition to the legal work, Mr. Jones was in charge of the corporate insurance program.

MARKETING AND SALES

Products. The company and its subsidiaries distributed a diversified line of about 100 organic and inorganic chemicals used as bactericides, cleaners, scale removers, and insecticides for industrial sanitation; and as oil absorbents, metal cleaners, floor waxes, and other products for industrial manufacturing and maintenance.

Cleaning compounds, including bottle-washing compounds Relion and Spec-Tak, accounted for approximately 60% of the company's dollar sales volume and were the major items in the company's line. Bactericides, of which Diversol, a chlorinated disinfectant, made up the major amount, represented approximately 20% of total sales. The balance of the business consisted of metal surface preparation chemicals, a field in which Diversey ranked as a leader; absorbent clays, used to spread over oil, grease, acid, and other hazardous spills in industrial plants; processed clays, used as bases, carriers, or binders by insecticide and fertilizer manufacturers, lubricating oil refineries, and processors of animal and mineral oils; and electronic equipment for measuring, testing, and controlling chemicals used in machines for washing milk cans, bottles, and dishes.

SALES BREAKDOWN BY INDUSTRIES SERVED, PERCENT

Industry	1945	1950	1955	1960
Dairy products	63.3	47.0	42.7	37.0*
Other food products (beverage, brewing, canning, baking)	21.3	30.6	31.4	33.0*
Total (foods)	84.6	77.6	74.1	70.0*
Miscellaneous (metal cleaning, moth products, clay products, electronic equipment)	15.4	22.4	25.9	30.0*
	100.0	100.0	100.0	100.0

* Estimated
SOURCE: Management Audit, American Institute of Management, Special Audit #129, Vol. 4, No. 20.

Although the food industry ranked as the company's most important market, its importance had been decreasing and in 1961 represented approximately 70% of total sales, whereas in 1945 it represented nearly 85% of sales.

Markets. The company had approximately 25,000 domestic customers. Most of the accounts were relatively small and averaged less than $500 per year. No single customer purchased as much as 5% of the total dollar sales volume. In order to service its customers, Diversey maintained warehouse and plants in about 100 different cities.

Sales Organization. The sales department of the parent company was decentralized geographically with 10 branch offices in the United States. Each branch office was headed by a divisional manager who reported to one of three regional managers (see Exhibit 3).

The parent company's sales organization consisted of approximately 280 salesmen and supervisors and was divided into four broad sales groups: the food industry, the metal industry, the institutional field, and miscellaneous.

In discussing the sales organization, Mr. Button, vice president in charge of sales, stated, "The biggest single problem confronting the company is finding and developing people." He went on to say that he believed the company salesmen should have some college training, since they called on college-trained bacteriologists, food engineers, and executives in charge of research manufacturing and similar activities in some of the largest food-processing plants in the world. "We do not have a formalized management development program," he remarked, "but we try to keep a certain number of men trained and in training for the new openings that constantly occur because of our world-wide operations and our constant expansion."

In discussing the problem further, Mr. Button remarked that one of the ways in which the top management group had been attempting ot improve the caliber of the management personnel was through its policy of decentralization. "Our aim is to bring the division manager closer to our customers and our field representatives. We have done this by making each division as autonomous as possible They do their own ordering, credit collection, billing, and are responsible for maintaining supplies and for inventory of finished goods." He remarked that the inventory position of each division was a problem because of the personal property tax which was levied by each state. He pointed out that it was important to reduce the inventory to as low a point as possible, compatible with current sales, to minimize the tax base. He commented further that the control on inventory was also needed because many of the divisional managers failed to keep their stocks in balance. He cited the situation in one of the eastern divisions, where stock shortages occurred in some items in several warehouses while other warehouses in the same area were overstocked in these items. "It was so simple for the division manager to merely order new supplies from one of our production plants in the territory instead of properly shuffling the inventory between warehouses under his jurisdiction. Normally, no one interferes with the placement of an order," he added, "but if, at the end of the month, an excess of any item is on hand, then action is taken by Mr. Perry or me."

Mr. Button felt that another major problem was in the area of forecasting and budgeting. He stated that the company was going to have to educate the regional, divisional, and district sales managers so that more and more of the planning responsibility could be placed on them. Originally, the various sales managers submitted their own sales estimates, which were always too optimistic, and this tendency carried over into other areas. He indicated that he, Mr. Kochs, and Mr. Perry had spent the past two years trying to get the managers to understand accounting and the analytical aspects of their jobs. "We have had to tread softly," he added, "and not give them too much at one time." He continued by stating, "Although most of our division managers are profit conscious, our district managers are more interested in sales than in profits."

Mr. Button agreed with Mr. Perry that communications was another major problem confronting the sales organization. "We don't have as much of a communication problem downward," he insisted, "as we do with communications coming up the line." Mr. Button admitted that part of the problem stemmed from the fact that the organization was so widely dispersed throughout the United States.

Mr. Button estimated that 20% of his time was involved in traveling and that Mr. Perry's traveling time was considerably more. He expressed concern over the fact that Mr. Perry had 14 men reporting to him. He felt certain that Mr. Perry was having a difficult time keeping up with the number of division managers who wanted to see him, even though they should have been covering their problems with the regional managers. "Mr. Kochs and I both realized the problem when I was general sales manager," he said. "There was too much to do. That's why we established the regional manager jobs." (See Exhibit 3.)

exhibit 3
DIVERSEY CORPORATION SALES ORGANIZATION

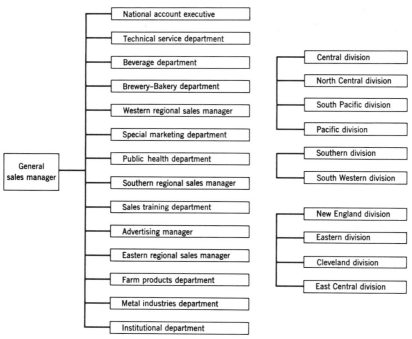

exhibit 4
DIVERSEY CORPORATION MANUFACTURING ORGANIZATION

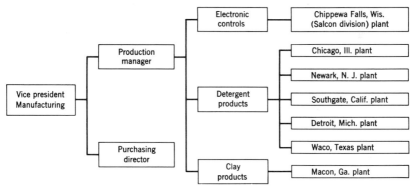

Mr. Perry had this to say about the problem: "I feel my job is to work with market men and do promotional work I am sure that our promotional campaigns would be more successful if I had the time to plan the details. My major problem is lack of time to get around and work with the people who report to me. I intend to bring in a trainee, or an assistant, for a couple of years to help work out planning with promotional men. After he is trained, I plan to move him out into the field and bring in another. I would like to cut down on the number of people reporting to me, perhaps get it down to five or six."

In discussing the regional managers, Mr. Perry commented, "I do have three strong regional managers and I meet with them once a month. We discuss ideas, problems, and product promotions, and they in turn discuss our conclusions with their divisional managers."

Mr. Perry observed that the three regional managers were appointed to their jobs when he was made general sales manager three years before: "At that time," he continued, "we had no clear-cut definition of duties."

The regional managers did not turn over any type of activity report to Mr. Perry. "I don't know how I would use one if I got one," remarked Mr. Perry, "although I occasionally ask for a special report on a phase of our business, or on a competitor's business, for my information and for use by our top management." He went on to say that he had a unique problem in that the business spanned so many industries. "I know I have a problem," he continued; "I am tied down with my job and I am afraid that if I continue to be a desk sales manager I will lose my feel and touch of the market."

Mr. Button agreed with Mr. Perry that the communication problem was improving. "We meet regularly with the regional and divisional managers each quarter for two days at a time," he said. "There has been a subtle change in the divisional meetings over the past two years," he continued. "Two years ago the individual managers were reluctant to speak up. We encouraged them to talk and to participate in the development of ideas leading up to decision making. We almost went too far. The division managers soon began expressing their opinions freely, even to the point of thinking that the business was going to be operated strictly on a democratic basis. But we emphasized that somebody had to take responsibility, which is contrary to the majority viewpoint. By encouraging them to participate in the conference, we have been obtaining suggestions and contributions from them." Similar meetings were held with the 45 district managers.

In 1960 a new compensation plan was introduced whereby Diversey salesmen received a guaranteed draw plus a percentage of each sale up to the draw. If total commission exceeded the draw the salesmen were paid the excess. A sliding commission rate ranging from 5 to 18% was paid based on the profitability of the products sold. In discussing the wage arrangements, Mr. Button remarked, "We don't have a set wage rule. We are leery of anything that smacks of rigidity." He went on to say that the district managers received a salary and additional compensation if the sales quota was exceeded. Divisional and regional managers were paid a salary plus a bonus based on the net profit of the company.

Mr. Button felt that the morale of his organization was comparatively good. We try to keep everyone completely informed. We encourage open discussion on all problems, but we discourage bypassing of subordinates. We insist on the proper chain of command." He commented further that he had a good line on his people and that he could tell when things were not going well by the conversation of the people, by their interests, their gripes, and their complaints. "On occasion we have problems," he continued. "About a month ago, while passing through New York, I phoned the division manager and asked him about the morale in his group. As a result of that call I received a four-page letter from him indicating poor morale. If I hadn't asked him about it, I would never have received any information."

Competition. The fields in which the company was engaged were highly competitive. No one company was a major factor. Diversey's products were sold in competition with similar products of other companies and with different products which could be used for the same purposes. The four principal competing manufacturers of industrial cleaning compounds in the field of food sanitation operating on a national scale were J. B. Ford Division of the Wyandotte Chemicals Corporation, Solvay Sales Corporation (a subsidiary of Allied Chemical & Dye Corporation), Diamond Alkali Company, and Oakite Products, Inc. There were also competitors operating on a regional or local basis who engaged in the distribution of bactericides, insecticides, and cleaners for industrial sanitation. A comparison with one of Diversey's principal competitors, whose operation was typical for the industry, showed the following for the fiscal year 1959:

Item	Diversey (Consolidated), %	Company "X" Competitor Consolidated, %
Sales and other income	100.00	100.00
Raw materials, supplies, advertising, and administrative costs	59.39	51.03
Salaries, wages, commissions	32.92	39.93
Cost of goods sold, expenses, et cetera	92.31	90.96
Profit before taxes	7.69	9.04
Net profit to net worth	15.41	20.33

MANUFACTURING

Production. Up to and including the World War II period, Diversey was strictly a sales organization and purchased all of its products from the Victor Chemical Works or from Dow Chemical Company. These companies blended finished chemical products according to Diversey's specifications. With the purchase of the Trojan Products and Manufacturing Company and the Nabs-Oyle Corporation in 1945, Diversey blended and packaged certain products formerly purchased from Victor and Dow. By 1960 it was producing a major portion of all its products (see Exhibit 4).

Diversey purchased its raw materials and finished goods on an annual contract basis from Dow, DuPont, Monsanto, and some 15 other national suppliers. The chief raw materials included caustic soda, soda ash, sodium metasilicate, hydrochloric acid, niter cake, sodium orthosilicate, alkyl benzene, sulphuric acid, and phosphates. Mr. Hannibal, director of purchasing, said that the company tried to have at least two suppliers for each item purchased. "We prefer to buy our supplies from a vendor who offers more than one raw material. The chances of making up a carload lot are greater if we are purchasing more than one or two items, and in that way we can limit our purchase and inventory on each item."

Most of the manufacturing process performed by Diversey in its plants consisted of the blending of raw materials. The finished product was not manufactured directly for the sales division but was placed in inventory. The sales division was, however, responsible for establishing inventory stocks and adequate controls of these stocks. All products were manufactured by the batch process, with the foremen keeping track of labor, raw materials, and containers on a batch basis. The finished product was packaged and shipped to one of the Diversey warehouses situated strategically in more than 100 different domestic locations.

In commenting on production costs, Mr. Foote, vice president of manufacturing, stated: "We have a standard cost system, but I feel the system has limitations. We receive a monthly manufacturing cost statement from the accounting office which relates total costs to standard costs and shows variances. The statement shows the breakdown of costs by products—labor, containers, and overhead—and is compiled from our work orders. Actually, standard costs are constantly under revision to keep pace with changes in formula and packaging. Hardly a month passes without revision of some costs."

Mr. Foote pointed out, "The bulk of our manufacturing costs are attributable to the cost of raw materials, over which we have no control because the price is administered nationally by the suppliers. Our purchasing department attempts to control the price of raw materials through time contracts with our major vendors. Our over-all problem is that we are a middleman. Many of our competitors or suppliers want to standardize detergents to the extent that they become commodities, so as to be able to mass produce the items and squeeze us and other small operators out of the market. We try to overcome this by offering something a little better both in quality and in service and specifically formulated for specialized purposes."

In reviewing the Diversey situation, Mr. Foote pointed out that the manufacturing division was not interested in taking over the few products still produced for it by the Victor Chemical Works or by Dow Chemical Company. He remarked that Diversol had become less profitable with time and that Relion sales had shrunk substantially because of new developments in Spec-Tak. Some of the raw materials for the latter were purchased from Dow and blended in Diversey plants. "As long as the operation is one of blending we will always do it. We do not want to get involved in making or producing the basic raw material because of the heavy capital investment required and freight penalties involved. Furthermore, we never know how successful a product will be, so it is best to buy rather than manufacture the raw materials."

RESEARCH AND DEVELOPMENT

The total research effort in Diversey was headed by Mr. Shere, president of the company. Some 30 chemists, bacteriologists, entomologists, and technicians under a research director conducted research activities at the company's laboratories in Chicago. The technical development department evaluated products generated by the research laboratories to determine their salability. Thus, when the company introduced a new product or changed the formula of an existing compound, the technical development department lined up customer plants in several districts to test the modified or new products. The tests were usually conducted for a six-month period. If the tests proved favorable, the new or modified product was distributed nationally and the old product withdrawn.

In 1925 Diversey chemists, working in the research laboratories of the Victor Chemical Works, developed the company's first new product,

Diversol, a solid form of cleansing agent and a bactericide. This product eventually became one of the best known sanitation products in the world. With acceptance of this product the company shifted its emphasis to products related to the food industries. In 1945, Relion, a bottle-washing compound, was developed, but because Victor was unable to produce it in flake form to Diversey's specifications, arrangements were made with the Dow Chemical Company for its manufacture.

Along with the development of Relion, Diversey introduced a new idea—that of providing a free service with the sale of the commodity. This was accomplished by the research and development department, which assembled a manual showing diagrammatic drawings of each type of bottle-washing machine in use. Mr. Shere, in commenting on this development, stated: "Previously, suppliers of this equipment offered little or no instruction on its use. With our manual we were able to show users how to change valves and nozzles for the unclogging of wash jets and rinse jets. This same philosophy, i.e., top service with quality products has continued to be the fundamental operating policy of the Diversey Corporation."

In 1961 Diversey had a research staff of 30 in its main research laboratories in Chicago. In addition, Diversey (U.K.) [1] Limited had established and expanded its research staff of chemists, bacteriologists, and technicians to 15, and Diversey Corporation (Canada) Limited employed 2 chemists on research. Each research facility operated independently. The expenditure on research activities by the United States parent company amounted to approximately $250,000 annually, with lesser sums expended annually for research by the English and Canadian subsidiary companies.

Mr. Shere estimated that approximately 20% of the company's research was basic and that 80% was applied. These research efforts had resulted in the granting of numerous patents annually, some of which had led to licensing arrangements for royalty income. In addition, substantial economies in production, as well as upgrading of product quality, had resulted from research efforts on new and less expensive materials which had given superior results.

FINANCE AND CONTROL

Diversey was incorporated as a wholly owned subsidiary of the Victor Chemical Works in August, 1923, with a paid-in capital of $10,000,

[1] U. K.: United Kingdom.

representing 101 shares of $100 par-value stock which were later con-
verted into 44,000 shares of no-par–value stock. In 1937 Victor sold
9,000 shares to Mr. Kochs, then president of Diversey, and 2,000 shares
to Mr. Shere, then vice president of Diversey, and retained 33,000 shares,
representing 75% of the company.

In December, 1950, Victor disposed of its 75% holdings in Diversey.
All the shares were reclassified into 220,000 common shares, Messrs.
Koch and Shere receiving 77,000 of the new shares for their original
holdings, thereby retaining their 25% interest in the company. The remaining 143,000 shares were offered to the public at $10 per share. In
order to accomplish this transaction, the Diversey Corporation entered
into an agreement with the Equitable Life Assurance Society of the
United States for a 12-year loan of $1 million at 3.92% interest, with
payments to be made annually at the rate of $100,000 per year.

In May of 1960 there was a 100% distribution of stock, having the
effect of a two-for-one stock split, and increasing the total shares outstanding to 527,238.

Mr. Soderberg, administrative vice president and treasurer, remarked
that the major problem confronting the treasure's office was to stay
financially ahead of the company's expansion needs. "The foreign expansion of the past five years has created money problems. We have been
trying to finance our expansion out of current income, but we can't
always do this." He cited the Diversey (U.K.) Limited acquisition in
1958 as an example; in that acquisition Diversey had had to supply
some $800,000 in advance. "When we need a large sum, we approach
the insurance companies and see what they have to offer, or we go
to our own bank and Mr. Kochs works out a deal."

Mr. Soderberg stated that Mr. Kochs was constantly searching for
new areas to move into, either by acquisition, which was more expensive,
or by starting from scratch. After Mr. Kochs decided on an area or
a new business possibility, the treasurer's office assessed the financial
needs. He went on to say, "We have decided in advance that acquisition
must meet our requirements, which we have placed at ownership of
at least 51% of the stock and working control of the company as well.
An exception to this had been Diversey-France, where we have a 50-50
relationship."

All international subsidiaries had separate accounts and were treated
as separate entities. Mr. Soderberg pointed out that tax considerations
were not the main reasons for maintaining separate entities. "It is true
that some advantages are had by keeping separate entities for each unit.

However, the main reason is to keep the morale and order of the existing organization, good will of customers, and continued identification on a local plane and with local flavor."

According to Mr. Soderberg, the parent company had good control over its domestic and foreign subsidiaries. "We have cash sheets and daily sales sheets which list the sales for the day and accumulated for the month, and monthly profit and loss statements on every subsidiary. If conditions are out of line in any one company, Mr. Kochs decides on the action to be taken." He indicated that the company had other controls which it used in all of its operations, such as stock inventory, semifinished-goods inventory, and accounts receivables. "We try to maintain a maximum of two months' inventory in each division, but we leave the division autonomous in that we are not interested in telling them what dollar amount of each product to have. The various production plants are limited in the amount of finished goods they carry, which may be as little as two weeks, depending on the lead time involved."

Mr. Soderberg emphasized that "each of the company's ten sales divisions issues its bills for sales and services and deposits the money collected in banks specified by the treasurer's office. The treasurer's office draws down the deposits several times per month. The bank balances for each division are never permitted to drop below $2,000 nor allowed to exceed $8,000 for any length of time." Mr. Soderberg pointed out also that if there was a surplus of funds in Chicago, larger amounts were allowed to accumulate in divisional office banks, and the reverse held true if money was tight in Chicago.

All financial and cost accounting reports, as well as sales reports, were issued from the controller's office headed by Mr. Horn. In addition, the controller initiated and reviewed all budgets, which were made out once a year, and analyzed all department performances in relation to planned estimates.

In commenting on his job, Mr. Horn stated: "Since 1953, I have reported directly to Mr. Kochs on all phases of the company's domestic and foreign accounting operations. In his absence I advise Mr. Shere." He went on to say that one of his chief problems was to determine how to obtain a better control system for the company's world-wide activities. "Since it is Mr. Kochs' philosophy to maintain local flavor in foreign operations by having the management on a local level, we have a job to educate the foreign accounting personnel in American managerial accounting techniques." Mr. Horn added that all foreign subsidiaries had been given the United States parent company's accounting procedures, but the difficulty had been to get them to change over from their less efficient systems to the parent company's system and still comply with local government regulations. "Last year I went to England to look over the accounting practices of Diversey (U.K.) Limited and its wholly owned subsidiary, Deosan Limited. Their system was so antiquated that I would say they were at least ten years behind us. They were hand-posting many forms of records. They had five people working overtime doing the costing work on operations of one plant, as contrasted with our three cost clerks handling the operations of seven plants." Based on his recommendations, the elaborate inventory lists and huge ledgers were eliminated, and expense control was greatly simplified with the introduction of fewer and simpler records and the beginning of department budgets.

Mr. Horn felt that one of the major functions of his job was to provide more usable information to the company's managers in the field. He expressed concern over the reluctance of some managers to stress the use of budgets emanating from his office; the job of budgeting left much to be desired. "I believe we are not generating enough questions about budgets," he added. "This is reflected in the day-to-day attitude of division and district managers toward their budgets. We could put their reports through with a $5,000 overstatement of expense, and it would not be questioned by them. Yet, in other instances, they get all steamed up over what they think is an overcharge and are embarrassed when they learn that they had earlier approved the expense in question. Some divisional men need quite a bit of education in accounting and control, particularly in budgeting."

INTERNATIONAL DIVISION

The international division of Diversey Corporation came into existence officially in 1955, when Mr. Kochs assigned Mr. J. R. Swihart, on a full-time basis, to look after the overseas operations other than the Diversey Corporation (Canada) Limited. However, its origins dated back to 1952, when the decision was made to move into the Hawaiian and Australian markets. "Actually, the conception of the foreign operations goes back to the early 1930's," remarked Mr. Kochs. "At the time I noticed the difference in economic conditions between countries. Some didn't have a depression while we had ours; others had a major depression before we did; others had the depression after ours. So I studied up on the foreign situation. We were growing so fast and were not affected much by the Depression because we were so small a part of the market. But I felt that when we got to be a larger company we would be affected by a major recession." He went on to say, "My thinking became crystallized in 1936, and I evolved a plan to establish foreign subsidiaries. Since we don't need a large force to produce our commodities, and since our type of business lends itself readily to smaller regional operations, I felt it would be smart for us to expand into foreign fields,"

The first foreign subsidiary was established in 1937 when the Diversey Corporation (Canada) Limited was organized. It was virtually independent of the parent organization except for research and top management consultation, for which it paid a fee to the parent organization.

The first major expansion of the Canadian company occurred in October, 1950, when it completed and equipped a plant and office building at Port Credit near Toronto at an aggregate cost of $150,000. The new plant processed products previously imported from the parent company. In 1953, the company constructed another plant at Clarkson, Ontario, to manufacture Diversol, formerly purchased from the United States parent company. At the same time it acquired a 65% interest in Sanitary Products Limited of St. Johns, Newfoundland, which became a distributor and local service organization for Diversey products on the island of Newfoundland. The total investment by the Canadian subsidiary in the two expansions amounted to $350,000. In 1956 the company sold its Port Credit plant, realizing a $133,000 capital gain. Two new plants were constructed at a cost of nearly a half million dollars. In 1958, the Canadian Company increased its holdings in Sanitary Products Limited from 65 to 68%.

Late in 1952 Mr. Kochs completed negotiations for the activation of the Australian company with headquarters in Sydney. Initial interest in the Australian market had occurred just before World War II, when the Diversey Corporation financed part of a study for an Ohio State University professor who was surveying the Australian dairy industry. Interest in the Australian market was renewed after World War II and culminated in an agreement in 1953 with J. B. Bryant and Co., a local manufacturer of bottle-washing machinery and equipment. The newly formed company became operational in that year and was 50% owned by the Diversey Corporation and 50% by the Bryant interests.

The original agreement called for the establishment of the Australian company to sell Diversey products imported from the United States parent company. However, when the Australian government introduced import restrictions in 1953, a change in plans became necessary, and Mr. Swihart was dispatched to Australia to start production on a local basis. In 1956 the company was reorganized, and Diversey purchased Bryant's share. The Australian Company borrowed $38,000 from the parent company to finance the transaction. Within two years the company's sales and profits climbed substantially, enabling the company to pay back its refinancing loan in full.

Early in 1953 Diversey purchased the Kills 'Em Chemical Company Limited, of Honolulu, Hawaii. The Hawaiian company was engaged primarily in the manufacture of disinfectants and insecticides in the Hawaiian Islands and operated one of the largest service organizations in the islands for the control of termites in homes and public buildings.

The Hawaiian plant was immediately rehabilitated and expanded, and the company began operating as an independent domestic subsidiary of Diversey Corporation. The company expanded rapidly, borrowing $30,000 from the parent company to improve its distribution and producing facilities. The name of the company was changed to Diversey Corporation (Hawaii) Limited in 1955. As sales and profits increased, the subsidiary paid off its earlier loan to the parent company. Two years later it borrowed an additional $60,000 from the parent company to purchase the Wilson Chemical Company of Hawaii, manufacturers of agricultural insecticides used primarily by the pineapple industry.

In 1955 Diversey decided to enter into the Latin American market and organized and incorporated Diversey Overseas Corporation. C. A., as a holding company. The new company was established as a tax haven, buying finished goods from the United States parent company for export to other countries in the Western Hemisphere. Shortly after it was established, the holding company purchased 50.9% of the assets of Industrias Consolidadas, C. A., Venezuela. In 1957 a revolution in the country interfered greatly with the business of the company, although there was no interference with the company's personnel or property.

In mid-1958 Industrias Consolidadas was faced with a serious situation in that the national competition influenced local authorities to withhold tariff concessions to which it was entitled. After considerable negotiations, Industrias Consolidadas obtained exoneration from tariff duties when it purchased a 60% interest in the local competitor, Technoquim

Venezolana, C. A. Upon acquisition of its competitor, Industrias Consolidadas transferred its production operations to the new firm and functioned solely as a sales organization selling the products produced by the newly purchased plant. The consolidation resulted in a profitable operation which more than offset all previous losses. In 1959, as sales and profits expanded, the company arranged to lease another plant to keep up with its growth. Late in 1960 Industrias Consolidadas acquired the balance of Technoquim stock.

The company's expansion efforts in Latin America were broadened with the establishment of a new holding company, Diversey Quimica Ltda., São Paulo, Brazil, in 1956. Its first official act was the purchase of controlling interest (53%, later increased to 78%) in Diversey Wilmington, S.A.—Produtos Quimicos, São Paulo, Brazil. The company experienced difficulty in the early months of 1958 as a result of the rapidly falling value of the cruzeiro, but it managed to strengthen its position by purchasing the assets of Industrias Quimicos Fosfaquima Ltda., the only manufacturer of complex phosphates and phosphoric acid in Brazil.

In 1957 Mr. Kochs carried his expansion into Puerto Rico through the purchase of the Diamond Alkali interests in Miles H. Fairbank, Inc. and Diamond Chemicals of Puerto Rico. Although the two companies constituted the principal source of industrial cleaning compounds and allied products in Puerto Rico, at the time that Diversey purchased 53% interest in them the companies were floundering.

Upon purchase, the names of the companies were changed to Diversey of Puerto Rico, Inc. and Fairbank-Diversey, Inc. The latter firm, which distributed the products produced by Diversey of Puerto Rico as well as heavy chemicals, machinery, and plating material, underwent a gradual transition from its former jobbing business to one of greater activity in the products produced for it by Diversey of Puerto Rico. A slight loss was sustained in the first year, but the combined operations showed a profit in 1958 and 1959.

In 1960, Diversey of Puerto Rico, which enjoyed a 10-year tax holiday on manufactured products sold by Fairbank-Diversey, Inc., increased its manufacturing facilities sizably. At the same time Diversey of Puerto Rico set up its own sales force and ceased selling to Fairbank-Diversey. The latter resumed its former position as a jobber for various lines of merchandise.

In 1955 Mr. Kochs decided to expand in the European area and established subsidiaries in France, England, and Italy in the next three years. Diversey-France was incorporated in Paris in December, 1955 by the United States parent company and a chemical complex headed by Saint Gobain and Progil of France. The company was capitalized at 200 million francs (approximately $400,000), with one half owned by the United States parent company and one half owned by the French chemical companies. Under the incorporation agreement, Diversey agreed not to buy out or control Diversey-France, and the French shareholders agreed not to enter into competition with the newly formed company for 20 years.

The new company began operations in 1956 with offices and laboratories in Paris and 12 warehouses located strategically throughout France. Key personnel from the United States parent company assisted in the establishment and operation of the company for the first year. In its second year of operation a profit was made, and two years later it began selling products in Belgium, Algeria, Morocco, and Portugal. In 1959 the company paid its first dividend to its shareholders and began construction of its manufacturing plant. Initially, French chemical companies manufactured the products for Diversey-France.

The second European subsidiary, Diversey (U.K.) Limited, was established by Mr. Kochs in London in 1958 with a capitalization of £296,000 (approximately $829,000). After protracted negotiations with Vick Chemical Company and the Milton Organization, Diversey (U.K.) Limited purchased Deosan Limited from the Vick Chemical Company for approximately $800,000. Deosan was principally engaged in the manufacture and distribution of cleaners and disinfectants to dairy farmers and supplied nearly 40% of the market. It also was one of the largest suppliers of commercial dishwashing compounds in the United Kingdom.

In 1959 the two companies were reorganized with Diversey (U.K.) Limited manufacturing and Deosan Limited selling the products. In addition, a research laboratory was established by Diversey (U.K.) Limited in London and was staffed with 15 chemists, bacteriologists, and technicians. The accounting was modernized and patterned after the parent company. Some $103,000 was spent on improvement of plant, equipment, and vehicles. Sales improved substantially during the year, and 42 sales and service personnel were added to the staff.

The third European subsidiary, Diversey Italiana, Sp.A., Milan, was organized in late 1958 and became operational in 1959 with the purchase of the industrial cleanser business of a local firm. The new company was organized with the Diversey Corporation owning 50.94% and the local interests, headed by the St. Gobain chemical firm, owning 49.06%.

In 1960 and 1961 Diversey initiated distribution of its products in Belgium, West Germany, Morocco, and Algeria, as it continued its expansion on a broad front. Only in the Cuban area did the company curtail direct sales activity. As the Cuban political and economic situation worsened, the parent company terminated credit arrangements with its Cuban agents, and sales were made only by confirmed letter of credit. When the United States government passed the Cuban Embargo Act the parent company terminated all direct sales activities with Cuba and the reduced volume of business transacted was handled through its Canadian subsidiary, the Diversey Corporation (Canada) Limited.

Control of International Operations. As Diversey expanded into overseas markets, each new unit added, whether established or purchased, was set up as a separate entity and permitted to operate with a minimum of direction from the parent company. By 1960, in addition to the Canadian company and its subsidiary, the international division consisted of 16 foreign subsidiary and affiliated companies operating on 5 continents (see Exhibit 5).

In his 1961 year-end report to Mr. Kochs on the activities of the international division, Mr. Swihart attributed Diversey's overseas growth to "a growing nationalism in many countries and a recognition of the United States as the world's technological leader." Mr. Swihart indicated that he was concerned about the organizational problems confronting the company when establishing overseas subsidiaries. "At times we get entangled in our operations. We will have to change our organization one of these days." He then went on to say that the international division had two problems: the recruiting and training of personnel and the general strengthening of the international department. "We prefer to draw our personnel from within the company," he remarked. "We have started to get young college people who have little or no industrial experience with the hope that they will make a career with us, particularly in our overseas subsidiaries. We use the export department in our Chicago office as an observation and training post for personnel we plan to send abroad."

In regard to the strengthening of the international department, Mr. Swihart remarked, "Actually, there is overlapping and semi-overlapping of authority. The Latin America subsidiaries report directly to me. However, the day-to-day operations come under the supervision of Mr. Noyes, formerly vice president in charge of sales and a consultant to the

United States parent company. Mr. Kaple, who is a director of the parent company, runs our Canadian companies and reports directly to Mr. Kochs, as does the manager of Diversey (U.K.) Limited and Deosan Limited."

Each foreign subsidiary was headed by a local board of directors, which included a local general manager as well as Mr. Kochs and in some cases other officers from the United States parent company. In commenting on managerial control of the subsidiaries, Mr. Kochs remarked that he did not want to do their managing and that he doubted the need for close supervision of the foreign subsidiaries. "The only controls we need to look at are the profit and loss statements." He stated further, "We go to these companies regularly, establish their budgets, and plan their programs, i.e., lay out each company's program for the year, decide on the number of salesmen, where and when to build a new plant or an addition, and where to establish new branch offices."

Mr. Kochs indicated that the foreign subsidiaries had been deliberately underfinanced. "It is the only way in which we can get local management to face up to their problems and solve them. If we did it the other way and bailed them out readily, giving them additional funds every time they thought they needed some, they would feel that they had a rich uncle in the parent company, standing ready to solve all their financial problems for them."

exhibit 5   COMPARISON OF 1960 SALES AND NET PROFIT OF FOREIGN OPERATIONS*

	Per Cent of Dollar Sales	Per Cent of Net Profit after Tax
Total Foreign Companies*	100.0	100.0
Diversey Corporation (Canada) Ltd.	31.4	35.0
Deosan Ltd.	14.3	7.5
Diversey-France	13.7	16.5
Diversey Corp. (Hawaii) Ltd.	10.4	11.0
Industrias Consolidadas	8.4	12.4
Diversey (Australasia) Pty. Ltd.	5.6	9.5
Fairbanks-Diversey	5.3	2.5
Sanitary Products	4.8	3.5
Diversey Wilmington	2.4	2.0
Technoquim Venezolana	2.1	
Diversey Italiana	1.2	†
Diversey of Puerto Rico	.3	

* Other than United States parent company
† Slight loss

exhibit 6 **THE DIVERSEY CORPORATION AND SUBSIDIARIES**
Consolidated statement of income and earnings (000 omitted)

	Parent Company with United States and Canadian Subsidiaries								Consolidated with World-wide Subsidiaries			
	1954	1955	1956	1957	1958	1959	1960	1961	1958	1959	1960	1961
Net sales	$11,564	$12,269	$12,738	$13,005	$12,891	$13,527	$13,585	$14,065	$14,409	$16,717	$17,798	$18,490
Dividends from foreign subsidiaries	.....	.....	.....	.....	.....	29	22	25				
Miscellaneous income	47	25	25	51	102	150	71	88	109	165	86	109
Total	$11,611	$12,293	$12,763	$13,055	$12,992	$13,706	$13,679	$14,178	$14,519	$16,882	$17,884	$18,599
Costs and expenses												
Materials, labor and manufacturing expenses	5,706	5,779	6,034	5,944	5,960	6,361	6,434	6,598	6,844	8,039	8,584	8,724
Selling, general, and administrative expenses	4,629	4,936	5,150	5,657	5,516	5,618	5,731	6,100	6,007	6,818	7,467	7,970
Depreciation depletion, and amortization	194	179	205	237	258	237	232	266	274	302	362	409
Research and development	231	252	269	285	248	244	233	237	248	268	287	289
Interest paid	44	39	42	47	81	97	90	107	86	98	101	128
Provision for Federal and state income taxes	373	532	536	415	477	573	459	414	485	631	508	462
Minority interest in net income of subsidiaries	.....	.....	.....	.....	.....	7	8	7	49	71	58	59
Total	$11,177	$11,716	$12,236	$12,584	$12,539	$13,136	$13,186	$13,729	$13,994	$16,227	$17,367	$18,041
Net income for the year	434	577	660	471	454	570	493	434	525	655	517	522
Earnings retained in the business at beginning of year	1,811	1,895	2,137	2,564	2,799	3,015	3,348	3,550	2,789	3,077	3,495	3,722
Total	$ 2,245	$ 2,472	$ 2,797	$ 3,035	$ 3,253	$ 3,585	$ 3,840	$ 3,985	$ 3,314	$ 3,732	$ 4,012	$ 4,243
Cash dividends (parent)	193	254	233	236	237	237	290	324	237	237	290	324
Stock dividends	157	81	.....	.....	.....	.....	.....	.....	.....			
Earning retained in the business at end of year	$ 1,895	$ 2,137	$ 2,564	$ 2,799	$ 3,015	$ 3,348	$ 3,550	$ 3,661	$ 3,077	$ 3,495	$ 3,722	$ 3,920

exhibit 7 DIVERSEY CORPORATION AND SUBSIDIARIES

Consolidated balance sheets: fiscal years ending December 31, (000 omitted)

Assets	Parent Company with United States and Canadian Subsidiaries								Parent Company with World-wide Subsidiaries			
	1954	1955	1956	1957	1958	1959	1960	1961	1958	1959	1960	1961
Cash	$ 645.4	$ 590.4	$ 550.1	$ 470.6	$ 782.5	$ 542.1	370.7	$ 361.1	$ 971.4	$ 635.3	$ 431.9	$ 394.2
Marketable securities—at cost	203.6	117.1	148.8	....	77.6	....	....	....	77.6	....	....	....
Accounts receivable—less allowances	910.9	1,117.3	1,145.8	1,213.2	1,390.5	1,470.1	1,514.7	1,656.0	1,864.7	2,038.0	2,112.2	2,251.5
Inventories—lower of cost or market (finished product, raw materials, etc.)	1,461.2	1,775.0	1,646.4	1,747.5	1,690.7	1,856.1	1,813.0	1,739.0	2,206.1	2,503.3	2,835.5	2,829.7
Prepaid expenses	49.4	38.2	43.6	64.0	85.2	71.6	77.0	93.1	97.6	96.0	113.2	140.2
Total current assets	$3,271.3	$3,638.0	$3,534.8	$3,495.2	$4,026.5	$3,940.7	$3,775.6	$3,849.2	$5,217.3	$5,272.6	$5,492.7	$5,615.6
Investments in foreign subsidiaries and affiliates—at cost	$ 26.7	$ 180.8	$ 322.8	$ 555.8	$1,353.1	$1,317.6	$1,300.5	$1,322.9	$ 148.4	$ 144.7	$ 128.4	$ 169.7
Fixed assets (land, building, equipment) at cost	1,890.2	2,055.2	2,607.0	3,429.4	3,612.7	3,701.9	4,391.4	4,658.1	4,200.8	4,455.1	5,413.0	5,868.1
Less depreciation and amortization	782.8	924.9	1,091.6	1,309.8	1,542.7	1,747.8	1,924.3	2,126.5	1,587.7	1,848.3	2,127.2	2,407.6
Total fixed assets (net)	$1,107.5	$1,130.3	$1,515.4	$2,119.6	$2,070.0	$1,954.1	$2,467.1	$2,531.6	$2,613.1	$2,606.8	$3,285.8	$3,460.5
Goodwill and other intangibles	....	....	....	....	....	....	....	162.2	277.2	277.8	290.6	438.3
Total assets	$4,405.5	$4,948.1	$5,373.0	$6,170.6	$7,479.6	$7,212.4	$7,543.2	$7,865.9	$8,256.0	$8,301.9	$9,197.5	$9,624.0
Liabilities												
Bank loans	$ 165.4	$ 198.0	$ 249.3	$ 154.5	$ 809.0	$ 357.5	$ 225.7	$ 369.3	$ 847.1	$ 371.2	$ 446.9	$ 622.7
Amounts due within one year on long-term debt	100.0	100.0	100.0	36.1	158.6	135.2	135.7	128.3	162.1	135.2	141.0	131.7
Accounts payable	752.3	903.1	881.8	935.6	909.0	820.6	813.0	847.8	1,234.3	1,355.1	1,646.2	1,639.2
Dividends payable	48.3	101.5	77.6	78.8	79.1	79.1	79.1	81.5	79.1	79.1	79.1	81.5
Accruals—payroll general taxes	67.3	85.6	103.7	105.6	122.2	141.9	153.4	134.9	145.2	174.7	204.4	175.4
Accruals—United States and foreign income taxes	72.0	114.9	132.8	283.8	336.8	381.6	287.3	265.7	360.6	453.2	391.2	359.4
Total current liabilities	$1,205.4	$1,503.1	$1,545.2	$1,594.4	$2,414.8	$1,916.0	$1,694.1	$1,827.6	$2,828.3	$2,568.5	$2,908.8	$3,009.7
Long-term debt	$ 700.0	$ 600.0	$ 500.0	$ 800.0	$1,100.0	$1,000.0	$1,400.0	$1,300.0	$1,100.0	$1,000.0	$1,400.0	$1,300.0
Installment contract and mortgage payable				157.8	111.1	75.9	39.5	10.4	126.1	89.9	45.4	10.4
Deferred income on service contracts		22.8	77.5	62.4	51.3	48.8	31.9	21.2	51.3	48.8	31.9	21.2
Minority interest in subsidiaries					30.1	67.0	70.3	72.6	316.7	342.9	332.8	390.0
Capital stock—par value $1	253.7	258.7	258.7	263.6	263.6	263.6	527.2	543.2	263.6	263.6	527.2	543.2
Capital in excess of par value of shares	351.2	427.3	427.3	493.3	493.3	493.3	229.7	429.7	493.3	493.3	229.7	429.7
Earnings retained in the business	1,895.2	2,137.2	2,564.3	2,799.0	3,015.4	3,347.8	3,550.4	3,661.2	3,076.7	3,494.9	3,721.8	3,919.8
Total liabilities and net worth	$4,405.5	$4,948.1	$5,373.0	$6,170.6	$7,479.6	$7,212.4	$7,543.2	$7,865.9	$8,256.0	$8,301.9	$9,197.5	$9,624.0

ELECTRIC
STEEL
CORPORATION

The Electric Steel Corporation was organized in New Albany, Indiana, in 1949 for the purpose of producing and selling high-quality steel using the Dornin process.[1]

Mr. John Chambers, a prominent Indiana industrialist, formed the original group which formulated the plans for Electric Steel and engaged in the promotion and financing of the company by public subscription.

At the first stockholders' meeting, held in early 1950, Mr. Chambers was elected President and Chairman of the Board of the newly formed corporation. At the same meeting four of the founding group who held large blocks of the outstanding stock were elected, along with Mr. Chambers, to three-year terms as Directors of the company.

The original plans of the company contemplated financing and expenditures as shown in Exhibit 1.

Late in 1951 it became apparent to management that the estimates of financial requirements necessary to place the company in operation were inaccurate. The actual costs of construction and preparation of

---

[1] After the steel is melted in an electric furnace the specially formed ingots are worked in a forging press to give a grain structure which insures an unusually high quality of steel. The Dornin ingots weigh 3.9 tons in contrast with conventional ingots which weigh from 6 to 16 tons. The specially designed ingot and the press shop are the heart of the Dornin process. The other facilities are largely conventional for the production of electric furnace steel.

exhibit 1   **ELECTRIC STEEL CORPORATION**
Original financing plan

Financing

Funds provided by common stock (400,000 shares)	$ 88,825
3½% debentures due 1961 (subordinate)	4,000,000
Reconstruction Finance Corporation loan	8,556,126
Total	$12,644,951

Expenditures

Acquisition of land and construction of steel plant	$ 9,035,657
Electric power transmission facilities	491,000
Preliminary expenses	100,000
Interest on debentures through June 15, 1956	700,000
Estimated interest on RFC loan	75,000
Financing cost	250,000
Working capital	1,993,294
Total	$12,644,951

the plant and equipment for production proved to be substantially in excess of estimated costs. The plant was built on a 130-acre tract of land, four miles from New Albany, Indiana, along the Ohio River.

Difficulties and delays encountered in the construction of this plant, which was originally planned as a highly efficient electric-furnace producing unit containing the most modern and efficient equipment avail-

exhibit 2   **ELECTRIC STEEL CORPORATION**
Comparative income statements and selected ratios for the years ended July 31, 1956–1954

	1956		1955		1954	
	Amount	*Per Cent*	*Amount*	*Per Cent*	*Amount*	*Per Cent*
Net sales	$17,273,275	100.00	$10,788,114	100.00	$5,413,155	100.00
Cost of goods sold	15,110,763	87.50	9,473,617	88.00	5,940,094	109.70
Gross profit or (loss)	$ 2,162,512	12.50	$ 1,314,497	12.00	($ 526,939)	(9.70)
Selling, general and administrative expenses	$ 743,866	4.30	$ 719,649	6.70	$ 621,239	11.50
Other expense (income)—net	76,891	.40	40,452	.40	24,098	.40
	$ 820,757	4.70	$ 760,101	7.10	$ 645,337	11.90
Net profit (loss) before interest, depreciation and taxes	$ 1,341,755	7.80	$ 554,396	5.10	($1,172,276)	(21.60)
Depreciation	$ 516,019	3.00	$ 507,345	4.70	$ 430,753	8.00
Interest	621,897	3.60	621,188	5.70	582,606	10.70
	$ 1,137,916	6.60	$ 1,128,533	10.40	$1,013,359	18.70
Net profit (loss) before income taxes	$ 203,839	1.20	($ 574,137)	(5.30)	($2,185,635)	(40.30)
State and Federal income taxes	–o–	–o–	–o–	–o–	–o–	–o–
Net profit (loss) for period	$ 203,839	1.20	($ 574,137)	(5.30)	($2,185,635)	(40.30)
Net profit before interest charges	$ 825,736		$ 47,051		($1,603,029)	
Cost of sales to fixed assets		1.50		.94		.62
Inventory turnover		13.00		12.00		9.00

able in the industry, were mainly responsible for the increase in costs over the estimated expenditures.

After several unsuccessful attempts to acquire additional financing the Board of Directors decided to drastically revise their original plans for the mills in an effort to conserve the company's rapidly dwindling working capital. As a result, less efficient equipment than originally contemplated was substituted in many parts of the plant, and certain equip-

exhibit 3   ELECTRIC STEEL CORPORATION
Comparative balance sheets, July 31, 1956–1953

	1956	1955	1954	1953
Assets				
Current assets:				
Cash	$ 295,691	$ 284,198	$ 85,663	$ 1,521,672
Receivables—net	1,870,046	974,021	852,061	1,113
Inventories	1,351,680	956,147	625,325	691,385
Other current	70,000	87,500	114,978	–0–
Total current assets	$ 3,587,417	$ 2,301,866	$ 1,678,027	$ 2,214,170
Other assets:				
Restricted funds	–0–	$ 122,500	$ 262,500	$ 480,535
Cash surrender value insurance	–0–	11,480	8,089	4,760
	–0–	$ 133,980	$ 270,589	$ 485,295
Plant and equipment:				
Cost	$10,591,627	$10,258,701	$10,149,118	$ 9,500,823
Reserve	1,462,573	951,036	443,692	–0–
	$ 9,129,054	$ 9,307,665	$ 9,705,426	$ 9,500,823
Deferred charges:				
Preoperating expenses	–0–	$ 1,033,885	$ 1,033,885	$ 1,033,885
Other	$ 296,943	325,754	365,628	407,871
	$ 296,943	$ 1,359,639	$ 1,399,513	$ 1,441,756
Total assets	$13,013,414	$13,103,150	$13,053,555	$13,642,044
Liabilities				
Current liabilities:				
Notes payable	$ 5,081,453	$ 2,966,876	$ 2,214,276	$ 700,000
Accounts payable	1,402,916	1,226,167	1,073,750	989,407
Accrued expenses and interest	1,177,164	743,906	375,112	87,041
Total current liabilities	$ 7,661,533	$ 4,936,949	$ 3,663,148	$ 1,776,448
Long-term debt	$ 8,898,522	$10,837,148	$11,487,217	$11,776,771
Capital and deficit:				
Capital stock	$ 6,625	$ 6,625	$ 6,625	$ 6,625
Capital surplus	82,200	82,200	82,200	82,200
Deficit	(3,635,466)	(2,759,772)	(2,185,635)	–0–
	($ 3,546,641)	($ 2,670,947)	($ 2,096,810)	$ 88,825
Total liabilities	$13,013,414	$13,103,150	$13,053,555	$13,642,044
Working capital	($ 4,074,116)	($ 2,635,083)	($ 1,985,121)	$ 437,723
Increase (decrease) in working capital				
over prior year	($ 1,439,033)	($ 649,962)	($ 2,422,844)	$ –0–

ment included in management's plans to obtain maximum operating efficiency was eliminated.

The company did not produce steel until the fall of 1953 and the first shipments were made in December of 1953. The unanticipated delay in starting production and the operating difficulties encountered resulted in substantial losses in the first two years of operation. In the third year of operation the company made a profit. The financial results for this period are shown in Exhibits 2 and 3.

INDUSTRY TRENDS AND THE POSITION OF ELECTRIC FURNACE STEEL

As indicated in Exhibit 4, steel production has fluctuated greatly over the past 20 years, ranging from a low of 31,752,000 net tons in 1938 to

exhibit 4 **ELECTRIC STEEL CORPORATION**
Steel industry production by furnace type, years 1936–1955 (thousands of net tons)

Year	Total Production in U.S.	Open-hearth		Bessemer		Electric	
		Production, Tons	Per Cent of Total	Production, Tons	Per Cent of Total	Production, Tons	Per Cent of Total
1936	53,500	48,761	91.2	3,873	7.2	866	1.6
1937	56,637	51,825	91.5	3,864	6.8	948	1.7
1938	31,752	29,080	91.6	2,106	6.6	566	1.8
1939	52,799	48,410	91.7	3,359	6.4	1,030	1.9
1940	66,983	61,573	91.9	3,709	5.6	1,701	2.5
1941	82,839	74,390	89.7	5,577	6.8	2,872	3.5
1942	86,032	76,502	89.0	5,553	6.4	3,977	4.6
1943	88,837	78,622	88.6	5,626	6.3	4,589	5.1
1944	89,642	80,364	89.7	5,040	5.6	4,238	4.7
1945	79,702	71,940	90.3	4,305	5.4	3,456	4.3
1946	66,603	60,712	91.2	3,328	5.0	2,563	3.8
1947	84,894	76,874	90.5	4,233	5.0	3,788	4.5
1948	88,640	79,340	89.5	4,243	4.8	5,057	5.7
1949	77,978	70,249	90.1	3,946	5.1	3,783	4.8
1950	96,836	86,263	89.1	4,535	4.7	6,039	6.2
1951	105,200	93,167	88.6	4,891	4.6	7,142	6.8
1952	93,168	82,846	88.9	3,524	3.8	6,798	7.3
1953	111,610	100,474	90.0	3,856	3.5	7,280	6.5
1954	88,312	80,328	91.0	2,548	2.9	5,436	6.1
1955	117,036	105,359	90.0	3,320	2.8	8,357	7.2

SOURCE: American Iron and Steel Institute.
NOTE: Crucible steel production included with electric steel. All production of steel for ingots and castings included.

a high of 117,036,000 net tons in 1955. Both open-hearth and electric-furnace steel production reached a peak in 1955. Electric-furnace steel production in that year amounted to 8,357,000 net tons, or 7.2% of total production. This figure was double the average electric-furnace steel tonnage of the 1947–1949 period. The year 1955 was an exceptionally good year for the steel industry in general and market conditions for all types of steel were more favorable than they had been in any previous period, including the war years.

exhibit 5 **OPERATING RATES IN STEEL INDUSTRY PRODUCTION AS PERCENTAGE OF CAPACITY**

Year	Total All Types of Furnaces, %	Electric Furnaces, %
1946	72.5	46.6
1947	93.0	74.6
1948	94.1	93.7
1949	81.1	61.9
1950	96.9	87.9
1951	100.0	94.5
1952	85.8	82.6
1953	94.9	71.2
1954	71.0	52.0
1955	93.0	77.3

SOURCE: American Iron and Steel Institute.

The market for high-quality steels for which the electric steel plant was designed constituted a relatively small part of the total market for all grades and types of steel. This market, however, had shown a much more rapid growth than the industry as a whole. The trend in the industry pointed toward a continued expansion of the market for a great variety of high-quality steels which can be produced only in electric furnaces.

Despite its more rapid growth, electric steel production has been subject to greater fluctuations than the industry in general. As indicated in Exhibit 5, the operating rates for electric furnaces are significantly lower than the total indusry.

During periods of low demand for high-quality steels it is possible, although not always economically feasible, to use excess capacity of electric furnaces to melt carbon and low grades of alloy steel normally produced by the open-hearth process. However, electric steel producers seek to melt only higher grades of alloy and stainless steels for which their furnaces were designed. The costs of producing low-quality steels in electric furnaces far exceed the costs of melting these steels in open-hearth furnaces.

As shown in Exhibit 6, approximately 90% of all steel produced from

exhibit 6 FIVE-YEAR ANNUAL AVERAGES OF GRADES OF STEEL (IN THOUSANDS OF TONS)

Average	Total	Carbon	Alloy	Stainless
1941–1945	85,410	74,978	9,994	438
1946–1950	82,990	75,700	6,695	595
1951–1955	103,065	93,577	8,488	1,000

SOURCE: American Iron and Steel Institute.

1941 to 1955 was of the carbon variety. High-grade alloy and stainless steels, however, showed growth throughout this period. From 1946 to 1955 the production of stainless steel increased at a rate of approximately 8.6% annually while that of alloy increased approximately 2.7% per year.

Because of the wide fluctuations in annual production and the frequent low-capacity operations of electric furnaces, successful producers in this area of the industry are required to have special skills and resources. Their product line must provide an adequate profit in a normal market and their sales organizations must be capable of competitively securing and maintaining profitable accounts for their specialized products. It is necessary to establish a sound reputation in the trade as a quality producer with a prime rather than secondary source of steel. Production facilities are of paramount importance and must be capable of producing the quality, grades, types and quantities of steel that permit an adequate return on investment.

PLANT FACILITIES

The main plant of Electric Steel consisted of five connected buildings with a total area of 150,000 square feet, as indicated in the following exhibit.

Exhibit 7   PLANT AREA OF ELECTRIC STEEL

		Area in
	Buildings	*Square Feet*
	Melt shop	20,500
	Teeming or pouring shop	21,000
	Soaking pit and press shop	23,000
	Rolling mill, finishing and shipping	67,000
	Change house and motor room	18,500
	Total	150,000

In addition to the main plant the company had the following auxiliary structures on the plant site:

Electric sub-station

Open crane runway extension to melt shop and part of scrap yard

Laboratory

Plant office, storeroom and first-aid station

Acetylene generator station

Oxygen storage facility

In addition to the main plant and auxiliary structures, the company had storage areas for scrap, ingot molds, refractories, and other necessary operating supplies. There were overhead cranes in all of the main plant buildings except the change house and the motor room. There was no maintenance or machine shop; however, there was one general-purpose lathe and one roll lathe.

The 130-acre plant site was close to barge facilities of the Ohio River and had a direct connection with a railroad. The property was not fenced and losses from pilferage frequently occurred.

OPERATING EQUIPMENT AND THE PRODUCING PROCESS

The company had five major producing departments. The operations and the facilities of these departments were as follows (see Glossary of Terms on page 340).

The *melt shop* operation included the loading of scrap and charging to furnaces, melting, pouring ingots and stripping ingots out of molds. Two basic types of arc electric furnaces were used for melting the steel. Each furnace had a rated capacity of 60 tons per heat and actual heat weights averaged about 62 tons. The combined annual capacity of the furnaces was 242,000 tons. The capacity of the furnaces varied, however, with different product mix and with the various tap-to-tap heat times for the different analyses of the steels produced. Electric Steel produced as much as 180,000 tons of ingots annually. On a 6-day, 18-turn basis, producing high-quality steels only, the plant capacity was rated at 135,-000 tons of ingots annually.

The ingots were poured in Dornin molds and in conventional molds. The conventional ingots weighed from 6 to 16 tons and the Dornin ingots weighed only 3.9 tons. The conventional ingots, because of their weight, had to be stripped from the molds by a 75-ton pouring crane. A 10-ton crane was used for stripping the lighter Dornin ingots. Because of the lack of space in the plant, however, there was interference between the pouring operation and the stripping of Dornin ingots. This sometimes resulted in a loss of ingot heat and required additional soaking pit time.

The *soaking pits* of Electric Steel were arranged in two batteries, each with four pits and one stack. The soaking pits were used twice in the processing of Dornin steel, first to heat the ingots prior to the forging operation and second to heat the forged blooms for the rolling operation. The heating time required in each case was dependent upon the steel analysis and also on the heat retained in the entering ingot or bloom.

Two 10-ton cranes serviced the soaking pits and the press shop. The cranes were not of the stiff-necked variety specified for the soaking pit operation and consequently slowed operations and increased the time during which it was necessary to have the soaking pit covers opened. The building which housed the soaking pits, press shop, and hot scarfing operation was too short to allow more than one crane to reach the soaking pit and the scarfing operation at one time.

There was only one damper for each battery of soaking pits, which made it difficult to maintain the degree of heating practice control necessary for high-quality steel. There were no recuperators to provide preheated air. The recapturing of heat through recuperators would have reduced fuel costs. One of the eight soaking pits was usually out of service for routine maintenance.

The *press shop* consisted primarily of a 2,500-ton hydraulic upsetting press and a 1,500-ton forging press. In addition there were manipulators for the forging press, a transfer car, and a hot scarfing station.

The Dornin ingot was pressed into a pear shape on the upsetting press, with a small cylindrical projection left at the top in which nonmetallic inclusions were concentrated. The ingot was then forged into a 16-inch-square bloom on the forging press, after which it was hot-scarfed to remove the entire skin in most cases. After this process the steel was returned to the soaking pits for reheating prior to rolling.

The *rolling mills* consisted of a single-stand 24-inch, 2-high reversing blooming mill and a 24-inch billet and bar mill. The billet and bar mill had a 3-high stand and a 2-high stand driven off the same shaft. In addition the mill was equipped with a bloom shear, a transfer table between the two mills, and a cooling bed.

It was found after the early operations that the blooming mill manipulators were not conventional and as a result the roughing operation was slowed down. This factor also made it difficult to roll slabs.

The mills were only capable of reducing blooms, billets, and rounds (and some sizes of slabs) down to $3\frac{7}{8}$ inches. It was not possible to produce sheets or bars in smaller dimensions. This limitation prevented the company from reaching the major portion of the high-quality steel market.

The finishing and shipping facilities were located in an extension of the mill building. These facilities included pickle and wash tanks, grinders, power hack saws, chipping hammers, a billet straightener, three annealing pits, and three car-type annealing furnaces. The annealing equipment was used principally to control the rate at which alloy, high carbon, and large-section, lower-carbon billets and blooms cooled. This operation was necessary to obtain the desired qualities of strength and ductility in the steel.

The company made shipments mainly by rail and truck, with a minimum of shipments by water. The shipping and finishing areas were overcrowded and caused extra handling of most of the finished goods.

Production Problems. The specially designed Dornin ingot and the press shop are the most important factors in the Dornin process of producing steel. Without these distinct features the other facilities are largely conventional for the production of electric furnace steel. The pressing of the Dornin ingot into a forged bloom introduces a cost into the processing of steel that is not present in conventional production. This additional cost is offset partially by a higher yield from the ingot to the finished product. However, to be profitable it is generally conceded in the steel industry that the Dornin process must be applied to the maximum extent possible to high-priced, high-profit alloy steels.

The production of high-grade steel through this process requires that a high proportion of the volume produced be control-cooled after roll-ing. This requires that there be a proper balance between forging and rolling facilities and the finishing and controlled cooling facilities in or-der to produce a profitable product mix.

The conservation of heat in ingots and forged blooms is an important production factor which reduces the soaking pit heating time. The maximum travel distances of hot steel between melt shop, soaking pits, and press shop should not exceed 100 feet.

Retention of heat is important because if alloy steel ingots are allowed to cool unduly, they will crack. These ingots cannot be "banked" with-out slow cooling. The slow-cooling process requires that once an alloy melt has started, subsequent processing must follow in regular se-quence. Consequently, each process must be accurately timed and scheduled to allow for a relatively precise assembly-line-type of opera-tion. This requires a correlation of the capacities of all the production processes.

In consideration of its production difficulties Electric Steel Corpora-tion hired a firm of engineering consultants in the fall of 1956 to make an analysis of its technical operations and particularly its capacity lim-itations. The analysis of the consulting firm is shown in Exhibit 8. The capacity analysis indicated that the slow-cooling facilities constituted the company's primary bottleneck in its attempt to produce high-priced, high-profit alloy steels. Only 29% of Electric Steel's melting capacity could be slow-cooled. The soaking pits were the cause of the secondary bottleneck. The capacity of the pits was only 84% of melting capacity. The excess of melting capacity over soaking capacity amounted to 2,392 ingot tons. The excess of soaking pit capacity over slow-cooling capacity was estimated at 6,412 tons per month.

It was estimated by the consulting firm that it would require approxi-mately $3.5 million to correct the unbalanced production facilities. This figure did not include supplementary finishing and shipping facili-ties, which would also be required.

SALES AND PRODUCT MIX

Exhibit 9 shows the sales of Electric Steel Corporation by dollar vol-ume and grades from 1954 to 1956. The company substantially in-creased sales volume in this period to where approximately 12,500 tons were shipped monthly. This was accomplished only by running on a

exhibit 8 ELECTRIC STEEL CORPORATION

Summary of analysis of Present facility capacity

Capacities	Tons Shipped per Month
Slow-cooling:	
Aircraft steel	1,500
Alloy steel	1,820
Total	3,320
Soaking pits:	
Aircraft steel	1,500
Alloy steel:	
Slow-cooled	1,820
Air-cooled	607*
Carbon and shell steel	5,805
Total	9,732
Press shop	9,732†
Mill	9,732†
Melt shop:	
Aircraft steel	1,500
Alloy steel	2,427
Carbon and shell steel	5,805
Excess	1,888‡
Total	11,620

Potential Product Mix at Capacity Operation	Tons Shipped per Month	Tons Shipped per Year
Product:		
Finished products		
Aircraft steel	1,500	18,000
Alloy steel		
Slow-cooled	1,820	
Air-cooled	607	
	2,427	29,124
Carbon and shell steel	5,805	69,660
Total	9,732	116,784
Ingots	2,392§	28,704
Total	12,124	145,488
Capacity ratios:		
Slow-cooling capacity to melt shop capacity	29.5%	
Soaking pit capacity to melt shop capacity	83.7%	

* Assumption that 75% of total alloy volume would be slow-cooled and that 25% would be air-cooled.
† Based on present operation of 14 turns per week. Could be increased materially with up to 21 turns per week.
‡ This is an excess melting capacity in terms of finished tons, including processing yields.
§ Excess melt shop tonnage converted to ingot tons.

exhibit 9 ELECTRIC STEEL CORPORATION

Net sales by grades of steel, 1954–1956 (in thousands of tons and millions of dollars)

Year	Period	Gross Sales (Less Freight)		Ingots		Total Finished		Commercial Carbon		Shell		Alloy*		Aircraft	
		Tons	Dollars	Tons	Dollars	Tons	Dollars	Tons	Dollars	Tons	Dollars	Tons	Dollars	Tons	Dollars
Total	1954 fiscal	53.1	$ 5.7	-0-	-0-	53.1	$ 5.7	N.A.	N.A.	N.A.	N.A.	N.A.	N.A.	N.A.	N.A.
Total	1955 fiscal	105.0	10.9	5.0	$ .3	100.0	10.6	25.0	$2.4	59.0	$5.8	16.0	$2.4	†	†
1956	1st quarter	35.8	3.8	8.7	.6	27.1	3.2	7.0	.7	11.7	.3	7.4	1.0	1.0	$ .2
1956	2nd quarter	37.7	4.3	11.7	.9	26.0	3.4	14.1	1.5	2.4	.3	7.5	1.1	2.0	.5
1956	3rd quarter	38.0	4.5	8.0	.7	30.0	3.8	15.7	1.7	5.0	.6	7.2	1.1	2.1	.5
1956	4th quarter	39.0	4.7	10.2	.9	28.8	3.8	9.4	1.12	10.4	1.2	6.9	1.0	2.1	.5
Total	1956 fiscal	150.5	17.3	38.6	3.1	111.9	14.3	46.2	5.0	29.5	3.4	29.0	4.2	7.2	1.7

N.A. = Not Available.

* Includes a small amount of miscellaneous sales.

† Included in alloy sales.

7-day, 21-turn basis. The increase in sales for the fiscal year 1956 was largely due to increases in carbon and ingot sales.

Ingots were first offered for sale by Electric Steel in June of 1955 in an effort to use excess melting capacity over that required for finished production. In 1956, 25.6% of the tonnage and 17.6% of the dollar volume of total sales were obtained from sales of ingots. All of the ingots that were sold were shipped to other mills for conversion to finished products.

While the Electric Steel plant was not designed to produce commercial carbon steel, the company produced as much as 40% of its total output in this grade in one quarter of 1956 and averaged over 30% of total output in the fiscal year. Because of strong market conditions in the second half of 1955 which carried over into 1956, Electric Steel was able to raise its price on carbon steel $9 a ton over the former going market price and add $7 per ton for freight charges which the company previously absorbed. These two factors enabled the company to realize in 1956 approximately $705,000 more than would have been possible in a normal steel market.

The sale of commercial carbon steel, however, proved to be the least profitable of all the grades sold. Exhibit 10 shows the gross profit per

exhibit 10   ELECTRIC   STEEL   CORPO-
RATION
Gross profits by grade of steel, 1956

	Gross Profit per Ton
Grade of Steel	
Carbon	($ 1.33)
Shell	10.63
Alloy	14.36
Aircraft	49.21
( ) Denotes loss.	

ton for the grades produced based on the company's standard cost system.

The production of shell steel by Electric Steel Corporation varied from nothing to 6,846 tons monthly. The average monthly sales in 1956 amounted to 2,460 tons. The company did not anticipate increased sales of shell steel in the next year of operation because of the closing of a number of ordnance plants and the reduction in the production schedule of others. The demand for this type of steel fluctuated greatly, since it was dependent upon the placement of government contracts.

The 1956 sales of high-quality steels for which the Electric Steel plant was designed accounted for 36,000 tons, or 25% of the total output. This amounted to 34% of the total dollar volume. In 1956 the company sold alloy steel, other than aircraft, for an average net price of $145 per ton. This price compared with the going market price for open-hearth quality steel, and was $20 a ton less than competitive electric furnace steel.

The equipment of Electric Steel Corporation limited it to the production of semi-finished products such as blooms, slabs, and billets. While these grades and forms of steel represented the most profitable products of the company, in the industry as a whole they accounted for only 10% of the alloy steel market. In 1956 there was no indication of the trend toward increased industry sales of alloy steel in these forms. In the preceding years blooms, slabs, and billets accounted for less than 10% of total alloy steel sales. Generally these forms of alloy steel were subject to greater fluctuations in sales than the industry as a whole. Specialty steels, particularly stainless steel and heat-resistant alloys, provided the most profitable and growing market. Up to 1956 Electric Steel had not entered this market.

The company sold all of its commercial products through 9 commission sales agents, with the exception of ingots which were sold by the Vice President of Operations, Mr. Dietrich. Shell steel was considered as a direct sale by the company since agents were not paid a commission for the sale of this grade and the bulk of the sales were made by company representatives. The agents had offices located in the following principal cities: Chicago, Illinois; Indianapolis, Indiana; Cleveland, Columbus, and Cincinnati, Ohio; New York; Philadelphia and Pittsburgh, Pennsylvania; New Haven, Connecticut; Tulsa, Oklahoma; Houston, Texas; and Los Angeles, California.

The remainder of the country not covered by agents, including the Detroit area, was covered by two employees of the sales department. The company formerly had contracts with agents covering Alabama, Detroit, Wisconsin, and St. Louis but canceled them in 1955 because management considered their performance unsatisfactory.

In 1956 a small number of agents accounted for the bulk of commercial sales. Sales were made to 123 customers and 65% of sales were made to 13% of the customer list. Two of the customers accounted for approximately 22% of total sales. The sales of the other 8 agents ranged from 0.2 to 9% of commercial sales, excluding ingots. Electric

Steel representatives made sales direct amounting to approximately 5.5% of sales, excluding ingots and shell steel. Shell steel sales accounted for 21% of commercial sales, excluding ingots.

The sales expenses of Electric Steel, as shown in the following exhibit, have been a small and declining part of total expenses of finished steel sales.

exhibit 11   **ELECTRIC STEEL CORPORATION**
Distribution of sales expense as a percentage of finished steel sales, fiscal years 1954–1956

	1954	*1955*	*1956*
Total selling expense	$ 142,988	$ 252,621	$ 320,199
Finished product sales	5,685,304	10,410,941	14,320,000
Expense as % of sales	2.426%	2.426%	2.236%
Breakdown of selling expenses:			
Salaries	19.22%	6.47%	7.47%
Travel and entertainment	14.80	5.01	5.11
Advertising	2.19	.02	.03
Payroll tax and insurance	.93	.27	.44
Commissions	62.58	87.83	86.86
Other	.28	.40	.09
Total	100.00%	100.00%	100.00%

As indicated in Exhibit 11 the agents' commissions constituted the principal part of selling expenses. They received commissions of 3% on alloy sales, 2½% on carbon bar, and 2% on all semi-finished carbon steel, but were not paid for any sales of shell steel.

ORGANIZATION

The organization chart of Electric Steel Corporation is shown in Exhibit 12. Mr. Chambers, one of the company's founders, was President and Chairman of the Board. Mr. Chambers was 65 years of age and had some 30 years of experience as an executive of one of the country's largest steel producers and was a member of the Board of Directors of several companies located in Indiana. Through several years of experimentation, Mr. Chambers developed what he considered to be satisfactory working relationships with his executive group. All department managers, with the exception of plant personnel, reported directly to him.

Mr. Chambers spent a good part of his time in attempting to establish the reputation of the company as a producer of high-quality specialty alloy steels employing the Dornin process. Because of initial difficulties

exhibit 12
ELECTRIC STEEL CORPORATION
Organization Chart, 1956

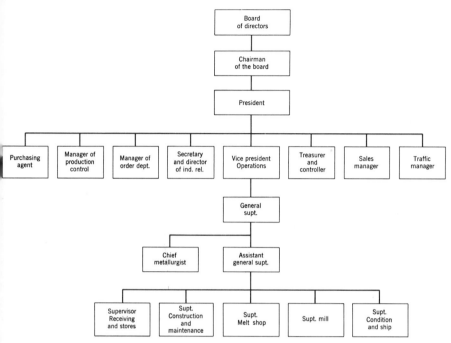

in getting the organization under way, he also found it necessary to spend much of his time on financial matters. The problem of utilization of plant capacity he considered necessary to the company's survival and as a result he felt that he frequently was forced to be "a peddler of steel in all its forms."

Because of the pressure of what Mr. Chambers termed "keeping the ship afloat," he found that he did not have the opportunity to spend as much time with his executive group as he thought was necessary. Mr. Dietrich, the Vice President of Operations, usually acted as the chief executive during Mr. Chambers' absence.

Mr. Chambers felt that his operating executives were very competent and resourceful individuals. He also expressed his confidence in his middle management group and department heads. He stated that they had frequently proved their competence by maximum utilization of the company's incomplete production facilities. He also frequently referred to the report of a personnel appraisal made by a management consulting firm which stated that the company "had been able to attract and retain higher-caliber personnel than could be reasonably expected under the circumstances." The report also stated that "the manufacturing organization had done a good job with the available equipment and facilities and had displayed considerable imagination in maintaining a schedule with the limited funds available for facilities and replacements."

Mr. Davis, the General Sales Manager, was 46 years of age. He had been brought into the company by Mr. Chambers to organize and develop a sales organization along the lines of a prominent specialty steel producer which had employed Mr. Davis as an Assistant Sales Manager. In addition to Mr. Davis, the sales organization was made up of an Assistant Sales Manager, a Traffic Manager, and nine commission sales agents.

Mr. Simmers was the Treasurer and Controller. He was 52 years of age and had previously worked for a large public accounting firm as well as a large steel producer as a head of an auditing section. Mr. Simmers installed a cost system, a sales and financial control system along the lines of the steel firm where he was formerly employed. His systems and handling of the Treasurer-Controller's function were frequently praised by both Mr. Chambers and Mr. Dietrich.

Mr. Dietrich occupied the important position of Vice President of Operations. He had 20 years' experience in various capacities with a producer of electric furnace steel. He was General Plant Superintendent when he left his previous company to come to the Electric Steel Corporation. Mr. Dietrich was 58 years old, and was considered in the industry to be a capable production man.

The other members of the executive group ranged from 34 to 57 years of age with an average age of 46. With the exception of the Purchasing Agent, who was with the company at the beginning of operations, the service of the other members averaged approximately 2 years.

FINANCIAL POSITION

Early in 1957 Mr. Chambers and Mr. Simmers expressed concern about the working capital problems of Electric Steel. They pointed out that companies similar to theirs in the industry considered minimum working capital requirements to be 15% of current sales. In 1956 six of the more successful electric furnace producers of specialty steels had from 15 to 38% of current sales in working capital and the average of the 6 producers was 24%. Mr. Chambers was of the opinion that if sufficient working capital could be obtained the day-to-day operations would eventually take care of themselves. He frequently pointed out that the original financing of the company placed it in a strained position from which it had never fully recovered. However, he felt that progress was being made and cited the 1956 profit figures as evidence of the company's potential.

The financial results for the first 3 full years of operation of the company are shown in Exhibit 2. Comparative balance sheets from 1953 to 1956 are shown in Exhibit 3.

GLOSSARY OF TERMS[2]

Annealing Heating steel and holding it at a suitable temperature followed by cooling at a suitable rate, with the object of improving machinability and coldworking properties.

Banked A charged furnace which is allowed to cool at a slowly diminishing rate until cold.

Billet A semi-finished product of a blooming or billet mill, either square or rectangular in section, and having a maximum cross-sectional area of 25 sq. inches.

Bloom Semi-finished products hot rolled from ingots and rectangular in shape with a minimum cross-sectional area of 25 sq. inches.

Heat One complete operation of a furnace from charging to tapping.

Pickling The process of chemically cleaning the surface of a metal object in preparation for further working.

Rolling mill In its simplest form a rolling mill consists of two rollers, one above the other, turning at the same speed, but in opposite directions so that the metal is drawn into them. Its purpose is to flatten metal objects.

Roughing The first phase of rolling or hammering a white hot ingot into blooms or slabs.

Scarfing The process of cutting out thin defective surface areas of ingots usually by the use of the oxy-acetylene method.

Skin A thin surface different from the main mass of a metal ingot.

Slab A semi-finished hot rolled product worked down from the ingot following the stage of the bloom but distinguished from the billet by its flat section. It has a minimum thickness of 1½ inches and a width generally more than twice the thickness.

Soaking pit A vertical reheating furnace for uniformly heating ingots to the temperature required for rolling.

Teeming The pouring of molten steel from the ladle into ingot moulds.

Turn A term denoting the amount of equipment utilization; i.e., a 7 day, 21 turn is necessary for maximum equipment utilization.

[2] *An Encyclopedia of the Iron and Steel Industry,* The Technical Press, London, 1956.

SEALED-FRESH
COMPANY

"In my opinion, our main problem today is getting consistency of earning power," said Mr. John A. Drake, president of Sealed-Fresh Company, in September of 1961. His company produced and sold fresh chilled orange juice to a 9-state midwestern area with the Detroit area as the major market.

"We are as conscious as anyone of the value of long-term goals," he went on. "Yet again and again we have consciously chosen courses of action which have had long-term detrimental effects to achieve short-term advantages. We have done so because at the time our reserves were so thin that we could not have taken the short-term disadvantage and survived as a corporation. This has been partly because of the industry we're in and partly because of our financial position. Important long-range objectives have on occasion received lower priority than the long-range goal of corporate survival."

With fresh chilled orange juice as its main product the company was vulnerable to crop failures and the subsequent price fluctuations for fresh oranges. For example, the freeze in Florida during the winter of 1957 had a profound effect on fruit prices of the orange crop of 1958–59 with prices increasing more than 400%.

Mr. Drake felt that as a practical matter, it was impossible to pass on all of the increased cost of raw material due to hurricanes and freezes in the selling price. He noted that products of inferior quality, including orange drinks and orangeades, were produced and sold at prices equal to or below their price before such events occurred. "It is apparent to us," Mr. Drake continued, "that the consumer is confused. What are these orange products in the dairy display case? Are they juice or drinks? Are they diluted? Are they freshly-squeezed oranges, or reconstituted frozen concentrate? This confusion and ignorance make it difficult for us to get the premium price to which we are entitled for our high quality product."

He remarked that the company management was working under constant pressure due to limited financial resources. Management believed that continued diversification into other food product lines would ease its problems and stabilize profits. "Our primary niche in the food industry will be the production and distribution of refrigerated (approx. 35°F) food products," Mr. Drake stated. Orange juice, he said, is basically a commodity, facing the intense competition and low profit margins common to such products. Sealed-Fresh intended to diversify into high quality, high priced "recipe" products which gave the consumer the benefits of labor saving plus skillful and exclusive seasoning, blending, cooking, etc. "I am convinced," said Mr. Drake, "that our management skill will make it possible for us to do a better job than our competitors in this area."

The company's first step in the diversification program was the acquisition in May of 1960 of Nitti Frozen Foods, a producer of frozen pizzas and hamburgers, and it was in the process of investigating the possibilities of acquiring other food companies. Sealed-Fresh produced other refrigerated products such as grapefruit juice, lemonade, two kinds of orange drink, pineapple-grapefruit drink, fruit salad, gelatin salad, potato salad, cole slaw, and bulk orange juice. However, the sales volume of these products amounted to less than 10% of the total sales and the contribution to profit was negligible. (See Exhibit 1.)

COMPANY BACKGROUND

Sealed-Fresh Company was formed on October 15, 1956, by consolidation of three interlocking chilled juice operations. The three predecessor companies, jointly managed by the same people, had encountered financial difficulties. The former president, who had a reputation for being a very competent salesman, had demonstrated little financial and organizational ability. Consequently, despite sales growth to approximately $1.1 million, the 1956 operations were unprofitable. The sizeable operating losses which the former management incurred resulted in part from heavy overhead and the lack of financial controls.

exhibit 1   SEALED-FRESH COMPANY
Sales analysis by type of product for typical summer week

Type of Product	Cases	Amount
Sealed-Fresh orange juice	14,430	$51,484
Private brand orange juice	235	815
Total Orange Juice	14,665	$52,299
Grapefruit juice	124	399
Sealed-Fresh lemonade	581	1,354
Private brand orange drink	285	699
Private brand lemonade	204	738
Sealed-Fresh fruit salad (quarts & pints)	52	283
Sealed-Fresh gelatin salad	177	528
Sealed-Fresh potato salad	170	499
Sealed-Fresh cole slaw	67	199
Nitti pizza (11″, 12″, & 14″)	172	2,344
Private brand herring	70	376
Private brand bulk orange juice (in gallons)	300	303
Private brand (dairy) orange drink deliveries	18	11
Total		$59,932

As financial problems increased, the former president was able to raise small amounts of funds from friends and associates, including suppliers. In addition, loans approximating $500,000 were made from several banks, the major participant being a state bank in a neighboring state. When bankruptcy appeared certain, the creditors turned to several investment bankers for assistance in raising funds through the flotation of a stock issue. However, most investment bankers were not interested because of the poor financial condition of the three companies. Finally, Sealed-Fresh turned to the Daniel L. Taylor Company, a Detroit investment banking house, for help. At first the Taylor Company was not interested, but when the state bank asked the Taylor group to try to work out a solution, it reluctantly agreed to attempt to reorganize the company.

Under the refinancing arranged by Mr. Taylor and the group of investors he represented the following arrangements were made:

1. Certain creditors, holding claims of $48,500 and $51,000 respectively, modified their claims and agreed to receive payment at the specified rate of 1/4¢ or 1/2¢ on each quart of orange juice sold by the company; other creditors, with claims aggregating $535,000, agreed to accept contingent certificates having no rights other than to participate in the earnings of the company to the extent of 50% of the net income in excess of $100,000 per fiscal year.

2. In exchange for the sum of $258,000, Sealed-Fresh on February 19, 1957, transferred to the Reiter Company, owned by Mr. Taylor and the group of investors he represented, substantially all of the real estate, machinery and equipment owned by Sealed-Fresh in Florida and Detroit, Michigan.

3. The Reiter Company immediately leased back the facilities to Sealed-Fresh for a term of ten years, at a monthly rental of $3,300 for the first sixty months, and $1,400 a month for the remaining sixty months.

4. Sealed-Fresh issued and transferred to the Reiter Company new common stock amounting to 51% of the total outstanding Sealed-Fresh common stock, for a cash payment of $22,500.

In order to protect its investment, the Taylor group immediately brought in Mr. John A. Drake as president of Sealed-Fresh. Mr. Drake, who was in his early thirties, had been a co-partner in an investment brokerage business with Mr. Taylor for several years. Mr. Drake had also successfully operated his own furniture and gift store in a suburban community of Detroit.

From the period of consolidation, October 15, 1956, through March 31, 1957, the company incurred an operating loss of $141,500, the bulk of which was sustained prior to February 1, 1957, the date when the new management took over. For the balance of the fiscal year ending September 28, 1957, the improvement in operations reduced the operating loss to $112,000. (See Exhibit 2.)

On December 4, 1959, a group of investors loaned Sealed-Fresh $65,000, receiving in exchange 8% subordinated convertible debentures due in 1964. This enabled the company to settle the contingent certificates by issuing 11,000 shares of common stock making a cash payment of $47,000, and issuing a promissory note for $165,000 due February 4, 1961. At the end of January, 1961, Sealed-Fresh issued an additional $65,000 of 8% convertible debentures due in 1965 and obtained a commitment for a loan of $100,000 from a Detroit bank, contingent upon the acquisition of the Reiter Company. On January 27, 1961, Sealed-Fresh purchased the Reiter Company by issuing 25,800 shares of $10 par, 8½% convertible preferred stock. The bank made the $100,000 loan and the $165,000 due the holders of the former contingent certificates was paid in full on February 4th.

With the acquisition of the Reiter Company Sealed-Fresh replaced an annual lease charge of $39,600 with a preferred dividend requirement of $21,950. The dividend requirement, although cumulative, was payable only if earned and, under the bank agreement, had to be earned better than four times on an annual basis before being paid. (See Exhibit 3.)

exhibit 2   SEALED-FRESH COMPANY
Income statements, 1957–1961, fiscal years ending September 30 (in thousands of dollars)

	1957	1958	1959	1960	1961
Net sales	$1,873	$3,021	$3,292	$2,978	$3,557
Cost of goods sold	1,392	2,104	2,394	2,095	2,451
Gross profit	$ 481	$ 917	$ 898	$ 883	$1,106
Selling, administrative and distribution expenses	593	801	893	973	1,048
Operating profit (loss)	$ (112)	$ 116	$ 5	$ (90)	$ 58
Other income	111*	6	1	24	15
Other expenses	27	23	—	18	55
Net earnings (loss)	$ (28)	$ 99	$ 6	$ (84)	$ 18
Special item:					
Provision for payments due creditors of predecessor corporations under deferred payment agreements	7	20	22	16	11
Net increase (decrease) to surplus	$ (35)	$ 79	$ (16)	$ (100)	$ 7

* Includes gain on sale of fixed assets of $103.

exhibit 3 **SEALED-FRESH COMPANY**
Balance sheets, 1957–1961, fiscal years ending September 30 (in thousands of dollars)

	1957	1958	1959	1960	1961
Current assets					
Cash	$ 19	$ 37	$ 19	$ 5	$ 44
Accounts receivable—net[1]	107	141	164	180	200
Inventories	69	120	68	107	106
Prepaid expenses	31	23	34	47	69
Total current assets	$226	$321	$285	$339	$ 419
Fixed assets—at cost					
Land, building, trucks and equipment	270	336	408	479	820
Less accumulated depreciation[1]	95	128	168	210	236
	175	208	240	269	584
Leasehold improvements—less amortization	56	59	63	56	8
Total fixed assets	$231	$267	$303	$325	$ 592
Other assets					
Deferred charges	36	36	25	42	48
Goodwill purchased	—	—	—	14	14
	36	36	25	56	62
Total assets	$493	$624	$613	$720	$1073
Current liabilities					
Notes payable to bank[1]	—	—	15	54	111
Current maturities of notes and obligations payable	100	137	63	202	77
Accounts payable—trade	39	52	106	171	199
Accrued liabilities	41	30	34	43	29
Total current liabilities	$180	$219	$218	$470	$ 416
Noncurrent liabilities					
Notes payable (collateralized by certain equipment)[1]	27	40	46	37	76
Notes payable to bank	—	—	—	—	45
8% convertible debentures due 1964[2]	—	—	—	65	65
8% convertible debentures due 1965[2]	—	—	—	—	65
4% subordinated note due 1964	—	—	—	22	22
Obligations payable to former contingent creditors—less current maturities	—	—	—	17	10
Total noncurrent liabilities	$ 27	$ 40	$ 46	$141	$ 283

[1] Notes Payable to Bank. Accounts receivable and inventories together with a chattel mortgage on certain assets in Florida are pledged as collateral for loans in the amount of $155,300 under an agreement dated January 27, 1961. At September 30, 1960, accounts receivable of $75,100 were pledged as collateral.

[2] 8% Convertible Debentures. At the option of the holders, the 8% convertible debenture bonds may be exchanged for common stock of the Company at any time prior to maturity on the basis of one share of common stock for each $1 of par value of the bonds.

exhibit 3 (continued)

	1957	1958	1959	1960	1961
Stockholders' equity					
8½% cumulative convertible pref. stock[3]	—	—	—	—	258
Common stock	61	61	61	70	70
Additional contributed capital	260	256	256	107	107
Retained earnings (deficit)	(35)	48	32	(68)	(61)
	286	365	349	109	374
Total liabilities and capital	$493	$624	$613	$720	$1073

[3] 8½% Cumulative Convertible Preferred Stock. The certificate of incorporation was amended to include the authorization of 50,000 shares of $10 par value preferred stock. This stock shall receive preferential cumulative dividends and is convertible to the common stock of the company at one share for each $1 of par value of the 25,800 shares of preferred stock issued and outstanding.

DIVERSIFICATION

"The chilled orange juice industry is a fairly new industry. It can be traced back only to 1952," said Mr. Drake, "but still it has passed the stage in its growth curve when the demand was skyrocketing, and it has now appeared to level off. It requires very little capital and skill to enter this field."

He went on to say that many people saw a chance to make quick money. The industry in 1961 was over-crowded with companies. Several of them had already been forced to go out of business and many of those which were left were on the verge of bankruptcy. It was the goal of Sealed-Fresh to become one of the survivors. Management strongly believed this aim could be achieved through a constant improvement of its merchandising and distribution skill. "We are now in a position to pick up those who fail," Mr. Drake continued. "The pressure on profit margins is severe and several of the companies I have talked to are considering selling out. Most of the owners, however, are still hopeful and want to wait and see." Mr. Drake was convinced it was only a question of time before some of them would have to sell.

Despite management's confidence in the future of the orange juice division in the long run, it did not want to put all its eggs in one basket. Violent price fluctuations of the raw material due to hurricanes and freezes could probably never be avoided. Management was constantly looking around for other companies with related product lines with which to merge. "Our financial position," said Mr. Drake, "is such that we cannot at the present time buy any good successful company. We have to search for 'sick' companies where we believe our better management skill can improve their earning power."

Three criteria had to be fulfilled before Sealed-Fresh would consider a merger with another company:

1. If possible, there should be an economic overlap in marketing and/or production with its present operation.

2. It had to be a food product, but a refrigerated recipe product rather than a commodity.

3. The product should move in reasonably good tonnage.

Several companies had been turned down because their product lines, such as fish and artificial cream, did not have enough tonnage. Sealed-Fresh preferred to seek a small specialized share of a big market rather than to fight for a large share of a small market. In this respect, further penetration of the egg and potato market was considered to be attractive with annual sales of $400 million, but Sealed-Fresh had not been able to find any suitable prospects in this area.

The acquisition of Nitti Frozen Foods in the spring of 1960 followed after an aggressive search. Nitti Frozen Foods produced and sold frozen pizzas and hamburgers in the Detroit market and had an annual sales volume of $400,000. The Sealed-Fresh management realized that any immediate economic overlap between the two companies would be of minor importance. Management felt, however, that many of the problems facing the pizza market were similar to those in the juice market and that the merchandising skill they had developed in their own business could be of value in reshaping Nitti into a profitable operation.

THE MARKET FOR CHILLED ORANGE JUICE
AND ORANGE DRINKS

The Detroit area was the company's major market. Since its product was highly perishable, Sealed-Fresh aimed for a 500-mile radius of the Detroit area. Delivery had to be limited to one or two days of the product's expected shelf-life of about 14 days. Consumption of orange juice and drinks was highest in urban areas. The competition within Detroit was intense. Differences in price and quality between various brands were significant. The Sealed-Fresh product was the

highest priced brand in the market, selling at retail for 43¢ a quart.
In the summer of 1960 a major chain outlet introduced its own private
brand, which sold at 29¢ per quart. The competitor who packaged
this private brand also produced another brand which retailed at 25¢
per quart in a second chain. In addition, the A&P brand was priced
at 29¢ per quart, and the remainder of Sealed-Fresh's competition in
the Detroit area included at least six other brands, most of which sold
from 25¢ to 35¢ per quart. Sealed-Fresh also had to meet competition
at the consumer level from various brands of frozen concentrated
orange juice and orange drinks.

Concentrated juice accounted for 75% of the total orange juice and
orange drink consumption in Detroit. It was priced at retail at about
20¢ per can. A reconstituted can of concentrated juice provided ¼
less juice than a quart of fresh chilled orange juice. Fresh orange juice
accounted for 16% of the total market while orange drinks had the
remaining 9%. There was a larger price spread between various
brands of chilled juice in the Detroit area than in the rest of the
country. It was recognized in the trade that large quantities of juice
were marketed in Detroit. According to figures compiled by Market
Research Corporation of America, the average price for the whole
country in August, 1961, for fresh chilled orange juice was 41.5¢ a
quart. (See Exhibit 4.)

A Detroit newspaper maintained a panel of families in the metropolitan area who kept diaries of their purchases of various food and
drug items. A study of these records was undertaken by Sealed-Fresh's
advertising agency. (The highlights of the findings are shown in
Exhibit 7.)

Market information similar to this about regional markets was not
available. According to Mr. Reynolds, director of marketing, the
study in itself did not reveal much new information, but primarily
confirmed previous general estimates of management. He admitted,
however, that he was surprised at the small population base for consumption of chilled orange juice. Also, the high turnover among
people who tried chilled orange juice and then went out of the market
disturbed him. He felt this might be due to special price offers in
various stores during the year, making people switch on a temporary
basis from tomato juice, grape juice, etc., or other forms of orange
juice, and when the price offer was over they went back to their
original consumption patterns. He believed that those few families

exhibit 4
CHILLED ORANGE JUICE
Consumer Purchases and Prices Paid

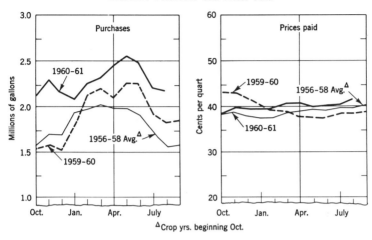

△ Crop yrs. beginning Oct.

FROZEN CONCENTRATED ORANGE JUICE
Consumer Purchases and Prices Paid

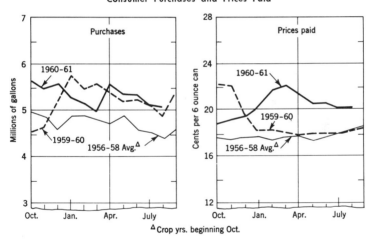

△ Crop yrs. beginning Oct.

SOURCE: U.S. Department of Agriculture, Economic Research Service.

who were regular users of chilled orange juice did so for the sake of convenience more than any other reason. A carton could be always at hand in the refrigerator and the housewife did not have to bother about opening a can and diluting the contents. The better taste of the chilled juice would also be a factor of importance, he felt, among more discriminating consumers.

SALES PATTERNS

Sales climbed to $3.3 million in fiscal 1959 from $3.0 million in fiscal 1958. Profits, however, dropped from $99,000 to $5,700, due primarily to higher fruit prices. The company lost approximately $50,500 during the first quarter of fiscal 1959, and earned approximately $56,000 during the last nine months of the fiscal year.

In the fall of 1959, management was optimistic about the near future. The new crop was being harvested at lower prices and it was quite evident that the total crop for the coming year would be considerably larger. The citrus concentrate industry had on hand the highest inventory in its history. Operations were expected to prove very profitable. More aggressive competition was expected, however, especially from competitors who would enter the company's marketing area for the first time.

The expected profitable operations failed to materialize. Sales dropped back to $2.9 million in fiscal 1960 and resulted in a loss of $84,000, of which the frozen food operation accounted for $14,900. The loss sustained by the parent company took place primarily over an 8-week period in May and June as a result of an increase in the price of oranges of more than 100%. In addition, several companies entered the industry during 1959 and attempted to secure a share of the market on the basis of low prices. To compound the problem, the principal competitors of Sealed-Fresh reduced their prices. By August, 1960, as some competitors went out of business and others withdrew from the midwestern market, the company again started to earn money. Sealed-Fresh increased prices on three occasions in the fall of 1960. Sales totaled $3.6 million in fiscal 1961, and profits amounted to $18,000. (See Exhibit 5 for an analysis of sales for a typical summer week during fiscal 1961.)

The company's share of the chilled orange juice market in Detroit had slipped from 60% in 1958 to 25% in 1961, due to the many brands introduced by competitors during the 4-year period. On the other hand, the company made substantial gains in sales to regional markets outside Detroit in 1960 and 1961.

"Of course, we will try to reverse the trend in Detroit," said Mr. Reynolds, "but I do not think our primary goal should be to recapture all of our lost market share in Detroit. In our type of business, with an easy entry and increasing acceptance of the product category by the trade, it is probably uneconomic to attempt to retain a 60% market share in a major market. Although we are always working to convert users of other chilled juice brands to our product, thus increasing our market share, absolute volume is more important than percentage of the market." Management was of the opinion that the major source of added consumption (i.e., extra sales) would be found in converting a small portion of the users of frozen concentrate. If promotions and advertising with this objective helped competitive chilled juice brands to some extent, Sealed-Fresh was confident that it would get more than its normal share of the new business.

The chilled orange juice industry, in the opinion of Sealed-Fresh officials, had done a very poor job of merchandising, advertising, and sales promotion in the past. They maintained that the consumer was confused. She was not fully aware of the differences in quality, quantity, etc., received for the higher price paid. Sealed-Fresh considered that it was its responsibility to inform and educate the public within the financial resources the company had available. "Sometimes, even if it sounds contradictory," said Mr. Reynolds, "I wish we had another high-grade competitor in the market, promoting broader usage of quality chilled orange juice as we try to do."

The Detroit City Sales Force. By September, 1961, the company had 18 trucks on the streets in Detroit handling store delivery. Each truck was operated by a driver-salesman. The system was similar to that used by major soft drink companies. The duties of a driver-salesman included: (1) soliciting accounts, (2) delivery, (3) collecting, (4) arranging displays, (5) rotating the stock, (6) fighting for cooler display space.

"Our route sales force has a reputation of being one of the best in the city," said Mr. Reynolds. "We need more routes, but the present profit margins do not permit this. To keep ahead of competition and maximize sales it is desirable to service most stores at least twice a week. City traffic and the number of accounts have grown to such an extent that this has become difficult with the existing number of routes. In addition, the introduction of the pizza line and the push we have given it has left less time for the driver-salesman to solicit new juice accounts. The driver-salesmen are members of the Teamsters' union, and are paid a union base salary plus 10¢ for each case of juice sold. They are guaranteed a minimum salary but there is no maximum."

Mr. Reynolds also stated, "The question of store delivery is a chronic problem in the industry. Many chains prefer warehouse delivery, while the union favors store-door delivery. Most dry shelf and frozen items are handled through the chain warehouses. On perishables such as orange juice, warehouse delivery gives lower initial costs to the supplier, but the store-door method affords better opportunity for in-store merchandising of the product and careful control of stock rotation. Sealed-Fresh has been generally successful in selling chain headquarters on the net advantage of store-door service, although the issue is always cropping up." (See Exhibit 5.)

exhibit 5	SALES ANALYSIS BY TYPE OF OUTLET FOR TYPICAL SUMMER WEEK

Area and Outlet	Orange Juice, %	Other, %
Detroit		
Corporate chains	14.7	16.9
Voluntary chains (cooperatives)	4.9	14.3
Independent stores	20.9	67.5
Dairies	25.9	—
Institutions	0.2	—
Total Detroit	66.6	98.7
Regional		
Total Regional	33.4	1.3
Grand Total	100.0	100.0

The Regional Sales Managers. "Soon after joining the company in January, 1960," said Mr. Reynolds, "I became convinced that our best growth potential was in the regional markets within a 500-mile radius of Detroit. These markets had been less developed for chilled juice than Detroit or major eastern metropolitan markets. Competition is primarily from Florida packagers, but is by no means as fierce as in Detroit. More than 500 miles west the population density becomes too low for profitable distribution of a perishable product, and on the east coast Florida producers with excess capacity and a large stake in holding the markets would fight back with the lowest possible prices."

In 1960 the Detroit area accounted for 76% of the company's total sales and the regional markets for 24%. Mr. Reynolds stated that the company's goal was to have more than 50% of total sales from its regional markets. In Mr. Reynolds' opinion the somewhat lower mark-up required by regional market retailers and the lower wage levels would more than offset the added freight cost to these areas. Sales in the regional markets were made through dairies which in turn delivered the juice to retail stores and direct to homes.

In fiscal 1961 the sales outside Detroit accounted for 32% of the company's total sales and Mr. Reynolds expected it to be 40% in fiscal 1962.

exhibit 6 COMPARISON OF SALES BETWEEN DETROIT AND REGIONAL MARKETS (FOR FISCAL YEARS 1960, 1961, AND 1962)

	1960	1961	1962*
Detroit	76%	68%	60%*
Regional	24%	32%	40%*

* Estimated.

"We constantly look for more imaginative merchandising methods," said Mr. Reynolds. "Our toughest marketing problem is to work effectively through a typical dairy organization and reach the consumer. A dairy wholesale route driver can earn as much as $15,000 a year. Orange juice to him is a secondary product to milk and can add little to his commission income. Yet, good store display is important to our sales, and it is highly desirable to keep track of juice which is about to exceed its expiration date and pull it from the stores. A consumer who gets old juice probably will not touch the product again for a long time. To get dairy drivers' cooperation in these tasks is difficult. The home delivery drivers are not so highly paid, but are generally moving too fast to cover their routes to be effective face-to-face salesmen for an individual item in their line."

"One step that helped us a little," continued Mr. Reynolds, "was to move the regional sales managers out of Detroit to live in their territories. Two of the regional sales managers were moved from Detroit and stationed in Pittsburgh and Indianapolis, and a new man was hired for northern Ohio. The dairies were pleased over having company representatives in their local areas. Six months after the moves were made a significant increase in sales was noticed in each of the districts affected."

Mr. Reynolds was very pleased with the regional sales force. He thought they were highly motivated men. He did not need to push them. "As a matter of fact," he remarked, "they are pushing us constantly, asking the home office for more and better working tools to be able to do a better job."

The Pittsburgh Market. In an effort to expand its sales the company entered the Pittsburgh area which was approximately one-third the size of the Detroit market. It had no entrenched competition and its potential appeared large enough to support a company route sales force similar to the one in Detroit. Most people in the industry felt it was impossible to take away the store delivery from the dairies and still get their cooperation in home delivery. They were convinced that Sealed-Fresh would not succeed in such an attempt. However, after one year of preselling the dairies on the idea, the latter agreed to let in the company's own route sales force and they agreed to continue to handle the home delivery for the company.

By October of 1961 Sealed-Fresh had five trucks on the streets in Pittsburgh handling orange juice and pizzas. After four months of operation it was still in the red. Mr. Reynolds expected it would take an additional six months before the company started to make money in the area. Sealed-Fresh had attained fair distribution but sales per store were low compared to Detroit. Ideally, the metropolitan area covered would require at least eight trucks instead of five to give proper service. The initial surveys undertaken indicated a promising outlook because of a lack of orange juice in the stores. But it was not fully realized until later the extent to which poor service by the dairies had ruined the store market. The consumers and the grocery trade had lost confidence in the product.

Marketing Proposal for Fiscal Year 1961–62. In his budget for the fiscal year 1961–62 Mr. Reynolds set forth as a major objective:

> to arrest and reverse the long-term sales decline of Sealed-Fresh brand orange juice in the Detroit market, by (1) increasing Sealed-Fresh's share of the chilled orange juice market, and (2) broadening the consumption base and volume of chilled orange juice.

The proposed plan called for an over-all increase in sales of 28% (from 790,000 cases in 1960–61, to 1,015,000 cases in 1961–62; each case contained 12 quarts). Sealed-Fresh's share of the chilled orange juice market was to be restored to over 30%. The objectives were to be accomplished through a combination of lower retail prices and increased advertising and promotion expenditures. A key element in the proposed budget was the assumption of a large, hurricane-free, freeze-free, Florida crop which would result in significantly lowered product cost.

Although management could not predict the danger point, it was certain that it had to reverse the sales trend in Detroit before it lost its dominant position in that market. Management further believed that if the Detroit market declined far enough it would become more attractive to a Florida producer for another invasion. Another reason for the recommendation was that Sealed-Fresh had never really tested what could be done by an effective 12-month campaign.

According to the marketing plan, the retail price would be reduced on October 1, 1961, from 43¢ per quart to 39¢. Past experience had shown that a retail price below 40¢ per quart could cause a significant increase in the company's sales volume. During the fall of 1960 Sealed-Fresh had been able to keep a retail price of 39¢ per quart, supported by extensive advertising and promotion. A substantial gain in sales was noticed. Unfortunately, the cost situation resulting from hurricane damage to the fruit crop forced Sealed-Fresh to increase the price to 43¢ per quart. In spite of the fact that the advertising and promotion program was carried on for an additional two months after the price increase, the sales volume dropped immediately about 15%. Furthermore, in one chain outlet where the price of competitors' products had been kept at 25¢ per quart, the differences in volume between chilled orange juice and concentrated orange juice were noticeably smaller than in other stores. "The present cost and profit situation does not actually justify a price reduction," said Mr. Reynolds, "but it has to go along with the proposed advertising program in hope that increased volume will make up the difference."

Estimated total advertising and promotion expenditures amounted to $263,000, or 7.8% of projected orange juice dollar volume of $3,360,000. This was substantially greater than the 6.6% rate spent in fiscal 1961 and the 6.4% and 4.3% spent in fiscal years 1960 and 1959 respectively.

RAW MATERIAL SUPPLY

Three sources of supply of freshly extracted orange juice were available to Sealed-Fresh. The supply could be drawn from Florida, California, or Texas. The Florida market was the most important, accounting for 70% to 80% of all oranges grown in the U.S.; California and Arizona accounted for 15% to 20%, Texas and Louisiana for the rest. The company had made it a policy to get its juice primarily from Florida and California. The Texas market was not used unless a shortage of fruit occurred in the other markets.

In Florida three principal crops could be distinguished. The early season started in mid-September and ended in November; the mid-season started in December and ended in mid-February, and the Valencia season lasted from mid-March to mid-June. Over this period of time the supply of oranges varied substantially. The peaks came normally during two six-week periods in January and May when 4 to 5 million boxes of oranges were moved per week as compared to the low in March when only 400 to 500 thousand boxes were moved per week. About 20 large producers of frozen concentrated orange juice usually did their buying during the two six-week peaks, when the fruit had its highest quality. They accounted for more than 65% of all purchases made and had a strong influence upon the market price. Sealed-Fresh and other chilled orange juice producers did their Florida buying over a 39- to 42-week period.

During the California Valencia season—which started in mid-May, reached its peak in August, and ended in October—Sealed-Fresh bought freshly extracted juice from California. However, since California oranges at this time of the season had a much higher acid content, the Florida oranges with low acid content were blended with the California oranges during the summer periods.

A very large percentage of all oranges from Florida were handled by grower-owned cooperatives, with the growers getting 75% of the price on delivery and the rest at the end of the season. The remaining "free market" fruit could be bought under three different contracts:

1. A spot cash price

2. A bulk contract (on a fixed date in the future the buyer agreed to buy all fruit produced by a certain orchard at a fixed price, regard-

less of quantity of fruit. The buyer took all the risks for freezes, hurricanes, etc.)

3. A future price contract (on a fixed date in the future the buyer agreed to buy a certain number of boxes at a fixed price per box)

In trying to avoid speculative profits or losses the Sealed-Fresh management had decided to buy on a day-by-day spot-price basis. It hoped to average out during a 5-year period. Only 10% of the orange crop in the state was sold on the free cash market. The company had so far been buying from broker-dealers (so called "bird-dogs") who moved about 12 million boxes a year. Sealed-Fresh was in this market for approximately 280,000 boxes per year.

The company faced three difficult periods during each year in the months of March, June, and September, when the fresh Florida fruit was immature and in short supply. In these periods it became vital to have concentrate at hand for blending. Concentrate had to be purchased during the peaks of the season. A decision about buying had to be made 3 to 6 months ahead, taking into account the expected future price, the start of the season which could vary from year to year, and the anticipated future sales volume of Sealed-Fresh. Management felt this to be the most important decision to be made in the company and very risky. "We can be the best managed company in the industry," said Mr. Haines, who together with Mr. Drake handled the buying of raw material, "but still lose money on a large scale depending upon how we choose to buy." The effect of a concentrate buying decision could be several times the normal operating profit for a year—for better or worse.

PRODUCTION AND PLANTS

The company operated two plants—one in Detroit from which it distributed its product to grocers and dairies, and one in Florida, where the juice was extracted and readied for shipment to Detroit.

The Florida plant operated 40 weeks of the year and employed 10 people, 2 of whom worked for the company the year around. The others were seasonal workers, mainly local housewives, who were glad to get an extra job at $1.25 per hour. The working hours varied between 8 hours per week early in the season to 60 hours per week during the peak season. The work involved was fairly simple. The oranges were carefully selected and passed through a series of cleansing processes before the machinery processed them. A perforated tube entered the orange from the bottom and a squeezing device came down from above. The juice was forced into the tube and drained away. It passed through a pulp remover and then, before it was chilled, it was subjected to six seconds of 186° temperature which arrested chemical change without disturbing the flavor.

Immediately thereafter it was chilled to about 28° to 30°F. and shipped in special trucks or rail tank cars which brought it to Detroit with a gain of not more than 5 degrees in temperature. There it was blended, packaged, and trucked out to stores and dairies. The Detroit plant employed 19 people, 8 of whom were involved in packaging, 5 in the warehouse, 4 in maintenance and sanitation, and 2 in quality control.

The Detroit plant could at most keep a "half a day" inventory which made proper delivery scheduling important. The company leased seven rail tank cars and two trucks for the shipments between Florida and Detroit. The trucks were more flexible but also more expensive than the rail cars. One problem that had been facing management was to find a reliable railroad. After several switches between various companies they finally felt they had found the "right" railroad. Despite the fact that the juice was transported 300 miles out of the way to get to Detroit from Florida, the delivery was faster than ever before.

NITTI FROZEN FOODS

Mr. Nitti started his business in 1954 and was one of the earliest producers of frozen pizzas in the Detroit market. By 1960, because of easy entry, the market was overcrowded with producers. Around 300 pizzerias of one kind or another, most of them restaurants, were competing for the consumer dollar in Detroit. Many were also supplying neighborhood grocery outlets, competing on a price basis selling frozen pizzas for 39¢ to 69¢ at retail. The profit margins were low and there was an average of one bankruptcy every month. Because of consumer taste preferences, there was much switching between brands. Most producers operated locally. The total market for pizzas in the U.S. was estimated at $50 million a year in 1960.

On May 1, 1960, Sealed-Fresh purchased Nitti Frozen Foods. The purchase price consisted of $15,500 in cash, Sealed-Fresh's $22,000 4%

subordinated four-year note, and 66,667 shares of Sealed-Fresh common stock. In addition, Mr. Nitti was given a two-year employment contract with Sealed-Fresh.

Prior to the purchase by Sealed-Fresh, Nitti frozen pizzas were sold from 39¢ to 49¢ at retail and the business was dependent primarily on two chain accounts and one large distributor. After the deal was closed it was found that since the fall of 1959 Mr. Nitti had been losing accounts, among them the National Foods account. In addition, in several stores where his product had been the only brand, there were now three or four other brands. Until October 29 of 1960, Nitti Frozen Foods was conducted as a division of the parent company and thereafter as a wholly-owned subsidiary company. Mr. Nitti had difficulty adjusting to the new philosophy of the Sealed-Fresh management and resigned from the business in June, 1961. Mr. Drake took over as general manager for the pizza division and assigned Mr. Haines as sales manager and Mr. Wayne as production manager, both from the parent company.

The Sealed-Fresh management soon became convinced that it was impossible to make a good tasting pizza selling from 39¢ to 69¢ at retail. At this price the cost of the crust and package became significant and left little room for good ingredients and a profit. It believed in an entirely different approach to the market which would avoid direct competition from low-priced items. Consumers had the opportunity of ordering good-tasting pizzas from restaurants at a price of $2 and up. "We see ourselves as the 'Sara Lee' of the pizza business," said Mr. Haines, "marketing a good tasting, high quality, high priced product, sold through grocery stores."

A market test was made in the summer of 1960 to find out what kind of pizza the public wanted with respect to price, size, and taste. Six items were introduced: two sizes, 14 and 12 inches in diameter, each either with cheese only, cheese and sausage, or cheese, sausage, and mushrooms (deluxe). From sales experience the number of items were cut down and in September of 1961 only two items were marketed —a 14-inch deluxe combination pizza and a 12-inch sausage and cheese pizza.

The high expectations placed by the food industry upon frozen foods in the early 1950's had not materialized. It had been forecast that by 1960 the frozen food business' share of the total food market would be 10%. The figure realized was closer to 5%, which had an effect upon the traffic passing the frozen foods displays in the stores. Sealed-Fresh intended to introduce and concentrate its operations on refrigerated pizza instead of the frozen variety. Management contended that refrigerated pizza could be placed in the dairy display in the store together with such items as eggs and milk, which were not impulse items and thereby avoid direct competition from other frozen food specialties.

The refrigerated line of pizzas accounted for more than 50% of the total Sealed-Fresh pizza business in September of 1961. The 14-inch deluxe pizza was sold at retail for $1.59 and the 12-inch sausage and cheese for $1.09. At the end of the summer of 1961 the company decided to expand pizza sales from local distribution within Detroit to a regional market including the same states as their market for chilled orange juice. The refrigerated pizza had a shelf-life of only six days, which required a fast turnover to keep down returns. Furthermore the large pizza, which accounted for a big share of the total sales, appealed particularly to lower-middle income families to whom it represented a complete meal. This had taught Sealed-Fresh to hand pick stores for distribution; the Nitti pizza was sold only in half of the stores of the major food chain in the Detroit area.

By September of 1961 the sales force of the pizza division consisted of Mr. Haines who handled the one major chain account in Detroit and was soliciting the others. Sealed-Fresh's largest account for pizzas had to be cleared through the central offices of the food chain for all 1,400 stores supervised by its midwest division. Mr. Haines intended to market frozen items in smaller cities and the refrigerated ones in larger cities. In addition, Mr. Haines was soliciting frozen food brokers outside Detroit, and Mr. Saxon, vice president, special sales, handled a certain number of major pizza accounts in Detroit along with his key orange juice accounts.

When Sealed-Fresh entered the Pittsburgh market it expected the pizza business to be secondary to chilled orange juice. Up to October of 1961 the reverse was true. At that time, management was also aiming for store-door distribution in the Chicago market with their refrigerated pizza. This market was twice the size of the Detroit market and had similar characteristics from a social-economic point of view. No refrigerated pizza was marketed in the area. Because of many failures the chains and the distributors were reluctant to try a new brand. Mr. Haines, however, was hopeful that he could offer them something new and get their cooperation. The company would then use its own trucks for delivery, and he estimated sales of $300,000 to $500,000 annually in the Chicago area.

When the large pizza first was introduced in the Detroit market it was sold at $1.40 retail; it became a success and the management raised the price to $1.59, which had no noticeable effect on sales. Management planned to enter the Chicago market with a $1.69 retail price for their deluxe pizza, which included an allowance for merchandising.

In promotion and advertising the company used mainly in-store promotion and price specials. Sales had been very responsive to the latter. For example, in July, with 20¢ off, sales increased 31% above the average for the preceding time period, and again in September with 10¢ off, sales showed an increase of 208%. This led Mr. Haines to suggest that a "10¢ off" promotion on the 14-inch pizza and "7¢ off" on the 12-inch pizza should be scheduled once during each six-week period commencing October 23, 1961, subject to an analysis of the results.

When Sealed-Fresh took over Nitti Frozen Foods, management realized that rigid quality control in production would be a key factor. Most complaints from consumers concerned the taste. With the high quality, high priced items that the new management intended to market, this control became even more important. This was an area of disagreement between Mr. Nitti and the new owners, and one of the reasons that led to the former's resignation from the business. The new man put in charge of production of pizzas was a graduate food technologist who had supervised the quality control of the juice division.

Pizza production consisted mainly of hand operations primarily performed by a work crew of 40 women and 3 male supervisors. Because of limited plant capacity, proper production scheduling was of significant importance. In October of 1960 an extra night shift had to be added to keep pace with production demand.

In October, 1961, Mr. Haines in commenting upon the operation, remarked that "sales had doubled since the same period last year and should approximate $560,000 for the 1961 fiscal year." He went on to say that "despite this good showing, we did not make any profit this year. Our present operation requires an average sales volume of $11,000 per week to break even. Sales have slacked off the past few months, but this is customary in this kind of business in the summer months." He stated further that he expected sales to grow to $1 million in 1962 and that he was confident that the business would become profitable from then on. He also pointed out that the company was seeking to buy other pizza producers in order to get their trade accounts. In addition, the company was searching for other recipe food products selling above $1 at retail to extend its product line. As an example, Mr. Haines mentioned fresh fruit pies. "Originally five producers of fruit pies had operated in Detroit," he said. "Today, only two are operating."

CORPORATE DEVELOPMENT

"To fill a vacancy," said Mr. Drake, "I would prefer to have a man with both brains and experience. If, for any reason, I cannot fill a job with a man possessing both, I would much rather choose a man with brains. Given time, the man with the brains will gain the experience." By 1961 Mr. Drake felt that he had gathered around himself a management team which, as a group, was comparable in quality to that of any company the same size. The average age of the management group was approximately 35 years.

In October, 1961, Mr. Drake, in addition to being the president of Sealed-Fresh, was in charge of production and acted as general manager for Nitti Frozen Foods. When Sealed-Fresh bought the latter company it was assumed that it could be run as a division and use a minimum of existing management's time. After Mr. Nitti resigned, management decided there was no longer any need to run the pizza operation as a subsidiary and it was brought back as a division of the Sealed-Fresh Company.

Mr. Drake strongly believed in giving as much freedom of action as possible to his management team. The officers met every two or three weeks to get away from day-to-day operations and discuss the long-term prospects of the company. Mr. Drake tried to schedule his activities in advance but found this difficult to do. In his opinion the need for a general manager for Nitti Frozen Foods had diminished after he had brought in his own people to take charge of production and sales, but on the other hand he realized the need for a man in charge of production of the orange juice division. Despite his belief in giving his subordinates independence of action, he found himself involved, because of the weak working capital position of the business, in assignments that preferably should have been carried out by others.

FUTURE PROSPECTS

Sealed-Fresh officials expected the orange juice business to continue to be competitive. They considered the long-term outlook for success to be enhanced by the fact that the major component of cost—oranges —was showing a downward trend. Many young orange trees had been planted in Florida in the past few years. In time the trees would contribute to an ever-expanding crop. Examination of the available data indicated that projected crops were increasing at a faster rate than population. Barring freezes or hurricanes, management expected this would lead to considerably larger orange juice sales because lower orange prices would lead to lower retail prices of orange juice. They expected the retail price to come down to 27¢ to 35¢ per quart by 1964, reducing the price spread between frozen and chilled juice to about 5¢ per quart on an adjusted quantity basis.

Mr. Drake contended that the expansion of the orange division would come primarily from consolidation with other orange juice companies and less from internal growth. Mr. Reynolds expected that the future distribution system would include company route sales forces in four to six key metropolitan areas within a 500-mile radius of Detroit. In those areas the company would probably keep branch warehouses for distribution to the dairies in the surrounding territory. This arrangement had been tried in Pittsburgh and found to be more profitable than the older method of having semi-trailers leave from Detroit to visit each dairy in the rural areas. Locations considered next in line for company route sales forces were Indianapolis and Cleveland. Sealed-Fresh also had plans to reach outside the 500-mile radius of Detroit by selling through dairies in New Orleans, Memphis, Houston, Fort Worth, and Dallas. Initially, the company planned to make shipments to these areas out of Detroit.

Sealed-Fresh also expected very rapid expansion in the pizza division through enlarged consumer acceptance and better coverage of distribution outlets within the Detroit area. The pizza division, according to Mr. Drake, had a larger potential than the juice division. He pointed out that steps had been taken to streamline pizza production. "With the introduction of automated equipment," said Mr. Drake, "we foresee the possibilities of increased productivity significantly greater than what can be accomplished in the production of orange juice."

Another company official remarked that the heavy returns from stores during the first year had substantially reduced profit margins, but that great strides had been made to standardize the quality of the product. In addition, efforts had been made to increase the shelf-life of the pizzas to 10 days or more. He emphasized that in view of the bright expectations for the pizza business, taste surveys were constantly being undertaken to find out consumer preferences, and that the management had decided to concentrate on this product in the immediate future.

exhibit 7   ORANGE JUICE CONSUMPTION PATTERNS AMONG THE FAMILIES IN A DETROIT CONSUMER PANEL
Highlights from a study undertaken by Sealed-Fresh's advertising agency

A. *Consumption of Orange Juice and Drink*
   1. Usage of orange juice and drink is almost universal among families in Detroit. Of the 258 families, 86% bought some orange juice and drink during the two year period.
   2. Incidence of purchase is higher among upper income and larger families but is over 70% in every population subgroup.
   3. While incidence of purchase is high in all groups, the rate of consumption varies markedly by group. The highest consumption rate occurs among upper income families ($8,000 and over) and larger families (five persons and over). Upper income families are 27% of the panel and consume 39% of all orange juice and drink. Larger families are 26% of the panel, and they account for 40% of all orange juice and drink consumption.
   4. As is the case with many products, a small segment of the population accounts for the bulk of the orange juice and drink consumed. Heavy users (those who used more than 6.5 quarts a month on the average) make up 9% of the panel and account for 44% of all orange juice and drink consumed. Medium users (2.6–6.5 quarts a month) make up 19% of the population and account for 36% of total consumption. Together, these two groups are 28% of the population and account for 80% of all consumption.
   5. Heavy and medium users of all orange juice and drink account for the bulk of each of the types of orange juice. They account for 72% of all Sealed-Fresh consumed, 72% of all chilled juice, 82% of all concentrated juice, and 79% of all chilled drink.
   6. Heavy users tend to be large, upper income, native white families.
   7. Concentrated juice is the dominant type of juice both in the incidence of use and in the heaviness of use:

exhibit **7** (continued)

73% of panel families tried concentrated juice in the two year period and they consumed an average of 54 quarts per family. Concentrated juice accounted for 75% of total orange juice and drink consumption.

8. Chilled juice ranks far behind concentrated juice in importance. While 48% of families tried chilled juice they consumed an average of only 17 quarts per user family in the two year period. Chilled juice accounted for only 16% of all orange juice and drink consumption.

9. Chilled orange drinks were tried by 25% of families who used an average of 18 quarts per user family in the two year period. Chilled drinks accounted for 9% of all orange juice and drink consumption.

B. *Changes in Usage of Orange Juice and Drink Between 1959 and 1960*

1. There was a total increase in the consumption of orange juice and drink between 1959 (September 1958–August 1959) and 1960 (September 1959–August 1960). Total quarts consumed rose 20%.

2. The expansion of the total market for orange juice and drink was due exclusively to an increase in the consumption of concentrated juice which rose 27% while chilled juice increased only 3% and chilled drink decreased 4%.

3. While total consumption of chilled juice did not change sharply between 1959 and 1960, the market was not a static one. While 34% of families used chilled juice in 1959, 12% dropped out of the market in 1960. These were counterbalanced by 14% who began to use chilled juice in 1960, making a total of 36% of users in 1960.

4. The monthly consumption of chilled juice was higher in the summer months than in the winter months in 1959 but the gap was eliminated in 1960.

C. *Usage of Chilled Juice*

1. Chilled juice constitutes a relatively small percentage of the total orange juice and drink market. While 48% of all panel families tried some chilled juice in the two year period, chilled juice accounted for only 16% of all orange juice and drink consumed.

2. The key group of heaviest users of chilled juice (consumers of 64 quarts or more) make up only 3.4% of all panel families but account for 57% of all the chilled juice used. An additional 3.4% accounted for an additional 18% of all chilled juice. Thus, 6.8% of families consumed 75% of all chilled juice.

3. Heavy users of chilled juice tend to use chilled juice rather than other types. Among families that consumed 63 quarts or more in the two year period, 80% of all their orange juice and drink consumption was chilled juice. Among fairly heavy users of chilled juice (17–63 quarts) chilled juice accounted for more than half their consumption. These findings indicate that chilled juice is directly competitive with other types of juice (particularly concentrated).

exhibit **7** (continued)

4. The heaviest users of chilled juice also tend to be heavy users of all orange juice and drink. These families tend to be larger families with higher incomes. They are of particular importance in the chilled juice market because their heavy use accounts for a high percentage of total consumption of chilled juice.

5. Home delivery was not very important among families that were the heaviest users of chilled juice who accounted for 57% of total consumption. Among these families, only 15% of all chilled juice consumed was home delivered.

D. *Usage of Sealed-Fresh*

1. Usage of Sealed-Fresh shows the same pattern as usage of all chilled juice. While 32% of families tried the brand, Sealed-Fresh accounted for only 6.5% of all orange juice and drink consumed.

2. Although Sealed-Fresh plays a relatively minor role in the total market for orange juice and drink, it plays a major role in the chilled juice market. Two thirds of all chilled juice users tried Sealed-Fresh in the two year period and Sealed-Fresh accounted for 40% of all chilled juice consumed.

3. Families that tried Sealed-Fresh generally had a high level of experience with other types during the two year period; 64% used other brands of chilled juice, 81% used concentrated, and 36% used chilled drink.

4. Sealed-Fresh has a higher share of market among heaviest users of chilled juice than among people who use less chilled juice.

5. A small group of families—2.1%—accounted for 57% of all Sealed-Fresh consumption.

6. Upper and middle income families account for a disproportionately high proportion of Sealed-Fresh consumption.

LANDMASTER, INC.

"The American project," said Mr. John H. Smeddle, president of Landmaster, Inc., the American subsidiary of Landmaster Ltd., London, in April, 1962, "originated with the natural desire of the management of Landmaster Ltd. for an export market so that the company could produce in larger volume."

Landmaster Ltd. manufactured farm implements specializing in rotary tillage equipment. At the end of 1959, after an extensive survey of the U.S. market made by Mr. Smeddle, the company decided to form an American subsidiary and introduce into the U.S. market three sizes of rotary tillers: The Mark 80, for small garden, lawn, and horticultural work; the Mark 150, for truck gardening, large lawn work and similar jobs; and the Mark 650, a 65-inch tractor-mounted, pto-powered [1] rotary tiller with either two- or three-point hitch for large field work. (See Exhibits 2, 3, and 4.)

Although roto-tilling as a tillage process was a commonly known practice by 1959, most farmers and gardeners still used the age-old traditional method of the moldboard plow, discs, and harrows. In the U.S. there had been recurring waves of interest in roto-tillers for several decades, but despite the apparent advantages and efficiencies of this type of equipment it had not found general acceptance among farmers. The small two-wheeled tractor type had, however, developed some popularity among gardeners and home owners.

In commenting on the operations in early June, 1962, Mr. Smeddle remarked, "Our business here has changed in character from what we

[1] pto: power take-off

originally planned. We expected the small machines, Mark 80 and 150, would become the money spinners. However, we faced unfortunate timing in introducing them to the market in the middle of a recession. The big machine, Mark 650, on the other hand, aroused great interest from the beginning and has so far taken all our time and energy."

LANDMASTER LTD. AND THE FIRTH CLEVELAND GROUP

Landmaster Ltd. was a member of Firth Cleveland Ltd. of London, England, known as the Firth Cleveland Group, a holding company which held control of 75 companies. The development of the Firth Cleveland Group had been the lifelong undertaking of Mr. Charles W. Hayward, a prominent English industrialist, who was chairman of the Board. "Our objective," said Mr. Hayward, "was to combine an entire group of companies to merge their individual skills, combine research, testing, and marketing facilities, and maintain a system of quality control that would extend from the production of raw materials through the manufacture of finished products."

The Group had plants and sales offices in 111 countries with 15,000 employees, and annual sales totaling $100 million. It operated steel and lead mills, produced a wide range of products (specialty nuts and bolts, electronic and radar instruments, computing machines, farm machinery, vulcanizing equipment), and in addition operated about 600 retail stores in England selling radio and television receivers, electric appliances, house and home furnishings, and toys.

The interest of Firth Cleveland in the manufacture of roto-tillers stemmed from the personal inclination of Mr. Hayward to extend his activities to the manufacture of agricultural implements. At the end of the 1940s, Mr. Hayward purchased Landmaster Ltd., then a small producer of tillers making only two models and no tractors. Under the new management Landmaster developed the Gardenmaster (Exhibit 5), a 1½ horsepower two-wheeled tractor tiller which gained considerable acceptance in England. It also developed several heavier models which were sold at home and abroad.

In their manufacturing activities the Firth Cleveland companies endeavored to pool their resources. The Landmaster staff was free to buy from any supplier it chose, following the rule of buying from the most advantageous and the most economical source. The purchase of all components and parts was submitted to the open market consideration of make or buy, with Firth Cleveland companies being given the right of first refusal. It was estimated that the majority of the component parts of Landmaster were made within the Firth Cleveland Group.

Landmaster's average production showed a reasonable upward trend toward satisfactory levels until 1956. At that time Landmaster came out with new models, a new management group took office, and a new export policy was developed in an attempt to expand sales.

THE IMPLEMENT INDUSTRY IN ENGLAND

In England the farm implement industry consisted of large manufacturers such as Ford, Massey-Ferguson, Nuffield, International Harvester, Allis Chalmers, and David Brown, none of whom produced a small tillage tool of the Landmaster type. There were also a number of other major farm implement manufacturers who were considerably smaller than the leaders, and there were numerous very small local and specialized manufacturers.

The pattern of distribution for farm implements in Britain consisted of the manufacturer selling to a distributor who sold to dealers who sold to the farmer. The distributor was sold on an annual-contract basis by which he agreed to take a certain quota of machines for delivery during the coming year. He received a 22½% to 25% discount from the list price and operated in a county-sized territory which was a closed territory, exclusively his. The contract required the distributor to buy a certain percentage, usually 10%, of the weight or value of his purchase in replacement parts for service. The manufacturer occasionally sold directly to a dealer if the dealer was large enough, in which event the distributor in that territory received a 5% over-ride on the order. The price of Landmaster equipment to the farmer was fixed by Landmaster Ltd. and no middleman was permitted to deviate from this price.

In England most of the land was in farms of about 80 acres, and many of these were made up of several small separated patches. Elsewhere in Europe a personal love of the land held many farmers to their ancestral farm despite the fact that higher earnings could be attained in industrial employment. In Britain this attachment to the soil was not evident, and there was a steady drift away from the land. In other industrial nations where the level of employment was high, such as the United States and Germany, sideline farming of small acreages by industrial workers had become popular, but this practice had not appeared in England.

In its English plants Landmaster had a total of about 500 employees, in addition to which many hundreds of other employees in Firth Cleveland factories were engaged in making Landmaster parts. The average weekly wage in the English plants was about £8 11/— ($24). The average wage of comparable American labor was $93. All of the Landmaster components (other than the engines) were made within the Firth Cleveland Group except the gearboxes for the largest tillers which were bought from an English firm specializing in these components. It was intended that the only facility needed in the United States would be for final assembly and storage.

THE DESIRE FOR EXPORT MARKETS

Landmaster Ltd. was a factor in the British small garden tractor industry, supplying about 35% to 45% annually of the total national British market. Management was of the opinion, however, that the home market potential was limited in spite of the prevalence of small farms, and its efforts at expansion were now being directed toward developing its export market.

Prior to 1956 Landmaster sold a small volume abroad through export managers and concessionaires. These concessionaires usually handled a number of varied lines of merchandise, not always ideally combined. They operated through a number of agents abroad, whom they contacted by mail. They seldom used traveling salesmen. Mr. Hayward was not satisfied that the exporters put forth enough sales effort. Often, he remarked, they became little more than a post office through which the manufacturer conducted a mail order business. He was convinced that the success of Landmaster depended upon developing an extensive foreign market, and decided upon a major reorganization of the business. This included the building of the company's own direct and exclusive representation abroad, including the engagement of several Landmaster representatives who traveled abroad for the purpose of establishing sales outlets. The company's long-range objective was to sell over 50% of its output abroad.

Mr. Smeddle had for several years been the chief engineer for one of the Far Eastern branches of the Harrison Crossfield Company, a large British mercantile organization. He and the directors of Firth Cleveland were well known to each other. Having served fourteen years in the Far East, Mr. Smeddle wished to relocate and, when his contract expired in 1958, the Landmaster management invited him to join them. He accepted their invitation with the understanding that his first assignment would be to make an intensive exploration of the foreign market potential of Landmaster. At this time the company had already entered markets in Australia, Southeast Asia, Scandinavia, and France.

Mr. Smeddle began his work in November, 1958, with a quick world survey of markets and countries with a view to deciding which was logically the next territory to develop as a part of the Landmaster expansion program. The survey, which was largely conducted in the Board of Trade offices in London, very quickly pinpointed the U.S. as being the most promising territory for consideration, with possible later expansion into Mexico and Canada, using Chicago as headquarters. Thereafter a more detailed survey was undertaken in the library of the United States Embassy in London and from this a picture of the American agricultural and farming pattern began to emerge. This study indicated to Mr. Smeddle that an additional survey was required. In the first half of 1959 Mr. Smeddle conducted an extensive survey of the U.S. market in an effort to determine the size of the market, the best selling techniques and system of distribution, potential modifications of Landmaster equipment to meet the needs of the American market, and the best location for the company's operations. The material for the survey took some four months to compile and the final report estimated the market potential and projected it through 1964, gauged the size of competitors, and analyzed the American distribution systems. In September, 1959, the Board of Directors of Landmaster and of Firth Cleveland Ltd. decided to form an American subsidiary.

THE WORLD MARKET

At the time of the formation of Landmaster, Inc., Landmaster Ltd. had already entered several other foreign markets. Landmaster Pty. Ltd. of Ballarat, Australia, had a plant in which it assembled the machines which were sold to farm equipment distributors, who in turn sold them to dealers. A Southeast Asian office was maintained under the administration of a Far East Marketing Director. He acted as Landmaster's representative, traveling for the company to select and train new dealers. In New Zealand, Landmaster had made arrangements to sell its small tractors through an old established family firm which was in the lawn mower business. No arrangements were made to establish a farm implement dealer in South Africa. While the company was exploring the South African market situation it placed, temporarily, distribution rights with its subsidiary, Stenor, located in Johannesburg.

To cover India, Landmaster was considering the possibility of licensing production by an arrangement with the East Asiatic Company, Ltd., a large and well-established trading company which acted as representative for Western exporting companies in India, Burma, Thailand, Singapore, and Malaya. Imports into India could be made only by an import permit issued by the Indian government which was making a studied effort to develop Indian industry and, therefore, was restricting the importation of finished industrial products. Landmaster Ltd. management believed that it would be necessary to make some modifications to enable it to sell its machines to the peasants of India, most of whom were illiterate. Unable to read instructions, these farmers would need to be instructed orally in the operation and maintenance of the machine. Consequently, machine parts would have to be painted in distinguishing colors, and the farmer would have to be taught to operate and service the tractor in terms of the color code.

Landmaster sold about as many small garden tractors abroad as it did in Britain. The bulk of these sales were in Scandinavia and France. Most of the 150's sold abroad were sold in Australia.

CONCLUSIONS FROM THE AMERICAN SURVEY

In his London survey, which was for the purpose of indicating the most suitable state in the U.S. in which to initially launch sales of the Landmaster rotary tillers, Mr. Smeddle took into account the following factors: farm wealth, mechanization, crop variability, farm density, geophysical/geographical suitability. "The answer that came out —the state of Illinois—was an uncompromising mathematical decision," said Mr. Smeddle, "influenced by nothing but recorded statistics." At the time he had been pleased to note that this area had been chosen by three of Landmaster's leading competitors as a place to center their operations.

After having studied statistics, technical journals, and market trends, Mr. Smeddle felt that, although some figures had been declining over the year and a lower level was projected for capital expenditures by farmers, the market for Landmaster's type of equipment would be dynamic. Farmers were changing the nature of their enterprises, enlarging their operations, specializing, consolidating, seeking greater efficiency and adopting new methods. Thus the market for capital items, he felt, was going into a period of flux and experiencing a changing pattern. Hence a lower level would not mean a slow or static market.

After having traveled extensively in the United States market, Mr. Smeddle concluded that his original intention of releasing the Landmaster products on a pilot scale using Illinois as a center needed to be modified. The accepted pattern of distribution he found was not quite what he had expected. It had been deemed most important that any tie-up with a distributor organization be with one of long standing and good reputation in the trade. Such organizations were all larger than he had counted on and instead of covering a few counties it was found that they covered several states.

MARKET POTENTIALS

From discussions with impartial and responsible people in all parts of the trade, Mr. Smeddle in 1959 had made the following estimates of market potentials:

Power Garden Equipment Estimated Sales for 1959

Total number of power garden equipment in use	40 million
Number to be sold in 1959	3.9 million
Number of manufacturers	315
Annual replacement	1.75%
Annual new sales	12.60%
Grass-cutters	75.00%
Tillers	17.50%
Sundries (snow-blowers, edgers, etc.)	7.50%

The number of manufacturers was starting to show a decrease, particularly in the case of grass cutters. The more successful manufacturers were increasing in strength and absorbing some of the smaller firms. Mr. Smeddle thought that the grass cutter market was nearing its peak, and making room for the tiller.

The total number of power garden equipment pieces in use had grown from 25 million in 1954 to 40 million in 1959 and Mr. Smeddle expected it to reach 55 million in 1964. While less than 1% of the machines purchased in 1954 were for replacement purposes, it was expected that in 1964 at least 50% of the machines sold would be for replacement with projected annual total sales of 5 million machines.

From the *Wall Street Journal* Mr. Smeddle had learned that garden tiller sales in 1959 would be between the broad limits of 325,000 and 525,000 units. A rule of thumb analysis would break this down to the following approximate figures:

Probable Total	*425,000 units*
Equivalent of Mark 80 type	300,000 units
Equivalent of Mark 150 type	125,000 units

Estimated Sales by Chain Stores and Mail Order Houses (in units)

Montgomery Ward	80,000	Goodyear Tires	5,000
Sears Roebuck	50,000	Aldens	2,000
Western Auto	20,000	McLeods (Canada)	1,300
Gambles	10,000	Marshall Wells (Canada)	1,300
Spiegels	8,000	Walter Woods (Canada)	1,300
Firestone Tires	5,000	Western Tires	500

Total: 184,400 units

This left approximately 241,000 which would probably be distributed through the following sources:

Principal farm equipment wholesale members (FEWA)	79
Balance (nonmembers FEWA) farm equipment distributors	641
Approximate total wholesalers (supplying about 65,000 hardware and farm equipment dealers throughout the country)	720

Independent of this there were probably about 30,000 lawn and garden specialists who, for the most part, bought direct from the factories.

Estimated Sales of Tractor Rotary Tiller Plows (Similar to Mark 650)

Total in use	17,000
Number to be sold in 1959	4,000
Number of makes offered	5
Annual replacement	4.4%
Annual new sales	23.5%

Percentage annual new sales was increasing rapidly and Mr. Smeddle felt it might easily rise to 100% per annum or more as interest in the tiller method gained impetus.

Mr. Smeddle recognized that the figures were subject to error, and care would have to be taken to keep the estimates as realistic as possible. He also felt that his projections might be off by as much as 30%. Also, any error that existed would most likely be an understatement, and a probable inaccuracy of 20% up and 10% down should be anticipated.

COMPETITION

"In a market that buys nearly four million garden power units a year, and whose economy is in a period of sustained prosperity," said Mr. Smeddle referring to Mark 80 and 150, "I felt there was room for any quantity of competitors providing the unit ceiling price was not exceeded. Obviously the nearer the new entrant's article is to the lower range of prices, the greater will be his measure of success."

Landmaster had always used Villiers and J.A.P. (J. A. Prestwich Co.) engines to power its tractors. As a result of his investigations, Mr. Smeddle in 1959 felt that as a condition of entering the American market it was necessary for the company to use American engines not only on the tractors to be sold in the United States but also on most others, including those to be sold elsewhere in the world. In persuading the Landmaster management to make this move, Mr. Smeddle explained that he had three considerations in mind.

The first of these considerations was the attitude of the American consumer, whom he termed "service conscious." Mr. Smeddle believed that he would meet too much consumer resistance if he tried to sell a foreign gasoline engine in the United States against the competition of nearby American producers whose engines were well-known and easily serviced.

Following the Firth Cleveland policy of making or buying component parts wherever most advantageous and economical, English sources proved noncompetitive. The entire British small engine industry produced only half a million engines a year. A single American producer, Briggs & Stratton, had a capacity of 100,000 a week. Although English labor costs were low, the British manufacturers did not have the efficiencies which were inherent in mass production and were unable to match American prices. Mr. Smeddle reasoned that if Landmaster Ltd. were going to buy abroad on the basis of price, it might as well shop in the world market and buy for its total requirements.

Lastly, Mr. Smeddle felt that it would restrict Landmaster in the American market if only one engine were used because it seemed that American customers had definite preferences. Therefore, he made arrangements with three leading producers and offered Landmaster distributors a choice of any one of three engines: Lauson, Briggs & Stratton, and Clinton. On any volume of less than 1,000 tractors a year, the option of choosing the engine would be Landmaster's. On a volume of over 1,000 the distributor would be permitted to specify his choice. It was expected that the distributor's choice would be conditioned by his knowledge of the preference of his dealers.

Except for the planned arrangement of using American gasoline engines, no additional modifications were deemed necessary to adapt the Landmaster to the American market. Mr. Smeddle had not expected to meet any significant amount of consumer resistance to his 80 and 150 machines because of the fact that they were foreign-made. He believed that this would be something of an advantage. "Foreign producers," he said, "are now riding high on the crest of American public opinion. Such things as foreign cars have created a snob appeal in this country, and there is a slop-over of this appeal from which we expected to benefit." Mr. Smeddle emphasized such sales points as Sheffield steel in his advertising copy. "No doubt there are many steels in this country," he said, "that are every bit as good as Sheffield, but nevertheless the Sheffield name has glamour." Mr. Smeddle used a decal label on his machine to carry out this theme. The label depicted a handsome yeoman spanning his bow and its message described the Landmaster as being made in Nottingham, in Sherwood Forest, the romantic home of Robin Hood.

Mr. Smeddle had anticipated that his Landmaster machines would be ahead of domestic competition in design, in the technical sense; and in eye appeal, in the domestic consumer sense. He had made samplings which indicated that only one property owner in ten would buy a tiller which was only a tiller. They would, however, he believed, be receptive to a tiller which could also do other jobs. Mr. Smeddle pointed out that the Landmaster had great versatility. It was a general purpose tool which could be used for all types of garden tillage and which could be used to power such attachments as lawn mowers, chain saws, hedge trimmers, orchard or paint sprayers, flexible shafts, water pumps, or electric generators. Mr. Smeddle stated that there was no parallel for this in the United States.

Price competition from machines of a quality comparable to that of Landmaster had not been viewed as a problem; however, the Landmaster management felt that it would also be competing with smaller machines which were cheaply made, the "back-yard scratchers," which were not designed with any thought of performance standards or durability. They estimated such machines sold at retail for as little as $80. The company determined to sell its equipment at a price slightly higher than the average price of all similar tillers on the U.S. market. Although long-term credit datings were already common in the implement industry, the Landmaster management offered credit terms that were even longer than those customary in the industry.

Landmaster management did not expect that the major American farm implement manufacturers would present any serious competition in the Mark 650 area. "Firms like International Harvester and John Deere," said Mr. Smeddle, "because of the resources at their disposal and the size of their operations can do things that would be impossible for us to do. We, however, intend to do things that International and Deere do not care to do. The large firms, as a matter of policy, seldom lead the industry with radical new departures or in promoting innovations. Tillage tools of our type are not yet fully accepted in the United States, and therefore the large firms have not added them to their lines. They will wait until there is a good solid consumer acceptance established before they are willing to undertake their production. The industry calls ours a 'short line' in contrast to the well-established multiple products of International and John Deere which are known as 'full lines.'"

CHANNELS OF DISTRIBUTION

When the Landmaster machines were introduced on the American market, Mr. Smeddle felt that three distinct systems of distribution were available to Landmaster:

1. Distribution through merchandising companies with their own stores using, at the same time, a factory representative to build up additional accounts.

2. Distribution through the national organization of Farm Equipment Wholesalers, backed up by a factory representative.

3. The use of an established direct factory agent who had connections among larger independent dealers, all farm distributors within his area, and some of the other channels of distribution.

Mr. Smeddle had considered that the initial choice of distribution channels was of critical importance. His impression had been that the direct factory agent would be the least attractive alternative because it was such an expensive form of selling. The large tillers, which the chain stores would not carry, were to be sold 100% through independent wholesale distributors of farm equipment. The intermediate size machines would be sold 50% through lawn and garden distributors and 50% through farm equipment wholesalers. On the small machines a decision had to be made whether to market them through chains or lawn and garden distributors. In general, he had planned to shift as many such functions as possible to the distributors.

SALES OBJECTIVES

In his original planning Mr. Smeddle was aiming for the following sales volume:

	Mark 80	10,000 units
October 1959 to December 1960	Mark 150	2,800 units
	Mark 650	300 units
	Mark 80	50,000 units
January 1961 to December 1961	Mark 150	10,000 units
	Mark 650	1,000 units

Gross margins after discounts to middlemen with respect to "landed cost" were expected to be 15–20% for Mark 80 and 150 and 30–35% for Mark 650. The status of the account and not the quantity was to determine discounts. Distribution price lists were to come under the following general headings:

Suggested list	Jobber	Drop shipments	Dealer
$X	$X–40%	$X–39%	$X–25%

In the case of the 80 and the 150, "List" would show a reduction by a percentage discount for the customer who attached his own engine. Mr. Smeddle forecast that sales volume for his third year would amount to 50,000 units for the Mark 80, 10,000 units for the Mark 150, and 3,000 units for the Mark 650, approximating a sales volume of between $16–20 million for the third year. The directors of Landmaster in London asserted that a number of times in the past they had aimed at goals of 10% of a foreign market within three years and had in every instance achieved that goal.

INTRODUCTION TO THE U.S. MARKET

The most effective and economical method of introduction, Mr. Smeddle determined, was to invite representatives from all groups of buyers, chain stores, mail-order houses, farm equipment wholesalers, dealers and lawn and garden specialists, to a central point for a two- or three-day period during the winter of 1960 to witness a well-planned demonstration of all equipment—a show which he called a "Tillerama."

"Our main objective was to get the people to the site and once we had done that, then it was entirely up to our demonstration and our showmanship to sustain their interest," said Mr. Smeddle. This kind of exposure had also been aimed to save Landmaster the sizable advertising expenditures which would otherwise have been necessary to gain recognition.

"In this manner we wanted to give clear indication to the trade of our intention to move into the market with force," Mr. Smeddle continued, "and not be labeled as just another one of those organizations which has sprung up and will undoubtedly disappear as have many others in the past." One other aim had been to indicate, by showing all three machines, that Landmaster was a manufacturer with agricultural experience.

A suitable site outside Phoenix had been selected for the "Tillerama" and about 150 potential buyers were invited. They traveled to Phoenix at their own expense but once there they were accommodated and entertained by Landmaster as its guests. Equipment, hand-out material, and two top demonstrators had been brought over from England for the show.

At the time, Mr. Smeddle was very pleased with the results of the Tillerama and the publicity the company received from it in various trade papers. He believed that it had helped him to sound the depth of the market, to judge the pricing policies to be adopted, the merchandising tactics and outlets of distribution to be used, and the product changes to be required. The introductory prices at the Tillerama had deliberately been set at a high level so that they could be adjusted. The original price schedule was as follows:

	Introductory price	Final market price
Mark 80	$ 165	$139
Mark 150	500	395
Mark 650	1,265	985

After the Tillerama it was decided to use (1) farm equipment wholesalers who would sell the big Mark 650 through dealers, both on an exclusive basis, and (2) independent distributors to sell the smaller machines. Chain stores and the mail-order houses would not be used at all.

Mr. Smeddle did not employ test markets. "For the big machine we at first intended to move out in circles from Chicago," he said, "but the Tillerama convinced us that we could cover the whole country immediately through 17 distributors at little extra cost. We would also gain broad experience much more rapidly. The market had already been tested by our competitors and we knew the demand was available."

Several thousand units of the smaller machines had been imported and over a period of 12 months independent distributors had been hand-picked in Birmingham, Detroit, northern Ohio, Utah, Missouri, Kansas, Oklahoma, and Arkansas. Because a difference in consumer acceptance was expected in different areas, Mr. Smeddle thought it was impossible to select any specific test area which would give him data to evaluate which could be applied across the country.

OPERATIONAL EXPERIENCE IN THE U.S. MARKET

"The Tillerama in itself was well timed," said Mr. Smeddle in March, 1962, "but when we started to sell the small machines we found ourselves introducing them in the middle of a period of recession." On the occasion of the 1960 fall buying season in which Landmaster was first introduced into the American market, it was found that dealers were heavily stocked with competitive products and were reluctant to take on a new unestablished foreign-made machine. A recession in America had much greater impact on the sale of these kinds of products than it would have had under similar conditions in England because the British market consisted primarily of professional people while in the U.S. the blue-collar workers were the most important buyers.

Contrary to experience with the small tillers, the big Mark 650 aroused interest from the beginning and immediately started to move in volume. This required much more of the energy and time of the Landmaster staff than had been anticipated. It also involved extensive traveling and left a minimum of time for the promotion of the small machines. Mr. Smeddle found that for the 650 almost all areas of the country were equally promising, each for different reasons, depending upon area characteristics. By March, 1962, a total of about 1,300 units of the 650 had been sold in the U.S., Canada, and Mexico, with area sales generally following farm population patterns.

"A tiller is not like a plow," said Mr. Smeddle. "The farmer has to be taught to use it properly." For this purpose a training school was organized. It consisted of two driver-demonstrators equipped with trucks to transport their tractors and implements. In cooperation with distributors in the various areas, these demonstrators visited farmers and dealers and showed the 650 in use. In the course of these demonstrations it became evident that the American farmer was much more careless in handling his equipment than the European farmer. Working in hard soils, using high-powered tractors and tilling big acreages, the American farmer desired speed and tended to use the 85-inch width in ways which were contrary to the company's recommendations. Certain components in the machine which were sufficient in strength for European use broke down under the hard usage to which they were typically subjected in America. Although damage due to careless handling was not covered by its warranty, the Landmaster management decided to redesign these components and replace them on all machines at no cost to the farmers. Over a period of one year this was done by a field force at a cost to the company of about $250,000.

"The American farmer likes to feel the wind blowing in his hair," said Mr. Smeddle. "Using the traditional method of the moldboard plow, discs, and harrows, he moves at a speed of about four miles per hour. With a roto-tiller he travels at only two miles an hour, which seems far too slow for him. But at the same time he is completely overlooking the fact that with our method he is doing four operations at once compared to the traditional method." In trying to overcome this psychological obstacle and get acceptance of its method as being more efficient, Landmaster during 1961 engaged five independent agronomists to do extensive research to evaluate existing differences between their method and the old one. Such an approach had never been taken before in the industry.

Before the research began the Landmaster management committed itself to a program of releasing data for publication regardless of whether the final results were favorable or not. Confident of the advantages of its method the company management, without hesitation, accepted these premises. In Colorado 22 farms were selected for test purposes, representing a cross-section of various crops raised in hard, medium, and light soils. The whole process of the two methods was studied, taking into account such factors as crop yield, speed, fuel usage, the proper application of fertilizers, and the amount of weeds. More than 2,000 soil analyses were made during various stages of the study.

The over-all result proved that the roto-tiller principle had significant advantages compared to the traditional method. In hard and light soils the two methods gave approximately the same crop yield, but the Landmaster method used only half the time and half the fuel to obtain these results. When an early application of fertilizer was used, the Landmaster method yielded a larger crop. In medium soil the differences between the two methods were not significant. The Landmaster method in general proved to be a better clodbreaker and had a higher ability to retain moisture in the soil. A cross-section of the results from the study was to be given to farmers as case histories to guide them.

The St. Lawrence Seaway turned out to be a disappointment for Landmaster. The company found itself encountering delays and higher freight costs which had not been expected. "I am not too happy with Chicago as a center for our operations," said Mr. Smeddle, "but on the other hand I do not know of any better place." He remarked that if Landmaster had to ship a big machine overland from Chicago to Portland, Oregon, this would eat up most of the profit. As a result the company decided to ship its machines from England directly to public warehouses in New York, Philadelphia, Houston, Savannah, Los Angeles, and Portland, which were used as distribution points.

By late spring, 1962, the major competition facing the company for its big machine (650) was Howard Standard Rotovator, an English firm in the American market. Others, like Agrotiller/Winpower, North Western, and Seaman-Andwall, appeared to be on a sales plateau without showing any marked sales increase. Some competitors, in fact, had already gone out of the market or were on the verge of doing so. Mr. Smeddle believed the failures were due to improper merchandising techniques and poor product design. He did not consider Howard a serious competitor. Its machine was built on a different concept than Landmaster's, and was less efficient. In addition, Howard offered 14 different types of machines while Landmaster had one type that could be used in 17 applications and its machine could do each job better. Farm dealers were much more inclined toward stocking one machine than fourteen. Howard's smaller sizes (50″) were about $50 cheaper than Mark 650. Its intermediate machines (70″) were $50 more than the 650, and its large ones (85″) sold at $1700–1800, or 60% higher than the 650 price of $985.

"Any foreign manufacturer entering the American market with highly specialized new products," said Mr. Smeddle, "has to be prepared to face financial losses during the first two years of operation. In our case they were higher than anticipated. The smaller machines did not move due to the recession. The big one got a good start and took all our time. We then made the decision to concentrate our effort on the 650 and come back to the smaller machines later when the big ones were in the black." At the same time minor product changes were under way in England on Mark 80 and 150, and to avoid being stocked with obsolete machines in the U.S. a large part of the inventory was shipped back to be sold in the profitable British market.

FUTURE EXPECTATIONS AND PLANS

"Farmers are by nature conservative which seems to stem from their spiritual bond with the natural elements," said Mr. Smeddle. He had found the American farming system to be a massive one with a cohesiveness and far less of individualism than in Europe. There the roto-tillage principle had readily been accepted as being more efficient than the traditional method. He was inclined to divide the American farmers into five groups according to their attitudes toward a new method:

Group 1: *The Innovators* (consisting of 5% of the total number). Fairly young or middle-age farmers who were leaders in their community, had capital to spend and were willing to take a risk. They worked in close contact with colleges and universities and were heavy subscribers to farm papers and magazines.

Group 2: *The Early Adopters* (consisting of about 5% of the total number). These were mostly younger than those in Group 1 and not as well-to-do but active in community work and in their relationship with scientific institutions. They were also heavy readers of trade papers.

Group 3: *The Early Majority* (consisting of about 25% of the total number). These attended farm meetings but were not the leaders. They showed a high awareness of what their friends thought about them and tended to follow the activities of those in Groups 1 and 2.

Group 4: *The Majority* (consisting of 60% of the total number). These were the followers. When a new method had been accepted by the members of the three groups above, the majority came along.

Group 5: *The Non-adopters* (consisting of 5% of the total number). Mostly older farmers with a fixed working pattern and an inborn resistance to change.

Mr. Smeddle felt that his present market was among the farmers in Group 1, and perhaps some in Group 2. He was convinced that the day would come when his method would get 95% acceptance but he admitted that it was impossible to estimate how many years it would take to reach this point. "At that time the market potential will be well above 100,000 machines a year," he remarked. "Of course, long before that happens, the big operators in the U.S. will produce them, and we expect that they will then pass us in production and sales volume. We do not expect to be a world leader in volume in the long run, but within a few years we will be well enough established to be able to set standards in the field, and to hold a share of the market."

Mr. Smeddle intended to start to push the small machines (Mark 80 and 150) again in the fall of 1963. However, no definite plans were made. "It's a highly competitive and rough market," he said, "and not very enjoyable to work in. It would be too costly to promote them now." The time to start, he believed, depended upon market conditions, the progress of the new development program in England, and the acceptance of the 650. A new market study was to be made. He hoped that the brand name and the reputation Landmaster was acquiring from Mark 650 could be carried over to the smaller machines especially among the trade people. He was aware of the fact that for a small machine of the Mark 80 type the biggest volume was probably in the $100 price range. Despite this, he expected that there would be a sizable market for a versatile, high quality, medium priced 150. In England the company had introduced a smaller, less expensive type of machine, Gardenmaster 34 (Exhibit 5), which had not been successful. The consumer entered the store to take a look at the 34, but came out having bought the more expensive Mark 80. There was a natural tendency among consumers to trade up, which he felt would also prevail in the U.S. The Mark 80 had 57 attachments but he expected the trade to be reluctant to carry all of them in stock and therefore the company had decided that, until it had more marketing experience, it would concentrate on only 10–15 of them.

"In summary," said Mr. Smeddle, "I would like to stress the flexibility of our company. We quickly recognized that our market survey did not reflect the change in buying patterns after 1959 and moved accordingly. The sales of small machines were dissolved leaving the door open for reentry. Operational expenses and the market outlook were trimmed. Our forces were regrouped behind the big Mark 650 and we are keeping our eyes open for new product ideas."

A NEW PRODUCT

In his close contacts with the trade and with farmers, Mr. Smeddle constantly came across the problem of cultivating soil in growing crops to kill weeds. Farmers felt that the existing methods were inefficient and could be improved with a new tool. Subsequently, Landmaster used its technical know-how, dynamic tilling as opposed to static, to develop a device which employed the mechanical principle of soil handling which the company understood best. "The result," said Mr. Smeddle, "was a high speed, large sized, and dynamic (in an engineering sense) corn, cotton, row crop cultivator capable of operating up to six miles per hour and completing up to ten acres per hour of finished work." He emphasized that the new product was to be priced within "the psychological barrier of $1,000 per unit for a tillage implement," designed to chop the weeds instead of turning them over, and equipped with regulating features so that it automatically followed the shape of the land.

Prototypes had been tested in the winter of 1961–62 and 100 "preproduced" samples of the machine were to operate in the U.S. during 1962. Based on the results of these tests a joint Anglo-American venture was to manufacture several thousands of units for 1963 using a combination of British and American components with all final fabrication taking place in U.S. factories.

"I am hopeful that we can completely control the future market for this product," Mr. Smeddle concluded, "because four important features of the machine are patented and it seems to me that it will be difficult for our potential competitors to go around them." By mid-'62 the company had received over 1,400 orders for the new machine but as a matter of policy had rejected them pending final development and testing of the product.

exhibit 1   **LANDMASTER, INC.**

Landmaster's conditions of sale

Payment for 50% of the machines of each model becomes due 180 days from the date of the invoice. For the purposes of dating and carryover, components and attachments ordered for a particular machine shall be considered a part of that machine.

Payment within:

> 10 days of invoice–40%–2%–4.50%
> 40 days of invoice–40%–2%–3.75%
> 70 days of invoice–40%–2%–3.0 %
> 100 days of invoice–40%–2%–2.25%
> 130 days of invoice–40%–2%–1.5 %
> 160 days of invoice–40%–2%– .75%
> 190 days of invoice–40%–2%
> and thereafter on agreed "carryover"
> Inventory up to a maximum of 360 days–40%

Statement of advertising policy

The following amounts are available for distributor/dealer use on a 50–50 cooperative basis:

Each Landmaster Tractor-Mounted Tiller	$20.00
Each Landmaster Mark 150 Universal Cultivator	7.50
Each Landmaster Mark 80 Lawn and Garden Power Tool	2.00

exhibit 1 (continued)

The Landmaster spare parts policy

It is the declared policy of the company that adequate parts for all their machinery are always available at all points where equipment is sold.

Up to a total of 100 units, 10% by value of parts must always be retained by the distributor, thereafter the percentage may diminish as the numbers of machines increase.

Discounts on spare parts will be at the rate of less 50%, less 10% for cash 10 days from date of the confirmed invoice, net 30.

exhibit 2
LANDMASTER MARK 80 AND MARK 150

exhibit 3
LANDMASTER GARDENMASTER 80

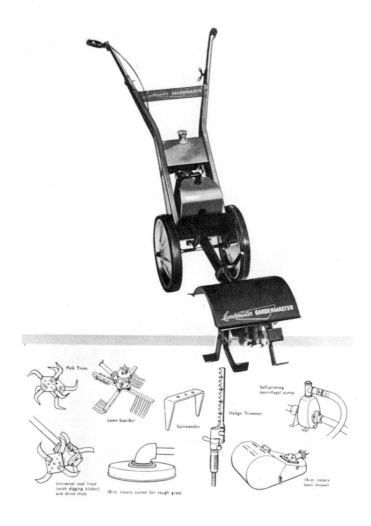

exhibit 4

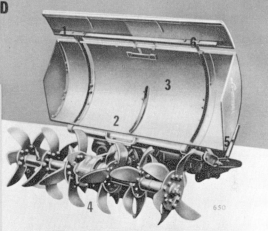

THIS IS THE LANDMASTER TRACTOR-MOUNTED ROTARY TILLER

1 SOIL TEXTURE CONTROL
Raise or lower the hood on Landmaster to leave the soil in any condition of texture you want. Blade bite is controlled by the tractor gear you select.

2 CENTERED POWER TRANSMISSION
Operating from standard PTO, power train is centered on rotor shaft, cuts down power losses, makes disc-changing or spacing easy.

3 TORQUE LIMITOR [SAFETY CLUTCH]
When load is exceeded, torque limitor disengages rotor automatically; it reengages after the PTO shaft has come to rest. This fully protects both tractor and implement.

4 FULL 65 INCHES OF TILLING WIDTHS
The Landmaster Mark 650 has 48 scimitar-shaped blades operating on total of eight discs that extend the full 65" of the shaft. For lighter work, this can be extended to 80". You can work right up to field margins, fence lines and roadways.

5 POSITIVE DEPTH CONTROL
"Touch Control" on tractor or adjustment of depth control wheels lets you vary depth of tillage from 0–9" in seconds, without use of tools.

6 LINKAGE TO FIT YOUR TRACTOR
Three-point linkage is standard on Landmaster. Available with two-point "fast hitch" at no additional cost. Either Landmaster rig is light enough for one man to handle and hitch without help.

Landmaster Ltd., Hucknall, Nottingham, England
Landmaster Inc., Evanston, Chicago, Illinois, U.S.A.
Landmaster Pty. Ltd., Ballarat, Victoria, Australia
Members of the Firth Cleveland Group

LANDMASTER TILLS THE SOIL AROUND THE WORLD!

Landmaster tilling equipment is at work right now in over 48 countries of the world. It has proven its worth and durability on every type of agricultural project . . . from English farms to Chinese rice paddies . . . and with a minimum of service required. The Mounted Rotary Tiller is only one of many Landmaster-engineered and Landmaster-built tools that have been serving the agriculture of the world since 1948. Over 75,000 have been sold. A complete spare parts depot is maintained in all territories. Your Landmaster dealer is ready and willing to demonstrate the range on your own farm to show you what Landmaster can do for you. Put a Landmaster to work on your soil, soon.

LANDMASTER SPECIFICATIONS-

Width of Cut	Weight	Number of Blades
Mark 350 (35" extendable to 50")	375 lbs.	24
Mark 500 (50" extendable to 65")	480 lbs.	36
Mark 650 (65" extendable to 80")	595 lbs.	48

Recommended for tractors up to 37.5 H.P.

Tilling Depth - - - - - - -	Adjustable 0" to 9"
PTO Shaft Speed - - - - -	540 r.p.m.
Rotor Shaft Speed - - - -	135 r.p.m.
PTO Shaft Size - - - -	1⅜"
PTO Shaft Size (alternate) - -	1⅜"
Minimum H.P. Required - - -	15
Linkage (standard) - - - -	3-point
Linkage (to special order) - -	2-point

exhibit 5
LANDMASTER GARDENMASTER 34

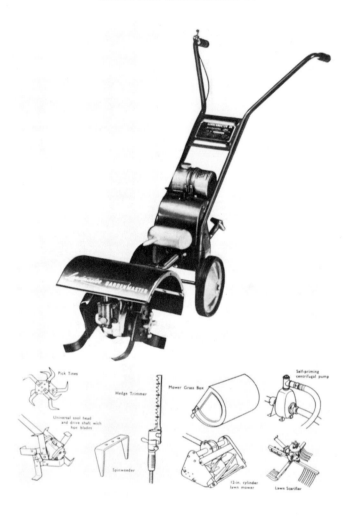

JAMES
TAILORS,
INC.

"Many buyers of men's clothing are unaware of the quality of fabrics and the fine points of tailoring in the higher-priced lines of suits and topcoats. Many of the qualities that make a fine suit are hidden inside the garment; but even if the buyer could see the inside, he would not be expert enough to judge the value of the materials and construction." Arthur James, vice-president of advertising for James Tailors, Inc., also felt that salesmen in retail stores often failed to educate the buying public. "More often than not the answer to a customer's objection to a price is a vague 'it's better quality.' " Arthur James drew up a list of more than thirty reasons why James clothes were superior to suits that could be made for $25 less. This list would serve as "talking" points for company salesmen, who could encourage retail store salesmen to pass on the information. A few of these "talking" points were as follows: (1) James fabrics[1] were made of fine Australian wool rather than domestic; (2) fabrics were carefully shrunk and finished rather than commercially shrunk; (3) the collar canvas was pure linen; (4) sewing thread was pure silk grade "1" rather than cotton; (5) buttonholes and buttons were sewed by hand rather than by machine; (6) stripes

---

[1] Quality of the fabric depends upon grade of wool, closeness of weave, number of plies in the yarns, and weight of cloth, as well as type of weave. Closeness of weave depends on "count" and is measured by the number of yarns to the inch in warp and weft. Satisfactory count in worsteds ranges from 64 x 60 up to 80 x 75, while for woolen flannel and tweed a count of 60 x 56 and 50 x 50, respectively, would be good. For worsteds and woolen suitings (winter wear), satisfactory weights would range from 13 to 15 ounces per yard. Worsted suitings have two-ply yarns running lengthwise (warp), and the better ones have two-ply in the weft. Woolen suitings usually have only a single ply.

and plaids were perfectly matched, etc. "The short cuts in making cheaper suits are many," said Arthur James, "but such garments will not hold their form and shape."

PRICE RANGE

In 1954 men's suits were manufactured to sell in certain retail classifications: (1) $40–$50; (2) $50–$60; (3) $60–$70; (4) $75–$85; (5) $85-over. James Tailors, Inc., located in Utica, New York, made suits mainly for class 5. James also made a line of evening clothes, which was priced in the same range as their other suits. Their summer suits retailed from $85 up to about $125. The company also made suits on special order, which retailed at a price above $100, depending on the fabric the customer wanted. In addition, James Tailors made a high-quality line of topcoats and overcoats.

COMPETITIVE PICTURE

Exhibit 1 shows industry sales in the various grades of men's clothing and total volume for the industry in recent years. The James Tailors

exhibit 1   SALES OF MEN'S AND BOYS' TAILORED
CLOTHING BY MANUFACTURER, 1947
(in millions of dollars)

Total	$1,485.7
Popular-priced	516.3
Popular- and Medium-priced	327.0
Medium-priced	296.8
Medium- and Better-priced	233.8
Better-priced	111.8

SOURCE: Market Planning Service, *Men's Clothing*, Report by Anglo-American Council on Productivity, 1950, p. 35.

RETAIL SALES OF MEN'S AND BOYS' CLOTHING, 1948–1951
(in millions of dollars)

	Men's Clothing	Boys' Wear
1948	$2,138	$818
1949	1,988	793
1950	2,107	809
1951	2,190	849

SOURCE: *Men's Wear Magazine*, 1952 Fact Book.

management regarded as their major competition about a dozen manufacturers of high-quality men's suits. These competitors sold their lines of products in the same price range and used comparable retail outlets. Annual sales volume for James was about $12 million and the firm had approximately 1,600 employees in 1954. Exhibit 2

exhibit 2 **NUMBER OF ESTABLISHMENTS IN MEN'S AND BOYS' CLOTHING INDUSTRY CLASSIFIED BY NUMBER OF EMPLOYEES, 1947**

No. of Employees	No. of Establishments
1–4	367
5–9	268
10–19	242
20–49	316
50–99	262
100–249	235
250–499	81
500–999	30
1,000–2,499	13
2,500–over	2

SOURCE: *Census of Manufactures*, 1947.

lists the number of manufacturing establishments in the men's clothing industry according to the number of employees.

CUSTOMER TRENDS

On October 1, 1953, Bertram J. Cahn, president of B. Kuppenheimer & Co., Inc., commented on trends in the industry in a speech before the Young Men's Group of the National Association of Clothiers and Furnishers:[2]

More buyer resistance has developed during recent years—it has been occasioned by the change in buying habits and customs and by the increased competition from the durable goods industries. Gone are the days of the tailcoat, the formal outercoat, the morning coat, the Sunday suit, and the clothes for all occasions. Now, one suit serves many men for all purposes. Sport jackets and their facsimiles, as well as slacks, are the substitutes. They now do valiant service and will continue to be over-indulged in, unless this trend is challenged effectively by you. Could we have predicted forty years ago that a shirt with its tails hanging outside, even though shortened, and overalls misnamed slacks, would be accepted

[2] B. Kuppenheimer & Co., Inc., of Chicago sold men's clothes in the same price ranges as James Tailors, Inc.

as substitutes? You must be aware that the shirt-maker and the overall-maker have entered the men's clothing business.

There is a definite trend towards comfort and convenience that is justified and welcomed, but there is a limit to the extent to which it should go. Every possible effort must be made to restore some regard, favor and respect for "Pride in Appearance."

Mr. Cahn also commented on the trend toward lighter-weight fabrics for spring and summer involving both the use of synthetic fibers and blends of worsted and wool yarns with synthetic fibers. He felt that the trend toward lighter suits, which included suits worn for three or four seasons, had its "unfortunate aspects," for it created "unbalanced production and decline in volume." Mr. Cahn voiced an optimistic note, however, by calling attention to tools, new and old, which the industry could use to encourage the consumer to increase his investment in the men's clothing industry. There were, he said, new fabrics, new colors, new styles and fashions,. modern designs, as well as the older selling tools of quality, good workmanship, and service. Exhibit 3 indicates the variety of style points that changed in some degree from year to year.

exhibit 3 **FALL TRENDS, 1954**

1. Color Trend	*Sold Fall '53*	*Will Buy Fall '54*
Light shades	20%	16%
Medium shades	41	40
Dark shades	26	27
Charcoal tones*	13	17
	100%	100%

2. Fabrics in Worsted Suits	*Sold Fall '52*	*Sold Fall '53*	*Will Sell Fall '54*
Orlon blend†	1%	3%	5%
Dacron blend†	1	8	9
Blue unfinished worsteds		6	7
Sharkskins		22	21
Checks		6	6
Fancy clear finished worsteds		28	29
Blue regular gabardines		8	6
Other colors—regular gabardines		4	3
Blue sheen gabardines		11	10
Other colors—sheen gabardines		4	4
		100%	100%

exhibit 3 (continued)

3. *Fabrics in Woolen Suits*	*Sold Fall '53*	*Will Buy Fall '54*
All-wool tweeds and shetlands	20%	20%
All-wool flannels	61	54
Orlon-blend flannels	7	8
Orlon-blend wool	3	3
Dacron-blend flannels	4	9
Dacron-blend wool types	5	6
	100%	100%

4. *Single- and Double-breasted*	*Sold Fall '52*	*Sold Fall '53*	*Will Sell Fall '54*
Single	77%	87%	88%
Double	23	13	12

5. *Button Type:* Regional preference for 3-button in Northeast, but relatively unimportant in Great Lakes area.
6. *Pocket Type:* Varies regionally.
7. *Vents:* Most popular in East.
8. *Vests:*

Year	3-piece with Vest‡	2-piece without Vest
1950	64%	36%
1951	51	49
1952	48	52
1953	25	75
1954 (est.)	26	74

9. *Overcoat:* Trend toward topcoat. Old-type heavy overcoat practically eliminated by zipper-lined or other.

Type	Fall '53	Fall '54 (est.)
Topcoats	70%	70%
Topcoats, zipper-lined	19	20
Overcoats (20–24 oz.)	6	6
Overcoats, regular	5	4
	100%	100%

* Most popular in Northeast—22% of total; least popular on Pacific Coast—12% of total.
† Largest increase in West and on Pacific Coast.
‡ 3-piece shows greatest preference in Northeast.
SOURCE: Clothing Manufacturers' Association of the United States of America, New York, N.Y.

The president of James Tailors, Mr. George James, commented:

> The recent trends toward synthetics haven't changed our operation very much. We gave synthetics a try several months ago but found that they just didn't fit into our way of doing business. For example, our buyers are wool buyers, not synthetic buyers. Furthermore, the synthetics are used mainly in summer suits where our market is limited anyway because of our $85-and-up price range. We know for a fact that many of our regular customers bypass us in the summer to buy cheaper suits made of synthetics. They're more interested in having a quantity of low-priced suits in the summer than having high-priced suits of quality like ours.
>
> The trend toward more casual clothes hasn't affected us too much either. The reason is that the customer is looking for low-priced goods in casual wear. We could make sport coats and slacks for $60 and $25 respectively, but that would be beyond his price range. Besides, he might as well get one of our suits for the same total price. We have tried a few of these new car coats, but they aren't too successful for the same reason. Our high-quality product commands a higher price than the customer will pay for casual clothes.

Mr. James felt that most of their major competitors had similar attitudes and policies toward synthetics and casual wear. "That kind of business is mainly for firms specializing in those items," he added.

One trend in men's clothing that had affected James Tailors, however, was the decline in popularity of the overcoat. James Tailors had at one time sold over 60,000 overcoats a year; in 1954 about 10,000 overcoats were sold by the company. Topcoat sales had increased considerably, but not enough to offset the loss of overcoat sales. The company also sold some zipcoats (a topcoat with a zipped-in lining). Mr. James said, "The trend is clearly toward topcoats and the zipcoat is just part of the transition. We haven't done too much in designing zipcoats for that reason."

CONSUMERS AND RETAIL OUTLETS

The principal consumers of James clothing were middle-aged men who resided in metropolitan areas and were employed in professional, business, or office occupations. They usually earned incomes in the upper-middle to high brackets. Management felt that, while people who worked in factories or as laborers also purchased some high-priced suits and topcoats to be worn when off the job, members of this group often found sport or casual clothing more to their liking and seldom purchased the more expensive suits.

Although every year brought new buyers into the market, replacement of worn garments was the prime cause for purchase of men's suits. Another important factor was the desire of certain buyers to enlarge their wardrobes for social or occupational reasons. Because men had been traditionally more conservative in dress than women, attempts to create obsolescence by changing styles had not been important on a year-to-year basis.

Men's clothing in the United States was distributed through a variety of outlets.

Retail clothiers operated primarily a men's specialty store, but sometimes carried women's and children's wear. The salesmen in these stores were usually experienced, well trained, and competent to assist a customer; good tailors were also employed to make what alterations were needed. A store usually offered a range of prices and stocked suits made by several manufacturers. Sometimes a store carried clothing bearing its own label. Private labels were often used by stores to obtain higher markups. Business was generated by window displays, advertising in local papers, and direct mail. Other media, such as radio, had also been used. James Tailors sold about 80 per cent of its volume through retail clothiers.

Department stores varied somewhat in the emphasis given to men's clothing. Some department stores had a "men's shop" or "store for men" which featured an attractive assortment of suits and overcoats bearing labels of a number of manufacturers and the store's own brand. These "stores for men" usually had expert salesmen and tailors. In other department stores, however, men's clothing was less important and was not offered in such variety, nor were the salesmen particularly expert. The importance of department stores as outlets for men's clothing varied to some extent between geographical areas. In big cities, the department store tended to be more important. James Tailors used department stores as a secondary channel of distribution and manufactured some suits to be sold under the private labels of certain high-grade department stores. The sales volume from private labels amounted to less than 5 per cent of total sales.

In some cases, chain stores were owned by a company which manufactured its own merchandise. Many of these chains sold suits and topcoats in the lower-price classifications. Even though their prices were low, these chains often found it necessary to extend credit. Since volume was important and price was the determining factor, salesmen had to strive for high sales and did not spend as much time in rendering the kind of service needed to build up a personal clientele as did salesmen in the men's specialty stores. Some manufacturers making high-grade men's clothing did own some stores in a number of large cities, but the stores did not necessarily bear the manufacturer's name or even a common name. One advantage of owning retail outlets was the ability to manufacture somewhat in advance with the knowledge that suits would be stocked. On the other hand, the problem of selling the garments was not solved simply by ownership of stores. James Tailors had a policy of not owning stores.

While most manufacturers sold direct to the retail store, there were some jobbers (116 of them in 1950) who bought from those manufacturers who did not have sales organizations. Jobbers might also buy up lots of clothing from broken lines, distress merchandise, or other assorted lots of clothing, such as cancellations. Jobbers played a relatively minor role in the 1950's.

Store location was an important matter in the merchandising of men's clothing. In spite of the trend toward suburban living, men seemed to prefer buying their suits and overcoats in downtown areas, where many men worked at their jobs. A survey conducted by Boston University confirmed this habit of purchasing in the Boston area and concluded that the suburban shopping center was apparently quite weak in the men's clothing department.[3] Some industry observers felt, however, that the development of the larger regional shopping centers would lead men to purchase more clothing in the suburbs.

SALES

Until 1925, James Tailors restricted its sales efforts to the territory east of the Mississippi. In this sales area, the company followed the practice of selecting an exclusive outlet in each city. It felt that better sales effort would result, that an exclusive outlet would enhance the prestige of its line, and that men who wanted the hand-tailored James clothing would seek out the store. This policy was continued after 1925, when the company expanded its sales west of the Mississippi. Each of James' major competitors also had the policy of granting exclusive distribution to a retail outlet in a specified geographical area. "Nowadays we have no choice but exclusive distribution," said Mr.

[3] *Fortune,* November, 1953, p. 230.

James. "The top-notch retailer has the power to demand exclusivity and we manufacturers have little choice but to give it to him."

As a matter of policy, James Tailors had always given much sales emphasis to small and medium-sized cities as well as concentrating on larger cities. Mr. James explained, "We like the stability of the smaller communities. Our kind of operation needs their stable influence as well as the business of the more fashion-minded customers of the big cities."

In 1954 James Tailors had about 800 accounts; these stores, however, did sell one or more lines of other clothing manufacturers. About 10 per cent of these outlets were department stores. In all sales territories, unwritten agreements between the company and the store management provided for meeting quotas based on experience with stores of similar size in similar communities. The relationship between the James company and these store managements was in most cases a very friendly and personal one.

Over the years James Tailors' outlets had experienced varying degrees of growth. Some had expanded with their area; others had remained in the same locations with the same floor space. In Washington, D.C., for example, the James Tailors' outlet had remained the same size for several years despite a sizeable population increase in the area.

Not all stores that carried the regular James line also sold James tuxedos. Some of the stores were located in areas where there was a demand for tuxedos only in the lower price ranges such as $50–$60. Another manufacturer specializing in evening clothes at those prices maintained a stock in many cities. This service made it easy for retailers to obtain quick delivery of stock sizes without carrying an inventory of tuxedos.

The company had sixteen salesmen who operated out of the New York and Chicago offices on extensive sales trips. Topcoats, overcoats and winter suits were sold March through June; visits for reorders were made at other times. The spring and summer lines were sold September through February, with other visits for reorders. The salesmen had periods when not much selling could be done. At these times, they did their missionary work, visiting stores and acquainting the store's selling staff with sales ideas.

They also tried to dispel false rumors, which were common in this industry, and counter the strategy of competitors' salesmen. One James salesman stated, "One of my biggest jobs is to meet competitive attempts to steal our accounts. One competitor, for example, advised my stores to drop our line of suits and take on his line with this clever approach: 'Mr. Retailer, I want you to carry James' overcoats because even I will admit that they are the best made. But be smart and carry our superior line of suits.'" The company's salesmen often tried to stimulate interest in pushing the James line by running contests among the retail salesmen, offering a suit as a prize.

The average length of company service among the James salesmen was 26 years. No new salesman had been added in ten years. Typically, a man was in training in the company's office for about ten years before getting a field assignment. The salesmen turned in weekly reports on their activities with information about sales, style trends, etc. They also submitted weekly expense accounts. Each salesman was given a quota for his territory and was paid on a salary-and-commission basis.

The vice-president in charge of sales, Henry James, was required to select a few new store outlets every year to replace the few stores that were dropped from the company's list. Sometimes a store was sold or liquidated when store owners decided to go out of business. Sometimes a franchise was taken away. For example, one store used the James trademark to get people into the store but then passed off its own brand as being of the same quality or even of the same manufacture. Before selection of a store, a careful check was made of its credit, management, location, and facilities. It was not difficult to find a store eager to sell James clothing which lent prestige to the merchandise line.

The James company from time to time had helped a new store get started in an area where there was no suitable outlet. Accommodation loans and open-book credit were extended. The company had also been under pressure recently from retail clothiers to assume responsibility for carrying a larger inventory. There had been suggestions by retailers generally that they should not be required to place firm orders for more than 50 per cent of their season's business in advance of the season. Manufacturers generally felt that such a practice would work to the disadvantage of the industry, and Mr. George James, president, concurred in this belief. He felt that James Tailors should resist the attempts of retailers to have the manufacturer increase his credit function.

The vice-president in charge of advertising, Arthur James, developed an advertising program that would assist the retail store owner in every season of the year. For many years, James Tailors had advertised in national magazines, but concluded in 1949 that most effective results were obtained by helping each store with advertising in its own area.

The company paid one-half the cost of advertising up to 3 per cent of sales in each store. The company furnished ideas, copy, and mats which a store could use if it desired.

Sales for the fall and winter business amounted to 60 per cent of the company's total business. The remaining 40 per cent represented sales in spring and summer. These percentages had changed very little over the past several years. Mr. James felt that the 60–40 relationship would remain relatively undisturbed despite manufacturers' efforts to minimize the seasonal production problems.

DESIGN AND PURCHASING

The company had an outstanding designer, Mr. Adams, who had created many new styles over the past several years. The designer attended conventions, visited style centers, and had new ideas translated into finished suits which were exhibited to top management for approval. When a new model was approved, the designer helped develop the patterns needed for cutting the various sizes that would be made. Designing required a most exacting knowledge of clothing manufacture, since new ideas on style could only be carried out if feasible from a manufacturing standpoint. An example of Mr. Adams' creativeness in design was a topcoat put together in such a way that it could be folded up without losing its shape or having wrinkles or creases appear. It was designed for the use of an automobile-driving public which was likely to throw the coat on the car seat or subject it to hard usage in other ways. Mr. Adams had designed coats and overcoats to hang with such balance that the garment seemed weightless to the wearer.

The designer worked closely with the woolens-purchasing vice-president, Mr. Brown, in developing ideas for patterns, shades, and types of fabric. Mr. Brown visited textile manufacturers to see new fabrics and also worked with one particular company in developing new fabrics. One recent innovation included a design in longer-wearing worsted which had the softness of tweed cloth plus a pattern with pleasing vitality. Since new designs and new fabrics could not be patented, it was expected that others would attempt to copy this development.

Purchasing was one of the key functions of the business. The woolens-purchasing vice-president, John Brown, had to follow the trends of the wool market as well as textile markets in this country and abroad. Some purchases were made in imported cloths from the United Kingdom and Ireland. Generally, in the men's clothing business imported fabrics tended to be used in the cheaper or more expensive suits, while suits in the middle ranges were usually made from domestic fabrics.

Since the company offered a wide selection of fabrics in many shades and patterns, some purchases involved small amounts, such as two or four "pieces" (40–80 suits), although there was usually a minimum-order quantity set by the seller. The company found that deliveries of small orders were apt to involve delays, since textile mills gave better service to large orders. In 1953, for example, poor deliveries coupled with labor shortages had necessitated considerable overtime.

Final decisions about the line to be offered were made by the top officials—the president, the vice-presidents of production and sales, the purchasing agent, and the designer. After his trip to the textile markets the purchasing agent usually knew in March what fabrics were good buys. Decisions were made in April. James Tailors followed the industry custom of reaching decisions about the next fall season's models in April, in order to provide sufficient time for designing, manufacturing and distribution. New models were always made up and inspected carefully before being added to the line.

Reports from the field by salesmen were useful in forming decisions on the line, since there were regional differences throughout the country with respect to preference for style and shades. In the Northeast tastes were more conservative—darker tones, narrower lapels, shoulders less pronounced. "In the West, men like clothes that 'glorify the man,' " said one James salesman, "broader shoulders, narrower waists, bolder colors."

In each of the two seasons, the company had about 700 to 1,000 different fabrics with about 100–200 being the same for both seasons. Probably 200 fabrics were the same from one fall line to the next. A typical breakdown of the number of fabrics used in the two seasons was as follows:

	Spring	Fall
Regular weight and tropicals	500	450
Topcoats	75	200
Overcoats	—	150
Sport coats	75	125
Slacks	100	75
	750	1,000

The company had about six basic models of suits in single-breasted styles. It also made a limited number of double-breasted suits to satisfy a small number of customers who still preferred this model. These basic models were given some regional differences to make some eighteen models—counting modifications. These eighteen were obtainable in an average of 152 different stock sizes and in some 450 different fall fabrics. The company had continued the double-breasted models even though this style had declined in popularity recently. "One of these years," Mr. James said, "the double-breasted suit will probably come back strong."

The company designed some lines to give service in a variety of situations and seasons. Some suits had enough pattern and vitality to make the coats useful as sport jackets when worn with slacks. Some suits were made of light-weight fabrics that permitted them to be worn in spring, summer and autumn.

In all lines of suits and topcoats, a variety of fabrics and styles was offered to suit a wide range of preference. For example, the summer line included suits of light worsted, fabrics of wool and dacron, 100 per cent dacron, fabrics of wool and silk, and pure silk in shantung weaves. The company also offered some highly-styled models in its line to appeal to those who liked distinctive dress.

Forecasting was an ever-present problem. As Mr. James put it, "We're like the rest in the industry. We do our forecasting by the seat of the pants." In 1952, the company misjudged the demand for summer suits made of new synthetics and at the end of the summer some 1,500 suits were still unsold.

PRODUCTION PROCESS

When fabrics arrived at the main plant, the bolts were stored close to the inspection and shrinking departments. Cloth was run over rollers and was inspected under fluorescent lighting by an operator who looked for irregularities and marked their location on the edge of the cloth with white string. Since wool is an animal fiber, it was expected that there would be some irregularities, although they were not always considered as flaws. If more than 10 per cent of a bolt was defective, it was returned.

After inspection the cloth was given alternate hot and cold baths, after which the cloth stayed wet for 24–48 hours before the final shrinking. Then the cloth was dried as it passed over rollers in a heated area. Although 3 to 5 per cent of the bolt of cloth was lost in shrinkage, fabrics given this treatment could go through countless dry cleanings without shrinking. Adequate shrinking was omitted by manufacturers of cheaper-grade suits. Tape and other material used in the inside construction were also shrunk, so that cleaning and pressing of a completed suit would not later cause shrinking that would pull the suit out of shape.

Shrunk fabrics were rolled on huge drums between layers of heavy, satin-smooth cloth; steam under pressure was forced through the layers to give the fabric a rich and lasting finish.

Cloth was then taken upstairs by elevator to the cutting room. Electric cutting knives could be used to cut as many as eight layers of cloth on which patterns had been marked out. Actually, the "lays" (layers cut) averaged around four because of many different patterns, sizes, and special orders. There were, of course, large powerful cutters able to cut up to fifty lays of cloth, but they were economical only with large volume. Also, union rules did not permit this kind of equipment for the better grade of suit. One worker commented, "We never cut more than 20 lays at a time." Peak cuttings for suits, separate coats, and trousers occurred in March through November with a low in July when the plant shut down for vacation. Peak cuttings for overcoats occurred in August and September with a low in January and February.

The company's designer worked with highly skilled draftsmen to create patterns for some 245 sizes. This work was performed in a special department, and over 19,000 patterns were stocked to make the company's line of models in all the various sizes. The company used separate patterns for each part of a suit, whereas concerns making cheaper grades might, for example, use the same size pocket for several different suit sizes. The cutters exercised great care in matching stripes and plaids, which was not done so carefully by makers of cheaper suits. Linings were also cut to specific patterns for each size, rather than using "averages" for several sizes, the latter being the practice for cheaper suits. Material used for linings was of high quality.

Men's clothing manufacture is a business requiring attention to a "thousand and one" details. There are close to 200 separate operations in making a suitcoat and over 100 in making a pair of trousers. After the cloth was cut to a pattern, the pieces were bundled and placed in boxes. Trimmings and findings were also bundled and placed in boxes. Buttons, thread and linings were, of course, carefully matched before being placed in the boxes. These boxes were then taken down in an elevator and placed in trucks for transportation to the No. 2 plant where the remainder of the manufacturing steps were carried out.

The company had long before outgrown the original plant, and a second building had been purchased four blocks away. In the No. 2 plant, the bundles from the cutting department were passed along a production line where the many operations were performed largely by hand, although some sewing machines were used. The linings were basted to the cloth—several thousand such basting stitches were used as a guide for hand-finishing tailors—and then the basting stitches were removed. Some 100 reinforcements were made in a suit at every point of strain. For example, stays and reinforcements prevented pockets from sagging; collars, lapels, edge seams, and armholes were carefully stitched with tape where needed. Only pure silk thread was used because of its strength and resistance to fading. At various stages there were many pressing operations to give the suit a lasting shapeliness. A suit coat had 36 pressings—every seam, reinforcement, and joining. Of these pressings, 29 were "under pressing" (performed on inside parts). Cheaper suits may have flat table pressing without the careful shaping of the hand-tailored suit and do not hold their form as well. James Tailors had special presses for collar and shoulders to give the suit proper form at those important points.

Buttonholes were sewn by hand, because machines could not match the strength and flexibility achieved by hand tailoring. Buttons were also sewn by hand to give greater permanence.

There were some 96 inspections along the way for each suit—over 70 of which were for tailoring operations. Twice a week top management inspected suits chosen at random from the line. The suits were modeled and were examined with great care. Following the completion of manufacturing, the suits were placed on hangers, hung on racks, and returned by truck to the main building where they were stored on racks, three levels high, prior to shipping. A movable ladder was used by the men who transferred the suits to these racks in building No. 1. Suits were shipped, still on hangers, in cartons reinforced with wooden strips and especially designed to protect the suits in transit.

The use of man-made fibers presented a number of manufacturing problems for the men's clothing industry. Since synthetic fibers, like orlon, had different properties from wool, it was necessary to reduce shrinkage in trimmings to a minimum, and cutting could not be done at great speed lest the layers of orlon cloth fuse. Sewing and pressing required extra care. For example, with orlon, light sewing thread tensions on machines were needed; high-speed sewing was not desirable; and, in pressing, temperature had to be carefully controlled lest the fabric fuse under heat.

In such a competitive industry as men's clothing, every step of the production process needed to be done efficiently. Lost opportunities for savings narrowed the profit margins. One of the officers pointed to some boxes containing scraps of cloth from the cutting room and said, "That's where we make our profit."

The James company also provided a special service for men who couldn't wear stock sizes or who preferred suits made to order. Each store selling James clothing was provided with forms on which measurements were to be indicated. A box of swatches was likewise sent to the store, containing some fabrics used in suits and coats and some special fabrics used only in special orders. The buyer could select a fabric that appealed to him. These special orders were handled by a special department that cut the fabrics and bundled them to be sent to the other building where sewing operations were carried on. The company doubted that this business was very profitable, but felt the service retained many buyers who liked high-grade clothing and who would buy some James clothing, such as overcoats and topcoats, in stock sizes.

Since orders for a particular season's output came in a relatively short period, the Production Control (Tracking) Department[4] scheduled production with greater efficiency during peak periods of manufacture than at other times. Reorders and special orders, which were difficult to anticipate, were scheduled during the off-peak periods. Orders were put on punched cards, which made it easy to accumulate orders for a particular model, size, and fabric. Tickets were made out showing specifications as to model, size, fabric, etc. Copies accompanied the bundles as well as strips of small numbered tickets which were torn off and kept by operators to show the number of pieces worked on.

[4] The Production Control Department was called the "Tracking" Department by many of the company's older employees. One of the officers commented, "We tried to use the more modern term—production control—but the old line employees still call it the Tracking Department; after all, one of the key workers in the department has been there 54 years."

Progress of manufacturing was noted by the return of copies to the production control department when an operation was completed.

Careful attention was given to inventory control over fabrics, trimmings, and findings. Inventory records for fabrics showed amounts on order, amounts received, totals on hand and issued; a swatch of each fabric was attached to the inventory record. Inventory of buttons, thread, trimmings, etc., presented some problems because of the large number of items that were kept on hand. A man formerly in charge of those items had devised his own system. After his death, however, no one else could follow his scheme and a new system was devised.

The company maintained a small laboratory for testing the fabrics purchased. Such factors as resistance to fading, the proportion of wool in mixed fabrics, wearing qualities, etc., were investigated by a skilled technician.

Plant facilities included some 150,000 square feet of space in the main building, and 120,000 square feet in building No. 2. The plants had been modernized with fluorescent lighting and air-conditioning in most areas. Open areas in most departments permitted the supervisors a good view of all activities under their guidance. The executive offices and home office personnel were located in the main building.

Exhibits 4, 5, and 6 show production and financial information on the industry.

exhibit 4 OPERATING CAPACITY OF MEN'S CLOTHING
INDUSTRY, 1950–1953 (AS A PERCENTAGE)

Month	1950	1951	1952	1953
Jan.	85	92	73	83
Feb.	95	98	85	94
Mar.	88	99	71	96
Apr.	86	79	56	84
May	89	69	68	88
June	76	69	67	84
July	—	—	—	—
Aug.	94	70	80	81
Sept.	78	63	76	72
Oct.	99	49	74	72
Nov.	91	58	80	76
Dec.	92	62	83	70

SOURCE: Clothing Manufacturers' Association of the United States of America, New York, N.Y.

exhibit 5   NET PROFIT ON SALES, MEN'S AND BOYS' CLOTHING
MANUFACTURE, 1933–1952 (AS A PERCENTAGE)

1933	1.70	1943	2.59
1934	0.78	1944	2.77
1935	0.94	1945	4.05
1936	1.28	1946	5.01
1937	0.15	1947	3.19
1938	0.21 loss	1948	2.47
1939	0.88	1949	1.38
1940	1.07	1950	2.09
1941	2.04	1951	0.76
1942	2.13	1952	1.25

SOURCE: Clothing Manufacturer's Association of the United States
of America, New York, N.Y.

exhibit 6   PRICE INDEX

Year	Men's Clothing	Woolens	Wool Price
	1947–1949—100		
1952	103.9	103.9	53.30 lb.
1951	104.4	112.8	97.0
	1935–1939—100		
1950	131.5	141.8	62.1
1949	131.8	140.0	49.4
1948	131.5	139.3	49.2
1947	127.4	134.7	42.0
	Jan. 2, 1931—100		
1946	107.8	110.2	
1945	106.0	108.1	
1944	105.9	108.1	

SOURCE: *Fairchild's Financial Manual Statistical Abstract, 1953.*

LABOR

The employees of the company were all highly skilled and were considered to be loyal to the company by the management. The average
age of the employees was rather high, and there was some difficulty in
recruiting new employees. The younger generation of clothing workers'
families seemed to prefer other occupations. Those already employed

in the men's clothing industry tended to stay, since they had acquired a skill valuable only in their own industry. The average employee had between 15 and 20 years of service with James Tailors and was considered by management as resistant to most changes. The proportion of women employees had been increasing.

Employees in the men's clothing industry were unionized for the most part, and wage negotiations on an industry basis set the pattern for wages in various manufacturing areas. Local negotiations with the union did not produce any important variations in the wage between firms in a specific area, although there were some differentials between New York, Philadelphia, Chicago, etc.

Union agreements provided for the closed shop and check-off. Employers paid for benefits involving sickness, accidents, old age and death. There was also a union social insurance program that gave limited payments for hospitalization, surgery, death, and retirement. One-week vacations were given for less than three years. In periods of low activity, work tended to be shared. While the terms of contracts specified a 36-hour week, in practice the week was 40 hours (8 hours for 5 days). The company operated a cafeteria at both plants. The officers and other employees joined the same line to buy food and ate in the same room in the main building.

The average hourly rate was close to the average for all manufacturing. Employees were paid according to a piece-rate system with about 85 per cent of the operations paid on that basis. The company was planning to add several industrial engineers to its factory staff, since none were presently employed.

FINANCE

Exhibit 7 includes financial information for the 1949–1954 period. In 1949 the company secured a loan of $929,500 at 2¾% for modernization of its plant and the building of an addition. All of the loan was not immediately used. The loan was to be liquidated at the rate of $71,500 per year until 1955, when the annual rate would become $165,000.

The company had a line of credit at several banks and was able to borrow without security. At peak periods of production for the fall and spring seasons, the company borrowed and then liquidated the loans over a period of several months. Purchase terms in the industry were

exhibit 7   JAMES TAILORS, INC.

Summary of financial position, October 31, 1949–1954

Balance Sheet

	1954	*1953*
Assets		
Cash	$ 216,847	$ 291,208
Accounts receivable (net)	2,309,341	2,612,775
Inventory	1,313,431	2,237,126
Est. tax credit	25,850	. . .
Sundry debtors	26,499	. . .
Total current	3,891,968	5,141,109
Investments	. . .	193,573
Fixed assets (less dep.)	1,275,090	1,362,617
Deferred charges	175,639	. . .
Goodwill	1	1
Total assets	$5,342,698	$6,697,300
Liabilities		
Notes payable	$1,397,000	$1,650,000
Accounts payable	234,644	658,431
Accruals	299,853	417,649
Federal tax, etc.	. . .	62,465
Total current	1,931,497	2,788,545
Notes payable	. . .	407,000
Common stock ($5 par)	396,000	396,000
Paid-in surplus	1,256,470	1,256,470
Earned surplus	2,011,699	2,102,253
Less reacquired stock	252,968	252,968
Total liabilities	$5,342,698	$6,697,300

Profit and Loss Statement

	1954	*1953*
Gross profit	$1,592,016	$1,805,436
Expenses	1,644,234	1,677,150
Profit or loss before taxes	* (52,218)	128,286
Federal income tax	. . .	60,500
Tax credit	25,850	. . .
Net profit or loss	* $ (26,368)	$ 67,786
Number of common shares	64,185	64,185
Earned per common share	$ .41d	$ 1.06

SOURCE: Company records.

* ( ) denotes loss.

1/10/n/60, and the company took advantage of discounts. Selling terms were the same.

The earnings in the preceding few years had been low due to a variety of factors. Adverse weather had slowed sales. Difficulties were encountered with synthetic fabrics that raised costs. In 1953 labor costs had gone up in May, but it had not been possible to pass the costs on to the consumer without the likelihood of hurting sales. The men's clothing industry was competing for the consumer's dollar in an en-

exhibit **7** (continued)

Balance Sheet

1952	1951	1950	1949
$ 241,407	$ 221,129	$ 104,936	$ 328,640
2,035,045	2,061,679	1,714,482	1,689,281
1,452,031	1,568,204	2,543,128	999,248
. . .	. . .	. . .	. . .
. . .	. . .	. . .	. . .
3,728,483	3,851,012	4,362,546	3,017,169
19,800	22,000	. . .	. . .
1,428,904	1,499,832	1,537,867	1,133,316
147,679	136,167	146,069	127,266
1	1	1	1
$5,324,867	$5,509,012	$6,046,483	$4,277,752
$ 715,000	$ 627,000	$1,221,000	$ . . .
241,237	274,622	390,948	164,758
311,609	353,055	449,692	314,835
96,867	272,428	79,510	66,030
1,364,713	1,527,105	2,141,150	545,623
462,000	517,000	649,000	550,000
396,000	396,000	396,000	396,000
1,256,470	1,256,470	1,256,470	1,256,470
2,098,652	2,065,405	1,856,831	1,782,627
252,968	252,968	252,968	252,968
$5,324,867	$5,509,012	$6,046,483	$4,277,752

Profit and Loss Statement

1952	1951	1950	1949
$1,656,384	$2,231,772	$1,760,818	$1,794,494
1,463,802	1,706,564	1,544,331	1,624,715
192,582	525,208	216,487	169,779
95,150	252,450	78,100	63,800
. . .	. . .	. . .	. . .
$ 97,432	$ 272,758	$ 138,387	$ 105,979
64,185	64,185	64,185	64,185
$ 1.52	$ 4.25	$ 2.16	$ 1.65

vironment where many new goods, appliances, and services were making demands on the consumer's pocketbook.

MANAGEMENT

The top management of James Tailors included eight men whose combined experience with the company totaled 261 years. With the exception of George James, Jr., the assistant to the president, each

exhibit 8
JAMES TAILORS, INC.
Organization Chart, 1954

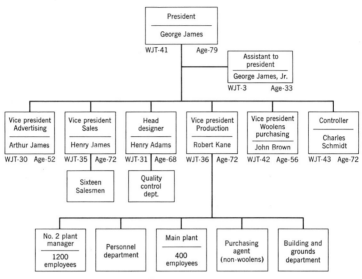

Note: WJT refers to years with James Tailors

man had served at least 30 years with James Tailors. This wealth of experience was considered by management as one of the most important assets of the company. Exhibit 8 shows the company's organization chart, listing the age and years of company experience of the firm's executives. George James, Jr., who drew up the chart, commented that "this is the first chart ever drawn up by the company and simply represents my view of the organization." He explained that "everyone has worked together so long that a detailed organization chart has always been considered unnecessary."

Mr. George James was the executive head of the business and held a position of great respect in the men's clothing industry. He had also been active for many years in civic affairs in the Utica area, but in recent years had encouraged his son, George James, Jr., to participate in many of these civic activities in his place. Mr. James continued, however, to perform his duties as chairman of the board and president of James Tailors. Every morning he was at his desk at 8 o'clock and worked steadily until 5 P.M. with an hour out for lunch. George James, Jr. commented that his father set a fast pace and expected his associates to keep up with him. "If I come in at 8:05 A.M., he'll quietly glance at his watch when I walk by his office and say hello," said George James, Jr.

Like his father, George James, Jr. was trained as a lawyer. It was expected that he would assume the role of executive vice-president as soon as his knowledge of the firm's customers, personnel, and mode of operations was sufficient. Mr. James felt that his son needed about one more year of experience before being given this additional responsibility.

Arthur James, vice-president of advertising, and Henry James, vice-president of sales, were brothers of the president and stockholders in the company. In addition to their responsibilities as department managers, both men did some field sales work with the company's larger accounts.

The other members of top management, while not members of the James family, were also department managers and held stock in the company. Robert Kane, the vice-president for production, and Charles Schmidt, the treasurer, were also on the board of directors. Other members of the five-man board were: Mr. George James, George James, Jr., and the president's other son, William James, a lawyer in private practice.

RECENT EVENTS

Mr. James pointed out that 20,000,000 men's suits were sold in 1954, out of a potential buyer total of 30,000,000 men—less than one suit per man per year. Average profits of men's clothing makers amounted to 1½ per cent that year. He felt that intense competition among men's clothing makers and the seasonal aspect of the industry also hurt business. Mr. James frankly admitted that the doldrums which had affected the men's clothing industry did not spare his company.

The James company reported a net loss in the fiscal year ended October 30, 1954, and Mr. James said at that time, "I'll be happy if we break even next year." He believed, however, that the industry might pick up in the future and pointed to the American Institute of Men's and Boys' Wear opening a five-year promotion to boost the sales of male clothing.

Later that year Mr. James learned that a small tailor shop in Utica, Sparkman's, was for sale. Sparkman's employed about thirty expert tailors and made high-quality men's suits that retailed for $185 and up. Distribution of the line had been limited to high-class local stores with the brand name of "Sparkman's" being featured.

Mr. James was attracted by the high-quality tailoring and felt that the "Sparkman's" shop, if purchased by James Tailors, could be used as an incentive to his firm's employees. The most expert James Tailors workmen would be promoted to making "Sparkman's" suits. Mr. James was also of the opinion that the high prices of the "Sparkman's" suits would make it easier to sell the James line to the retailer. "Our regular line wouldn't seem nearly so expensive," he said.

APPENDIX: ARTICLE IN WALL STREET JOURNAL, JANUARY 12, 1955

New York. An unusual masculine sensitivity to fashion's whim is help-ing turn gloom to cheer in the factories that turn out men's suits, coats, slacks and sport jackets.

Many a male is snapping up apparel in the newly-popular dark tones, such as black and charcoal gray and brown. As a result, retail sales of men's clothing have pulled out of a decline; they've outrun the year-ago pace ever since last June, by a generally widening margin. And they've been running ahead of production for more than a year, with a conse-quent paring of once-heavy stocks on retailers' racks.

After watching their sales and production skid steadily downward from May, 1953, until last October, men's wear makers feel the tide has defi-nitely turned in their favor.

The Production Tumble. While the men's-store sales were trailing 1.5% behind a year ago in 1954's first 10 months, production of men's suits was down much more steeply—by 14%. But in November, responding to the retail upturn, the manufacturers began to wield their needles faster; average weekly cuttings of men's suits rose $2 above those of November, 1953. In a more-than-seasonal gain, the industry's operating rate climbed to 77% of capacity in November from 69% in October.

The upturn has been felt most in suits, but they still have a long way to go to reach past popularity. Production of men's suits hit a record high of nearly 26 million in 1947, in response to pent-up wartime demand. Since then, production has been trending down. For the past five years, suit output has averaged under 20 million annually. As long ago as 1940, production was nearly 24 million.

Sportswear Surge. Meantime, the trend to casual living sent sportswear sales soaring. Manufacturers are now turning out nearly 8 million sport coats annually, up from only about 3 million in 1947 and from less than 1 million annually before World War II. Many, but not all, men's suit manufacturers also make sport coats. Now, while sport coats are still gain-ing, suits are making a comeback.

The sudden upsurge has not been as good for manufacturers as it ap-pears on the surface. It reflects, they say, inadequate anticipation of fall needs by retailers when they did their initial buying last spring, in a super-cautious frame of mind. Officials of H. Daroff, Hammonton Park and Joseph H. Cohen agree retailers bought only 50% to 60% of their expected needs when they placed initial orders, whereas a 70% figure is regarded as normal.

What's more, there was apparent under-estimation of the demand for the new styles, which generally call for a more conservatively-cut, single-breasted coat with narrow lapels and unpadded natural shoulders, in addition to the darker hues. Manufacturers are inclined to blame the miscalculation on retailers, while retailers tend to pin it on manufacturers. In either case, the result was what one manufacturer calls a "terrific jam-up of re-orders in November."

The Time Lag. Most clothing makers keep no stock of either cloth or clothes on hand; they work to order and plan production months ahead. According to Jerome Udell, chairman of New York City's Max Udell Sons & Co., it takes six months from the time a worsted fabric is ordered from the mill until a suit is completed. The minimum production time after a clothing maker receives his fabric is about six weeks. This time lag has made it hard to fill the unexpected demand.

One of the few firms that does maintain a stock of finished apparel is Joseph H. Cohen & Sons. Its merchandise manager says: "Retailers were completely unprepared for the color demand, and they hit our stock hard."

A different kind of company, Robert Hall Clothes, which is both a manufacturer and a retailer, has had a similar experience. "Like everybody else, we experienced a squeeze on charcoals," says an official. "It's been the biggest season yet on this merchandise."

And Meyer Kestnbaum, head of Chicago's famed Hart, Shaffner & Marx, reports: "We have had to turn down some business on dark gray and brown flannels or worsteds because of inability to produce enough to meet demand."

A Topcoat Sag. Held back last fall by the scarcity of wanted fabrics, men's suit production in 1954 lagged about 10% behind 1953, Mr. Udell figures. And besides the loss of some potential business, the industry is feeling the loss of some very real sales; production of topcoats and overcoats last year, it's estimated, sagged as much as 27% below 1953 output. Retailers indicate why.

In Dallas, E. M. Kahn's topcoat sales in December lagged 25% behind a year ago. "Who wants a topcoat in 70-degree weather?" asks another Dallas merchant, referring to the area's mostly mild winter.

The Silverwood chain in and around Los Angeles reports sales of topcoats and overcoats this season about the same as a year ago but around 10% below the previous pace. Says Vice-President Smith: "I think more men are leaving their overcoats home and turning on their car heaters."

OLYMPIA
WERKE

HISTORY

Olympia Werke began its existence as the Union Typewriter Company, which was organized in 1903 by the AEG, the Allgemeine Elektrisches Gesellschalt (the General Electric Company of Germany). It had been the intention of the parent company to produce an electrically operated machine, but by the time production plans materialized it had been decided that it would be more practical to make a manual machine. The acceptance of the original machine prompted the company to expand its factory in Erfurt (now a part of East Germany). The company's progress was interrupted by World War I; after the war the company changed its name to the Europa Typewriter Company, and the brand name Olympia was adopted. In 1942, the company produced its millionth typewriter.

In April of 1945 the Erfurt plant was heavily damaged by bombing, and the Russians confiscated what production facilities remained. The Olympia top management group, however, remained intact and quietly proceeded to search for a new location in West Germany. This was found in the abandoned German Navy barracks on the harbor at Wilhelmshaven. During the summer of 1946 a new production facility was arranged there, based upon a complete set of microfilmed plans and blueprints of the company's products, plants, and facilities, which had been daringly smuggled across the East German border in a single suitcase by three company officials.

The stay in the Navy barracks was temporary. Soon a new and modern plant was built a few miles inland in Wilhelmshaven. Shortly thereafter a second new factory was built in the neighboring city of Leer to undertake the production of a new lightweight portable typewriter. During the early 1950's Olympia developed a four-function calculating machine, and the management was considering building a plant to manufacture the new machine. Instead of building, it merged with Brunsviga Werke of Brunswick, which had two plants, 1,200 experienced employees, and long experience in making calculating machines. The emergent company was called Olympia Werke AG. In the ensuing years, Olympia added to its line a variety of adding and calculating machines, bookkeeping machines, and a limited line of data-processing equipment, but typewriters continued to dominate its operations. During the period from 1951 to 1963, Olympia's sales increased tenfold, and it extended its market to include all of the globe. By 1963, it had produced over 5 million office machines.

From its inception Olympia had operated fairly independently of the AEG, which continued to own all of Olympia's invested capital in 1963 of 68 million DM ($17 million). From time to time, at critical junctures, the AEG made major policy decisions directly affecting Olympia's future, and in some instances these were not in keeping with the thinking of the Olympia management.

Throughtout its history, Olympia had been a successful and profitable operation.

OLYMPIA WERKE IN 1964

In 1964, the bulk of Olympia's production was concentrated in its huge plant at Wilhelmshaven, which produced mainly typewriters. The branch plant at Leer manufactured small portable typewriters; Brunsviga Werke produced other office machines. Its labor force in Germany approximated 16,000 employees. Olympia's only other manufacturing facilities were assembly operations in Chile and in Canada which were relatively insignificant in size.

The typewriter line of Olympia included standard manuals, standard electrics, regular portables, and flat portables. To complement the typewriter line the company also manufactured transistor dictation machines and transcribers. Its line of office machines included manual and electric four-function machines, automatic bookkeeping machines, hand-operated and electric calculating machines, and a limited line of programming equipment.

THE GERMAN MARKET

Roughly 40% of Olympia's production was sold in Germany, where it supplied approximately 50% of the domestic requirement of typewriters. Its only significant competitors in Germany were Adler and Triumph, both of which, Olympia officials conceded, had maintained their share of the market by making a good product, by good management, and by their well-established reputations. American typewriter producers tended to concentrate their efforts on the United States market, which was the largest in the world. Some competition was experienced from Olivetti of Italy and from the subsidiaries of American companies which operated production facilities in the Netherlands, where labor costs were lower than in the United States or Germany. Even in Germany, Olympia did not compete on a price basis. As elsewhere, its policy was to compete on the basis of high quality and dependable service and to sell at prices which were moderately high.

Olympia distributed in Germany through branch houses and subsidiaries which were 100% company-owned sales and service operations. Its branch house operations were limited to the home market, where the company had an installation in every principal German city. All of the branches were staffed by Germans who had been trained by Olympia at Wilhelmshaven. Branch house operations were tightly controlled by the inland sales department of the sales division at Wilhelmshaven, which virtually dictated all policies with respect to personnel, pricing, retailer standards, service, advertising, and branch house operations. In Germany the wholesaling function was handled by Olympia. However, in all other parts of the world Olympia sold to wholesalers. Outside of Germany Olympia sold strictly for cash at wholesale prices, which were fairly uniform, on a world-wide basis. In Germany its terms of sale varied a great deal and were the subject of negotiations between the Olympia branches and the retailers. In Germany there was a single fixed retail price established for every Olympia machine, and strict controls by the branch houses permitted no deviation from this price.

Olympia believed that the German share of world consumption would increase during the coming years because of Germany's continually expanding economy and the growing popularity of portable typewriters (which were often used by business concerns as office machines). Olympia also expected its share of the German market to increase with the introduction of new models: electric, flat, and electric portable machines.

MANUFACTURING

The concentration of Olympia's production in its Wilhelmshaven plant permitted long, uninterrupted runs of single models with a minimum of setup changes and changes in tooling. The production process was highly mechanized, and wherever possible, it was automated. The plant management aimed at the ultimate in smooth work flows, using highly efficient mechanized, belted, or conveyorized carriers.

The Olympia headquarters management looked upon its efficient mass production methods as being integrally linked to its policy of producing typewriters which were high in quality. High-quality standards added heavily to production costs in the use of materials of premium technical specifications; in the use of many high precision instruments; in numerous inspections against tight tolerances; and in performance tests that allowed margins far beyond the requirements encountered in normal usage. The management aimed to have its low-cost, efficient production more than offset the high costs of producing a premium-quality product.

One of the advantages which had attracted the Olympia management to Wilhelmshaven was the fact that this sector of Lower Saxony in northern Germany was largely a rural area which, in the immediate post-World War II period, had a surplus of labor of the type used by Olympia. Only a small percentage of the employees were veterans from the Erfurt plant, and most of these were in supervisory capacities. About half of the work force were women. Within a few years the Wilhelmshaven plant had exhausted the local labor supply, drawing from a radius of 50 kilometers (30 miles). Thereafter refugees were attracted from Eastern Europe. On 1964 over 80% of the Olympia work force consisted of local residents, and approximately 20% were refugees.

Most of Olympia's work force were young people; the average man was 33, the average woman 29. Many who were from peasant homes and those who were refugees and had suffered difficult times considered themselves to be fortunate to be working under such favorable conditions. Their attitude generally was appreciative. Union conflicts were negligible, and occasional grievances of employees were settled in a friendly manner in negotiations between the management and the

Workers' Council. The management took pride in the good spirit of the work force and their high productivity.

DISTRIBUTION

Olympia divided its sales into domestic, European, and export. The management stated that it had organized these sales divisions because (1) it believed that the whole sales function was too large for a single administration; (2) the approach to the European market was different, Europe being more uniform and more like a single market; (3) the documents involved in overseas business varied a great deal in nature; and (4) European transactions tended to be more refined and more stable. "Overseas business," said Mr. Heinz A. Krueger, director of overseas sales, "is rougher. Sometimes it is actually volatile."

In Germany, Olympia sold to retailers through its own chain of wholly owned branches. In Paris, Milan, Brussels, Stockholm, London, Zurich, Luxembourg, Bogota, and Santiago, Olympia wholesaled its machines through wholly owned subsidiaries. Europe was looked upon as an extended German market. The European subsidiaries were operated on the same basis as the German branches and were staffed by German nationals trained at Wilhelmshaven. The company had no partnership arrangements anywhere. In all other territories outside of Europe sales were made through wholesalers which were independently owned agencies of the company. Olympia did not have any administrative offices between the headquarters level at Wilhelmshaven and the wholesalers. "We feel no need for any embassies abroad," said Mr. Krueger. "We might need them some day, but not yet."

The subsidiaries had been established in some instances because the management felt that it would be dangerous to entrust a very large market to an independent agent. In other instances it did so because no one with enough capital was found to finance a large agency. "The typewriter business is neither exciting nor romantic," said Mr. Krueger. "No fabulous quick fortunes are made selling typewriters. It takes substantial capital to finance a large agency . . . sometimes several million dollars . . . and since we make no flowery promises to potential agents, venture capital tends to find other activities more attractive."

PRICING

"Ten years ago," said Mr. Krueger, "when the reborn company was still young, out first agents had a lot to say about pricing. Now headquarters virtually dictates price levels, especially in the large markets. In fact, all marketing policy making has swung to Wilhelmshaven."

In the open market there were six firms selling on a world-wide basis which informally established the world price level. On low-price models, a field in which Olympia did not participate, costs were a factor in setting prices. Olympia's prices were moderately higher than those of most competitors.

In the open market prices did not generally fluctuate much in the short run. There was no need to guarantee agents against losses from price reductions, which simply did not occur. Prices abroad were intended to be competitive, and the Olympia management stated that its agents were reliable and had little inclination to cut prices. Retail margins were not large enough to permit much deviation from the normal price structure. No agent would cut prices as a matter of routine strategy, and in those rare instances in which one did temporarily drop prices, he would do so only after consulting headquarters. Wilhelmshaven suggested the retail price on newly introduced models and sometimes urged agents to raise their prices on going models. Agents regularly reported to Wilhelmshaven their prices and the prices of their competitors. Olympia machines were never permitted to get into the hands of discount houses. "Violations of our pricing policies simply do not happen," said Mr. Krueger. "No agent would be inclined to be headstrong and go his own way. Our relations with our agents are friendly and helpful. They consider themselves to be part of the 'Olympia family.' "

The f.o.b. price was fairly uniform on a world-wide basis, with a few exceptions to meet competition. Consumer prices varied widely, however, because of the costs over f.o.b., such as freight, licenses, and duties. In exceptional instances Olympia made allowances for this to keep agents alive in particularly distant and competitive markets, but this rarely occurred. Markups were f.o.b. plus 6 to 7% for cif,[1] plus duties, taxes, and licenses, which varied widely. Landed cost to the agent was marked up 40 to 60%, depending upon local competition. Thus the typical pricing structure would be:

F.o.b.	100
Cif	6
Duties, fees, etc.	34
Landed price	140
50% markup	70
Final price	210

[1] cost, insurance, freight

Markups were the same in each territory for all competitors. They varied widely, however, from one territory to another, generally varying inversely with the volume sold in that market; in high-volume territories markup tended to be lower. Sales costs, such as advertising and the local level of salesmen's salaries, also affected the final price.

Olympia's wholesale prices in the open market tended to be fairly uniform, but in the government market, where thousands of typewriters were bought on a single purchase contract, prices tended to fluctuate. Government business was looked upon in the industry as prestige business, which was jealously sought after for its advertising value. Prices were tendered in sealed bids, and to the government purchaser, price tended to be the determining factor, with quality playing a secondary role. School and institutional business tended to follow the government pattern.

Olympia did not, as a matter of policy, engage in promotional price deals. Olympia was established in most markets, and management felt no need to cut prices to gain entrance into any new market, except possibly such markets as Spain and parts of Africa. If this expedient were to be used, it would be a very temporary thing. The only other instance in which headquarters cut prices was, in case of distressed stocks or outmoded models, and these were sold off quietly in the home market through the branch house organization. This rarely happened, however.

"We have seriously considered," said Mr. Krueger, "the possibility of charging higher prices. We came to the conclusion that charging the highest price possible would be shortsighted. Volume in individual markets fluctuates widely from year to year, but aggregate sales do not fluctuate greatly and show a steady increase. We decided that our best strategy would be to charge a moderately high price and push ahead on all fronts equally."

ADVERTISING

Olympia machines were advertised in practically every type of medium all over the world. On national advertising within a sales territory the local Olympia agent handled the program. Olympia took little part in these programs unless Wilhelmshaven contributed to a local campaign; in these instances it retained the right of approval on all advertising matters. International advertising costs were paid for by Olympia, national costs by the agents. The bulk of Olympia advertising was centered on typewriters in local and national campaigns, and national advertising costs were typically 4 to 5% of the retail sales dollar. Wilhelmshaven provided many promotional materials, such as leaflets, slides, school calendars, and posters, without charge. The advertising appropriation varied only with the over-all trend in sales volume. The advertising effort varied widely from country to country. In general the free markets, where all competitors met on a par, required more advertising than the restricted markets.

Olympia advertising was beamed mainly at consumers, and, since only a very small percentage of any population used typewriters, perhaps as little as 5%, the ad campaigns were designed to meet this segmented market. Advertising themes emphasized quality, reliability, and the availability of service. All advertising was low-pressure. In Germany, Olympia headquarters took the initiative in originating ad themes, and some of these proved suitable for export to other markets. It was the management's experience, however, that no single ad theme was suitable in all markets, because of language and cultural differences. Two popular slogans were: "Olympia typewriters don't cost—they pay" (Australia) and "Olympia writes best of all—because Olympia is best of all" (United States).

Advertising agencies were used extensively by Olympia agents abroad, but not in all territories. The headquarters management believed that they proved particularly helpful in Anglo-Saxon areas. Ad agencies did market research, selected media, created mottoes, slogans, and themes, and wrote copy. They also did consumer sampling, in which Olympia usually rated well.

MARKET RESEARCH

Olympia's overseas agents sometimes used consultants for market research at their own volition and at their own expense. The Olympia headquarters never did so. In its early years at Wilhelmshaven it had used consultants occasionally before entering new overseas markets, but when the company attained world coverage it discontinued this practice. Olympia's market research was conducted by a staff group at Wilhelmshaven which did all of the data collecting for the entire company. There were also four men in the overseas department who did "desk work," analyzing the data collected by the research group.

The main objective of the research group was to collect figures on world market movements. For the overseas department it gathered import figures on every country in the world, even very small ones. On typewriters the company aimed to know what every country had imported and from whom, by models. These data were collected from Olympia's own organization and from government statistics. The data on its own sales were gathered by its sales and service representatives from a standard questionnaire designed by Olympia headquarters. Government information was obtained through the German Federal Statistical Office, which had information on virtually every area of the world. It was the company's experience that sufficient statistical data were available on most areas. Even countries which were underdeveloped economically often had good statistical information because of the efficient government services that had been developed for them in their colonial days.

Based upon the data Olympia collected it made forecasts, one per country per year. These forecasts became the basis for all company planning, including production. "Our Wilhelmshaven operation was once definitely production-minded," said a sales executive. "That was understandable, since in our early years here we were rebuilding our production facility from nothing, and that took all of our attention. Lately, however, more and more attention is being paid to sales, even though we have been oversold for a number of years."

The Olympia research staff felt that it was not difficult for them to make accurate forecasts. The over-all volume of typewriter sales in most markets was stable and sudden market shifts were rare. The Olympia management felt that it had its finger on the market pulse much better than most of its competitors.

SALES

In 1963 about 60% of the Olympia unit volume was sold in the export market. World production of typewriters had been about 5 million units in 1963. The United States produced 27% of this total, West Germany 22%, Italy 15%, and the Netherlands 10% (which included production by subsidiaries of United States manufacturers). Out of the total production, 2.4 million were sold in export markets. In 1962 the German consumption was about 6% of world consumption, whereas its share of the typewriter export market (which was largely the Olympia share) was 25%. In 1963 it was 27%. This 2% rise represented an 8% increase in the amount of Olympia's export sales. By comparison

Italy's (Olivetti's) share had increased from 21 to 22%. Olympia's typical market share in most established areas of the world market was 20% or more. Its principal competitors for overseas business were Remington, Royal, Underwood, Smith-Corona, and Olivetti. The largest single market was the United States, which consumed about 40% of total world production, or 2 million machines, but United States producers usually confined their sales efforts to the American market and did not play any significant role in the export field. Germany consumed about 500,000 units, the rest of Europe 1.3 million, and the rest of the world 1.2 million.

Olympia believed that not only its volume of export sales but its percentage share of the total export market would continue to rise. The world typewriter market had been growing lately, at the rate of 12 to 15% every two years, and the German share of the market had been keeping pace. Olympia's typewriter exports had been rising faster than other German exports, and the Olympia management believed that the introduction of new models in the near future, such as the electric, the flat, and the electric portable, would increase its market share. The management was confident that the world demand for typewriters would accelerate, especially the demand for portables. Portables were increasingly in demand for home use, and in some markets were used both in homes and in offices. Electrics were also increasing in popularity.

In the export market it was the aim of the Olympia management to compete on the basis of high quality, which it considered basic and fundamental; on the basis of thorough and dependable service; and on the basis of prices which were moderately high rather than low. "We are the Mercedes of the typewriter industry," said an Olympia executive, "but where the Mercedes price is twice or more than that of a Volkswagen, our prices are only about 15 to 20% above those of our competitors."

In the German market Olympia's terms of sale varied considerably, but its terms for export sales were fairly uniform. In general, it sold on some basis in which no credit risk was involved: letters of credit, advance payments, or documents against acceptance, and certain exporting companies in the free cities of Hamburg and Bremen handled payment of Olympia's bills on presentation. Olympia's overseas receivables averaged about 30 days.

Olympia concentrated on selling its typewriters, mostly the manual ones, in the export markets, other office machinery and equipment being

considered secondary products. Its grand market strategy was to push
ahead uniformly on all fronts at the same time rather than to concentrate on selected markets. World typewriter sales followed general economic trends, with few cyclical swings that were significant. Neither
were there seasonal variations, even in the Christmas period. Olympia
planned a future hard push of the sale of newly designed electric typewriters in the high-potential and well-developed areas, such as the
United States and England.

THE OVERSEAS SALES STAFF

The overseas division of Olympia was headed by Mr. Heinz Krueger,
director of overseas sales, who held the title of *Prokurist,* which was
just below the level of board member. He had formerly answered directly to the board, but in 1963 the AEG had approved a change in the
headquarters organization, as a result of which a new office of general
sales manager was created. Herr Mossner was appointed to it and made
a *Vertriebsdirektor* and a member of the board. Although the overseas
division accounted for two-thirds of Olympia's sales volume and demanded much attention because of fluctuations in individual markets,
distances, and its lack of homogeneity, the entire division had less than
50 people. Of these, only four people, including Herr Hubert Fleige,
reported directly to Mr. Krueger (see Exhibit 3).

The link between Wilhelmshaven and its agents abroad was Olympia's sales and service representatives. A typical representative joined
the company at about the age of 20. He would spend about two years in
the headquarters office as a clerk, learning in general the operations of
an overseas territory. This would be followed by a period of six months
of technical training in the plant, after which he would spend some
time working for one of the German branches. He would then represent
Olympia in one of its overseas areas. The representative traveled a circuit, regularly visiting Olympia agents. His duty was to assist agents in
every way, along Olympia policy lines, in achieving their share of the
market. "It is our belief at Olympia," said Mr. Krueger, "that an agent
should not need to experiment. Therefore we give our agents, through
our sales and service representatives, methods and practices which have
already been tried and proven elsewhere." The representatives were
prepared to handle service questions, advertising plans, credit policies,
the management of agent inventories, training of agency personnel, the

layout and decor of showrooms, and any matter at all in the whole-saling operation. Sales and service representatives were well paid in comparison with Olympia representatives in Germany. Olympia usually had five or six such representatives on its staff. In 1964, however, there were only two.

It was Olympia policy to leave most of the sales activities in the hands of its agents. In keeping with this policy, the company's sales and service representatives, after a few years of traveling their circuit and a short refresher course at Wilhelmshaven, would leave the employment of Olympia and join one of the company's agents as a sales and service representative. The agency employing the representative would be chosen by Olympia headquarters and he would work for it on a contract basis, the terms of the contract and his remuneration being suggested by Wilhelmshaven. At the agency the representative would carry on the same activities he had formerly performed for Olympia, concentrating on his particular agency and carrying his help further down toward the retailer level. In 1964 there were over 20 such Olympia-trained representatives at various overseas agencies. In addition to these there were innumerable sales representatives who were nationals employed by the agents and trained by Olympia's sales and service representatives or in classes conducted by headquarters at Wilhelmshaven.

In addition to these sales and service men, there were four group leaders at headquarters who had general responsibility for the sales activities in their respective territories (see Exhibit 3). Their responsibilities were limited, however, to the administrative handling of sales. They were not charged with generating sales volume. Generating sales volume was considered to be the responsibility of the agent.

AGENCIES

For purposes of distribution Olympia divided the world into over 100 market areas. In over 80% of these areas Olympia sold through agencies. In most of the world, agencies were Olympia's liaison between Wilhelmshaven retailers and the ultimate consumers.

It was the responsibility of the agencies to generate sales through advertising and through promotion. Agencies performed the wholesale function, selling mostly to retail dealers, but occasionally to consumers. They imported stocks and maintained inventories. They granted short-term credit to retailers. They sold to several types of customers: to retailers, to consumers, to governments and governmental institutions, and to schools. Agencies did repair work, cleaning, and maintenance work and performed guarantee work on behalf of Olympia, in which case they acted in the name of Olympia in making good Olympia's guarantees.

In large-volume markets, where large capital investment was required to establish an agency (perhaps several million dollars), agencies were usually corporations; in middle-sized markets they were often partnerships and sometimes proprietorships; and in small markets most of them were proprietorships. Most of the capital investment in an agency would be used to finance inventories. The requirement of Wilhelmshaven was that an agency have on hand at all times a three-month stock, plus one month on order, one month in transit ("on the water"), and the accounts receivables of its retail dealers.

The character of the concerns which *wholesaled* Olympia machines varied. Most of them were wholesalers of office equipment and supplies, but where these were not available Olympia might use trading firms, which handled many products and operated somewhat in the manner of a mail-order house. The Wilhelmshaven management was selective in its choice of agencies and was only interested in agencies which would actively promote the sale of Olympia products. In most parts of the world it could afford to be selective, for the internationally advertised Olympia line was considered to be attractive, and many wholesalers were eager to secure a franchise. Olympia would not do business with the 'agency-hunter', the trading company which was always eager to add either items or sources to its catalogue. Olympia used trading houses only in such areas as parts of Africa and Asia, where, as an Olympia executive put it, "the geography is big, but the sales potential is small."

In general, Olympia had one agent in each market area, and in most instances a market area consisted of one country, but there were some exceptions. A country like Saudi Arabia was large in area but contained two trading areas which were distinct and far removed from each other, in which case two agencies were granted franchises. In any event, each agent was strictly limited to doing business only in his own market area, and his contract with Olympia guaranteed him exclusivity in his territory. Olympia itself was not permitted to sell directly in that territory. At the same time, agencies were not required to be exclusively Olympia agencies. They usually handled many other products, including the office equipment and machinery of other manufacturers. They were not permitted, however, to handle lines of typewriters and calculating machines which were directly competitive with Olympia.

The agencies were not compensated directly by Olympia in the sense of being paid a commission on sales. They were independent businesses which purchased and resold Olympia products and they received their compensation in the form of markups. It was a stated policy of the Wilhelmshaven headquarters that Olympia would take a direct interest in fostering the profitability of its agencies. Wilhelmshaven furnished them with advertising advice and materials, sometimes at no cost, and at times on a shared-cost basis. International advertising was done by Olympia at no cost to the agencies. Olympia often deliberately set manufacturer's prices at a level which would enable the agents to earn a reasonable profit; it gave them technical assistance; and at times it lent them people from headquarters, in which case the agency assumed the salary expense involved.

Wilhelmshaven trained the agency's marketing men, in most instances at no cost to the agency. This was done in two ways: (1) Olympia's sales and service representatives did on-the-spot training in the course of their routine calls upon agencies; (2) for longer and more intensive training programs the personnel of the agency were sent to Wilhelmshaven at the expense of the agency. Once there, Olympia provided the training free of charge.

Olympia did not have any capital invested in its agencies. None of them were joint ventures. Occasionally Olympia might provide an agency with short-term credit in the form of bills of exchange or extended credit terms, but this was limited to agencies which were young and was only a temporary expedient. Extended credit was never granted to an established agency.

The pattern of distribution in each agent's marketing area evolved out of the circumstances existing in the territory. In a territory like Australia, which covered a vast area, there were several city-centered trading areas, each separated from the other, in which the agent might operate from branches of his own. Again, a market like Burma meant only Rangoon, the port city, and was virtually a single-city operation. Agents were free to determine their own best method of distribution. If an agent were new and green and did not have an insight into the typewriter business, Olympia would instruct and advise him, in which case Olympia would expect that the agent follow its advice.

Retailers might be granted a local franchise by their agency. If they were, they would normally be required by the agent to carry a minimum inventory of machines in stock. Sometimes agencies granted retail dealers consigned stock arrangements. Exclusiveness at the retail level was not common; most retailers carried several brands of office machinery. Agencies were free to make whatever inventory arrangements they wished with their retailers. They also set their own credit terms and sometimes even supplied long-term capital to a promising new retailer. In general, the burden of financing, including the carrying of inventories, was on the agency.

All agency relationships were governed by a legal contract between Olympia and the agency, and the contract specified that any dispute arising from the contractual agreement would be settled according to German law in the Court of Wilhelmshaven. The Olympia management stated that such disputes were virtually nonexistent. The management at Wilhelmshaven extended itself to cultivate the friendship of its agents, and it claimed that it had been so successful in that its sales organization had come to be known as "the Olympia family."

EXPORTING PROBLEMS

In selling in the export market Olympia faced several obstacles: there were other large producers who sold in the world market, whose production costs were lower and who sold at lower prices; there were large producers who operated branch plants in local markets; there were import duties which ranged from 0 to as much as 40%; there were preferential duties; there were preferential quotas and preferential treatment; there were those nations which were nationalizing production; there were free trade areas; and there were nonquality machines being sold on a very low-price basis.

Remington, Royal, Underwood, Smith-Corona, Olivetti, and certain Japanese producers all had large-scale production facilities. All except the latter two produced quality machines which they sold at normal price levels. While American producers tended to concentrate upon the American market, some were now operating branch plants abroad.

Since Germany consumed less than 10% of the world typewriter requirement, the Olympia management believed that any large producer had to look to the world market to obtain enough volume to make possible mass production of a quality machine at reasonably low cost. Furthermore, Olympia believed that its own production should be concentrated in its one huge plant at Wilhelmshaven. It reasoned that this enabled the production management to make the fullest use of its expert engineering talents, which it thought would be weakened if spread to other locations. It made possible the strict policing of quality controls. The labor force at Wilhelmshaven was experienced and stable, and there was good morale. Long runs of single models were practical, using the ultimate in cost-saving equipment. The Olympia management did not believe that any typewriter factory producing less than 50,000 machines a year could operate efficiently and turn out a satisfactory machine.

The Olympia management believed itself to be strongly handicapped in the Commonwealth areas because of their system of preferential duties. In countries like Australia, Canada, New Zealand, and Rhodesia the preferential difference ranged from $7\frac{1}{2}$ to 22%. In Australia, Underwood was able to sell its machines for £70, and Olympia, despite its higher costs and duties, was forced to match this price. There was a tendency, however, toward equalization in recent years. Brazil, for example, had reduced its duty from $17\frac{1}{2}$ to $7\frac{1}{2}\%$. New Zealand, on the other hand, still maintained a duty of 25%.

Quotas were also tending to disappear from year to year, but in 1964 Olympia still had to contend with many. The French had a system which gave preferential treatment to certain countries, such as Algeria. Imports into these countries would typically favor France, giving the French perhaps 40% of the total allotment and parceling out the remaining 60% to all others.

Another allotment system which restricted Olympia was the "oldest established importer" system. This system aimed to maintain the status quo, preference being given to imports from companies which were already established in the market. This worked strongly against Olympia which was a relative newcomer in almost all world markets, dating to the post-World War II period. Olympia's serious exporting effort was even more recent, having begun only in the late 1950's.

Some countries set quotas which were intended to protect and to foster national production. These countries took either of two means to implement their resetrictive policies: (1) they assessed import duties at restrictive or sometimes prohibitively high levels; or (2) they simply forbade imports. Argentina, for example, permitted no imports at all. Brazil, Mexico, and India were severely restrictive. "Some countries," said an Olympia executive, "are so unrealistic that they prefer to produce within their own borders at any cost no matter how high. Others blindly shut out all imports. We do not believe that any country can maintain this exclusion policy permanently. Others, like the Australians, have policies which are more refined, but are nevertheless rather impractical. The Australians have invited us to set up a plant in Australia. They would require, however, that our Australian-produced typewriter be restricted to a factory cost which we would guarantee would not be over 20% higher than the cost of comparable imported machines. How can we possibly guarantee this? We don't see the economies of setting up factories in the various world markets at the present time."

In Canada and the United States Olympia believed that it faced two hurdles: (1) duties and (2) the effect of the United States fair-trade laws. In Canada, Olympia had to contend with both preferential duties and the carry-over effect of United States fair-trade laws. "I cannot understand," said Mr. Krueger, "what the German price has to do with the United States price. The end eect is that the fair-trade laws hamper free trade, and this is generally not in keeping with American foreign trade policies. Olympia is one of the few foreign companies which has been successful in selling in Canada, but we have done so at the cost of profits. Our price must have added to it all the expenses to land our machines in Canada plus duties of 17½%." Underwood, Remington, and Olivetti all manufactured within the Commonwealth. Olympia did not.

In the Philippines, the United States was given preferential treatment. Olympia had been charged a duty as high as 20% on its machines, whereas the United States producers paid no duty. In turn, the United States reciprocated by buying up the cane sugar production of the Philippines. The Philippines had lately been leveling their duties, reducing them by stages from 20 to 15 to 10%. In doing so they were torn between their wish to get away from their colonial status and their wish to maintain the income which accrued to their government from the import duties. Olympia, following its policy of covering all markets, even the low-profit ones, kept its foothold in the Philippines.

Foreign aid programs tended to work against Olympia. Those countries which received substantial United States aid tended to give preference to United States-produced goods. In Egypt, which had close trade ties with the Russians, Nasser did business on a bartering basis, trading Egyptian cotton for Russian Bloc radios, refrigerators, typewriters, or canned milk. This preferential treatment to others resulted in a landed cost to Olympia that was prohibitive. "It would have cost us a loss of 25

DM per typewriter to sell our machines in Egypt," said Mr. Krueger, "therefore in this instance we abandoned our policy of pushing ahead on all fronts, and we gave up the Egyptian market."

The Olympia management believed that there were some slight advantages accruing to it in the operation of the Common Market. French and Italian duties, which had been high compared to those of Germany, were now leveling. Olympia had once paid 40% duty to export to Italy, whereas the Italians could export to Germany at 15%. Olympia saw distribution and costs as being a second Common Market advantage. Europe would become an extended German market. Selling in Paris, Rome, or Amsterdam would become the same as selling in Bremen, Frankfurt, or Munich. In the European Free Trade Area, however, Olympia believed the outlook was somewhat different. "It has been our experience," said an Olympia executive, "that England thinks England first, and Commonwealth second, and then EFTA." Mr. Krueger said that some knowledgeable authorities believed that the totally free trade era was as far as 30 years away. He himself believed that it would be realized within 10 years.

The free trade areas which were developing in other parts of the world affected Olympia. Argentina had closed its borders to the importation of typewriters entirely, and Brazil had imposed strong restrictions on imports. Together, Argentina and Brazil had enough manufacturing capacity to supply all of Latin America. The end result, according to Olympia, was high-cost production that resulted in a low-quality machine which was sold at a high price. "A typewriter," said Mr. Krueger, "is not the kind of product with which a developing nation should start its manufacturing. A typewriter is highly technical, has about 3,000 precision parts, requires skilled industrial labor, and a high degree of organization in the flow of materials and the assembly process. Neither do these countries have a large enough mass market for typewriters to enable them to manufacture in mass at low cost. The Indians are turning out typewriters today, but they are definitely shoddy products. They would be better off if they had chosen products which are relatively simple to make . . . like furniture or shoes."

Every major producer of typewriters which competed with Olympia in the world market had branch plants and local assembly facilities at strategic points abroad. Olympia had none, except for token assembly operations it had established in Chile and Canada, nor was there any inclination to shift production to foreign locations. Olympia's AEG parent company had committed Olympia to a one-large-plant policy, the thinking of the parent management being that Olympia had a huge manufacturing facility at Wilhelmshaven now, and it had consistently had a backlog of orders which kept the huge facility operating at capacity. Since typewriters were postponable purchases, AEG did not wish to have any general economic recession, with the accompanying accelerated slump in typewriter sales resulting in idle plant capacity and high overhead costs. Furthermore, in terms of AEG policies, although Olympia was doing very well on the present basis, it had enough current problems to deal with to keep it fully occupied, and it had neither the time nor the manpower to establish facilities abroad.

In general, the Olympia management agreed with the thinking of its AEG parent. However, Olympia management believed that at times it was faced with a choice of (1) dominating a market or (2) abandoning it totally. They also expected that the coming free trade era would tend to emphasize this kind of choice. There was a chronic labor shortage in Germany. Olympia had pressed for further expansion of the Wilhelmshaven plant to work off its chronic backlog, but the AEG had not approved, citing that it was easy to add bricks and mortar but impossible to secure more workers. Olympia had never resorted to the expedient used by other labor-hungry plant operators in Europe, who sent missions abroad to import workers on a contract basis from such places as Portugal, Morocco, Malta, and Turkey.

The Olympia management had from time to time made studies of the possibilities of establishing plants in South America, Central America, and the Far East. On the basis of these studies it had prepared detailed plans which would enable it to start construction of plants in any of these areas on very short notice. The management of Olympia often debated the advisability of establishing plants abroad. The question frequently asked was "when and where?"

OTHER CONSIDERATIONS

"I think that our major problem," said Mr. Krueger, "is one faced by the entire typewriter industry. It is the same situation which faced the American automobile industry an era ago, and from which the present auto industry evolved. During the 1920's there was a great shake-out process going on in the auto industry, and in the end there remained only a few large producers. The typewriter industry today is a mixture of many large, small, and intermediate companies. There are big swings in production . . . occasional dumping . . . some producing largely for export . . . some not interested in exporting at all. All of this would have regulated itself except for Olivetti, which had its own unique policy. This policy seemed to be: dominate the world market; Olivetti-ize the world. In carrying out this policy Olivetti sold machines at half its factory cost to get into some markets. The Olivetti American manager said, 'Put an Olivetti in every butcher and baker shop . . . and don't worry about whether it's ever paid for . . .'

"The fights, the slashing, are gradually disappearing. Little producers are selling out before they go broke. The business which remains is conducted on a fairly reasonable basis. If in the end only five large producers remain, and each is satisfied with his market share, the entire business will be more orderly. Then we can still be strong competitors, but within economic limits. Olympia selling is low-pressure, dignified. We do not believe in hard selling at any level, nor in using credit as an inducement. Olympia does not mean to monopolize the world. We have been consistently oversold, but we are not expanding production. Olympia wants only its fair share of the market. It means to let others live. We set goals which are reasonably attainable, and we attain them.

"I often wonder whether we are not too preoccupied with our policy of high quality. People are becoming less interested in products which last a long time. Our machines have an average life of 15 years. Our machines have cast and pressed parts, like the frame, which are machined, drilled, tapped, and threaded and are screwed together. This permits precision, and the resulting typewriter is highly accurate and durable. Now the Japanese have commenced to make a typewriter which has a plastic frame which is so designed that it can simply be clipped together by hand . . . no drilling, tapping, screwing involved. Their machine is produced at very low cost, it sells for a very low price, and there is no intention that it give quality performance. It is sold with a three-year free service guarantee, and after that length of time the consumer can dispose of it.

"This leads me to wonder whether there might be some much simpler means of writing mechanically than the conventional typewriter. A typewriter performs a fairly simple function—it translates writing by hand into a mechanical means of writing. In the form that current typewriters take, this means producing a precision machine which has over 3,000 parts, making it so that it will perform precisely, making it so that it will last, and making it so that it can be sold for about $100. I should think that mechanical writing could be done by some device that would be much simpler, less precise, and less costly. But there has been no change in the basic idea of the typewriter since its invention. No one has come up with any revolutionary new principle. There has been some experimentation with photoelectric and chemical-reaction writing, but nothing useful has emerged. And we at Olympia are continuing on the assumption that there is not going to be any radical change in the current method of mechanical writing.

"I think that Olympia now has certain advantages over its competitors in the export market. We have an established, accepted line of high-quality machines. We have a reputation for giving good service. We are loyal to our agents and have their loyalty. Our agents know they will receive fair treatment from us. They also know that our policies and our prices change only very slowly. The 'Made in Germany' label still has the connotation of high quality abroad, although others are now catching up to us. And our associates in business know that we believe in conducting our business systematically, that we believe in knowing our limits, and that we do not believe in trying to overdo.

"Our long-range objectives are to increase and consolidate our market share; to achieve more co-ordination of manufacturing and sales and more sales orientation; to produce machines in the most rationalized way for profitability; to do more research to keep pace with developments; to reliably determine what our optimum program ought to be. . . .

"Perhaps we ought to be thinking more about other office machines. Olympia is now, in a sense, the primitive in the industry, and this segment represents a small part of our business. We have chosen to concentrate on what we call consumer items . . . principally mechanically operated office machines and mainly typewriters, which we produce in mass volumes. Office machinery ranges all the way from flat portable typewriters ($40) to computers ($250,000). The whole product line includes calculating machines, check writers, bookkeeping machines, adding machines, dictating machines, comptometers, data-processing equipment, and photocopy machines. Olympia now makes most of these, in a limited way, and we are expanding our line. All of these are within the sphere of our interest, but we cannot make all of these on a volume basis. Where should we draw the line? Electric and electronic machines are becoming popular, but we have no such department worth speaking of. Should Olympia follow the trend? Should we copy IBM or Remington?"

exhibit 1 OLYMPIA WERKE
Balance sheet, 1954–1963 (in thousands of dollars)

Assets	1954	1955	1956	1957	1958	1959	1960	1961	1962	1963
Current assets:										
Cash	$ 589	$ 84	$ 102	$ 78	$ 509	$ 738	$ 1,008	$ 808	$ 924	$ 1,022
Accounts receivable	4,561	4,732	5,722	6,290	9,617	9,972	4,153	4,774	7,660	8,067
Realized payments on account	15	11			16	4	12	7	20	26
Received from subsidiaries		163	278	192	116	382	859	1,010	1,680	942
Demands from payments on account							2,989	2,497		
Other receivables	315	465	528	730	1,129	869	915	1,020	903	804
Inventory:										
Raw, auxiliary, and working materials	964	1,405	1,732		2,638	2,241	3,089	3,694	3,139	2,566
Work in process	1,903	2,588	3,334		5,921	6,045	6,708	6,388	6,104	5,707
Finished goods	616	903	1,081	6,776	3,011	2,145	2,515	3,342	4,253	4,244
Other	8	33	90	127	221	262	135	259		
Total current assets	$ 8,971	$10,384	$12,867	$14,193	$23,178	$22,658	$22,483	$23,799	$24,683	$23,378
Fixed assets:										
Improved property										
Business buildings	44	74	71	212	537	519	504	453	425	420
Factory buildings	3,067	5,606	7,152	8,104	11,312	10,790	10,435	10,204	11,240	10,900
Unimproved property	47		27	13	9	9	4	54	247	512
Buildings under construction	231	750	149	607	841	450	536	1,499	877	524
Payments on account	47	151	127	258	139	53	163	246		
Machines	3,285	3,410	3,998	4,775	6,806	6,133	5,809	6,281	6,722	5,992
Tools, factory, and business equipment, vehicles	855	1,412	1,463	1,669	2,083	2,000	1,866	1,874	1,810	1,848
Shares, patents, and valuable papers	129	174	962	3,430	1,077	1,029	2,184	2,184	2,940	3,010
Total fixed assets	$ 7,605	$11,577	$13,949	$19,068	$22,804	$20,983	$21,501	$22,795	$24,261	$23,206
Total assets	$16,577	$21,959	$26,816	$33,260	$45,984	$43,642	$43,987	$46,597	$48,946	$46,584

451

exhibit 1   (continued)

Liabilities	1954	1955	1956	1957	1958	1959	1960	1961	1962	1963
Current liabilities:										
Installment credits	1,690	1,750	1,750	1,750	3,931	4,277				
Liabilities for export							6,815	7,987	16,507	13,392
Bills of exchange	661	1,147	1,866	2,498	3,125	3,125				
Other short-term bank liabilities	1,711	219	957	715	4,237	2,846				
Accounts payable	871	1,114	766	1,258	1,249	837	1,106	1,320	1,080	835
Liabilities through acceptance of bills	804	1,995	2,378	3,628	3,542	2,545	3,707	3,361	2,750	2,378
Down payments from customers	34	26	69	55	48	113	70	57	109	42
Liabilities to subsidiaries			1,250	157	966	178	151	183	455	375
Other short-term liabilities	592	712	949	1,097	1,535	1,578	1,821	1,887	1,903	2,162
Total current	$ 6,363	$ 6,963	$ 9,985	$11,158	$18,633	$15,499	$13,670	$14,795	$22,804	$19,184
Long-term notes and credits from banks	4,081	5,297	5,951	7,561	9,219	8,645	8,998	9,534	2,275	1,949
Allocated reserves	1,203	2,162	3,066	3,669	4,349	5,631	7,565	7,945	7,594	9,451
Items that limit-restrictions					15	15	25	24		
Capital:										
Required reserve funds	400	625	625	875	1,250	1,250	1,375	1,375	1,375	1,375
Optional reserve funds	250	250	375	375						
Supply										500
Basic capital	4,000	6,250	6,250	8,750	11,250	11,250	11,250	13,750	13,750	13,750
Total capital	$ 4,650	$ 7,125	$ 7,250	$10,000	$12,500	$12,500	$12,625	$15,125	$15,125	$15,625
Net profit for the year	280	410	562	854	1,262	1,350	1,575	1,575	1,146	1,375
Total liabilities	$16,577	$21,959	$26,816	$33,260	$45,984	$43,642	$43,987	$46,507	$48,946	$46,584

exhibit 2 OLYMPIA WERKE

Profit and loss statements, 1954–1963 (in thousands of dollars)

	1954	1955	1956	1957	1958	1959	1960	1961	1962	1963
Proceeds from manufacturing activities (Net of CGS)	$11,446	$14,564	$18,862	$22,131	$26,629	$29,158	$34,247	$35,902	$36,734	$37,956
Proceeds from non-manufacturing activities	30	36	245	487	798	347	722	1,336	1,389	672
Gross yield	$11,476	$14,600	$19,107	$22,618	$27,427	$29,505	$34,969	$37,238	$38,123	$38,628
Less:										
Salaries and wages	6,456	8,358	11,087	12,663	15,889	17,001	19,175	22,183	23,823	23,327
Social dues	606	857	1,092	1,467	1,861	2,090	2,331	2,661	2,841	2,773
Other social expenditures	3	3	6	9	8	8	697	655	781	762
Depreciation:										
Fixed capital	1,774	2,517	3,644	4,717	4,656	4,824	4,336	4,515	4,405	4,113
Floating capital							409	58	5	171
Maintenance expenditures	195	410	408	474	534	654	1,109	1,271	1,194	1,529
Interest expense	653	713	1,029	1,000	1,439	1,597	1,653	1,343	1,463	1,287
Taxes:										
On profits	950	1,104	1,134	1,258	1,374	1,964	2,219	1,820	1,311	1,719
Other taxes							1,069	1,000	1,123	1,045
Property adjustment for refugees-capital levy							395	30	29	28
Correction for interest-free loan	160		18	21	27	15				
Other expenditures										
Annual profit	$ 679	$ 638	$ 691	$ 1,009	$ 1,634	$ 1,352	$ 1,576	$ 1,702	$ 1,148	$ 1,874
Allotment to required reserve		225		153	375			125		
Allotment to free reserve	400		125							500
Net profit	$ 280	$ 410	$ 562	$ 854	$ 1,262	$ 1,352	$ 1,575	$ 1,575	$ 1,148	$ 1,375

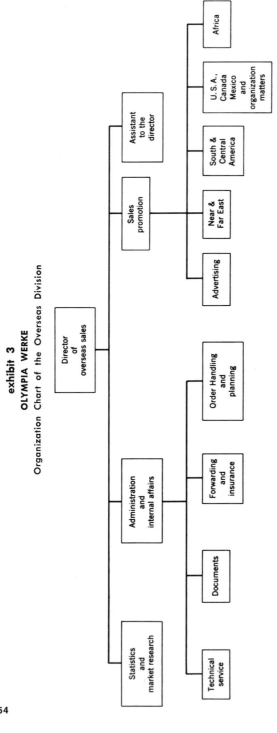

exhibit 3
OLYMPIA WERKE
Organization Chart of the Overseas Division

454

LEATHERCRAFT
CORPORATION

EARLY HISTORY AND DEVELOPMENT

The Leathercraft Shoe Corporation was founded in Davenport, Iowa, in 1905 by George Meyer and Randolph Langford to engage in the jobbing of men's shoes and rubbers in Iowa, Nebraska, and northwestern Illinois. In 1909, after a series of profitable years, the partners decided to go into the manufacturing of men's shoes to assure a supply for their constantly increasing sales and to gain the profit advantages of a manufacturing operation. To accomplish this objective they purchased the machinery and equipment of a bankrupt Chicago shoe manufacturer and installed them in a warehouse near their sales office.

In 1912 the shoe manufacturing facilities were expanded and the sons of the founders, John Meyer and Kurt Langford, were brought into the business. John Meyer was 22 years of age. He had an engineering degree from Iowa State University and two years of experience in construction engineering. Kurt Langford was 21 years of age with two years of liberal arts education in a small Iowa college and one year of work experience.

In 1915 a new factory was built in Davenport to replace the original manufacturing facilities contained in the warehouse building. In the same year the company purchased a Davenport tannery to gain cost advantages and further integrate the firm's operations. The operation of a tannery by a shoe manufacturer was contrary to normal industry practice. Most manufacturers purchased their leather from independent tanneries.[1]

[1] This practice was still true in the industry in 1956.

In 1916 the original partnership of Meyer and Langford was dissolved and the firm was incorporated as the Leathercraft Corporation in the state of Iowa. At this time Kurt Langford was given the responsibility for shoe manufacturing and John Meyer took charge of tannery operations.

From the time he entered the company John Meyer conducted experiments in the tanning of horsehide in an effort to find a tough leather for bicycle shoes which would have advantages over cowhide. In 1917 he perfected a tanning process for horsehide and by 1918 the entire capacity of the tannery was utilized for the tanning of horsehide.

The use of horsehide as a leather for shoe manufacturing, instead of traditional cowhide, produced particular market advantages. Horsehide had a "tough shell" which gave the leather excellent wearing qualities, strong resistance to water, and the ability to dry soft. These advantages were incorporated into Leathercraft's main product line— a heavy-type work shoe. The characteristics of horsehide leather in a work shoe had strong appeal to farmers. As a result, within a few years after the conversion to horsehide, the company was concentrating its entire sales effort in rural areas. The company also found that the favorable characteristics of horsehide, which aided in selling its work shoes in rural markets, also applied to the Leathercraft line of work gloves which were produced from offal, the residue resulting from work shoe manufacture.

The concentration of the sale of Leathercraft's horsehide work shoes and work gloves in the rural markets proved to be successful. By 1930 the company was producing and selling over 1 million shoes annually. While Leathercraft experienced some losses in the early depression years of the 1930's, operations were profitable enough to allow the company to maintain its market position and to provide for the construction of a new plant. From 1941 to 1944 the company's main production effort was concentrated on manufacturing shoes for the armed services.

POSTWAR PROBLEMS AND MARKET CHANGES

The sales of Leathercraft Corporation increased substantially in the postwar period, rising from $5.4 million in 1945 to a peak of $12.1 million in 1951. Operating profit also showed a corresponding increase in this period, rising from $.5 million to $1.4 million. In 1952, however, the upward trend was halted and sales dropped to $10.2 million and continued to decline each year to a low of $8.7 million in 1955. Operating profits also decreased in this period from $.8 million to a deficit of $.3 million in 1955. (See Exhibit 12.)

The management of Leathercraft attributed the decline in sales and profits after 1952 to external factors beyond their control. They believed that a major reason for the decline was the dwindling farmer market caused by the shift of population from rural to urban areas. This shift, they pointed out, was decreasing the farm labor force and increasing the number of industrial and white-collar workers. There were also indications that the heavy-type work shoe produced by Leathercraft was not suitable for the average industrial worker who preferred a semi-dress type of work shoe. The company did not have a shoe in its line to meet this requirement.

In anticipation of the loss of sales in the work shoe and work glove markets the company introduced a line of dress shoes in 1950 and a line of dress gloves in 1953. In 1954 a semi-work shoe named the Lightweight was added to the product line in an effort to bolster sales in the industrial work shoe market. In a further effort to reverse the trend of declining sales the company placed a line of golf shoes, hunting boots, and other specialty shoes on the market.

In addition to the changing marketing conditions for its products, Leathercraft was also confronted with the rising price and diminishing supply of horsehide. At the same time farm population was decreasing, the nation's horse and mule population was also decreasing. The demand for horsehide, however, remained relatively constant in the face of a diminishing supply, which caused the price of horsehide to increase from $1.40 per butt in 1941 to $3.81 in 1954, representing an increase to the company of 171% in leather cost.

In an effort to cope with this situation Leathercraft gradually reduced its soaking of horsehide (the preliminary preparation of the hide for tanning) and looked for another type of hide as a substitute which would be low in cost and plentiful in supply.

MARKET CHANGES

Four main reasons were advanced by management for the shift in the company's market: (1) population shifts; (2) occupational shifts; (3) changing income patterns; (4) changes in the white-collar working group. They pointed out that the number of rural places, those under

2,500 in population, had declined 2% from 1930 to 1950, while the number of towns and cities (2,500 population and over) increased 16% in the same period.[1]

In addition, the farm population decreased 16.6% from 30 million to 25 million, from 1930 to 1950. In this same period the urban population increased 17% from 117 million to 137 million.[2]

The shift in population was accompanied by occupational changes. From 1940 to 1955 the farm labor force decreased 25%, from 8 million to 6 million. The industrial work force increased 56% in this period, from 14 million to 22 million.[3]

A study of national income statistics by management revealed that the median income of industrial workers increased from $1,000 annually in 1939 to $3,000 in 1952. In contrast, farm labor increased its median wage from $340 a year in 1939 to $675 in 1952.[4]

The white-collar group of salesmen, office workers, professional and technical men also fared better than the farm group in growth and income. In the period 1940–1955, urban white-collar workers increased from 12 million to 17 million, a 45% gain. Their median wage rose 150% in the period 1939–1952, from $1,500 to $3,750.[3]

RAW MATERIAL SUPPLY—INTRODUCTION OF PIGSKIN

Because of the diminishing supply and rising price of horsehide, Leathercraft gradually reduced its soaking of horsehide. In 1941 the company soaked 623,721 hides and in 1954 had reduced its soaking to 239,932. The percentage of Leathercraft's soakings to the national horsehide soakings declined from 56% of the total to 26% in 1954. Throughout this period the company was experimenting with other hides in an effort to relieve its dependence on a basic raw material which was high in price and low in supply.

Leathercraft's location in the heart of the hog-producing and pork-processing area of the nation directed the attention of management to pigskin as a possible answer to their leather problem. The supply of pigs was large and the price of pigskin was low, which seemed to offer the advantages formerly obtained with horsehide. In the period of

[1] *Statistical Abstract of the United States*, 1954, p. 29.
[2] *Ibid.*, p. 13.
[3] *Ibid.*, p. 208, and *Monthly Labor Review*, July, 1955.
[4] Data derived from the *Statistical Abstract of the United States*, 1940–1953.

1945–1948 pigskin averaged about 6.5¢ per pound as contrasted to 12.75¢ per pound for horsehide. In addition pigskin appeared attractive because Leathercraft had experience in processing the leather for work gloves.

The first tannery runs of pigskin which were made into work shoes in 1948 and 1949 were considered to be unsatisfactory. The leather proved to be too porous and did not have the quality of horsehide or cowhide leathers. As a result the company abandoned temporarily the use of pigskin in its line until it could produce a better product.

Upon investigation it was found that pigsides rather than bacon rinds, which the company used in its first attempts to tan pigskin, offered a more satisfactory hide for shoe manufacture. However, a problem of supply confronted the company because a large percentage of pigsides, as furnished by meat packers, were damaged by burning and knife cuts as a result of the skinning process.

In an attempt to improve the quality of pigsides the company developed a skinning machine. In 1950 Leathercraft was successful in getting three meat-packing firms to install its machine. In order to persuade the packers to accept the skinning machine, however, it was necessary to pay them a premium of 3.5¢ a pound over the market price of pigsides and guarantee to purchase the entire output of pigsides processed by the machines.

The packers who initially accepted the skinning machine and agreed to furnish pigsides to the company gave it up after a trial run. They felt the operation was too uncertain and they were not assured of a market for the pigsides if Leathercraft suddenly decided to abandon the idea. This action forced Leathercraft to seek other packers to install the machine. While the company was successful in finding others to use the machine, the supply of pigskin was not produced in uniform quality.

In 1951 Leathercraft resumed the tanning of both bacon rinds and pigsides and began the manufacture of both dress and work shoes out of this leather. During 1955 approximately 40% of the work shoe line was produced from pigskin. Although the leather had improved in quality, it had not reached a uniform quality which would make it entirely acceptable for use in shoes. The company, however, believed that the leather could be successfully tanned in the future to meet uniform quality requirements for shoe manufacture.

Leathercraft shoes produced from pigskin were reported to be acceptable in the market. However, members of the trade stated many objections that were raised by customers. The primary complaint concerned the inability of the leather to resist water and to hold its dye or color. The company stated that an improvement in tanning techniques made in 1955 would correct this fault.

PRODUCT LINES AND SALES POLICIES: WORK SHOES

Extent of Line. Leathercraft manufactured a broad line of work shoes in both horsehide and pigskin. In 1955 the company substantially increased the numbers carried in both the horsehide and pigskin lines to include 140 horsehide numbers and 90 different pigskin numbers, as indicated in Exhibit 1.

exhibit 1   LEATHERCRAFT SHOE LINE, 1955

Year	Horsehide Numbers	Pigskin Numbers	Average Price per Pair	
			Horsehide	Pigskin
1946	40	—	$5.40	—
1947	38	—	6.30	—
1948	40	3	6.40	$3.70
1949	28	3	6.00	3.70
1950	38	—	7.50	—
1951	40	15	7.25	5.40
1952	52	10	7.10	5.00
1953	37	30	7.80	5.90
1954	98	60	7.10	5.80
1955	140	90	7.30	5.50

Exhibit 2 shows Leathercraft's work shoe production in relation to production of the industry.

Sales Practices. In calling upon prospective customers the salesmen usually carried five or six sample cases for display. However, when they called on regular customers, usually only one case of samples was shown to the dealers. This case contained what the salesman considered his best sellers or basic numbers. The numbers usually found in this case would vary according to the sales representative's territory, but generally included many of the same numbers. In addition to carrying in the single sample case, several sales representatives carried one to four numbers in their hand which they hoped the dealer would add to his line. Usually these numbers were shown first to the dealer, followed

exhibit 2

Leathercraft and Industry Work Shoe Production,
Excluding Military, 1946–1954 (Thousands of Pairs)

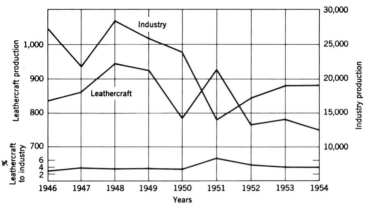

by opening the sample case on occasion for a few more numbers. In some instances as many as ten shoe samples were shown, but there were instances when the sample case was not opened at all. Occasionally a sales representative carried in a second sample case, or returned to his car for it when a special number was requested by the dealer or the salesman wished to impress the dealer with the size of the line.

Dealers in general expressed little interest in the Hunter styles, a line of hunting boots, the Sportsman line of golf and sports shoes, or the safety shoe line. Both dealers and sales representatives stated that there was little demand for two of these styles in their stores, since the Hunter styles and Sportsman were shoes which sold through sporting goods stores, particularly those stores in the larger cities. As a routine practice the salesmen did not make calls on sporting goods stores. Safety shoes, on the other hand, were generally either not in demand, or the dealer refused to handle them because of severe competition in this line from other sources.

The horsehide work shoe was generally acceptable as a line, although several dealers commented on the fact that farmers and industrial workers were demanding a lighter-weight shoe and were refusing to buy the heavy type of Leathercraft shoe. Although no specific objections were encountered concerning the pigskin line, some dealers expressed strong general prejudice against it. It was observed that the broadening of the work shoe line of horsehide and pigskin apparently failed to stimulate any interest on the part of the dealer to add additional numbers to his stock.

Pricing. The company believed that the rise in horsehide prices was gradually pricing its work shoes out of the market. One purpose of introducing the pigskin was to overcome this handicap and at the same time compete with cowhide. When the sales manager made field calls on dealers, he found that those located in the small towns and crossroad centers would usually sell a shoe at a lower gross profit than those located in the larger cities. The difference in gross profit averaged about 7%. Dealers in the less populated areas seemed satisfied with a lower profit because shoes generally represented a relatively small part of their business. In contrast, shoes represented the major or entire part of the city dealer's business. The city dealer found that when he marked up the price of Leathercraft shoes to obtain the gross profit he required, the price of any particular Leathercraft shoe would usually be considerably higher than competitive shoes of similar quality. He either was faced with reducing his margin on the Leathercraft shoe or pushing the sale of other competitive brands. The dealers usually chose to push the competitive brands since they could obtain a higher markup at a lower selling price. Exhibit 3, which follows, indicates the cost and price relationship of Leathercraft and two competing brands of shoes of similar or superior quality.

exhibit 3 COST-PRICE RELATIONSHIP PER PAIR OF SHOES OF
LEATHERCRAFT TO COMPETING BRANDS

	Cost to Dealer	Recommended Markup by City Dealer	Retail Selling Price
Leathercraft (horsehide)	$6.70	37%	$9.25
Brand A	5.70	40%	8.00
Brand B	6.05	30%	7.85

Country dealers, because of their lower markup, were not as reluctant to handle the Leathercraft shoe because the competition of price was not as severe and their low markup made the retail price of the shoes more acceptable to the customer.

Dealer markup practices affected pigskin shoe sales in the same manner. However, when dealers compared pigskin shoe prices with competitive cowhide shoe prices, they raised questions over price differentials. For example, it was pointed out that the features of one number of Brand A were so superior that they were unable to sell the competitive pigskin shoe at the same markup. In instances where smaller dealers handled Leathercraft exclusively, the pigskin line was used as the price leader over the horsehide. In larger stores where competitive work shoes were also handled, dealers pointed out that Leathercraft pigskin shoes competed with its own horsehide rather than good-quality cowhide shoes of competitors.

In the larger stores where price was the primary factor, the price leaders in cowhide shoes ranged from about $4.00 retail to $7.00. The most popular retail prices were $5.00 and $6.00. Dealers generally refused to consider Leathercraft's pigskin shoes, which cost them $5.00, as a strong competitor with cowhide shoes in the same price range.

Style. Style in work shoes did not change as often as in other types of shoes, and work shoes were frequently viewed as a staple product. Fit, comfort, and wear were stressed rather than style in the company's advertising. Many comments, however, were made about Leathercraft's style by dealers and sales representatives.

In an effort to determine the competitive standing of Leathercraft products, early in 1955 the company hired an independent marketing consulting firm to review the market with dealers, sales representatives, and other sources. The following summarizes the adverse comments obtained by the consultants about Leathercraft's styling of work shoes:

1. Customers want a lighter, trimmer-looking shoe. Leathercraft has never changed its basic, nineteenth-century style.

2. Although older customers still buy the same Leathercraft shoe year after year, younger men want a lighter, dressier work and safety shoe, something they can wear on the street.

3. Men in light industry want dressier and lighter safety and work shoes. Men in heavy industry are also asking more and more for a lighter shoe. Leathercraft shoes still look, feel and are heavy.

4. Horsehide and pigskin will not take a shine like cowhide.

5. White-collar people and foremen in the steel plants are urged to wear safety shoes. They need dressier safety oxfords for white-collar people and lighter, dressier safety shoes for foremen.

6. Leathercraft shoes are sloppy-fitting. Quarters are loose.

7. Leathercraft shoes are uniformly oversized and customers cannot get the same fit in the size they are wearing in a competitive shoe.

8. Competitive shoes in the same price range look like a neater shoe. Leathercraft shoes are not finished as well. Both the exteriors and interiors are rough.

Quality. Many comments were also made about the quality of the shoes. The reports of sales representatives and dealers indicated that, for all the quality its name once signified, Leathercraft shoes were generally below the quality standards of its competitors. Some common references to the quality of Leathercraft shoes were as follows:

1. Counters are made of paper.
2. Shanks are too light in weight.
3. Vamps are too soft.
4. Insoles are of inferior quality.
5. Welt strips on some shoes are too narrow and when the shoes are resoled they have to be rebuilt.
6. Welt stitching breaks or rots out is a typical comment from the dealers who sold to farmers.
7. Pigskin sponges water and cannot be worn where a man may run into bad weather.
8. Shoes do not meet the company's description. In one case the black sole of the wedge oxford was described as not marking the floor; however, it did. In another case the midsole of a safety shoe was described as being composed of rosin and cork; it was found to be made of rosin and sawdust upon analysis. Steel shanks had also been eliminated from shoes that were supposed to have them.
9. Typical dealer reaction to Leathercraft as compared with competitive shoes is found in this statement: "My Brand A selling at $8.00 looks better made than the comparable Leathercraft horsehide."

Workmanship. Workmanship had also received frequent adverse comments, such as:

1. Because of poor stitching, cork soles have come loose on some numbers.
2. Some shoes had poor heel seats.
3. Cemented cushions have come loose.
4. In one order of safety shoes the nails had not been cut off; the shoes had to be fixed before they were sold.
5. Quarters were sewn together wrong, resulting in a poor fit.
6. The leather in the toe of the soft-toe shoe is so poorly fitted that there were wrinkles in the toe.
7. The leather on some shoes is of noticeably different thicknesses.

Some of the samples sent to the salesmen were so poor that they had to be returned for new ones. Several dealers cited instances when they had to return shoes because of poor workmanship.

Deliveries. Another common complaint made by both salesmen and dealers concerned the slow delivery of work shoes. Sales representatives were reluctant to show new numbers for which future orders had to be placed. Several representatives did not display the new numbers at all or did so in only a few instances. One salesman said, "Why should I show the new shoes when I can't get good deliveries on current numbers?" Slow deliveries were reported on the basic fast sellers—often these took from three weeks to a month for delivery. Several salesmen reported that they often had to write special requests to get service in critical cases. Field trips by the consulting firm revealed the following common complaints:

1. Smith's Shoe Shop of Dubuque, Iowa, placed its 1954 fall order on September 28 for October or November delivery. The order was not shipped until February 25, 1955, at least a three-month delay. Seven days later the spring shipment arrived. The store returned the spring shipment to the factory at its own expense. This is typical of similar cases reported by salesmen where a slow delivery of an order for immediate shipment created an inventory problem for the dealer.

2. Williams Shoe Store, located in a small Illinois town, complained about the "lousy" deliveries, pointing out that deliveries had been "especially bad the last two months." The store's July order for fill-ins was delayed and then size $9\frac{1}{2}$ was sent instead of 9. There were still outstanding two other orders which should have arrived by the time of the sales call. The manager commended two competing lines for their prompt deliveries and for their use of pre-printed cards on which fill-in orders could be written. This case is typical of slow deliveries on fill-ins.

3. Another dealer in southwestern Illinois ordered 12 pairs of work shoes in August, 1955, and waited three weeks for the shipment. Size 11 was not included and he was still waiting when the call was made in October for the filling of his special order for this one size.

4. A Wisconsin dealer ordered dress shoes and complained to the sales representative that he had not received them after two weeks.

5. A dealer in Ohio buys about four dozen Leathercraft shoes a year and a like amount of a competing brand. After commenting on how bad Leathercraft deliveries had been earlier, the dealer said the service still does not compare with competitive lines.

6. A general store in Indiana complained about Leathercraft deliveries for fill-ins. A chief competitor supplied a printed postcard to dealers for reorders and ships the shoes within three days after receiving the order.

7. A prospective Wisconsin dealer placed his first order in October ·for about $200; the order was almost canceled when the new dealer learned that the four pairs of field boots could not be delivered for six weeks. Only when the sales representative promised to make a special request for immediate shipment did the dealer reinstate the order.

Sales Territory Coverage. Leathercraft followed a sales program with work shoes of having sales representatives cover their territories by working one county at a time and completing it before moving to the next county. Each salesman was expected to make ten calls a day. Many of the sales representatives did not follow the company's program. However, the newer salesmen tended to adhere closely to the schedule set for their respective territories. The more experienced salesmen scheduled themselves on loop routes which enabled them to make calls in the territory going out and returning. Their routes were planned on a basis which provided time and frequency of calls in relation to the size and importance of the dealer or area. Considerable travel was necessary for all sales representatives regardless of whether they followed the company's program or not, since the majority of Leathercraft's dealers were located in rural areas and small towns.

Sales representatives considered it very difficult to sell industrial shoes because of the time involved in selling various key members of a plant before their product would be accepted. Many of the salesmen did not feel that the commissions justified the effort, compared with the commissions received from their sales to dealers.

Sales representatives also pointed out that specialized wagon jobbers with well-stocked trailers called regularly on plants where they sold and fitted shoes to employees on the spot. In several plants management made special arrangements with the jobber to absorb 10% to 20% of the shoe list price so that the employee could purchase work shoes at prices lower than the local dealer could offer them. In other plants certain employees acted as part-time agents of shoe manufacturers by conducting a mail-order business.

Leathercraft measured the sales performance of its sales representatives by the number of dealers sold in a territory and the volume sold to each dealer.

Exhibit 4 gives an analysis of the selling efforts of a sample of ten work shoe sales representatives by size of town. Exhibit 5 gives an indication of the company's sales per capita. Exhibit 6 provides an analysis of sales to work shoe dealers for 10 selected representatives covering 14 territories.

exhibit 4 **LEATHERCRAFT CORPORATION**
Work shoe dealers and sales by size of town, 1954—14 territories, 10 sales representatives

Size of Town	Dealer		Sales		Average Sales per Dealer
	Number	Per Cent of Total	Dollars	Per Cent of Total	
Urban					
1,000,000 or more	18	.5	$ 12,460	1.0	$692.22
500,000–999,999	24	.6	18,120	1.5	755.00
250,000–499,999	12	.3	4,460	.4	371.67
100,000–249,999	34	.9	15,360	1.2	451.76
50,000– 99,999	52	1.3	17,030	1.4	327.50
25,000– 49,999	71	1.8	25,800	2.1	363.38
10,000– 24,999	191	4.8	79,530	6.4	416.39
5,000– 9,999	217	5.5	95,750	7.7	441.24
2,500– 4,999	330	8.3	132,050	10.6	400.15
Rural					
1,000– 2,499	644	16.3	228,510	18.4	354.83
999 and under	2,363	59.7	611,840	49.3	258.92
Total	3,956	100.0	$1,240,910	100.0	$313.67

exhibit 5 **LEATHERCRAFT CORPORATION**
Work shoe sales per capita, 1954–14 territories, 10 sales representatives

Territory Numbers	County Population	Total City in County	Per Cent of Total	Total Work Shoe Sales	Work Shoe Sales per Capita
5	1,483,700	548,831	37.0	$ 69,440	$.05
10	2,565,600	1,392,811	54.3	138,370	.05
15	7,144,000	4,932,068	69.0	170,420	.02
20	117,800	49,324	41.9	21,810	.19
25	8,241,500	3,559,324	43.2	122,930	.01
30	2,781,000	1,290,627	46.4	83,360	.03
35	3,304,100	1,583,363	47.9	105,190	.03
40	1,311,300	357,801	27.3	78,850	.06
45	1,720,500	359,783	20.9	84,030	.05
50	4,674,800	2,084,966	44.6	207,840	.04
55	6,659,200	517,122	7.8	53,810	.01
60	5,041,600	2,303,647	45.7	22,900	.0045
65	2,312,000	685,900	29.7	17,590	.01
70	1,226,800	424,647	34.6	64,370	.05
Total	48,583,900	20,090,214	41.4	$1,240,910	$.026

exhibit 6 **LEATHERCRAFT CORPORATION**
Analysis of sales to work shoe dealers, 1954—14 territories, 10 sales representatives (number of dealers sold)

Territory Number	Total Work Shoe Dealers		Work Shoe Only		Work Shoes and Dress Shoes		Work Shoes and Gloves		Work Shoes, Dress Shoes, and Gloves	
	No.	Per Cent	No.	Per Cent	No.	Per Cent	No.	Per Cent	No.	Per Cent
5	291	100.0	139	47.8	26	8.9	95	32.6	31	10.7
10	430	100.0	173	40.2	60	14.0	131	30.5	66	15.3
15	437	100.0	180	41.2	44	10.1	153	35.0	60	13.7
20	56	100.0	28	50.0	8	14.3	18	32.1	2	3.6
25	357	100.0	118	33.1	125	35.0	48	13.4	66	18.5
30	372	100.0	196	52.7	30	8.1	93	25.0	53	14.2
35	372	100.0	222	59.7	35	9.4	89	23.9	26	7.0
40	222	100.0	81	36.5	18	8.1	80	36.0	43	19.4
45	275	100.0	132	48.0	37	13.5	74	26.9	32	11.6
50	538	100.0	248	46.1	128	23.8	98	18.2	64	11.9
55	245	100.0	118	48.2	36	14.7	72	29.4	19	7.7
60	102	100.0	62	60.8	9	8.8	24	23.5	7	6.9
65	71	100.0	42	59.2	8	11.3	16	22.5	5	7.0
70	188	100.0	75	39.9	13	6.9	78	41.5	22	11.7
Total	3,956	100.0	1,814	45.9	577	14.6	1,069	27.0	496	12.5

WORK GLOVES

Extent of Line. The number of work gloves offered to the dealer annually from 1946–1955 was as shown in Exhibit 7.

exhibit 7 **LEATHERCRAFT'S LINE AND AVERAGE PRICE OF WORK GLOVES**

Year	Numbers Horsehide	Numbers Pigskin	Average Price per Dozen	
			Horsehide	Pigskin
1946	40	Na	$13.00	Na
1947	90	40	13.75	$15.00
1948	70	50	19.10	15.10
1949	60	45	19.00	12.00
1950	55	90	21.00	14.90
1951	50	55	22.00	14.50
1952	52	85	20.00	15.00
1953	100	Na	17.40	Na
1954	60	100	18.50	16.00
1955	50	60	19.00	15.00

Na—not available.

In addition to the above lines the company offered 12 goatskin and buckskin gloves including two new dress buckskins.

Exhibit 8 shows Leathercraft's production of work gloves and the

exhibit 8
LEATHERCRAFT CORPORATION
Leathercraft and Industry Production of All-grain and Leather Fabric Gloves, 1946–1954
(Thousand Dozen Pairs)

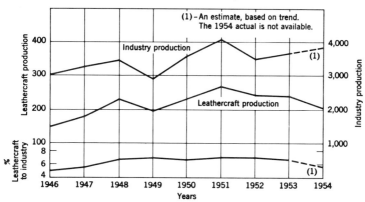

glove industry production of all-grain leather and leather-fabric gloves.

Sales Practices. In contrast to work shoes, work gloves were a point-of-purchase sale. The work gloves in most stores were usually displayed on small racks or on shelves, generally in small quantities. The glove racks were designed to hold a dozen numbers and were used by dealers for their entire line of work gloves, including their all-cloth numbers. These racks were generally located near the greatest movement, such as the cash register, wrapping counter, or other busy part of the store.

After checking on the present stock and getting reorders on the numbers the dealer was carrying, the sales representative usually showed about 6 or 8 numbers, infrequently as many as 10 numbers, from the 100 or so glove samples in his case. These were generally new numbers, numbers the dealer had not been carrying, or Leathercraft styles which could replace competitive styles the dealer was handling. The salesmen concentrated on showing two or three horsehide and pigskin drivers from the 18 numbers they carried in this line. They usually followed this style by showing the leather palm safety cuffs in one or two styles of horsehide and pigskin. The leather palm drivers in both horsehide and pigskin were usually shown, although some salesmen made no effort to push this line.

Additional lines were shown depending upon the store and the nature of its trade. Examples of the variation that the sales representative might show included:

Horsehide with knit wrist
Pigskin with knit wrist
Buckskin drivers
Goatskin drivers
Plastic-coated gloves

Generally sales representatives showed about 6 from 38 style numbers out of a total of 115 samples. Some of the sales representatives reported that they left as many as 15 to 20 style numbers at home.

Several salesmen expressed the view that some of the gloves designed for retail stores did not fit in with the stores they generally called on. Almost none of the dealers who were called upon in either urban or rural areas expressed interest in ski mittens, ladies' utility gloves, or dress buckskin gloves. The dealers usually stated that gloves of this nature were for sporting goods stores, department stores, or haberdashery stores.

Pricing. Price was not stressed in Leathercraft's promotion of its work glove line. The company placed the emphasis on the quality of the glove, pointing up such features as its durability, comfort, and ability to dry soft.

Dealers usually sold Leathercraft gloves at one-third gross margin. Aside from a few truck terminal stores where the markup was somewhat greater, no major differences in markup existed in either urban or rural areas. In the rural hardware or feed store where Leathercraft gloves were handled exclusively, the question of price was not usually raised. But in urban areas where competitive gloves were usually handled, the price question was of prime importance.

Field work by the sales manager uncovered the fact that in many truck terminals where Leathercraft's all-leather number had good acceptance, a competitive fabric-back glove was sold as a substitute. In other stores competitive gloves with cloth backs and split-cowhide palms were pushed by the dealer because they sold at $1.00 a pair and provided the dealer with a 50% markup. If the Leathercraft glove were to be sold for $1.00, the dealer's gross margin would amount to only 20%.

The proprietor of a large Army and Navy store, which was one of the best accounts in the area, stated that, "Customers will pick up anything for 95¢ but resist paying more. Leathercraft can't compete with the average glove." This dealer stated that he had hoped to feature Leathercraft as a quality item but could not because of the price. After handling the line five years he discontinued it, stating, "You can't sell quality, even at 10 or 15 cents more." This customer purchased $10,000 of Leathercraft gloves in 1951, and averaged about $6,000 in purchases annually in his five-year period as a customer.

Some sales representatives believed that competition had the advantage over all styles of Leathercraft gloves. Others believed that Leathercraft could compete favorably on the leather drivers but not on the leather palm line. Many salesmen felt that the pigskin glove competed with their own line rather than with the cowhide gloves of other producers.

Styling and Quality. Contrary to the reactions that work shoes appear too heavy and too rugged, dealers and sales representatives commented that work gloves had too much of a dress glove appearance.

A summary of the reactions of sales representatives and dealers to Leathercraft styling and quality obtained in the field work of the marketing consulting firm employed by the company is as follows:

1. A work glove must give the appearance of ruggedness and quality at a price. Leathercraft gloves look too dressy to take the abuse a work glove gets.

2. Industrial concerns refuse to buy Leathercraft gloves for their workers; not only are they too costly, but the gloves look and fit so much like dress gloves that workers pilfer them.

3. Leathercraft gloves are too good to be realistically competitive in industry. Plants buy cheap split cowhide gloves for their workers. These gloves are thrown away when they get greasy; the longer-wear feature of Leathercraft gloves does not count. In some cases Leathercraft gloves are purchased for plant foremen, as a prestige item for them.

4. In industrial areas, the traditional color of work gloves is gray. The Leathercraft yellow is hard to sell. One key dealer who refused to handle any more Leathercraft gloves reported that he had tried to feature Leathercraft gloves for five years but his customers preferred gray gloves.

5. Special gloves are often introduced too late in the season. As an example, the two dress buckskins were introduced July 15, 1955, after the customary time for the purchase of fall gloves by dealers.

6. Special gloves which have been added to the line do not fit into the line. As examples, the women's garden gloves, the ski mitten, and the two dress gloves. These special items were turned down by work glove dealers as items for other types of stores. It was frequently said of the two buckskin dress gloves, "They are beautiful, but we can't sell them. They belong in a haberdashery shop."

7. The buckskin dress gloves are not fully patterned after the usual dress glove. The shirred back runs counter to the open-cuff trend in dress gloves.

8. In industrial areas Leathercraft gloves appeal primarily to truck drivers. The truck driver who is reported to be a free spender buys the Leathercraft glove for driving because of the fit and softness. However, he buys a competitive, cheaper glove, either all fabric or fabric and split leather, for his heavy work.

9. The special quality of dry-soft has limited appeal in industry. Leathercraft gloves are bought by plants for the small percentage of workers who handle wet objects or chemicals.

10. The wearing quality of Leathercraft gloves was not universally accepted. Many dealers stated that cowhide split gloves wear better; some did believe that the Leathercraft glove outlasted cowhide.

11. At least in the urban communities, the intrinsic qualities of the Leathercraft gloves had not won customers. As one dealer said, "I have had no complaints, but not enough men who buy them come back for another pair."

12. In the rural market the buying habits of farmers have changed. They, too, are buying cheaper gloves, especially fabric. Now that they no longer use their hands for such jobs as corn shucking, they buy fabric gloves at 49 cents.

Workmanship. The complaints received by the sales representatives about the workmanship in Leathercraft's work gloves followed the same pattern as those on work shoes. The chief complaints were:

1. Some gloves are not properly sized. One company is returning an order because they are not properly sized.

2. Some gloves have poor seams. On several occasions, it was found that the pigskin seams, particularly, ripped out.

3. There were several instances where dealers complained that the glove fingers were too long.

4. The fact that the gloves in a pair were not matched was another fairly common criticism.

5. The leather is uneven.

6. The color is not uniform.

Deliveries. As in the case of work shoes, Leathercraft had improved its delivery of work gloves in 1955. Both the dealers and salesmen had noticed the improvements, and comments were generally favorable.

Many dealers stated that the speed of delivery was not too important in work gloves purchased from Leathercraft. Since the company did not use jobbers it was necessary for the dealers to place large orders well in advance of their need. The dealers also pointed out that they purchased most of the competitive lines from jobbers who provided almost continuous service and did not require large-quantity purchases.

Territory Coverage. The company sales program concerning territory coverage on work gloves generally followed the selling policy of the Work Shoe Division. In the field, sales representatives either followed the company program or scheduled loop routing as was found with work shoes. Many dealers who purchased Leathercraft work gloves also handled Leathercraft work shoes or dress shoes, or all three lines. (See Exhibit 6.)

Work glove representatives sold work gloves to dealers other than Leathercraft shoe accounts. These were gas stations, hardware stores, super markets, Army and Navy stores, grain and feed stores, implement dealers, clothing stores, and similar types of retail outlets. The sales representatives mentioned that it was practically impossible to sell more than three of these dealers in any one town due to the objections of dealers over others underselling them on the same Leathercraft brand glove. Competitive glove manufacturers, on the other hand, attained maximum dealer coverage by selling their own brand and unbranded gloves through jobbers, and private brand-name gloves through manufacturers of brand-name work clothes. A competitor of Leathercraft, for example, was able to sell five or six or more dealers in the same area or shopping center without creating dealer objections.

TERMS AND DISCOUNTS—WORK SHOES AND WORK GLOVES

The company believed that its terms to the trade were satisfactory on both work shoes and gloves. Most dealers believed them somewhat better than others in the trade. Some country and smaller dealers took advantage of the Leathercraft Term Plan which allowed a 5% discount on six dozen pairs of shoes. Competitors did not offer any discount on small orders. Small dealers were usually not too conscious of inventory turnover nor did they conduct their business on an inventory control basis. The larger dealers generally were not interested in the Term Plan because they claimed that they lost money when overstocked. Usually these dealers maintained strict inventory control. Some competitors offered larger dealers an annual rebate plan. For the first $1,000 of shoe purchases, the dealer received a 1% rebate, which increased 1% for each additional $1,000 of annual purchases up to $5,000.

In the case of work gloves, the discounts on volumes from 12 dozen pairs and up did not seem to appeal to most dealers, whether located in small or large towns.

Sales representatives were of the opinion that the volume discounts were satisfactory for larger-dealer accounts, but pointed out that their commission payments on net purchases made it unprofitable for them to go after volume accounts. They stated that they could sell three separate dealers 12 dozen pairs of gloves each and make more commission than selling one big account 48 pairs of gloves on one order. The sales representatives, in order to take advantage of maximum commissions, were calling on dealers only once a year rather than twice. This was done in order to write one order which carried a proportionately higher commission than the commission on two single smaller orders.

DRESS SHOES

The company had manufactured dress shoes for only five years and had never made a field analysis of its sales and retail outlets. From 1951, when the company started to produce dress shoes, through 1952, national production had an upward trend. Since 1952, national production and Leathercraft's output dropped. In 1952 Leathercraft produced 0.24% of the national production and in 1954 it produced 0.17%. (See Exhibit 9.)

exhibit 9
LEATHERCRAFT CORPORATION
Leathercraft and Industry Production of Men's Dress Shoes, 1951–1954
(Thousands of Pairs)

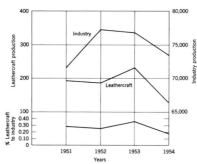

SOURCE: *Facts for Industry,* Department of Commerce, Series M68D and Leathercraft Records.

The work shoes and dress shoes were sold in the same manner with little, if any difference. Many of the work shoe dealers also carried the dress shoe line. (See Exhibit 6.) The dealers in larger towns and cities usually carried larger stocks of the semi-dress and dress shoes and less of the work shoe line. The more important the dealer, the larger was his dress shoe stock, and he often displayed his small stock of work shoes in the back room.

TURNOVER OF SALESMEN

A review of the 49 work shoe sales representatives covering the length of time each had been employed with the company as of August 1, 1955, revealed that one third of them had been with the company under one year, about another third between 1 and 5 years, and that the remaining third had been employed by the company over 5 years. The number of salesmen leaving in any one year varied between 5 and 24 and averaged 14.2 for the period 1948–1955. The average income of the 24 men who left the company in 1954 amounted to $4,164 compared to the industry's average annual earnings of $7,500 for footwear and clothing sales representatives.

When company sales representatives were questioned in the field concerning whether income was a possible reason for turnover, they thought that the 5% and 7% commission rates were fair and satisfactory. However, they felt that new men were unable to earn an adequate income because of the difficult task in selling sufficient volume against better competition and the more than usual resistance of many dealers to the Leathercraft line. They also mentioned the poor recruiting and selection and the fact that the position was oversold.

MANUFACTURING CAPACITY

The company operated a single plant at Davenport, Iowa, from 1903 to 1935. This plant had a production capacity of 1,050,000 pairs of shoes annually and was known as Plant 1. In 1935 Plant 2 was erected in Des Moines with an annual capacity of 210,000 pairs of shoes. Plant 3 was constructed in 1948 at Moline, Illinois, with an annual capacity of 375,000 pairs.

Shoe production capacity of Leathercraft by 1950 had increased from 1,050,000 pairs to 1,635,000. This production capacity was reduced to 1,425,000 pairs in late 1950 when Plant 2 was closed. Plant 4, however, was opened in 1951 at Rock Island, Illinois, with a capacity of 300,000 pairs of shoes, which was increased to 600,000 in 1954 to give the company a total capacity of 2,025,000 pairs of shoes. (Exhibit 2 indicates the annual production of Leathercraft and the shoe industry for the period 1946–1954.)

The company explained its decentralization of plants in the Tri-City area as a move to take advantage of the labor supply offered in each of the separate cities.

Prior to 1945 Leathercraft's tannery produced sufficient leather for the manufacture of 1,645,800 pairs of shoes annually. In 1950, in the expectation of pigside tanning, capacity was increased to provide leather for the production of 3,276,120 pairs of shoes. The cost of the new tannery building and the machinery and equipment amounted to $110,000.

INVENTORIES

Leathercraft employed a first-in-first-out (FIFO) method of inventory valuation. During the last ten years the company had gone through an upward trend in over-all material prices followed by a period of stabilization and in late 1955 a downward trend of over-all prices. The company's pricing policy reflected the changes in raw-material prices.

As indicated in Exhibit 12, Leathercraft's inventory turnover averaged 4.9 from 1946 to 1951. The average rate of inventory turnover for all shoe manufacturers in this period was 6.4. In 1953 and 1954 turnover dropped to an average of 3.5.

The relationship of inventory to working capital of Leathercraft and two of its chief competitors are indicated below in Exhibit 10.

exhibit 10   INVENTORY TO WORKING CAPITAL RATIO

Year	Leathercraft	Leathercraft (Excl. Hides Inv.)	Competitor A	Competitor B
1951	.74	.65	.64	.72
1952	.56	.51	.52	.56
1953	.85	.75	.66	.67
1954	.89	.79	.59	.59

Exhibit 11 shows the relationship of finished goods inventories in dozens of pairs (shoes and gloves) to production and shipment in dozens of pairs.

FINANCIAL POSITION

The trend of Leathercraft's operations are indicated in the following exhibits:

Exhibit 12. Financial and Operating Ratios
Exhibit 13. Detailed Listing of Manufacturing Expenses
Exhibit 14. Selling and Advertising Expenses
Exhibit 15. General and Administrative Expenses

exhibit 11 **LEATHERCRAFT CORPORATION**
Operating statistics, 1945–1954 (dozens of pairs)

	Work Shoes				Gloves				Dress Shoes			
	Shipments	Production (Packed)	Finished Goods Invent.	Invent. Production Ratio (%)	Shipments	Production (Packed)	Finished Goods Invent.	Invent. Production Ratio (%)	Shipments	Production (Packed)	Finished Goods Invent.	Invent. Production Ratio (%)
1945	75,922	77,585	9,115	.117	131,056	132,010	3,080	.023				
1946	71,550	69,823	7,680	.109	146,441	151,446	7,992	.053				
1947	72,435	71,917	7,476	.104	179,580	178,590	9,083	.051				
1948	77,642	78,859	9,213	.117	213,254	233,326	33,266	.143				
1949	76,850	78,094	16,239	.208	197,988	194,901	35,069	.180				
1950	70,107	65,162	6,733	.103	239,999	230,243	27,784	.121				
1951	73,997	77,621	11,649	.150	260,145	265,654	37,527	.141	18,008	15,910	3,165	.199
1952	66,890	64,738	10,510	.162	254,216	238,057	27,548	.116	15,899	15,328	2,903	.189
1953	64,504	65,945	15,923	.241	223,397	238,828	45,278	.190	17,111	19,494	5,908	.303
1954	61,241	66,266	22,639	.341	222,270	206,638	36,216	.175	13,184	11,043	3,933	.356

exhibit 12 **LEATHERCRAFT CORPORATION**
Financial and operating ratios, 1945–1955 (in millions of dollars)

	1945	1946	1947	1948	1949	1950	1951	1952	1953	1954	1955
Sales	$5.4	$5.8	$7.2	$8.5	$8.8	$9.8	$12.1	$10.2	$10.0	$9.0	$8.7
Operating profit	.5	.6	.9	1.2	.9	1.1	1.4	.8	.9	.3	(.3)
Net working capital	2.5	2.4	2.6	2.8	2.9	3.2	3.8	3.9	3.7	3.5	3.2
Balance sheet ratios											
Current ratio	4.6	4.7	3.9	3.2	3.2	3.0	3.5	4.2	3.8	4.1	4.3
Quick ratio	2.7	3.0	2.3	1.5	1.4	1.4	1.6	2.4	1.4	1.3	1.4
Inventory to net worth	39.5%	34.4%	39.9%	51.0%	52.6%	56.2%	58.2%	42.9%	61.4%	63.4%	72.9%
Fixed assets to net worth	13.9%	19.2%	22.9%	27.9%	26.1%	24.2%	23.7%	24.1%	26.2%	25.3%	27.0%
Total debt to net worth	21.7%	19.6%	24.2%	28.9%	31.4%	34.7%	42.1%	30.6%	30.0%	24.9%	39.4%
Operating ratios											
Cost of sales to fixed assets	9.0	6.9	6.8	5.6	6.2	6.7	7.5	6.4	5.5	5.5	5.5*
Net sales to avg. inventory	4.9	4.8	5.9	5.2	4.4	4.2	4.6	4.3	3.9	3.0	2.7*
Net profit to net sales	4.9%	5.4%	7.3%	7.5%	4.5%	4.8%	3.7%	3.4%	3.3%	1.4%	(2.2)%
Operating profit to net sales	9.1%	9.8%	12.5%	13.0%	9.1%	10.1%	11.0%	7.0%	7.7%	2.9%	(2.5)%
Inventory to working capital	51.2%	47.0%	56.2%	79.3%	79.9%	82.3%	73.8%	55.9%	85.4%	89.1%	89.1%

( ) indicates loss.

exhibit 13 LEATHERCRAFT CORPORATION
Analysis of manufacturing expenses, 1945–1954

	Total		Supervision		Other Salaries and Wages	Lasts, Dies, and Tools	Repair and Maintenance Materials	Heat, Light, Power and Water	Insurance	Provision for Depreciation	Rent
	Amount	% of Unadjusted Sales	Amount	% of Unadjusted Sales							
1945	$ 616,400	14.3%	$ 52,700	.0122%	$242,200	$10,300	$ 69,800	$ 51,200	$ 7,500	$ 31,700	$ 5,200
1946	731,900	15.2	76,600	.016	290,100	15,600	80,100	62,500	9,400	40,300	2,800
1947	945,500	15.1	48,100	.008	409,100	12,100	118,700	80,400	10,600	52,800	3,100
1948	1,131,900	14.6	87,800	.011	436,800	19,200	139,900	118,300	15,400	69,000	3,200
1949	1,233,000	14.7	101,600	.012	473,800	20,700	137,900	107,100	19,500	89,000	1,800
1950	1,311,000	14.4	98,800	.011	516,200	20,300	128,400	118,900	19,800	100,000	2,000
1951	1,564,500	14.1	113,500	.010	617,900	25,800	167,600	134,400	12,100	106,000	9,000
1952	1,539,200	16.0	121,600	.013	608,100	29,000	136,500	131,100	14,600	108,800	8,900
1953	1,696,000	17.9	142,100	.015	590,800	62,900	149,800	146,500	15,800	110,600	17,050
1954	1,628,200	18.2	144,500	.0162	582,400	42,400	120,700	139,600	15,800	123,000	17,300

	Freight, Express, and Cartage	Truck Expense	Supplies	Factory Office Supplies	Property Taxes	Telephone and Telegraph	Payroll Taxes	Travel	Engineering Services	Membership Dues and Subscriptions	Miscellaneous
1945	$ 7,500	$1,500	$29,900	$4,600	$17,500	$1,400	$27,900	$ 1,800	—	$ 700	—
1946	8,100	1,100	38,200	4,800	20,800	1,800	31,900	3,100	—	900	$ 4,200
1947	16,500	2,100	49,100	4,700	28,000	2,400	40,700	3,500	$2,000	1,500	4,900
1948	24,300	2,000	53,700	4,100	25,200	3,600	48,600	5,700	2,500	900	7,500
1949	29,800	900	43,700	4,900	30,500	4,500	51,400	4,900	300	1,900	11,100
1950	32,300	2,900	52,500	4,600	30,200	4,800	63,500	8,300	600	2,200	9,200
1951	39,400	2,600	76,400	8,500	30,100	5,800	74,800	10,000	600	2,900	14,300
1952	37,100	900	69,600	6,400	45,500	5,300	70,300	10,700	1,400	2,000	16,400
1953	52,900	100	78,400	6,000	48,600	6,400	77,800	16,600	9,900	2,100	21,800
1954	41,200	600	67,900	5,900	65,400	5,500	79,800	13,200	1,900	2,000	25,900

exhibit 14 LEATHERCRAFT CORPORATION

Analysis of shipping, advertising, and selling expenses by year, 1945–1954

	Total (Not Incl. Advertising)	Salaries and Wages	Commission	Repair and Maintenance	Heat, Light, Power, and Water	Insurance	Provision for Depreciation	Machine Rentals	Misc. Supplies	Stationery and Printing	Postage	Telephone and Telegraph	Payroll Taxes
1945	$ 439,758	$138,977	$206,916	$ 3,161	$2,132	$1,354	$ 5,221	—	$ 1,405	$ 2,634	$ 5,079	$1,635	$ 5,259
1946	524,394	150,464	260,943	1,632	2,177	769	4,595	—	456	5,592	5,369	2,010	6,671
1947	701,685	188,411	369,821	2,776	2,623	901	5,981	—	1,425	11,396	7,894	1,926	6,607
1948	866,038	219,288	433,379	28,179	4,301	1,040	8,587	—	1,020	14,827	8,690	2,523	7,566
1949	1,038,341	270,746	481,414	4,163	5,042	809	11,928	—	5,143	18,367	11,158	2,873	9,602
1950	1,165,589	320,445	406,958	4,031	5,126	1,230	12,666	$11,159	8,082	23,071	11,358	4,498	13,314
1951	1,494,801	393,096	527,697	5,655	5,440	1,688	13,189	15,742	18,820	36,721	16,372	5,885	15,003
1952	1,414,278	410,794	438,066	8,520	7,359	1,775	13,931	22,257	12,467	19,511	20,098	5,782	16,182
1953	1,441,634	435,332	429,105	6,762	6,808	2,154	14,481	23,456	18,504	31,946	21,251	6,006	15,796
1954	1,446,363	427,693	401,978	4,641	7,809	1,777	15,733	23,924	16,718	29,711	20,417	6,168	16,969

	Provision for Doubtful Accounts	Salesmen's Traveling Expense	Credit Information Rating Books	Collection Expense	Salesmen's Samples	Salesmen's Educational Expense	Legal and Other Professional	Misc.	Advertising				
									Salary and Wages	Magazine Advertising	General Advertising	Dealer's Helps	Total Advertising
1945	$ 893	$ 49,891	$ 5,096	$ 890	$ 541	$ 8,094	—	$ 580	$ 6,729	$ 66,543	$ 3,499	$16,959	$ 95,701
1946	—	67,973	5,216	1,257	1,351	7,257	—	663	9,990	69,791	4,061	20,753	108,303
1947	7,594	77,477	6,975	1,677	2,610	5,336	—	255	13,638	105,501	4,930	19,498	148,050
1948	6,523	107,089	5,745	3,967	4,104	8,496	—	715	14,303	122,595	7,765	19,434	168,621
1949	17,065	162,228	7,395	7,189	2,947	19,481	—	790	18,797	146,365	13,036	23,859	209,449
1950	37,573	262,958	9,669	11,633	1,138	18,865	—	1,813	17,591	143,261	22,620	23,211	214,695
1951	46,216	337,152	12,963	14,416	7,657	22,896	—	1,192	28,638	220,108	30,058	41,685	331,619
1952	13,023	364,146	13,097	17,656	5,950	21,613	—	2,049	36,084	204,394	26,332	51,980	330,435
1953	3,073	360,100	13,055	18,302	3,478	27,257	$2,068	2,699	33,801	191,672	33,585	33,712	306,597
1954	10,326	390,625	14,204	15,703	10,285	28,514	95	3,075	28,387	188,403	26,636	31,672	290,315

SOURCE: Audit reports.

exhibit 15 **LEATHER CORPORATION**

Analysis of general administrative expenses, 1945–1954

	Total	% of Un-adjusted Sales	Salaries and Wages	Stationery and Printing	State Taxes	Telephone and Telegraph	Payroll Taxes	Group and Other Insurance	Legal and Audit	Travel, Postage, Gifts, Dues, Etc.	Miscel-laneous
1945	$32,348	.0075	$12,497	$ 803	$7,290	$1,519	$ 199	$ 837	$4,855	$1,498	$2,850
1946	43,760	.0091	27,471	202	7,114	1,730	298	18	4,012	1,892	1,035
1947	65,332	.0104	41,232	1,058	7,770	2,059	1,941	584	6,600	2,306	1,722
1948	75,984	.0098	52,818	1,431	8,509	1,970	2,047	696	2,578	3,827	2,108
1949	114,736	.0137	65,031	1,693	10,583	3,427	2,166	686	6,439	22,761	1,949
1950	127,801	.0141	96,456	1,410	10,867	3,700	4,378	1,889	4,174	2,491	2,435
1951	222,565	.0201	135,699	2,133	16,735	3,628	3,651	21,457	28,488	8,889	2,884
1952	249,866	.0260	138,765	2,355	19,926	3,456	3,792	30,096	32,473	17,469	5,489
1953	288,519	.0305	147,284	3,285	28,545	3,522	4,023	71,736	9,183	15,466	5,470
1954	315,544	.0353	139,580	3,397	29,435	3,122	4,879	76,915	42,411	8,209	7,537

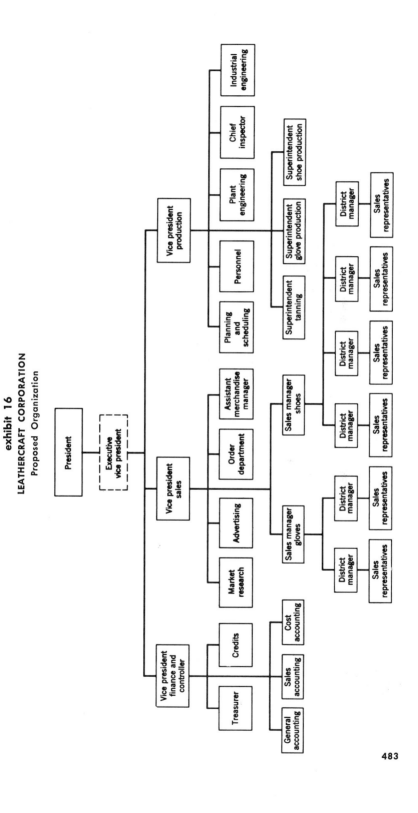

exhibit 16
LEATHERCRAFT CORPORATION
Proposed Organization

ORGANIZATION

Leathercraft's nine-man board of directors was composed of family members and employees. The informal executive committee was composed entirely of family members. This committee had difficulty in agreeing on company policy. Within the company organization individuals tended to operate independently of each other generally with little regard to co-operative effort. The organization charts of the company, which were developed at considerable expense and effort, were not being followed. (See Exhibit 16.)

The president did not operate as the chief executive officer because of his ineffectiveness in dealing with the board and the executive committee. He was unwilling to take a firm stand with the rest of the family.

A great deal of money had been spent for gathering and recording accounting and statistical information to provide facts for formulating policy and making decisions. This information was rarely used and management often did not believe it. (See, for example, Exhibits 12–15.)

A comparison of base salaries with a normal salary curve, developed from the American Management Association Executive Compensation Survey, indicated that top executive salaries of the company were above those being paid in similar size companies. Contrariwise, a tendency to underpay the lower and middle management group was indicated.

RALEIGH
INDUSTRIES

Raleigh Industries started in business in 1888 under the ownership and direction of Frank Bowden, a young man of means, who had become a cycling enthusiast because he believed that cycling had so improved his health that it had saved his life. His venture coincided with the great cycling boom of the late 1800's, and by the beginning of the twentieth century his plant in Nottingham was turning out 30,000 cycles a year. Bowden adopted Dunlop tires, which made cycling more comfortable; the Shurmey-Archer variable three-speed gear, which made riding less strenuous; and the lightweight English-style frame. Over the years he acquired the rights to such famous cycle names as BSA, Humber, Rudge-Whitworth, Triumph, Sunbeam, and Brooks Saddles. Raleigh achieved such a reputation for its dependable and fashionable cycles that by 1950 its Nottingham plant had grown to be the largest cycle factory in the world, and Raleigh was selling in every world market.

During the period from 1950 to 1959 both domestic and export demand fell so drastically that production was reduced from 4 million to 2 million cycles a year. Describing the situation in his 1959 report to shareholders, Chairman George Wilson said:

> The prospects for the bicycle are difficult to foresee. For the past three years sales in both our home and export markets have continued to decline. There are several reasons for this, and the reasons which apply in the case of the home market differ from those which apply in our export markets.
>
> In the home market it is a fact that never since the war has the sale

of pedicycles in this country ever equalled pre-war levels. There are many factors to which this development can be traced. Foremost among them is the improved standards of living of the population, which has given rise to an enormous increase in motorized transport on the roads of this country. You have only to be outside the gates of any large factory at closing time to have ample evidence of this. The incidence of purchase tax, the restrictions on hire-purchase and the competition the bicycle is facing from the recent introduction of so many forms of heavily advertised domestic appliances, are all further factors. For these reasons I do not expect to see the demand for pedal cycles in this country ever again achieve post-war levels.

In the case of our export markets, however, I see the position very differently. In many of our large overseas markets there has been an inevitable, albeit sporadic, rise in the standard of living which is introducing into the range of potential cycle purchasers many thousands of people who are for the first time in their lives able to acquire a personal means of transport. It is a fact that in the large native territories a bicycle is one of the most sought-after and prized possessions. However, on the export side, we are meeting increasing embargoes on imports into some of our principal markets.

ACQUISITION BY TUBE INVESTMENTS

Tube Investments Limited was a major British industrial company which controlled numerous iron, steel, and aluminum producing and manufacturing subsidiaries (see Exhibit 1). It was a large producer of tubing, an activity which led it into the manufacturing of cycles. Its cycle division, the British Cycle Corporation, operated plants in Birmingham, close to Nottingham, and produced such well-known brands as the Phillips, Hercules, Sun, Armstrong, and Norman. British Cycle was second in size only to Raleigh, and both companies competed actively in both home and foreign markets.

There had always been close cooperation between Raleigh and Tube Investments. Tube Investments supplied Raleigh with its requirements for tubing for cycle frames and brought many of its own components from Raleigh. Both firms looked on it as an economically natural relationship that had been built up over the years. The coordination of the two operations was so close that for many years the managements had entertained the thought of combining them.

When Raleigh was experiencing the drastic decline in sales during the latter fifties, Tube Investments was having the same experience. Both companies found themselves vying for the potential which remained.

exhibit 1   TUBE INVESTMENTS LTD.

History: Registered in England in 1919.

Business: Manufactures precision tube, cycles and components, aluminum electrical engineering and iron and steel products. Company and subsidiaries operate following divisions: Steel Tube, Cycle, Aluminum, Electrical, Engineering and Iron and Steel, General and overseas.

Subsidiaries: British Aluminum Co. Ltd. (appended statement—51% owned by company and 49% by Reynolds Metals Co.—see general index) which in turn controls Canadian British Aluminum Co. Ltd. (appended statement). Also has a number of subsidiaries and affiliates in England, Argentina, Australia, Canada, New Zealand, Pakistan, So. Africa, Eire, India, Italy, Kenya, Norway, Southern Rhodesia, U. S. A., France, Germany and Holland.

Also Raleigh Industries Ltd., (100%).

Board of Directors: Lord Plowden, Chmn.; Sir I. A. R. Stedeford, Pres.; Lord Clitheroe, Vice-Chmn.; Sir William Strath, L. Dobson, Man. Dir.; Sir David C. Watherson, E. D. E. Andrews, W. Hackett, Jr., A. J. S. Aston, L. L. Roberts, E. L. Burton, C. H. T. Williams, E. G. Plucknett, R. G. Soothill, Lord Normanbrook, M. L. G. Boughton, B. S. Kellett, J. W. Menter.

Secretary: H. A. Woodroffe.

Annual Meeting: In December.

No. of Stockholders: July 31, 1964, 7% preference, 1,455; 4½% preference stock, 3,964; ordinary, 48,213.

No. of Employees: July 31, 1964, 60,600 (incl. British Aluminum).

Head Office: T. L. House, Five Ways, Birmingham 16.

Consolidated income account, years ended July 31

	1965	1964
Sales (net)	£215,800,000	£194,100,000
Trading profit	22,817,843	20,279,539
Dividends and interest income	1,116,728	1,125,554
British Aluminum Co.	3,633,829	2,982,630
Total	27,568,400	24,387,723
Depreciation	7,112,203	6,369,182
Taxation, net	5,936,767	5,068,825
Minority interest	1,369,437	929,837
Loan interest	1,361,302	1,065,923
*Extraordinary expenses	1,293,836	2,595,645
Net profit	10,494,854	8,358,311
Preference dividends	168,618	173,334
Ordinary dividends	3,325,216	3,250,046
Retained by subsidiaries	1,141,414	1,661,556
Balance for year	6,859,606	3,272,375

* Concentration of production, pre-production and commissioning of new steelworks (Park Gate).

exhibit 1   (continued)

Consolidated balance sheet, as of July 31

Assets	1965	1964
Inventory	£ 60,496,000	£ 56,514,806
Debtors	54,443,000	46,928,953
Other current	1,386,000	1,635,632
Total current	£116,325,000	£105,079,391
*Plant machinery, etc.	93,272,000	92,736,176
Trade investment	9,122,000	8,745,695
Subsidiary advances	4,394,000	5,569,592
Shares subsidiaries not consolidated	7,908,000	7,907,576
†Other assets	7,272,000	7,481,945
Total	£238,293,000	£227,520,375
Liabilities		
Creditors	£ 28,650,000	£ 23,094,943
Tax payable	4,887,000	6,473,120
Banks	3,327,000	3,035,008
Other current	2,766,000	5,478,518
Total current	£ 39,630,000	£ 38,081,589
7% preference stock	828,000	828,487
4½ preference stock	5,000,000	5,000,000
Ordinary stock	35,375,000	35,374,646
5¼% loan stock	7,500,000	7,500,000
Capital reserves	33,262,000	33,108,786
Revenue reserves	51,546,000	46,524,508
Subsidiary debentures	15,007,000	15,254,317
Future tax	7,438,000	5,572,570
Minority interest	26,710,000	25,660,870
Profit and loss	15,997,000	14,614,602
Total	£238,293,000	£227,520,375

* Net after depreciation.
† Difference between cost of subsidiary shares and book values of net
assets attributable to such shares, less writeoffs.
SOURCE: *Moody's Manual of Industrials, 1966.*

This situation brought to a head the merger which had long been under
consideration. Tube Investments and Raleigh each had subsidiaries
which operated factories in Ireland and South Africa. In 1959 these were
merged and their production and distribution facilities amalgamated.
It was generally recognized that this was a pilot run which contemplated
a later merger of the full-scale cycle interests of both companies.

In 1960 the cycle interests of Tube Investments and Raleigh were
combined by an exchange of ordinary shares. Tube Investments became
the emergent parent company, with Raleigh Industries Limited a subsidiary operating as a division. At the same time, the board of directors

of Tube Investments asked the board of Raleigh Industries, enlarged by the addition of two Tube Investment executives, to assume responsibility for the combined cycle, component, and motorized divisions of the group, with Mr. Wilson continuing as chairman of Raleigh. As a result of the merger, Raleigh Industries came into control of 80% of the total cycle production capacity of the United Kingdom, with its only competition a few small producers. During the next several years the Raleigh management rationalized the combined production and distribution facilities of the group; it diversified by adding wheeled toys and a reeled safety belt to its product line; it revitalized its motorized cycle activities by developing new mopeds and scooters; it developed a new small-wheeled bicycle of revolutionary design; and it devised new strategies in a determined effort to hold its substantial export markets which were being pre-empted by foreign competitors.

ORGANIZATIONAL CHANGES

Mr. George Wilson had been managing director and chairman for 20 of his 40 years with Raleigh, having succeeded Sir Harold Bowden, the son of the founder, Sir Frank Bowden, in 1955. Mr. Wilson was nearing retirement age at the time of the merger, and although he was still very active and well-liked wihtin the company, he felt that the new challenges facing Raleigh might better be met by a man who was younger and more vigorous. Mr. Wilson continued to serve as chairman until his death in 1963; in January, 1962, he retired as managing director to be succeeded by Mr. Leslie Roberts, who had been brought into the company to head the production activities. During the next several years there were numerous changes in the Raleigh personnel.

The board was increased from seven to eight members, six of whom were new as executives of the company and as members of the board. The new board acted in two roles: it met as a main board for policy-making purposes once a month; and acting as an executive committee it met weekly to act upon operating matters (see Exhibit 2).

In 1965 Mr. T. E. Barnsley, formerly a financial executive with Tube Investments, was brought into Raleigh as deputy managing director, a newly created position. Most of the former managing directors of small subsidiary units which had been liquidated as a result of the merger were worked into the new organization. Of the middle and top management staffs of the combined group, 38 out of 50 people were replaced.

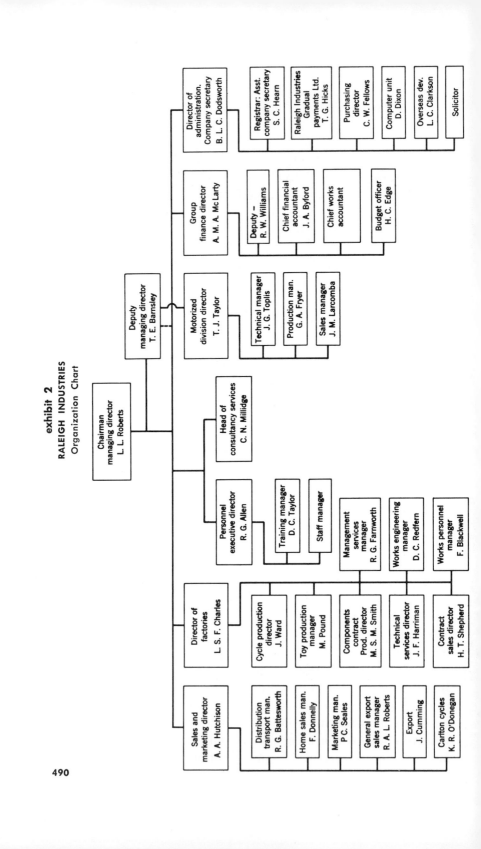

exhibit 2
RALEIGH INDUSTRIES
Organization Chart

Chairman managing director L. L. Roberts

Deputy managing director T. E. Barnsley

Head of consultancy services C. N. Millidge

Sales and marketing director A. A. Hutchison
- Distribution transport man. R. G. Battesworth
- Home sales man. F. Donnelly
- Marketing man. P. C. Seales
- General export sales manager R. A. L. Roberts
- Export J. Cumming
- Carlton cycles K. R. O'Donegan

Director of factories L. S. F. Charles
- Cycle production director J. Ward
- Toy production manager M. Pound
- Components contract Prod. director M. S. M. Smith
- Technical services director J. F. Harriman
- Contract sales director H. T. Shepherd

Personnel executive director R. G. Allen
- Training manager D. C. Taylor
- Staff manager
- Management services manager R. G. Farnworth
- Works engineering manager D. C. Redfern
- Works personnel manager F. Blackwell

Motorized division director T. J. Taylor
- Technical manager J. G. Toplis
- Production man. G. A. Fryer
- Sales manager J. M. Larcomba

Group finance director A. M. A. McLarty
- Deputy – R. W. Williams
- Chief financial accountant J. A. Byford
- Chief works accountant
- Budget officer H. C. Edge

Director of administration. Company secretary B. L. C. Dodsworth
- Registrar: Asst. company secretary S. C. Hearn
- Raleigh Industries Gradual payments Ltd. T. G. Hicks
- Purchasing director C. W. Fellows
- Computer unit D. Dixon
- Overseas dev. L. C. Clarkson
- Solicitor

490

RALEIGH—THE WORLD'S LARGEST CYCLE MANUFACTURER AND EXPORTER

In 1966 the British cycle industry was the largest in the world and sold about 65% of its production abroad. Raleigh commanded a leading position in the industry, exporting over 70% of its total production, which comprised nearly all of the cycle exports from the United Kingdom and represented nearly half of all of the total bicycle exports of the whole world. Raleigh exported cycles to 140 different markets. Its closest competitors, the Japanese, sold in only about half as many export markets. (See Exhibits 7 and 8 for statement of financial condition.)

exhibit 3   SPREAD OF BICYCLE EXPORT MARKETS 1962–1964

Exporting Country	Number of Markets Served*		
	1962	1963	1964
United Kingdom (Raleigh)	138	140	140
Japan	31	83	77
France	39	35	34
Western Germany	24	18	22
Austria	19	21	22
Netherlands	8	11	11
Poland	17	25	n.a.

* Minor markets are not shown.
SOURCE: Company's records.

Of Raleigh's manufactured products of bicycles, bicycle components, mopeds, wheeled toys, and a reeled safety belt, the export sales of bicycles and bicycle components consistently formed over 70% of the company's turnover. In the period from 1951 to 1965 there had been shifts of great magnitude in the whole bicycle trade, and the world export market had been declining, but Raleigh's share of world exports had been increasing, as shown by the most recent figures available:

exhibit 4   NUMBER OF BICYCLES

Year	Raleigh Exports	World Exports	Raleigh Exports % World Exports
1961	1,322,000	3,006,000	44.0
1962	1,343,000	2,796,000	48.0
1963	1,542,000	2,981,000	51.7

SOURCE: Company's records.

Raleigh accounted for nearly all of the United Kingdom exports of bicycles:

exhibit 5   EXPORTS OF BICYCLES, UNITED KINGDOM, 1962–1964

Year	Raleigh Exports	U.K. Cycle Industry	Raleigh % of U.K. Cycle Exports
1962	£10,956,000	£11,405,000	96.1
1963	12,786,000	12,816,000	99.8
1964	9,338,000	9,523,000	98.1

SOURCE: Company's records.

exhibit 6   EXPORTS OF BICYCLES TO THE U. S. A., 1962–1964

Year	Raleigh Exports	U.K. Industry Exports	Raleigh % U.K. Industry	Raleigh U.S. Cycle Exports % Total Raleigh Cycle Exports
		By Value		
1962	£4,881,000	£4,577,000	100.0+*	44.6
1963	5,299,000	5,740,000	92.3	41.4
1964	3,200,000	3,365,000	95.1	34.3
		By Units		
1962	636,000	596,000	100.0+*	47.4
1963	695,000	753,000	92.3	45.0
1964	395,000	415,000	95.2	35.0

* The Raleigh figures are of goods involved; the United Kingdom figures are of goods shipped. This accounts for the anomaly of 1962.
SOURCE: Company's records.

Since 1951 there had been a rapid and steady decline in the world trade in bicycles, as import duties and restrictions had their effect and as developing nations nationalized their production. In 1951, the all-time year for bicycle production, the total British output was some 4 million machines. In 1965 it was 1,740,000 of which 1,128,000 were exported.

exhibit 7 RALEIGH INDUSTRIES LIMITED AND ITS SUBSIDIARIES

Consolidated balance sheet, 31st July, 1965

		31st July, 1965 £			31st July, 1964 £
Share capital (Note 3)	5,722,505			5,722,505	
Capital reserves (Note 4)	7,395,249			7,339,500	
Revenue reserve					
Unappropriated profit	987,529			543,311	
	14,105,283			13,596,316	
Future income tax					
1965–1966 assessment				540,500	
Overseas tax 1966–1967	31,500			39,000	
Corporation tax					
Payable 1st January 1967	860,500				
6% debenture stock 1978–1983 (Note 5)	3,283,857			3,332,618	
Loan from tube investments limited	3,771,013			4,934,668	
Total capital employed	**£22,052,153**			**£22,434,102**	

	31st July, 1965 £	£	31st July, 1964 £	£
Fixed assets (Note 6)				
Freehold land and buildings	4,179,571		4,324,335	
Leasehold land and buildings	153,777		166,644	
Plant and machinery	1,324,102		1,631,127	
Other equipment	430,993		421,281	
		6,088,443		6,543,387
Goodwill (Note 7)		1,817,237		1,817,237
Investment in associated companies (at cost)		376,024		376,024
Current assets				
Stocks (Note 8)	6,259,665		6,421,611	
Debtors	10,674,563		10,153,237	
Current accounts with fellow subsidiaries	82,659		86,782	
Quoted investments				
(market value £26,231 (£28,580))	25,068		25,068	
Cash in banks and in hand	742,243		587,168	
	17,784,198		17,274,366	
Deduct:				
Liabilities and provisions				
Trade creditors and accrued charges (Note 9)	2,598,442		2,658,400	
Current accounts with fellow subsidiaries	84,254		111,174	
Current taxation	726,610		607,706	
Preference dividend accrued	4,443		4,652	
Proposed ordinary dividend	600,000		195,000	
	4,013,749		3,576,912	
Net current assets		13,770,449		13,697,454
Total net assets		**£22,052,153**		**£22,434,102**

L. L. ROBERTS
B. L. C. DODSWORTH } *Directors*

493

exhibit **7A   RALEIGH INDUSTRIES LIMITED AND ITS SUBSIDIARIES**
Notes on accounts

1. Directors' emoluments

The emoluments of the Directors of Raleigh Industries Limited were as follows:

	1965	*1964*
	£	£
Fees	500	*333*
Other emoluments	57,259	*61,916*
Payment on cessation of employment	8,500	*10,000*
	£66,259	*£72,249*

2. Taxation

	1965	*1964*
	£	£
Based on the profit of the year:		
Income tax	(105,290)	*446,138*
Corporation tax	860,500	
Profits tax		*177,132*
Overseas tax	98,979	*67,145*
Exceptional items:		
Additional income tax 1965–1966	34,000	
Prior years' overprovisions	(17,944)	*(70,826)*
	£870,245	*£619,589*

Taxation is stated after estimated relief of £27,000 (*£56,000*) from investment allowances. Corporation tax has been calculated at 40%.

	At 31st July, 1965	
		Issued and
	Authorized	*Fully Paid*
3. Share capital	£	£
6 per cent cumulative preference shares of £1 each	1,000,000	1,000,000
Ordinary shares of £1 each	6,500,000	4,722,505
	£7,500,000	£5,722,505

There has been no change during the year.

4. Capital reserves	£	£
Share premium account		
At 31st July, 1964 and 1965		77,838
Debenture redemption reserve		
At 31st July, 1964	167,382	
Appropriation from profit and loss account	48,761	
At 31st July, 1965		216,143
Surplus on realization of fixed assets		
At 31st July, 1964	597,122	
Surplus on sale of land and buildings	15,988	
At 31st July, 1965		613,110
Surplus on revaluation of buildings in 1948		
At 31st July, 1964 and 1965		160,926
General reserve		
At 31st July, 1964 and 1965 (being the total other reserves of Raleigh Industries Limited at the date		

exhibit **7A** (continued)

of acquisition in 1960 by Tube Investments Limited)	6,306,496
Total capital reserves of Raleigh Industries Limited at 31st July, 1965	7,374,513
Total capital reserves at Raleigh Industries Limited at 31st July, 1964	*7,309,764*
General reserve—subsidiary companies At 31st July, 1964 and 1965 (being the total other reserves of subsidiary companies at the date of acquisition in 1960 by Tube Investments Limited)	20,736
Total capital reserves of the group at 31st July, 1965	£7,395,249
Total capital reserves of the group at 31st July, 1964	*£7,330,500*

5. 6 per cent debenture stock 1978–1983

£3,500,000 6 per cent debenture stock 1978–1983 was issued at £97 per cent during 1957–1958 and is repayable at par on 31st July, 1983, or at the option of the company after 31st July, 1978. There are provisions for annual sinking fund payments, commencing in the year ended 31st July, 1961, designed to secure the repayment of one-half of the principal amount of the stock at par by 31st July, 1983, through annual drawings or purchases by the company in the market. The sinking fund payment this year amounted to £47,281 and this has been used to redeem £48,761 of stock. The relative sum has been transferred from profit and loss account to debenture redemption reserve.

6. Fixed assets

Italic figures relate to the previous year.

	Valuation or Cost at 31st July, 1964, £	Acqui- sitions, £	Disposals, £	Valuation or Cost at 31st July, 1965, £	Accumulated Depreci- ation, £	Net Book Value, £
Freehold land and buildings	5,604,446	28,707	177,155	5,455,998	1,276,427	4,179,571
	6,106,750	*48,439*	*550,743*	*5,604,446*	*1,280,111*	*4,324,335*
Leasehold land and buildings	241,964	3,280	31,508	213,736	59,959	153,777
	252,941	....	*10,977*	*241,964*	*75,320*	*166,644*
Plant and machinery	6,233,525	86,738	197,161	6,123,102	4,799,000	1,324,102
	6,290,983	*266,587*	*324,045*	*6,233,525*	*4,602,398*	*1,631,127*
Other equipment	1,301,097	137,577	85,871	1,352,803	921,810	430,993
	1,237,040	*148,392*	*84,335*	*1,301,097*	*879,816*	*421,281*
Group totals	£13,381,032	256,302	491,695	13,145,639	7,057,196	6,088,443
	£13,887,714	*463,418*	*970,100*	*13,381,032*	*6,837,645*	*6,543,387*
Raleigh Industires Ltd. totals	£13,093,583	242,706	485,875	12,850,414	6,878,874	5,971,540
	£13,592,044	*460,423*	*958,884*	*13,093,583*	*6,667,676*	*6,425,907*

exhibit **7A**   (continued)

The detailed figures for Raleigh Industries Limited do not differ materially from those shown above for the group.

The net book value at 31st July, 1965, includes £182,284 for assets which were independently valued on 1st July 1948. Otherwise fixed assets are stated at original cost to the companies now forming the group.

Depreciation is calculated separately for each fixed asset (excluding freehold land) on the straight line basis to amortize the cost of the asset by the end of its useful life.

The accumulated depreciation includes provisions made by certain companies before they joined the group.

7. Goodwill

This comprises the cost of goodwill, trade-marks, etc., purchased together with the excess of the purchase consideration of shares in subsidiary companies over the book value of their tangible assets at the date of acquisition.

8. Stocks

Stocks, comprising raw materials, work in progress, finished goods and stores, are stated, consistently with previous years, at the lower of:

(a) Cost (including an appropriate proportion of overhead expenditure), and

(b) Net realizable value.

9. Outside shareholders' interest

Outside shareholders' interest in the share capital and reserves of subsidiary companies, £555 (£555) has been included in trade creditors. Such shareholders' interest in the profit of the year £35 (£35) has been excluded from the account on page 6.

10. Contracts for capital expenditure

There were commitments for capital expenditure at 31st July, 1965, of approximately £142,000 (£50,000) not provided for in these accounts.

11. Foreign currencies

Assets and liabilities have been converted at rates of exchange ruling at the date of the balance sheet.

MANUFACTURING

In 1952 the Raleigh management had expected sales to continue to rise, and Raleigh made a £1.5 million ($4,260,000) addition to its plants. In 1957 it built another 20-acre, £5 million ($14,200,000) addition, which had been planned in 1953, but by the time this addition was completed sales had fallen sharply. In 1957, for the first time in 20 years, Raleigh was constrained to reduce the work week for three months. In 1958 it introduced a four-day week.

In 1959 Mr. Wilson, chairman, brought into the company as head of factories Mr. Leslie Roberts, a dynamic manager, who had been a manufacturing executive with Rootes Motors. Later Mr. Roberts became managing director. Mr. Roberts' first major objective was to rationalize manufacturing. The new combined group employed 14,500

exhibit 8 **RALEIGH INDUSTRIES LIMITED AND ITS SUBSIDIARIES**
Consolidated profit and loss and appropriation accounts, year ended 31st July, 1965

			31st July, 1964	
	£	£	£	£
Profit of the group	2,742,515		2,189,111	
Deduct: depreciation of fixed assets	568,035		601,234	
		2,174,480		1,587,877
Other income				
From associated companies	19,591		748	
From quoted investments	1,995		1,746	
		21,586		2,494
		2,196,066		1,590,371
Interest payable				
On debenture stock	197,031		200,695	
On loan from parent company			11,228	
		197,031		211,923
		1,999,035		1,378,448
Exceptional items				176,470
Profit before taxation		1,999,035		1,201,978
Taxation (Note 2)		870,245		619,589
Net profit of the group for the year				
carried forward (Note 9)		1,128,790		582,389
Net profit of the group for the year of which £1,059,356 (£500,732) is dealt with in the accounts of Raleigh Industries Limited)		1,128,790		582,389
Unappropriated profit brought forward from previous years				
Raleigh Industries Limited	248,241		24,206	
Subsidiary companies	295,070		231,413	
		543,311		237,619
Profit available for appropriation		1,672,101		820,008
Appropriations				
Capital reserves (Note 4)	48,761		44,947	
Dividends (*less* income tax)				
On 6 per cent preference shares	35,811		36,750	
Proposed on ordinary shares	600,000		195,000	
		684,572		276,697
Unappropriated profit carried forward				
Raleigh Industries Limited	623,025		248,241	
Subsidiary companies	364,504		295,070	
Total unappropriated profit of the group as shown in the consolidated balance sheet		£987,529		£543,311

people in nine widely separated factories, each with its own management, with a total floor area of 4.5 million square feet.

During the years which followed the merger, the number of plants was reduced from nine to five by disposing of those Birmingham plants which duplicated Raleigh's Nottingham operations. All tubing, saddle, and replacement parts manufacture was concentrated in the remaining Birmingham plants. All cycle manufacture (intermingled with toy production) was concentrated in the 60-acre Nottingham plant complex, which remained intact. The number of employees was reduced to 9,000.

Mr. Roberts' rationalization program was continued by Mr. L. S. F. Charles, whom Mr. Roberts brought into the company. Mr. Charles introduced more automatic processing in plating transportation, in heat treatment, and in enameling. On the premise that bicycle costs consisted of about 50% materials and 15% labor, Mr. Charles scrutinized intensely those processes which tended to be wasteful of materials. He introduced electrostatic spraying; brazing of tubing joints; scintering moulding; the use of plastic where possible; and cold instead of hot forging. Time study and piece rates were critically reviewed; factory layout and material handling were under constant study; and design engineers focused their attention on economies in product designs. As a result, the over-all consumption of material per unit was reduced by 10%.

In 1966 production was still at such a low level that there was 20% excess plant capacity at Nottingham. The excess was spread throughout many departments of the plant and therefore could not be sold or leased. To utilize the excess capacity the company sought custom manufacturing jobs. These consisted of straight machine work for some leading auto makers, forming tubing for a perambulator manufacturer, and a variety of small jobs. In 1966 contract work accounted for about 10% of the company's total turnover.

COSTS AND PRICES

Raleigh prices were determined by a factory-cost formula, and the resulting price was shaded to meet competitive prices, aiming to earn a minimum 10% net profit. The Raleigh management had statistics which indicated that in a three-year period the retail price index showed a rise of 14%, and wage rates in the engineering industry increased 22%. Abroad, pricing policies tended to be dictated by distributor competition, and United Kingdom cost increases could not be passed off to foreign customers via raised prices in countries where no cost-price rise had taken place. Although Raleigh's long line of models included several price categories, all Raleigh cycles were high quality, and its prices tended to be 8 to 10% above competitors'. As the company's sales turnover fell from year to year, it was observed that the fall was greatest in those products which had the highest margins.

Raleigh had statistical data which indicated that bicycle prices on an index basis in Great Britain (1954 = 100) were standing at 131.4 in 1963. This compared with 119.8 for all manufactured products, 70.9 for refrigerators, 97.4 for washing machines, and 112.6 for vacuum cleaners. Although these products were not directly competitive, they were a call on the consumer's disposable income, and they possibly had more attraction than a bicycle. Research indicated that children were eager to buy bicycles, and most objections to buying came from parents, mainly on price.

Purchase tax in England constituted 14.8% of the retail price. This meant that in every £20 ($56.80) the customer paid about £3 ($8.52) in purchase tax.

THE UNITED STATES MARKET FOR BICYCLES

The United States was by far the largest single bicycle market in the world. It had been Raleigh's largest export market for years. In the United States Raleigh had popularized the lightweight, "sport," English-style bicycles so successfully that these models took the market away from the old-style, heavy-framed American cycles.

Between 1950 and 1956 the Raleigh share of cycles imported into the United States decreased by over 60% and Raleigh's sales there declined every year thereafter, in spite of the fact that total cycle sales in the United States rose steadily throughout the period from 2.5 million in 1960 to 5 million in 1965.

The United States was essentially a "price" market, and Raleigh's major customers were mail-order houses and chain stores which bought in mass quantities on a price basis. Raleigh's declining sales resulted from a sharp increase in the activity of America's own cycle makers, who were now contesting the market Raleigh had pioneered there for lightweight cycles. Most of Raleigh's mass-volume customers had switched their purchases to local producers or to other importers who were making cycles to the customers' specifications under their private labels and doing it for prices which were sometimes below Raleigh's factory cost. To Raleigh, with its premium-priced line, this was marginal business, but nevertheless valuable. As recently as 1954 Raleigh had sold about 1 million cycles in the United States.

The United States duty was $22\frac{1}{2}\%$ for a cycle with less than 26 inch wheels and weighing less than 36 pounds. For larger cycles the duty was $11\frac{1}{4}\%$. This meant that Raleigh typically paid a duty of $11\frac{1}{4}\%$ plus about 5% for freight costs, giving the local manufacturer making the same cycle an advantage of $16\frac{1}{4}\%$.

In 1966 Raleigh management made a policy decision to limit its volume in the general United States market and to concentrate on the sale of its Raleigh-labeled cycles and the premium-branded lines, which were to be sold through the retail dealer trade. Raleigh also planned to continue to sell to the smaller chain stores and the minor mail-order houses. In doing this, Raleigh realized that it would be cutting in half its potential United States dollar sales volume.

Raleigh had always sold substantial quantities of components in the United States. Increasing emphasis was to be placed on this component business.

THE EUROPEAN MARKET FOR BICYCLES

A major market area of the world in which Raleigh bicycle sales had been minimal was western Europe, particularly in the countries of the Common Market. The recent sharp drop in bicycle sales had been in the United Kingdom, but not in Europe generally. In 1966 it was estimated that Germany had a sales potential of 1.5 million cycles versus 600,000 for the United Kingdom. Raleigh's lack of sales in western Europe was due partly to tariff barriers, which were generally about 20%, and partly, the management admitted, to sheer neglect.

In 1965 Raleigh had a market survey of western Europe made by international consultants, and it followed this with a survey made by its own staff. Based upon its findings, a European sales promotion tour was undertaken, featuring the slogan, "Go Gold Medal Cycling." The tour covered Belgium, Holland, Germany, Switzerland, Denmark, and Sweden, and promoted the RSW 16 and the Compact (see following sections of the case).

Raleigh did not now have a plant in the Common Market, and the

management looked upon Europe as a whole as an unexploited territory. The failure of the Common Market negotiations had been a disappointment to the Raleigh management. Pending the possible entrance
of the United Kingdom into the ECC, Raleigh planned to make every
effort to become established in the Common Market as soon as possible,
in spite of the 20% tariff hurdle. The thinking of the management was
that if this could be done, then if England did join the Common Market, Raleigh would already be established and have a 20% advantage.
There were also long-range plans to establish a plant in Germany, but
the plans were still in the discussion stage.

THE MOULTON

There had been no change in the basic design of the bicycle since
the turn of the century. The lightweight English sports model had become the predominant design in the bicycle market. Its large-size wheels
were considered to be an engineering necessity, since large wheels took
up road shocks.

Alex Moulton was a British Motors Corporation design engineer who
had developed the famous BMC Hydrolastic Suspension shock absorbers. In about 1960 it occurred to Mr. Moulton that there would be many
advantages in a small-wheeled bicycle if it were not for the shocks due
to the small wheels. Moulton designed a short-based, 16-inch-wheel bicycle with unique rubber suspension shock absorbers in both forks and
with handle bars and seat which were adjustable to accommodate riders
of all sizes.

Moulton brought his design to Raleigh, which saw possibilities in it
and permitted Moulton to use their design laboratory to do further
developmental work. Raleigh finally decided against producing it;
Moulton took his cycle to his employers at British Motors and persuaded
them to manufacture it.

Moulton Cycles Limited's first cycle to be marketed appeared in 1963
bearing the brand name Moulton (see Exhibit 9). It found immediate
consumer acceptance and was hailed by the industry as the first new
bicycle design in 70 years. Selling in only a limited area around London,
the Moulton achieved an estimated turnover of 40,000 units in its first
year, and volume increased each year thereafter. In succeeding years
Moulton added several other models to his line, including one model

exhibit 9

constructed largely of aluminum alloy, another with a six-speed gear-shift, another which was collapsible for stowing in a car trunk, and another with an automatic gearshift.

It was expected that Moulton's sales in the 1965 cycle year would be about 75,000 units.

RALEIGH'S MARKET RESEARCH ON BICYCLES

In 1963 Raleigh commissioned a study of basic motivation and atti-tudes towards bicycles. The profile of the English cyclist which emerged characterized him as associated with poverty, low social status, and hard times. The bicycle was seen as the poor man's useful and valuable friend. Bikes were usually pictured as old and worn, and their dilapidated con-dition did not matter to the owner.

In 1964 Raleigh carried out the most comprehensive product research regarding bicycles that had ever been undertaken in the United King-dom. The project included product testing of both 16- and 20-inch models.

From this research project it was found that 75% of all bicycles were bought for children under 15, whereas 62% of Moulton owners were over 25 years of age. Only 25% of Moulton owners were children in the 8 to 15 age group. Some 58% of Moulton owners came from car-owning families and 13% from families owning two cars. Prior to the introduction of the Moulton, only 55% of the Moulton owners had wanted a bicycle, yet 95% of the owners were pleased that they had bought one.

Commenting on the research findings, Mr. Peter Seales, Raleigh's marketing manager said, "For years the two people who rang the bell on the bicycle shop most have been the school child and the working-class adult. They wanted something just to take them to school and work. The profile of today's cyclist is quite different: highly educated, with sophisticated ideas concerning dress, style of living, and careers. We believe we have discovered a market segment heretofore uncatered for."

THE RSW 16 AND THE COMPACT BICYCLES

Based upon its research findings, Raleigh developed what it described as an entirely new concept in cycling, the RSW 16—from Raleigh Small Wheel 16. (The names Elite and Citizen had been considered but discarded because it was thought that they might eventually lose their identification with Raleigh.) (See Exhibit 10.)

The RSW 16 was extremely compact, being 4 to 6 inches (10 to 15 centimeters) lower in height and 11 inches (28 centimeters) shorter in over-all length than the typical standard cycle. This greatly enhanced handling, maneuverability, and storage characteristics. The same design was equally suitable for men or women, boys or girls. The handle bar and saddle bar positions were adjusted to permit use by children of eight or nine years, and adults up to 6 feet 4 inches (1 meter 93 centimeters) in height. This made it a cycle which could be used by the entire family.

The RSW 16 had specially designed 16-inch (41 centimeters) balloon tires of 35# pounds per square inch (2.44 kilos per square centimeter) to give a smooth, comfortable ride. It was equipped with a three-speed Sturmey-Archer gearshift, dyno hub-operated lighting, a prop-stand, carrier, and a large detachable carrier-bag, yet was considerably lighter than any standard cycle. Brake and lighting cables were almost entirely concealed.

exhibit 10

Along with the RSW 16 the company developed the Raleigh Compact, a folding bicycle with no loose components, whose folding actions required only 10 seconds (see Exhibit 11). The main frame member folded in the shotgun manner, providing instant locking and perfect rigidity. It was necessary to press only one lever to release the mechanism and fold the bicycle. The specifications of the Compact were identical to that of the RSW 16, except that the cables did not pass through the frame, and lighting was not included as standard equipment. When folded, the size of the cycle was 38 × 30 × 15 inches (97 × 77 × 38 centimeters), permitting it to be easily fitted into the average car trunk.

PROMOTION OF THE RSW 16 AND RALEIGH CYCLES

Mr. Peter Seales had proposed that Raleigh exploit the developing leisure market, pointing out that camping, caravaning, boating, and other leisure sports were collecting an increasing amount of consumer

exhibit 11

spending each year. Raleigh salesmen and retail dealers were puzzled at the thought of projecting their cycles, with their old-fashioned image, into this leisure-society spending picture (see Exhibit 12).

It was believed that the bicycle was underpublicized as a product and that it was meeting progressively more skillful competition from other consumer items such as tape recorders, transistor radios, and record players. Raleigh had information which indicated that producers of these products were spending up to 8% of their sales dollar on advertising. Raleigh was spending 4%. The United Kingdom cycle industry spent less than 1%.

With the launching of the RSW 16 in 1965, the leisure-market theme was revived. "To help place our bicycles in the leisure-society picture," said Mr. Seales, "we need the assistance of the trend-setters, the people who already have four-stroke motor mowers, the *Sunday Times* readers, the people who have had movie cameras for years. These are the people who can set the lead with the RSW 16, and tens of thousands of people will be willing to follow. All of our RSW 16 marketing launch is aimed at people who would not normally be in the market for a cycle. We

exhibit 12
THE NEW PROMOTION THEME
"All sorts and sizes of people can ride a horse; so it is with the Raleigh RSW 16."

mean to increase our business, and not merely provide a substitute shape which would still limit the number of bicycles sold each year in this country."

Mr. Seales asserted that his own usage of advertising was not intuitive but was on an actuarial basis. Raleigh's future advertising was to use "glamour" themes to combat the social inferiority of the bicycle. Pictorial advertisement featured beauty queens, stage and screen celebrities, equestrians in riding costume, golfers, hunters, and airline hostesses, all riding the RSW 16. Typical of these celebrities were Leslie Langley,

Miss World; Peter Thompson, 1965 British Open Golf Champion; Uffa Fox, world-famous yachtsman; Graham Hill, noted racing driver; and Mary Quant, the "darling of the smart fashion set."

The question of the price of the RSW 16 was strongly influenced by the research findings, which indicated that Moulton owners had been willing to pay a high price. Since Raleigh was aiming its new promotions at the upper-income groups, it believed that it could raise the price considerably above conventional bike prices. The RSW 16 was introduced at £30 9s ($86.46). The Moulton price was £30 ($85.20).

The projected sale of the RSW 16 was 75,000 for the first year. At the end of an eight-month period in 1965–1966, 80% of the quota had been achieved.

MOTORIZED PRODUCTS

The Raleigh management had been observing the moped (motorized pedicycle) market with interest for a number of years, because motorized cycle sales in the United Kingdom had been very small in comparison with the business on the Continent, where sales were flourishing. In 1958 Raleigh entered the field with a low-priced utility vehicle which raised the United Kingdom industry sales from 46,000 in 1958 to 115,000 in 1959 (see Exhibit 13). Pleased with this initial success, the management stated that it saw a bright future for mopeds and that eventually the production of mopeds might become just as essential to the company's economy as the production of pedicycles. It also envisioned the growing demand spreading to Africa and Asia.

In 1960 Raleigh's moped sales fell sharply. Technical difficulties had developed in a crankshaft in the engine, which was purchased from a French manufacturer. Furthermore, the government had reinstituted credit restrictions in the form of tighter hire-purchase requirements. "There can be no doubt," said Mr. George Hamilton Wilson, then chairman of Raleigh, "that the moped has yet to be accepted in this country as it has been on the Continent, for a number of reasons. For one thing, until recently, no United Kingdom manufacturer has produced a moped to a quality specification and price capable of competing with the machines produced on the Continent. We have restrictive legislation governing licensing, driving tests, and the minimum age at which the tests may be taken. In recent years our government has pursued a "stop-and-go" policy with respect to hire-purchase terms. Finally, we have

exhibit 13

Automatic Mk II

A more powerful version of the RUNABOUT.
Engine power output is increased by 30% (1.7
B.H.P. at 5,000 R.P.M.) and a telescopic front
fork is fitted to provide extra comfort; Automatic clutch; Adjustable handlebar and saddle;
Double dipping headlamp; Full width hub
brakes, front and rear; 1⅜ imp. gallon (6.2 litre)
fuel tank with reserve tap; Electric horn.
Colour finish: Pearl grey and charcoal grey
enamel. Bright chromium plated fittings.

Supermatic

This is the high performance
machine in the range. Engine output is increased to 2.66 B.H.P. at
5,500 R.P.M.; Automatic clutch;
Automatic transmission; Swing-
ing arm front and rear suspension;
Adjustable handlebars; Dual seat
and pillion foot rests.   Electric
horn. Colour finish: Carmine Red
enamel, bright chromium plated
fittings.

RUNABOUT

An elegant machine, fitted with the 1.39 B.H.P.
version of the basic two-stroke engine; Automatic clutch; Adjustable handlebar and saddle;
Sturdy, bicycle type front forks; 1⅜ imp. gallon
(6.2 litre) fuel tank fitted with reserve tap;
Single beam headlamp; Calliper front brakes
with full width hub brakes at the rear. Colour
finish: Pearl grey and Raleigh green enamel.
Bright chromium plated fittings.

RALEIGH

MOPEDS

exhibit 13 (continued)

RM6
Runabout

RM8
Automatic MKII

RALEIGH ™

a highly efficient and co-ordinated public transport system in this country."

Although United Kingdom industry sales in general had fallen, regardless of make, Raleigh's sales had not dropped as much as others, and Raleigh continued to gain in market share. Mr. Wilson was convinced that mopeds and scooters would remain relatively unpopular in the United Kingdom, because Continental competitors were far ahead in development and design. To match Continental standards Raleigh entered into agreements with the Société des Ateliers de la Motobecane to manufacture under license the Mobylette type of moped, a leading world seller, and with the Società per Azioni Edoardo Bianchi to make a Bianchi-type scooter, one of the most attractively styled. Both were to sell in the popular price category.

Total industry demand in the United Kingdom fell to 42,000 in 1962. At this time Raleigh was nearing completion of a moped design and development project on which its engineers had worked for several years. In 1963 Raleigh re-entered the moped market with a range of four new machines, designed for specialized applications suitable for post-office, police, and other service duties. Only two major components, the engine and frame pressings, were imported from France; the wheels, brakes, lighting equipment, and all other components were designed and manufactured in Nottingham and Birmingham. The new Raleigh moped, called the Runabout, was low-priced, and with it Raleigh again proceeded to lead the field in the United Kingdom. In 1965 the United Kingdom industry consisted of a number of small assemblers of imported components and Raleigh, who was the only major producer. Raleigh was turning out over 40,000 mopeds a year, which was 66% of the industry turnover.

In 1964 Raleigh exported about 1,500 mopeds; in 1965 about 3,000. This was at a time when a single major European manufacturer was exporting 140,000 mopeds a year. Early in 1966 Raleigh launched a full-scale sales drive aimed at capturing the untapped markets in Britain's Commonwealth countries, the Americas, and certain European markets. It was expected that a greatly increased output would go to those markets where, through the cycle side of its business, Raleigh had long-established distribution outlets. Some dealers were not convinced that this strategy was sound, believing that it was a mistake to mix bicycles and powered machines under the same roof. The thinking was that if bicycles predominated, moped customers would not be attracted; if powered cycles predominated, bicycle sales would suffer.

In 1966 the United Kingdom license age for motor bikes was still 16, versus 14 in Europe generally. Stiff driver tests were compulsory. Licensing costs were high enough to discourage low-income customers. Hire-purchase regulations continued to fluctuate, with the required deposit seesawing between 10 and 20% of the purchase price. Abroad, many developing nations, whose people found cycles attractive, were nationalizing manufacture.

In 1966 mopeds and toys accounted for about 10% of the company's turnover.

TOYS

Raleigh's first major departure from cycle manufacture came in 1960 with the introduction, under the Sunbeam label, of a line of wheeled toys (see Exhibit 14). The line included tricycles, bicycles, toy wheelbarrows, scooters, gocarts, and roller skates. There were sizes to accom-

exhibit 14

TODDLERS TO TEN-YEAR-OLDS

THEY ALL WANT A

RALEIGH made SUNBEAM

Says Dr. Sunbeam

modate children of all ages. Additions to the toy range were constantly being studied. In doing so Raleigh worked with nurseries, where new toys were "play-value" measured. These practical tests showed, for example, that the coaster feature on a chain-driven tricycle frustrated small children, who would drive up to an obstruction and then find themselves unable to reverse. Elimination of the coaster and substitution of a direct drive allowed the child to back up. It also lowered the cost of the tricycle.

For many years Lines Brothers had been the major producer of toys in the United Kingdom. Lines made complete ranges of all kinds of toys. It was believed that many retailers welcomed the entrance of Raleigh into the toy field, for they resented the dominance of Lines. Raleigh toys received good initial acceptance from toy dealers.

The Raleigh management eventually came to believe that their original toys had too much built-in quality. The high-quality features had been deliberate as an introductory strategy: ball and roller bearings, chromium and nickel finishes, high-quality paints and finishes. "Our tactic," said a Raleigh sales executive, "was to build 8 shillings worth ($1.12) of extra quality into each toy and sell it for a price that was 3 shillings (42¢) higher." From year to year the company retreated from that policy. By 1966 its quality was still somewhat better than that of competition, and its prices were only slightly higher. Retail dealers were still of the opinion that Raleigh's high-quality toys lasted too long.

In the United Kingdom, Sunbeam toys were sold through the same retailers who handled Raleigh cycles. The attempt was made to use cycle distribution channels abroad, but the toys proved too bulky for their relatively low value to permit shipment to be made economically over long distances. Consideration was given to shipping them completely knocked down, which would permit the nesting of parts compactly. This, however, would require design changes, such as substituting nuts and bolts for many rivet applications to permit their reassembly abroad by simple means. This meant adding to production costs at home. "To gain 9,000 unit sales in Nigeria," said a Raleigh export executive, "might cost us our profit on the sale of 90,000 units in the United Kingdom."

THE BROOKS SAFETY BELT

In August of 1962 Raleigh's subsidiary, the Brooks Saddle Company, entered into an agreement with Teleflex Products Limited to produce and market under the Brooks trade name a safety harness on the inertia reel principle for motorists. During the war the Brooks firm had produced substantial quantities of harnesses for parachutists, and the new belt was a modified version of the inertia harnesses used by military air crews and commercial pilots. The unique feature of the new belt was an inertia reel which permitted freedom of movement yet locked and secured its wearer into the seat upon impact or violent deceleration. By virtue of the reel principle, the belt automatically adjusted itself to persons of any size; there was no feeling of being "trussed up," to which many motorists objected, but the belt would lock securely under any sudden forward movement. When uncoupled, the surplus belt would automatically rewind into the reel (see Exhibit 15).

After considerable developmental work, Raleigh agreed to produce the belt. Research among auto and accessory dealers had indicated that there was a demand for such an accessory. The Minister of Transport had indicated his intention of making safety belts standard required fittings on all new motor cars, although he had no authority to compel motorists to wear them.

The Brooks Company did not market its belts through Raleigh cycle channels; the entire output was sold to a distributor who wholesaled both auto and bike accessories. Attempts to get new car manufacturers to adopt the belt were unsuccessful. British Motors had been on the verge of adopting them but had finally decided not to do so. In 1966 the only sale of the belts was to individual consumers, who bought them through auto accessory retailers and had to have them fitted to their cars.

The Brooks belt retailed for £6 15s. ($19.14). Its chief competitors were the Romack at £4 7s. 6d. ($12.43) and the Raydyot at £4 4s. ($11.93). The Raleigh management conceded that the Brooks belt had not made much of an impact upon the market but had given the Raleigh management some experience in diversification.

CYCLE COMPONENTS

A bicycle could be divided into two basic kinds of parts: (1) parts which were technically simple to make, involved little engineering, and were relatively low in cost, such as frames, fenders, spokes, handle bars, and carriers; and (2) intricate parts, which required sophisticated product engineering, exacting metallurgy specifications, and precision manu-

EXHIBIT 15

AFTER a period of great secrecy extending over several years, a revolutionary type of car safety belt incorporating an inertia reel which permits complete freedom of movement, yet which locks and secures its wearer safely into the seat upon impact or violent deceleration, was demonstrated in public for the first time on August 13th.

The new belt, introduced by J. B. Brooks Ltd., can be used in every type of road vehicle ranging from family saloon and sports car to high speed touring coaches and heavy commercial vehicles.

Mr. Ernest Marples, Minister of Transport, has indicated his intention to make safety belts standard fittings for new motor cars, but also that he has no power to compel motorists to wear them. Because it allows complete freedom of movement, the Brooks belt will be welcomed by many people who have previously been averse to wearing safety belts because of a feeling of restriction.

BROOKS INTRODUCE CAR SAFETY BELT

This new belt is a modified version of the well known inertia harness currently used by the military air crews and pilots of leading airlines, such as BEA and BOAC. The patent inertia reel is the product of Teleflex—a firm which has had a vast amount of experience in the aircraft equipment field. Research on the car inertia reel included tests up to 26 G retardation.

Brooks have also had experience in the exacting aircraft equipment field, for during the war they were responsible for supplying the harness of thousands of parachutes.

One of the outstanding characteristics of the Brooks Reel Safety Belt is the freedom of movement allowed. There is no feeling of being 'trussed up', all controls can be easily reached and the driver can lean forward (at halt signs, for example) without restriction. But under impact or violent deceleration, the reel immediately locks.

A feature of the belt is the two-way buckle which is completely foolproof, being fully operative whichever way it is fastened and which is easily released by a flick of the finger.

exhibit 15   (continued)

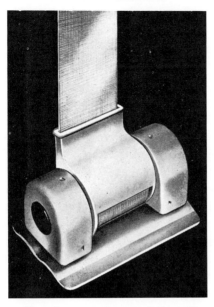

The other great advantage is that when
not in use the reel automatically winds the
surplus webbing away, but keeps it always
ready to hand, and also avoids entangling
the feet or trapping the harness in the door
thereby keeping the webbing clean and free
from 'scuffing'. Due to its flexibility, it does
not crease clothing and it is immediately
adjustable to any man, woman or youngster.
In fact, 'Brooks take Reel care of you!'

facturing, such as gears, hubs, generators, brakes, gearshifts, sprockets,
and wheel rims. A single cycle had well over 1,000 individual parts,
which could be combined into some 8,000 differentiations in the completed cycle. Most components were standardized and interchangeable.

For decades Raleigh had sold not only completed cycles but also component parts to other cycle manufacturers. In a period of fifty years,
this business had grown to such proportions that by 1960 almost every
country in the world which had local cycle manufacture imported Raleigh components. In the course of the growth of its components business, Raleigh had developed solid and friendly relationships with virtually every manufacturer of bicycles in the world. Raleigh completed-
cycle sales had been declining, partly because many emerging nations
were building their own cycle plants and partly because importers in developed countries were discovering that they could produce Raleigh-type

cycles of their own manufacture at lower cost. In each of these instances the new cycle manufacturers looked to Raleigh to supply them with at least a portion of their component parts.

The simple components were typically large in bulk, heavy in weight, and relatively low in value, making them economically unsuited for shipment over long distance. The intricate components, on the other hand, were small in size, light in weight, and high in value. Local manufacturers found it easy to make the simple components. The intricate components, however, required a large investment in product engineering, machinery, and equipment. Furthermore, Raleigh, with its huge production, was able to utilize mass production techniques to turn out its quality components at costs which small producers could not match.

Threatened with the permanent loss of overseas completed-cycle sales, Raleigh decided to put concentrated effort behind the sale of components. Its objective was to have every cycle manufacturer in the world use components manufactured by Raleigh. This was to be achieved by (1) a considerable advertising expenditure allocated to advertising components; (2) a royalty agreement with the local manufacturer giving him the right to use the Raleigh names and trademarks on his completed cycles, conditional upon certain specific components and a certain percentage of the total components per cycle being Raleigh components made in the United Kingdom; and (3) Raleigh, where necessary, engaging in local manufacture itself, drawing supplies of components from the United Kingdom to the extent that this was allowed by the local government. Raleigh believed that by this strategy it could permanently sustain production in its United Kingdom plants. Especially promising were certain components which were already world-famous, such as the Sturmey-Archer range of gears, brakes, and lighting equipment (see Exhibit 16). The percentage of profit was also higher on these types of components than on the simple low-value parts.

The Raleigh management was aware that component sales and completed cycle sales might become competitive with each other. A local producer might assemble a cycle largely from Raleigh components and market it, using the Raleigh brand names, in the same markets where Raleigh was itself selling its completed cycles manufactured in Nottingham. Sometimes foreign competitors sought deliberately to capitalize on the Raleigh brand names. A Malaysian distributor, for example, assembled cycles from components bought from many companies. He used

exhibit 16

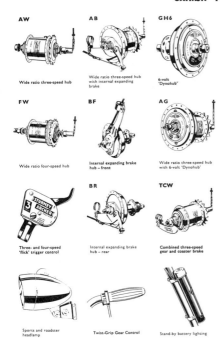

AW — Wide ratio three-speed hub

AB — Wide ratio three-speed hub with internal expanding brake

GH6 — 6-volt 'Dynohub'

FW — Wide ratio four-speed hub

BF — Internal expanding brake hub – front

AG — Wide ratio three-speed hub with 6-volt 'Dynohub'

— Three- and four-speed 'flick' trigger control

BR — Internal expanding brake hub – rear

TCW — Combined three-speed gear and coaster brake

Sports and roadster headlamp

Twist-Grip Gear Control

Stand-by battery lighting

Modern Bicycles

need

Modern Equipment

GEARS – that are fully enclosed, and designed and built to give years of trouble-free service.

HUB BRAKES – to make cycling safe.

LIGHTING EQUIPMENT – A 'Dynohub' offers the best in dynamo lighting with something **extra**. Built in – streamlined – frictionless – trouble free, and always in position. Can also be combined with three or four-speed gear in one compact unit. Stand-by battery lighting available for all models.

STURMEY ARCHER

GEARS · BRAKES · LIGHTING EQUIPMENT

only the Raleigh frame, but he used the Raleigh nameplate. Through legal action Raleigh stopped him from doing so.

Although Raleigh knew of no means of completely eliminating the danger of intracompetitive conflicts, it attempted some measure of control by regulating the use of its brand names. On all Raleigh-produced assembled cycles the components were Raleigh brand-name labeled. Its Phillips subsidiary had long been engaged in the production of components under the Phillips name, which was continued, and the Phillips name was also permitted on Raleigh-produced cycles. Sturmey-Archer parts and Brooks saddles everywhere bore their brand names, whether on Raleigh cycles or competitors' cycles, but all other components sold to competitors bore no labels at all. Neither would Raleigh put another cycle maker's name on Raleigh-made parts, but under pressure from very large customers, Raleigh was beginning to make exceptions to this rule.

The production of completed cycles made up the majority of Raleigh's turnover, but its sale of components in the export market was growing steadily. Raleigh produced components and accessories for its own com-

pleted cycles, for the replacement market, and for sale to other manufacturers. Of those components which were not made for use on Raleigh
completed cycles, the ratio of production was one part for replacements
to three parts produced for other manufacturers.

DISTRIBUTION CHANNELS

Raleigh sold its products in the world markets through independent
wholesale distributors, and in some instances through its own selling
companies or agents. Occasionally it sold directly from its Nottingham
headquarters to mail-order houses, chain stores, or department stores,
but this was exceptional; most Raleigh sales in the world markets were
made through wholesalers.

Distributors were usually of necessity fairly large-sized trading firms,
since they were required to carry costly inventories of cycles and components and had to finance extensions of credit to their retail customers,
often for a year at a time in those export markets where the economy
depended upon a single farm crop. In Mauretia a whole year's sales
might depend on whether there was a good sugar crop; in another area
it might be maize. Many distributors in Africa, the Far East, and the
East Indies were old, established trading companies which handled general merchandise. Distributors were permitted to sell to anyone. Since
historically individual brands had come to be well-established and identified with certain distributors, the same retailer might buy Phillips from
one wholesaler, Raleigh from another, and BSA from a third, a practice
which Raleigh Industries believed to be to its advantage. In the United
Kingdom and in Europe generally, wholesalers handled bicycles only, or
bicycles were their main product line. In Europe Raleigh had a much
closer relationship with its distributors, every one of whom it knew intimately. In some export areas it knew no more about its distributors
than the knowledge it gained by doing business on a mail-order basis.

In many areas, even where Raleigh had distribution channels, components were sold through separate channels. Motorized equipment was
commonly sold through cycle wholesalers but often to separate retail
outlets. Sunbeam toys were sold by all Raleigh cycle dealers and were
also sold through other channels which handled only toys.

Raleigh believed that a major current problem was to change the
attitude of its distributors, to arouse them to enthusiasm in the new
Raleigh sales methods, and to persuade them that it was to their interest

to generate the same kind of excitement in their retail dealers. Until 1960 there had been no innovation in the industry. There had been no research, and distributors were ignorant of their own market potentials. They tended to be conventional-minded about the bicycle as a product, about its uses, about their retail dealers, about advertising, and about their markets. This was especially true of many old, established trading firms which handled a wide variety of merchandise. Many distributors did little to generate sales to retailers and were satisfied to take what business came their way.

RETAILERS

Raleigh believed that its retailers in the United Kingdom could be classified in four categories.

One-man shops were very prevalent. These often had their own unique and highly individualistic ways of doing business. Raleigh thought the best of them to be very good, but most of them led a doubtful existence.

There was the Limited Company type of retail shop, often a solid family business, employing three to ten people and sometimes more. Here individuals tended to specialize, customers were better served, and the business was conducted more efficiently.

Still another class was represented by the "multiples," typically chain specialty stores or chain department stores, which operated anywhere from ten to several hundred stores. These outlets sold huge volumes of accessories, but Raleigh believed that they could sell a much greater volume of cycles if they had more sales drive. They bought ahead, maintained good stocks, had well-informed sales personnel, and maintained high standards of store cleanliness, all traits which Raleigh believed educated nearby small retailers and "kept them on their toes."

Last, there were what Raleigh called the "big boys." These supermarket-style retailers were a postwar phenomenon. They were well capitalized, were shrewd traders, and set up huge retailing establishments in population centers, with plenty of room for well-lit displays of merchandise in mass quantities.

In the character of its retail dealers, Raleigh recognized a chronic problem. Many individual cycle dealers had gotten into the business by starting a home repair shop, later getting into the selling of cycles. They tended to forever remain service-oriented. "The Depression spawned a whole generation of cycle retailers who were good at repairing but not good at selling," said a Raleigh sales executive. "They are not sales-minded and not merchandise-minded, and in today's modern marketing world, they are an anachronism. They are not good business managers and are often just hanging on. Most of them have been pushed off the high streets onto the back streets, into shabby shops with old-fashioned fronts where they have an odd cycle or two lying about. Many of them will be quick to tell you that the cycle business is a dying trade, that everyone wants cars."

Before the merger British Cycle Company retailers and Raleigh retailers competed across the street from one another. Raleigh and British Cycle vied with each other for the dealer's loyalty, standards for dealerships degenerated, and there was little attention given to the ultimate customer. Retailers handled cycles from both companies, and since most dealers were usually short of money, they bought consecutively from one manufacturer after another, in round-robin fashion, until they had accumulated enough money to pay the overdue bill of the first supplier, whereupon they would proceed to make the rounds again. When Raleigh and British Cycle merged, most small dealers suddenly found themselves owing all their bills to the new Raleigh Industries. With their accounts past due, their only remaining source of supply consisted of small local cycle makers, whose offerings were not as attractive. As a result of this incident Raleigh lost sales volume and also lost dealers who switched to small manufacturers. Dealer ill will for Raleigh was generated in such proportion that the retail dealers' association came to carry on a virtual vendetta against Raleigh.

In 1962 Raleigh had 12,000 retailers in the United Kingdom, served by 14 distribution centers. In 1964 the number of distribution centers was reduced to 6, and the number of retailers was reduced to 7,500. Retailers were guaranteed once-a-week deliveries, with fully assembled cycles delivered to them by trucks.

The number of outlets for retail sales of cycles in the United Kingdom declined 35.97% between 1950 and 1961, compared to a decline of 0.51% for retail outlets for all types of trade. During the same period retail outlets for household goods increased 12.0% and radio and electrical outlets increased 59.42%. The number of retail outlets for cycles continued to decline after 1961, but at a less drastic rate.

At the time when Raleigh was reducing the number of its retail dealerships, it also decided to sell to chain stores and mail-order houses. These outlets had been difficult to serve because of a general problem: there were so many bicycle variations needed to suit each individual customer's needs. There were men's and women's bicycles; sizes from 19½ to 23 inches; gears or no gears; lights; accessories; colors. There were 28 basic models, and in all there might be some 18 possible combinations of a single model. Mass retailers balked at carrying the inventories required to support such an operation. Individual retailers stocked only the fast-moving models and depended on fast delivery service from Raleigh to obtain variations, but chain merchandisers were geared only for forward buying.

In the RSW 16 Raleigh was now able to offer mass retailers a single, unvarying product suitable to buyers of either sex and all sizes: an all-purpose cycle which was fully equipped. The prospect had attraction for the chains as well as for Raleigh.

SALES TRAINING

"Training in the two-wheeler trade," said a Raleigh sales executive, "is either nonexistent or haphazard. Each new entrant muddles along until he learns how they do it in the particular firm where they joined the business. Since our trade is characterized by widely differing forms of outlets, the employee 'trained' with one firm might be astonished at how differently another firm operates, even though both are in the same town."

Until the early 1960's Raleigh had provided no training within or outside of the company. With the reorganization of the home sales market, a training manager was introduced into the home sales department. His function was to teach Raleigh salesmen who called upon retailers how to conduct their sales calls more efficiently. No training was provided by Raleigh for retailers or distributors. If retailers received any training from distributors, it was at the volition and expense of the distributor, but this seldom occurred. Occasionally a nearby overseas distributor might bring a group of his retailers to Nottingham, at their own expense, for a visit of a day or two. There they might view the plant but not do much of anything else.

PROBLEMS OF EXPORT

"The export potential for bicycles is best," said Mr. R. A. L. Roberts, Raleigh's export sales manager, "in those underdeveloped regions of the

exhibit 17 GROUP BICYCLES AND TRICYCLES*

Calendar Year	Basis	Total Production		Production for Home Market		Exports	
		Units	Value £	Units	Value £	Units	Value £
1963	Actual	1,723,805	15,597,000	314,932	3,947,000	1,408,873	11,650,000
1964	Actual	1,415,406	12,872,450	321,865	3,689,450	1,093,541	9,183,000
1965	Estimated sum of firm's present expectations	1,329,143	12,167,566	327,600	3,754,296	1,001,543	8,413,270
1966	Estimated	1,257,972	11,581,151	332,200	3,807,012	925,772	7,774,139
1967	Estimated	1,238,400	11,418,064	338,400	3,878,064	900,000	7,540,000
1970	Estimated	1,258,800	11,606,848	358,800	4,111,848	900,000	7,495,000
1970	National plan	1,769,258	16,090,563	402,331	4,611,813	1,366,926	11,478,750

* Bicycles with frames not less than 15 inches and tricycles with wheels not smaller than 14 inches.
SOURCE: Company's records.

world where the standard of living is still comparatively low. There, most people would be eager to buy a bicycle, but the irony of it is that most of them cannot even afford shoes. There would be many good export markets in countries which would like to import bicycles, but which cannot afford to do so. But the current general world prosperity is reaching even these people." (See Exhibits 17 and 18.)

exhibit 18   RALEIGH PROJECTED BICYCLE EXPORTS BY UNITS

Sales Areas	Raleigh Actual Sales, 1964	Raleigh Projected Sales, 1967	Raleigh Projected Sales, 1970
Europe	107,082	107,000	107,000
Africa	216,718	178,000	108,000
North America	450,415	400,000	490,000
Central America	42,346	40,000	42,000
South America	69,998	35,000	35,000
Pacific	21,850	20,000	21,000
Asia	194,180	120,000	97,000
Miscellaneous	140		
Total	1,102,729	900,000	900,000

SOURCE: Company's records.

In exporting, Raleigh had tended to do better in the East, where there were vast underdeveloped areas of population, than in the West, which was more industrialized. Mr. Roberts felt that Raleigh had a hard core of export business which tended to stay with it, but the cream of the export business was in those markets which tended to fluctuate. In many of these the bicycle business depended on short-term agricultural prosperity and whether the current major national crop matured well. Farmers were especially good potential in many emerging nations, where they were, for the first time, earning enough cash to afford a bike. In some, like Nigeria, there were government boards which controlled agricultural marketing, and in these the bicycle business depended directly on governmental regulations.

There were great differences in the level of import duties in the various world markets. The duty to Raleigh ranged from zero in EFTA (European Free Trade Area) countries to 200% in some Latin American countries.

There was a growing tendency for many of Raleigh's traditional African, Middle Eastern, and Asian export outlets to prohibit or to greatly restrict their imports because of a shortage of sterling or of foreign exchange of any kind. Many of these would have continued to be desirable export markets if they could only have found a means of paying for their imports.

Nationalization of production, dictated by either economic or political pressure, was making severe incursions into Raleigh's export trade, with countries often closing their borders completely to imports. Nottingham could no longer ship to many regions which had formerly been prime Raleigh markets but now had their own production facilities: Indonesia, India, South Africa, Eire, Brazil, Argentina, and Mexico. As a general practice, if Raleigh saw such a threat in time, it tried to work up enough volume in the market on an export basis to make it feasible to locate a plant within the market (see Exhibit 18).

Raleigh was losing some markets to producers behind the Iron Curtain and in the Far East. Russia and Eastern Bloc countries were selling British-type lightweight bicycles in world markets at what appeared to be artificial prices. Japan and China were taking over mass-volume "price" markets, where their low wage and cost levels permitted them to sell at prices which Raleigh could not match.

Wherever it could do so, Raleigh intended to continue to export from Nottingham. If this proved impossible, Raleigh would consider overseas production. Failing either of these alternatives, Raleigh would try to insure that overseas manufacturers obtained their components from Raleigh's United Kingdom plants.

implementation through organization and control

BAY
LABORATORIES

In 1935 Mr. Richard J. Haines and Mr. Stewart Cord left their jobs as tool and die makers at the Pringle Radio Company to set up a shop of their own. Their business began as a job shop with some stamping presses, and for several years their largest customer was the Standard Amplifier Corporation for which they made loudspeaker stamping. Standard Amplifier was subsequently bought out by a competitor; so Mr. Haines and Mr. Cord hired Standard Amplifier's speaker engineer, Mr. Thomas Priestly, and started to produce amplifiers. Within a year they were producing 2,000 loudspeakers a day. Sales were $102,729 in 1938 and $225,227 in 1939. Profits exceeded 8 per cent of sales in both years and the partners' interest increased rapidly, reaching $40,000 in 1940.

The partnership was incorporated July 31, 1941, as Bay Laboratories with $50,000 capital stock, held by Mr. Haines, who became president, and by Mr. Cord, who acted as executive vice president. The business continued to grow during World War II, with sales exceeding $2.5 million in 1945.

CORPORATE DEVELOPMENT, 1945–1952

In 1945 Bay Laboratories secured contracts with the United States Electronics Corporation (U.S.E.C.), the largest radio-phonograph manufacturer, to produce record changers. When long-playing machines began to appear in 1948, Bay Laboratories became one of U.S.E.C.'s principal suppliers of 45-rpm units. Contracts to build record changers for other nationally distributed radios were also secured. A wire recorder for office use was added in 1948.

As new items were added to the line, the organization of the company developed primarily on a product division basis. From 1941 to 1945 the company had essentially two operating divisions—metal fabrication and loudspeakers. Finance, sales, and engineering were handled largely by Mr. Thomas Priestly under the direction of Mr. Haines as president and Mr. Cord as general manager. Mr. Davis Stanfeld was in charge of speaker production. With the advent of the record changer and wire recorder business, another separate division was added. (See Exhibit 3, part *a,* for outline of the organization in this period.)

Toward the end of 1947 Mr. Priestly suffered a heart attack and found it necessary to relinquish most of his duties. Before he left the company, he hired Mr. Alan Deems, who had had seventeen years' experience in the radio business, including three years as vice president in charge of sales and engineering at the Western Transmitter Company of Los Angeles. Mr. Deems was placed in charge of sales in order to utilize to the best advantage his intimate acquaintance with the managers of leading radio companies.

Bay Laboratories was located in Jersey City, New Jersey, until 1950 when a large new plant with 137,000 square feet of space was built in Hoboken, New Jersey. About 1,500 people were employed, most of them relatively unskilled women. The company's products included a variety of loudspeakers, a 45-rpm record-changer mechanism for U.S.E.C., the 45-rpm phonograph which was sold to U.S.E.C., the same 45-rpm machine sold to the public under Bay Laboratories' own name, an elaborate all-speed changer for Mars Radio Corporation (third largest producer of radio phonographs), a three-speed phonograph of Bay Laboratories' own design, a general-purpose tape recorder, and a wire recorder for office use.

The company also had a press department with a capacity which was greater than that needed for Bay Laboratories' own work. (Exhibit 1 gives the dollar volume of the various departments for 1951 and 1952. Exhibit 2 shows monthly income statements by departments.)

Nearly 2,000 units per day were being built for U.S.E.C. in 1953. However, U.S.E.C. was building a plant of its own at Dearborn, Michigan, to manufacture a 45-rpm unit. The U.S.E.C. plant was expected to be producing up to capacity by the end of 1953.

ORGANIZATION CHANGES, 1952–1953

In February, 1949, Lewis Haines, eldest son of the president, finished college and came to work for the company. The management was of the opinion that the product division type of organization, together with the lack of clearly defined lines of authority and responsibility (which carried over from Bay Laboratories' early years), militated against efficient operation and effective control. For example, although the multiple responsibility for sales had been unified under Mr. Deems, no one person was in charge of finance, and purchasing was done independently by the metal fabrication, speaker, and record changer divisions. Lewis Haines was given the job of making a study of the existing organization and of developing a plan for changing it into a *functional* system. Within two and one-half years he had made specific

exhibit 1 **SALES BY DEPARTMENTS**

	1952	1951
Record changers	$4,448,904	$ 6,495,232
Loudspeakers	2,089,449	3,510,420
Wire recorders	447,632	704,779
Color scanner	111,920	—
Consumer	18,149	—
Stampings	526,878	1,659,807
Dies	219,832	106,075
Other	100	1,020
Total	$7,862,864	$12,477,333

SOURCE: Auditor's report, 1952. All statistical information is from the various auditor's reports unless otherwise noted.

recommendations regarding the distribution of overhead, sales goals, cutting costs, daily reports, and systematizing procedures. In August, 1950, Mr. Richard J. Haines informed his son that in the future he was to confine himself to industrial engineering; there had been some complaints that he (Lewis) was trying to dominate Bay Laboratories' management.

Nevertheless, Bay Laboratories continued to move in the direction of a functional organization. Lewis Haines was consulted and assisted in hiring the necessary personnel to effect the change in organization. In August, 1950, Mark Torren was hired as comptroller. In December,

exhibit 2 BREAKDOWN OF INCOME STATEMENT AND COST OF GOODS SOLD BY DEPARTMENT FOR APRIL, 1952

	Speaker Department	Record Changer Department	Wire Recorder Department	Stamping Department	Tool and Die Department	All Departments
Net sales	$162,786	$562,689	$ 30,479	$ 93,472	$ 14,873	$864,299
Less cost of goods sold						
Direct materials	99,294	369,378	15,506	54,467	5,391	544,036
Direct labor	21,601	53,811	4,901	26,164	13,522	119,999
Factory expense	22,673	55,412	7,726	24,707	11,185	121,703
	$143,568	$478,601	$ 28,133	$105,338	$ 30,098	$785,738
Less selling and admin. expense	14,729	39,763	7,092	6,340	1,174	69,098
Operating profit	4,489	44,325	(4,746)	(18,206)	(16,399)	9,463
Other income and expense (net)	821	2,847	153	471	74	4,366
Net profit before taxes	$ 5,310	$ 47,172	$(4,593)	$(17,735)	$(16,325)	$ 13,829

1950, Victor Brown, formerly of Symes Electric, was hired as plant superintendent; the intention was to centralize manufacturing under his direction. Frank Parks was hired in February, 1951, to organize a consumer sales department. Mr. Parks was a former executive vice-president of the Towne Phonograph Company, a large independent producer. A chief engineer, William Johns, was also hired; but he resigned later after having designed the Bay Laboratories' three-speed record changer which, in the opinion of management, was an excellent changer with great potentiality. Mr. Parks was named general manager in September, 1952, to co-ordinate the new functional organization. Mr. Brown, the plant superintendent, was fired in October, 1952. (See Exhibit 3 for a listing of organizational changes from 1947–1953.)

Lewis Haines then focused his attention on the company's complete lack of material and production control. He drew up a system and put together a manual to facilitate its installation. In this effort he had the assistance of Bruce Ward, the assistant manager of consumer sales, who had set up material and production control systems at the Towne Phonograph Company. Systems analysts from four business-machine corporations were brought in. Lewis Haines continued through 1952 to press for the adoption of his system, and approval was given by the end of the year.

Thus, in early 1953 the organization was, as Mr. Richard Haines put it, "very confused." The new material and production control system had been inaugurated and personnel hired to run it, but the basic organization was neither divisional nor functional. Mr. Richard Haines returned in February from a winter vacation to discover that Bay Laboratories had an operating loss of $131,000 for the last 5 months of fiscal year 1953. Some of the officers thought the loss was actually much greater. In any case, the need for strictest economy was obvious in view of Bay Laboratories' weak financial condition. Mr. Richard Haines decided that the most immediate savings could be effected by eliminating the expense connected with the proposed organizational changes and the adoption of the material and production control system. Accordingly, some 160 people were dismissed, including the nine people who had been hired to set up the new control system. The organization reverted to its pre-1952 form with three product divisions and four functional departments. Mr. Stanfeld was put in charge of speaker production. Mr. Deems retained his control over industrial sales and engineering and was also placed in charge of record changer and recorder produc-

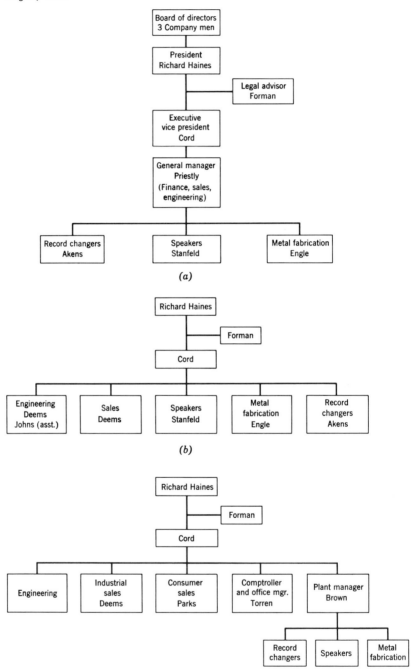

(a)

(b)

(c)

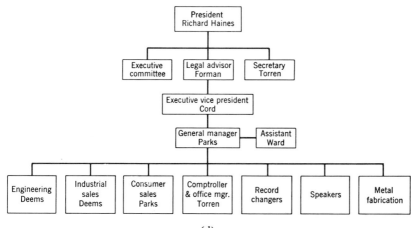

(d)

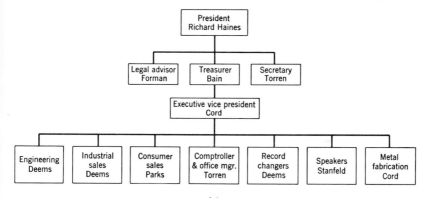

(e)

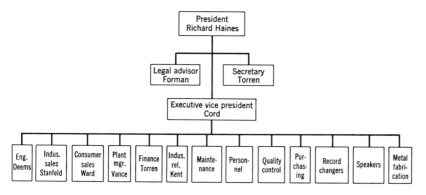

(f)

tion. Mr. Parks was demoted from general manager to his former position as head of consumer sales. (See Exhibit 3, part *e.*)

On June 15, 1953, Mr. Richard Haines announced at a meeting of the principal department heads that he would assume the function of general manager for two months to try to put the company in the black. If he were not successful, he said he would bring in someone else to run the whole show. The decision was made to consolidate the production of record changers, phonographs, and wire and tape recorders. This was necessary to "simplify our inventory and to avoid overlapping of authority," Mr. Haines explained. Thus, the functional arrangement which had been adopted and abandoned in February was to begin another trial.

After the February dismissals, a treasurer had been hired; he resigned in August, recommending that a production expert of his acquaintance be brought in to straighten out the company. His advice was followed, and Daniel Vance, a man with sixteen years' experience in production at Dorn Aviation and in a job shop of his own, was hired as plant manager in September. At the same time, a functional arrangement was adopted throughout the organization: Mr. Stanfeld was moved from speaker production (which was under Mr. Vance) to industrial sales; Mr. Deems was to be in charge of engineering only; Mr. Torren remained head of finance. Mr. Parks resigned, and his assistant, Mr. Ward, was placed in charge of consumer sales. Thus, the organization of the company as of October 1953 was as shown in Exhibit 3, part *f.*

Mr. Vance's initial orders to his foremen and recommendations to the president were put in the following memoranda:

GENERAL FOREMEN AND FOREMEN   July 29, 1953
Subject: Assignment of Duties

1. For a long time many discussions have taken place to determine ways and means of getting all supervisors to assign the functions and details of their assistants; also the necessity of educating supervisory employees to hold their assistants responsible for their assignments, and to follow up to see that their assistants carry out their assignments.

2. Considerable progress has been made in this respect, but there is still room for improvement. There is set forth below briefly a few of the principal methods by which these objectives can be reached. It is expected that you will carefully consider them, apply them to your department or section, and see that copies are given to your principal assistants for their observance and execution.

a. It should be the objective of each department head to assign the responsibility for the execution of each function assigned to him to a single person, and, insofar as it is physically possible, the work of each function should be done in a single place.

b. As soon as any activity or function of a department becomes sufficiently crystallized to permit its definition and description it should immediately be assigned to an assistant for performance. Department heads will thus constantly strip themselves of duties and pass them down the line so that the heads may devote their attention to new problems and the discovery of new functions which can likewise be delegated, and thus leave themselves with time to follow up and see that their assistants are carrying out the duties assigned to them.

c. When the responsibility for carrying out a function is assigned to any person, such person must be given complete responsibility for carrying out the duties assigned to him.

d. In selecting assistants for carrying out a function or duty, extreme care must be exercised to see that the person to whom the duty is assigned is qualified by experience and intelligence to readily handle the assignment.

e. Each department head should see to it that there are men next to each key position who are receiving the necessary training to qualify them as replacements so that organizational changes may easily be made.

f. Each department head should advise his subordinates that the selection of their assistants can only be made after consultation with and approval of the department head.

g. Definite lines of supervision and tapering of authority should be set up so that each person has definite and clear-cut responsibilities, so that he reports to only one person, and so that he is subject to orders from only one source.

h. No change should be made in the scope of the responsibility of a position without a definite understanding as to the effect of such change on the part of all persons concerned.

i. In assigning responsibilities for carrying out the duties assigned to assistants, authority should be granted that any decision in connection with the duties assigned shall be made at the lowest point in the organization at which the decider possesses all the facts necessary for a sound decision.

j. In assigning work as outlined above and in issuing daily orders, there is one cardinal rule which the department head and his principal assistants must keep before them constantly:

THE AUTHORITY TO ISSUE AN ORDER INVOLVES A RESPONSIBILITY TO SEE THAT IT IS PROPERLY EXECUTED.

In order to follow up and be at all times completely familiar with the performance of the persons to whom functions have been assigned, each department head should set up a regular system of reports which would flow to him regularly from his subordinates.

3. Many able men in this plant are failing as supervisors because they

do not properly delegate their functions and are making the fatal mistake of reserving final judgment to themselves on every matter of even minor importance. As a result, many of their assistants who are able and competent become mere "office boys" who dare not assume the responsibilities which have been assigned to them because of limitations in the authority conferred on them.

4. Everyone must realize that an organization as large as the organization at this plant can only function when each department head delegates authority and then makes it his business to see that the authority he delegates is exercised reasonably and efficiently.

All department heads are directed to study carefully the provisions of this letter and to carry out the instructions contained therein.

D. Vance

INTER-OFFICE CORRESPONDENCE   *Bay Laboratories, Inc.*
To: Richard J. Haines   Sept. 10, 1953

It has been told to me that as of the ending of the fiscal year, July 31, 1953, there was a total sales of approximately $14,000,000, and no profit. The actual inventory figure is not yet available, but Mark Torren has informed me that it does not look like any gain over the past three years' performance.

After carefully analyzing your operations for the past eight weeks and obtaining all the facts, I am listing below those recommendations which I strongly advise:

Item #1. All personnel, who are in the employ of Bay Laboratories on a salary basis, should start to work at 8:00 A.M. and go home at 5:00 P.M., with one hour for lunch. I am well aware of the fact that this does not meet with everyone's approval, but on the other hand, we cannot have plant personnel drifting in at all hours from 8 to 12 o'clock.

Item #2. Eliminate all but one salesman in the Speaker Department.

Item #3. Eliminate all but one salesman in the Industrial Sales.

Item #4. Eliminate export sales and the personnel connected with it.

Item #5. Take the necessary steps to get material control quickly.

Item #6. Take the necessary steps to get labor control quickly.

Item #7. Eliminate all personnel from the payroll who cannot get along with fellow employees. In other words, any feuding which has gone on during the past year or more should be eliminated by having all persons involved terminated. This is one of the most important steps in these recommendations. It is impossible to arrive at good, clean operation as long as any employee is trying to protect his own personal feelings rather than to help progress in Bay Laboratories.

Item #8. Eliminate the present service setup, which is inadequate, expensive, and again has all the earmarks of a personal empire.

Item #9. Eliminate all but twelve people in the Tool Room. Discontinue at once the practice of making dies for other concerns. Should a stamping contract be obtained, dies are easily purchased for less money than it would cost us to make them.

Item #10. Scrutinize each and every department in the plant with the view of eliminating indirect labor.

Item #11. Get a realistic forecast from the Sales Department, one that is ample for their needs, also, one that does not increase our finished goods inventory, which we cannot stand financially. It seems that our only objective would be to manufacture those items which were already sold until such a time as we have financial strength enough to stock all items.

D. Vance

FINANCIAL DEVELOPMENTS, 1947–1952

From its banner year in 1947, Bay Laboratories' earnings plunged in 1949 to a loss in excess of $100,000; in 1951 sales soared to more than $12 million with earnings of only $51,275. As sales expanded the company sought additional working capital. Capital stock increased from $187,000 in 1945 to more than $1 million by 1952. Additional capital was obtained in 1951 by a $410,000 ten-year mortgage loan at $4\frac{1}{2}$ per cent. This was payable in quarterly installments of $10,000 and the terms of the indenture placed limitations on the payment of dividends.

Bay Laboratories had not been able to secure a regular line of bank credit. In 1945 an agreement with a bank was executed which provided up to $250,000 credit, but the agreement placed restrictions on dividends, compensation of officers, and the acquisition of fixed assets. As security the bank held a first-mortgage installment note which was backed by a trust deed covering the company's fixed property; the bank also held some $25,000 of government bonds belonging to the company.

The pressure of mounting inventories required to carry the increasing volume of sales led the company in 1952 to assign its receivables and inventories, valued at $2,284,734, to a finance company. Up to July 31, 1952, $820,464 had been advanced against receivables and inventories at an interest rate of $\frac{1}{32}$ per cent per day on the outstanding daily balance.

THE MANAGEMENT PERSONNEL AS OF OCTOBER, 1953

David Stanfeld. Mr. Stanfeld was vice president in charge of industrial sales. He came to Bay Laboratories in 1939 as head of production

exhibit 4 BAY LABORATORIES

Income statements, 1944–1952, fiscal year ending July 31 (in thousands of dollars)

	1952	1951	1950	1949	1948	1947	1946	1945	1944
Net sales	$7,824	$12,393	$6,156	$4,143	$4,802	$5,519	$2,954	$2,527	$1,963
Cost of goods sold									
Direct materials	4,723	8,315	3,776	2,514	2,647	2,786	1,414	1,034	722
Direct labor	1,737	2,554	1,417	999	1,136	1,081	751	532	447
Factory expense	786	774	496	365	409	393	262	235	181
Total manufacturing cost	7,246	11,643	5,689	3,878	4,192	4,260	2,427	1,801	1,350
Inventory variation increase (decrease)	(129)	(1)	(54)	(71)	23	(16)	(10)	(10)	(5)
Total cost of goods sold	7,117	11,642	5,635	3,807	4,215	4,244	2,417	1,791	1,345
Gross margin	707	751	521	336	587	1,275	537	736	618
Selling and admin. expense	628	733	426	506	469	497	252	265	229
Operating profit (loss)	79	18	95	(170)	118	778	285	471	389
Other income and expense	(27)	53	7	8	15	19	12	3	6
Federal taxes	5	20	35	58*	55	304	155	349	290
Net profit (loss)	47	51	67	(104)	78	493	142	125	105
Retained earnings August 1	100	369	308	798	725	261	176	181	101
	147	420	375	694	803	754	318	306	206
Adjustments									
Renegotiation payments				(6)	(1)	(29)	(53)	(42)	(21)
Taxes prior years								(4)	
Additional amortization emergency facilities								(5)	
Capitalized surplus		(310)							
Dividends									
Cash	(10)	(10)	(6)	(380)	(4)		(4)	(4)	(4)
Stock								(75)	
Retained earnings	$137	$100	$369	$308	$798	$725	$261	$176	$181

( ) indicates deduction or loss.

* Rebate for previous loss.

538

exhibit 4 (continued)
Income statements, 1944–1952, fiscal years ending July 31 (percentage analysis)

	1952	1951	1950	1949	1948	1947	1946	1945	1944
Total manufacturing cost	100	100	100	100	100	100	100	100	100
Direct materials	65.0	71.0	66.0	65.0	63.0	65.0	58.0	57.0	54.0
Direct labor	24.0	22.0	25.0	26.0	27.0	25.0	31.0	30.0	33.0
Factory expense	11.0	07.0	09.0	09.0	10.0	10.0	11.0	13.0	13.0
Net sales	100	100	100	100	100	100	100	100	100
Total cost of goods sold	91.0	94.0	91.5	92.0	88.0	77.0	82.0	71.0	68.5
Gross margin	09.0	06.0	08.5	08.0	12.0	23.0	18.0	29.0	31.5
Selling and administrative expense	08.0	05.9	07.0	12.2	10.0	09.0	08.4	10.5	11.7
Operating profit (loss)	01.0	00.10	01.5	(04.2)	02.0	14.0	09.6	18.5	19.8

( ) indicates deduction or loss.

exhibit 5 **BAY LABORATORIES**

Balance sheets, 1944–1952, fiscal year ending July 31 (in thousands of dollars)

	1952	1951	1950	1949	1948	1947	1946	1945	1944
Current Assets									
Cash and U.S. bonds	$ 36	$ 22	$ 16	$ 21	$ 74	$ 147	$ 72	$116	$234
Receivables (net)	599	687	619	383	332	549	298	292	209
Inventories	1,680	1,024	759	450	442	378	271	134	107
Investments: life ins.	37	30	24	24	16	14	10	8	5
Prepaid expenses	21	17	15	76	30	24	15	10	11
Total	$2,373	$1,780	$1,433	$954	$894	$1,112	$666	$560	$566
Current liabilities									
Loans and notes	$ 883	$ 635	$ 89	$ 81	$ 39	$ 9	$ 9	$ 50	$ 50
Accounts payable	786	668	627	190	151	77	177	66	49
Accrued liabilities	258	90	151	93	117	82	75	41	66
Provision for Federal taxes	9	20	35	5	55	310	170	234	323
Dividends payable	4	9	4	4					
Total	$1,940	$1,422	$ 906	$373	$362	$ 478	$431	$391	$488
Working capital	$ 433	$ 358	$ 527	$581	$532	$ 634	$235	$169	$ 78
Fixed assets									
Buildings, land, machinery	1,145	1,117	587	436	410	271	259	204	186
Other assets: patents, investments	4				69	33	10		39*
Less mortgage	(320)	(360)	(88)	(112)					
Less other notes	(90)	(43)			(26)	(26)	(46)		
Less minority interest							(10)	(10)	(10)
Net assets	$1,172	$1,072	$1,026	$905	$985	$ 912	$448	$363	$293
Capital stock									
First preferred	$ 200	$ 162	$ 157	$ 97	$ 62	$ 62	$ 62	$ 62	$ 62
Junior preferred	825	800							
Common	10	10	500	500	125	125	125	125	50
Retained earnings	137	100	369	308	798	725	261	176	181
Total capital	$1,172	$1,072	$1,026	$905	$985	$ 912	$448	$363	$293

* Postwar excess profits tax refund.
( ) indicates deduction or loss.

and purchasing, when the company was in the speaker business only. His previous experience had been in production with three other companies making speakers. In December, 1950, when Mr. Brown was brought in as head of all manufacturing, Mr. Stanfeld was transferred to sales. He explained that the company then had production well under control but needed more sales.

Mr. Stanfeld had no preference as to the divisional or functional organization of the company. Bay Laboratories' difficulty resulted from erratic management, not from an unsuitable organization. Since mid-1952 Lewis Haines had shown much ability and energy in his work in industrial sales; but Mr. Stanfeld, while recognizing that many of his ideas were really good, believed that the organizational changes had caused difficulty because "Lewis pushed them too fast." The situation was also aggravated, Mr. Stanfeld thought, by the ambitions of Mr. Parks, who, after his appointment as general manager in September of 1952, had brought in many outsiders to run Bay Laboratories.

While Mr. Stanfeld attached no great importance to any particular form of organization, he declared that the rapid changes had damaged speaker production by stripping it of engineering. The result was that both quality and production suffered.

Mr. Stanfeld said that sales were no problem in his own department; Bay Laboratories could sell everything it could make. In fact, production was well behind commitments and one of the unpleasant problems was to satisfy impatient customers. This also created problems between the industrial and consumer sales departments because of appeals to fill the commitments of one from the supplies of the other. Mr. Stanfeld stated that he and Mr. Ward co-operated well in this situation, but felt a single head of sales should be the one to make that kind of decision. He did not know whether or not the management contemplated creating such a position.

Mr. Stanfeld further thought that the new Bay Laboratories' three-speed record changer could be pushed and exploited much more than it had been. He felt that too much of the company's effort was devoted to satisfying the demands of U.S.E.C. and The Mars Corporation.

Bay Laboratories' biggest single problem, Mr. Stanfeld believed, was that costs and profits were not known. "For five years," he declared, "the company did not know whether or not it was making money. I have not seen operating statements for August or September, if they are available, and I wouldn't trust them anyway." He said candidly, but without rancor, that Mr. Richard Haines had been getting bad advice from Mr. Torren and Mr. Deems. He had told the president that if some sound decisions were not forthcoming soon, Bay Laboratories would have another competitor in loudspeakers.

Bruce Ward. On September 15, 1953, Mr. Ward was made sales manager of the still-new consumer sales department. He had been with Bay Laboratories for one year; his previous experience had been with the Towne Phonograph Company and a large electronics company, primarily in sales, though for a time he had been in charge of establishing a production control system at both places.

Three separate sales channels operated under Bay Laboratories' consumer sales department. Most important was jobber sales which went via manufacturers' representatives to distributors like United Radio of Boston, and from them to retailers. Jobber sales amounted to about $250,000 in the last half of 1952. A second sales channel was the Secretariat Corporation, a separate distribution organization set up to handle Bay Laboratories' office wire recorder. There were six regional managers in the Secretariat Corporation who sold to office machine dealers. The Secretariat Corporation was a wholly-owned subsidiary of Bay Laboratories, established in part to ease the burden of taxation. Its sales volume for 1952 was about $150,000. A third sales channel was exports, a category which included a small amount of private label business. The volume of export sales was relatively insignificant.

Mr. Ward said that the company could sell everything it could make —at that time there was an $850,000 backlog of consumer sales. Bay Laboratories' problem, he believed, was in production. Mr. Ward declared that he thought the lack of a material and production control system was the key production problem and explained that he had worked with Lewis Haines in developing such a system for Bay Laboratories and regretted that it had been abandoned. He also observed that Mr. Richard Haines thought that all his son knew "came out of books." Mr. Ward did not agree.

Bay Laboratories' principal competitors were the Towne Phonograph Company and the Hawk Company of Des Moines, Iowa. The Towne Company did about $22 million worth of business annually— about $4 million was in laminations for industrial electric motors, $10–$15 million was consumer products, and the remainder was government business. The Towne Company had recently abandoned industrial sales, except for laminations. The Hawk Company had taken over much of the Towne Company's industrial business, but it had recently embarked on a million-dollar program to promote consumer sales. Mr. Ward thought that consumer sales would become increasingly important to Bay Laboratories, and he wished he could spend more on advertising. Bay Laboratories split local advertising 50–50 to a maximum of 2 per cent of the dealer's volume.

Alan Deems. Mr. Deems was a vice president; he explained that he was chief engineer and head of Industrial Sales. He came to Bay Laboratories in 1947 from the Maine Radio Company where he had been for seventeen years. The Maine Company absorbed several smaller com-

exhibit 6   **THE TOWNE PHONOGRAPH COMPANY AND BAY LABORATORIES**
Comparison of cost of goods sold

	The Towne Phonograph Company			Bay Laboratories
	Total	Bloomingdale	McLean	
Sales (100%)	$950,404	$837,535	$112,869	$801,167
Material	50.7%	49.7%	58.1%	53.76%
Labor	10.5	11.6	2.1	12.54
Overhead	20.0	20.5	16.2	11.65
General and admin. expense	20.1	21.6	8.6	11.30
Net profit before taxes	(1.3)	(3.4)	15.0	10.75

( ) indicates deduction or loss.
SOURCE: "Report of a Special Meeting of the Advisory Board," March 11, 1952.

panies, and later was itself absorbed by the Western Transmitter Company, which went bankrupt. For three years before coming to Bay Laboratories, Deems had been a vice president in charge of sales and engineering.

Normally, the engineering design section worked exclusively on new products, but Mr. Deems explained that under the pressure of emergency conditions, the entire engineering staff was working on production problems. He was spending most of his time on the tape recorder production line and had been concerned particularly with the amount of run-out admissible in the tape recorder drive pulley before a noticeable "wow" resulted when the machine was played. Usually, Mr. Deems spent about half of his time on sales and divided the rest evenly between new product development and production problems on current products.

Mr. Deems said that the old departmentalized production organization had been too rigid but, on the other hand, he felt that the change to a functional arrangement had been pushed too fast by Lewis Haines who he said had good ideas, but he couldn't put them across. During the change the company had been over-staffed and much opposition had developed. When in February the decision had been made to return to a divisional organization, he thought that the management had gone too far. "The organization had to have flexibility," Mr. Deems said. For example, it was necessary for him to remain in industrial sales because he knew the important people at U.S.E.C., Mars, and other large manufacturing and retailing companies. "Bay Laboratories could get a chief engineer to do this work at half my salary," he added.

Mr. Deems further said that U.S.E.C. orders would certainly drop to a low level after the end of the year. However, this was scarcely a problem because Bay Laboratories could easily have absorbed the released capacity on its other production lines. In fact, he had a compilation of man-hours per thousand units on the tape line. He estimated the efficiency of the line at 75 per cent and concluded that one-third more labor was needed to achieve its scheduled production.

The source of most of Bay Laboratories' difficulty, Mr. Deems concluded, was the failure to define clearly the areas of responsibility and authority. He called attention to the vagueness of his own position and to that of Lewis Haines. He said that Mr. Richard Haines had been advised to have his son learn the business from the ground up but that the advice had not been heeded.

Daniel Vance. Mr. Vance came in as plant manager on September 1, 1953. He had had sixteen years' experience in production at Dorn Aviation and had also owned his own job shop.

Mr. Vance stated that his immediate aim was to show a profit for two months by getting the most billings with the least personnel. As of early October, he did not know whether or not he had succeeded in this goal because August and September statements were not ready.

After being satisfied that the company was not in immediate danger, he felt he could attack Bay Laboratories' production problems. Production control was, he believed, the foremost problem. No one in the plant knew, he declared, when material was delivered, where it was stored, or how much of each item was on hand. Returned goods were accepted without inspection; damaged goods were not accounted for; and worst of all, orders were not processed in any systematic way, which occasionally caused embarrassing situations with its customers. Mr. Vance had a production control system. The necessary personnel was all set to be installed as soon as the company had been in the black long enough to safely stand the production slowdown involved in making such a change. Besides production control, Mr. Vance was responsible for purchasing, maintenance, personnel, and the foremen of the various product lines.

Mr. Vance thought that on the basis of his initial estimate of the situation the Bay Laboratories' organization was thoroughly confused. He thought the main trouble was that Mr. Deems would not relinquish the authority over industrial sales and production. "None of Bay Laboratories' problems," he declared, "can be solved without running afoul of Mr. Deems." He observed that the Mars Corporation was a good customer, but that Bay Laboratories could not be expected to respond to their every whim at the behest of Mr. Deems and at the expense of other customers.

Mr. Vance also emphasized that he had been hired to secure results in production. Mr. Richard Haines had ordered him to fire a foreman for something Mr. Vance did not believe was the foreman's fault. He said he would ignore the order since personnel and organization of his department were up to him and he added that Mr. Richard Haines could fire him if he did not approve of the results.

Mark Torren. Mr. Torren was comptroller and secretary of the board of directors and had come to Bay Laboratories in August, 1950. He had been general manager of Downes and Company, a rendering firm in Dayton. He explained that the organizational changes in process during the summer, while not affecting his department directly, made it impossible to allocate costs. Mr. Torren said the company's break-even volume was about $750,000. He presented departmental estimates (made by him) with allocations of fixed and variable charges. (See Exhibit 7.) He received daily reports from all foremen giving cost of material used, fixed charges, cost of labor, operating profit and over- or underbudgeted for his department. Mr. Torren said that under the new organizational arrangements these reports would be different, although the exact form was still uncertain.

Mr. Torren thought Bay Laboratories' financial problem resulted from a zeal to increase sales on the assumption that volume beyond the break-even point was all pure profit. He pointed out that additional sales required more inventory and increased accounts receivable.

exhibit **7**   **BAY LABORATORIES**

Estimates of operating results at various volumes (in thousands of dollars)

Sales per year	$ 4,512	$ 5,640	$ 6,768	$ 7,896
Sales per month	376	470	564	658
Variable costs				
Direct materials	$ 226	$ 282	$ 338	$ 395
Direct labor	75	94	113	131
Prime cost	$ 301	$ 376	$ 451	$ 526
Variable expenses (see Analysis below)	30	38	45	53
Total variable	$ 331	$ 414	$ 496	$ 579
Fixed expenses (see Analysis)	88	88	88	88
Total operating costs	$ 419	$ 502	$ 584	$ 667
Loss on operations	$ 43	$ 32	$ 20	$ 9
Income from operations				
Factoring expense	3	3	4	5
Net loss	$ 46	$ 35	$ 24	$ 14
Net income				

Variable expenses				
Social Security taxes	$ 2,960	$ 3,700	$ 4,440	$ 5,180
Light and power	816	1,020	1,224	1,428
Maintenance and repair	632	790	948	1,106
Factory supplies and expense	1,864	2,330	2,796	3,262
Office salaries	2,636	3,295	3,954	4,613
Sales salaries	524	655	786	917
Freight and delivery	1,232	1,540	1,848	2,156
Advertising	800	1,000	1,200	1,400
Stationery and postage	1,712	2,140	2,568	2,996
Telephone and telegraph	1,848	2,310	2,772	3,234
Dues and subscriptions	640	800	960	1,120
Sundry supplies and expenses	1,208	1,510	1,812	2,114
Entertainment and travel	2,200	2,750	3,300	3,850
Cafeteria	544	680	816	952
Insurance	4,568	5,710	6,852	7,994
Legal and audit	256	320	384	448
Bad debts	920	1,150	1,380	1,610
Other expenses	3,256	4,060	4,854	5,668
Employee's welfare	1,584	1,980	2,376	2,772
Total variable expenses	$30,200	$37,740	$45,270	$52,820

*Fixed expenses**	
Management salaries	$46,608
Jig and fixture salaries	3,655
Maintenance labor	8,808
Traffic	2,542
Research and development	8,002
Depreciation—manufacturing	7,500
Rent	1,465
Heat	920
Officers' salaries	6,000
Taxes	1,500
Depreciation—office	1,000
Total fixed expenses	$88,000

exhibit 7 (continued)

$ 9,024	$10,152	$11,280	$12,408	$13,536	$15,792	$18,048
752	846	940	1,034	1,128	1,316	1,504
$ 451	$ 508	$ 564	$ 620	$ 677	$ 790	$ 902
151	169	188	207	225	263	301
$ 602	$ 677	$ 752	$ 827	$ 902	$ 1,053	$ 1,203
60	68	75	83	91	106	121
$ 662	$ 745	$ 827	$ 910	$ 993	$ 1,159	$ 1,324
88	88	88	88	88	88	88
$ 750	$ 833	$ 915	$ 998	$ 1,081	$ 1,247	$ 1,412
$ 2	$ 13	$ 25	$ 36	$ 47	$ 69	$ 92
6	6	7	8	8	10	11
$ 4						
	$ 7	$ 18	$ 28	$ 39	$ 59	$ 81
$ 5,920	$ 6,660	$ 7,400	$ 8,140	$ 8,880	$ 10,360	$ 11,840
1,632	1,836	2,040	2,244	2,448	2,856	3,264
1,264	1,422	1,580	1,738	1,896	2,212	2,528
3,728	4,194	4,660	5,126	5,592	6,524	7,456
5,272	5,931	6,590	7,249	7,508	8,026	8,544
1,048	1,179	1,310	1,441	1,572	1,834	2,096
2,464	2,772	3,080	3,388	3,696	4,312	4,928
1,600	1,800	2,000	2,200	2,400	2,800	3,200
3,424	3,852	4,280	4,708	5,136	5,992	6,848
3,696	4,158	4,620	5,082	5,544	6,468	7,392
1,280	1,440	1,600	1,760	1,920	2,240	2,560
2,416	2,718	3,020	3,322	3,624	4,228	4,832
4,400	4,950	5,500	6,050	6,600	7,700	8,800
1,088	1,224	1,360	1,496	1,632	1,904	2,176
9,136	10,278	11,420	12,562	13,704	15,998	18,282
512	576	640	704	768	896	1,024
1,840	2,070	2,300	2,530	2,760	3,220	3,680
6,472	7,236	8,040	8,844	10,048	12,446	14,854
3,168	3,564	3,960	4,326	4,752	5,544	6,336
$60,360	$67,860	$75,400	$82,910	$90,480	$105,560	$120,640

* These figures are the same for all volumes.

Bay Laboratories simply did not have the working capital, for such expansion and borrowing was proving expensive. As Mr. Torren put it, borrowing working capital "eats up profits faster than they can be made." The company's condition had become crucial in the latter part of 1952 when it lost $200,000 in four months, but the situation improved thereafter. He said he would like to have seen sales level off at about $15 million until earnings provided capital for further expansion.

Stewart Cord. Mr. Cord was executive vice president of Bay Laboratories. He had been Mr. Richard Haines' partner in the original enterprise, and owned 40 per cent of the stock. Under the former divisional organization, he had been primarily concerned with metal fabrication, which included the tool and die shop and the stamping presses.

He observed that the company had had organizational difficulties, but apparently believed the new arrangements would work out satisfactorily.

Lewis Haines. Mr. Lewis Haines had come to Bay Laboratories after finishing college in February, 1949. His initial concern had been with the company organization, and later with production control; nominally his position was head of industrial engineering. In the summer of 1952 he shifted to industrial sales under Mr. Stanfeld, and traveled extensively, dealt with the company's customers, and sought new ones. In the summer of 1952 he returned to industrial engineering and the problem of production control where he was to assist Mr. Vance, the new plant manager.

Mr. Lewis Haines had concerned himself at one time or another with all of Bay Laboratories' general problems. In fact, he conceived of his job as that of an executive assistant or trouble-shooter, in which capacity he, along with those responsible, worked on a specific problem until it was solved. From time to time he wrote reports to his father about these problems, together with his recommendations. He felt that although his ideas were sometimes taken with apparent seriousness and even occasionally adopted officially, they were never actually enforced and tested in practice.

For example, he had repeatedly urged the adoption of a group of daily and weekly reports as a control measure. Suggestions for daily reports included direct labor hours, orders received, cash receipts and disbursements, total of accounts receivable and payable, and a quality control statement for the day's production. Suggestions for weekly reports included administrative overhead (actual and budgeted), material costs by department, indirect factory expense, and estimated cash requirements and sources. Some of these were adopted.

Mr. Lewis Haines had also frequently emphasized the necessity of establishing sales quotas for each department. He had pointed out that to absorb the overhead of the tool and die department, sales of other departments would have to increase $350,000. Yet he believed the tool and die department could break even on sales of only $35,000. The

failure to set up sales quotas meant that the comptroller could not prepare a budget. Mr. Lewis Haines believed that total sales were a decep-
tive measure of how well Bay Laboratories was doing, and that it was
necessary to have sales quotas meet the overhead of each department.
He believed that monthly sales of $400,000, properly distributed, would
enable the company to break even. All the officers put the break-even
point at between $650,000 and $750,000. A management consultant
hired in the spring of 1953 investigated and found on a basis of total
expenditures that the break-even point was about $700,000.

Mr. Lewis Haines was also critical of the product diversification and
experimentation which had been promoted by Mr. Deems. He claimed
that the speaker line had been enlarged from 51 models in 1947 to 365
models in 1952, that daily production had dropped, and that Bay Laboratories had lost money and market position in the process. He also said
that a variety of product ideas had been pushed by Mr. Deems. These
included automobile rear-view mirrors, television focusing magnets, a
television pay-as-you-go coinbox, color television scanning wheels, and
parts for a telephone answering device. Mr. Lewis Haines said losses on
these items aggregated about $350,000. The following report, summariz-
ing his analysis of the company's operations, was submitted to his father, Mr. Richard Haines.

  Production. In slack periods inventory was too high. On the other hand,
  in busy seasons shortage of materials caused shutdowns. Because of these
  shutdowns, which were due mainly to poor scheduling and control, direct
  labor costs exceeded estimates. Obsolete machinery also contributed to
  high costs.
  Recommendation. The company should install production control and
  planning and scheduling departments under Lewis Haines and these
  would be under the supervision of the general manager. This would reduce direct labor costs 15 per cent to 20 per cent and reduce indirect
  labor costs 15 per cent from the May, 1953, level. It would also reduce
  inventory to a twenty-day supply.
  Engineering. Most of Bay Laboratories' sales problems were in reality
  engineering problems. Eleven potential customers for record changers
  awaited engineering modifications. A four-pole motor, a raised mounting
  pan, and an aluminum tone arm also needed engineering work. Four
  products in the regular record changer line needed changes and improvement. Of particular importance was the new Bay Laboratories drive assembly which offered special advantages to the consumer and was cheaper
  than the assembly then being sold. Loudspeaker also needed designing and
  improvements in production.

Recommendation. An immediate engineering program enforced from the top be adopted to carry through these changes, with the new three-speed unit getting top priority.

Sales. Five elements entered into the problem of industrial sales—salesmanship, engineering service, quality, price, and delivery. Bay Laboratories had no real sales organization. The usual procedure was for the sales personnel to sell hard when business was slow and then to help out in production when orders poured in during the busy season. Mr. Stanfeld had been in and out of sales a half dozen times in the past four years. While Bay Laboratories had two salesmen for their entire line, the Hawk Company, one of Bay Laboratories' two principal competitors, employed eight full-time salesmen on their three-speed unit alone. The quality and price of Bay Laboratories' products compared favorably with those of competitors, but industrial users were reluctant to adopt an unknown brand of record changer for their radio and television sets.

Recommendation. Regular and continuous sales efforts be backed by prompt engineering service. Advertising and promotion were also considered necessary to get acceptance of the Bay Laboratories' name by dealers and the public.

Richard Haines. Richard Haines had been president of Bay Laboratories since its incorporation in 1941 and was the dominant member of the partnership. He owned 60 per cent of the company's stock.

He said that the board of directors, which had always been made up of company officers, consisted of himself, Mr. Cord and Mr. Torren. He put the company's break-even point at $700,000 monthly sales, but did not know offhand how this broke down among Bay Laboratories' products; he remarked that Mr. Torren had that information. He said his goal for the company was an annual volume of $20 million divided more or less equally between industrial and consumer sales. Latest addition to the Bay Laboratories' line was a new and larger tape recorder which would be built for a large manufacturer under Bay Laboratories' own label.

Mr. Haines felt that production was always the biggest problem. He was out on the line every day attempting to discover the reason why production was always so far behind schedule. "Sales, on the other hand, seem to take care of themselves," he said. He pointed out that in the new organization he intended to separate consumer and industrial sales.

When asked which of his officers he relied upon most Mr. Haines observed that it was a tough question; he declared that he relied equally upon them all.

PROPOSED MANAGEMENT CHANGES—OCTOBER, 1953

In the middle of October, 1953, the inventory for the fiscal year ending July 31 was complete enough for management to be certain that Bay Laboratories had sustained an operating loss of about a quarter of a million dollars for the year. Mr. Haines wrote a note to his son directing him to find someone to finance and manage the company. "I'll be glad to relinquish my duties as president," he concluded. "However, I must be assured before I take such a step."

Lewis Haines approached this assignment by seeking three leading businessmen in the fields of finance, manufacturing, and sales to serve on Bay Laboratories' board of directors with Mr. Richard Haines and Mr. Cord. The new board of directors would choose a general manager who would also be on the board.

Lewis Haines promptly interviewed three such men: one was a banker, another a manufacturing executive from one of Bay Laboratories' competitors, and the third a recognized sales manager. The three lunched together; two tentatively accepted the proposal but the third wanted time to consider. Lewis Haines thought the most important consideration was to assure the new board members that their advice would be taken seriously by putting actual control of Bay Laboratories in their hands through some legal device such as a voting trust.

SUBURBAN BANK AND TRUST COMPANY

HISTORY

The Suburban Bank and Trust Company was chartered in the state of Indiana in 1916 and was incorporated in 1920. The bank was located in an outlying area of Indianapolis and was generally considered to be a specialized institution, catering mainly to local businessmen of the area. Suburban, however, ranked as one of the larger outlying banks in the Indianapolis section. At the end of 1955 deposits totaled about $120 million.

The special services and aggressive management of the bank resulted in rapid growth and established an excellent reputation for the institution. In the late 1920's many new banks were organized throughout the Indianapolis area. The competition for deposits became intense and Suburban soon found itself in direct competition with six new neighborhood banks which had opened during this boom. Suburban lost ground steadily to these institutions, because its ultra-conservative loan policy had alienated many business depositors, who withdrew their funds from the bank. "Why should I keep my money here?" was the general question. "I need a loan. Your bank won't grant it, but the new bank will. I'm going to put my money in one of the new, more progressive banks." This story was heard many times by loan officers at Suburban.

Henry Davidson, the chief loan officer, was determined to maintain a strict loan policy despite pressure from other bank officers and influential depositors. The name of "No Loan Davidson" was soon well known among the hard-pressed business depositors. As a result of Davidson's attitude there was constant bickering between him and the other bank officers. This period of disagreement was short-lived, however.

The stock market crash and the ensuing depression of the 1930's resulted in a period of moratorium for banks. Many of the "easy loan banks" never reopened.

Suburban reopened, the only one of the seven in the area to do so. The depositors who had left Suburban suffered severe monetary losses when the other banks in the area failed to reopen, while those depositors who had stayed with Suburban suffered no losses. Because of Davidson's determination to maintain high standards and a strict loan policy despite the pressure from members of his own staff, the bank survived. This firmly established the bank's reputation for soundness and subsequently was one of the chief factors responsible for its steady growth.

ORGANIZATION

Henry Davidson, the strong-willed force which kept the bank from "going under," was made president in 1949 at the age of 54. In fact, however, he had been directing the bank's operations since 1928 in his capacity as chief loan officer. He was considered by bankers throughout the state to be an exceptionally able administrator. One of his close friends in the banking fraternity remarked:

> He works just as hard today as he did thirty years ago when the bank was in its infancy. He is a man of boundless energy with the ability to make quick decisions. There is little doubt about his being the hardest-working person at Suburban. Banking hours are from 9:00 A.M. until 2:00 P.M. You'll always find Davidson at his desk opening the daily mail at 7:00 A.M., and he rarely leaves before 5:00 P.M.

Every department came under the personal supervision of Mr. Davidson. Very few decisions, whether important or merely routine, were made without his approval. Edward Frey, head of banking and deposits, stated:

> We have the utmost confidence in Mr. Davidson, but on many occasions he appears to try to show his authority by reversing decisions of others. A perfect example is the time I refused to authorize a check presented by a woman customer who had forgotten to have her husband en-

dorse the check as required. It was a clear-cut case. I'm sure that Mr. Davidson would have refused to cash the check had he been approached originally. However, even after I had refused to cash this check, which was in line with a policy he had established, he went right ahead and approved it anyway. It made me look foolish.

It's getting to the point where even the girls who work in my department go to him directly—they don't even bother with me. I'm supposed to be in charge, but you'd never know it. Other department heads will tell you the same thing, so it can't be that I'm always making the wrong decisions. Just take a look at him during banking hours; he has a long line of employees behind him and a long line of customers in front of him. He just has to have his say about everything.

Mr. Randall, executive vice-president, was sixty years old. He had been with the bank since its second year of operation. Most of the bank's customers preferred to talk to him. In contrast with Davidson, whose answers were abrupt and sometimes blunt, Randall was more discreet and had a milder manner of speaking. One of the larger accounts stated, "He has a wonderful personality and takes an honest interest in each one of his customers." Randall was considered by the other officers and employees of the bank as a good administrator capable of handling the bank's affairs in Mr. Davidson's absence. However, he was usually so busy with customers during banking hours that he was often unaware of the bank's management problems unless he stayed after banking hours and discussed them with subordinates.

Harper Young, the assistant vice-president, was forty-three years old. After twenty-five years in the real estate loan department, he was made manager. He had little to do with the bank's general management and policy decisions.

Dennis Tanner had the title of assistant cashier; however, he was more of a replacement officer and trouble-shooter. One day he worked in the commercial department; the next day he helped out in the real estate, the savings, or credit departments. He knew the general operations of the bank very well, but he had never had the opportunity to learn much about such special areas as investments, duties of a loan officer, or policy administration.

The board of directors was composed of seven members. They had monthly meetings but were dependent on Mr. Davidson for most of their information. In addition to Davidson and Randall, the board consisted of two real estate operators, an attorney, a president of a manufacturing firm, and Mr. Reynolds, the largest stockholder, who was the president and owner of a small chain of hardware stores. Mr. Reynolds summed up the board's operation in these words: "We have faith in Mr. Davidson so we usually follow his recommendations. There isn't much sense in trying to upset his apple cart. He's here every day; we meet only once a month."

Suburban had 290 stockholders. Many of them were local businessmen, employees, or demised employees' families. The largest stockholder, Mr. Reynolds, owned only 8 per cent of the total. The board members owned a total of about 40 per cent of the stock, which assured them of continuous control. The board members had served for the past sixteen years.

FINANCIAL

Earnings had risen steadily for the past ten years. Dividends had been modest—most of the earnings had been plowed back into the capital account.

EARNINGS AND DIVIDENDS PER SHARE, 1951–1955*

	1951	1952	1953	1954	1955
Earnings	$23.50	$22.00	$40.00	$46.00	$37.00
Dividends	7.00	7.00	7.00	7.00	7.00 †

* Based on number of shares outstanding each year end.
† Plus stock dividend: 50% declared at year end.

Deposit growth had been moderate but steady. Deposit growth for the nation had been increasing at a rate of about 4 per cent per year. Suburban's annual growth rate had been about 3.5 per cent for the past five years. Savings deposits made up the greater share of Suburban's deposit total. Savings deposits were also growing at a faster rate than demand deposits (checking accounts). Statistical data for selected years follow:

DEPOSIT DATA FOR 1953–1955 (IN MILLIONS)

	1953	1954	% change	1955	% change
Savings	$70.0	$73.5	Plus 5.0	$76.0	Plus 3.42
Checking	42.0	42.6	Plus 1.5	44.0	Plus 3.30
	$112.0	$116.1	Plus 3.7	$120.0	Plus 3.36

Although Suburban was not keeping pace with the national growth average for deposits, the management of the bank had not expressed concern. They refused to actively seek new business.

Davidson stated: "If a customer walks through the door we're glad to serve him, but we're definitely not going outside to try to get him in here."

The bank did not have a new business department. No effort was made to visit businessmen at their establishments and give them information concerning the various services offered by the bank. This method of solicitation was practiced by most of Suburban's competitors. George Daniels, president of the Exmoor National Bank, one of Suburban's chief competitors, made the following statement:

> We went out and hustled a million dollars' worth of new accounts last year. New business departments are as important as loan departments these days. Competition for the deposit dollar is intense. Besides competing with banks for commercial business, we're faced with a new threat for the savings dollar. Savings and Loan Associations are hurting our savings business, because they pay a higher rate of interest. So we just have to get new commercial accounts to pick up the slack.

Suburban, however, had one distinct advantage over most of the outlying banks. It had a trust department that was comparable to those of large mid-city banks. In describing the importance of the trust department Mr. Randall stated:

> A lot of our new commercial and savings business arises indirectly as a result of our trust department. We have the only bank trust department available to people who prefer to do business outside of the downtown area. Most people like to do all of their banking in one place, so when we get their trust business we usually get their checking and savings business as well.

INVESTMENT POLICIES

Investment policies were formulated by Mr. Davidson. Short-term and intermediate-term government securities comprised the bulk of the investment portfolio. Municipal bonds and equipment trust certificates also represented sizable holdings. Statutes permitted the holding of only certain types of high-grade securities. To this extent all banks were somewhat limited in what they could do investmentwise.

Mr. Davidson displayed unusual skill in selecting investments which provided a relatively high yield from a restricted group of high-grade securities. The bond account of Suburban had always shown better than average results. Mr. Davidson's record compared very favorably with that of the professional staffs of larger banks.

LOAN POLICIES

All loan policies were formulated by Mr. Davidson. He believed that the bank should not make a loan unless it was sure, beyond a reasonable doubt, that all principal and interest would be repaid as scheduled. He refused to take borderline risks. The criteria which he set up were considered to be very rigid by the members of the staff. Davidson had frequently stated: "We're in business to loan money, not to give it away and then hope for default and foreclosure or legal action." The bank's policy limited maximum loanable funds to about 25 per cent of deposits, or about $30 million. In 1955 the bank had $26 million outstanding in loans. The average bank in Suburban's class usually set its maximum loan limit at about 35 to 40 per cent of its total deposits.

PROMOTION POLICIES

The bank's stated policy was to promote from within. In recent years, however, two key positions had been filled from outside the organization. This was considered necessary because the two positions required experienced men and no one within the organization was considered qualified to take over.

Suburban did not have an active formal training program. From time to time an effort had been made to hire "trainees," but because of a personnel shortage they were rapidly placed in a particular job and usually left there.

The bank operated with a minimum of personnel. However, salaries were generally higher than for most banks the size of Suburban. This seemed to be the main factor in maintaining a stable work force. There had been a very low turnover rate among the male employees of the bank. Recently, however, two young men of recognized potential left the bank for other jobs. One of them explained:

> I'll have to go to work for less money, but at least I'll have a chance to learn and to progress accordingly. They're so busy and have so little help

at the bank that it's practically impossible to learn anything except what a person's particular job calls for. As a result, when a better job does "open up," it's necessary to bring in someone from the outside. There are plenty of good people here, but they can't get experience toward better jobs unless they are given the chance.

A veteran of twenty years said:

> I'm stuck here. I can't afford to go somewhere else and take a salary cut. I have to think of my family. Most of us get promoted in order as jobs open up. But they pass all of us up on the big jobs in favor of an "experienced outsider." Sure I'm disgusted, but what can I do?

THE ARCHER-DANIELS-
MIDLAND COMPANY

The Archer-Daniels-Midland Company had its origin in a firm founded in 1902 by George Archer and John Daniels to "manufacture flax and other oil producing seeds and cereals into their natural products, and to sell the products so manufactured by it." In 1923, after a number of firms had been acquired by the parent company, the Archer-Daniels-Midland Company was organized to take over their combined assets. During its first ten years the company's investment in plant increased from $130,000 to $1 million; by 1923 its combined properties were carried on its books at $7 million. At that date the company had become the largest producer of linseed oil in the world.

In 1927 a grain division was formed to operate four terminal elevators. Two years later the company became a producer of foundry core oils and an importer and processor of foreign and marine oils. Soybeans were added to its crushing activities and the company expanded into extensive new lines of food, livestock feed, and chemical products. In the early 1930's it acquired the Commander-Larabee Corporation, the nation's third largest flour miller, which operated 14 flour mills.

By 1962 the company had developed hundreds of new products through refining and modifying raw linseed oil, crude soybean oil, and marine and whale oils. Its expanded operations covered the United States and extended into Latin America and Europe. (See Exhibit 1.) The company had reported earnings every year since its incorporation

559

and had paid quarterly dividends without exception for more than a quarter of a century.

"Our business," said Mr. John Daniels, president of the company, "is best described in general terms as the processing of agricultural and chemical products. While we are primarily an agricultural processing company, we are growing in the chemical field. We are expanding overseas. Our objective is to achieve a more even balance of profits from agriculture, chemicals, and foreign operations. About 99% of our products go to other industries for further processing into finished goods. We have virtually no consumer products."

CORPORATE DEVELOPMENT

John Daniels and George Archer had been personal friends long before they became partners to organize the Archer-Daniels Linseed Company in 1902. In 1903 they hired Samuel Mairs, then twenty-four years old, as a bookkeeper and he was successively promoted to secretary and director. In 1909 he succeeded John Daniels as treasurer. Together this trio managed the business for over twenty years.

Mr. Daniels and Mr. Archer occupied facing roll-top desks in an office in the crushing mill. They gave close supervision to every detail of the business even to supervising such minute matters as the opening of the morning mail so that the envelopes could be saved to provide the day's scratch paper. Mr. Mairs supervised the bookkeeping, handled bank relations, and accumulated numerous small day-to-day administrative responsibilities. It was said of the partners that their personalities made a fortunate combination—Mr. Daniels was a bear, Mr. Archer was a bull, and Samuel Mairs acted as modifier.

In 1911 Shreve Archer, the twenty-three year old son of George Archer, joined the company. While he was given the title of treasurer, he was put to work at manual labor. In 1914 Thomas L. Daniels, the son of John Daniels, joined the company as treasurer and Shreve Archer became vice president. In November of 1924 Mr. John Daniels, then sixty-seven, became chairman of the board and turned the presidency over to Shreve Archer, who was thirty-six years old at the time. Samuel Mairs meanwhile had been made vice president, and under Shreve Archer became executive vice president.

Under the presidency of Shreve Archer the company went into a period of great expansion. Shreve was reputed to be a canny trader with an intuitive sense for recognizing a bargain. It was during his term in office that the company merged with other linseed crushers to become the nation's largest operator; it added soybeans to its line, and this grew to be a larger item than linseed; it bought and built terminal elevators; it purchased the Commander-Larabee Mills; and it added numerous smaller lines, such as core oils, foundry products, the flax fiber mill, and the alfalfa division.

Shreve Archer occupied a corner office next to Thomas Daniels, then a vice president, and Mr. Mairs. The doors of these offices were left open and the executives walked in and out of each other's offices freely. If one of them felt the need for discussion, he stepped into the next office. Some matters brought them all into Shreve Archer's office. After such a discussion a decision was usually made at once. Among the rank and file personnel in the company Mr. Mairs came to have the reputation of making most of the decisions. "Actually," said one of his contemporaries, "this was only because Mr. Mairs had little inclination to travel, was the one who could always be found at his desk, and therefore had gathered to himself the supervision of many small day-to-day operating details. Even as executive vice president he insisted that all capital expenditures over $25 be presented for his approval. Shreve Archer, Thomas Daniels, and Samuel Mairs generally agreed on policy issues and acted as a team. But it was Shreve who called the big turns, and he did that personally. He was a power in his own right."

In 1947 Shreve Archer died suddenly at the age of fifty-nine. Mr. Mairs, then sixty-eight, became chairman of the board, and Thomas Daniels, fifty-five, was elected president. In January of 1955 Mr. Mairs passed away, and with his passing Thomas Daniels, then sixty-two, was the only one of the old top-management trio who remained.

During the spring months of 1955 Mr. Thomas Daniels carried on alone all of the activities that had formerly been performed by Shreve Archer, Mr. Mairs, and himself. He became acutely aware of the organization problems that had developed over the years. There were few formally organized divisions. Management tended to be along product lines, and plants were the operating units. "The company," said an executive, "was literally one big pool. People worked in specialized areas, but often they weren't sure who their boss was, except at the very top."

There was an executive committee, but it was inactive. There was a central accounting department, which served most branches. Accounting staffs existed at only some of the outlying plants and divisions. There was no central engineering department to serve all of the mills, nor was there any central coordination of production. The mills had done most of their own buying under the supervision of the top management trio. Sales strategy was developed at the product level, and research, which had been no more than tolerated a generation ago, had become of critical and pressing importance. Purchasing, transportation, and quality control were not under the specific direction of any one executive in the home office. Warehousing and distribution were handled at the plant level. There was no systematic salary administration or job evaluation.

During his first year as president Mr. Thomas Daniels actively supervised financial matters and kept in close hourly touch with the grain markets. The executives in charge of the linseed and soybean business reported their activities to him daily. Eighteen senior executives, including the treasurer and the controller, reported directly to him. In a typical week he read between 50 and 60 detailed reports on markets and on operations. "Besides all this," said Mr. Thomas Daniels, "the business had become much more complicated. We were no longer simple producers of linseed oil. I felt I could no longer carry the burden alone." During the summer of 1955 the executive committee agreed upon the need for a reappraisal of the management, and for that purpose the services of a firm of management consultants, Richardson, Henry, Bellows and Company, were retained.

While the original study made by the consultants was intended to be primarily a personnel audit to evaluate the management resources of the company, the consultants reported that their comprehensive analysis of the company's operations definitely pointed to the need for improvement in certain areas of operations and organization. Therefore they were engaged to make a further study of all of the elements of the organizational structure, its planning, and staffing. There emerged definite recommendations regarding organizational structure, positions, and position relationships. The Archer-Daniels-Midland executive committee studied the recommendations and decided to adopt most of them.

A new office of administrative vice president was established. This office was to coordinate the service staff functions of purchasing, traffic, employee relations, warehousing, and quality control. Another new office with the title of assistant to the president was created for the purpose of relieving the president, as much as possible, of his routine duties. The office of director of marketing, originally established in 1953 for the purpose of coordinating all sales and merchandising activities of the company's numerous product lines, was reaffirmed and given new emphasis.

Until this time the executive committee had been composed of those men in the top management group who were considered to be important in directing the affairs of the company, and they had been chosen without regard to their particular positions or functions. In the reorganization the composition of the committee was changed to include both general and staff executives. Also, one young executive was appointed to the committee to act as its secretary for a six-month period on a rotating basis, for the benefit to be gained in observing the proceedings of the committee. The executive committee was again reactivated, it met weekly, and reviewed all matters of major importance.

The size of the board of directors was increased to nineteen members. Four of the younger executives were placed on the board for the experience it would afford them. The board included five outside directors whose detached viewpoint was considered valuable.

All jobs were evaluated and a system of salary administration was installed. A standard cost system was adopted and accounting figures were refined to give division managers more details of their operations. In production, each division appointed a production coordinator and the responsibility for manufacturing was shifted to the divisions. Commodity buyers, who formerly answered to top management in Minneapolis, reported to the managers of their divisions. Policy making on trading in commodities, formerly centralized in top management, was set daily by each division head.

"The effect of our reorganization," said Mr. Thomas Daniels, "was to shift the major responsibility out of my office and down the line. The division managers are now our key people, and they make the critical decisions."

In 1958 Mr. Thomas Daniels became chairman of the board and his son, John Daniels, then 37, became president, chief executive officer, and chairman of the executive committee.

RESEARCH AND PRODUCT DEVELOPMENT

"I believe," said Mr. Thomas Daniels, chairman of the board, in 1961, "that the major problem facing our company is clearly defined: many activities of former years no longer yield a profit. The crushing of oilseeds, which once gave our organization bread-and-butter income, must be replaced with the production of chemicals and other products which yield a higher profit. We hope to achieve this by skill-ful research."

Archer-Daniels had carried on research for many years, but until 1946 it had been only a limited effort. "Until a few years ago," said Mr. James Konen, vice president and director of research, "if any research project took more than six months, management had a tend-ency to get nervous and say, 'Look, this is costing a lot of money. How about quitting?' And if I ever presented a requisition for a new piece of laboratory equipment that cost over a thousand dollars, I knew that I'd better be prepared to explain exactly how that expenditure was going to pay off."

In the earlier days the entire cost of any research project had been charged to the division concerned. Accounting methods were not re-fined enough to reflect the benefits, and therefore, division managers often did not fully appreciate research. Efforts were made by division managers to maintain the profit position of their respective divisions and to keep expenditures under control in so far as possible. Manage-ment was also intensely interested in maintaining expense control but at the same time furthering product development and research in all of the divisions.

In general, the new tactic was to take the research effort one step further than the basic product stage. "We still have in mind that we expect practical results from our projects," said Mr. Konen. "Our ap-proach is about half way between practical and pure research."

During the period following World War II Mr. Konen, head of research activities, had been promoting to management the idea of a development department which would take the results of the experi-mental research done by the laboratories and bring it closer to the market-production stage. He considered the idea as a possible way to aid research and sales. "There's more to research than just producing new products," he said. "New products have to be developed to the application stage. They have to be produced, and they have to be sold." On the consideration that these developmental activities were taking place anyway, and that it would be more efficient to perform them systematically under central direction, the executive committee approved the creation of a development department.

"My job," said Dr. George Nelson, who headed the department, "is to analyze any new product for commercial acceptance. We relate all items to a profitability base, measuring profitability as profit related to capital investment." It was intended that the department would have three general objectives:

The Evaluation of New Products. Determining the probable demand, the most lucrative markets, and the economic worth of products. The appraisal of similar products and the competitive position of ADM regarding manufacturing facilities and raw materials.

Market Research. Objective analysis of new products and the markets for them through market surveys. Market research activities were divided into three main groups: Industrial chemicals, resins and plastics, and agricultural products.

The Acquisition of New Companies. The investigation of any existing companies or processes which ADM had the opportunity of acquiring.

In working out the marketing of a new product, the development department tried to determine where the product might be useful. Then they approached leading manufacturers in that industry and presented it to them. If the prospect was interested, the development department worked closely with their engineering and production people until the new product was well under way to achieving consumer acceptance. At that point the funds to put it into full production would be allocated, and the production and sale of the product would be shifted to the division which would produce it.

THE SOYBEAN DIVISION

ADM made its entrance into the growing soy products industry in 1928 when it started to process soybeans by using the same hydraulic presses that it used for flaxseed. At that time the industry was in its infancy, having been born during the first World War when the demand for fats, oils, and proteins spurred the production of soybean products. The first large scale use of soybean oil was in such products as margarine, shortenings, and salad dressings. Consumer acceptance was so strong that during the decade of the thirties production increased sixfold, and by 1940, 80% of the half-billion-pound annual output went into these products. Livestock and poultry feed producers found that soybean oil meal served as an excellent high protein feed supplement in poultry mashes and hog feed supplements. In 1955 the bulk of the 6½-million-ton production of soybean oil meal was used in livestock feeds, and most of the balance went into soy flour which was used in bakery goods, pancake and waffle flours, and protein bread. Since 1940 ADM had been known as the largest and most efficient producer of soybean products in the world. During the fifties it added to its product lines edible soybean oils, which it sold to the producers of cooking and salad oils and to the canners of tuna and sardines.

"During World War II," said Mr. Thomas Daniels, chairman of the board, "the soybean industry was cradled in the lap of luxury by the demand for fats and oils. After the war life became real and earnest. Overexpansion plagued us. Every processor had excess capacity and tried to get his share of the market—and a little more. Add to this a good deal of speculation and the result was chaos in the market place." After the war, ADM's soybean plants had been operating at about 75% of capacity. During only 10% of the year did soybean oil and meal bring a better price than the soybeans themselves.

As a mater of company policy ADM did not process its basic products into ultimate consumer products. It did not engage in the manufacture of paints for fear of offending paint manufacturing customers. For the same reason it refrained from making salad oils, shortenings, and margarines. Management reasoned that the company's name was not known to the retail public; neither did the company have retail marketing skill or experience. The trend, however, was toward further refining of its products to bring them closer to the state of the ultimate consumer's products, but stopping just short of the finished commodity. Less than half of the company's volume was in basic products. The balance was refined and modified into what the management called "upgraded" products.

Mr. Thomas Daniels believed that the soybean industry could not match the petrochemical industry in resources for research; that industry was making competitive inroads into the ultimate soybean markets. Mr. Daniels also believed that the federal government should properly undertake the "pure" research into the basic nature of soybeans, their composition, component separation, and fundamental reactions. Thereafter private industry could avail itself of the findings and develop new products such as adhesives, binders, foaming agents, and emulsifiers. "A few million dollars spent by the government in such research," he said, "would forestall many millions presently spent for price supports in the soybean market."

Mr. Daniels was of the opinion that the industry should press expansion into foreign markets. In European markets generally soybean oil was discriminated against as an inferior product in favor of the scarcer olive oil, even in margarines. He also believed that the American market had not been fully exploited. "Americans are a value-conscious and diet-conscious people," he said, "and the soybean is our finest source of low-cost vegetable protein. Both home and abroad we have to do a good deal of old-fashioned American selling."

In 1961 soybean products amounted to 34% of ADM's aggregate sales. In the prewar period they had accounted for 14% of the company's volume.

CHEMICALS

George Archer, one of the founders of the company, had often said in his day that linseed oil was good enough as a vehicle for any paint, and that he was satisfied to produce high quality linseed oil, produce it at low cost, and sell it on a price basis. He had little use for chemists. In its early history the company had done no refining. It sold its basic linseed oil to refiners who processed it according to paint manufacturers' specifications. As late as 1923 ADM had offered a limited line of only 18 grades of linseed oil.

Over the years the demand for refined oils grew, while the use of crude linseed oil declined. Before the days of paint chemistry the average gallon of exterior house paint contained about five pounds of linseed oil. This was the standard unit of sale, and to compete the manufacturer could do one of two things: sell the same product at a lower price, or sell a superior product at the same price.

The extraction of linseed oil (or soybean oil) was a simple process which required little technical knowledge. "Beyond requiring a pretty good sense of market timing, which our people had," said an Archer-Daniels executive, "it was no trick at all to operate as a processor." The result was that many small marginal producers entered the field and competition between them forced all of the profit out of the conversion operation. Inferior oils added to the deterioration of the market. For as little as 4¢ a pound industrial users might switch from linseed oil to soybean oil.

Early paints had been simple products: an oxide or lead base, a pigment for color, and linseed oil for a vehicle. Competition forced manufacturers to seek new and superior ingredients. The trend was to odorless paints that were fast drying, had greater covering quality and more opacity. A gallon of typical modern paint contained three pounds of refined special-purpose linseed oil, and the remainder was in other ingredients.

Previously, a linseed salesman had been a salesman, not a technician, and he sold on a friendship basis and for price. With the transition to the vehicle business, selling was no longer on a "wining and dining" basis. Selling came to be strictly on a technical specification, low-pressure basis. Salesmen were technicians who could go into a customer's laboratory and discuss technical matters with purchasing agents who were generally paint chemists. The conversion operation also changed with the new technology. Common laborers were replaced by trained operators, and the modern mill foreman was a college graduate with a degree in chemistry.

ADM was first drawn into the field of industrial chemicals by its wish to sell a larger portion of its oil production as a refined, finished product, commanding a better margin than that derived from the sale of the basic crude oil. In a series of acquisitions, dating back to the early thirties, ADM acquired concerns which processed various types of oils, such as core oils, Chinawood (tung) oil, oiticica, perilla, menhaden, sardine, sperm, and herring oils.

In a foreign venture with Peruvian partners, ADM constructed a land-based whaling station near Lima, Peru, at a cost of $1.5 million. From this base three whaling ships killed about 2,000 whales a year, producing about 7,000 metric tons of sperm oil. ADM was the largest marketer of sperm oil in the U.S. Sperm oil was unique among all other oils in that its viscosity did not change with extreme changes in temperature. This property made it ideal for use in cosmetics, watch lubrication, and automatic transmissions.

In 1930 a subsidiary of ADM was organized to produce fatty acids, which led to the production of many new products not previously manufactured by the company. ADM also produced glycerides, glycerine, and saturated or fully hydrogenated oils, contrasted to partly hydrogenated products such as Crisco and Fluffo. Nineteen different grades were produced, many in the form of flakes, and they were used in a wide variety of products including rubber, leather, tin-plate, plastics, lubricating grease, cosmetics, and detergents.

Early in 1954 the ADM management decided upon a major expansion into the field of fatty alcohols, and for that purpose it built a plant which used the sodium reduction process, which produced either saturated or unsaturated alcohols. The expected volume for these products did not develop, and during its early years the plant never operated at more than 25% of its 12 million pound annual capacity, which resulted in substantial losses. After considering converting to other processes, or converting the plant to other uses, either of which would be costly expedients, the company finally sold the plant.

Although the total dollar volume of ADM's chemical production had multiplied several times during the postwar period, the operation had not been consistently profitable. The profit pattern tended to be similar to that of proprietary drugs: any new product which found acceptance would earn high profits until competition entered the field, when profits might disappear abruptly. Peak profits were not as high because chemical users balanced costs against performance, and because there was a high degree of substitutability in industrial chemicals.

RESINS AND PLASTICS

ADM's gradual movement toward plastics started in the early thirties when the company began to expand its limited facilities for the production of special and refined linseed oils. In 1931 the research laboratory developed a new product made from linseed oil which it called ADM 100 Oil. This product was marketed continuously from that time on as a nitrocellulose lacquer plasticizer. (A plasticizer is an ingredient that softens and lends flexibility to hard, resinous material.) ADM 100 Oil found a ready market among manufacturers who sought a permanent film-forming lacquer plasticizer for furniture finishes, metal lacquers, and automotive primers. Nitrocellulose, as a basic ingredient of all lacquer, is classified as a plastic, and with the production of ADM 100 Oil, Archer-Daniels entered the plasticizer industry. Since 1931 ADM had developed through research three additional lacquer plasticizers for specific uses and the company followed with active interest any developments in the lacquer industry.

In 1947 the research laboratory became interested in developing a plasticizer for the rapidly growing polyvinyl chloride or "vinyl" resins field.[1] From the company's research there emerged, in 1953, its first vinyl plasticizer, Admex 710, which found extensive applications in such products as raincoats, garden hose, wall coverings, shower curtains, and seat covers. During the period 1955–57 the company introduced five more vinyl plasticizers which were used in floor tile, electrical insulation, wall coverings, infants' wear, foam for cushions, footwear, rainwear, weatherstripping, and molded products.

The Resins and Plastics Division was generating an increasing share of ADM's annual total sales volume and contributing a relatively high percentage of the company's net profit. It had earned a net profit every year since its establishment and, next to the grain division, was the most stable operation in the company. It was, of all the divisions, the heaviest contributor to the company's research program. As much as 4% of its sales dollar was allocated to research activities. It was generally believed that most of the division's future expansion would be based on the results of continuing research.

Early in 1958 the division bought Crosby Aeromarine, a producer of fiberglass boats. "It was not our intention to get into the boat business in a big way," said Mr. Walter Andrews, head of the Plastics Division, "but we were interested in acquiring the molding facilities and manufacturing knowledge of the company so that we could apply it to other shapes and forms." Three years later ADM sold the boat company, stating as its reason that it did not provide the expected market for plastic resins, and that it was a drain on manpower and resources.

THE TERMINAL ELEVATORS

The Archer-Daniels Grain Division was formed in 1927 with the original intention of acquiring elevators to provide storage for flaxseed

---

[1] Polyvinyl chloride is a hard, brittle resin which has little value when used alone. However, when a plasticizer is added and the mixture is processed with heat, the result is a finished, flexible vinyl material which can be made into a variety of calendered, extruded, or molded consumer products.

and soybeans. During the next few years, by new construction and by additions to existing elevators, ADM expanded its elevator capacity at Minneapolis to 14 million bushels. During the next two decades there was considerable expansion into other parts of the country, particularly the Southwest, the Midwest, and the Pacific Northwest. At the start of World War II the grain division had a capacity of 37 million bushels. In 1962 it was operating 29 terminal and subterminal elevators, with a total capacity of 97 million bushels.

The grain division performed two principal operations: Storage of grain owned by others, and the merchandising of grain. As much as 30 million bushels of the elevator capacity had been used to store grain for the Commodity Credit Corporation. About 10 million bushels of the capacity was used by the Commander-Larabee Mills, about 12 million for other processing raw material storage, and most of the balance was used for the division's merchandising activities. These merchandising activities were extensive and were carried on in both national and international markets. Although wheat constituted about 70% of the grain handled, all kinds of grain were handled, including corn, barley, soybeans, oats, and flaxseed. To secure the highest practical grade the elevators were equipped to clean, dry, mix, and blend grains. Customers included flour mills, feed manufacturers, maltsters, and grain exporters. All grains purchased by the company were hedged.

In 1960, to improve its grain procurement facilities throughout the upper Midwest, Archer-Daniels bought the J & O Grain Company, which had 12 grain-buying offices in the North Central states, an office in Chicago, and a seat on the Chicago Board of Trade. Management believed that by this move it would enhance the efficiency of its grain merchandising activities by improving its grain buying and originating facilities. Early in 1962 it purchased the Norris Grain Terminals which operated 11 terminal elevators with 12 million bushels capacity in four midwestern states. The Norris terminals complemented the existing Archer-Daniels terminals.

Mr. Carl Farrington, vice president in charge of the grain division, reported directly to Mr. Thomas Daniels until 1958. About once a week Mr. Farrington called on Thomas Daniels in the president's office to discuss affairs, and occasionally Mr. Daniels phoned him to ask the reason for having taken some market position even though it was hedged. Mr. Farrington said that over the years there had been a trend toward giving him more and more independence due, he believed, to the satisfactory relationship he had established with top management and to the fact that his division was consistently one of the most profitable in the company. The grain division seldom posed problems of a critical nature to the executive committee or the board. During the decade of the 1950's it had earned a higher return on its investment than any other division in the company.

For many years grain storage had been a profitable activity. However, in recent years there had been a reduction in the storage fees paid by the Federal Government. In view of this trend management decided upon a program of reducing the storage part of its business. At the same time it mounted a campaign to intensify its merchandising activities and to expand its exportation of grain with the thought that this would maintain the over-all profitability of the grain division.

THE COMMANDER-LARABEE MILLS

Early in the 1930's Archer-Daniels bought, at a fraction of its face value, the defunct Commander-Larabee Corporation. The purchased company operated 14 mills which had a daily capacity of over 3 million pounds of flour, and owned over 5 million bushels of elevator capacity. Under ADM management the operation became profitable within a few years.

Since the beginning of the century the per capita consumption of flour in the United States in the form of bread had been declining, but total consumption had remained constant. Making up for the decline in bread consumption was an increase in the consumption of flour in what millers called "the more glamorous forms," such as crackers and cookies, spaghetti, macaroni, and noodles. There was a sharp rise in the popularity of macaroni products in their convenience food forms—canned spaghetti, ravioli, canned chicken and noodles, or tuna and noodles, and cheese mixes. All forms of macaroni (paste goods) were made from semolina flour which was milled from durum—a hard, high-protein wheat. Commander-Larabee's durum products department was one of the country's largest producers of semolina flour.

In the 1950's many flour millers and bakers had been converting to bulk flour systems. The bulk system abandoned bags in favor of transportation of flour in bulk trucks. The flour was conveyed within the mills by augers or pneumatic tubes. Bulk handling proved an efficient operation for the small mill whose customers were within trucking range, and it was especially advantageous to the large miller who happened to operate the only mill in a large metropolitan center. Commander-Larabee's mills were in neither situation, and in the middle 1950's their profits began to decline. The division then began to ship bulk flour in railroad cars, and the mills convenient to water transportation shipped sacked flour in barges. Despite this move many long-standing customers switched to mills which had converted to bulk handling at an earlier date.

Except for bulk handling there had been no revolutionary developments in flour milling. No better way of milling wheat flour had been discovered since the age-old method of pressing the grain between rollers. During the past few decades, however, there had been a constant succession of small improvements in processing and refining.

There had been little research in the industry on the basic chemistry of flour, but there had been a good deal of experimentation with the types of wheats and flours which could be used for special baking purposes, such as crackers, cookies, breads of various compositions, and cakes. Commercial bakers tended to produce more specialty breads and pastries, and their changing technology was forcing the milling industry to change its technology. There was more classifying of streams of grain particles and streams of flours, more nutrition tests, and an increased demand on commercial mills to do "prescription milling."

"The Commander-Larabee Division," said Mr. English, the division manager in 1957, "has been one of the most independent divisions in the company. Headquarters furnishes us with money and with borrowing power. We make monthly reports and are always available for consultation, but we consult on only the broadest of policy matters. The home office does not direct our operation. We have generally been profitable, and therefore they feel quite easy about it."

THE ALFALFA DIVISION

By the end of World War II Archer-Daniels' was a leading supplier of protein supplements to the livestock feed industry through its production of soybean oil meal, linseed oil meal, and mill by-products. An important ingredient it did not produce was dehydrated alfalfa meal. The company entered this field in 1951 by purchasing the Small Company of Neodesha, Kansas, the nation's leading producer of alfalfa meal.

The Small Company operated 55 dehydrating plants located in 10 of the plains states. Alfalfa was purchased from farmers within a radius of 10 miles of each mill. It was chopped and blown into wagons at the time it was mown, and it was transported to the mill where it was dehydrated by a hot-air process, ground into meal by hammer-mills, and bagged.

During the years immediately following the acquisition the ADM management reduced the number of Small plants to 36, modernized them to reduce production costs, and undertook to improve the product. The important ingredient in alfalfa meal was vitamin A, which was highly perishable under ordinary storage conditions, and for this reason the Small Company had stored its finished inventory in cold storage plants. The ADM management developed a new method of pelleting the meal which made for easier handling, and reduced the surface exposure subject to vitamin loss. These pellets were then stored in an inert gas in huge storage tanks, each having a capacity of over 10,000 tons, and also in standard concrete tanks of smaller size. This preserved 95% of the vitamin A content against 55% formerly saved.

FLAX FIBER

In 1939, Shreve Archer bought a flax fiber plant in Winona, Minnesota. Archer-Daniels had never owned any flax straw facilities of its own, and it was only a coincidence that the Winona mill which it acquired at this particular time processed straw from flax, and that Archer-Daniels was a major producer of linseed oil made from flaxseed.

Until 1940 the bulk of American cigarette papers were made principally from linen rags that were imported from Europe. When World War II halted foreign imports cigarette makers turned to improving American papers, which had previously been considered inferior. Until 1941 the Winona mill had never processed more than 7,400 tons a year. Under Archer-Daniels' management the method of processing was revised so that, by blending several grades of straw, it was able to produce a tow that made a satisfactory cigarette paper.

As a result production was increased several fold. The entire output of the plant was sold to a paper mill, which in turn sold the paper to the major American tobacco companies.

The Flax Fiber Division plant usually had 100 employees. Forty per cent of its product by weight was in tow, which was sold to the Ecusta Paper Company. The principal other products of the division were shives, the woody portion of the straw, which were sold to a maker of wallboard.

The investment in the fiber mill was carried on the company's books at a nominal figure. The paper mill which purchased most of the output maintained a close business relationship with the fiber mill management. Routine and special reports on the fiber mill operation were mailed to the ADM executives in Minneapolis. Under ADM's management the fiber mill had returned a profit every year. Since the operation was on a cost-plus contract basis, the risk of unprofitable operations was minimized.

CORPORATE CHANGES UNDER JOHN DANIELS

Prior to election as president in 1958 John Daniels had been one of 17 vice presidents. As such he had taken an active part in the reorganization activities and had earned a reputation for being deliberate and methodical. John Daniels was convinced that the narrowing margin between costs and prices and the resulting decline in profits was a trend that could be arrested only by drastic action. Therefore, in June, 1959, he announced the following program:

1. To determine the most efficient form of organization for ADM.

2. To set objectives and policies and communicate them effectively.

3. To appraise each operation for return on investment, and profit outlook.

4. To dispose of operations which did not meet profit standards.

In a second major reorganization within a decade, all operations were consolidated into two domestic groups: an Agricultural Division, and a Chemical Division. (See Exhibits 2, 3, and 4.) To this was added a third group: the Overseas Division. "You might say," said John Daniels, "that Archer-Daniels today is two entirely separate and decentralized businesses—an agricultural processor and a manufacturing chemist. The fact that they exist side by side is important because each strengthens the other."

"In the second step," said Mr. John Daniels, "we set objectives and formulated policies, and communicated them to all management personnel. These spelled out, among other things, areas of concentration, rate of growth, and standard return on investment."

In the third step, Mr. Daniels said, each individual operation was appraised in terms of objectives, taking into account promise of future growth and fitness with the long range objectives of the company. Return on investment studies were made for each profit center and a standard rate of return was established. New ventures were also evaluated on the basis of payout and projected return on investment. As a rule of thumb, any new venture to be considered had ultimately to produce at least 20% return before taxes.

Finally, those operations which were marginal, or showed little promise of future growth, or whose character was not considered to fit the pattern of ADM's business, were disposed of. Included in the various dispositions were several major divisions of the business.

For many years linseed products had been declining in relative volume, while soybean and chemical volume had been increasing. In 1941 linseed products had represented 36.38% of total sales volume; in 1961 it was only 8.92% of the total. In the most dramatic move in its program of dispositions, the company closed its last remaining linseed oil plant in 1961. Linseed oil, the product on which the company had been founded, was henceforth produced for ADM by others under toll contracts.

ADM entered the growing livestock feed business in 1930. Using linseed oil meal, soybean oil meal, and alfalfa meal (the principal ingredients of livestock feeds) which it produced in its other divisions, the company compounded a rounded line of poultry and livestock feeds which it sold under the brand name Archer Booster Feeds. In the early 1960's it was marketing about 100,000 tons of formula feeds a year, which was about $\frac{1}{3}$ of 1% of the estimated national consumption of 35 million tons. At that time ADM also was the nation's largest producer of linseed oil meal, soybean oil meal, and alfalfa meal, of which it produced over a million tons a year. The latter it sold to the major livestock feed producers of the country.

"The feed business," said John Daniels, who had once been vice president in charge of the feed division, "had always been treated as an orphan child in our company. We had difficulty deciding to what extent we wanted to be in the business. We were afraid that if we got into it in a big way, we might offend major customers in the raw ingredients end of our business."

In 1960 management disposed of the feed business. "This had been our largest consumer business," said John Daniels, "and, in general, we would rather be suppliers of raw materials." He added that the business had been relatively unprofitable.

When ADM acquired the Commander-Larabee Flour Mills the acquisition included a chain of some 80 small country grain elevators. These elevators, located in the plains states, had acted as wheat collecting stations for the flour mills. When trucks replaced horse transportation, these elevators became obsolete as grain collection stations, and the company disposed of all but 40 of them. These 40 still collected grain, but they were largely converted into farm supply stores which sold a rounded line of seeds, feeds, fertilizers, insecticides, herbicides, fungicides, and light farm tools and equipment. The country elevators had always been profitable. Nevertheless, in the early 1960's, the company sold them. "The elevators," said John Daniels, "were poorly located for the type of grain merchandising we envisioned for the future."

When Archer-Daniels bought the Small Company (which became the Alfalfa Division) the purchase included a machine shop in which Small had designed and manufactured most of the equipment it used to harvest and process alfalfa. The Archer-Daniels management expanded the machine shop operation and placed its services at the disposal of all of the ADM divisions on a competitive basis. The intention was that the machine shop would fabricate and service for all of the company's mills such equipment as hammermills, pneumatic and mechanical conveying systems, dust collectors, and bulk flour and feed bins. In 1960, however, the management sold the machine shop. John Daniels announced that ". . . this operation did not fit into the pattern we had cut out for ADM. . . ."

In the period following World War II chlorophyll became an extremely popular product. Premium quality alfalfa was the richest source of chlorophyll and Archer-Daniels was the world's largest producer of high quality alfalfa meal. Impressed with the possibilities, Archer-Daniels bought, in 1952, two small concerns which produced chlorophyll, and management made plans to expand their capacity. However, the company's 1953 Annual Report stated that the expected demand for chlorophyll had failed to materialize. By the end of that year the company disposed of its chlorophyll plants, asserting that the operation had proved to be unprofitable, and showed no promise.

Some of the foregoing disposals were profitable. However, the company's 1960 report described in detail a $7 million net write-off of assets to cover losses anticipated from the disposal program.

In the same year, 1960, John Daniels announced that $40 million was being budgeted during the next three years for an expansion program. "We will pursue every justifiable growth route in our expansion," said Mr. John Daniels. "At this stage we are utilizing four such routes: Plant construction; plant lease; plant purchase, including acquisition of established businesses; and joint ventures."

In May of 1962, in one of the most spectacular moves in its expansion program, the first processing unit of the company's new Peoria Chemical Center went into production. This plant, which had been under construction for 18 months, was the first unit of a plant complex which would consolidate many of the company's far flung chemical operations. Included in the comprehensive plan was the moving of some plants, the closing of leased plants, and the sale of others. The Peoria Chemical Center had been conceived as a basic plant for industrial and specialty chemicals and plasticizers. It was designed to permit expansion as new products and technologies were developed by Archer-Daniels' research laboratories. The new plant covered 33 acres and consisted of 21 buildings and a 150-unit tank farm for storage of raw materials and finished products. The Peoria plant produced its own hydrogen, nitrogen, inert gas, and compressed air. It pumped and treated its own water from five wells, and had a complete waste purification and disposal system that eliminated pollution of nearby streams. Its network of processing equipment included chemical reactors, distillation units, a molecular still, high pressure splitting columns, automatic deionizers, pressure autoclaves and centrifuges.

exhibit 1
ARCHER-DANIELS-MIDLAND COMPANY

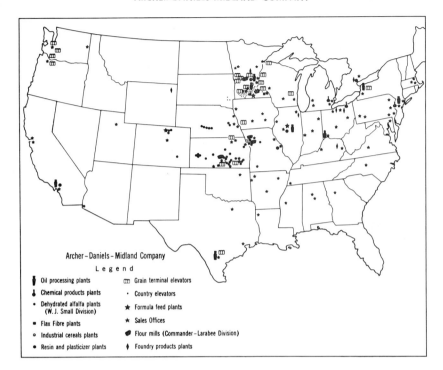

Archer – Daniels – Midland Company

L e g e n d

▐ Oil processing plants	⊞ Grain terminal elevators
▼ Chemical products plants	· Country elevators
• Dehydrated alfalfa plants (W. J. Small Division)	★ Formula feed plants
▪ Flax Fibre plants	★ Sales Offices
○ Industrial cereals plants	◆ Flour mills (Commander – Larabee Division)
• Resin and plasticizer plants	♦ Foundry products plants

exhibit 2
ARCHER-DANIELS-MIDLAND COMPANY
Organization August 1, 1962

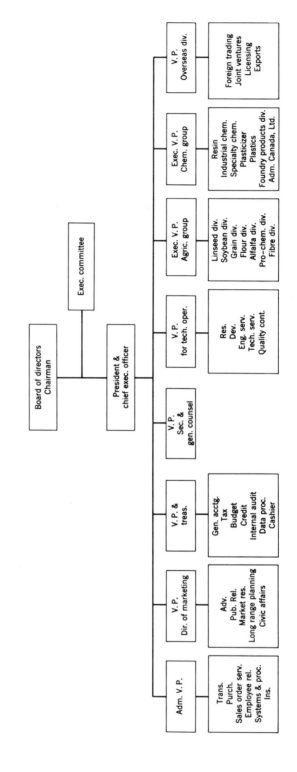

exhibit 3   ARCHER-DANIELS-MIDLANDS COMPANY
Major operating groups

CHEMICAL GROUP

Departments and Products	Principal Industries Served
Foundry products—Core oils, binders and washes, foundry supplies, bentonite	Foundry, oil well drilling, taconite
Industrial chemicals—Fatty acids, hydrogenated oils, sperm and marine oil products, spermaceti, glycerine, pitches	Protective coating, soap, rubber, lubricant, textile, leather, cosmetics, detergent, metal working
Specialty chemicals—Fatty nitrogens, fatty alcohols, olefins, hydrocarbons	Textile, detergent, cosmetics, petroleum, ore separation
Resin—Synthetic resins, resin solutions, specialty resins, esters	Industrial and architectural paints, varnish, ink, adhesives, gum bases
Plastics—Polyester and urethane resins, Freight Liner products	Reinforced plastics, marine, building materials, furniture, transportation
Vinyl plasticizers—Epoxy, polyester and monomeric plasticizers	Vinyl plastics for flooring, upholstery, films, coatings, extrusions, moldings
Coated chemicals—Coated plant food	Lawn, garden, commercial horticulture

Plants

Cleveland, Ohio; Colony, Wyoming; Decatur, Illinois; Elizabeth, New Jersey; Los Angeles, California; Newark, New Jersey; Pensacola, Florida; Peoria, Illinois; Valley Park, Missouri

AGRICULTURAL GROUP

Divisions and Products	Principal Industries Served
Grain—Wheat, barley, corn, grain, sorghums, oats, rye, flaxseed, soybeans	Milling, malting, distilling, oilseed processing, formula feeds
Flour—Wheat flour, durum flours, millfeeds	Bakery, macaroni, formula feeds
Alfalfa—Dehydrated alfalfa	Formula feeds
Linseed—Linseed oil, linseed oil meal	Paint, chemical, formula feeds
Soybean—Soybean oil, soy flours, soybean oil meal, lecithin	Margarine, salad oils, bakery, specialty food, formula feeds, adhesives, paper, paint, chemical and pharmaceutical
Flax fiber—Flax tow, shives	Fine paper, foundry, formula feeds
Prochem—Starches, isolated soy proteins, protein supplements	Paper, building materials, explosives, adhesives, foundry, ore separation, oil well drilling, paint, bakery, specialty foods

Plants

Soybean plants: Decatur, Illinois (2); Mankato, Minnesota; Fredonia, Kansas
Flour mills: Minneapolis, Minnesota (2); N. Kansas City, Missouri; St. Joseph, Missouri
Flax fiber plant: Winona, Minnesota
Prochem plants: Evendale, Ohio; St. Joseph, Missouri

exhibit 3 (continued)

Terminal elevators: Illinois—Chicago, Joliet, Morris, Ottawa, Peoria, Sheldon, Spring Valley; Iowa—Burlington, Council Bluffs; Kansas—Hutchinson, Wellington; Louisiana—*Destrehan; Minnesota—Minneapolis (6), St. Louis Park, St. Paul; Missouri—Clinton, St. Louis; Nebraska—Murray, Omaha; Oregon—Portland; Tennessee—Memphis; Texas—Kenedy; Washington—Tacoma, Vancouver; Wisconsin—Superior
* Under Construction

OVERSEAS DIVISION

Foreign Operations

Wholly-owned subsidiaries: Canada: Archer-Daniels-Midland, Ltd., Toronto—resins, foundry products, chemicals, isolated proteins, industrial cereals; Holland: N. V. Archer-Daniels-Midland, Verkoopmaatschappij, Rotterdam—commodity trading; Panama: Archer-Daniels-Midland, S.A., Panama City—overseas licensing

Affiliates and associates: Belgium: Oleochim, S.A., Brussels—fatty acids and derivatives; Colombia: Productos Quimicos Admicol, S.A., Bogota—resins, plasticizers, foundry products; Germany: Scado-Archer-Daniels GmbH & Co., Rühle—resins, plastics; Holland: Nederlandsche Castoroliefabriek Necof, N.V., Geertruidenberg —paint vehicles, castor oils; Scado-Archer-Daniels, N.V., Zwolle—resins, plastics; Alchemica, N.V., Schoonebeek—phthalic anhydride; Mexico: Productos Api Aba, S.A., Gomez Palacio, Guadalajara, Mexico City—formula feeds; Admex, S.A., Mexico City—resins, plasticizers; Peru: Cia. Ballenera del Norte, S.A., Lima—sperm whaling; Spain: Oleotecnica, S.A., Castro-Urdiales—resins, foundry products, fatty acids, soaps, margarine; Sweden: Scado-Archer-Daniels, A/V, Vallakra—resins, plasticizers; Australia: Jordan Chemical Works (A'sia) Pty., Ltd., Sydney—resins, paint vehicles, foundry products

exhibit 4   **ARCHER-DANIELS-MIDLAND COMPANY**
Organization, operations, plants and affiliations, 1962

PLANTS

ADM operated the following plants in 20 states and Canada. Processing plants were strategically located in raw material producing and importing areas and when practical close to their markets.

29 terminal elevators; total grain storage capacity of approximately 95 million bushels	3 chemical plants
	2 vinyl plasticizer plants
	3 foundry products plants
4 soybean processing plants	2 bentonite mining properties
5 vegetable and marine oil refineries	1 industrial cereals plant
4 flour mills	1 isolated soy protein plant
30 alfalfa dehydrating, blending, and storage plants	1 flax fiber plant
	4 pilot plants
5 resin and plastics plants	

exhibit 4 (continued)

RESEARCH AND SERVICE LABORATORIES

These were located at Minneapolis; Newark, New Jersey; Los Angeles; Wyandotte, Michigan; Cleveland and Evendale, Ohio; and Toronto, Canada, and assisted production and sales by finding new uses for existing materials and developing new products. A new Central Research Laboratory was under construction in suburban Minneapolis.

Pilot plants tested new products under actual plant conditions. Control laboratories were maintained at each major manufacturing plant to assure uniformity of products.

ORGANIZATION

The company's activities were organized into three marketing units—the Agricultural and Chemical Groups and the Overseas Division.

Agricultural Group

The Agricultural Group was engaged in the processing, storing and marketing of agricultural commodities.

1. *Linseed Division.* ADM was a major marketer of linseed oil which was produced from flaxseed and was used in the manufacture of paint, varnishes, and other products. After the linseed oil had been removed from the flaxseed, the remaining linseed oil meal became an excellent source of vegetable protein for livestock feed.

2. *Soybean Division.* ADM was one of the largest processors of soybeans, which yield soybean oil and soybean oil meal. The oil was widely used in the food industry as a salad and cooking oil and in margarine and vegetable shortening. It also had many industrial uses. Lecithin, a derivative of soybean oil, had applications in foods and pharmaceuticals. Soybean oil meal was a valuable livestock and poultry feed ingredient. ADM also was the largest producer of industrial and edible soy flours. Important industrial applications were plywood adhesives, boxboard, wallboard, paints, and pet foods. Edible uses included icings, meringues, baby foods, specialty foods, bread, pastries, and macaroni.

3. *Flour Division.* ADM was one of the largest flour millers in the United States, with a daily wheat flour capacity of 43,500 cwt which included 4,000 cwt semolina used in the manufacture of spaghetti and macaroni. Its products were sold primarily to the baking and macaroni industries.

4. *Grain Division.* One of the nation's largest grain merchandising companies, ADM bought and sold grain in all of the principal markets and carried on export trade throughout the world. It also purchased large amounts of grain for its own milling and processing operations. ADM operated 29 terminal elevators which cleaned, handled, and stored grain. The company's total grain storage capacity was approximately 95 million bushels. A new export terminal was being built at Destrehan, Louisiana.

5. *Dehydrated Alfalfa Division.* ADM was one of the largest producers of high quality dehydrated alfalfa, an important ingredient of many formula

feeds. It operated 30 plants located in Arizona, Colorado, Kansas, Missouri, Nebraska, and Utah.

6. *Flax Fiber Division.* ADM was a major processor of flax straw from which it produced flax fiber and shives. The fiber was used to make cigarette paper, air mail stationery, fine printing papers, and U.S. currency. Shives were used in wallboard, in livestock feeds, as fillers for agricultural fertilizers, and for other industrial purposes.

7. *Industrial Cereals Department.* These products derived from grain sorghums and corn were used in several segments of the paper industry, building materials, dynamite, wallboard adhesives, core binders,- ore flotation and oil well drilling mud.

8. *Isolated Protein Department.* Isolated proteins extracted from soybeans were important ingredients of many industrial products. They had basic applications in the coating of fine printing papers, water dispersible paints, adhesives, and building products.

9. *Ardex Department.* Marketed Ardex 550, a protein supplement and milk solids replacement for use in spaghetti and macaroni products, bread, and other foods.

10. *Productos Api-Aba, S.A. ADM,* in partnership with a group of Mexico City industrialists, manufactured and marketed livestock and poultry feeds.

Chemical Group

The Chemical Group manufactured and marketed broad lines of resins for protective coatings and plastics, industrial chemicals, hydrogenated oils used as intermediates by many industries, and vinyl plasticizers for plastics. The group also refined and processed marine oils and sperm whale oil for protective coatings and special industrial uses.

1. *Resin Department.* Marketed more than 300 synthetic resins and resin solutions primarily for the protective coating and printing ink industries. Specialty resins also had been developed and were sold in volume to the chewing gum and adhesives industries. Products included chemically modified oils, alkyd resins, water reducible resins, rosin esters, modified esters, and pure and modified phenolics.

2. *Plastics Department.* Marketed laminating polyester and urethane resins for reinforced plastics, urethane foam and elastomers. These resins had many applications in the production of boats, corrugated plastic sheeting, lining of bulk storage tanks, seat cushions, automobile crash pads and insulation. Also marketed adhesives, calking compounds and protective coatings sold under the Freight Liner trade name for use in repair of freight cars and other equipment.

3. *Industrial Chemicals Department.* Marketed fatty acids, hydrogenated oils, sperm and marine oil products, spermaceti, glycerine and pitches. These had a variety of uses, including paints, soaps, printing inks, rubber, lubricants, textiles, leather, cosmetics, and detergents.

4. *Vinyl Plasticizer Department.* ADM's line of Admex epoxy plasticizers

exhibit 4 (continued)

was used by the plastics industry for such products as garden hose, vinyl fabrics, toys, shower curtains, foot wear, and floor tile.

5. *Specialty Chemicals Department.* Marketed a line of fatty nitrogen chemicals which find their principal applications in fabric softeners, detergents, petroleum additives, corrosion inhibitors, bactericides, printing inks, waterproofing formulations, and ore separation processes. In addition, offered a line of fatty alcohols and derivatives, including fatty olefins and hydrocarbons. Principal markets for alcohols were in detergent and viscosity index improvers for motor oils. Olefins were used as chemical intermediates, while hydrocarbons were used as functional fluids.

6. *Foundry Products Division.* Largest processor of core oils and other additives for the foundry industry, it offered a binder for every type of core practice. Made a line of parting compounds, air setting binders, shell molding and hollow core resins.

7. *Archer-Daniels-Midland (Canada) Ltd.* A wholly owned subsidiary, it processed core oils and binders, resins and special linseed, soybean and marine oil products that were distributed throughout Canada.

Overseas Division

ADM's foreign operations were handled by this division with the exception of the formula feed business in Mexico and diversified businesses in Canada. Overseas activities included export sales, fats and oils trading, licensing, and joint ventures.

1. *Export Sales.* Many ADM products were sold in nearly every country. Sales representatives were located in more than 35 markets abroad.

2. *Foreign Trading Department.* In addition to world-wide trading in vegetable and marine oils, fats, and meals, ADM also purchased commodities on world markets for its own domestic needs.

3. *Licensing.* ADM S.A. Panama, a wholly owned subsidiary of ADM, had entered into a number of licensing agreements on a royalty basis for the manufacture and sale of ADM products in specific foreign markets. Licensing agreements were in effect with the following companies:

Scado-Archer-Daniels N V, Zwolle, Holland—for plasticizers, phenolic, alkyd, urea and other synthetic resins for the plastics and surface coatings industries.

Scado-Archer-Daniels GmbH, Rühle, Germany—for plasticizers, phenolic, alkyd, urea and other synthetic resins for the plastics and surface coating industries.

Nederlandsche Castoroliefabriek NECOF N V, Geertruidenberg, Holland—NECOF processed castor oil and produces paint vehicles, core binders and foundry specialties, as well as a full range of PVC stabilizers.

Holtz & Willemsen, KG, Krefeld-Uerdingen, Germany—for soybean meals, flours, and specialties.

Azienda Lavorazione Colori Resine e Affini, Milan, Italy (ALCREA)— for plasticizers, plastics, resins, copolymer oils, and foundry binders.

exhibit 4 (continued)

Bunge Corporation, New York City, New York—General exchange of know-how was provided for products manufactured by ADM and the Bunge Group in Argentina, Brazil, Paraguay, Peru, and Uruguay. Specific licensing agreements covered soybean flours, soy protein specialties and lecithin with Bunge's Brazilian associate, Samrig of Porto Alegre.

Jordan Chemical Works (PTY) Ltd., Sydney, Australia—for all types of resins, surface coating oils and materials for the plastic and foundry industries.

4. *Joint Ventures.* ADM had entered into partnership with a number of companies in foreign countries. Licensing agreements also exist with most of them.

Admex, S.A., near Mexico City, Mexico—Admex, S.A. distributed resins and plasticizers manufactured on a toll basis by Quimica Organica S.A.

Oleochim, S.A., Brussels, Belgium—This company operated a plant in Ertvelde which manufactured fatty acids and their derivatives. Oleochim S.A. was owned jointly by ADM and Palmafina, a Belgian company.

Nederlandsche Castoroliefabriek NECOF, N V, Geertruidenberg, Holland—The capital of this company was made up in majority of Netherland interests. ADM owned a small equity. In addition to the products manufactured under ADM S A licenses, NECOF processed linseed and castor oils.

Scado-Archer-Daniels, N V, Zwolle, Holland.

Scado-Archer-Daniels, GmbH, Rühle, Germany—In addition to licensing contracts, ADM had a capital investment in these two companies. They produced resins and plasticizers.

Alchemica, N V, Schoonebee, Holland—Owned by Scado-Archer-Daniels group, this company produced phthalic anhydride, an important raw material for coatings resins.

Scado-Archer-Daniels, Vollakra, Sweden—Owned by the Scado-Archer-Daniels group, this company manufactured resins and plasticizers.

Oleotecnica, S.A., Castro-Urdiales, Spain—Production included margarines, shortenings, soap, detergents, PVC stabilizers, wire drawing compounds, core binders, fatty acids, hydrogenated triglycerides, specialty oils, and other derivatives from fats and oils.

Cia Ballenera del Norte S.A., Lima, Peru (BALNOR)—This company operated a land based whaling station near Paita, Peru. BALNOR was owned generally by an ADM Peruvian subsidiary (Consorcio Peruano del Norte S.A.) and Peruvian interests (Sindicato de Inversiones Industriales S.A.).

Productos Quimicos Admicol, S.A., Bogota, Colombia—Admicol distributes resins, plasticizers and foundry products manufactured for it on a toll basis in Colombia.

exhibit 5   **ARCHER-DANIELS-MIDLAND COMPANY**
Statements of consolidated earnings and reinvested earnings, Archer-Daniels-Midland
Company and subsidiaries, years ended June 30

Earnings	1962	1961
Income:		
Net sales and other operating income	$245,896,523	$213,115,452
Dividends received and interest earned	426,664	399,178
Profit on sale of securities (less provision for		
possible loss on investments)	1,136,987	947,468
Other	257,318	288,059
	$247,717,492	$214,750,157
Costs and expenses (including provision for		
depreciation: 1962—$2,598,740; 1961—		
$2,497,307):		
Cost of products sold and other operating costs	$221,410,793	$191,228,627
Selling, general and administrative expenses	16,221,615	16,258,606
Interest expense	1,701,882	887,145
Other	165,883	107,581
	$239,500.173	$208.481.959
Earnings before taxes on income	$ 8,217,319	$ 6,268,198
Taxes on income	3,796,051	2,520,468
Net earnings for the year	$ 4,421,268	$ 3,747,730
Reinvested earnings		
Balance at beginning of year	$ 59,781,738	$ 59,209,598
Net earnings for the year	4,421,268	3,747,730
	$ 64,203,006	$ 62,957,328
Deduct cash dividends paid—$2 a share	3,195,208	3,175,590
Reinvested earnings at end of year	$ 61,007,798	$ 59,781,738

exhibit **5** (continued)

Consolidated statement of financial position, Archer-Daniels-Midland Company and subsidiaries, June 30

	1962	1961
Current assets:		
Cash	$ 5,326,593	$10,788,460
Receivables	20,662,401	18,294,983
Inventories	50,950,276	43,930,985
Prepaid expenses	1,098,282	1,380,839
Total current assets	$78,037,552	$74,395,267
Current liabilities:		
Notes payable	$11,000,000	$ —
Accounts payable and accrued expenses	15,133,546	23,459,685
Taxes on income	1,547,834	902,058
Anticipated replacement cost of inventories	242,000	344,000
Total current liabilities	$27,923,380	$24,705,743
Net current assets (working capital)	$50,114,172	$49,689,524
Investments and other assets	5,808,222	5,865,900
Property, plant and equipment	58,172,752	38,275,323
Term bank loans	(18,000,000	—
Deferred liabilities and credits	(1,636,452)	(2,404,170)
Net assets	$94,458,694	$91,426,577
Shareholders' equity		
Common stock	$33,382,734	$33,382,734
Additional paid-in capital	595,304	523,960
Reinvested earnings	61,007,798	59,781,738
Common stock in treasury	(527,142)	(2,261,855)
	$94,458,694	$91,426,577

exhibit 5 (continued)

Ten-year summary of financial and operating data (fiscal year ends June 30th) (in thousands of dollars except per share figures and others)

	1961	1960	1959	1958	1957	1956	1955	1954	1953	1952
Financial:										
Working capital	$ 49,690	$ 50,815	$ 50,978	$ 47,954	$ 46,737	$ 50,645	$ 48,380	$ 50,201	$ 47,610	$ 49,091
Per share	31.26	32.06	31.75	30.15	30.19	31.10	29.38	30.52	28.95	29.85
Inventories	43,931	33,312	39,084	33,320	36,668	41,368	26,506	31,283	39,634	44,164
Net property and plant	38,275	37,774	42,435	43,118	41,535	41,949	42,419	38,392	38,319	37,872
Net additions to property and plant	4,430	4,160	3,298	5,452	3,179	3,082	7,559	3,001	3,314	6,033
Total assets	118,536	107,644	115,226	111,716	108,803	111,550	105,350	105,261	100,146	102,969
Shareholders' equity	91,427	90,708	98,698	95,953	92,914	93,987	92,116	89,591	87,867	88,619
Per share	57.51	57.24	61.48	60.32	60.02	57.71	55.93	54.47	53.42	53.88
Operating:										
Net sales and other operating income	213,115	239,895	239,370	225,812	231,869	221,378	230,793	216,425	227,520	240,189
Payrolls	24,858	27,631	25,634	24,523	22,476	21,421	20,846	19,987	21,127	21,310
Depreciation	2,497	3,233	3,729	3,869	3,593	3,552	2,380	2,928	2,866	2,617
Provision for income taxes	2,520	2,878	5,750	3,607	5,353	6,061	6,317	5,044	2,365	6,368
Total taxes	4,626	5,181	7,840	5,548	7,125	7,842	8,000	6,549	3,784	7,774
Net income	3,748	3,665	5,435	3,904	5,204	5,872	5,750	5,013	3,853	7,413
Per share	2.35	2.31	3.38	2.45	3.36	3.60	3.49	3.05	2.34	4.51
Cash dividends	3,176	3,196	3,206	3,189	3,194	3,270	3,292	3,289	4,605	4,577
Per share	2.00	2.00	2.00	2.00	2.00	2.00	2.00	2.00	2.80	2.80
Retained in business	572	469	2,229	720	2,010	2,602	2,458	1,724	(752)	2,836
Other:										
Outstanding shares (in thousands)	1,590	1,585	1,605	1,591	1,548	1,629	1,647	1,645	1,645	1,645
Number of shareholders	9,196	8,598	7,787	6,837	6,315	6,197	5,449	5,102	4,941	4,764
Number of employees	3,706	4,661	5,038	4,903	4,652	4,674	4,651	4,940	4,930	5,424
Common stock:										
Price Range*	43-33	40-30	49-38	44-29	39-28	41-35	43-32	46-32	52-30	60-48

* Fractions omitted.

589

BOSSART'S

In the spring of 1957, Mr. James Johnson, the executive vice president of Bossart's, was reviewing the company's position. Located in a large eastern city, Bossart's had opened its fifth retail store in the city the previous fall. Mr. Johnson was particularly interested in the overall effects of the firm's new department store on the company's operations. He noted that Bossart's net sales had increased appreciably and that the new store was more than achieving its predicted volume. While this performance was gratifying, Mr. Johnson was nevertheless concerned with two major problems which he felt the new store had created.

> We expected the D store [the symbol used by management to identify its new store located in a recently constructed shopping center called People's Plaza] to take some business from the First Street and A stores because they are located within the same general shopping area. However, D has been so successful that both the First Street and A stores are experiencing a squeeze on their profit margins. These reductions in volume are making it hard for the First Street and A store managers to keep costs in line.
>
> The D store has created another problem because our longstanding policy of the same store hours for all outlets had to be changed. The D store broke the established tradition by setting hours more suited to the shopping habits of its customers. Then the C store wanted to open and close at still another set of times. In the case of the D store, the different time schedule was necessary and has undoubtedly helped the store's volume. The new hours at the C store haven't materially affected their volume and have created some operating and personnel difficulties. Attracting and retaining competent sales people who have to work at least two evenings is difficult.

EARLY HISTORY AND DEVELOPMENT

In the early 1880's, when the city's population was about 250,000, Daniel Bossart arrived in America from Switzerland. After one year's work in a small dry goods store, he joined with a friend, Leslie Scherer, in a retail business venture called Bossart's. The store's location in a resi-

exhibit 1
BOSSART'S
Rough Map of the Metropolitan Area

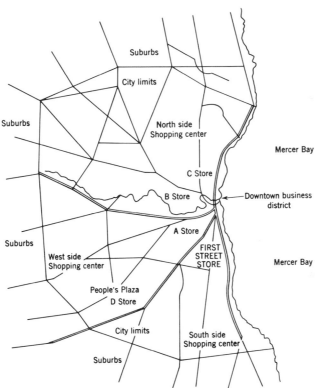

dential area of the city outside of the downtown business district was regarded as a key factor in the company's early success. When new stores were added in 1900, 1917, 1924 and 1956, management continued to choose neighborhood areas located between the center of the city and the suburbs. (See Exhibit 1.)

The first and second Bossart stores (called First Street and A by the management) were located on the south side of the city. They were both about two miles south of the center of the downtown business section and separated by approximately a half mile. The third store opened by Bossart's (called B) was located about two miles west of the center of the downtown business district, and the C store was a mile north of the downtown center. The D store, opened in 1956, was located in the southwest section of the city on the edge of the suburbs. It was about five miles southwest of the First Street and A stores. In 1957 the city's population was about 750,000 and the metropolitan area had well over a million people.

When the first four Bossart stores were established, each of their neighborhoods was considered to be on the outskirts of the city. However, as the city grew and the suburbs became more mature, the stores became surrounded by the growing populations, and neighborhood shopping areas developed at each location. Bossart's sales volume climbed as the city's residents found Bossart's stores conveniently located and competitive with the large downtown stores with respect to price, service and quality of merchandise.

As the four stores grew with their neighborhoods, Bossart's management endeavored to keep the four units operating essentially as one store. It was their thought that if Bossart's had uniform stores, the company would derive many advantages of a centralized (one-store) operation. Furthermore, the public would have one, not four, images of what a Bossart store was.

On the occasion of Bossart's 50th anniversary, the firm's president, Mr. Leslie Scherer, explained the company's major characteristics as follows.

> Few department stores in America are like Bossart's. Some are single stores in a central part of the city or the district. Others have a parent store with branches. Others are organized like a chain group. Bossart's four stores are organized on yet a different plan. They are under one ownership and control, have certain functions in common, and yet are managed as four distinct stores. Each store has its own manager, who is responsible for the unit's operation, yet the Bossart name is one; the reputation and good will are one; Bossart's contact with the market in buying merchandise is one. In advertising, which is done from a central bureau, the same items are offered at the same time in the four stores. Each Bossart store is a community store, having its entire stake in the community it serves. Yet in spirit, in policies, in reputation, and in operating methods, the four Bossart stores constitute one merchandising activity.

THE POSTWAR PERIOD (1945–1957)

During the postwar period management carried out a program of expansion and modernization of all existing facilities. Each of the four stores and the warehouse building were improved, as Bossart's sought to maintain its position as the city's leading retailer both in terms of volume and quality.

Keen competition was felt from several sources within the trading area served by the Bossart stores. (See Exhibit 1.) There were two large department stores and several specialty stores in the downtown business district. One of the large department stores was a unit of a large national chain of department stores, while the other was part of a large eastern retailing organization. Three Sears stores, seven Penney's stores, several specialty stores and numerous variety stores were also affecting Bossart's share of the retail business in the city. Of particular concern to the management was the opening in 1951 of the large North Side Shopping Center, three miles from Bossart's C store. A unit of one of the large downtown stores (the national chain) was the major retail outlet at the North Side Shopping Center. Two large variety stores and several specialty stores were also located there. In view of the changing competitive picture, Bossart's undertook plans for further expansion. Originally, the firm's directors had in mind a single outlying store located near the growing suburbs; but as time passed and they observed the country-wide interest in shopping centers, the directors found more and more attractive the notion of developing a complete shopping center with the Bossart unit as the dominant store.

In the spring of 1954 ground-breaking ceremonies took place for the new shopping center on the southwest side of the city. People's Plaza, as the center was called, was planned as the city's largest and most modern shopping center. Its total cost was to be about 15 million.

Bossart's failed in its efforts to negotiate a deal with a major downtown department store to have it establish an outlet at People's Plaza. Bossart's did manage, however, to get Penney's and one of the city's leading specialty stores to join them at the new center. In 1956 the center was opened with total building area of nearly one million square feet, parking facilities for 7,000 automobiles, and a complete range of stores and service organizations.

In 1956 Bossart's total sales volume was close to $60 million. It had more than 5000 employees and the floor area in the five stores totaled over a million square feet. The A, B, C, and D stores had equal floor areas and accounted for three-quarters of the company's total floor space.

While management felt that Bossart's competitive position in the city had been strengthened due to the new D store in People's Plaza they were concerned about recent announcements made by the two large downtown stores. The eastern firm had announced its plan to lease a store in an established shopping center in a suburb immediately south of the city. The store would be about five miles south of Bossart's First Street and A stores and four miles southeast of the new D store. Prior to this announcement, Sears had been the only major retailer at the South Side Shopping Center, which was considerably smaller than both People's Plaza and the North Side center.

The national chain also announced plans to develop another shopping center on the west side of the city. It revealed that a well-known Philadelphia retailing concern had already agreed to lease one large retail unit while the national chain would occupy the other area. This new center, which would not be completed for a few years, was to be located about three miles from People's Plaza in a west side suburb. In size and style, it was planned to be at least on a par with People's Plaza.

GENERAL ORGANIZATION

Throughout Bossart's history, a member of the Bossart family had been president of the firm. When Daniel Bossart died in 1907, his partner and son-in-law, Leslie Scherer, became president and general manager. Leslie Scherer passed away in 1937 and his son, Leslie Jr., succeeded to the presidency. In 1948, Leslie Jr. died and his brother, Steven, became president.

In 1957 the Bossart organization was largely a mixture of two distinct groups: those with over twenty-five years of service with the company and those who had joined the firm within the past twelve years. Reporting to Mr. Steven Scherer, the president, were two men, each a representative of one of the above-mentioned groups.

Mr. Harry Gargill, who had been with Bossart's for more than 40 years, was a vice president and treasurer. He was principally interested in the financial aspects of the company. In recent years he had concerned himself largely with the financial planning for the construction and leasing at People's Plaza.

Mr. James Johnson, on the other hand, had been with Bossart's less than twelve years. He had joined the firm as a vice president following successful retail experiences with an eastern retailing concern and a well-known department store in the West. As the executive vice presi-

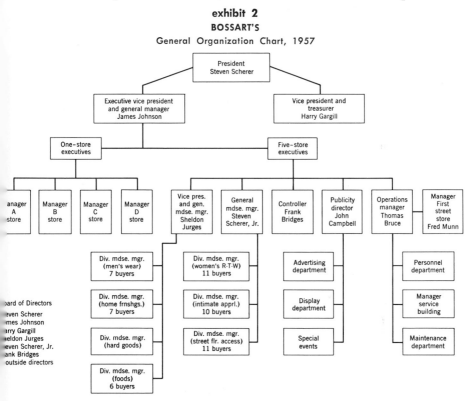

exhibit 2
BOSSART'S
General Organization Chart, 1957

dent and general manager of Bossart's, he was primarily responsible for all the operations affecting the company's retail business. Mr. Johnson had eight people who reported directly to him. As shown in Exhibit 2, these eight men were divided into two groups—the A, B, C, and D store managers and the heads of the functional divisions (merchandise, control, publicity, and operations). The store managers were usually referred to among the Bossart management as "one-store executives," while the heads of the functional divisions were called "five-store executives."

The responsibilities of the First Street store manager were considerably different from those of the managers of the other stores. In the latter stores, each manager was responsible for both the selling and the operating phases of the store. Each of these stores had a superintendent who handled the operating problems and five divisional supervisors who had charge of the selling floors. These relationships are shown in Exhibit 3. The A, B, C and D store managers reported directly to Mr. Johnson.

exhibit 3
BOSSART'S
A, B, C, and D Stores, Organization Chart, 1957

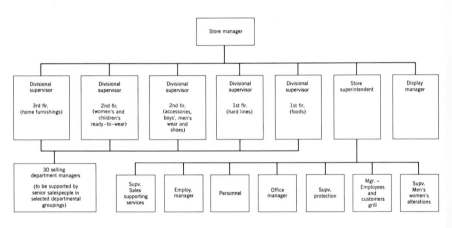

The First Street store manager, on the other hand, reported to the operations manager and was directly responsible for only the operating aspects of his store. The buying organization under the two general merchandise managers was responsible for the selling function in the First Street store. Each division merchandise manager acted as a divisional supervisor at the First Street store and was responsible for a number of selling departments. The buyers under each division merchandise manager acted as department managers at the First Street store. Mr. Johnson summed up their dual roles in saying, "The buyers have line responsibilities at the First Street store and staff relationships with the other four stores." The executive offices and the buying organization were all located at the First Street store.

Mr. Munn had been store superintendent at the First Street store until February 1, 1957, when the new position of store manager was created and he was selected for the job. No one was appointed to fill the position Mr. Munn vacated. Mr. Munn continued to report to the operations manager, whose office was next to Mr. Munn's.

Each store manager received regular reports from the controller's office on the operations of his store. Copies of the operating reports of each store were also sent to Mr. Johnson and the "five-store executives."

THE "FIVE-STORE EXECUTIVES"

There were two general merchandise managers who reported directly to Mr. Johnson. Mr. Sheldon Jurges, a vice president of over forty years' experience with the company, was the general merchandise manager in charge of four major classifications of merchandise. These lines were men's wear, home furnishings, hard goods, and foods. Under Mr. Jurges were four division merchandise managers and 30 buyers. Mr. Steven Scherer, Jr., a son of the president, was the general merchandise manager in charge of the remaining "soft" goods. These were women's ready-to-wear, intimate apparel, and street floor accessories. Mr. Scherer had three division merchandise managers and 32 buyers under him. Mr. Scherer, who was under 40 years of age, had been with the company approximately ten years.

The merchandise divisions had the buying responsibility for the five Bossart stores. Each buyer specialized in a line of merchandise such as women's hosiery and was in constant contact with the manufacturers of these products. This often involved considerable traveling to trade shows and manufacturers' showrooms. Each buyer operated within the limits of a predetermined budget and Bossart's established merchandising policies of price and quality. Still he was allowed considerable flexibility in his buying program and his personal income depended to a great extent on the success he had in purchasing the "right" merchandise.

Each buyer's performance was measured with respect to his sales, gross profit margin, and inventory composition and amount. The buyer was also responsible for the supervision of the selling force at the First Street store.

With their offices in the First Street store, the buyers tried to visit each of the other Bossart stores once a week. During these visits a buyer attempted to work out any problems that related to his particular line of merchandise. At the A, B, C, and D stores the buyer set prices, ordered markdowns, determined assortments and planned promotions, and in these matters he had direct authority. In such things as the location or arrangement of merchandise displays, however, he would make suggestions, and his suggestions were generally but not always accepted by the department manager in charge of the department which sold the buyer's merchandise.

At the First Street store, where the buyer was responsible jointly with the store manager for the selling function, it was much easier for the buyer to put his ideas into immediate practice. The sales people reported directly to him, and as department manager he always knew the status of the department's budget.

Each buyer also spent a great deal of time each week controlling the inventory of his merchandise. In many departments this required a trip once a week to the service building (warehouse) and a detailed review each week of reports showing the sales and inventory by product classifications for each store.

The publicity division was under the direction of Mr. John Campbell. Under his supervision were the advertising department and the display and special events department. Advertising for the five stores was handled by a centralized staff at the First Street store location. Advertisements were run in the local papers under the Bossart name and carried a message that applied equally to all stores. It was a rare occasion when one of the Bossart stores advertised independently in the local papers. Sales promotion and display were handled in the A, B, C, and D stores by a person at each location who reported directly to the store manager. The First Street store's sales promotion and display were handled by an individual who reported to a five-store display director, who, in turn, reported to Mr. Campbell.

The operations division, which was managed by Mr. Thomas Bruce, was responsible for all merchandise-handling functions, store services, and personnel. The company had a service building where all the merchandise was received, marked, stored, and eventually shipped to the five Bossart stores. The maintenance department was responsible for maintaining the interiors and exteriors of all Bossart stores at the high levels always associated with the company's reputation.

Each of the stores had a personnel office which hired the line employees, such as sales people, for that store. The First Street store also hired the five-store maintenance and warehouse employees. Buyers were hired by the general merchandise managers, and five-store staff personnel were hired by the five-store executives, who also supervised executive training programs.

Mr. Bruce's main function was the determining of the amounts and types of operating assistance that should be administered to each store. He worked closely with the store superintendents at the A, B, C, and D stores and the store manager at the First Street store on the operating problems of each unit. He was also in daily contact with Mr. Johnson, to whom he reported directly.

The controller's office was under the direction of Mr. Frank Bridges. Mr. Bridges had been with the firm for over forty years and was a member of the board of directors. He had been promoted to his present position from assistant controller several years previously. His office gathered and distributed the accounting and statistical information relative to the stores' operations. For instance, sales and inventory records of each store were consolidated by lines of merchandise and reports were sent to each buyer relative to his line.

COMMITTEES

"Bossart's was not managed by committees," said Mr. Johnson, the executive vice president and general manager, "but we use them as a means of focusing attention on management problems, co-ordinating thinking and action, and as a means of top-level communication." The company had four committees: the General Management Committee (GMC), the Expense Control Committee, the Division Merchandise Managers' Committee, and the Wage Committee.

The General Management Committee had 18 members, which included five functional division heads, the five store managers, and the seven merchandise division managers. Mr. Johnson regarded this committee as a "communications get-together." The group met whenever Mr. Johnson felt the need to discuss general policy matters. He often used these meetings to present major policy decisions that top management had reached.

The Expense Control Committee was composed of the five functional division managers and the five store managers. This group met once a month with Mr. Johnson. At these meetings budgets were determined and later reviewed. Current trends affecting the stores' operations and any problems relating to expense control were also discussed.

The Wage Committee was made up of five store managers. This group was originally brought together to establish wage programs that could be administered uniformly in all Bossart stores. However, it developed that the store managers found it convenient to discuss at these meetings any common problems they wished brought to Mr. Johnson's attention. One store manager said, "I like these meetings because each store has an equal vote on problems facing a manager. When a decision is reached, even if I am opposed to the idea, I don't mind going along with the group. We all respect the judgment of each other on the store manager's problems, which are many."

The Division Merchandise Managers' Committee was made up of the two general merchandise managers, the seven merchandise division managers, the five store managers and the publicity director. Their meetings were concerned mainly with the merchandising and publicity problems of the company.

Decisions reached at the merchandising, store managers, and expense control meetings were often announced at the General Management Committee meetings.

In addition to the use of committees, Mr. Johnson kept in close contact with all Bossart operations by means of personal observation and direct contact with the management personnel. He tried to visit the A, B, C, and D stores at least every two weeks and met with their store managers about as often. He also exercised control of management activity through a system of operating reports that came to his desk regularly. "I follow these reports closely because it gives me the opportunity to raise key questions. When something seems out of line I contact the person responsible and expect to get a reasonable explanation," said Mr. Johnson.

"A great deal of my control problems," he went on, "are simplified by our unique organizational set-up. We have both five-store and one-store executives. Therefore, if there is some difficulty relating to a certain line of merchandise at a particular store, I can contact the merchandise people right in this office or I can get in touch with the appropriate store manager."

INTERSELLING

Mr. Johnson explained that "the internal organization of the Bossart stores is in a state of transition because we are adopting a plan of interselling.' Until now the organization of each store paralleled the traditional merchandising organization in that each department manager and his salespeople were responsible for selling a line of merchandise which had been procured by one buyer. Recent steps have been taken, however, to establish fewer selling units within each store."

"Interselling" meant that several units formerly classed as departments were grouped together as one selling unit under one department manager. Sales people assigned to the selling group might sell at any sales area within the selling unit. The department manager shifted the personnel to the selling areas where the sales efforts were most needed at particular times. Prior to interselling a salesperson was assigned to a certain station and sold only the products at that station. These items of sportswear were a typical example: Better sportswear, better blouses, and better casual dresses were each a separate line, and each was bought by a different buyer. Although in each store their stations were adjacent, each line had its own salesperson who sold only the items at her station. The buyers had often helped instruct the sales people assigned to the stations where their merchandise was sold.

Interselling did not originate at the D store; Bossart's had tried the plan elsewhere on a trial basis, and while results had shown promise, the management found that some resistance was encountered from buyers and sales people who were reluctant to change their ways. When the D store was opened, however, its entire organization was based on interselling and its success there was helping to break down the resistance of the merchandising organization at the other stores.

In the spring of 1957, Mr. Johnson noted that the organizational set-up at the D store was operating to his satisfaction and that he hoped to follow the same basic pattern of interselling at the other stores. "We've already begun forming new selling groups at the A, B, and C stores, and before long we will have interselling in full swing at all of these stores. It will take longer to put this principle into practice at the First Street store because the buyers are still very much in the picture at that location."

THE FIRST STREET STORE

The First Street Store was the first Bossart store opened and was traditionally the leader in sales volume. For several years it had contributed a larger share of sales than the other stores. Although this percentage dropped significantly with the opening of the new D store, in 1957 it was still the largest volume unit. In terms of net sales, the D store ranked a close second, while A, C, and B followed in that order.

The First Street store was unlike the other stores in that there were no department managers directly responsible to the store manager. The buyers acted as department managers for their respective lines of merchandise, or in many cases delegated this responsibility to the assistant buyer.

One of the division merchandise managers expressed the opinion that most of the 62 Bossart buyers regarded the selling responsibilities of the merchandise organization at the First Street store as an essential aid to them in their merchandising function.

> Every buyer tries to spend some of his time each day on the selling floor. He uses this time to instruct the salespeople in his department, and to make a few sales himself. In that way our buyers get close to the customer. They find out just what the customer wants and how he can best be sold.
>
> There are other reasons why this arrangement is valued by our buyers. A buyer has full authority at all the stores in setting prices, ordering markdowns, planning advertising and promotions. But only at the First Street store can he order such details as the location and arrangement of merchandise.
>
> The buyers also feel that control of the selling responsibility at the First Street store helps their overall showing. The buyers feel that at the First Street store, where they have full authority over the selling function, they have an opportunity to test their ideas, and those which prove out at the First Street store, they feel, should be equally successful at all of the other stores. Thus the buyer's supervision of his selling department at the First Street store becomes a proving ground that he feels will enable him to increase his sales volume at all the stores, and thereby increase his income, too.

THE B STORE

Mr. Mason, the manager of the B store said that his time was divided as follows: 50% acting as a liaison for his store's organization in its relations with people located at the First Street store, 40% on exclusively B store problems, and 10% on general company business.

> I probably should spend more time on B store problems exclusively. There are enough of them. The new D store has hurt our volume, our

neighborhood has gotten old and is declining, and our expenses have been increasing all the time.

The changeover to interselling should help to get our expenses back in line. However, I wonder if it will increase our problems in dealing with the buyers.

BLAW-KNOX

In 1961 the management of Blaw-Knox considered that they had finally integrated their numerous subsidiaries and divisions into a single corporate unit. "But," said Mr. Snyder, president of the company and chairman of the board, "only the initial objectives of our program have been accomplished so far. We've correlated the divisions, and succeeded in getting the people at the divisional and plant level to think as one company. We've re-asserted the staff functions and put new life into them. The big job now is to upgrade our profit picture. We're working at that by hammering away at costs and weeding out the poor earners in our product lines. We also need more long-range planning. We've got to learn to think years ahead. We've also got to be thinking about bringing up our younger people so that eventually we have better executive personnel."

Mr. Cordes Snyder Jr. was elected president of Blaw-Knox in 1951 following a working capital crisis which had resulted from the independent action of the company's subsidiaries and division managers. Mr. Snyder started his career with Blaw-Knox as a shop metallurgist and through a series of quick promotions became manager of a division which he operated profitably for nine years. Feeling that his opportunities with Blaw-Knox were limited, he left to become president of Continental Foundry and Machine Company. Later he accepted a position as vice president of Koppers Company. In 1951 Mr. Snyder was offered the presidency of Blaw-Knox. Knowing that the company needed, as he put it, "a helluva lot of attention," he deliberated a full month before accepting, considering what had to be done and discreetly exploring the management's attitude toward him, especially certain people whose cooperation he felt he would need. When he did accept, it was with the tacit understanding that he was to plan and execute a drastic and far-reaching reorganization of the entire company.

CORPORATE DEVELOPMENT

Blaw-Knox had its origins in a sewer contracting business started in 1906 by Jacob Blaw based on the use of collapsible steel forms. A few years later Luther Knox pioneered a business which produced pressed and welded foundry equipment. These businesses combined to form the Blaw-Knox Company in 1917. The operations of the newly formed company were consolidated in a new plant built at Pittsburgh. During the ensuing decades Blaw-Knox, by merger and purchases, entered into numerous other industries and added many new products to the company's line: foundry equipment, road-paving machinery, steel towers, gas cleaners, steel buildings, high-alloy castings, rolls for the metals industry, cast-steel plant equipment, and rolling mills and machinery. In addition, Blaw-Knox developed within its existing facilities such products as clamshell buckets, open steel grating for flooring, and numerous other steel and foundry products.

During World War II Blaw-Knox became an important producer of heavy armament. Its most significant wartime activity, however, was the establishment of a standard design for synthetic rubber plants for the Defense Plant Corporation. From this experience the company established one of its major divisions, the Chemical Plants Division.

Moses Lehman, the first president of Blaw-Knox, was a prosperous Pittsburgh shoe merchant who had supplied the newly founded company with financing and given it the benefit of his business acumen. He was followed by his son Albert, who was president until 1934. Three years of interim officeholders followed until William Witherow, who had been a board member for four years, was elected president. His administration was characterized by extreme. decentralization, diversification, and independent operation of the subsidiaries and divisions. During this era the function of headquarters was described as that of a holding company in which the divisional vice presidents acted with the independence of subsidiaries, and the president limited his activities to listening to their reports at the monthly meetings of the board of directors.

As Blaw-Knox had expanded through the years into new product lines and new industries, each unit added was allowed to operate as it did prior to acquisition. Since most acquisitions involved products which were different from anything the company had previously produced, individual plant operations were continued with little change and with a minimum of direction from the home office. The personnel acquired were also retained, including the executives. It was assumed that they had proven their competence by successful performance and they brought with them strong sales followings. The Blaw-Knox management saw no reason to change their method of operation as long as it was profitable.

The board of directors consisted of seventeen members, fourteen of whom were division managers, staff executives, or presidents of subsidiary companies, and the others represented banking connections. When Mr. Witherow was president, he was said to have looked upon his executive function as that of a coordinator, leaving the major decisions to be made by division managers, whom he saw only at board meetings. Each division manager acted as though he was the head of an independent company, and he made his own plans with the assurance that there would be little interference from the corporate executives at Pittsburgh. Operating authority rested with the division managers and the board usually approved whatever recommendations they made. "Controls were loose," said a division manager. "As long as you were in a profit position, nobody bothered you very much." The division managers, however, felt themselves to be in competition with each other, on a rivalry basis, and they measured their success by their sales volume, the spectacular contracts they captured, and the profits of their divisional operation.

After coming into the Blaw-Knox organization each unit continued to handle its own sales, production, industrial relations, and research. There was no central coordination of staff functions. The executives in the Pittsburgh office who carried on the staff activities had no authority over their corresponding staff functions at the division level, and the division staff personnel answered to the vice president in charge of their division.

The controller of the company, who had been a company lawyer, assumed the controller function because of the necessity for someone at headquarters to consolidate division reports. He did not exercise authority over division accounting staffs which operated independently and without uniformity. Accounting was on a completed contract basis, which meant that it was not taken into sales figures until the contract was completed. This was criticized as distorting sales figures, for it occasionally happened that several large contracts might be 90% completed at statement date, but would nevertheless be entirely excluded from sales figures.

Purchasing was done independently by each division. Each division had its own credit manager who was responsible to the division manager for credit granted and for the policing of accounts receivable. Accounts payable were also treated as a divisional responsibility, with each division setting its own standards and procedures.

Eleven different design groups were scattered throughout the company and these were concerned primarily with adjusting products to the needs of individual customers. Research efforts were entirely at the division level and each project was considered separately rather than as part of a company-wide program. Only two divisions had laboratory facilities for exploring new fields, and their efforts varied, requiring little more than one professional man per year.

The legal department reviewed all of the company's contracts, including sales and union contracts. While the substance of the contracts was determined by each division, there was criticism to the effect that business tended to be done on a legal basis.

Personal salesmanship had become a company tradition. Division heads cultivated the patronage of the top executives of the steel companies and other large organizations that presented a potential market for Blaw-Knox products. Much of the business was done on a reciprocity basis. Sales personnel were mainly engineers who directed most of their efforts toward obtaining big and spectacular contracts to satisfy the prevailing thinking among division managers that large and special orders were the key to a profitable operation.

The treasurer, who had been in office for many years, had accepted the pattern of the treasury department as it had developed. Elderly and due to retire soon, he showed no inclination to disturb the system which, until 1951, had functioned well enough. There was no coordination of the company's over-all finances, and the treasurer's staff performed such duties as compiling company reports for statement and tax purposes. The director of safety reported to the treasurer because his efforts had a direct effect upon insurance premiums, which were paid by the treasury department.

Financial planning was done at the division level with each manager arranging for his own requirements. Plant expenditures were not formally budgeted. Each division manager simply discussed his major projects with other division managers at the monthly board meetings. It was this practice which precipitated the change of management which took place in 1951. That summer a number of unusually large contracts had suddenly increased the company's bank credit requirements from the usual $10 million to $18 million. The banks finally consented to the full amount of the credit but imposed restrictions upon any further consolidations, acquisitions, and capital expenditures. Following this, those Blaw-Knox directors who represented its banks persuaded the board to seek new leadership for the company, an action which culminated in the election of Cordes Snyder in 1951. When Mr. Snyder became president, Mr. Witherow assumed the position of chairman of the board. At this date the Blaw-Knox organization consisted of the parent company and three principal subsidiary companies which operated ten plants through nine divisions and had foreign subsidiaries in London and Paris. The structure of the company had never been reduced to an organization chart.

REORGANIZATION UNDER CORDES SNYDER

By the time Mr. Snyder took office he had decided that, while his reorganization promised to be thorough and far-reaching, it would be a gradual and slow-moving process which might take years to accomplish. He stated that several reasons led him to this decision: he did not wish to alarm Blaw-Knox industrial customers by setting off an internal upheaval; he did not wish to antagonize the skilled employees, who were loyal to their managers and old systems; and finally, he wished to retain as many division managers as he could, for he valued their talents and wished to enlist their help.

One of Mr. Snyder's early moves was to change the size of the board of directors. The board had seventeen members, several of whom were in their seventies and five of whom were division managers. Mr. Snyder was convinced that the deliberations of a small board of younger men who were not company executives would be more constructive. "I want somebody who can beat me over the back," he said, and within a year he induced the board to reduce its membership to eleven. Three of those who left the board were division managers who had been requested to resign their directorships.

Mr. Snyder also merged the company into a single corporate unit. It had consisted of four corporations that operated eleven different businesses.

Mr. Snyder outlined the following objectives for the unified company:

> To establish a more centralized management system by a program of integration which would serve to effect better control.
>
> To make an engineering study of manufacturing facilities and management organization, looking to a strengthening of both.
>
> To make a marketing survey to determine which markets the company was in the best position to serve profitably.
>
> To make a technical study to serve as a guide in establishing a research and product development division or department, and a corresponding program.
>
> To prepare for increased participation in the national road-building program, and in the construction of public works.
>
> To increase the company's penetration and impact on the chemical and food processing markets. The aim would be to become a factor of substance in this field, not merely a fringe participant, and strive to make a real contribution.
>
> To lower production costs and increase the profit ratio. Any segment of the business not responding to upgrading and offering no promise of profitability was to be considered a subject for elimination.

During his first several years in office Mr. Snyder gradually proceeded to place controls upon the divisions. "My objective," he said, "was to re-establish a certain amount of centralized control and coordination of divisional activities while still remaining essentially a decentralized operation. This meant re-emphasizing certain staff functions, such as sales, production, industrial relations, accounting and finance, and making them uniform throughout the company. At the same time I wanted to allow the divisions to retain most of their independence."

Mr. Snyder replaced the staff executives in the finance, legal, and accounting departments, and he created four new staff offices: sales, production, development and research, and industrial relations. Most of the new staff executives were brought in from outside the company and were younger men, typically in their early forties. Each of them was made a vice president of the company, a point which Mr. Snyder considered to be of importance, for he felt that this would give them equal status in dealing with division managers.

To replace the treasurer, early in 1952, Mr. Snyder chose George Langreth, who had achieved a reputation for financial reorganizations. Reflecting the new status to be accorded the office, Mr. Langreth was elected vice president of finance and treasurer. In 1953 William Rodgers, who had previously conducted a successful business of his own, was brought into the company to fill the newly created position of vice president and general sales manager. Howard Winterson came into the company as vice president of industrial relations, and George Kopetz was promoted to another newly created position—vice president of production. In 1953 Mr. Snyder brought into the company a former commander of naval ordnance, Captain Eugene Rook. In 1955 Capt. Rook was appointed vice president of fabricated products operations. In 1956 Dr. D. F. Jurgensen was brought into the company as vice president of development and research, and in 1957 J. Sterling Davis joined the company as controller. (See Organization Chart, Exhibit 1.)

An early move under Mr. Snyder was the compilation of an organization manual, the writing of job descriptions, and a manual of procedures. Since the new formal organization structure was something new that many of the old executives would be meeting for the first time, Mr. Snyder set up a Control Section to coordinate the activities between the divisions and between the line and staff executives. Mr. David Tomer, an engineer who had extensive experience in organizational work, was placed in charge of the control section. Mr. Snyder brought Mr. Tomer, whom he had known at Koppers, into the company. Mr. Tomer was to counsel and advise executives on the initial phases of the new coordinated practices. He was given the title of assistant to the president.

In the course of changing operating procedures, Mr. Snyder took away from the division managers two authorities: the first was their authority over financial appropriations in two areas—capital additions and improvements in plant and equipment, and research. Requests for appropriations which were over $1,000 were now required to be submitted to an appropriations committee which analyzed them and either submitted them for approval to the operating committee or held them. The operating committee consisted of the heads of all the divisions and the staff executives. Major appropriations took a further step to the board of directors. All appropriations were coordinated by the financial executive of the company. In addition, control over the employment of management personnel and the setting of their salaries was taken away from the division managers and placed under the supervision of a salary committee which worked out a management compensation plan. All new personnel came under the plan, and the salaries and positions of all current personnel were systematically reviewed and realigned.

In his contacts with management personnel, Mr. Snyder constantly emphasized the importance of using the guidance of the staff people.

PRODUCT LINES AND PRODUCT DEVELOPMENT

In 1951 the list of products produced by the company was the largest in its history. (See Exhibit 2.) Diversification had become a well-established tradition within the company and division managers took pride in the widespread array of products and dissimilarity of the product lines turned out under the Blaw-Knox name. Mr. Snyder looked upon this as an item of concern that deserved his special attention.

"Long ago," he said, "we achieved a record for quantity in the matter of identifying products with our name. I am not implying criticism of past management policy in creating this complex picture. Definite gains were achieved by putting our eggs into many baskets. But this diversified activity led to a pride in mere numbers of products. I am proud of our product mix and happy that we are diversified, but there is a danger in depending too much on the variety of our activities. It is my judgment that we are at a crossroad in this company's history where the emphasis must be placed on the performance of each product line, rather than on pride in quantity, especially if the quantity does not add to our quality and profit performance. We may have to conclude that some of the company's present products no longer fit the future picture. We must be sure that we aren't keeping any 'sacred cows.' If any product no longer meets the full needs of our customer, or cannot be produced efficiently enough to return a profit, we must acknowledge that fact and agree that it is time to do something about it."

In examining the widespread array of sizes and models within each product line, Mr. Snyder noted that a single item like clamshell

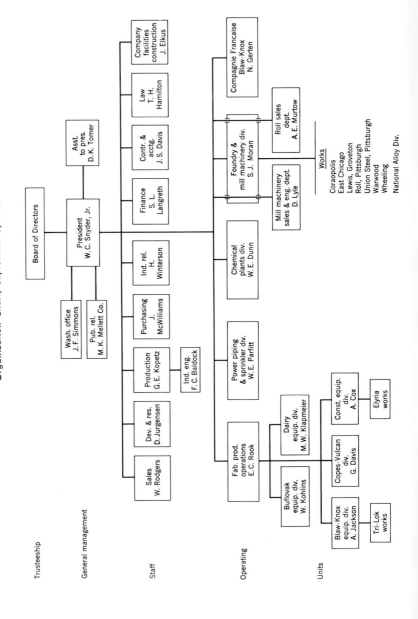

exhibit 1
BLAW-KNOX COMPANY
Organization Chart, September 6, 1957

Trusteeship

General management

Staff

Operating

Units

Board of Directors

President
W. C. Snyder, Jr.

Asst.
to pres.
D. K. Tomer

Wash. office
J. F. Simmons

Pub. rel.
M. K. Mellett Co.

Company
facilities
construction
J. Elkus

Law
T. H.
Hamilton

Contr. &
acctg.
J. S. Davis

Finance
S. L.
Langreth

Ind. rel.
H.
Winterson

Purchasing
J.
McWilliams

Production
G. E. Kopetz

Ind. eng.
F. C. Baldock

Dev. & res.
D. Jurgensen

Sales
W. Rodgers

Power piping
& sprinkler div.
W. E. Parfitt

Chemical
plants div.
W. E. Dunn

Compagnie Francaise
Blaw-Knox
N. Gerten

Foundry &
mill machinery div.
S. J. Moran

Roll sales
dept.
A. E. Murtow

Mill machinery
sales & eng. dept.
D. Lyle

Fab. prod.
operations
E. C. Rook

Dairy
equip. div.
M. W. Klapmeier

Const. equip.
div.
A. Cox

Elyria
works

Buflovak
equip. div.
W. Kohlins

Copes-Vulcan
div.
G. Davis

Blaw-Knox
equip. div.
A. Jackson

Tri-Lok
works

Works
Coraopolis
East Chicago
Lewis, Groveton
Roll, Pittsburgh
Union Steel, Pittsburgh
Warwood
Wheeling
National Alloy Div.

612

buckets might include over a hundred models and sizes; a cement-mixing truck might be equipped with a costly device for adjusting the pouring chute; and if the stock sizes in the evaporator line included 45-gallon and 50-gallon models, and a customer tendered an order specifying that he required a 47-gallon model, he would probably be accommodated.

Mr. Snyder emphasized the need for standardization. "We should not only establish stable items," he said, "but we should develop

exhibit 2 **BLAW-KNOX COMPANY**
Divisions and subsidiary companies and partial list of products in 1951

Blaw-Knox Company
Blaw-Knox Division
(Blawnox, Pa.)
Concrete finishing machines
Concrete paving spreaders
Clamshell buckets
Truck mixers
Concrete buckets
Subgraders
Steel bins
Concrete-mixing plants
Open steel flooring
Transmission towers
Radio and television towers
Gas cleaners
Steel forms for concrete
construction
Chemical and process equipment
Water-cooled furnace equipment
for high-temperature furnaces
Buflovak Equipment Division
(Buffalo, N.Y.)
Vacuum rotary dryers
Double-drum dryers
Evaporators
Pilot-plant equipment
Gray iron castings
Miscellaneous equipment for the
food processing and chemical
industries
Lewis Foundry and Machine
Division (Groveton, Pa.)

Rolling mills and auxiliary machinery for rolling ferrous and nonferrous metals
Rolls for steel and nonferrous rolling mills
National Alloy Steel Division
(Blawnox, Pa.)
Alloy steel castings for highest resistance to extreme temperatures, abrasion and corrosion
Pittsburgh Rolls Division
(Pittsburgh, Pa.)
Rolls for steel and nonferrous rolling mills
Union Steel Castings Division
(Pittsburgh, Pa.)
Heavy alloy steel castings for general industrial use
Blaw-Knox Construction Co.
Power Piping Division
(Pittsburgh, Pa.)
Prefabricated piping systems for high pressures and temperatures
Blaw-Knox Sprinkler Division
(Pittsburgh, Pa.)
Automatic sprinkler systems, fog nozzles, water curtains and deluge systems for fire protection
Chemical Plants Division
(Pittsburgh, Pa.)

exhibit **2** (continued)

Complete plants for the chemical and process industries

The Foote Company, Inc.
(Nunda, N.Y.)
Black top road pavers
Concrete road pavers

Buflovak Midwest Co.
Buflovak Midwest Co. Division
(Mora, Minn.)
Specialized equipment for the

dairy industry including dry milk elevators and flakers, pulverizers, dryers, evaporators, hotwells, etc.

Foreign Affiliates
Blaw-Knox Limited
(London, England)
Compagnie Française Blaw-Knox
(Paris, France)

standard sizes, standard designs, standard construction, standard sequences of repetitive production, and even standard costs. We should also develop standardization of parts and components, so that small inventories will serve wide categories of products on a company-wide basis."

In keeping with this aim, a group called the Fabricated Products Operations was organized. Any product which required burning or riveting, cutting or welding, or the fitting or assembling of components into finished products was considered a fabricated product. Fabricated products production had previously been carried on in six unrelated divisions, each of which produced several lines of fabricated products. One division, the Blaw-Knox Division, produced some 15 major product lines, most of them unrelated. The objective of the new department was to coordinate fabricated products operations and screen them for profitability. A production coordinator scheduled all orders and analyzed every product for its prospective profit. As a result, a number of lines were integrated, some lines were dropped, and emphasis was placed on those lines which were considered to have growth or profit potential.

The management of Blaw-Knox looked upon the over-all product mix which it had accumulated over the years as diversified strength against recessions. Management was aware that most of its products were capital goods and especially sensitive to fluctuation in the general economy, but it pointed out that short recessions would not affect business until one to three years later, except in new orders taken and backlog figures. Management felt that over the long run the completed-contract basis of accounting tended to level out cyclical fluctuations.

In the latter part of 1955 Mr. Snyder arranged to buy Continental Foundry and Machine Company, a large rival steel mill equipment producer with a more complete line of rolling mill machinery and facilities. It was a major acquisition, doubling the company's foundry production, which already represented the largest single segment of its sales.

In earlier years sales to steel makers had represented half of Blaw-Knox's volume, but experience with the cyclical nature of the steel business during the depression years had persuaded the Blaw-Knox management to lessen their dependence on steel and expand in other directions. In 1951 the Foundry and Mill Division contributed only 36% of B-K sales, and by 1955 the percentage was down to 25%. By that date, however, Mr. Snyder's management had come to look upon the steel industry as having growth possibilities, and it was this thinking that resulted in the purchase of Continental in November, 1955.

Ten years previously, in 1945, Mr. Snyder had been president of Continental for one year and consequently was well acquainted with the company's situation. Blaw-Knox foundry plants had been concentrated in the Pittsburgh area, and in Continental's huge East Chicago Works Mr. Snyder saw an opportunity for a strategic advance into the growing midwestern market. Continental also had the facilities to make a full range of rolling mill equipment, including the larger sizes. "During the war Blaw-Knox built a big mill for Kaiser," Mr. Snyder recalled, "but the castings were too big for our shops and we had to subcontract them." Continental also had ample facilities for making the largest size castings, which Blaw-Knox could not produce. "Now we can spread our production, and manufacture equipment at the plant nearest the customer," said Mr. Snyder, "and eventually there are certain to be economies through plant consolidations."

Blaw-Knox emerged from the Continental acquisition as the nation's second largest supplier of mill equipment. In 1956 the Blaw-Knox share represented one-third of the market available to the three largest producers and Mr. Snyder expected B-K's share to increase. Early in 1959 Mr. Snyder made the arrangements for Blaw-Knox to purchase the assets of the Aetna-Standard Engineering Company, which manufactured seamless and buttweld pipe mills, cold drawing equipment, and related auxiliaries for sheet, tinplate, and other flat mill products supplemental to Blaw-Knox rolling mill machinery and other lines.

Nearly $12 million was spent for this acquisition to acquire annual sales of approximately $20 million.

In 1960 total sales of all Blaw-Knox products reached $193 million, an all-time high, and of this amount nearly one-third came from the Continental and Aetna operations.

Mr. Snyder did not think that the steel industry's cyclical nature would pose a problem for Blaw-Knox for some years to come. "We are witnessing the most creative era of steel's development and growth," he said. "There is every reason to believe that for the next several years steel will continue to be one of the economy's fastest growing segments. The emphasis so far is on additional ingot tonnage. But eventually the industry is going to need new blooming and slabbing mill facilities, together with additional plate and structural mills to meet the increasing demand for finished products. Beyond that, in the coming years, there should be capacity for these steel products in new regions."

MARKETING AND SALES

It was intended in the reorganization that Mr. Rodgers, the new general sales manager, would establish broad general sales policies that would apply throughout the company. He was to assist the division sales managers in their appraisal of markets and in interpreting the performance of certain segments of their markets. This was to be accomplished from the feedback information he received from large accounts of Blaw-Knox and from other industry sources. From this information he was to advise and assist the divisions in establishing new areas for sales and to aid the divisions in the selection of sales personnel and in the selection of distributors and agents. Although it was intended that Mr. Rodgers would act mainly in an advisory capacity as a staff executive, the function proved to be flexible and at times Mr. Rodgers participated actively in helping the divisions obtain new customers.

During the postwar period a sizable portion of the company's volume each year had been comprised of government work. In 1954 defense work contributed 58% of net income. In 1955 less than 20% of net income derived from that source and a strong effort was made to further decrease defense work. By 1957 it contributed only about 10% to net income. Management was of the opinion that long-term defense contracts were not likely to be switched abruptly to other companies and therefore would become a stabilizing influence.

In the summer of 1959 the company entered into fixed price contracts with the U.S. Government covering construction of Atlas missile launching complexes and the manufacture of related equipment. Due to changes in specifications and mistakes in the original bids on the construction contracts, actual costs greatly exceeded anticipated costs. The total missile contract amounted to $31.9 million, with total direct costs amounting to $40.5 million, or nearly $8.6 million greater than contract receipts. Late in 1959 the company initiated and obtained some relief action with the Government. Other relief action was not obtained until 1961 when the Government agreed to an adjustment of nearly $7.9 million. The company adjusted its annual profit and loss statements by charging excess costs of $4.5 million in 1959, $4.1 million in 1960, and credits of $7.9 million in 1961, causing corresponding adjustments in the profit picture for each year.

Early in Mr. Snyder's administration he established annual company-wide sales conferences. "I am not surprised," said Mr. Snyder, addressing a sales conference, "that some of you have admitted that you learned about some of our products for the first time at these meetings. Many of our customers, too, identify us with just one line of goods. Very few people associate the name Blaw-Knox with all of the activities in which we are engaged. I guess we have to live with this matter of being unable to achieve an over-all product identity in people's minds. But there is a way of helping it. Know your company and its products. Know the big picture—and serve the *total* opportunity."

Salesmen were urged, regardless of division affiliation and primary responsibility, to interest themselves in uncovering sales leads for all products. They were urged to tip each other off to new sales possibilities and where such cooperative effort resulted in new business, they were assured that credit would be given to "the beagle who nosed it out."

The familiar Blaw-Knox diamond set against a rectangular background was adopted under Mr. Snyder as the official company emblem to provide a distinctive designation for the company and its products. On those products of acquired concerns which still used their original names, emphasis was gradually shifted to the Blaw-Knox name, and it was intended that eventually all products would bear the Blaw-Knox name alone.

It was Mr. Snyder's intention to continue defense work on a reduced scale and to keep the company in a position to operate on a much larger defense basis in the event of a national emergency. "We have no intention," said Mr. Snyder, "of becoming another General Dynamics." In 1961 less than 15% was government work.

The 1961 annual report indicated that income from foreign sales in 1961 amounted to $219,000 as contrasted to $275,000 the previous year. In commenting on the decline in foreign income, Mr. Snyder explained that the decrease was due principally to a reduction in the dividends received from Blaw-Knox Limited. In his letter to the stockholders in April, 1962, Mr. Snyder called attention to the problem of overseas operations and the probable growing importance of such operations. He stated:

> The rapid growth and increasing potency of overseas trading blocks, the most noted being the European Common Market, dictates continuing reappraisal and realignment of your company's foreign operations and marketing activities. Overseas business for Blaw-Knox has increased steadily with volume of export sales ranking second only to those of our largest domestic market area, namely the iron and steel industry. Maintaining this position in markets abroad, under the developing competitive circumstances, will probably require expansion in manufacturing arrangements as well as in marketing procedures.

Foreign subsidiaries and associates of Blaw-Knox included Blaw-Knox Chemical Engineering Company, Limited, London, England; Blaw-Knox Limited, London, England; Copes Regulators Limited, London, England; Compagnie Française Blaw-Knox, Paris, France; and Blawknox Japan Company Limited, Tokyo, Japan.

RESEARCH AND DEVELOPMENT

In 1954 Mr. Snyder engaged Arthur D. Little Company, industrial research consultants, to make a comprehensive survey of the research effort of Blaw-Knox. As a result of this survey Dr. Jurgensen was appointed staff vice president of research and development to build up and coordinate research programs in the divisions.

Dr. Jurgensen immediately established a central research and development group. He explained to the division managers that the function of this group was to impart an over-all understanding of the research activities to the operating units, emphasizing that the talents, abilities, and knowledge in one group were to be made available to all other groups so that units might mutually reinforce each other.

In reviewing the tradition of spontaneous initiative and imagination that had given Blaw-Knox an impressive record of invention, Dr. Jurgensen said:

> Industrial research is no longer a case where one fertile mind sits, thinks, and works in some obscure garret. It's a team effort—it's the combined, incessant pounding of many minds: the director of research; the research engineers; the technical experts in various fields; the designers and engineering department; the sales manager and his organization; the marketing and sales promotion specialists; the industrial engineers; the manufacturing people; the finance organization.

A central task force was organized to review projects and impart an over-all knowledge of research to the operating divisions. The group consisted of Dr. Jurgensen, a metallurgist, a mechanical engineer, and a chemical engineer. Projects reviewed by the committee included a pilot plant for gravel benefication; the design and construction of antennae structures for radio telescopes for astronomical and astral-physical exploration; an aluminum foil mill which would yield a thinner sheet in a width 50% greater than ever before accomplished at double the previous maximum speed; a basic research project on "temper brittleness" in metals; a pilot plant for disposing of waste pickle liquor; and a new technique for computing pipe stresses by electronic computer.

PRODUCTION AND PLANTS

"One of my most trying problems," said Mr. Snyder, "was to dilute the historical concept of full autonomy at the divisional level." This, he found, was specially true of plants whose managements had long been accustomed to thinking in terms of their own operations. Mr. Snyder was convinced that maximum efficiency in production could be achieved only by coordination of the production operations in all plants through a staff executive in charge of all production. Expecting to meet vigorous opposition from plant managers whose independence would be curbed, Mr. Snyder sought a man of strong convictions for the office. On January 1, 1956, George Kopetz was elected to the newly created post of vice president of production. Kopetz, who had been vice president in charge of the chemical plants division, had not had extensive manufacturing experience but Mr. Snyder thought that he had shown strong managerial judgment.

For the foundry and mill machinery group, a central planning department was established in the headquarters office in Pittsburgh. This department allocated jobs to plants, worked out the backlog of orders according to machine loads and plant capacities, and also allocated the work geographically. Over-all plant loads were assigned to plants from Pittsburgh, but particular details, such as machine assignments and scheduling, were left to the plant management. In other divisions this was done informally.

Purchases of components, supplies, and small quantities of steel, which had previously been made independently by each plant, were consolidated in the Pittsburgh office under the vice president of purchasing. Purchases of basic raw materials and large quantities of steel had always been made centrally. Inventories were also controlled. The over-all aim was to keep inventories at one-sixth of the sales volume of each line.

Kopetz was convinced that proper planning and scheduling were the most effective means of saving money and maintaining a stable work force. He believed that a good standard cost system was the only effective way to show up variances in such factors of production as inefficient machinery, defective materials, and bottlenecks. "My job, in a nutshell," said Mr. Kopetz, "is to see to it that the work gets done on time, and on budget."

The foundry and mill machinery plant managers generally went along with the new system without objection. They found that the central scheduling made for flexibility. By proper scheduling a large rush order could now be worked on simultaneously by several plants, making it possible to meet the customer's requirements. It made it possible also to take the large contracts which no single division previously could have accepted. Under the new system, however, these plant managers knew less about the orders they were producing. They knew the estimated costs they were expected to meet, but selling prices were deliberately withheld from the plants.

New technical developments turned up by one plant were thoroughly worked out and tested by that plant and then passed along to all other plants. The foundry plant managers and the fabricated products managers had meetings once a month to exchange technical information.

In 1955 Blaw-Knox invested $3.5 million in the construction of a new plant at Mattoon, Illinois, to consolidate all of the company's production of road-building equipment. This was the company's first new construction since Blaw-Knox had built its original facilities at Blawnox, Pennsylvania, in 1919. The remainder of its plants were those it had acquired from merged concerns.

When Blaw-Knox bought the All-Purpose Spreader Company of Elyria, Ohio, in 1954, it was already producing similar equipment at Nunda, New York, in the Foote Construction Division, and at Blawnox in the Blaw-Knox Equipment Division. In the new plant at Mattoon all production of road-building machinery was combined under one roof and the organizations of the three operations were combined in a newly-formed Construction Equipment Division.

INDUSTRIAL RELATIONS

Prior to 1951 each division of the company handled its own labor relations and each plant made its own labor settlements, with the result that the unions played one division against another, and also played Blaw-Knox against some of its steel customers which also contracted with the same unions. The latter situation was not only a source of embarrassment but at times lost customer good will.

When Mr. Howard Winterson was brought into the company as vice president of industrial relations in 1952, Mr. Snyder charged him with setting up a department which would operate effectively as a staff function. Under Mr. Winterson's direction a centralized industrial relations department was established which handled all union contract negotiations, including the authorization of all arbitration settlements. In addition, the department introduced a company-wide wage and salary administration plan in which all jobs were evaluated and the positions of all current personnel were systematically reviewed and realigned. A strict policy of promotion from within was inaugurated. Division managers were no longer free to hire new key management personnel or to make promotions. The addition of personnel, transfers, and promotions within the management group were screened by the office of Mr. Winterson, and division managers were expected to follow his recommendations unless they had serious objections. Mr.

Winterson was pleased with the results of the new promotion policy. "During one year," he said, "out of 214 promotions in the management group, 194 were from within the company. This is approximately nine out of ten."

FINANCE

When Mr. Langreth was appointed vice president of finance in 1952, working capital shortage was a critical problem. Mr. Langreth instituted a methodical program of financial controls aimed at increasing cash balances and reducing bank loans, inventories, and accounts payable.

All bills, which previously had been paid independently by divisions, were now paid by the central finance office in Pittsburgh. Accounts receivable were also centralized and supervised from the office of the treasurer. Commitments for all funds, including capital expenditures, were made subject to review and approval of the treasurer.

There was a tradition in the company of growth from retained earnings, rather than from the sale of capital stock, and Mr. Langreth intended to abide by the tradition. The company's stock had been selling at high prices and Mr. Langreth did not wish to generate a group of unhappy stockholders by selling them stock at the current high prices. To retain funds in the business, stock dividends were declared in all years from 1953 to 1961, except 1955.

In an effort to acquire substantial funds to carry out Mr. Snyder's planned capital expansion program to modernize the company's plants, and to take advantage of favorable conditions in the lending market, Mr. Langreth arranged to obtain a 3.5%, $15 million loan with a maturity date of 1975. Under the loan agreement $10 million was borrowed at the end of 1954, and the balance was required to be borrowed in 1955. Temporarily the borrowed funds were invested in U.S. Government securities. In 1954, when the loan agreement was executed, management believed that the funds acquired would be adequate to carry to completion all expansion plans then contemplated. One year later, in an attempt to further improve working capital and to accommodate new expansion plans, new lines of credit totaling $20 million were arranged with the Mellon Trust Company —$10 million for financing defense business and $10 million for commercial requirements. By the end of the year more than $7 million was borrowed for defense work. Despite sizable acquisitions, through the period 1955–1962 funds were acquired from retained earnings. Long-term debt in this period decreased from $21 million to $15.4 million. (See Exhibit 3.)

ACCOUNTING AND CONTROL

In April of 1957 Mr. J. Sterling Davis came to Blaw-Knox at the invitation of Mr. Snyder to fill the position of controller which had been vacant since the former controller had retired in mid-1955. For 30 years Mr. Davis had been an accounting and financial executive in utilities and in industry. He came to Blaw-Knox with the understanding that he was to revamp and unify the accounting procedures of the entire company.

"My primary job," said Mr. Davis, "is to collect data and report the facts of the operations to management in such form that management can make proper decisions. These facts must be reported quickly and must include past, present, and future operations. Decisions can be good only if they are based on accurate facts, and the accounting must be geared to collect those facts. Management cannot produce better decisions than the quality of the information it receives."

One of the first moves made by Mr. Davis was to establish what he called "true responsibility accounting," whereby results, whether good or bad, might be assessed against the responsible individual. "Whenever a profit went sour," said Mr. Davis, "we got two answers: the sales department claimed the manufacturing costs were too high, and the production department said that the sales department gave the material away." Under the previous accounting system, management could not be sure who was right.

Mr. Davis proceeded to install a standard cost system directed toward enabling management to measure individual responsibility. Manufacturing operations were judged on the extent of variance from standard cost and sales efforts were judged on the amount of profit above standard cost. The new system started in 1957 was still in the process of adjustment and correction in 1961.

Mr. Davis also established a system of budgetary controls. Previously sales forecasts had been based upon past performance. The emphasis was now shifted to sales potential. In 1956, before Mr. Davis was connected with the company, Blaw-Knox elected to adopt the last-in, first-out method of valuation of prime material inventories so that current costs would be matched against current revenues.

Accounting records were, as far as practical, reduced to standard forms. Invoicing had previously been done by each division independently, some of them using their divisional name rather than the name of the company. A standard invoice form featuring the name Blaw-Knox was now designed for use throughout the company. Company-wide policies were established governing the granting of credit, the collection of receivables and the payment of accounts payable. Accounts receivable and accounts payable were adapted to machine accounting methods so that data might be sorted and summarized to produce more detailed statistics.

MANAGEMENT CHANGES

In a message to management personnel on May 28, 1959, Mr. Snyder outlined his plans for strengthening the company organization through further integration of the company's operating units and through the establishment of group management and the realignment of top management positions of these groups. Effective June 1, 1959, all operating units were consolidated into two groups—the Foundry and Mill Machinery Group, and the Fabricating, Engineering and Construction Group—with the newly acquired Aetna-Standard Engineering Company listed as a Division and operating as a third group. Mr. A. E. Murton was appointed vice president and general manager of the Foundry and Mill Group; Mr. Kopetz, vice president and general manager of the Fabricated, Engineering and Construction Group, and Mr. Coffey, vice president and general manager of the Aetna-Standard Division.

On September 28, 1959, Dr. Jurgensen, who had headed the company's research and development department for three years, was named vice president and general manager of the Construction Equipment Division headquartered in Mattoon, Illinois. With this change, responsibility for research and development was transferred to the individual operating units. (See Exhibit 4.)

In a further effort to streamline the organization Mr. Snyder, on December 27, 1960, appointed Mr. Winterson to a newly established position of vice president-administration, with general supervision of the executive staff accounting, administrative and productive services, industrial relations and personnel, law, marketing, purchasing, and traffic departments.

In mid-July, 1961, when Mr. Kopetz, who had been vice president and general manager of the Fabricated Products and the Engineering and Construction Services Group, resigned, the direction of these two groups was added to Mr. Winterson's responsibilities.

Early in 1962 Mr. George Langreth died suddenly and the position of treasurer and vice president of finance remained vacant for more than six months. In discussing a replacement Mr. Tomer, assistant to the president, remarked, "Mr. Snyder believes in promoting from within where competent people are available. However the company does not have enough men trained to take over." Consequently, the company hired Mr. Charles Strange to fill the position.

In March, 1962, Mr. Snyder established a new central staff department—the marketing services department—and hired Mr. Frank Farnum, formerly of the Raytheon Company of Lexington, Massachusetts, as director. (See Organization Chart, Exhibit 4.) Duties of the newly established department included the conducting of studies to determine the most profitable markets for the company's products, the need for redesign of products and product lines to meet customer requirements. These functions were formerly performed by the staff sales department headed by Mr. Rodgers.

In discussing these changes Mr. Tomer remarked that the company had a good management training program in operation and that 26 college graduates were currently undergoing training. He also emphasized that most supervisory and management positions had been filled by qualified personnel promoted from within the company.

In summing up the operations, Mr. Tomer went on to say that, "As the company matures under the leadership of Mr. Snyder the managers become more adept at carrying out their functions according to Mr. Snyder's wishes. Thus, all our managers today have much more of the Blaw-Knox philosophy as espoused by Mr. Snyder than they had ten years ago."

exhibit 3 BLAW-KNOX COMPANY

Comparative statistics (in thousands of dollars, except share figures)

Operations:	1961	%	1960	%	1959	%	1958	%	1957	%
Net sales of products and services	$174,518	100.0	$192,810	100.0	$161,295	100.0	$167,709	100.0	$182,663	100.0
Costs and operating expenses	170,774	97.8	180,558	93.5	144,881	89.5	152,155	90.7	167,780	91.9
Operating income	$ 3,744	2.2	$ 12,252	6.5	$ 16,414	10.2	$ 15,554	9.3	$ 14,883	8.1
Missile contracts—excess costs (recoveries)	(7,892)	(4.5)	4,101	2.6	4,500	2.8	—	—	—	—
Non-operating income	1,741	1.0	1,580	.8	1,424	.8	1,248	0.6	1,279	0.7
Interest expense	775	.04	880	.4	742	.4	820	0.4	1,055	0.6
Income before taxes	$ 12,602	7.2	$ 8,851	4.6	$ 12,596	7.8	$ 15,982	9.5	$ 15,107	8.2
Provision for taxes on income and renegotiation	7,150	4.1	4,604	2.4	6,765	4.2	9,050	5.4	8,100	4.4
Net earnings	$ 5,452	3.1	$ 4,247	2.2	$ 5,831	3.6	$ 6,932	4.1	$ 7,907*	4.3
Depreciation and amortization included in costs	3,498	2.0	3,623	1.9	3,156	1.9	2,510	1.5	2,520	1.4
Repairs and maintenance included in costs	4,171	2.4	4,421	2.3	4,188	2.6	3,618	2.1	4,610	2.5

exhibit 3 (continued)

Financial position:

Cash and equivalent	$ 20,480	$ 12,537	$ 9,662	$ 25,278	$ 12,108
Total current assets	72,470	75,958	63,461	68,799	74,082
Total current liabilities	29,756	36,057	24,731	21,766	32,037
Net current assets (working capital)	42,714	39,901	38,730	47,033	42,045
Total assets	112,810	117,313	105,399	99,725	106,047
Long-term debt	15,450	16,625	17,800	18,725	19,650
Capital stock	19,768	19,211	18,671	18,056	17,546
Other capital	10,885	9,658	8,785	6,777	5,608
Retained earnings	36,951	35,762	35,412	34,401	31,206
Total capitalization	83,054	81,256	80,668	77,959	74,010

Property, plant and equipment:

Before depreciation and amortization	$ 66,630	$ 65,084	$ 63,709	$ 50,626	$ 49,812
After depreciation and amortization	38,427	39,391	40,586	29,888	30,926
Expenditures for property, plant and equipment	2,749	2,575	14,013	1,563	1,755

Dividends:

Amount paid in cash	$ 2,696	$ 2,620	$ 2,543	$ 2,196	$ 2,021
Per share outstanding at time of declaration	1.40	1.40	1.40	1.25	1.20
Stock dividend—percent	2½%	2½%	2½%	2½%	4%

* Includes non-recurring credit of $900,000.

exhibit 3 (continued)

Operations:

	1956	%	1955	%	1954	%	1953	%	1952	%
Net sales of products and services	$167,009	100.0	$109,161	100.0	$101,128	100.0	$120,068	100.0	$99,941	100.0
Costs and operating expenses	151,791	90.9	103,493	94.8	92,250	91.2	104,068	86.7	88,086	88.1
Operating income	$ 15,218	9.1	$ 5,668	5.2	$ 8,878	8.8	$ 16,000	13.3	$ 11,855	11.9
Missile contracts—Excess costs (recoveries)	—	—	—	—	—	—	—	—	—	—
Non-operating income	676	0.4	635	0.6	584	0.5	523	0.4	537	0.5
Interest expense	1,028	0.6	439	0.4	28	0.0	290	0.2	460	0.5
Income before taxes	$ 14,866	8.9	5,864	5.4	$ 9,434	9.3	$ 16,233	13.5	$ 11,932	11.9
Provision for taxes on income and renegotiation	7,900	4.7	3,420	3.2	5,310	5.2	12,095	10.1	7,743	7.7
Net earnings	$ 6,966	4.2	$ 2,444	2.2	$ 4,124	4.1	$ 4,138	3.4	$ 4,189	4.2
Depreciation and amortization included in costs	2,601	1.5	1,975	1.8	1,691	1.6	1,474	1.2	1,363	1.3
Repairs and maintenance included in costs	4,730	2.8	2,198	2.0	2,100	2.1	2,705	2.7	2,631	2.7

exhibit 3 (continued)

Financial position:

Cash and equivalent	$ 12,768	$ 12,635	$ 24,471	$ 14,183	$ 9,928
Total current assets	71,323	56,046	50,126	46,120	45,615
Total current liabilities	35,754	26,282	16,077	26,123	28,613
Net current assets (working capital)	35,569	29,764	34,049	19,997	17,002
Total assets	104,571	89,872	68,105	63,986	64,032
Long-term debt	20,575	21,000	10,000	—	—
Capital stock	16,761	15,694	15,694	14,468	14,115
Other capital	4,474	2,010	2,010	784	537
Retained earnings	27,007	24,885	24,324	22,611	20,767
Total capitalization	68,817	63,589	52,028	37,863	35,419

Property, plant and equipment:

Before depreciation and amortization	$ 48,699	$ 47,715	$ 31,228	$ 29,375	$ 28,799
After depreciation and amortization	31,796	32,725	17,258	16,719	17,090
Expenditures for property, plant and equipment	3,580	17,597	2,269	1,162	1,088

Dividends:

Amount paid in cash	$ 1,891	$ 1,883	$ 1,831	$ 1,694	$ 1,764
Per share outstanding at time of declaration	1.20	1.20	1.20	1.20	1.25
Stock dividend—percent	5%	—	1½%	2½%	—

exhibit 4
BLAW-KNOX COMPANY
Organization Chart, April 2, 1962

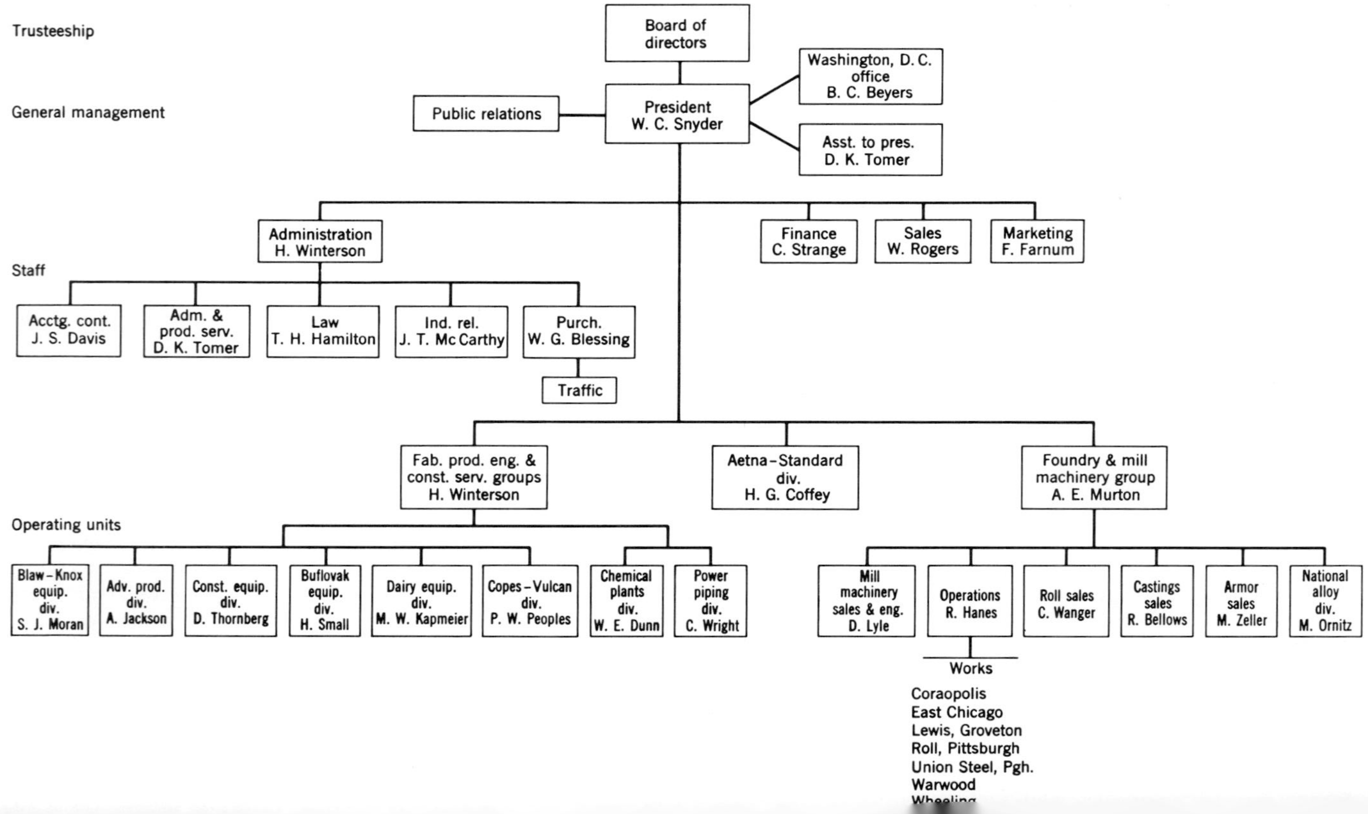

Trusteeship

Board of directors

General management

President
W. C. Snyder

Public relations

Washington, D. C. office
B. C. Beyers

Asst. to pres.
D. K. Tomer

Finance
C. Strange

Sales
W. Rogers

Marketing
F. Farnum

Staff

Administration
H. Winterson

Acctg. cont.
J. S. Davis

Adm. & prod. serv.
D. K. Tomer

Law
T. H. Hamilton

Ind. rel.
J. T. McCarthy

Purch.
W. G. Blessing

Traffic

Operating units

Fab. prod. eng. & const. serv. groups
H. Winterson

Blaw–Knox equip. div.
S. J. Moran

Adv. prod. div.
A. Jackson

Const. equip. div.
D. Thornberg

Buflovak equip. div.
H. Small

Dairy equip. div.
M. W. Kapmeier

Copes–Vulcan div.
P. W. Peoples

Chemical plants div.
W. E. Dunn

Power piping div.
C. Wright

Aetna–Standard div.
H. G. Coffey

Foundry & mill machinery group
A. E. Murton

Mill machinery sales & eng.
D. Lyle

Operations
R. Hanes

Roll sales
C. Wanger

Castings sales
R. Bellows

Armor sales
M. Zeller

National alloy div.
M. Ornitz

Works
Coraopolis
East Chicago
Lewis, Groveton
Roll, Pittsburgh
Union Steel, Pgh.
Warwood
Wheeling

630

exhibit 5   **BLAW-KNOX COMPANY**
Divisions and subsidiary companies and partial list of products in 1962

OPERATING GROUPS	MAJOR PRODUCTS BY INDUSTRY CATEGORIES
Foundry, mill machinery and metal processing equipment	*Metal processing and fabricating*
Continental	Rolling mills and accessory equipment, shears, tables, lathes, and straighteners
Lewis	Pipe and tube mills, cold drawing equipment; annealing, tinning, and galvanizing lines; sheet and strip finishing equipment
National Alloy	
Rolls	
Union	
Medart	
Aetna-Standard	Iron and steel rolls
Plant Locations	Water-cooled doors and frames, valves, charging boxes, ladles, slag pots, dolomite machines; heavy steel, armor, and high alloy castings
Blawnox, Pa.	
Coraopolis, Pa.	
East Chicago, Ind.	
Groveton, Pa.	*Highway, public works, and general construction*
Pittsburgh, Pa.—2	
Wheeling, W. Va.—2	Bituminous and concrete pavers, spreaders, finishers, subgraders, road forms, truckmixers, and aggregate concrete mixing equipment
Ellwood City, Pa.	
Warren, Ohio	
Fabricated products	
Blaw-Knox Equipment	Heavy forms for subways, tunnels, dams; clamshell buckets
Buflovak Equipment	
Copes-Vulcan	*Chemical, petroleum, and food process*
Construction Equipment	Design, procurement, and erection of plants for the chemical, food, gas, petroleum, petrochemical, nuclear, and other process industries
Dairy Equipment	
Plant Locations	
Blawnox, Pa.	
Buffalo, N. Y.	Design and fabrication of evaporators, dryers, welded pressure vessels, digesters, mixers, and milk and food processing equipment
Erie, Pa.	
Mattoon, Ill.	
Mora, Minn.	
Engineering and construction services	*Public utilities and general*
	Fabrication and erection of pressure piping and pipe hangers
Chemical Plants	
Power Piping	Metal grating, running boards, stairs, and walks
Engineering Locations	
Pittsburgh, Pa.—2	Communication and transmission towers, radio telescopes, tracking and scatter antennas
Plant Locations	
Pittsburgh, Pa.	
Jackson, Miss.	Steam boiler accessories and gas cleaners

exhibit 5 (continued)

FOREIGN INVESTMENTS

Blaw Knox Limited, London, England

Blaw Knox Chemical Engineering Company, Limited, London, England

Copes Regulators Limited, London, England

Compagnie Française Blaw-Knox, Paris, France

Blawknox Japan Company Limited, Tokyo, Japan

exhibit 6   **BLAW-KNOX COMPANY**

Statement of operation and retained earnings year ended December 31, 1961

	1961	*1960*
Revenues:		
Sales of products and services	$174,517,781	$192,809,582
Other income	1,741,188	1,579,653
	$176,258,969	$194,389,235
Costs and expenses:		
Cost of products and services	$141,954,566	$148,929,820
Selling and administrative	17,545,409	20,211,591
Repairs and maintenance	4,170,680	4,421,322
Depreciation and amortization	3,498,410	3,622,668
Retirement plans	3,605,557	3,371,549
Interest	774,779	880,039
	$171,549,401	$181,436,989
	$ 4,709,568	$ 12,952,246
Recoveries in 1961 of costs in excess of contract amounts—missile contracts Excess Costs in 1960 and 1959	(7,892,058)	4,100,828
	$ 12,601,626	$ 8,851,418
Taxes on income:		
Federal	6,708,000	4,278,000
Pennsylvania	442,000	326,000
	$ 7,150,000	$ 4,604,000
Net income for the year	$ 5,451,626	$ 4,247,418
Retained earnings at beginning of year	35,762,537	35,411,594
	$ 41,214,163	$ 39,659,012
Dividends:		
Cash—$1.40 per share	2,696,187	2,619,622
Stock—2½% each year		
1961—48,215 shares at $32.50	1,566,988	—
1960—46,857 shares at $27.25	—	1,276,853
1959—45,540 shares at $50.00	—	—
	$ 4,263,175	$ 3,896,475
Retained earnings at end of year	$ 36,950,988	$ 35,762,537

exhibit **6** (continued)
Statement of financial position December 31, 1961

	1961	*1960*
Current assets:		
Cash	$14,522,376	$12,536,858
U. S. Treasury bills	5,958,075	—
Receivables, less estimated doubtful accounts	28,715,738	36,331,879
Manufacturing inventories	20,779,191	21,970,621
Contracts in progress—costs less billings	1,541,089	4,456,855
Prepaid expenses	953,607	661,359
Total current assets	$72,470,076	$75,957,572
Current liabilities:		
Note payable to bank	$ —	$ 6,000,000
Accounts payable	11,128,620	16,443,550
Salaries, wages and other employee compensation	4,262,703	3,777,592
Federal taxes on income	4,714,268	2,093,515
Long-term debt payable within one year	1,175,000	1,175,000
Other current liabilities	8,475,061	6,567,162
Total current liabilities	$29,755,652	$36,056,819
Working capital	$42,714,424	$39,900,753
Property, plant and equipment (net)	38,427,417	39,390,936
Investment in foreign affiliates and other assets	1,912,624	1,964,742
Total assets less current liabilities	$83,054,465	$81,256,431
Long-term debt	15,450,000	16,625,000
Excess of assets over liabilities—stockholders' equity	$67,604,465	$64,631,431
Stockholders' equity:		
Capital stock—authorized 3,000,000 shares. $10 par value—issued 1,976,788 and 1,921,133 shares	$19,767,880	$19,211,330
Other capital	10,885,597	9,657,564
Retained earnings, excluding amounts transferred to other capital accounts	36,950,988	35,762,537
Total stockholders' equity	$67,604,465	$64,631,431

QUAKER OATS
IN EUROPE (A)

Speaking of the complete change that had taken place in the character of Quaker Oats' foreign business during the past forty years—most of which had been under his direction—Mr. Earle Muzzy, retired vice chairman of the Board, remarked, "There was a time when we exported payroll in the form of products manufactured here, and we collected profits. After that we exported dollars in the form of know-how, and we get our return in the form of dividends."

During the second quarter of the twentieth century the Quaker Oats Company had converted largely from selling its American-made products abroad through sales agencies to the manufacture of its products by foreign subsidiaries staffed entirely by nationals. Throughout the twenties the entire output of some of Quaker's American mills had been shipped to Europe. In 1960 the amount of American-made products it shipped abroad was insignificant. During that period foreign sales volume had risen to a point approaching $100 million a year.

THE QUAKER OATS COMPANY OF CHICAGO, ILLINOIS

The Quaker Oats Company was incorporated in 1901 to succeed the American Cereal Company, which had been composed of a number of merged cereal companies. The oldest of these had begun operation in 1832. Rolled oats was originally the company's chief product.

Prior to the merger the industry had overcapacity, causing acute competition. At that time oatmeal was sold in sacks or barrels, no miller's brand had achieved retail preference, and retailers bought for price. The Quaker management was one of the first to realize the possibilities of packaging and branding their products. This permitted aggressive advertising and merchandising, and price maintenance, functions which, from that time forward, became traditional company policies. (See Sales Promotion, page 537.)

During the decades which followed the turn of the century the company expanded its product line to include a full line of oat, corn, wheat, rice, and barley cereals. Livestock and poultry feeds, first manufactured from milling by-products, grew to be a major activity. By purchase the company acquired the Aunt Jemima label, which was originally used only on a line of pancake mixes. The use of the label was gradually expanded to include many other "convenience" foods, such as baking mixes, corn meal and grits, cooky mixes, and others. The milling of semolina flour led the company into the production of macaroni, spaghetti, and egg noodles. The prepared food line was expanded to include pie crust, cheese cake, muffin mix and corn bread mixes, chili con carne and tamales. Quaker also acquired, by purchase, Ken-L-Ration dog food and Puss 'n Boots cat food.

The company's laboratories were successful in developing furfural and tetrahydrofurfuryl alcohol from waste products such as oat hulls and corn cobs. Both chemicals were widely used in industry. From this beginning the Chemical Division added numerous other products to its line. By 1950 it was a major division of the business.

Early in its history the business had expanded to operate on a nationwide basis. In 1902 the company built a sizable mill at Peterborough, Ontario, from which it sold oat products to all of Canada and exported them to the British Empire. Exportations of finished products gradually gave way to the establishment of plants at strategic foreign locations in Europe and Latin America. This trend was especially pronounced in the 1950's when the number of Quaker plants outside of the United States grew from 7 to 21.

In 1960 the Quaker Oats Company had four major product lines: (1) food products, (2) livestock and poultry feeds, (3) dog and cat foods, and (4) chemicals. Its activities were directed from central headquarters offices in the Merchandise Mart, Chicago, Illinois. In the United States it had 27 plants and 50 country grain elevators, employing 6,300 men and women. It had 19,000 stockholders, assets in the United States carried at over $160,000,000, and a domestic sales volume approaching a third of a billion dollars. Abroad it had 21 plants in 10 countries, employing 3,600 people, and it had sales offices covering the globe. Its product line included hundreds of items. It was a factor in the oat milling industry, and several of its brand names, principally Quaker and Aunt Jemima, had achieved international recognition.

THE DEVELOPMENT OF SALES IN EUROPE

In 1899 the British operation, which had been functioning as a sales agency for about five years, was incorporated as Quaker Oats Limited, and Frederick Pleasants, the former agent, was made managing director. Concurrently, Ernest Noell, a star salesman from Quaker's Akron mill, who had been sent to Rotterdam in 1896, was working in various capacities with Mr. Voorhoeve, the Dutch manager. The Rotterdam office did business with almost every country in central and southern Europe and Noell gained extensive experience. In 1906 he was made vice president, European sales, with responsibility for all of Europe except the British Isles, which became the United Kingdom Division. Prior to World War I an office was established in Christiania, Norway, to serve Scandinavia. Later this was moved to Stockholm, where it became a Swedish stock company, Quaker Oats, A.B., directed by Mr. Gustav Runesham, a former salesman from the Hamburg, Germany, plant. This company supervised sales in Norway, Sweden, Denmark, Finland, Estonia, Latvia, Lithuania, and Poland. These territories were transferred to Copenhagen when Quaker purchased the Ota Company of Denmark in 1930. Throughout this period matters of policy were controlled from the United States, the foreign managers answering to Mr. Earle Muzzy, vice president, export, and Mr. Gaylord Whipple, manager, Foreign Department, who actively directed foreign activities. The U.S. Quaker plants sold their goods to the foreign subsidiaries, which in turn sold to Quaker dealers. The foreign subsidiaries were given a commission on their sales.

Ernest Noell, the vice president, European sales, who had moved the European headquarters office to Berlin, passed away just before the outbreak of World War II. He was succeeded by his son, James Noell, who moved the headquarters to Rotterdam, from which he was forced to flee during the German invasion in 1941. Shortly thereafter James Noell became totally disabled in an accident and there followed a period when the European business as a whole had no resident executive director.

EUROPEAN ADMINISTRATIVE COMMITTEE

The Chicago headquarters hired a Dutch citizen to replace Mr. Noell as vice president of European sales. The new executive officer proved to be domineering and uncooperative. The managers of the European plants were forced to channel all communications to Chicago through the Rotterdam office for approval by the vice president of European sales. To aid in correcting this situation and to provide more effective communications between the European plants and Chicago office, Mr. Earle Muzzy, then executive vice president of Quaker, organized the European Administrative Committee. The original committee consisted of the managers of each of the European companies with Mr. White, then managing director of Southall (London), as chairman. The committee met every sixty days in London to discuss and pass upon policy matters, personnel, and capital expenditures. The chairman reported to Mr. Whipple, then manager of Foreign Operations. Mr. Whipple, in turn, answered to Mr. Muzzy.

The vice president of European sales failed to cooperate with the EAC and was dismissed by the Chicago office. Over-all supervision of European operations was then placed under the EAC as a coordinating body. Originally limited to $10,000 in capital appropriations, the EAC's authority was increased to $40,000. It was empowered to review all matters of policy, personnel, and capital expenditure.

In 1960 the chairman of the EAC was Mr. B. C. L. Summers, former managing director of London, who had been elected to the newly created office of vice president, Europe. As such he answered to Mr. Augustin Hart, vice president, Foreign Operations. At this date the EAC consisted of Mr. Summers; Mr. Towler, general manager, Southall; and Mr. Boesen, managing director, Copenhagen. Mr. Pitkeathly, export manager, Southall, was recorder. Other managers met with the committee when their affairs were under consideration. Meetings were held every sixty days and were rotated to a different plant for each meeting. The function of the committee was to discuss any items of importance, such as capital expenditure appropriations (CEA's). It did not act as an executive committee in making formal approvals, nor did it ever vote on issues brought to it.

An example of a typical policy matter discussed by the EAC was the building of additional grain silo capacity proposed by the Danish Ota Company. A miller had asked to use some of its storage capacity on a rental basis, which proved a profitable operation for Ota. The customer then proposed to Ota that it build an addition to its elevator which would increase its capacity to 10,000 tons, the increase to be leased to the customer on a long-term basis, which would include not only storage, but grain conditioning services to be furnished by Ota. Since Quaker was a miller, not a storer of grain, this was a departure from policy and therefore the matter was reviewed with the EAC, which found it attractive and recommended to U.S.A. headquarters Executive Committee that it approve the capital expenditure appropriation involved.

Personnel matters were handled less formally. In matters of staff personnel, any new addition, any transfer, promotion or dismissal would be discussed with the committee. Likewise any change of magnitude at lower level, such as increasing a sales force by 40%, would be brought before the EAC. It was also required that any such changes be approved by Mr. Summers, not as EAC chairman, but in his capacity as vice president, Europe.

Similarly, capital expenditure appropriations were reviewed by the committee, but required executive approval. For this purpose the manager of a small plant had a relative approval power of 1; the managers of the larger plants had a power of 5; while Mr. Summers, as vice president, Europe, had a relative authority of 25. Above this amount, proposals went to Mr. Hart, who presented them to headquarters Executive Committee.

The Executive Committee, the Chicago executives, or the Board of Directors seldom injected themselves into the foreign operations, other than to elect the executives at the highest level and to pass upon major investments. The only notable incursion had been the vetoing of a proposal by the EAC to buy a plant in France, a move which the management in Chicago had disapproved because of the unsettled situation of the Common Market. "Our aim," said Mr. Summers, vice president, Europe, "is to achieve centralization of planning and policy formulation, and at the same time decentralization of operating responsibility. This is a company-wide objective. It holds true not only for the European operation, but for the whole of Quaker."

THE FOREIGN ORGANIZATION IN 1960

In 1960 the Quaker Oats Company owned twenty-one plants located in ten countries in Latin America, Canada, and Europe. (See Exhibit 9.) Mr. Augustin S. Hart, Jr., vice president, International Operations, was responsible for the direction of foreign activities. Foreign operations were decentralized into three areas:

1. Europe, under the direction of Mr. B. C. L. Summers, vice president, Europe. Mr. Summers, whose office was in London, was responsible for the business done in the United Kingdom, and for the existing companies in Denmark, Germany, Holland, and France. He also directed the development of Quaker business in the balance of Europe, as well as in Africa, the Near East, India, Australia, and New Zealand.

2. The Latin American Group was under the management of Mr. A. J. Dimino, manager, whose office was in New York. He coordinated the activities of five Latin American subsidiary companies in Mexico, Colombia, Argentina, Brazil, and Venezuela. Mr. Dimino was also responsible for export sales from the United States to more than twenty countries in the Latin American, the Pacific Far East, and Caribbean areas.

3. Canada, in which all activities were the responsibility of The Quaker Oats Company of Canada, Limited. Mr. R. C. Faryon, then chairman of the Board of the Canadian company, was also a member of the Board of the parent company. Mr. J. C. Wharry was its president and chief executive officer. The Canadian company was Quaker's oldest and largest subsidiary, operating eleven plants, producing a larger line of products than any other Quaker company, and had a sales force large enough to cover the Canadian Commonwealth. Operations were directed from a plant at Peterborough, Ontario. Also, from an office in Vancouver, British Columbia, the Canadian company shipped the products of the Saskatoon, Saskatchewan, plant to the Far East and the Orient.

Quaker's foreign sales volume for the fiscal year ended June 30, 1960, at the going rates of foreign exchange, was $85,000,000 compared to United States sales of $321,800,000. Earnings of the foreign companies were over $2,000,000 and dividends paid to the parent company were $1,064,696. Domestic earnings, after taxes, were $10,670,000.

In its plants and sales offices outside of the United States the Quaker Oats Company had over 3,600 employees. While the products it made abroad varied from country to country, rolled oats were sold in all markets, and some of the foreign companies marketed products not sold in America, such as Sugar Puffs, Oat Krunchies, Frescavena, Chocavena, and Baby Quaker.

THE FOREIGN DEPARTMENT IN THE CHICAGO HEADQUARTERS

The Foreign Department in Chicago acted as liaison between the foreign operations and the headquarters office in Chicago. "My job," said Mr. Robert McGorrin, coordinator, International Operations, "is to keep in communication with each of our foreign subsidiaries so that they will be sure to know, in a general way, what headquarters here is thinking and doing. We also collect and screen information from abroad, and pass it along to any people in this office who might be interested."

Mr. McGorrin was a part of the staff of Mr. Augustin Hart, Jr., vice president, International Operations. As such, Mr. McGorrin acted in an advisory and communications capacity. Mr. Hart had direct line authority, did the long-range planning of the entire foreign operation in production, sales, finance, and the expansion of facilities. Mr. Hart answered to the president, and to the executive committee, for foreign operations.

At the Chicago headquarters office the "president's staff"—of which Mr. McGorrin was a member—met once a month. At these meetings, at which the president presided, the secretary of the company reported all items of major importance to the entire group. Each member of the staff also reported any development of interest within his sphere. Mr. McGorrin watched for any item that was of interest to the foreign subsidiaries. Included in the American "know-how" sent abroad was information on technical research, market research, market research techniques, production processes, merchandising methods, product development, promotions, innovations in advertising, and general information which might be useful to the foreign companies.

Although the scope of the information sent abroad was very broad, a great deal of it had to do with product research and development. The Foreign Department in Chicago received reports bi-monthly from the American Research and Development groups. These reports were coordinated and from them it transmitted a comprehensive report to the foreign groups. The Foreign Department also received bi-monthly information of product development from the foreign operations which it reviewed and passed along to the American personnel.

In previous years, when Mr. Earle Muzzy had been vice president, export, he actively directed foreign operations from his office in Chicago. He was the final authority on foreign matters, and made the operating decisions on any matters of relative importance. At that time the foreign department, headed by Mr. Gaylord Whipple, received voluminous reports from abroad, which were analyzed and passed up the line. Mr. Muzzy himself spent hours reading letters and reports.

In November of 1959 there was a major reorganization of the Foreign Department, brought about by a general decentralization program which had been in progress throughout the company during the post World War II period. By this time the authority and the initiative for foreign operations had already been shifted to the managing directors of the foreign subsidiaries. As a result fewer reports from abroad came to the Foreign Department. Formerly the Foreign Department had received monthly sales reports, estimated monthly profit and loss figures, cost statements, inventory position reports, and reports on product development and any sales promotions in progress. The transmission of information on product research and development was continued but the amount of detail the reports contained was reduced sharply. Chicago formerly received copies of all orders, a practice now dispensed with entirely. Sales reports, from which the Chicago headquarters might previously have criticized any monthly recession, were now made only quarterly, and rather than questioning any short-term fluctuation, the Chicago office looked only at long-term trends. Many of the other reports from abroad were transmitted by the Foreign Department, without analysis, directly to the Chicago departmental counterpart. Thus cost reports and inventory reports were turned over directly to the Chicago controller's office. Most of the reports which no longer came to the Foreign Department were now being sent to Mr. Summers in London who passed the important matters on to Mr. Hart. The Foreign Department worked with staff departments on the preparation of special reports for foreign subsidiaries. It was intended that eventually these reports would go directly from the staff department concerned to the corresponding department of the foreign subsidiaries.

COMMUNICATIONS

Before World War II there had been little direct personal contact between Chicago executives and the European managers. Only a few American executives had visited Copenhagen between 1930 and 1949. The German plant was incommunicado during World War II and for over a year after its close. Mr. Stuart, the chairman, and Mr. Muzzy visited Germany in 1947. After this date no Quaker executive visited the Grevenbroich plant for over ten years. The German and Dutch managers had never been to the United States. This was during a period when ocean passage was by ship, a time-consuming and expensive means of travel. Cablegrams were expensive and so were transoceanic phone calls, which took days to arrange and were limited to matters of utmost urgency. During this era the foreign managers often felt that their propositions to Chicago headquarters received inadequate attention. The Chicago executives, in turn, felt inadequately informed, in spite of a sizable exchange of correspondence.

In the late 1950s the pattern of communications changed significantly. Mr. Hart visited each company twice a year and spent a good deal of time with each management group. Every year several other senior Chicago officials made random visits to Europe. Mr. Summers came to Chicago three or four times a year, and also visited American plants, and he passed along the information he gathered to the other European managers at the frequent meetings of the European Administrative Committee. Lower level European executives also visited the United States. Thus the English production manager might spend two weeks with the Cedar Rapids plant superintendent studying the flow of production. On his return to Europe he would then transmit his findings to the other European production managers at the regular meetings of the production committee. Other means of communication also came to be used much more. Night cablegrams became inexpensive, and a daytime phone call which had formerly cost hundreds of dollars now cost only $4 a minute and could be arranged in a few hours. The European managers now felt well informed on all of the European situation, as well as on developments in the United States.

ADVERTISING AND SALES PROMOTION

In the early days of Quaker, oatmeal was a homogeneous product, the milling process was elementary and standardized, and there were few refinements. It was sold in sacks or barrels to grocers who measured it out. No attempt was made to identify its source. Competition was on the basis of price, which eventually forced prices down to unprofitable levels.

Soon after the Quaker Oats Company was formed the management introduced family-sized packages labeled with the company's brand. Branding the product made it worth while to refine the ingredients. The grain was more strictly graded at purchase and tested for moisture, weight of groat, nutritional content (fat, protein, carbohydrate, vitamins, and fiber), for flavors and off-color. A process of steel cutting of the groats was developed and the streams of cut groats were sorted for size to produce various thicknesses of rolled flakes (Quick Quaker, Regular). Packaging was in cardboard packages, foil bags or tin cans to suit the end destination and to keep the oatmeal fresh and vermin- and insect-free. With labeled packages Quaker adopted a policy of fixed retail prices.

Branding and product refinement were followed by aggressive promotion through advertising and merchandising. The picture of the benign Quaker and cheerful Aunt Jemima gradually appeared on a multitude of showcards, posters, window displays, and in myriad advertisements in newspapers and magazines. Introductory bonuses were offered to grocers; premium merchandise, such as china and silver, was offered to housewives; tops and games for children were inserted in packages. There were contests for consumers and sales contests for salesmen. In 1960 the company was spending several million dollars a year for advertising and sales promotion. By that time, in America, the word oatmeal had become synonymous with Quaker.

"The oatmeal business," said Mr. Whipple, "is not a 'flashy' business. It takes a lot of promoting to increase oatmeal sales. Even with hard-hitting sales drive a 2% gain a year is quite respectable. It takes a long time and a lot of money in promotions to open a new territory. That is why we have gone to great lengths to hang on to these territories in Europe where our name has become established. We mean to capitalize on the advertising and promotion money we have spent."

exhibit 1   **QUAKER OATS LIMITED**
Southall, Middlesex and London, England

Corporate form:
    A limited-liability corporation
Ownership:
    100% voting power held by Quaker Oats Company, Chicago
Employees:
    About 1,200
Executives:
    B. C. L. Summers, vice president, Europe, manager director
    R. M. Towler, director and general manager
    R. D. Kennedy, financial director
    J. E. Pope, secretary
    A. R. Wilks, comptroller
    G. F. Kendall, production manager
    W. F. Cooper, marketing manager, Cereals
    N. H. Beeston, marketing manager, Feed and Pet Foods
Plants and properties:
    Manufacturing, storage and office facilities.
    The largest cereal plant in the British Isles.
    Road, rail and canal facilities. Grain silo 2,000 ton capacity.
Products manufactured:
    Oat products   Livestock feeds
    Rice products   Pet foods
    Cold cereals   Paste goods
    The Southall plant produces the full Quaker line of products with the
    exception of chemicals.
Principal products sold:
    The full Quaker line. This includes cake and pancake mixes im-
    ported from the United States.
Brand names:
    Quaker, Sugar Puffs, Oat Krunchies, Ful-O-Pep, Ken-L-Ration
Marketing area:
    The British Isles   India
    Africa   Pakistan
    The Near East   Burma
    Australia   Ceylon
    New Zealand   The Mediterranean countries
Sales force:
    200 travelers; a cereal marketing manager; a feed marketing manager;
    sales and advertising managers in each division.

exhibit 2   AKTIESELSKABET "OTA" DE FORENEDE HAVRE—OG—RISMOLLER
Copenhagen, Denmark

Corporate form:
  A limited-liability corporation
Ownership:
  99.91% voting power held by the Quaker Oats Company, Chicago
Employees:
  About 275
Executives:
  Gerhard Boesen, manager director
  Per Lorenzen, general manager
  Alfred Christensen, superintendent
  Sven Boeck, prokurist
Plants and Properties:
  Head office in Copenhagen.
  Manufacturing and storage facilities at Nakskov, Lolland.
  Six warehouses for finished products covering Denmark.
Products manufactured:
  Oat products
  Rice products
  Sugar Puffs
Principal products sold:
  All Quaker cereals.
  Aunt Jemima cake mixes (from United States).
Sales force:
  14 salesmen; 2 supervisors
Brand names:
  Dana—used on corn flakes. (Derived from Danamark.)
  Sol Gryn—used on rolled oats. (Means sun grain.)
  Ota Gryn—used on rolled oats. (Ota is a word derived from oats.)
  Pama Rismel—used on rice products.
  Guld Korn—used on Sugar Puffs.
  Kala Puffer—used on Sugar Puffs in Sweden.
  Mexi—used on corn flakes in packages.
  Quaker—used on corn flakes in bags.
  Lif—used on Oat Krunchies in Denmark.
  Frass Kudder—used on Oat Krunchies in Sweden.

exhibit 3   QUAKER OATS GRAANPRODUCTEN, N.V.
Rotterdam, The Netherlands

Corporate form:
   A limited-liability corporation
Ownership:
   99.56% voting power held by Quaker Oats Company, Chicago
Employees:
   About 130
Executives:
   T. Zaaijer, manager
   M. H. L. Van Gemert, mill superintendent
   A. J. Vivjerberg, chief accountant
Plants and properties:
   Plant and office at Rotterdam. These facilities are directly on Rotter-
   dam harbor. Quaker has a small 300 ton silo, which stands adjacent to
   the largest grain elevator in Europe.
Products manufactured:
   Rolled oats (including oats in tins for export)
   Paste goods
   Vigour (a chocolate flavored oat drink)
Principal products sold:

Oat products	Puffed Wheat (from London)
Paste goods	Sugar Puffs (from London)
Vigour	Cake mixes and pet foods (from
Corn Flakes (from Copenhagen)	U. S. on a very small scale)

Brand names:
   H-O (from Hecker Oats, predecessor company)
   Vigour
   Quaker
Marketing area:
   The Benelux countries
Sales force:
   15 salesmen

exhibit 4   **QUAKER NAHRMITTEL GESELLSCHRAFT, M.B.H.**
Grevenbroich, Germany

Corporate form:
  A limited-liability corporation
Ownership:
  100% owned by the Quaker Oats Company, Chicago
Employees:
  About 80
Executives:
  F. Scherz, manager
  W. Beyerling, marketing manager
Plants and properties:
  Manufacturing, storage and office facilities. Has fully pneumatic oat
  milling equipment installed new in 1953. Said to be the most modern
  oat milling plant in Europe. Adjacent to highway and railway siding.
  Grain silo has a capacity of 2,500 tons.
Products manufactured:
  Rolled oats only, in two forms:
      1. Rapidflocken (Quick Quaker)
      2. Vollkernflocken (full kernel—Quaker Regular)
Principal products sold:
  Rapidflocken   Corn flakes (from Copenhagen)
  Vollkernflocken   Honigkorn (Sugar Puffs from Copenhagen)
  Rolled oats in bulk   Puffed Wheat (from Copenhagen)
Brand names:
  Rapidflocken
  Vollkernflocken
  Honigkorn
Marketing area:
  Parts of West Germany
  Berlin
  The Saarland
Sales force:
  17 salesmen, 1 sales supervisor

exhibit 5   **QUAKER OATS FRANCE, S.A.**
Paris, France

Corporate form:
   A limited-liability corporation
Ownership:
   99.88% owned by the Quaker Oats Company, Chicago
Employees:
   10
Executives:
   R. A. Chretien, manager
   O. de la Brosse, sales coordinator
Plants and properties:
   A sales office only. Has no manufacturing facilities.
Products sold:
   All Quaker products, but principally rolled oats. Imports its merchan-
   dise from Rotterdam, Copenhagen, and London.
Brand names:
   Quaker
Marketing area:
   France and Algeria

exhibit 6　THE QUAKER OATS COMPANY

Domestic and Canadian companies statement of consolidated income, year ended June 30

	1960	*1959*
Net sales	$321,842,899	$322,162,721
Cost of goods sold	235,902,811	240,810,357
Selling, general and administrative expenses	59,706,373	57,481,834
Income from operations	$ 26,233,715	$ 23,870,530
Other income	3,152,065	3,935,292
Income charges	1,514,739	1,433,492
Income before federal and foreign income taxes	27,871,041	26,372,330
Federal and foreign income taxes	14,347,909	13,205,480
Net income	$ 13,523,132	$ 13,166,850

Statement of earnings retained in the business

Balance at beginning of the year	$ 53,066,369	$ 48,297,346
Net income	13,523,132	13,166,850
Total	66,589,501	61,464,196
Cash dividends: Preferred stock	994,312	1,019,613
Common stock	7,378,214	7,378,214
Total	$ 8,372,526	$ 8,397,827
Stock dividend on common stock		
Earnings retained in the business at end of the year	$58,216,975	$53,066,369

Notes to financial statements

The consolidated balance sheet includes the following net assets in Canada at the dates indicated:

	June 30, 1960	*June 30, 1959*
Current assets	$ 9,977,887	$11,092,587
Current liabilities	1,909,799	1,530,259
Net current assets	$ 8,068,088	$ 9,562,328
Other assets	346,076	389,145
Properties, less reserves for depreciation	4,151,549	4,267,958
Total	$12,565,713	$14,219,431

Properties have been converted at U.S. dollar cost at dates of acquisition; net current and other assets have been converted at the lower of cost or current rate of exchange.

The reserves for possible loss on uncollectible accounts deducted from accounts receivable amounted to $1,648,745 at June 30, 1960 and $1,657,543 at June 30, 1959.

Provisions for depreciation for the year ended June 30, 1960, included in the statement of consolidated income aggregated $4,978,767.

exhibit 7 **THE QUAKER OATS COMPANY**
Domestic and Canadian companies consolidated balance sheet

Assets	*June 30, 1960*	*June 30, 1959*
Current assets:		
Cash	$ 9,383,632	$ 10,337,391
Securities of the U. S. Government and its instrumentalities, at lower of cost or market	32,763,625	28,585,147
Accounts receivable, less reserves	26,725,730	26,486,936
Inventories of grain, materials, products and supplies, at lower of cost or market	31,448,488	33,974,435
Total current assets	$100,321,475	$ 99,383,909
Investments in and advances to affiliates (European and Latin America), at cost	$ 4,027,032	$ 2,908,897
Other receivables and investments	344,041	438,971
Prepaid expenses	1,401,260	1,613,717
Property, plant and equipment, at cost:		
Land	2,674,394	2,671,273
Buildings and improvements	37,889,965	36,342,406
Machinery and equipment	58,537,596	54,567,104
Country elevators	7,037,319	6,407,084
	$106,139,274	$ 99,987,867
Less—reserves for depreciation	43,658,032	40,744,988
	$ 62,481,242	$ 59,242,879
Patents, trade-marks, trade rights and goodwill—less amortization	1,148,279	1,325,548
	$169,723,329	$164,913,921

exhibit **7** (continued)

Liabilities

Current liabilities:

Accounts payable	$ 6,481,581	$ 7,530,901
Accrued federal and Canadian income taxes	10,085,310	9,281,063
Other accrued liabilities	8,125,050	7,739,238
Dividends payable	2,092,541	2,096,288
Total current liabilities	$ 26,784,482	$ 26,647,490

Funded debt:

2⅝% debentures, due July 1, 1964	7,719,000	7,929,000
3½% notes, due February 1, 1977	20,000,000	20,000,000
	$ 27,719,000	$ 27,929,000

Capital stock and earnings retained in the business:

Preferred, $100.00 par value, 6% cumulative, authorized 250,000 shares; issued 180,000 shares	$ 18,000,000	$ 18,000,000
Common, $5.00 par value authorized 6,000,000 shares; issued 3,689,107 shares	18,445,535	18,445,535
Amount in excess of par value	22,469,783	22,469,783
Earnings retained in business	58,216,975	53,066,369
	$117,132,293	$111,981,687

Less stock held in treasury—June 30, 1960, 14,675 shares of preferred, at cost	1,912,446	1,644,256
	115,219,847	110,337,431
	$160,723,329	$164,913,921

exhibit 8

THE QUAKER OATS COMPANY

Organization Chart

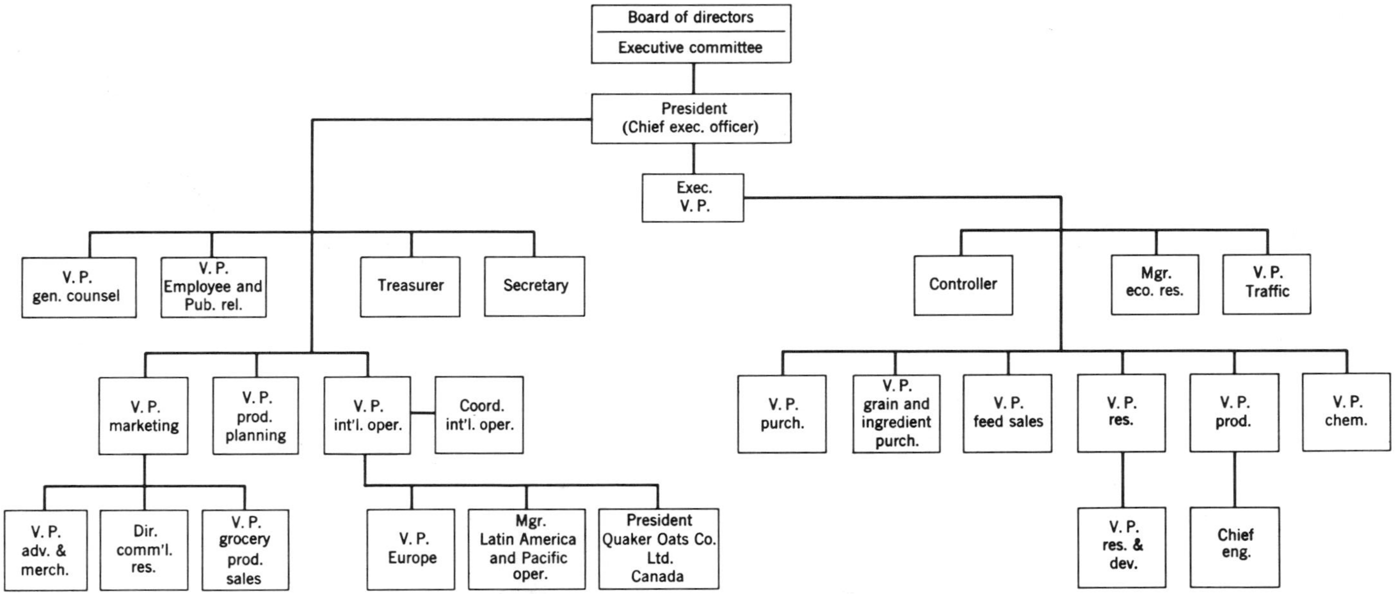

exhibit 9   **QUAKER OATS COMPANY**
Foreign subsidiaries

Europe
Quaker Oats Limited
  Southall, Middlesex, England
  Whitehaven, Cumberland, England
A/S "Ota"
  Nakskov, Denmark
Quaker Oats–Graanproducten, N.V.
  Rotterdam, The Netherlands

N.V. Vleeschwarenhandel "Equinox"
  Rotterdam, The Netherlands
Quaker Nahrmittel Gesellschaft,
  m.b.H
  Grevenbroich, Germany

Canada
The Quaker Oats Company of
    Canada, Ltd.
  Brampton, Ontario
  Dresden, Ontario
  Edmonton, Alberta
  Norwood, Ontario
  Peterborough, Canada
  St. Jerome, Quebec

  Saskatoon, Saskatchewan
  Smithville, Ontario
  Swift Current, Ontario
  Trenton, Ontario
  Wallaceburg, Ontario

Latin America
Elaboradora Argentina de
    Cereales, S.A.
  Buenos Aires, Argentina
Productos Quaker, S.A.
  Cali, Colombia
Produtos Alimenticios Quaker, S.A.
  Porto Alegre, Brazil

Productos Quaker de Mexico, S.A.
  de C.V.
  Mexico City, Mexico
Productos Quaker, C.A., Venezuela

exhibit 10 QUAKER OATS COMPANY
Selected economic statistics

Item	England	Denmark	Holland	Germany	United States
Population	50,225,224	4,448,401	9,625,499	50,974,500	179,323,175
Pop. per sq. km.	214	106	350	213	19
Employment including agriculture (1953=100)	105	N.A.	115 (1957)	128	105
Employment in mfg. (1953=100)	105	N.A.	108	131	94
Hrs. of work	46.1	N.A.	48.9	45.8	40.3
Percentage of unemployed	2.3	6.1	1.8	2.4	5.5
Industrial production (1953=100)	110	109	116	113	104
Agricultural production (1952/53–1956/57=100)	105	110	110	108	112
New building (buildings completed)	281,568	28,202	1,040	625,400	1,607,473**
Consumer price index (1953=100)	120	N.A.	119	112	109
National income	18,931,000,000 (pounds)	31,165,000,000 (kroner)	31,860,000,000 (guilders)	70,428,000,000 (Deutsche marks)	396,600,000,000 (dollars)
In dollars	$53,764,000,000	$4,674,000,000	$6,372,000,000	$17,607,000,000	

SOURCE: *Statistical Yearbook of the United Nations*, 1960.
** Permits issued.

QUAKER OATS
IN EUROPE (B)

ENGLAND: THE LONDON OPERATION

Quaker's first entrance into the British market was in 1893 through a selling agent whose six offices and warehouses had sales territories which covered the British Isles. The British market proved to be so promising that, in 1899, Quaker established its own sales subsidiary there, Quaker Oats, Limited. An American salesman, noted for his ingenuity in advertising and sales promotion, was sent to England to direct the campaign of the new company. The English company's first product was oatmeal and rolled oats, which it imported from a Quaker plant in Ravenna, Ohio. Under the aggressive sales drives of its first managers the company expanded rapidly.

The first Quaker executives sent to Europe by the American headquarters were chosen for their promotional flair. One of the early extravaganzas of Frederick Seymour, an early Quaker executive sent to England, was a giant Quaker package mounted on a van. It was so large that British police did not permit it to be driven on English streets. Seymour then mounted a poster campaign, and was soon brought into court, charged with defacing His Majesty's royal telephone poles. Seymour then proceeded to erect Quaker billboards of heroic proportions on the White Cliffs of Dover, visible to all passing ships. An act of Parliament was required to effect their removal, and in the course of the litigation the name Quaker received widespread publicity in the British press.

Impressed with the prospect of a sizable export business, the management of Quaker in the United States decided to build a plant to serve the export trade. In 1902 the company erected a sizable mill at Peterborough, Ontario, a strategic site in line with the flow of grain from the American West and the Canadian Northwest, and close to the ocean seaport of Montreal. Peterborough was the largest cereal mill in the British Empire. At that time Canada was called the breadbasket of Britain, and in the following decades all of the production of the Peterborough mill was shipped to member states of the British Empire. Preferential tariff rates permitted the Canadian plant to export freely to England. Its export volume grew to be over two million cases a year, making Quaker the largest cereal company in England. During the first World War the Peterborough mill operated at full capacity to supply England with oat products as well as cold cereals and flour.

In 1937, by which time tariff levels had become prohibitive, Quaker erected a major plant at Southall, Middlesex, a suburb of London, to manufacture ready-to-eat cereals, macaroni, and livestock feeds. Oatmeal continued to be imported until World War II, when the British government shut off all imports from North America. Quaker's chief competitor in oatmeal, a domestic firm named Scots, absorbed all of Quaker's business. The Quaker management proposed to buy Scots but the asking price was so high that it was declined. There followed a period of eight years during which Quaker oatmeal products were off the British market.

The production of livestock feeds had also been halted, but for a different reason. There had been a general pooling, in wartime England, of all resources, including technical information. In the livestock feed industry, all firms made their feed formulas available to the industry as a whole. Southall was not prepared to publish its formulas, and chose instead to withdraw from the business from 1941 to 1945.

After the war imports were still banned because of the dollar shortage. "England was broke," said Mr. Towler, general manager of Southall. "We had no dollars with which to buy—not even Canadian dollars." Thereupon the Quaker American management decided to install oat milling facilities in England and to make Southall a fully autonomous plant. This move was again blocked by governmental restrictions, which did not permit the building of a new plant in the

London area, where there was a pressing labor shortage, because the government wished to disperse the heavy London population concentration. Industry was being encouraged to build in such "distressed" areas as Manchester, in England's industrial Midlands, where a severe unemployment problem existed. The Quaker management, however, considered Manchester to be a poor location for distribution purposes. Instead, the Quaker management received government permission to add an extension to its Southall plant, which was permitted, and in this "warehouse" the company was allowed to install a "workhouse." In the workhouse was installed oat rolling and packaging machinery transferred from the Peterborough plant, a move which was also entirely legal. The Southall plant secured its oat supply from Patterson's, a competitive mill at Whitehaven, Cumberland, near the Scottish border, whose entire output of groats was bought by Quaker. Quaker purchased the Patterson business which increased its capacity to 2,000 barrels of oatmeal a day. Through aggressive campaigning Quaker was able to capture 70% of the business it enjoyed in the prewar period. In 1960 Quaker was once again established as the leading cereal producer in England. The Southall plant produced the entire line of Quaker products, with the exception of chemicals.

The English management was convinced that it had to buy local grains. "It would be suicide not to," said Mr. Towler, "we cannot rely on imports. We must support our home grain market, and keep the British farmer raising oats." Canadian oats were considered to be too high in price. The Southall management also felt the need to be cautious of foreign crop failures, pointing out that Australia, for example, had little surplus to ship abroad in 1959. American oats tended to be dry, light, and had a higher protein content because they received more sunshine. The Scottish oats used by Southall were bigger, plumper, and had more fat content. The English management stressed the importance of the yield factor. "The price of a bushel of oats is meaningless," said Mr. Pitkeathly, Southall's export manager, "it is the oat groat content, and the art in our milling process is to try to extract from the kernel the maximum amount of edible material. If we can get a 10% higher yield than a competitor like Scots, then we are in a strong position to compete with any similar mass-producing competitor."

The English management considered the highly varied character of its export market to be an extremely complicating factor. "We sell to 78 different markets," said Mr. Pitkeathly. "In many of them we encounter tariffs and import restrictions. Often we cannot package in economic sizes—there are areas where our products are still sold and eaten by the spoonful . . . as medicine, or as health foods. Although, in general, packaging is cheap in terms of paper and print, our production is for a multi-lingual market, which means that even running an identical product we have to use packages in different languages, resulting in short runs and high costs. In many countries inserts are not permitted. Some markets require tin containers for insect-proofing, and others require packages in six or eight languages. Sugar Puffs, because of the hydroscopic nature of the product, requires aluminum wrapping."

Impressed by the success of the Danes in educating the Danish public to eat oatmeal in its raw state, the Southall management tried to promote the same effect in England. Birmingham, a heavy industrial section, was chosen as a test area. The program was launched with expensive television shows in which popular British film stars performed dramatic skits portraying father, setting out to cook oatmeal "the old-fashioned way," being corrected by mother, who showed him the "modern way" to eat oatmeal cold and raw. The campaign failed to make any noticeable impression upon the British public, and the company experienced sizable advertising expenses which were not recovered.

At the close of World War II the English management was considering the introduction of cake mixes, and in this connection the English sales manager made a trip to the American headquarters to gather facts and discuss the project. He was particularly interested in learning more about the experience of the American company, which had just retired from a similar attempt to become a factor in the cake mix business in the United States where Pillsbury, the leading cake flour manufacturer, had already been well established. Pillsbury had spent close to a quarter of a million dollars in a single week to introduce its mixes, in such advertising barrages as six consecutive pages of full-color ads in the *Saturday Evening Post*. Mr. Muzzy and Mr. Whipple, then directing foreign operations, pointed out that Southall would have to buy its cake flour from England's principal flour miller, who was already the leading producer of cake mixes in Britain. Although the Quaker headquarters management was a firm believer in extensive advertising and accustomed to allocating substantial expenditures for that purpose as a routine thing, it was not in favor of trying again in England a venture that had not succeeded in the United States. The American headquarters, however, left the decision to the English management, which, on the basis of the information it had collected, decided firmly against it.

The English management had also considered adding Sugar Puffs to its product line. Word had come to them that Kellogg was on the point of introducing sugared corn flakes in England, where sugar rations had just been lifted and the British people were hungry for sweets. Although the British sales manager had some misgivings about the effect on his Wheat Puff sales, he decided to try Sugar Puffs. The Chicago headquarters management authorized a $200,000 expenditure for machinery—funds which the British generated themselves. Sugar Puffs were introduced one day after Kellogg's Sugar Corn Flakes. The puffs were a success from the start, building up to a sales volume of over a million cases a year, and puffed wheat sales showed no sign of diminishing. All of this action had taken place outside of the formal channels of the European Administrative Committee, the decisions having been made by the British executives directly involved.

Mr. Summers believed that it was too early to assess the effect which the Common Market and the Free Trade Area would have upon the the Quaker companies in Europe. Most countries tended to jealously guard their own agricultural economies and generally favored the retention of import duties to keep the prices received by their own farmers at relatively high levels. The general objectives of both trade areas were to eliminate many tariffs or to adjust those which remained to a common level, but certain exceptions were made. Agricultural products were one of these exceptions. "As to agricultural products," said Mr. Summers, "we are still on the fringe area. Neither market area had yet made a firm decision as to whether the products of our plants will be considered agricultural products or, because of the degree to which we have processed them, will be considered industrial products. It might be that corn flakes and some dry cereals which are made from grains not grown in this country would be classified in the industrial category, while the oat products made from our home-grown grains would be considered agricultural products."

It was the prospect that oats and oat products would continue to be subject to import duties, and that these duties would, like most dutiable goods, be subjected to the gradual process of leveling among the several nations in each area. "This leveling," said Mr. Summers, "might help us, or it might hurt us, depending upon the final tariff level upon which the market areas settle. Some of our European plants import most of their grain." Holland, which had good seaports, good storage facilities, and low tariffs, had been importing huge supplies of grain which it trans-shipped into the interior of the Continent. France, on the other hand, had such high tariffs that imports were virtually excluded. If the end result was a general raising of the tariff level in the Common Market, Mr. Summers believed that the over-all combine of Quaker operations in Europe would be hurt. The leveling program was to be a gradual one (10% per year for the first several years) and in 1960 the ultimate direction of the trend was not yet predictable. "As to the placement of our plants," said Mr. Summers, "we are very fortunate. In the Common Market we have plants in Germany, and our plant at Rotterdam is at the gateway to the Continent. In the Free Trade Area we have plants strategically located in Britain and in Denmark." In the meantime, until future developments were more indicative, Mr. Summers had people in the marketing department of the London plant making continuous studies of the situation and maintaining files of any new information which developed. Mr. Summers himself followed the situation closely from day to day.

exhibit 1   **QUAKER OATS LIMITED**
Southall, Middlesex; London, England

Corporate form:
    A limited-liability corporation
Ownership:
    100% voting power held by Quaker Oats Co., Chicago
Employees:
    About 1,200
Executives:
    B. C. L. Summers, vice president, Europe, manager director
    R. M. Towler, director and general manager
    R. D. Kennedy, financial director
    J. E. Pope, secretary
    A. R. Wilks, comptroller
    G. F. Kendall, production manager
    W. F. Cooper, marketing manager, Cereals
    N. H. Beeston, marketing manager, Feed and Pet Foods
Plants and properties:
    Manufacturing, storage and office facilities.
    The largest cereal plant in the British Isles.
    Road, rail and canal facilities. Grain silo 2,000 ton capacity.
Products manufactured:

Oat products	Livestock feeds
Rice products	Pet foods
Cold cereals	Paste goods

    The Southall plant produces the full Quaker line of products with the
    exception of chemicals.
Principal products sold:
    The full Quaker line. This includes cake and pancake mixes imported
    from the United States.
Brand names:
    Quaker, Sugar Puffs, Oat Krunchies, Ful-O-Pep, Ken-L-Ration
Marketing area:

The British Isles	India
Africa	Pakistan
The Near East	Burma
Australia	Ceylon
New Zealand	The Mediterranean countries

Sales force:
    200 travelers; a cereal marketing manager; a feed marketing manager;
    sales and advertising managers in each division.

QUAKER OATS
IN EUROPE (C)

DENMARK: THE OPERATION AT COPENHAGEN

The Danish company—A/S Ota—was founded in 1898 as an oat mill by Gerhard Boesen, Sr. At that time only imported rolled oats were used for human consumption. The original plant was a windmill, and a farm tractor was used for auxiliary power when the wind failed. The business made slow but steady progress, and added rice products to its line in the early 1920's. The Quaker Oats Company bought the business from Gerhard Boesen, Sr. in 1930. The name Ota was retained because it had become so well established, and because it was a period in which there was a strong feeling of nationalism in Denmark. The Ota name was still being used in 1960. While no deliberate effort was made at secrecy, most Danes were not aware of the Quaker ownership of the company, which was now managed by Gerhard Boesen, Jr., son of the founder.

In 1960 Ota was the leading cereal company in Denmark, selling over 50% of the total consumption of both hot and cold cereals. It was the only producer of rice products, which it made in a variety of forms. Ota was the only manufacturer of Quaker corn flakes in continental Europe which it supplied to all of the sterling and some of the dollar areas. Ota's corn flakes were sold under a variety of brand names such as Guld Korn, Mexi Corn Flakes and Dana Corn Flakes. Almost all of the corn for the corn flakes line was imported from the United States or from La Plata, Argentina. Corn, known in continental Europe as maize, was not native to Denmark, nor did the temperately cool climate of most of Europe permit its cultivation.

The land area of Denmark consisted of a peninsula and a number of large islands separated from the peninsula by straits. In the days of Gerhard Boesen, Sr., both the office and mill had been in the town of Nakskov, on Lolland, a large island about 100 miles from Copenhagen. Since it was necessary to go to Copenhagen to transact business with most of Ota's principal customers, the headquarters office was eventually moved there. In 1960 Ota had its head office at Copenhagen and manufacturing and storage facilities at Nakskov. In addition to the storage facilities at Nakskov, Ota rented six warehouses for storing finished products. These were so located that when the straits froze in winter, making the islands inaccessible, the company was still able to supply its customers from its local inventory. Deliveries were made by company-owned trucks. The Danish railways were state owned and offered a rebate of 10% to any shipper who shipped all of his goods by rail, but Ota found this impractical and chose to forego the rebate. There was some prospect that the government might bridge some of the straits. In that event, the Ota management planned to dispose of its warehouses.

At the Nakskov mill Ota had grain silos which had considerable capacity. Ota usually had excess grain storage capacity and in 1957 when a miller asked to use some of this capacity on a rental basis, the company agreed. The Ota management found this to be a profitable practice, and the miller found it a convenient arrangement. The miller asked Ota if it would be willing to build additional capacity for rental purposes. Mr. Boesen presented the proposition to the EAC, which approved it. The Nakskov elevator was enlarged to a capacity of 12,000 tons, some of which was leased to the Danish government, but 90% was rented to the miller.

Ota was one of the few Quaker companies in Europe which used native oats. If Danish oats had a good growing season they were given preference because their yield was high and their flavor was good. If, however, the quality was affected by poor weather, such as by excessive rain at harvest time, Ota imported its oats. Its first choice on the world market would be Australian oats, and after that it bought according to the price-yield ratio, with the source of supply shifting from year to year. Hard wheat was imported, mostly from Canada, because Danish wheat was soft. It was the experience of the management of Ota that the lack of uniform and permanent grading standards among the several grain-exporting nations made purchasing difficult. Some countries changed their grading standards abruptly and without notice. At times the grain which Ota bought as Grade No. 1 turned out, on delivery, to be what it had previously purchased as Grade No. 3.

In Denmark there was an exceptionally high consumption of oatmeal, estimated to be close to eight pounds per capita annually (compared to less than one and two-thirds pounds in the United States). Part of the high consumption was due to the fact that about 60% of it was eaten uncooked and cold, just as it came from the package. During World War II, the Germans did not permit enough fuel for heating, and gas and electricity for cooking was also rationed. The practice of eating rolled oats uncooked was said to have been started then by the Danish Boy Scouts, who had been taught to do so on camping trips, and once it caught on, Ota helped to boom the idea by extensive advertising. The practice had an added advantage to Ota: when oatmeal was eaten cold, people tended to eat twice as much as in the cooked form. In Denmark, oatmeal was not considered a winter cereal; in fact, more oatmeal was sold in summer than in winter.

Until 1958 it had been impractical to import almost any food product into Denmark. Denmark was a rich agricultural country and food products were plentiful and cheap, especially dairy products. Imported food products were relatively high in price, and the Danish people, known for their thrift, were price conscious. Until the late 1950's, the importation of most any foodstuff had been virtually prohibitive. Ota imported only a few cake mixes from the United States, and its sales of these, which were sold as a luxury food, were insignificant.

Ota produced a number of rice products: regular whole rice, minute rice, flaked rice, rice meal and puffed rice. Rice was not a native Danish grain, and Italy was the only significant producer on the Continent. Ota bought most of its supply on the world market, from whatever source was most advantageous. In the summer of 1960 finished Italian rice products were being imported into Denmark at prices low enough to enable retailers to sell them at half the price of Ota rice products. To meet this competition the Ota management had considered several alternatives. Meeting the competition by cutting the price of Ota rice products was hardly possible, since Ota's prices had to be kept relative to the price of rice on the world market. Management believed that it might have some success in placing emphasis in its advertising and merchandising on the theme that Ota rice products were of superior quality, and by this strategy, maintain its higher prices. Lastly, it could buy some Italian production, which it would market through its own distribution channels. At late summer, 1960, the Ota management had not yet made any move, but was waiting to see what would happen to competitive prices in fall and winter.

The economy of Denmark had been highly regulated by the government since 1930. The trend had been toward socialization of certain facets of the economy, such as the granting of free medical care, unemployment insurance, government care of the aged, and government ownership and control of railroads, schools, and utilities. However, 90% of the country's industries remained privately owned and operated. Labor unions were national, all employers belonged to a single association, and these groups met for the purpose of negotiating wages and such matters as working hours, holidays, vacations and working conditions, once every three years, largely following price indexes. No strike ever occurred, but there was a shortage of labor and some black marketing of wages.

The Danish government also regulated some prices, and since agricultural products were considered a national necessity, food prices received special attention. As far as Ota was concerned the price regulations applied to rolled oats only, this being considered an essential basic food product. The government, through its Monopoly Board, had the legal right to inspect the company's books and to review their financial statements, which it did with regularity. The aim of the government was to allow the producer only a modest margin of profit. If grain prices rose, Ota was not permitted to raise the price of its rolled oats without specific permission from the Monopoly Board, which necessitated filing an application and showing cause and awaiting the decision of the board. The Ota management found the price controls hampering to their freedom of action, and there was some feeling that the basis for revisions was changing and unpredictable.

There was no legal restriction, however, against collusion in marketing, and the producers had combined in an Oatmeal Organization which allocated the bulk business. The estimated consumption was divided among the members of the industry, and any member who sold more than his allotted share was assessed a per-ton fine for each ton sold above his quota. There were only a few oat millers in Denmark, each knew what the others were doing, and the millers believed that, because of this, the quota system had worked well.

The Danish government levied a tax upon dividends, but the regulation permitted the first 5% of dividends paid on share capital to be tax free. To Ota, with its capital of 3½ million kroner ($525,000), the first 175,000 kroner ($26,250) in dividends paid were tax free. Income taxes were substantial; the rate fluctuated annually between 30% and 50%. Ota had recently formed a subsidiary company to which it sold all of its assets, which were reappraised and increased in value to allow for 5 million kroner ($750,000) in appreciation, and depreciation was permitted to be taken on the new increased carrying value.

Mr. Boesen was concerned about the growing popularity of retailers' co-operatives in Denmark. The Danish co-ops enjoyed tax advantages not available to an independent producer or wholesaler; they sold to their own stores only, their member stores were required to purchase all of their goods from the co-op, and some of the co-ops operated their own milling facilities. Together, they did about 14% of the retail grocery business in Denmark, and their share of the market was growing. About 25% to 30% of the retail sales of oatmeal were made through their stores. Their oatmeal products were sold to their stores at prices which were about 5% below those of Ota. Those co-operatives which did not have their own manufacturing facilities were Ota's biggest customers, taking about 10% of Ota's total output. The Ota management was concerned because these co-ops were in the position of being a wholesaler with a captive following of retailers, giving them strong bargaining power. Also, the co-ops' main concern was low price.

Mr. Boesen was of the opinion that the coming Free Trade Area would hurt Danish trade through the leveling of tariffs, which would probably result in the raising of the low Danish tariffs. Danish tariffs averaged only 4% on total imports, England's average was 26%, and about 40% of Danish industry would be affected by any increase in the rate. Duties and import restrictions were already a handicap to Ota on its sales abroad. Sweden levied a customs duty of 10% ad valorem on Ota's products, and Norway, Finland, and Iceland all had high rates. Ota had already lost some markets to local nationals who manufactured under licensing agreements from other producers.

In Denmark, Mr. Boesen pointed out, the consumption of rolled oats was declining, but the total consumption of all cereals was rising. He believed, therefore, that his major problem was to add new products to his line to retain his share of the market. These could even be in other lines than foods.

The Ota operation was consistently profitable. Under the direction of Mr. Boesen and his father, the company had had only one loss year since 1920. From 1955 through 1960 both the unit volume of sales and the rate of profit had risen steadily.

exhibit 1   AKTIESELSKABET "OTA" DE FORENEDE HAVRE—OG—RISMOLLER
Comparison sales units and earnings as of June 11, 1960

Financial Year Ended	*Sales Units, %*	*Income Before Taxes, %*
April 30, 1957	100.0	100.0
April 30, 1958	100.8	120.8
April 30, 1959	103.3	127.5
April 30, 1960	106.5	126.5

exhibit **2** **AKTIESELSKABET "OTA" DE FORENEDE HAVRE—OG—RISMOLLER**
Copenhagen, Denmark

Corporate form:
    A limited-liability corporation
Ownership:
    99.91% voting power held by the Quaker Oats Company, Chicago
Employees:
    About 275
Executives:
    Gerhard Boesen, manager director
    Per Lorenzen, general manager
    Alfred Christensen, superintendent
    Sven Boeck, prokurist
Plants and properties:
    Head office in Copenhagen.
    Manufacturing and storage facilities at Nakskov, Lolland.
    Six warehouses for finished products covering Denmark.
Products manufactured:
    Oat products
    Rice products
    Sugar Puffs
Principal products sold:
    All Quaker cereals.
    Aunt Jemima cake mixes (from United States).
Sales force:
    14 salesmen; 2 supervisors.
Brand names:
    Dana—used on corn flakes. (Derived from *Dana*mark.)
    Sol Gryn—used on rolled oats. (Means sun grain.)
    Ota Gryn—used on rolled oats. (*Ota* is a word derived from oats.)
    Pama Rismel—used on rice products.
    Guld Korn—used on Sugar Puffs.
    Kala Puffer—used on Sugar Puffs in Sweden.
    Mexi—used on corn flakes in packages.
    Quaker—used on corn flakes in bags.
    Lif—used on Oat Krunchies in Denmark.
    Frass Kudder—used on Oat Krunchies in Sweden.

QUAKER OATS
IN EUROPE (D)

HOLLAND: THE ROTTERDAM OPERATION

Quaker's first direct selling effort on the continent of Europe occurred in 1896 when the United States management engaged a Hollander to represent Quaker in the Netherlands on an agency basis.
Within a year the company's star Akron, Ohio, salesman—Ernest Noell
(who eventually became vice president, Europe)—was sent to join the
Hollander. A sales office was established in Rotterdam, and this office
supervised a selling effort that covered the Netherlands, Switzerland,
Italy, and a portion of central Europe.

During the early decades of the operation of the Rotterdam agency
Dutch tariffs on imports were raised from time to time until, by 1930,
import duties reached prohibitive heights. At this point the United
States management organized a Dutch corporation, the Quaker-Oats
Graanproducten, N.V., and the Dutch company proceeded to mill oats
in a plant building which was rented for the purpose. Not long thereafter the Dutch company bought from the Hecker Oats Company of
Rotterdam the brand name H-O and the H-O sales rights to the Netherlands, continental Europe, and the Dutch East Indies. The Quaker
management decided to retain indefinitely the H-O brand, which at
that time outsold the Quaker brand three to one in Holland and its
colonies.

Eventually, during World War II, the Dutch Quaker Company
purchased the Hecker Company's plant. The Hecker plant, located

directly on the shore of Rotterdam harbor, was situated where it could receive grain from ships with a minimum of transportation cost. Quaker's Hecker plant was adjacent to the N.V. Graansilo Company, an 80,000-ton grain elevator, which was the largest single grain storage facility in Europe. Quaker's grain imports were transferred from incoming ocean ships into Graansilo's elevator from which they were drawn as needed by tube directly into the Quaker plant. The location of the plant was considered by management to be a natural advantage, providing easy access for incoming grain shipments, and being equally well located for outgoing shipments of finished products, since Rotterdam was a focal point from which overland traffic fanned out to inland Europe. Rotterdam shipped its finished products by cartage carriers, which were efficient and economical.

In the purchase of their grain supply each of the European Quaker companies formulated its own policies independently, and each of them acted differently because of the different conditions and types of their home-grown grains, and because of import duties, regulations, and government controls. The Rotterdam plant bought virtually all of its oats from America, and most of these from Canada. Dutch oats were almost never used because they were too dark in color, the moisture content was too high, and they tended to be strong-flavored. In other years the Dutch plant had, at times, bought either Argentina Plate oats or Australian oats, and the choice was made mainly on price considerations. Australian oats gave a better net yield in final product, but even taking this into consideration, the 1960 price had been too high to make them economical.

The Dutch government levied a special duty on imported oats. This duty was somewhat similar to the German import duty by which the German government fixed the domestic prices of oats at a high level, and levied a tariff on any lower-priced imported oats which equalized the price. The Dutch duty, however, was not directly related to a fixed pegged price of domestic Dutch oats. The Dutch tariff was determined by the relationship of the price of Dutch domestic oats and the price of oats on the world market. Since the German fixed domestic price was higher than the price of Australian oats, the German management might just as well buy the high-yielding Australian oats, regardless of the fact that their price on the free world market was high. To the Dutch manager, however, the higher yield of the Australian oats was not sufficient to justify the higher price; for his purposes Canadian or

Argentine oats were more economical. Also, where the German price was fixed annually, the Dutch price was subject to change at any time and was, in fact, sometimes changed daily, a circumstance which made it impossible for the Dutch purchasing agent to methodically place his purchase orders to best advantage.

The Dutch tariff regulations had been in effect for many years and there was little prospect for any change. Mr. Thomas Zaaijer, the Dutch general manager, after years of trying to persuade the govern-ment to amend the tariff, had succeeded in obtaining some measure of relief. The company was now given a refund of 75% of the tariff if the finished product was sold on the home market, and it paid no tariff at all on oats imported for product sale abroad.

Mr. Zaaijer was considerably more concerned about the import duty policies of the Belgian government for he feared that, through the operation of the Common Market, Belgian tariffs would have the ad-verse effect of raising the general level of Dutch custom duties. It was a particular feature of the Common Market plan that goods entering any of the member nations' countries from nonmember na-tions were to be charged a duty which was to be the same in any member nation. The amount of this duty was to be determined by arranging a leveling of the current duties of the several member na-tions, this leveling to be effected over a period of ten years. By July, 1960, there had been two 10% decreases in these tariffs between the Common Market countries, and under an acceleration of the original program, there was to be another 5% decrease by the end of 1960. Nevertheless, Mr. Zaaijer believed that the final effect of Belgian tariff policies would be to raise tariffs above the current Dutch levels. The Belgian tariffs had been considerably higher than those of the Dutch and, unlike the Dutch tariffs, the Belgian tariffs were used as a source of revenue to finance the operations of the Belgian govern-ment. Where the Dutch tariff varied inversely with world oat prices, the Belgians might raise their prices at a time when world prices were rising. After studying the proposed Common Market policies, Mr. Zaaijer wrote his reactions in a paper which he transmitted to the Dutch government, and he encouraged the German management to make similar representations to the German government. By this ac-tion it became the responsibility of their respective national govern-ments to protect their interests in negotiations for the coming Com-mon Market. "To be directly represented at the Brussels headquarters of the Common Market," said Mr. Zaaijer, "we would have had to organize the oatmeal millers from all six countries as a group. This would not have been practical. We are not going to organize a European Union of Oat Millers."

Oatmeal, Mr. Zaaijer believed, had been fairly well accepted by Dutch consumers, but the Dutch people had not accepted cold cereals. Taste, he believed, had been the factor which had, in the past, determined their choice of food, and the time of preparation was secondary. With the trend toward working housewives, the importance of the first factor was diminishing in favor of the second.

Prior to World War II there had been a great many small retail shops in Holland. After the war there were only about half as many and, of those which remained, 80% had affiliated with some type of chain organization. Originally these were buying co-operatives, giving their members the benefit of their mass purchasing power and profit sharing. Later they expanded their activities to give their members advice about advertising, merchandising, bookkeeping, and business management. By 1960 such co-op names as Spar, Vivo, and Konsum, which had started in Holland, were commonplace all over Europe. Retailers bought only from their own organizations which, in effect, were wholesalers with a captive trade following, and were in a position to make demands upon food producers.

Faced with this market condition, Mr. Zaaijer believed that the Dutch management had to choose between these three alternatives: (1) selling the co-ops the Quaker H-O brand of rolled oats; (2) selling them bulk oats packaged under the co-op label; (3) abandoning this segment of the market. By quota agreement with the other Dutch millers the Rotterdam plant, like all other Dutch millers, agreed to try to sell as much of its product as possible in the packaged form. It sold very little of its output as bulk oatmeal because of the small profit margin in bulk oatmeal. The H-O brand had for many years been the most popular packaged oatmeal in the Dutch market and currently accounted for 53% of Dutch domestic packaged oatmeal sales. Mr. Zaaijer believed it was a vital necessity for his company to maintain its leading market position and every effort was being made by the Dutch sales department to hold its lead.

In Holland, instant dehydrated soups had been very popular, a circumstance which persuaded Quaker's Rotterdam management to install a small but modern and highly efficient paste goods plant which manufactured vermicelli, popularly used in packaged dehydrated soups, for the Holland market only. The plant consisted of a single one-man machine which was operated three shifts a day. The Dutch company also sold packaged elbow macaroni imported from London.

An unusual product made by the Dutch plant was Vigour, a powder used to make a chocolate quick-energy drink. The Dutch people were very fond of chocolate, which was one of their colonial products. They ate it in various forms and at any meal of the day including breakfast. Vigour consisted of oat flour to which was added vitamins, chocolate and some powdered milk. It was sold domestically and as an export product to markets in Africa, Portugal, Malta, the Caribbean region, Panama, and Colombia.

In 1942 the headquarters company in Chicago purchased the dog food business of Chappel Brothers of Rockford, Illinois, makers of the well-known Ken-L-Ration brand of dog food. At the same time Quaker also purchased the N.V. Vleeschwarenhandel "Equinox," of Rotterdam, Holland, because it was affiliated with Chappel Brothers and was available. Equinox produced horsemeat for human consumption and the headquarters management of Quaker had in mind that Equinox would be used to introduce the company into the pet food business in Europe.

The attitude of Europeans toward human consumption of horsemeat was very different than that of Americans. In Holland, as in most of continental Europe, horsemeat was looked upon as an economical form of meat fit for human consumption. Doctors stated that horsemeat was wholesome and had a protein value that was higher than that of beef or pork.

Equinox produced high quality smoked and salted horsemeat for human consumption. The horsemeat was imported from Argentina, and the operation was conducted in a small plant in Rotterdam by six employees who answered to Mr. Zaaijer. Government regulations required that all of the product be sold as horsemeat; none of it could be processed into any other form such as sausage or meat loaf, and the regulation was enforced to the extent that a sausage packer would be subject to prosecution if the presence of any horsemeat were discovered on his premises. In 1960 Equinox was operating profitably under Quaker management without change in its traditional business.

Although there was an overemployment situation in Holland, Dutch wage rates were low in comparison with almost every other country in Europe, which gave the Rotterdam plant some labor cost advantage. Typically, where a German factory worker would earn three marks an hour, the Dutch worker would be paid only the equivalent of two. Both the employers and the unions were associated as groups, but each had to negotiate its claims with the Dutch government, which made the final decisions on wage rates and working conditions. Residential rentals were government regulated, and so were retail prices. Although the government followed a rigid policy of permitting wage increases only to the extent of increases in productivity, the trend was one of increasing wage rates. In view of this, Mr. Zaaijer tried to mechanize the plant as much as possible. There was no shortage of labor at the Rotterdam plant. The work force was 65% unionized, and relations with the union had been good. The Rotterdam plant had ample capital and its operation had been consistently profitable. Mr. Zaaijer felt that his major problem was to add more products to his line, a need that he felt was critical. He was convinced that cold cereals would, in due time, be fully accepted by Dutch consumers.

Mr. Zaaijer was pleased with operation of the EAC. He felt that through its operation he was in much closer touch with both the United States headquarters and the other European companies. He felt that the committee of production superintendents and sales managers was particularly helpful. His management had never been in disagreement with any EAC policies, nor had the EAC ever attempted to direct the affairs of the Dutch company.

Mr. Zaaijer looked upon Dutch government controls as a chronic problem that would always be with him. The imposition of import duties, the fixing of prices and wage rates and rent levels, he felt, were often on an unrealistic basis and in general made it difficult to do business in an orderly manner. "Just last week," said Mr. Zaaijer, "we had a government man in here going over our cost records to see whether our prices might possibly be reduced. We are faced often with higher costs and duties and taxes, and lower retail prices fixed by the government." The Dutch firm had sufficient capital for its operation, and the operation had been consistently profitable.

"I am always pushing for new products to add to our line," said Mr. Zaaijer. "I am sure that, in time, dry cereals and other convenience foods will come to be accepted in Europe. Completing a broader line will take time, but we have a good sales force that covers the Benelux countries, and we also produce for the French sales office. We should be ready when the time comes. I feel that more new products are critical to our success here."

exhibit 1   **QUAKER OATS GRAANPRODUCTEN, N.V.**
Rotterdam, The Netherlands

Corporate form:
   A limited-liability corporation
Ownership:
   99.56% voting power held by Quaker Oats Company, Chicago
Employees:
   About 130
Executives:
   T. Zaaijer, manager
   M. H. L. Van Gemert, mill superintendent
   A. J. Vivjerberg, chief accountant
Plants and properties:
   Plant and office at Rotterdam. These facilities are directly on Rotterdam harbor. Quaker has a small 300-ton silo, which stands adjacent to the largest grain elevator in Europe.
Products manufactured:
   Rolled oats (including oats in tins for export)
   Paste goods
   Vigour (a chocolate-flavored oat drink)
Principal products sold:

Oat products	Puffed Wheat (from London)
Paste goods	Sugar Puffs (from London)
Vigour	Cakes mixes and pet foods (from
Corn flakes (from Copenhagen)	U. S. on a very small scale)

Brand names:
   H-O (from Hecker Oats, predecessor company)
   Vigour
   Quaker
Marketing area:
   The Benelux countries
Sales force:
   15 salesmen

exhibit **2**   **QUAKER OATS FRANCE, S.A.**
Paris, France

Corporate form:
   A limited-liability corporation
Ownership:
   99.88% owned by the Quaker Oats Company, Chicago
Employees:
   10
Executives:
   R. A. Chretien, manager
   O. de la Brosse, sales coordinator
Plants and properties:
   A sales office only. Has no manufacturing facilities.
Products sold:
   All Quaker products, but principally rolled oats. Imports its merchandise from Rotterdam, Copenhagen and London.
Brand names:
   Quaker
Marketing area:
   France and Algeria

QUAKER OATS
IN EUROPE (E)

GERMANY: THE OPERATION AT GREVENBROICH

Quaker's Akron, Ohio, plant had exported oatmeal to a Hamburg wholesaler as early as 1908, and the Rotterdam office also sold a small volume of packaged goods in Germany. At about the time of the first World War, to avoid rising import duties, milling was begun in rented quarters in Hamburg, a strategic seaport location close to Berlin, whose population concentration was looked upon as the market of greatest potential in Germany. After the close of World War I, following two years of litigation to settle claims that arose from the operation of the plant by the German government, the Hamburg mill was closed.

In 1914 Quaker had a German sales volume of 68,000 cases of packaged oatmeal, plus some bulk rolled oats, and sales offices at Hamburg, Bremen, Berlin, Frankfurt, and Magdeburg. During the war years sales dropped sharply; by 1917 sales volume was insignificant and all of the sales offices, except Hamburg, had been closed. This was due in part to the effectiveness of the British blockade, but even more to the encouragement which the German government gave to the domestic makers of oatmeal and rolled oats. There was a shortage of all foodstuffs, especially meats and dairy products. People were urged to eat more grain and, since Germany produced little wheat, the emphasis was on rye, barley, and oats. Under an official guarantee of a sufficient supply of raw oats and the promise of an attractive profit, almost three hundred oatmeal mills were established in Germany by the close of the war. Most of these went out of business after the Armistice, but the poor quality of their product and the duress under which the German people had been forced to eat oats left them with an aversion to oatmeal that still lingered generations later. At the close of World War I Quaker had distribution only in the Rhineland area in north-western Germany, and this was being supplied from nearby Rotterdam. This arrangement was continued until 1922, when Quaker purchased all of the capital stock of the Grevenbroicher Mühlenwerke Gesellschaft, m.b.h., to provide facilities for the manufacture of Quaker oatmeal. This was the inception of the Grevenbroich operation which remained the source of Quaker's sales in Germany from 1922 to 1960. The markets lost during the first World War were never recovered, and in 1960 the Grevenbroich mill had sales only in two provinces of West Germany.

During World War II the Grevenbroich plant was theoretically under control of the German government but actually its management continued as usual under the direction of Mr. F. Scherz, who had never been a party member and was respected as a lifelong Quaker employee. The plant went undamaged throughout almost the entire war, but one month before VE Day a single stray bomb made a direct hit upon the main plant building, gutting it.

After the end of the war there was a period of over a year during which the German plant was entirely out of touch with the American headquarters. During this time the German staff, acting on its own initiative, under the direction of Mr. Scherz, proceeded to rebuild the plant. The rubble was cleared, the building partially reroofed, the machinery was dissembled, cleaned, and reassembled, and by the end of 1946 the plant was again turning out some product, but this was only a fraction of its former capacity, and in the form of bulk rolled oats. During the rebuilding no American funds had been added to the German capital. Neither had the German management borrowed money from its bank, the Komerzbank of Düsseldorf, where it had a line of credit of 1 million Deutsche marks. The employees worked twice as long as their normal working hours during the rebuilding and, although wage rates were very low, management paid for all building labor and solicited no donations of labor from its employees—a practice which was common at that time. In the year following its rebuilding the company earned a net profit after taxes of 800,000 DM ($200,-000) on its capital of 1 million DM ($250,000).

For several years the Quaker United States headquarters management debated the future of its German operation but it withheld any decision until its plans were complete, its attitude being that it was to be either a comprehensive action or nothing at all. During these years the German management, alarmed at the advances being made into the market by its competitors, appealed to headquarters for fast action. In 1948 the American management made its decision to rebuild the plant on the same scale, but equipped entirely with modern machinery. Rebuilding proceeded at once, using the shell of the original building, and by the end of 1949 the new Grevenbroich mill was said to be the most modern on the Continent, and the first fully pneumatic mill in Europe.

In the course of the rebuilding there were a number of instances in which the American headquarters and the German management were not in agreement. The first of these concerned the location of the new plant. The Grevenbroich mill had adequate land transportation but its oats, which were imported from Australia, had to be transported overland at a cost of about 11.50 DM ($2.87) per ton, plus 1.50 DM (38¢) unloading fees. Most of the finished product had to be shipped back across the same route and Grevenbroich was, in general, considered to be poorly located with respect to its marketing territory. In 1938 and 1941 Mr. Scherz had bought from the City of Neuss two adjacent parcels of land fronting on the Rhine River, with a view to eventually relocating the plant. The terms of the sale contract included a clause which required the buyer to build upon the land within one year, a provision which could not possibly have been fulfilled during the war years. Mr. Scherz strongly desired to relocate and the City of Neuss was willing to make concessions on the point, but the American management was convinced that it would be impossible to obtain government permission to rebuild and that insufficient capital funds were available locally. The sale was rescinded. Two years later the city resold the land.

During the course of the rebuilding, work was halted on four occasions due to changes in plans suggested by the home office. Each of these became a subject for discussion by trans-Atlantic mail, with the result that several of them were compromised or withdrawn entirely, but the completion of the construction was considerably delayed. At one point the German management received a letter from the home office suggesting that it might be well for them to consider liquidation or sale of the business before it became hopelessly insolvent. The German management staff received this message with resentment and at a meeting of the staff unanimously agreed to demonstrate how well they could perform. During the next ten years, however, the German company operated at a profit only part of the time, and in 1960 its share of the German oatmeal market was $5\frac{1}{2}\%$, compared with its leading competitors, Peter Köln with 62%, and Knorr AG, Heilbronn 25%.

Peter Köln went all through the war without suffering any damage. The plants of Knorr and Quaker were destroyed. As a result, Peter Köln won almost the bulk of the German oat business from its competitors. In the years following the close of the war packaging materials were scarce, and so was the foreign exchange with which they might be bought. When rationing ended in 1949 Köln was the only oat miller in Germany able to produce packaged goods, and in 1960 Köln made *only* packaged and branded goods. Until 1949 Quaker, with its makeshift mill, could produce only bulk rolled oats and when it was able to package its output the management decided to use paper bags with a moisture- and vermin-proof laminated aluminum foil lining of a type which had become popular during the war when they were used extensively by the Reichswehr. Quaker's sales of packaged goods were growing, and had been for years, but in 1960 Quaker sold over 50% of its output in bulk form due, mainly, to its weak position with respect to chain stores and co-operatives.

The larger co-ops and chains, which operated on a national or international basis, tended to take on only one or two products in a line, and for these they chose the fastest selling brands which had national distribution. Quaker had direct distribution in only a minor portion of West Germany, and in many parts of the country the Quaker name was hardly known at all. Commenting on this situation Mr. Wilfried Beyerling, sales manager at Grevenbroich, said: "Housewives who are over 45 know Quaker from their former experience but they have almost forgotten it, and have long since become accustomed to using some other oatmeal, mostly Peter Köln. The younger housewives— those under 25—have never met Quaker at all, and almost all of these have been systematically introduced to Köln. There was practically no oatmeal marketed in most of Germany under the Quaker name from 1939 to 1949. Quaker has no goodwill left in large areas of Germany, where the name has died out. There is a great need for missionary work. . . ." The Grevenbroich management made every effort to obtain greater package sales and continued to accept whatever bulk business it could get from smaller chains and co-ops. Most bulk buyers bought for price, with the result that competition forced profit margins to unattractively low levels. Quaker management tried to persuade its bulk customers to permit packaging of their products on a custom basis, but most co-ops preferred to do the operation themselves, believing that they could do it at lower cost.

For many years Peter Köln had been advertising by using extensive direct mailing. Using public government records of births, Köln sent every new mother a brochure on baby care, a booklet that had achieved general acceptance as a sound and useful instruction manual. With it she was sent a small sample of Köln oatmeal, which she was invited to use. Thereafter at certain age intervals Köln again sent the mother similar booklets and advised her that it was now time to change to a different type of oatmeal. This continued from infancy to high school age. Doctors and midwives were also furnished with instructive literature. This advertising was so successful that most German housewives automatically associated oatmeal with the name of Köln. Doctors and midwives did not simply prescribe oatmeal, but prescribed Köln oatmeal. "When Germans think of oatmeal," said Mr. Beyerling, "they think of Köln, just as Americans think of Quaker."

Mr. Beyerling, who had been engaged by the European Administrative Committee to launch an aggressive long-range sales campaign, admitted that Quaker could not attempt to duplicate the program of Köln, which was already too well established. Neither did he believe that Quaker could undertake a single gigantic introductory promotion, as had been successfully done by Corn Products Refining, Kellogg's, Coca Cola, and other American firms. Such promotion might cost a million Deutsche marks, and Quaker had neither the sales staff nor the nationwide distribution facilities to follow it up. Instead, with the approval of the EAC, Mr. Beyerling had laid out a six-year step-by-step promotional program, beginning with the expenditure of 250,000 DM ($62,500) in 1960. Mr. Beyerling believed that the potential was excellent, for the German yearly consumption of oatmeal averaged 1.3 kilograms (2.73 pounds) of oatmeal per person. He envisioned the program achieving a 30 million DM ($7½ million) cereal business, plus 10 million DM ($2½ million) in livestock feeds. During the next few years all earnings were to be retained and directed toward the sales drive. It was expected that additional funds would be needed and these were to be obtained from the company's banks, or from the money markets.

As part of the new long-range program, a new advertising agency was engaged for Grevenbroich. This was an English concern, chosen by Mr. Summers because it had done a good job for Quaker in England and Canada. This was the first time it would be working in Germany and there was some feeling at Grevenbroich that the agency was learning while working there. It had already made several mistakes because it was not familiar with German culture.

A new sales portfolio was arranged for salesmen in the form of a large showcard-sized illustrated book which salesmen exhibited as they presented a standardized lecture to a prospective customer. The talk emphasized particular sales points, such as Quaker's new package design on which the illustration had been made more prominent and the text simplified in accordance with the advice of the Institüt für Selbst-Bedienung (The Institute for Self-Service); samples of the product itself; an account of television, radio, magazine, and newspaper advertising backing the product; a copy of at least one local morning paper, containing a Quaker ad, which the salesman left with the prospect; and an introductory order offer of two free bags with every 24-bag case.

Mr. Beyerling intended, beginning in 1961, to use some television advertising, but could use it only to a limited extent. There was only one German television station which covered the Westphalian, Rhenish, and Palatinate territories in which the company had sales representatives. The station was on the air for only a few hours a day and it was difficult for an advertiser to purchase time.

Although newspaper advertising was used wherever feasible, Mr. Beyerling felt that this was not a good medium for his products. Market research had shown that oatmeal, in Germany, was definitely a children's food, and as such it should be advertised in such a way that the message would reach mothers. There were only a few papers in Germany which had national distribution, such as *Die Welt* and the Frankfort *Allgemein,* which had the character of the *New York Times* or the London *Times;* or the *Deutsches Wirtschaftszeitung,* which was the businessman's paper, comparable to the *Wall Street Journal.* The advertising carried by these papers was directed at their male readership and consisted of ads for tobacco, commercial air travel, liquors, and prestige automobiles. In addition to these papers, Germany had a system of Gebietliche Zeitungen (regional newspapers), each serving an area, such as the *Köln Staatsanzeiger,* which served the Cologne area, or the *Hessische Zeitung,* which circulated in the Hessian provinces. Each of these had a circulation of about 100,000 and a readership of about 400,000 (hand-me-downs) but German housewives were not accustomed, as were American housewives, to regularly reading a newspaper for food news.

Mr. Beyerling believed that magazines would be one of his best mediums. There were picture-news magazines comparable to America's *Life* magazine, some of which were regional, such as the *Münchner Revue* (Munich Review), and some of which were national, such as *Krystall* (Crystal). Each of these magazines had a circulation of about 500,000 and a readership of 3 million, whereas the nationals had a far greater circulation. The nationals were also circulated by an organization called Der Less Zirkel (The Reading Circle), which passed a stated package of magazines down a reader list. The magazines might come to a reader a month or six weeks late, but this was a circumstance which was of no concern to Zirkel readers. Quaker also intended to advertise in Radio Program, a radio-program listing comparable to TV Guide. The advertising appropriation granted to Grevenbroich in recent years had been only about 150,000 DM a year ($37,500). This figure was based on a standard allowance per case of goods sold during the previous year.

The Grevenbroich mill used Australian oats which, although high in price on the world oat market, were not as high priced as German oats, which the government pegged at a high level. To support the price of domestic oats the German government charged an import duty that was equal to the difference between the two. Thus, when the free price of Australian oats was 210 DM ($52.50) eif Rotterdam, and the price of German oats was 320 DM ($80), the duty was 110 DM ($27.50).

There was a shortage of all kinds of help in Germany—unskilled, skilled, and managerial. In June, 1960, the government reported 130,000 unemployed in all West Germany which had a population of 70 million. It was estimated that there were 500,000 jobs in Germany which were going unfilled. Unions and employers were associated on a nationwide basis and bargained at the national level. Throughout the postwar recovery period the German government had made strenuous efforts to keep wages from rising. In 1960 a typical German factory wage was between 2 DM and 3 DM (49¢ to 73¢) an hour. The Greven-broich mill, although not unionized, paid union wages.

The German mill had had only a few profitable years during the postwar period. During that time it had never paid a dividend.

exhibit 1   **QUAKER NAHRMITTEL GESELLSCHAFT, M.B.H.**
Grevenbroich, Germany

Corporate form:
> A limited-liability corporation

Ownership:
> 100% owned by the Quaker Oats Company, Chicago

Employees:
> About 80

Executives:
> F. Scherz, manager
> W. Beyerling, marketing manager

Plants and properties:
> Manufacturing, storage and office facilities. Has fully pneumatic oat milling equipment installed new in 1953. Said to be the most modern oat milling plant in Europe. Adjacent to highway and railway siding. Grain silo has a capacity of 2,500 tons.

Products manufactured:
> Rolled oats only, in two forms:
> 1. Rapidflocken (Quick Quaker)
> 2. Vollkernflocken (full kernel—Quaker Regular)

Principal products sold:

Rapidflocken	Corn flakes (from Copenhagen)
Vollkernflocken	Honigkorn (Sugar Puffs from
Rolled oats in bulk	Copenhagen)
	Puffed Wheat (from Copenhagen)

Brand names:
> Rapidflocken
> Vollkernflocken
> Honigkorn

Marketing area:
> Parts of West Germany
> Berlin
> The Saarland

Sales force:
> 17 salesmen, 1 sales supervisor

WESTERN SOAP PRODUCTS

Western Soap Products was a large producer of soaps, detergents, edible oil products, and toilet articles like shaving soap and tooth paste. There were eight plants throughout the country, with the largest one in Newark, where the company employed around 3,000 people. Company headquarters were located in Chicago, Ill.

Steady growth of the Newark works had posed some problems of organization at the plant manager level. It seemed as if the organization structure had no sooner been defined and charted than some new change evolved that required further examination of relationships between the plant manager and the department heads under his control. In 1940, the plant manager had an assistant, who acted primarily as a staff man, while the 12 department heads reported directly to the plant manager (Exhibit 1). As staff activities were added the number of departments increased to 16 in 1954, and the assistant manager gradually became, in fact if not in name, an operating man to whom 6 department heads reported directly while the others reported to the plant manager (Exhibit 2). Continued growth of the company put further strain on the plant manager, since his office was a channel through which flowed a growing stream of communication from the home office to various departments of the plant. The pressure was partly relieved by direct dealing between headquarters staff and plant staff on technical matters affecting a plant department, but the plant manager still had to keep informed about such events.

Between 1942 and 1952, there had been a succession of plant managers at the Newark works. Jim Powell, president of Western, reminisced about this period:

We've been through a lot of changes at Newark. John Edwards, who became plant manager in 1942, held things together, but some major projects lagged. To some extent, he pushed what he was interested in,

exhibit 1
WESTERN SOAP PRODUCTS
Organization Chart, 1940

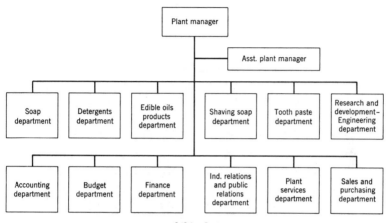

exhibit 2
WESTERN SOAP PRODUCTS
Organization Chart, 1954

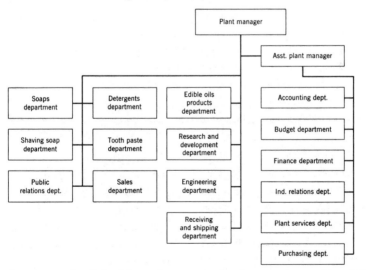

but he was overloaded with 14 department heads reporting to him. Edwards was succeeded in 1944 by Homer Jacks, who was primarily concerned with plant expansion that was needed. Jacks did consolidate some activities to simplify the organization. For example, accounting, budgeting and finance were placed under one man. This arrangement worked so well that industrial relations and plant services were combined (Exhibit 4).

These changes helped, but didn't cure. Jacks found that he couldn't

exhibit 3
WESTERN SOAP PRODUCTS
Organization Chart, 1942

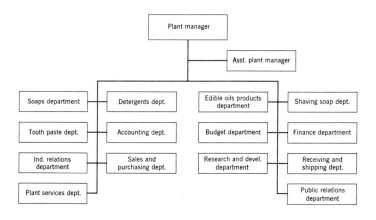

exhibit 4
WESTERN SOAP PRODUCTS
Organization Chart, 1944

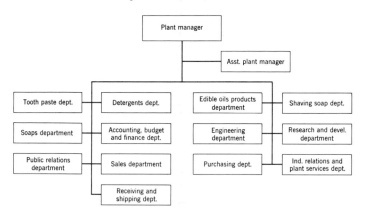

push many decisions down to department heads, which he wanted to do. Too many decisions were being thrown up to him, in part because he had a lot of new people who hadn't been seasoned in their jobs—also in part because a lot of projects needed coordination with numerous departments. Jacks just had to take first things first, and some department heads saw very little of him.

When Jacks moved up to a position at company headquarters, he was succeeded by Bob Stevens, who, as assistant plant manager, had long felt that the organization needed an overhaul. He feared that he would be smothered by administrative detail, while important projects would languish. As the new plant manager, Bob Stevens discussed his ideas with management at the home office as well as with members of his own team. Briefly, Stevens thought that three administrative coordinators ought to be introduced into the line so that each administrator would have five or six department heads reporting to him. These three would

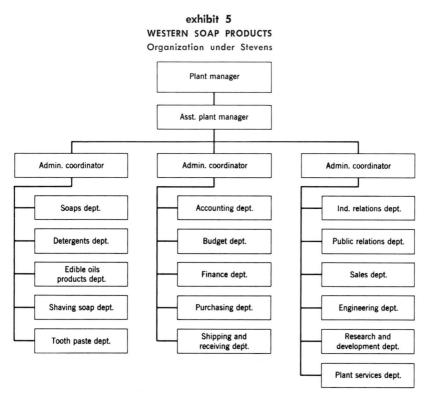

exhibit 5
WESTERN SOAP PRODUCTS
Organization under Stevens

take a big load off the shoulders of the plant manager and his assistant (Exhibit 5). While there were mixed reactions to Stevens' proposal, he decided to give the system a try. Some of the views expressed in discussions about the problem were as follows:

CLIFF EDSON (chief engineer): Our present setup, with 14 men reporting to the manager and his assistant, hasn't been working out. Some department heads hardly every get a chance to see the boss.

ART JOHNSON (v.p. of industrial relations): We could try introducing another

level of management, but I'm not happy with that suggestion. I think
the industrial relations department head at the plant should be able
to go directly to Bob Stevens on important matters.

BOB STEVENS: Your I. R. man could still come to my office if he couldn't get
satisfaction from his administrative coordinator. Of course, I would
expect most problems to be ironed out at the administrative coordinator's
level. If that didn't happen, there'd be no sense having an administrative
coordinator.

ART JOHNSON: Will the theory really work out in practice? You say a department head can see the plant manager, but won't a department head be
reluctant to go topside and run the chance of alienating the administrative coordinator? Either the administrative coordinator is line or
staff, and if he's line, he's going to be the boss. You are actually pushing
department heads farther down the line with one more level in the
channel of communication. Why not push more decisions down to department heads?

BOB STEVENS: Department heads already have the authority to clear with each
other on programs affecting more than one department. The number of
decisions that must be made after this preliminary clearance has been
taken care of is still so large that some screening is needed to relieve me.
These administrative coordinators will get to know my way of doing
things. I'm going to work very closely with them; we'll meet several times
a week. They'll be in a position to tell department heads whether to go
ahead, whether to drop a project, or whether a meeting with me is
necessary.

SAM SMITHIES (v.p. of production): These assistant managers will be walking
a tight rope. We're interested in decentralizing authority, but the administrative coordinator will be tempted to keep the reins in his hands.
How can they keep from making decisions that we'd like the department
heads to make?

BOB STEVENS: At present the department heads are relatively new. If you throw
problems down at them, they won't know what to do. They'll do
nothing. Some guidance is needed, but I can't handle them all.

Ultimately, the proposal for three administrative coordinators was
approved by top management, and the organization at the Newark
plant was changed accordingly. Stevens held a number of meetings
with department heads and the three administrative coordinators. One
of the most frequent questions that came up was this one. "If we as department heads still have the right to take some matters up to Mr.
Stevens, how do we know what to bring up?" To this question, the answer was as follows: "We can't spell out all the situations. The best we
can do is to give a general guide. Whatever you feel you can handle
yourself, go ahead and take care of it. All our department heads have
now had long experience in the company. It isn't like 1940, when so
many of us were new. I think you'll have no trouble making decisions."

After a year of trial, Stevens made a study of how his organization was working. On the plus side of the ledger, he felt that he had been relieved of a lot of administrative detail. He felt department heads had been doing a good job in planning a variety of projects. On the minus side was the realization that too many plans were not being translated into action. The administrative coordinators were sometimes holding up decisions. Instead of counseling, advising and giving a go-ahead or passing a tough decision up the line, they sometimes acted as bottle-necks. If this continued, the initiative of department heads would be killed. Stevens wondered whether he was responsible for this result. Had he been too critical of his administrative coordinators, so that they were reluctant to make decisions? Perhaps some change in the organizational relationship would be necessary. Stevens noted that the administrative coordinators were presenting and explaining programs coming up from department heads. Very often the administrative coordinator was not as familiar with the details as the men who had worked them out. A number of times an administrative coordinator would make a poor showing because he lacked this knowledge. Perhaps the bottleneck was caused in part by the belief that an administrative coordinator should be an expert on all matters relating to his area of interest.

There seemed to be two alternatives that might help the situation. The administrative coordinators were in the main channel of communication and authority. Possibly the present arrangement put too much pressure on an administrative coordinator; he would find it almost impossible to stay in the background. If administrative coordinators were placed in an advisory position, with direct lines of communication going to department heads, then the relationship between department heads and administrative coordinators would develop into a more consultative arrangement. At any rate Stevens was concerned with the role the administrative coordinator was playing. One other explanation for the administrative coordinator's dominant role occurred to Stevens. He had picked men who had come up the ladder within one of the departments they'd supervised. Possibly from habit the administrative coordinators were getting into too much detail.

Stevens also reflected on the size of his operation: better results might be obtained if he could spin off some activities. For example, some of the research activities had little immediate relationship to plant operations. Edible oils and toilet articles were also product groups that might be managed separately.

COASTAL CHEMICAL COMPANY

The Coastal Chemical Company was organized during World War I for the purpose of manufacturing chlorine and other war gases. After the war it began to manufacture sulfuric and nitric acids for industrial use. The company survived the Great Depression of the 1930's and diversified its lines greatly during World War II, particularly in the field of industrial plastics. The development of petrochemicals, which first became of importance during the decade of the 1930's, began to offer increasing competition to the nonpetrochemical companies, particularly after new and inexpensive methods of obtaining hydrogen from petroleum were invented.

In addition, the demands being made on the chemical industry for new synthetic materials, fuels, and lubes in connection with the missile rocket and space programs being conducted after World War II by the U.S. Department of Defense and later for the National Aeronautical and Space Agency offered new and lucrative markets for fundamental chemical research and development. Because of the intensive heat encountered on the re-entry of the missile or space craft into the earth's atmosphere and other hostile environmental factors encountered in space, all material for hardware, fuels, and lubes had practically to be revolutionized, and this required vast amounts of scientific research.

The chemical industry had been research-minded from its inception, and the Coastal Chemical Company was no exception to the rule. As was stated in a company history, "The company's top management became convinced that expenditures for research and development had cash value, and to lag behind in technical development was likely to cost heavily."

Management's interest in chemical research and development is indicated by the increase in the number of professional personnel employed in the department as the company grew. In 1920, one Ph.D. in chemistry was employed. By 1925, two chemists and one chemical engineer were employed. In 1930, this number had increased to about 50. Ten years later, the number had doubled to 100. By the end of World War II the number of professional employees engaged in research and development reached 2,250, supported by 625 technicians. These numbers were reduced after the war to a total of 1,101 research and development employees in 1950.

SCOPE OF COASTAL CHEMICAL R&D ACTIVITIES

Up to 1950, the basic R&D policy of the company was:

1. To help the manufacturing department solve problems resulting from the tremendous demand for industrial chemicals of all kinds.

2. To learn how to make these products in improved quality from lower-grade raw materials as high-grade raw materials became scarce.

The Coastal Chemical Company did not enter the petrochemical field until after World War II, when it purchased a small petrochemical company. The petrochemical company was a wartime project and had purchased its raw material from a nearby oil refinery, converting it into a limited range of synthetic resins. This petrochemical company had already established a small research laboratory for the purpose of helping customers find uses for its products. After the purchase the laboratory was put under the parent company's R&D department.

After the acquisition of the petrochemical laboratory, the scope of the Coastal Chemical R&D department was expanded to include petrochemical research and development. The director of research felt this expansion to be justified, as the company's over-all objective in the 1950's was understood by top management to be: ". . . in the development of any technically based operation or product which our capital, manufacturing, marketing, or technical assets render commercially attractive."

GROWTH OF R&D DEPARTMENT, 1951–1960

Acting under this general policy, the scope of both the chemical and petrochemical research of the Coastal Chemical Company was rapidly expanded with heavy emphasis on petrochemical research (see Exhibits 3 and 4). The director of research was elevated to the rank of director-general when petrochemical research and development were placed under his jurisdiction. He was also made a member of the board of directors of the Coastal Chemical Company.[1] The growth in Coastal Chemical's R&D department from 1954 through 1962 is shown in Exhibit 4.

COMMERCIAL VALUE OF R&D ACTIVITIES

In early 1963, the director-general of the parent company's R&D department had the economic section of the main laboratory prepare a five-year study of the estimated economic value[2] to the company of all chemical and petrochemical R&D. The study found that the economic value of the R&D work to the company averaged $60 million per year for the period 1958 to 1962. (See Exhibit 5.)

The report further pointed out that the estimated economic value to the company did not and could not show the intangible values derived from enhancing the R&D stature of the company by the publication of professional papers, co-operative studies made either through the committees of professional societies or with other companies, or patents obtained as a result of either company or individual research.[3] The director-general of the R&D department felt that it had achieved an outstanding reputation with respect to its professional capabilities. (See Exhibit 6.)

Although the company had never considered the procuring of United States or foreign patents as a primary objective of the R&D activities, such activity was bringing in a relatively small but steady income from

[1] Coastal Chemical Company had long had an "inside" board of directors. Other members included the president, executive vice president, and the heads of the manufacturing, marketing, finance, and legal departments.

[2] That amount of business activity created as a result of the activities of the R&D department. Net economic value is the total economic value minus the developmental costs involved. The value derived from R&D activities may not be traceable directly to a specific amount of sales increase or other indicator and/or a specific product. Other exogenous and endogenous variables, such as a new use created by the general public for the product in question, may have caused the observed increase.

[3] The policy of the department was to allow every professional employee up to 10% of his time for private research on any subject in which he was interested. It was not required that the private project have prospects of immediate economic value to the company, but the project had to be related to the general field of chemical product and process research. Many times private projects, if and when they showed promise of success, became company-sponsored projects.

licensees amounting to approximately $1.5 million (Exhibit 1), of which two thirds came from chemical patent licenses and one third from petrochemical patent licenses. Income from royalty payments was treated as an offset to R&D expenditures.

Another direct source of income to the R&D department was the reimbursements received under Federal government contracts for expenses incurred in connection with the government research projects. Such payments averaged about $750,000 annually during the 1950's and covered both synthetic materials and lube research work.

CHANGES IN THE COASTAL CHEMICAL COMPANY'S ORGANIZATION, POLICIES AND PROCEDURES IN 1963–1964

In the spring of 1963, the board of directors of Coastal Chemical Company announced a major corporate reorganization and realignment of operating functions of the consolidated group of companies, one of which was the newly formed Coastal Petrochemical Company. The purposes of this reorganization were (1) to reduce the number of subsidiary companies and (2) to realign the operating activities to increase the return on investments and increase profits. (See Exhibits 1 and 2.)

The corporate reorganization was designed to create what the parent company called "two primary profit centers: (1) manufacturing and marketing of chemical products and (2) manufacturing and marketing of petrochemical products." The parent company retained direct financial control over the consolidated group of companies. The further expansion of the company into the petrochemical field was to be limited for the ensuing five years. The directors anticipated a dearth of corporate capital for this period.

In connection with the second objective, the board of directors announced a new corporate policy for the consolidated group of companies. In brief, this policy stated for the ensuing five years (unless changed by action of the board of directors of the parent company) the over-all objective of the consolidated companies would be to lift the chemical business to a satisfactory return on investments. Product diversification and exploitation of new products would be held at a minimum during the five-year period.

A national authority[4] on research and development programs stated

[4] The "authority" is a highly placed official of a large industrial company who prefers to remain anonymous. The material quoted in the following paragraphs was taken from two unpublished speeches he made before business forums.

that it was his belief that the first step toward planning of R&D activities was a thorough re-examination of the company's own corporate objectives. This should be done before the R&D departments attempted to plan their own activities. He further said that his experience showed that company objectives should be reviewed periodically and that when company objectives were changed, R&D objectives should be re-evaluated. He proposed that top managements of long-established chemical companies ask and answer for themselves at recurring intervals of 5 to 10 years three questions on general corporate objectives. These were:

1. Should the company try simply to maintain its present level of business and to become more and more efficient and profitable in its chosen field?

2. Should it try to expand within its current field and increase sales of existing products, at the same time developing new uses and new products in its basic line?

3. Should the company broaden its interests and move into entirely new fields, presumably of higher profitability?

Depending on the answer arrived at by the top executives, or perhaps the board of directors of the company, the R&D department should then be able to tailor its own objectives to meet the company objectives. As this authority saw it, there were four principal directions in activities that chemical R&D departments could take. The four directions were:

1. Concentrate a more limited research on those cost-reduction and product-improvement projects with the greatest remaining potential for profit.

2. Search for new uses for existing products.

3. Diversify through R&D into new fields.

4. Seek government research contracts in fields to which the technical skills of the department were particularly well adapted.

In another speech this same authority noted a growing tendency for top management to measure R&D results more and more from a short-run monetary viewpoint. This was done by placing R&D activities under more rigid budgetary control. With respect to the effect that budgetary control had on R&D activities, he said: "The R&D budget, when it serves to stimulate a penetrating analysis of the needs of the company, can be a valuable aid in research effectiveness. When it provides a convenient and concrete schedule for the guidance of an evaluation judgment, it can be a powerful instrument in departmental control. If it is superficial in information and rigid in application, it can be a soporific to management and a monkey wrench in the wheels of technological process."

OBJECTIVES OF R&D DEPARTMENTS

Three months after the new corporate policy was announced, a new directive stating the objectives and function of the R&D departments of the parent and petrochemical companies was issued. The essential items in the directive were:

1. The research and development operation throughout the consolidated companies would be a "limited growth" operation for the next several years, or until modified by action of the parent company.

2. Technological research by the parent company would be maintained at a level sufficient to capitalize on present patent assets and service licenses. Diversification and exploitation of new chemical fields arising from new research would be minimized for the next five years.

3. The R&D department of the parent company would restrict its research primarily to relatively short-term product and process work[5] and would aim it primarily at cost and profit improvement. Such long-term efforts as were appropriate should be directed primarily toward new concepts and uses for industrial chemicals.

4. The government contract division of the parent company's R&D department would continue to conduct government contract research at its own laboratory or elsewhere as required.

5. The R&D department of the parent company no longer had any responsibility to conduct research for subsidiaries[6] *unless* specific project budgets were provided by the subsidiary company, even if the subsidiaries were doing R&D work for the parent company.

6. The R&D department of the parent company should complete its review of the R&D needs for manufacturing and marketing non-petro-industrial chemicals and should establish programs at its laboratory which would satisfy the requirements of promoting non-petroleum based business.

7. The R&D department of the Coastal Petrochemical Company (now independent) would be commensurate with the needs of the present product lines and level of sales.

8. The Coastal Petrochemical Company's R&D department was

[5] For definitions of the various categories of research, see Appendix A.
[6] After the 1963 reorganization there were four subsidiary companies, including foreign subsidiaries.

charged with defensive research and technical service, but with a minimum of long-range or fundamental research.

9. The Coastal Petrochemical Company's research on behalf of licensee support should be of two categories: (a) defensive work designed to fulfill existing commitments and (b) offensive research explicitly pointed toward royalty income from new licensees.

10. The management of all subsidiaries should give serious thought to their technical needs and, for the present, should put their R&D work on a contract basis with the existing parent company's R&D department or if necessary with outside research institutions. (No more research laboratories were to be established.)

With reference to point 6 in the above directive, the Coastal Chemical Company's director-general of R&D had initiated, prior to the issuance of the R&D directive but with the approval of the president of the company, a departmental study of his own. The purpose of this study was to determine the changes required in research activities by the new company objectives. After the research directive was received, the director-general suggested and received the approval of the Coastal Chemical Company's board of directors to hire an outside business consulting firm which had specialized in studying R&D operations and objectives in order to check the department's own study and conclusious. This firm was immediately employed and started its studies in the late fall of 1963.

The consultant's report recommended somewhat more drastic and speedier action than the departmental report, although it was highly complimentary with respect to the caliber of the professional staff of the Coastal Chemical Company's R&D department and the laboratory space and equipment provided by the company. The criticisms in the consultant's report were leveled at (1) the over-organization of the R&D department; (2) the lack of over-all control provided under the program system, resulting in unnecessary increases in costs and delays in completing specific projects; (3) the lack of effective and rapid communication between the lower supervisory and working levels of the R&D department and the users of the research results.

The consultant recommended (1) that the maximum number of departmental supervisory levels between the professional worker and the director-general of the department be reduced from seven to four and (2) that a "project" method of operation be substituted for the "program" method.

Under the project method a "project leader" would be appointed for each proposed project. He would be provided with an adequate professional staff to perform the various phases of the work required, regardless of the location of the workers in the department's formal organization structure. For each project team a "user representative" or "client" would also be appointed to insure direct and continuous contact between the using department or client company and the project researchers. The "project" method of operation would, therefore, satisfy both the second and third objections made by the consultant to current methods of organization.

Cost control would be exercised by monthly reports of actual project expenditures compared to budget authorizations. Copies of these monthly cost statements would be furnished to the director-general, the project leader, and the client representative. If it appeared that the objectives or budget of the project needed revision, it would be the responsibility of the project leader to prepare recommendations of such changes for the director-general and the client. This in effect would give continuous control over the project and enable client users to have a better understanding of the precise problems being encountered by the workers on the project. It was thought that this would decrease the criticism of "using" departments that the research process was so slow that the results had lost their timeliness before the program was completed.

In addition to these three main points in the consultant's report, it recommended a 25% cut in professional staff of the Coastal Chemical Company's R&D department. (The consultant's report to the parent company did not indicate what the organization of an independent R&D department of the Coastal Petrochemical Company should be.)

While the departmental and consultant studies were being made, it had been decided that the branch laboratory at the petrochemical plant which had been maintained by the parent company's R&D department would be closed as soon as possible, leaving the Coastal Petrochemical Company with only a small R&D department whose duties would be confined to assisting customers or licensees. It was also agreed between the Coastal Petrochemical Company and the Coastal Chemical Company that the former would contract with the parent company's R&D department for any long-range fundamental or exploratory research it needed performed. Therefore, the parent company's R&D department would retain its Petrochemical section, albeit with a reduced staff, at its main laboratory.

The parent company's research directive had authorized its R&D department to continue its United States government contract work and either perform it in its "propulsion" laboratory or subcontract it out to others, as required. Therefore, no changes were made in the laboratory facilities for this purpose.

The petrochemical laboratory at the petrochemical plant was closed on June 1, 1964. A few of the professional personnel remained to operate the customer and licensee research laboratory authorized to the petrochemical company. Some of the surplus professional personnel were moved to the main chemical laboratory, and a few were released. Surplus equipment no longer needed at the petrochemical laboratory was either sold or shipped to the parent company's laboratory.

Since the chemical product and process research and development work would be both reduced in quantity and changed in direction, a departmental reorganization plan was proposed by both the departmental and consultant studies. Differences between the proposals were adjusted, and a departmental reorganization plan was announced and made effective as of July 1, 1964 (see Exhibit 7).

At the same time the new departmental organization plan was put into effect, the operating technique was changed from the "program" to the "project" method. Departmental officials had some skepticism as to how well a project system would work for a long-range fundamental or exploratory research problem. On the other hand, they felt that the department had in fact been using the project method of operation for short-range product or process research and hence had no objection to the change in nomenclature. (For the form in which a research project was to be presented to the director-general for approval, see Appendix B.)

With respect to budget retrenchment, no serious attempt was made to rewrite the 1963 parent company's R&D departmental budget, although it had been made up six months prior to the corporate reorganization. The consultant did, however, use the 1963 departmental budget as the basis for recommending both the changes in direction and total amount of expenditures to be made under the new parent company directives. The over-all decrease recommended for chemical research was quite small (5.4%), but as to how and where the money was to be spent, there was considerable change in direction (see Exhibit 8).

In his annual report to the president of his company and the board of directors for 1963, the director-general stated that chemical research expenditures had increased about 3% over 1962 expenditures but that, owing to the removal of petrochemical research activities at the petrochemical plant, petrochemical research costs had declined 87.5%. After adjustments due to the transfer of the chemical laboratory at the petrochemical plant to the Coastal Chemical laboratory, the parent company's research department had lost 43 men during the year but had taken on 31 (mostly new employees) so that the net change was a decrease of 12. At the end of 1963, the professional staff of the R&D department numbered 386 and the technical and supporting staffs 629.

In his annual report for 1964, the director-general reported a decline in net R&D expenditures for the year of approximately 6% and a further reduction in professional manpower of 12% plus 18% in nonprofessional personnel, leaving a total of 341 professional and 516 nonprofessional personnel as of December 21, 1964.

In a preliminary budget forecast for the years 1965 and 1966, the director-general forecasted a 10% decrease in research expenditures by his department between 1966 and 1967, with little or no future decrease to occur in 1968. Manpower would also be reduced to what the director-general felt was an irreducible minimum of 300 professional employees. The technical staff had been reduced to a minimum in 1964 and might have to be increased slightly in 1965 to offset in part the reduction of professional workers.

exhibit 1 COASTAL CHEMICAL COMPANY

Consolidated statement of net earnings, year ended December 31, (1,000)

	1954	1956	1958	1960	1962	1963	1964
Net sales and operating revenues	$405,445	$419,189	$488,931	$490,961	$526,919	$548,206	$569,000
Miscellaneous revenues	767	824	1,383	1,521	1,784	1,988	2,274
Total revenues	$406,212	$420,013	$490,314	$492,482	$528,703	$550,194	$571,274
Cost and expenses:							
Cost of products and services sold	$253,596	$261,752	$317,971	$318,610	$343,788	$359,721	$374,055
R&D expenses	9,279	11,751	12,898	16,104	16,854	14,276	13,417
Selling, administrative, and general expenses	65,469	67,669	73,207	73,599	80,114	85,199	89,893
Depreciation of property, plant, and equipment	28,627	39,501	43,104	44,817	46,618	47,073	48,569
Pension plans	6,447	6,331	6,913	6,986	7,871	6,477	5,997
Interest	46	1,416	2,904	3,623	2,650		
Provision of bonus	1,811	1,300	1,678	1,768	1,995	2,149	2,296
Loss on disposal of property and equipment	68						21
Federal taxes on income	20,000	19,400	15,000	13,000	14,000	17,500	18,500
Total expenses	$385,343	$400,120	$473,675	$478,507	$513,890	$532,395	$552,748
Earnings from operations	$ 20,869	$ 19,893	$ 16,639	$ 13,975	$ 14,813	$ 17,799	$ 18,526
Extraneous gains or losses (after taxes)	2,481						
Net earnings	$ 23,350	$ 19,893	$ 16,639	$ 13,975	$ 14,813	$ 17,799	$ 18,526

exhibit 2 COASTAL CHEMICAL COMPANY

Consolidated balance sheet, year ended December 31, ($1,000)

	1954	1956	1958	1960	1962	1963	1964
Current assets:							
Cash	$ 49,783	$ 16,271	$ 17,053	$ 26,183	$ 18,623	$ 20,130	$ 16,206
United States Government securities—at cost and accrued interest (approximate market)	1,178	20,714	18,501	398			
Marketable securities—at cost and accrued interest (approximate market)					14,359	10,813	10,136
Trade accounts receivable—net	42,799	46,551	37,115	59,872	52,925	60,536	65,907
Other accounts and claims receivable—net	1,947	2,964	3,364	3,056	1,782	1,746	2,988
Inventories							
Finished and in-process products and raw materials	47,741	48,499	69,157	61,861	62,084	62,546	66,597
Shipping materials, repair parts, other supplies	6,695	6,767	7,491	7,496	7,896	8,109	7,910
Total inventories	$ 54,436	$ 55,266	$ 76,648	$ 69,357	$ 69,980	$ 70,655	$ 74,507
Prepaid taxes, insurance and other expenses	1,825	9,316	8,839	9,145	9,121	10,231	11,007
Total current assets	$151,968	$151,082	$161,520	$168,011	$166,790	$174,111	$180,751
Investment and other assets:							
Long-term sulfur properties sale contract	$ 644	$ 545	$ 446	$ 347	$ 248	$ 149	
Refundable Federal taxes on income	2,791	2,791					
Miscellaneous investments and other assets including investments in foreign affiliates—at cost	4,333	4,313	3,311	2,747	4,412	9,302	19,551
Total investments and other assets	$ 7,768	$ 7,649	$ 3,757	$ 3,094	$ 4,660	$ 9,451	$ 19,551
Property, plant and equipment at cost, less accumulated depreciation:							
Land	$ 19,461	$ 20,706	$ 24,182	$ 27,809	$ 28,826	$ 29,315	$ 29,259
Buildings, machinery, and equipment	585,561	680,395	826,482	861,704	981,009	1,026,096	1,065,561
Construction in progress	82,581	102,464	19,379	62,129	10,158	13,991	9,911
Total	$687,603	$803,563	$870,043	$951,642	$1,019,993	$1,069,402	$1,104,731
Less accumulated depreciation	365,860	407,572	487,919	575,938	667,610	714,683	762,431
Total property, plant, and equipment	$339,743	$395,993	$382,124	$375,704	$352,383	$354,719	$342,300
Total assets	$490,479	$554,724	$547,401	$546,809	$523,833	$538,281	$542,602

exhibit 2 (continued)

	1954	1956	1958	1960	1962	1963	1964
Current liabilities:							
Trade accounts payable	$ 33,685	$ 30,508	$ 28,695	$ 27,382	$ 26,286	$ 27,806	$ 21,087
Accrued pension plan costs	4,872	7,045	6,568	8,071	7,804	6,076	7,244
Salaries, wages, and amount withheld from employees	10,827	10,624	12,078	14,716	16,031	16,189	16,593
Payroll, property, and other taxes	11,007	13,632	20,482	22,222	22,110	23,898	20,651
Provision for laying up and fitting out steamships	1,863	1,856	1,855	1,675	1,584	1,618	
Taxes on income	14,057	7,206	14,351	9,569	14,306	12,260	15,593
Portion of term loans payable within one year			11,011	29,183			
Total current liabilities	$ 76,311	$ 70,871	$ 95,040	$112,818	$ 88,121	$ 87,847	$ 81,078
Term loans payable to bank less amount due within one year	$	$ 56,601	$ 72,542	$ 32,242			
Shareholders' investment:							
4% preferred stock, $100 par value to be redeemed Dec. 31, 1955	$ 73,617	$ 72,101					
Common stock, $1 par value*	7,897	7,907	7,907	7,951	8,100	8,108	8,117
Additional paid-in capital	160,206	160,974	160,974	162,116	170,439	171,031	171,773
Revaluation of sulfur properties	2,461	2,084	1,702	1,324	942	564	564
Earnings retained for use in business	169,987	184,186	209,236	230,358	256,231	270,731	281,634
Total shareholders' investment	$414,168	$427,252	$379,819	$401,749	$435,712	$459,434	$461,524
Total liabilities	$490,479	$554,724	$547,401	$546,809	$523,833	$538,281	$542,602

* 10,000,000 shares authorized between 1952 and 1961; 50,000,000 shares authorized in 1962.

704

exhibit 3   PETROCHEMICAL PRODUCTS AND THEIR AREAS OF USE, 1964

	Products								
	Oxides		Glycols				Glycol Ethers	Glycerin	
Industries	Ethylene	Pro-pylene	Ethylene	Di-ethylene	Poly-ethylene	Polypro-pylene	Glycol Ethers	Sur-factants	Chlor-inated
Agriculture	x		x	x				x	x
Automotive			x	x	x	x	x	x	x
Building and construction							x	x	
Chemical	x	x	x	x	x	x	x	x	x
Cosmetic				x		x	x	x	
Dyestuff	x		x	x	x	x	x	x	x
Ferrous metal						x		x	
Food and beverages					x		x	x	
Fuel and power	x		x	x	x		x	x	x
Glass and ceramic					x			x	
Highway construction and maintenance			x		x				
Leather processing						x		x	
Nonferrous metal				x		x	x	x	x
Paint		x	x	x		x	x	x	x
Paper		x	x	x			x	x	x
Petroleum	x	x		x	x	x	x	x	x
Pharmaceutical	x	x	x	x	x	x	x	x	x
Plastics, resins, and film		x	x	x	x	x	x	x	x
Printing		x	x	x		x	x	x	x

exhibit 3 (continued)

Industries	Oxides		Glycols				Glycol Ethers	Glycerin	
	Ethylene	Pro-pylene	Ethylene	Di-ethylene	Poly-ethylene	Polypro-pylene		Sur-factants	Chlor-inated
Refrigeration and air conditioning			x	x	x		x	x	x
Rubber			x	x				x	x
Sanitation	x							x	x
Soap and surfactant	x	x		x		x	x	x	x
Textile				x	x	x		x	x
Water treating								x	x

End products
1. Basic chemicals:
   a. Hydrogen
   b. Chlorine
   c. Hydrogen peroxide
   d. etc.
2. Foams, both rigid and flexible
3. Fertilizers
4. Solid rocket fuel binder
5. Gasoline additives
6. Dry cleaning chemicals
7. Rocket lubricants
8. Synthetic fibers
9. Hydraulic fluids
10. Cleaning compounds for machinery
11. Caulking compounds
12. Detergents and soaps
13. Swimming pool disinfectants
14. Cosmetics
15. Dye
16. Wrapping materials

exhibit 4   TOTAL R&D EXPENSES AND PERSONNEL, 1954–1962

Year	Chemical R&D Expense, $ Million	Petrochemical R&D Expense, $ Million	Combined R&D Expense $ Million	R&D Personnel*		
				Professional† Number	Technical Number	Supporting Number
1954	8.48	0.80	9.28	380	640	165
1956	10.90	0.85	11.75	467	730	187
1958	11.70	1.20	12.90	476	730	178
1960	13.55	2.55	16.10‡	510	778	174
1962	13.45	3.40	16.85	459	608	140

* Includes the home and subsidiary plants' R&D department personnel.
† The majority of professional workers had their Ph.D.'s in chemistry or chemical engineering. All were college graduates with at least a bachelor's degree in these fields.
‡ For the last three years of the period, 1960 through 1962 inclusive, total research and development expenditures, including production research, were from $16 to $17 million per year. Of this amount about 80% was spent on chemical and 20% on petrochemical research and development.

exhibit 5   PERCENTAGE BREAKDOWN OF ECONOMIC VALUE TO THE COMPANY FROM TOTAL RESEARCH ACTIVITIES, 1958–1962

	Company's Estimated Breakdown of the Economic Value to the Company Derived from Each Type of Research	R&D Department's Claimed Share of the Estimated Economic Value to the Company
Products improvement research	16.64	25.2
Process improvement research	13.00	85.0
Product specification services	44.74	6.5
New product research	5.35	65.7
New process development	16.10	98.6
Investment analysis studies	3.91	65.0
Supporting activities	0.26	11.1
	100.00	40.0 (weighted average)

exhibit 6   OUTPUT OF PATENTS GRANTED, PAPERS PUBLISHED
AND REPORTS ISSUED DURING THE PERIOD 1954–1962

	1954	*1956*	*1958*	*1960*	*1962*
Patents issued	62	87	131	118	122
Papers published	27	35	34	42	66
Reports issued	18	28	66	40	48

exhibit 7   COASTAL CHEMICAL COMPANY'S R&D DEPARTMENT BEFORE AND
AFTER DEPARTMENTAL REORGANIZATION

As of 7/1/63	As of 7/1/64
Director-general	Director-general
Manager of chemical research laboratory	
Director of chemical research	Director of chemical research
Director of product research	
Area director	General supervisor
Division director	
Section leader	Project leader
Group leader	
Professional worker	Professional worker

exhibit 8   CHANGES IN DIRECTION OF RESEARCH

	5-Year Average 1958–1962, %	*Recommended Distribution,* %
Product improvement research	16.75	30.7
Process improvement research	11.10	51.1
Product specification services	8.00	6.7
New product research	21.25	2.8
New process development	20.80	4.1
Investment analysis studies	9.90	3.0
Supporting activities	12.20	1.6
	100.00	100.0

Based on an offensive-defensive classification, the recommended distribution of the budget was:

	%
Fundamental and/or exploratory research	4.0
Defensive research	49.0
Offensive research	5.6
Research technical service	6.4
Technical services (development)	28.5
Patents and licensing	6.5
	100.0

APPENDIX A

CLASSIFICATIONS OF RESEARCH AND DEVELOPMENT PROJECTS

R&D projects are classified in many different ways. Most industrial researchers tend to use the following threefold classification. Each classification overlaps the others, so the qualifying adjective(s) used is not necessarily the only one that could be applied.

1. *By length of time likely to be consumed in carrying out the research assignment*
   a. *Short-term*. A project likely to be completed in not more than one year, and certainly in less than two.
   b. *Long-term*. A project which is likely to take from five to ten years to bring to completion.
2. *By type of competitive advantage sought*
   a. *Offensive*. Research that is directed toward finding entirely new products or processes including both manufacturing and marketing aspects.
   b. *Defensive*. Research that is directed toward improving present products and/or processes for the purpose of keeping the company competitive in the existing market place.
3. *By objective of the research*
   a. *Pure or basic research*. This is research undertaken solely for the purpose of increasing the scientific knowledge of mankind, regardless of whether or not the project has economic or social value. It is the domain of the universities and scientific foundations. Little or no pure research is undertaken in industrial laboratories, but industrial firms can and do participate through grants and donations to universities and engineering schools.
   b. *Fundamental research*.[7] It is sometimes known by empirical experience

[7] Fundamental and exploratory research are sometimes linked together under the name of "advanced technical" research.

that certain results can be attained under specified conditions, but why
or how they happen is not known. Fundamental research is undertaken
to find why or how the known result is obtained. It is generally long-
term research, with a high degree of uncertainty as to the results which
will be obtained from the project.

c. *Exploratory research*[7] takes the results of purse research and attempts to
apply them to known products or processes to find out what will happen
through the application of the pure research results to existing products
or processes. It is considered to be somewhat more commercially oriented
than fundamental research and to have somewhat better chances of
profitable results. It is generally long-term research.

d. *Product and/or process research* may be for the purpose either (1) of
discovering entirely new products or processes of commercial value; or
(2) of improving existing products and processes. This type of research
is closely allied to "offensive" research for (1) and "defensive" research
for (2). Numerically speaking, most projects are short-term of themselves,
but there is a continuing flow of projects, so that product or process
research usually is the bread and butter work of many industrial research
departments.

e. *Government research*[8] for the past 15 years has been sparked by the
national rocket, missile, and space programs. Some of the government-
sponsored projects have been in the pure research field, but almost all
lie in the fundamental or exploratory fields. The original program in
this field was the atomic bomb research program during World War II.
Whereas the Manhattan project was entirely operated and financed
under military supervision, the government is now inviting the co-opera-
tion of private industry. In some instances the project is wholly govern-
ment-financed, but the tendency is for the government to ask private
industry to finance part of the costs, on the ground that industry reaps
the "commercial fall-out" from the research projects, which can be used
by the private contractor for his own profit in connection with civilian
products.

[7] See note, page 709.

[8] *Note:* Research appropriations for all United States government purposes have
been running between $15 and $20 billion per year, mostly for defense and space
research. This is the largest chunk of research funds that can be definitely traced.
Civilian ways of accounting for research and development funds are so diversified
that it is impossible to definitely determine how much American industry is
spending annually on privately financed research and development, but it is
definitely accepted that the government has been financing more than 80% of
the "advanced" research being carried on in industrial laboratories.

APPENDIX B

PROJECT PROPOSAL

R&D department—Coastal Chemical Company

| Project Title | Project No. |
| | Project Leader |

Starting Date: Estimated Controllable Costs $M_____

                        Estimated Overhead Costs $M_____

Target Date: Total $M_____

                        Estimated Capital Costs $M_____

Urgency of Completion:

Technical Objective: (The technology to be acquired.)

Approach: (Main steps with key personnel and any major new equipment required.)

Prepared By: Date:

Commercial Objective and Benefits Expected:

Alternatives:

___

Our Strengths and Weaknesses:

___

What would be required for commercialization if technically successful:

___

Prof. Team Members:

___

Client Department:
Client Representative:

___

Schedule of Reviews and Reports: (Types; Dates; To Whom Made)

___

PART FIVE

---

basic
day-to-day
administration

BARRETT TRUMBLE

Professor Floyd Hall of Bristol University was visiting his old friend Barrett Trumble, president of Green & Richards, the leading quality department store in Gulf City, one of the fastest-growing metropolitan centers of the South. Hall read at breakfast of Trumble's election as president of the Community Fund.

Trumble said, "You might wonder, Floyd, why I would accept this job. I've already done my stint as general campaign manager for the Fund. I guess most people consider this kind of work an important community responsibility but, at the same time, enough of a headache to expect others to take over after you've done your share. I feel differently about it. Unless business leaders continue to spearhead the private sponsorship of needed community agencies, their functions, which must be performed by someone, will more and more be taken over by the Federal, state, and municipal governments."

Trumble went on to say, "I played hard to get for quite a while. I told the boys I wouldn't take the job till we had firmed up our plans to raise funds for the next three years, including agreement on and acceptance by three executives who will take over successively as general campaign managers. Also, I insisted on the Fund setting up an advisory council of business executives, consisting of company presidents. I find that if we are going to get anything done around Gulf City, the way to do it is through the top brass. Now we have twenty business leaders on this council and I am sure there is nothing we want to have done that we can't swing through this group. Then again, I think it's good

715

for G & R for me to be out front in this type of job. As you can see from the morning's paper, we get pretty good publicity. In addition, I intend to have all meetings of the council and some meetings of the more important committees in our executive dining room in the store. And I am sure it won't turn out to be too much work. A job like this is just a job of getting it organized."

TRUMBLE'S OUTSIDE ACTIVITIES

Professor Hall suggested, "It sounds as though you have it well organized. However, don't you think you will still be harassed by personal appeals and requests from all the other agencies in Gulf City and from others who are interested in community welfare?"

Trumble replied, "Frankly, Floyd, I wouldn't tell this to anyone else, but I must confess that if I didn't have these outside interests, I'd just be twiddling my thumbs down at the store."

Hall was surprised. He knew that Trumble served on the boards of five other businesses: the First Federal Savings and Loan Association, the Commercial National Bank, the Equitable Casualty Insurance Company, Intercontinental Textile Products Corporation, and National Laboratories. He was also a trustee of the Franklin Museum of Modern Art, the Gulf City Symphony Orchestra, Hambletonian College, and the National Retail Merchants Association. Barrett was also a member of the business advisory committee to the Department of Commerce and the treasurer of the Gulf States' Republican Committee.

Barrett explained, "But these other activities don't really take much of my time. Most of these boards have no more than one meeting per month, and they are not very active during the summer months. Of course, when I am on any board committees, it takes a little more time. Then, down at the store, we have things so well organized that the operation pretty well runs itself. Ever since I brought in Tom Jenkins as executive vice-president, I only find it necessary to get into things at the overall policy level."

TRUMBLE AND HIS VICE-PRESIDENTS

Hall recalled that when Jenkins joined Green & Richards, the vice-presidents in charge of customer relations and store operations had resigned to go with other merchandising firms. Trumble pointed out, "Of course, their resignations made it possible for us to promote two out-standing junior executives who were coming along so fast that we couldn't have kept them in the business if we hadn't been able to move them up the ladder. We now have eight vice-presidents reporting to Jenkins; one each for ready-to-wear merchandising, home-furnishings merchandising, store operations, personnel relations, cutomer relations, control, advertising, and research. Tom and his eight vice-presidents constitute an executive council which meets twice a week. I sit in on all the meetings and have an opportunity to keep in touch with major policy questions. Once in a while I find it necessary to step in where there is a strong difference of opinion, but I can usually rely on Tom to straighten things out without my intervention."

Hall asked, "Don't you find it necessary, as president, to meet with the heads of other businesses in town on questions which involve all the stores in town? For example, don't you have common problems like retaining the importance of the central business district as a shop-ping center or instituting charges for customer services which you can no longer render free of charge?"

"Yes, you have a point there. I could spend a lot of my time doing this, but the other boys are really better qualified than I am to make a contribution to joint meetings with other stores. For example, take the question of charging for deliveries, which is a hot subject right now. I think it is something all the stores must consider seriously. But why should I spend the time sitting in on the series of harangues among the other merchants in town when Jack Ogleby (vice-president for store operations) is really up to date on this question and can quote chapter and verse when they get down to brass tacks in their discussions? Any-way, before anybody does onything about this, the question will come before our executive council, and I will get in on it at that point."

HOW TRUMBLE SPENDS HIS TIME

Hall wondered how Trumble used the rest if his time in directing the operations of Green & Richards. "Well, I guess I spend a good 10 per cent of my time with the board of directors—in regular meetings of the board, in preparing for these meetings, and in individual confer-ences with some of the more interested members of the board. For exam-ple, Frederic Pellham (senior partner of the leading law firm in Gulf City) is on my neck now, pressing us to come up with a ten-year plan for our business. He thinks we should be looking to the future growth and development of G & R rather than concentrating on today's profits alone. However, the board as a whole now has enough confidence in me so that the others don't needle me the way Fred does.

"Also, the Green family is concerned with maintaining a good steady return on their investment. They aren't interested in spending the kind of money we would need over the next few years if we were going all out to become the largest department store in the South, which is what Fred would like to see.

"Then, I meet with the executive council twice a week. I have a regular meeting every Monday morning with Tom Jenkins. I am always available to talk with the other vice-presidents about any of their problems. They know that I won't make any decision on the matters they bring to me, but I am always glad to toss ideas around with them for whatever help that may be. But I guess I would have to say that most of my time in the store is spent just going through the business as much as I can. I spend between three and four hours a day walking through the store, particularly in the sales departments, just seeing how things are going, chatting with the people as I go, doing everything I can to help give people a lift. It helps keep me in touch with the way things are moving out on the selling floor, and I am sure that the people down the line feel better to see me around, because they know that I am not trying to run things from an ivory tower."

OPERATING RESULTS OF G & R

"How has the store been doing the last couple of years, Barrett?"

"I certainly can't complain, Floyd. I would say our sales and profits are excellent. Every quarter, for the last three years, we have done better than our budgeted dollar sales, gross profit, and net profit. By the way, I have always found it useful to present to the board of directors a highly conservative sales and profit plan so there won't be any unpleasant surprises when the final reports are in. Our reports are better than the Federal Reserve reports for Gulf City as a whole and better than the National Retail Merchants Association averages. Looking ahead, with defense spending the way it is, creeping inflation, population trends in general, and the growth curve for Gulf City, I don't see how we can miss. Sometimes I wonder if we might show even better results if I put a little more pressure on the boys or if I spent a little more time myself in some of our major problem areas. But here we are, the major downtown store, with three suburban stores (two of which we did not have six years ago) and with our sales increasing every year somewhere between 4 and 6 per cent. Our operating profits before income taxes have averaged 7.6 per cent of sales for the last five years."[1]

DELEGATION AND MANAGEMENT DEVELOPMENT

"And now I have built a team. As I see my job, it is to help select and develop competent people for our key jobs and then let them go ahead and do the things they are qualified to do and for which they are being well paid. It seems to me you either delegate responsibility and authority or you don't. The trouble with most store heads with whom I am familiar is that they talk a lot about delegation but they spend a lot of their own personal time going around and asking the department heads why they bought this, what they think of that, why don't they do so and so. One of our mutual friends, who runs a store up North, tells me that he thinks his job is one of constantly impressing department heads with the fact that he is thoroughly familiar with the way things are going in each department. He watches each department's figures like a hawk and calls people on the phone or on the carpet to discuss what they have in mind to correct things in the future. I don't see why we spend a lot of time developing people and pay them the money that we do if we don't rely on them to take the kind of action that is good for business and therefore for themselves."

Floyd asked Barrett if he was satisfied with his executive staff. "I would think you would have problems from time to time, humans being what they are."

Trumble replied, "Sure, like any other big happy family, we have our troubles from time to time. For example, Malcolm Donaldson (vice-president for personnel) gets himself steamed up on a special training course for executives and makes the mistake of bringing it up cold at the executive council meeting. The boys kick it around but finally decide that department heads have too many pressing problems confronting them; that it would be unwise to take them away from their operations for extended training sessions. Mal's idea gets voted down. Then, later in

---

[1] The National Industrial Conference Board had reported that the previous year's operating profits of large department stores averaged 5.6 per cent of sales.

the day, he comes to me to see if he can get my backing for the idea, knowing that I am all for more and more executive training.

"What Mal ought to do is talk with some of the other vice-presidents ahead of time and get them interested in the idea and at least briefed to the point where they understand thoroughly what Mal has in mind. Most things get settled in our business outside of council meetings; the interested executives are covered individually or in small groups ahead of time, so that when the issue comes to a vote at the council meeting, it is pretty much a matter of rubber-stamping the proposal.

"Mal really needs a lot of help, anyway. We have just employed a personnel consulting firm, with an annual retainer of $20,000. They keep us in touch with what is going on in other businesses, union trends, etc.; they work with Mal on employee training courses and do a lot of other things for us. For example, I learned the other day that one of their communications specialists is helping Mal write employee bulletins before they come to me for my signature."

BOARD RELATIONS

"You were saying, Barrett, that you don't have much trouble with the board of directors."

"No, except for Fred Pellham, who is a little troublesome from time to time. He has made it a point to dig into our business more deeply than the other directors. He gets his own industry figures direct from the Fed, National Retail Merchants, and Harvard Business School, so that he can compare our operations with what others are doing. As I told you, he is trying to get us to think further ahead and anticipate the changes that are likely to happen ten years from now, so that we will be able to make the necessary moves today in terms of what is going to happen then, instead of struggling year by year to keep abreast as things shift. Of course, most merchants realize that department store business is, at best, a ninety-day business; we have to be quick on our feet to meet day-to-day changes. No one has a good enough crystal ball to be able to forecast several years ahead.

"The other directors now accept almost anything I propose as a sound idea. Over the last five or six years, I have been careful to make sure that the things that I brought before the board were thoroughly explored and based on conservative projections. As a result, I no longer find it necessary to justify most of the things I want to do. Sometimes I wonder if they are a little too easy on me. However, I don't know; it is certainly a lot more comfortable this way. I can't say that I would like to repeat the struggles that I had in selling the board this idea or that idea during the first year or two I was in this job. I guess no president wants a board of directors that is as active in the business as their own stockholders expect them to be. From my own experience in serving as a director on these other boards, I find it pretty easy to put the management on the spot by raising questions which are not self-evident from the figures presented to the board. Before every board meeting in these other concerns, I spend a lot of time going over the material they send us ahead of time, because I think I have the responsibility, both legal and moral, as a director to serve as His Majesty's loyal opposition, so to speak."

OTHER ACTIVITIES

"By and large, it looks to me as though things are in pretty good shape at Green & Richards, but every once in a while I wonder where I am going. Here I am, close to fifty, doing well financially—my directorships alone give me a pretty good income. Of course, income is not important in my tax bracket, and I definitely feel that my serving on these outside boards is a good thing for the store. Too many of my retailer friends aren't in touch with the methods and viewpoints of other businessmen. I think I have the advantage over them as a result of these contacts outside our own trade.

"Apart from these business and community activities, I seem to have plenty of time for golf; I get in three rounds a week on the average, except when Jane and I are away on vacation. I guess I told you that we are leaving the middle of next month for a cruise around the world. In a way, this will combine business and vacation. It will give me an opportunity to touch base with some of our important resources from whom we import in the Far East and Europe. Our merchants are over there regularly, but I think it means something from time to time to have the head of the business pay them a visit. I get a real kick out of meeting their families, going through their operations, and talking about the problems they are up against. It seems to me that they get something out of it, too. In one sense, it does the same thing I try to do when I walk around the store each day—and maintaining good relations with our key resources, both domestic and foreign, is almost as important as good employee relations, I think. I also try to spend as much time as I can in our domestic markets—especially in New York and on the West Coast."

Since Trumble was thoroughly wound up, Hall continued to listen without comment.

SATISFACTION THROUGH CONTRIBUTION

"I get a good deal of satisfaction out of things I am doing. I thoroughly enjoy my regular job. I feel that Green & Richards is making an important contribution to our growing community.

"I am convinced we help raise the cultural standards of Gulf City through our emphasis on quality merchandise and good taste; through constantly making available to our customers exciting new items, many of them exclusive with us; through concerts, Christmas and Easter festivities, art shows, and many other events throughout the year. I think our reputation for courteous service (and there is nothing more important), for making good on all commitments, for integrity and fairness in all dealings with customers, resources, and employees, sets an example for others in the community. And I believe that my chief contribution to Green & Richards is to help other people understand, believe in, and apply these principles to their day-to-day problems. My job is to help our executives grow and develop to the full limit of their capacities, to the point where they can operate on their own, within our guiding policies and principles. To the extent I am successful in doing this, I not only improve the sales and profits of the store but also feel, in some degree, the kind of satisfaction you derive from your teaching—the satisfaction which one gets from helping others.

"I would hate to give up any of my outside business interests or directorships. As for the Community Fund, the Museum, and the other community service activities, I consider them too important to give up—they make it possible for me, in a small way, to repay the community for my own good fortune. You said you wanted to talk with me, Floyd, about the kind of problems I find most troublesome. I guess my problem is that I don't have any real problems at the present time. Of course, if we had a real recession, I would have my hands full down at the store without any of these outside interests. However, from the looks of things, there isn't going to be too much for me to sink my teeth into in the near future."

EARLIER PROBLEMS AS GENERAL MERCHANDISE MANAGER

"Sometimes I find it hard to look back to nine years ago with G & R. I'm sure you remember how Jane used to complain about the way I worked around the clock and never had any time for her or the youngsters. At that time, we were in really bad shape. During the preceding five years, the store had slipped from position to a shaky fourth in relation to the other stores in Gulf City. Someone had to get in and work closely with the buyers, one after another. I practically lived with each merchant, helping him get his department back on its feet. In some cases, we found it necessary to replace them with seasoned buyers from other stores. I hated to bring in so many executives from the outside, but we simply didn't have enough good people coming along at the lower levels to do much promoting from within.

"And the store had developed such a poor reputation in some markets that I was forced to work personally with many leading apparel, accessories, and home-furnishings resources before we were in a position to carry their lines again. With conditions as they were and with our competitors doing everything they could to keep us from regaining our No. 1 spot, this was a job I had to tackle myself, as general merchandise manager. The divisional supervisors and buyers just weren't strong enough to deal with the presidents and owners of some of the finest manufacturing establishments in this country and abroad. It was hard work, but it was also a lot of fun."

WHERE DO I GO FROM HERE?

"I can't help wondering what the next stop should be. Young Barrett and Sheila are well along in college and, except for summers, have flown the nest. The only way I can continue to grow is to keep on tackling new, challenging problems. I know that some of my friends think I'm already spreading myself too thin. From the look on your face, Floyd, it may be in your mind, too. I think I am pretty close to the boys down at the store, but it may be that they, too, think I am becoming an absentee president. However, as I have already said, I believe thoroughly in the significance of the causes for which I am working outside of the business, and I also believe each of them, in one way or another, helps contribute to the success of Green & Richards. Besides, I just can't see myself sitting in the office down at the store, reading a newspaper and waiting for someone to come in with a problem.

"Every so often, I have thought about trying a few years of government service. Through my work on the business advisory council of the Department of Commerce, I am in touch with a good many of the key people in the Administration. If they knew that I might be available, I suspect there would be an opportunity for me to move in at a level challenging enough to be more than just another bureaucratic job. Several of my friends have even had the temerity to suggest my name for governor, but in this state, a Republican candidate has lost the race before he starts. I think what I would really like to do is talk with you a little bit about your own experiences as a teacher. Perhaps, at this point in my career, I could get the greatest satisfaction from helping pass on to young people coming along some of the things I think I have learned in business. What do you think, Floyd?"

Hall arose as the two wives entered the room and said, "Why don't we let things soak a bit? You've given me so much to think about I hardly know where to begin."

TRUMBLE'S BACKGROUND

Floyd Hall recalled that Trumble had graduated from Hambletonian College. With business conditions as they were at the time, he had gone on to take his M.B.A. at the Tuck School of Business Administration at Dartmouth. All of his business life had been spent in retailing. Barrett had started as an assistant buyer of women's ready-to-wear at Fisk Brothers in Buffalo, New York. He progressed rapidly to the place where he was merchandising their entire ready-to-wear line. After eight years, he left Fisk to become divisional merchandise manager of a leading Southeast department store. Four years later, he became assistant general merchandise manager of a nationally known high-quality store on the East coast. He joined Green & Richards as vice-president and general merchandise manager and became president two years later. Hall recalled that Trumble had always been active in community affairs, wherever he worked. In the twenty-odd years Hall had known him, Trumble had never shown any evidence of being under pressure. Hall considered this unusual in an industry noted for heavy demands it made on its executives. Trumble had always had time for a full social life and an opportunity to take advantage of his consuming interest in golf. Barrett had been runner-up twice in the national intercollegiate golf championship while in college. He continued to play top-drawer golf after graduation, reaching the quarter finals of the National Amateur in his midforties. Two years earlier, he had been runner-up for the Gulf State Championship and had been club champion of the Jefferson Davis Country Club for six years running.

THE "SERMON"

Floyd Hall remembered that Trumble had sent him a copy of a talk he had given before the Parkville Presbyterian Church shortly after he became president of G & R. When he returned to Bristol, he found it was still in his files.

THE OPPORTUNITIES AND RESPONSIBILITIES
OF THE CHRISTIAN LAYMAN
IN THE COMMUNITY

Excerpts from Barrett Trumble's Talk

Parkville Presbyterian Church
Wednesday Evening—November 28

It is very good to be with you, and I am sure that you understand that I am not here to preach. . . . But I thought that perhaps we could all think out loud, in an informal way, about the subject at hand, namely, the layman's opportunity and responsibility in the community.

The first thing we should ask ourselves is: What is a Christian layman? Obviously, a Christian layman is a follower of Jesus Christ and, in essence, stands for and believes, with his heart, in the teachings of Jesus. In this conjunction, it might be interesting to point out that Jesus Himself was a layman. Although he was called Rabbi (that is to say, teacher), there is no record of His attending a theological school. Further, Jesus surrounded Himself with laymen from the common walks of life, and although the message came down out of Heaven through Christ into the church, it was carried out of the church into life by laymen who preached the Gospel. There was really no other way to do this. . . .

. . . We might stress the qualities Jesus stands for and the kind of person He wants the Christian layman to be.

Taking great liberties with Matthew: In Chapter 5, Verse 3, which begins, "Blessed are the poor in spirit for theirs is the kingdom of Heaven" and goes on through the various beatitudes that Jesus mentioned, it seems quite clear that (1) kindness and consideration for

others—giving the other fellow a second chance, (2) aggressive courage
—going the second mile for good causes, (3) courtesy—coming from the
heart, (4) thoughtfulness and understanding, (5) fairness, (6) integrity
and vision, and (7) faith are some of the vital qualities that we should
strive to possess in our everyday living if we would measure up to Jesus'
standards.

. . . These very same qualities that Christ taught us to strive and
stand for are the ones that make for true success in everyday life. I think
it important to emphasize here that I am talking about inner spiritual,
rather than material, success—the sort which would lead a man such as
Disraeli to want to be a great *man* rather than a great *lawyer*. These
qualities make for true success in every walk of life, whether one is engaged in teaching, farming, a profession, business, or household duties.
The old idea that to be successful one had to be ruthless, unscrupulous,
and tough with people just doesn't stand up today and it is my honest
opinion that the inability to handle, work with, and influence people is
probably the cause of the greatest number of personal failures in life.
Time and time again, I have—and I am sure you have—seen brilliant
people who appeared to have just what it takes for success fail utterly
because they overlooked the fact that one rarely succeeds alone but
rather succeeds because others make one successful. . . .

I have been very fortunate in my life to have met and watched a great
number of prominent people at work. I think you will agree with me
when I say that a Charles Wilson or a George Marshall or a Dwight
Eisenhower exemplifies fully these qualities that I have listed. I have
never met a more humble, homespun, or thoughtful man than Charles
Wilson; nor a more kind, considerate, and honest one than Marshall;
nor a more thoughtful, fair, or courageous man than Eisenhower. As a
matter of fact, it seems to me that the greater the man, the fewer the
pretenses and the more down-to-Christian-fundamentals he is. . . .

Let me quote, again, from the text: Ephesians 4:32—"Be ye kind one
to another, tender-hearted, forgiving." In Barrie's play, *Little White
Bird,* a young husband is waiting at the hospital for his child to be born.
He has never been unkind to his wife, but he wonders if he has been as
kind as he might have been. "Let us make a new rule from tonight," he
says, "always to be a little kinder than is necessary." . . . "Somehow, I
never thought it paid," said Lincoln, when his friends urged him to
make a stinging reply to a bitter, untrue word spoken about him. In the
end, kindness, even to those who have been unkind to us, is never regretted. "A little kinder than is necessary" is the finest of the little arts
of life, if not its final joy. The only things we are never sorry for are the
kind things said and done to others. They make a soft pillow at the end.

. . . What are the obligations of the layman to his business or profession? In this regard, we have a great obligation to attempt to do the
best possible job that we can in the field we are in, whatever that field

might be. I believe it was Plato who said, "The source of the greatest happiness is in a job well done." Furthermore, by doing a good job in our field, whether it be as a mother in a home, a teacher in the school, a doctor in the hospital, or a businessman, we raise the standard of living and happiness of all those around us, and I am sure you will agree this is a most worthwhile goal.

Then there is the obligation of the layman to his fellow worker. To realize the dignity of man, to make his working and living conditions as pleasant as possible, to treat him with inner courtesy—coming from the heart. . . .

More directly and to the point of our subject, there is the obligation of the layman to his community, and I mean this in the large sense—the community being either local, national, or worldwide. Now, this interest in the obligation to the community can take the form of helping to improve the school system, of working with the sick and needy through the hospitals and in other ways helping to take care of the less fortunate. It can take the form of interest in striving for better, more enlightened, and honest government or in working for world peace. And finally, it can take the shape of interest in the church and in what the church stands for. Certainly, in some small way to help improve the lot of one or all of these five community efforts would be a most Christian thing to do—certainly something that Jesus urges us to pursue. Schools need better facilities, and teachers need more pay; the sick need care—the needy, relief from want; the government needs to understand and work for world peace and tolerance. And, certainly, the church, of all these community needs, should always be in our minds as an ever-present source of spiritual guidance, helping us to live every day a better and more Christian life. As I see it, going to church once a week isn't enough. We must also strive in our everyday living to *live* by the examples and teachings of Jesus. . . . It is not enough to just accept these teachings of Jesus. We must make these teachings work for us in our daily life.

. . . A Christian church is not a religion of monuments, but a religion of life. Of course, all of us must work for the physical needs of the church. But we must realize that the human race can never be saved by priests and monks and ministers alone, but rather by the Christian layman courageously setting a living example and aggressively selling, if you please, the teachings of Christ in his community. Every great idea must express itself in form. There must be an organization, but organization alone is not enough. Any religion worth having must demonstrate a power that makes changes in the lives of people who profess it. . . .

In conclusion—so many times I have heard people say that working for all these causes is fine, but what can I do about it—I am only one individual. . . . Of course, if everyone lived as Jesus taught us to live, there would probably not be need for helping other people. . . . If we solve our problems from a Christian and spiritual standpoint, we have taken a great step toward helping to solve the world's problems. Secondly, one doesn't have to head up organizations to be helpful. There are all levels of responsibility in community work for . . . anyone who wants to help. Finally, the argument that one is too busy would seem highly unjustified when the old expression, "When you want a job done, give it to a busy man," is so true.

INTERNATIONAL MINERALS
AND CHEMICAL
CORPORATION

In the proxy statement issued by the management of the International Minerals and Chemical Corporation in September, 1961, notice was given to the stockholders that they would be requested to vote on a "Deferred Compensation Plan for Directors." In brief, the plan proposed by management was to increase the annual compensation of directors from $3,000 to $10,000 per annum, and to give the directors the option of receiving their compensation in cash or of deferring payment until either (a) they retired from their principal occupation, or (b) until they retired from the Board of IMC. Management was in favor of the proposed plan and in support thereof gave the following explanation:

> The Management has determined that it is in the best interests of the Corporation and its stockholders to provide more substantial compensation for the individuals serving as members of the Board. It is believed that the effect thereof will be to encourage the present members of the Board to continue to serve the Corporation in such capacity, and to aid the Corporation in securing the services of properly qualified men in the future as vacancies occur or the number of directors is increased.

As soon as the proxy statement was received by the public press, both the proposed amount of director compensation and the deferred payment proposal were commented upon in the financial columns as being somewhat unusual. The company, however, gave out no additional information until the annual meeting (held in New York on October 24, 1961) when Mr. T. M. Ware commented to the stockholders in attendance along the following lines:

> During the past few years it has become apparent that the *work, time* and *effort* required of the directors has increased at an ever-accelerating pace. To illustrate, IMC directors have been asked to authorize capital expenditures of more than $55 million in the last 30 months. They have approved four acquisitions by exchange of stock, a $40 million financing, major disposition of idle property and other matters of consequence involving the future of the Corporation. In the last twelve months, written material appended to monthly agendas has exceeded 1,000 pages. Six members of the Board are on active committees and others will be on special projects as time passes.
>
> The Proxy Statement has given you the background on the men proposed for membership on your Board of Directors. I am sure that you see outstanding individual capability and see how together they can help us in our business—domestic and foreign. Looking at them as individuals, I am sure that you can see why I take advantage of their abilities in individual consultation a countless number of times each year. Consultation has been heavy in the past and it will be more so in the future.
>
> Once it was determined that compensation was inadequate for past duties and as we looked forward to an acceleration of demand in the future, it became obvious that simple fairness indicated an adjustment in the retainer was necessary. With this background, we began a broad study of director compensation. We found that there is no pattern among corporations in the United States. Companies vary in policy on "inside" versus "outside" directors. Some corporations pay annual retainers and others pay by the meeting. The total compensation varies from $1,000 to well over $10,000. Some pay nominal retainers but high fees for committee assignments, and some even have the directors participate in employee benefit programs, pension insurance, etc. In other words, you can find support in the figures for any position you wish to take.[1]
>
> However, we did find that there is a trend toward annual retainers, and there is a trend toward higher pay for outside directors. Considering our Company, its policies and its plans, it was determined that $10,000 per annum was a fair figure in relation to the work and risks involved. The trend is up and what seems high today may well be at median a few years from now. We believe that we are right in taking a leadership position in this matter. . . .
>
> The deferred feature of the plan is relatively common in industry. Deferral does not increase cost to the Corporation. As a matter of fact, there is benefit because participants in these programs acquire a con-

[1] For supporting evidence see Appendix.

stantly increasing stock interest with corresponding incentive to work harder for the best interest of their investment.

Some months after the annual meeting of 1961 an official of International Minerals and Chemical Corporation gave this additional explanation of the reasoning behind the executive thinking about the directors' compensation plans:

Competition in the agricultural chemical field in the past years has been sharply increased by the entrance of several of the major petroleum companies. This competition has become particularly acute since the oil companies are producing nitrogen at a low cost in a form suitable for agricultural fertilizers. This competition is affecting IMC's position in the basic agricultural fertilizer market and may bring about some reduction in the basic product sales volume of the corporation.

In order to meet this growing competition IMC executives have formulated a three-fold plan:

1.   To modernize and enlarge existing plant facilities.

2.   To intensify their research program in agricultural chemicals in order to develop new products.

3.   To seek out opportunities to acquire other companies who are successfully producing complementary but noncompeting products to the line already being produced by IMC.

As anticipated by the chairman in his remarks to the stockholders' meeting, the burden being placed on this year's Board members has already been increased. Every member of the Board has been appointed to at least one committee. Among the more important of the 1961–62 committees are: Audit and Budget, Finance, and Stock Option and Compensation. Also since the 1961 annual meeting a new $50 million development program to cover a two-year period has been approved by the Board. Each project authorized under the general program will be subject to final review by an appropriate Board committee before work starts. On March 26, 1962, IMC announced three new acquisitions of small companies.[2] It has also entered into a joint venture with Standard Oil Company of California and the Indian government to study the feasibility of a new chemical plant in India.

[2] The three companies were Alamo Lumber Co., San Antonio, Texas; May Brothers, Inc., LaFayette, Louisiana; and Mud Control Laboratories, Oklahoma City. All three firms are concerned with the oil well drilling mud industry.

It has been estimated that, under the new plan, in addition to the time spent at the nine or ten monthly Board meetings, and the preparation therefor, each Board member will be expected to attend anywhere from three to five additional committee meetings, and be available at almost any time for individual consultations with respect to matters he is most familiar with.

Inasmuch as it was the policy of management to have the Board of Directors review and approve each major project proposed under the general investment program, and since the over-all program was large, members of the Board on the Finance Committee were certain to be called upon for more than normal amount of their time.

In order to properly direct the research program, the company's management wished to add to the Board of Directors men from the university field who were noted in the chemical research field.

Similarly, the management desired advice upon possible acquisitions by IMC and was looking for men who were in positions to direct the corporation's attention to likely areas.

The following is a summary of the Board compensation plan:

1. Each management member of the Board is to receive an annual compensation of $10,000. Management members who are directors will receive no additional compensation nor be eligible for the directors' deferred compensation plan.

2. Each nonmanagement member of the Board of Directors may elect at the beginning of his service to defer receiving all or any part of his director's compensation (a) until such a time as he has retired from his principal occupation, or (b) until he retires from the Board of Directors of IMC. Once made, this decision is irrevocable and cannot be changed, except that the amount of compensation to be deferred may be increased at the will of the director.

3. The amount of the compensation deferred by the director is to be allocated to the participant's deferred compensation account each month. At the end of each calendar month all cash received from such deferrals, or from dividends on stock units already held in participant's deferral account, shall be converted into common stock units at the closing price on the last trading day of the calendar month on the N.Y.S.E.

4. When the deferred account becomes due it may be paid by the corporation either in common stock or in cash *at the option of the corporation*. The normal method of distribution will be in ten equal annual installments, but the participant may shorten this period to five

years by filing a written request with the secretary of the corporation six months before the first installment of the deferred account becomes due.

5. Stock payments for either the management bonus plan or the directors' deferred compensation plan cannot be made by issuing additional stock, but must be made from prior issued stock held in the treasury of the company.

6. The Board of Directors can terminate or amend this plan at any time, but such action cannot be made retroactive once a participant has had deferred compensation credited to his account.

After the chairman read his statement at the stockholders' meeting there was a brief debate on the resolution from the floor. One woman objector said in effect that she felt $10,000 a year to attend ten or twelve luncheons (paid for by the company) was rather high remuneration, and she would like to have a job like that. The second objector, a man, said that while he could see no fault with the plan as applied to IMC, he felt that the company was establishing a dangerous precedent for other companies to follow, inasmuch as the calls made upon the time of the directors of IMC appeared to be somewhat unusual.

When the vote was taken on the resolutions they were approved by greater than a 15:1 margin.

The new Board of Directors for the ensuing year was also elected at the annual meeting of the stockholders. Out of the eleven men elected, only one was a company executive—the President, Mr. Thomas M. Ware.[3] The other ten elected were all outsiders. Only two of the nominees were up for stockholder election for the first time—Dr. Earl L. Butz, Dean of the School of Agriculture, Purdue University, and Mr. Robert W. Purcell of the International Basic Economy Corp. Mr. Purcell had already been elected by the Board to fill a vacancy occurring in the summer of 1961.

The proxy statement, in addition to the names of the nominees and their stockholdings, gave a brief description of their principal business connections. In the following tabulations, this latter listing has been amplified to include all directorships held in profit-making enterprises.[4]

[3] The Chairmanship of the Board, since this position does not carry the responsibility of being Chief Administrative Officer, is not considered by IMC to be a management position. Hence the Chairman, Mr. Louis Ware, is now considered to be an "outside" member of the Board.

[4] This information was obtained from the 1962 edition of Poor's *Register of Directors and Executives.*

The Eleven Nominees (in Alphabetical Order)

Name	*Common Stock Owned as of 8/15/61*	*Occupation & Directorships Held*
Austin, Edwin C.	227	Partner, Sidley, Austin, Burgess and Smith (attorneys-at-law), Chicago Director of: Brooks-Scanlon, Inc., also V.P. and member of Exec. Comm. Harris Trust and Savings Bank Hoover Co. Leath & Co. A. C. Nielsen Co. G. D. Searle & Co. Int. Minerals & Chem. Corp.
Budinger, John M.	1,000	Chairman of advisory committee, sr. V.P. and director of Bankers Trust Co., N.Y. Director of: Thomas J. Lipton, Inc. Mavibel International, N.V. Rockwell Standard Corp. N. V. Becuny Amer. Mutual Liberty Ins. Co. Federal Paper & Board Co. Int. Minerals & Chem. Corp.
Butz, Earl L.	100*	Dean, College of Agriculture, Purdue Univ. (former Asst. U.S. Sec. of Agriculture)
Dunlap, Jack Wilbur	500	Chairman and president, Dunlap & Associates, Inc. (business consultants) Director of: International Minerals & Chem. Corp. Carmody Corp. Chart-Pak, Inc. Clark Channel, Inc. Agri Research, Inc. (Chairman & Director) Public Service Research, Inc.
Johnson, Glover	2,000	Attorney-at-law and partner, White & Case (N.Y.) Director of: International Minerals & Chem. Corp. F & M Schaeffer Brewing Co. Genung's Inc.

* Purchased prior to election to Board of Directors.

The Eleven Nominees (in Alphabetical Order) (continued)

Name	*Common Stock Owned as of 8/15/61*	*Occupation & Directorships Held*
		Chock Full O'Nuts Corp.
		Gevaert Co. of Amer., Inc.
		Federal Paper Board Co., Inc.
		Howland Dry Goods Co.
Meers, Henry W.	300	Resident partner, White Weld & Co. (investment bankers)
		Director of:
		North American Life Insurance Co.
		Lennon Wall Paper Co. (Joliet, Ill.)
		Kroehler Manufacturing Co.
		Continental Bearings Corp.
		International Minerals & Chem. Corp.
Purcell, Robert W.	1,000*	Chairman of board of directors, International Basic Economy Corp. (promotional organization)
		Director of:
		Brightwater Paper Co.
		Investors Syndicate of Canada, Ltd.
		Investors Diversified Service, Inc.
		Chemway Corp.
		Vitro Corp. of America
		Transoceanic-AOFC, Ltd.
		Industrial & Mining Dev. Bank of Iran
		Pakistan Industrial Credit & Inv. Corp. Ltd.
		International Minerals & Chem. Corp.
Ryan, John T., Jr.	100	President and director, Mine Safety Appliances Co. (manufacturing organization)
		Chairman, Federal Reserve Board, Cleveland
		President and director, Mine Safety Appliances of Canada
		Chairman, board of directors, Callery Chem. Co.
		Chairman of Auergesellschaft, W. Berlin, W. Germany
		President and director, MSA Research Corp.
		Director of:
		Blaw-Knox Co.

The Eleven Nominees (in Alphabetical Order) (continued)

Name	Common Stock Owned as of 8/15/61	Occupation & Directorships Held
		Mine Safety Appliances Co., Africa, (Pty) Ltd., South Africa
		Thorofare Markets, Inc.
		Heppenstall Co.
		Catalyst Research Corporation
		Elastic Stop Nut Corp.
		International Minerals & Chem. Corp.
		H. J. Heinz Co.
Taylor, Vernon F., Jr.	500	Vice president and director, Peerless Oil & Gas Co. (petroleum company)
		Director of:
		International Minerals & Chem. Corp.
Ware, Louis	30,000	Chairman of the board of directors, International Minerals & Chem. Corp.
		Director of:
		First National Bank of Chicago
		Air Reduction Company
		Illinois Central R.R. Co.
Ware, Thomas M.	6,000	President and director, International Minerals & Chemical Corp.
		Director of: **
		Dunlap & Associates, Inc.

** Also member of Advisory Committee, Bankers Trust Co. of New York.

The proxy statement had the following comments to make on the two men who were being presented for the first time to the stockholders as nominees for the Board of Directors:

> During the last five years Mr. Purcell has been a director and since 1959, Chairman of the Board of Directors of International Basic Economy Corporation, a company engaged in the development and financing of basic business enterprises abroad. Dr. Butz has been, since 1957, Dean of the School of Agriculture, Purdue University. For three years prior thereto he was Assistant Secretary of Agriculture in Washington, D.C.

APPENDIX

The *Wall Street Journal* carried two news articles within the past few years with respect to the modern trend toward "working directors." The first of these appeared on November 30, 1960, and was entitled "Working Directors—Many Companies Give Boards a Bigger Role, Add More Outsiders." The second article appeared on March 15, 1962, and was entitled "Study Finds 'Outside' Directors Dominate More Firms' Policies." Both articles were based on reports issued by the National Industrial Conference Board relating to corporate directorship practices.

After describing a meeting of the "working directors" of the Hupp Corporation, Cleveland, Ohio, the article of November 30, 1960, stated:

> . . . more companies are making the "working" board an increasingly important tool of management. Tightly squeezed profit margins, mounting competition and diversification into unaccustomed fields are all spurring companies to make better use of the sometimes almost untapped store of top talent in their board rooms.
>
> "Many American companies are becoming increasingly aware of the value of alert, active boards of directors and are making special efforts to step up their effectiveness," reports the National Industrial Conference Board, a private research group.
>
> How can companies put their boards to work? Many are doing it by arming directors with more facts, and bringing them in earlier on developing problems. They're seeking more outside directors with specially needed knowledge and fresh viewpoints, and are taking directors on more trips for firsthand looks at company facilities. Some firms are using their directors as supersalesmen who can influence big companies, and many are gingerly but determinedly making room for new blood by easing out the old-timers. In turn, these companies are paying the newcomers more for their extra time and trouble.
>
> The trend toward working boards is important not only to top management and to directors themselves, but to the millions of Americans owning stock in corporations and working for them. Carefully chosen boards with more facts at their disposal are better equipped to make the right decisions on vital corporate matters and thus enhance prospects for improved sales and profits. What's more, the knowledge that directors are hard at work can spur on employees all down the line.
>
> Much more so now than a decade or two ago, directors' duties only begin with attending a formal meeting every month. "I recently joined the boards of two companies," complains a Chicago executive, "and as a result, I haven't had dinner with my family one night in the last two weeks." Besides the monthly meetings, there are meetings of an operating committee, an executive compensation committee, and a long-range planning committee, plus frequent telephone calls, conferences stretching over long lunch hours, dinner meetings lasting well into the night, and even weekend sessions.

Because of the new emphasis on keeping the board informed, today's directors probably talk about "homework" as much as any schoolboy. "Our directors can't come in fully informed unless they spend two or three days on their homework," says Edward K. Thode, vice president and secretary of General Mills, Inc., Minneapolis. Their "homework" consists of studying "one or two packets of information mailed to them every week," he says. . . .

As they demand more of their directors' time, companies are also compensating them a bit better. One of every six companies surveyed by the National Industrial Conference Board has increased fees "moderately" in the past two years, but $100 a meeting is still the most popular fee. However, Chicago's Fairbanks Morse Co. not long ago dropped the $100-a-meeting fee for a $3000-a-year retainer, and one steel company recently went to $750 quarterly from $625. While contending that directors usually aren't paid enough to fairly compensate them, one philosophizes that raising fees is foolish "since most of it goes to taxes anyhow," and that service and the opportunity to learn are the chief motives for taking on the job.

Companies adding outside directors often find they get a bonus through the director drawing on the skills of specialists on his firm's staff. "There are many times that a company gets the benefit of experts in a director's company," says David M. Kennedy, chairman of Continental Illinois National Bank & Trust Co. of Chicago. When a matter calling for specialized banking knowledge comes up in one of the firms of which Mr. Kennedy is a director . . . "I'll have people in our bank take a look at it," he says. . . .

The second article in the *Wall Street Journal* on March 15, 1962, added statistical proof of the recent trend toward increasing the number of outside directors and increasing their compensation. The pertinent remarks in this article are:

In 1961 . . . outside directors were a majority on the boards of 61% of the manufacturing companies studied, compared with 57% in 1958 and 54% in 1953.

. . . the companies also have raised the compensation of these outside directors. The payment averaging $200 a meeting is still largely symbolic in nature because of the tradition that directors are men of substantial means who accept directorships as an honor. Some 28.5% of 554 companies have boosted the payment since 1958, and a few companies pay over $1000 per meeting, plus travel expenses.

Possibly in recognition of outside directors' increasing responsibilities, more corporations are paying them a yearly retainer, with the median payment running $2500 per year. . . . For half, the retainer is the sole form of compensation, while about half the companies combine per-meeting fees with retainers. . . .

SURENESS COMPANY

The Sureness Company produced and distributed nationally a complete line of large and small appliances, such as dishwashers, laundry units, dryers, refrigerators, home freezers, electric stoves, air conditioners, irons, toasters, blenders, beaters, and squeezers. The company was one of the largest in the industry and sales had doubled since 1946. As a result of this expansion the company had made a number of important organizational changes. In 1955 the company employed the services of an outside consulting firm to study the productivity of its executives.

As part of its study approach, the consulting firm assigned one of its senior account executives, Phillip Harms, to interview all company executives to determine their views on how their productivity could be improved. Prior to interviewing each executive the consultant studied the man's personnel record, the general nature of his work, his position in the organizational structure, and the number and type of persons reporting to him. Following is an interview with the sales manager.

STALEY: I'm glad that top management has decided to study the productivity of its executives. This company can certainly use some help on this subject. We're all working too many hours—and I, for one, don't see any relief in sight. In my own case I know I work a lot longer than forty hours each week and so does my boss, the vice-president of marketing.

HARMS: How much time would you guess you put in each week? Could you break this down by type of work activity?

STALEY: Both of your questions are tough to answer, since some weeks I spend a majority of my time in the field. There's one stretch around the first of the year when I'm in the field for better than a solid month. That's the time when we introduce our new models.

HARMS: Well, I can see why your problem is a little different from some of the

other executives I've talked to—but why not tell me what you did
last week. You were here all last week, weren't you?

STALEY: Yes, I was here last week, but I'm not sure that it was a typical
week. Well, O.K., let's try it on for size and see what happens. You'll
want to make some notes, won't you? Should I have my secretary record
our discussion?

HARMS: No, I'll just do a little scribbling from time to time. Go ahead.

STALEY: I usually get to the office about 8:00, which is a half hour before
the bell rings. By the time my secretary gets in, I have her work pretty
well lined up for the day. From about 8:30 or 8:45 to nearly 10 I'm
dictating and handling papers. I feel that paper work is important in a
big company like this and if I don't keep on top of it I'm really in
trouble. Of course, I do a lot of my work over the telephone—especially
with my district sales managers.

   After 10 o'clock I don't have any prescribed routine. It all depends on
where the fire is and what's going on in the vice-president's office. I'd
guess I average an hour a day with him. He wants to know everything
that goes on in this department so I find that I spend a lot of time brief-
ing him on our activities. When I was new on this job I was glad that he
was there with a net to bail me out, but I've had this job for almost
two years and he still seems to worry about everything I do. Say, I assume
that whatever I tell you is confidential. I have a note here from the
president which says that I'm not to hold anything back.

HARMS: That's right. Nothing you tell me will ever be revealed. That's why
I didn't want your secretary to take any minutes of this meeting.

STALEY: Well, don't misunderstand me—I've got a swell boss—but the company would be a lot better off if he spent more of his time working on
over-all company problems instead of worrying about my operations.
He does the same thing with the advertising manager and the sales engineering manager. I can't speak for them, but in my case it's like he was
still running the department and I was the assistant manager.

HARMS: What kinds of matters do you discuss with him?

STALEY: Everything. About once a day he asks me to come up for a meeting.
He then asks how things are going, and the first thing you know he's
got me telling him about all my problems. Also, he remembers them
and asks me later what I did about them. Of course, sometimes he tells
me what to do—and how to do it. He's got a sharp memory and wants
me to report back on the action I took. But heck, I'm a big boy now
and can make most of my own decisions. Also, he gets a copy of all my
sales analysis reports.

HARMS: What kinds of reports are these?

STALEY: These are reports which come out weekly from our sales analysis
unit showing sales by product item, by distributor, by sales district, and
so on. They show sales for the week, sales cumulated for the year, sales
for the same period last year, and the quota. Boy, when I'm off quota

he's really on my back. I suppose in some cases he's got a right to be. I'll say one thing, though; he's a guy you can talk to. He'll listen to me, and for the most part he'll let me do what I want. Of course, we've been working together for over ten years now.

One problem with trying to keep him fully informed is that I have to be on top of everything. This means that I do many of the things that probably should be left to some of my staff. I think one of the problems that this company has is delegation. My boss should delegate more, and if he would, then I could do more delegating.

HARMS: Could you be a little more specific about this matter of delegation?

STALEY: Well, delegation is an abstract subject, but take the matter of signatures. When I was assistant sales manager no one could sign a letter except the boss. When I took over, I studied the situation and found that four members of my staff wrote 80 per cent of the letters in this office. Therefore I told these people that they could sign for me, but that before the letters were mailed I would check them. I was told by the V.P. that it wouldn't work, but it's worked fine so far.

HARMS: If you check all the letters, then how does this save you any time?

STALEY: I don't really read them—I just glance at them. From this I can tell what's important—and these I read more carefully. It only takes me about 15 or 20 minutes a day to check these letters, but before I delegated responsibility it took me almost an hour. Also, I've noticed that I find fewer errors. People know they've got the responsibility, whereas before they could rely—or thought they could—on me to catch their mistakes. Now they have the responsibility.

HARMS: Do you have any other thoughts on delegation?

STALEY: Well, we have a tough situation here which prevents me from doing all the delegation I'd like. My assistant is an old-timer—been with the company for over 20 years. He's a nice guy and a real salesman. Trouble is he can't administer. He used to be a district manager, but his health went bad and the doctor said he'd have to get an office job with regular hours and no traveling. He knows all the salesmen and many of our big accounts. If I want any information about the history of a salesman or a big account, I just ask him and the chances are he'll give me a quick and accurate fill in.

But he's no administrator. I find that I have to do part of his job. He's terrible about answering correspondence or even routing things. About twice a week I sit down with him at his desk and go over the stuff in his "in" basket. He doesn't seem to mind. I don't know what he'd do if he had a really tough boss.

HARMS: Do you have any other people on your staff to whom you feel you can't delegate?

STALEY: Yes, I do. I have a research director who at times drives me nuts. He's a smart technologist who knows his statistics—but he can't see the forest for the trees. Research isn't any good unless it's problem-oriented.

It's got to help serve a marketing problem. Well, I have to practically tell this research specialist what the study objectives should be. What's more, I have to suggest the kinds of information he should get in order to solve the problem. But after that he's a good man. He does have difficulty writing a final report. Several times I've had to take his reports home and rewrite them so that my boss will be able to understand them.

HARMS: Can you tell me more about how you spend your day?

STALEY: Let's see—we were up to about 10 in the morning just after I'd finished dictating to my secretary. Well, as I said, I don't have a regular schedule after that. I spend about an hour a day with my boss and probably average about another hour a day working with our advertising manager and the head of our sales engineering department. Then there are always several long-distance phone calls from the field from salesmen or customers. Some of these I can turn over to my assistant, but usually I figure if it's important enough to warrant a long-distance call that it's important enough for me to answer. I always have some personal visitors —salesmen, product men, and so on. I like to talk with them if only for a few minutes since it gives me a feeling of knowing what's going on in the market. There are also plenty of committee meetings—production coordination, styling, incentives, and so on. The higher one gets in an organization, the more committees he's on. But I don't mind too much—I learn a lot. By the time 5 o'clock comes my "in" basket is filled up again and so I load a lot of things in my brief case and head for home. I do all my magazine reading at home—they'd think I was loafing if they caught me reading on the job. I know I'd feel that way if I found any of my men doing it. I never get a chance to do any really good reading. At times I worry about this, because if I ever get promoted I probably ought to know about such things as the tariff, the national debt, the important trends in business, and so on. I even come down here on Saturdays and work trying to get caught up. When we're planning our activities for the next year I find I'm head over heels in work—days, nights and week-ends. My wife hardly knows me and soon I'll need an introduction to my kids. Speaking of the time, I'm afraid I'll have to beg off for today. I've got to make a meeting date. I'm late now.

HARMS: You've been very cooperative. Would you object to my talking to any of your staff?

STALEY: No, just as long as you arrange a time which is convenient for them.

After Staley had left, Harms paid a visit to the company's research director, Don Hartwig. He explained who he was and what he wanted and asked when he could get together with Hartwig. The latter replied that now was as good a time as any.

HARMS: Delegation is always a big problem in a company as large as this. Still there are always ways in which it can be improved. Do you have any suggestions as to what can be done about it within this office? You probably got a note from the president saying I'd be around. Everything will be kept absolutely confidential.

HARTWIG: Gee, this is something I haven't thought about for quite some time. All in all, I think things run pretty smoothly around here. I have some problems with my boss, Mr. Staley, but they're not too serious. His biggest trouble is that he works too hard and expects everybody who works for him to do the same. Generally speaking he's a real good guy, but he insists at times on spelling things out too much. Sometimes he spells things out so much that I'm boxed in. Also, he tries to tell me how to make surveys. He's way out of touch with the latest research techniques. He hasn't been in research for ten years and a lot has happened since then. But I guess it's natural for a guy to be interested in a field he used to be pretty good in.

I have a relatively small section here—only about a half dozen people. We farm out any big stuff, and our advertising agency helps a lot. They have a research man full-time on this account. I don't really have many delegation problems. I'll tell you a guy you really ought to talk with who has this problem. He's Matt Keerney, Staley's assistant. He's a wonderful guy and in his day was probably the best salesman in the company. His health got bad and they gave him a desk job. He really knows his stuff and advises Staley on just about everything. In fact, I'm not sure he doesn't make most of his decisions. Staley treats him O.K., except he's always after him for not following company procedures. Matt isn't a paper hound, but he can get more done with a phone call than any of the rest of us could with a dozen letters. You ought to talk with him. Trouble is he's on vacation right now and won't be back for a couple of weeks.

HARMS: It's just about lunch time and I've a luncheon date with somebody from the advertising department. Can I come back sometime and talk again?

HARTWIG: You sure can. Any time.

Sometime later Harms talked at length with the vice-president of marketing, Fred Kroll. Part of the interview dealt with the problem of delegation. On this subject Kroll said:

In my job I don't have much of a problem of delegation. I have only about five people who report to me. Take my sales manager, for example. He's one of my boys. We've been together for a long time, but despite all this there are times, I'm sure, when he feels that I won't get off his back. But this is a "dog eat dog" business. You have to keep the pressure on day and night. I'm responsible for the total marketing operation which runs well over one hundred million dollars a year. If I'm not on top of the latest price cut, the latest merchandising gimmick, the latest "deal," I don't feel that I'm doing my job. You have to push your men—drive them, because if you don't you'll wake up some morning and find that some competitor has stolen part of your market. I'm considered by some people to be old-fashioned—I won't delegate my life away—but I get results and that's what counts.

Harms then asked what he thought about the delegation in the sales department. Kroll replied:

I don't pay much attention to whether Staley delegates or not. I figure that's his business. I don't tell him how to run his people. I never hear any complaints so I guess he's probably doing O.K. Staley has one problem though—he brings me too damn many problems. For example, yesterday he wanted my advice on what to do with a San Francisco department store which had refused delivery of their last order. How should I know what he should do. I know what I'd do because Bob Scope, the buyer in the Frisco store, is an old friend of mine. Another thing about Staley is that he's not out in the field enough. You don't sell appliances by sitting in the home office. He ought to be out there on the firing line. But Staley's a good man—we all have some faults. He's one of the best in the business. Sometimes I wish he knew just how good he really is.

THE CASE OF THE
MISSING TIME

At approximately 7:30 a.m. on Tuesday, June 23, 1959, Chet Craig, manager of the Norris Company's Central plant, swung his car out of the driveway of his suburban home and headed toward the plant located some six miles away just inside the Midvale city limits. It was a beautiful day. The sun was shining brightly and a cool, fresh breeze was blowing. The trip to the plant took about twenty minutes and sometimes gave Chet an opportunity to think about plant problems without interruption.

The Norris Company owned and operated three quality printing plants. Norris enjoyed a nation-wide commercial business, specializing in quality color work. It was a closely held company with some 350 employees, nearly half of whom were employed at the Central plant, the largest of the three Norris production operations. The company's main offices were also located in the Central plant building.

Chet had started with the Norris Company as an expediter in its Eastern plant in 1948 just after he graduated from Ohio State. After three years Chet was promoted to production supervisor and two years later was made assistant to the manager of the Eastern plant. Early in 1957 he was transferred to the Central plant as assistant to the plant manager and one month later was promoted to plant manager, when the former manager retired.

Chet was in fine spirits as he relaxed behind the wheel. As his car picked up speed, the hum of the tires on the newly paved highway faded into the background. Various thoughts occurred to him and he said to himself, "This is going to be the day to really get things done."

He began to run through the day's work, first one project, then another, trying to establish priorities. After a few minutes he decided that the open-end unit scheduling was probably the most important; certainly the most urgent. He frowned for a moment as he recalled that on Friday the vice president and general manager had casually asked him if he had given the project any further thought. Chet realized that he had not been giving it much thought lately. He had been meaning to get to work on this idea for over three months, but something else always seemed to crop up. "I haven't had much time to sit down and really work it out," he said to himself. "I'd better get going and hit this one today for sure." With that he began to break down the objectives, procedures, and installation steps of the project. He grinned as he reviewed the principles involved and calculated roughly the anticipated savings. "It's about time," he told himself. "This idea should have been followed up long ago." Chet remembered that he had first conceived of the open-end unit scheduling idea nearly a year and a half ago just prior to his leaving Norris's Eastern plant. He had spoken to his boss, Jim Quince, manager of the Eastern plant, about it then and both agreed that it was worth looking into. The idea was temporarily shelved when he was transferred to the Central plant a month later.

A blast from a passing horn startled him but his thoughts quickly returned to other plant projects he was determined to get under way. He started to think through a procedure for simpler transport of dies to and from the Eastern plant. Visualizing the notes on his desk, he thought about the inventory analysis he needed to identify and eliminate some of the slow-moving stock items; the packing controls which needed revision; and the need to design a new special order form. He also decided that this was the day to settle on a job printer to do the simple outside printing of office forms. There were a few other projects he couldn't recall offhand but he could tend to them after lunch if not before. "Yes sir," he said to himself, "this is the day to really get rolling."

Chet's thoughts were interrupted as he pulled into the company parking lot. When he entered the plant Chet knew something was wrong as he met Al Noren, the stockroom foreman, who appeared troubled. "A great morning, Al," Chet greeted him cheerfully.

"Not so good, Chet; my new man isn't in this morning," Noren growled.

"Have you heard from him?" asked Chet.

"No, I haven't," replied Al.

Chet frowned as he commented, "These stock handlers assume you take it for granted that if they're not here, they're not here, and they don't have to call in and verify it. Better ask Personnel to call him."

Al hesitated for a moment before replying. "Okay, Chet, but can you find me a man? I have two cars to unload today."

As Chet turned to leave he said, "I'll call you in half an hour, Al, and let you know."

Making a mental note of the situation, Chet headed for his office. He greeted the group of workers huddled around Marilyn, the office manager, who was discussing the day's work schedule with them. As the meeting broke up Marilyn picked up a few samples from the clasper, showed them to Chet and asked if they should be shipped that way or if it would be necessary to inspect them. Before he could answer Marilyn went on to ask if he could suggest another clerical operator for the sealing machine to replace the regular operator who was home ill. She also told him that Gene, the industrial engineer, had called and was waiting to hear from Chet.

After telling Marilyn to go ahead and ship the samples, he made a note of the need for a sealer operator for the office and then called Gene. He agreed to stop by Gene's office before lunch and started on his routine morning tour of the plant. He asked each foreman the types and volumes of orders they were running, the number of people present, how the schedules were coming along, and the orders to be run next; helped the folding-room foreman find temporary storage space for consolidating a carload shipment; discussed quality control with a pressman who had been running poor work; arranged to transfer four people temporarily to different departments, including two for Al in the stockroom, talked to the shipping foreman about pickups and special orders to be delivered that day. As he continued through the plant, he saw to it that reserve stock was moved out of the forward stock area; talked to another pressman about his requested change of vacation schedule; had a "heart-to-heart" talk with a press helper who seemed to need frequent reassurance; approved two type and one color order okays for different pressmen.

Returning to his office, Chet reviewed the production reports on the larger orders against his initial projections and found that the plant was running behind schedule. He called in the folding-room foreman and together they went over the line-up of machines and made several necessary changes.

During this discussion, the composing-room foreman stopped in to cover several type changes and the routing foreman telephoned for approval of a revised printing schedule. The stockroom foreman called twice, first to inform him that two standard, fast-moving stock items were dangerously low; later to advise him that the paper stock for the urgent Dillon job had finally arrived. Chet made the necessary subsequent calls to inform those concerned.

He then began to put delivery dates on important and difficult inquiries received from customers and salesmen. (The routine inquiries were handled by Marilyn.) While he was doing this he was interrupted twice, once by a sales correspondent calling from the West Coast to ask for a better delivery date than originally scheduled; once by the personnel vice president asking him to set a time when he could hold an initial training and induction interview with a new employee.

After dating the customer and salesmen inquiries, Chet headed for his morning conference in the executive offices. At this meeting he answered the sales vice president's questions in connection with "hot" orders, complaints, the status of large-volume orders and potential new orders. He then met with the general manager to discuss a few ticklish policy matters and to answer "the old man's" questions on several specific production and personnel problems. Before leaving the executive offices, he stopped at the office of the secretary-treasurer to inquire about delivery of cartons, paper, and boxes, and to place new orders for paper.

On the way back to his own office, Chet conferred with Gene about two current engineering projects. When he reached his desk, he lit a cigarette, and looked at his watch. It was ten minutes before lunch, just time enough to make a few notes of the details he needed to check in order to answer knotty questions raised by the sales manager that morning.

After lunch Chet started again. He began by checking the previous day's production reports; did some rescheduling to get out urgent orders; placed appropriate delivery dates on new orders and inquiries received that morning; consulted with a foreman on a personal problem. He spent some twenty minutes at the TWX[1] going over mutual problems with the Eastern plant.

By midafternoon Chet had made another tour of the plant after which he met with the personnel director to review with him a touchy personal problem raised by one of the clerical employees; the vacation schedules submitted by his foremen; and the pending job evaluation program. Following this conference, Chet hurried back to his office to complete the special statistical report for Universal Waxing Corporation, one of Norris's best customers. As he finished the report he discovered that it was ten minutes after six and he was the only one left in the office. Chet was tired. He put on his coat and headed through the plant toward the parking lot; on the way he was stopped by both the night supervisor and night layout foreman for approval of type and layout changes.

With both eyes on the traffic, Chet reviewed the day he had just completed. "Busy?" he asked himself. "Too much so—but did I accomplish anything?" His mind raced over the day's activities. "Yes and no" seemed to be the answer. "There was the usual routine, the same as any other day. The plant kept going and I think it must have been a good production day. Any creative or special project work done?" Chet grimaced as he reluctantly answered, "No."

With a feeling of guilt, he probed further. "Am I an executive? I'm paid like one, respected like one, and have a responsible assignment with the necessary authority to carry it out. Yet one of the greatest values a company derives from an executive is his creative thinking and accomplishments. What have I done about it? An executive needs some time for thinking. Today was a typical day, just like most other days, and I did little, if any, creative work. The projects that I so enthusiastically planned to work on this morning are exactly as they were yesterday. What's more, I have no guarantee that tomorrow night or the next night will bring me any closer to their completion. This is a real problem and there must be an answer."

Chet continued, "Night work? Yes, occasionally. This is understood. But I've been doing too much of this lately. I owe my wife and family some of my time. When you come down to it, they are the people for whom I'm really working. If I am forced to spend much more time away from them, I'm not meeting my own personal objectives. What about church work? Should I eliminate that? I spend a lot of time on

[1] Leased private telegram communication system using teletypewriter.

this, but I feel I owe God some time too. Besides, I believe I'm making a worthwhile contribution in this work. Perhaps I can squeeze a little time from my fraternal activities. But where does recreation fit in?"

Chet groped for the solution. "Maybe I'm just rationalizing because I schedule my own work poorly. But I don't think so. I've studied my work habits carefully and I think I plan intelligently and delegate authority. Do I need an assistant? Possibly, but that's a long-time project and I don't believe I could justify the additional overhead expenditure. Anyway, I doubt whether it would solve the problem."

By this time Chet had turned off the highway onto the side street leading to his home—the problem still uppermost in his mind. "I guess I really don't know the answer," he told himself as he pulled into his driveway. "This morning everything seemed so simple but now. . . ."

exhibit 1
NORRIS COMPANY
Organization Chart

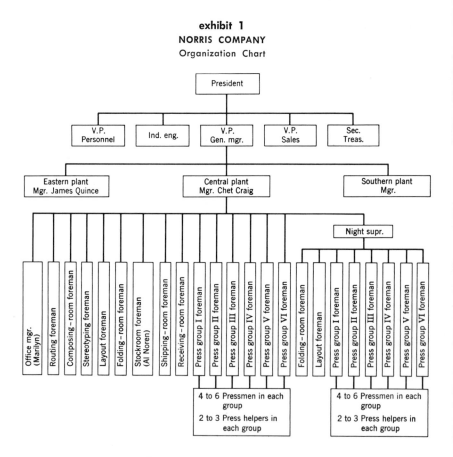

reapraising
and
recharting
courses of action

ELGIN NATIONAL
WATCH COMPANY

INTRODUCTION

Elgin National Watch Company for the fiscal year ended February 28, 1962, experienced its most profitable year since 1957 and reported a net income of $1.4 million, equal to $1.52 per common share as contrasted with $114,000, or $.12 per share in the previous year. Net sales for the year amounted to $40.4 million, representing a gain of 21% over sales of $33.3 million for 1961. (See Exhibit 1.)

In reporting the improved performance of the company in the 1962 annual report, Mr. Margolis, chairman of the company and chief executive officer, stated that the improved earnings for the year reflected operating efficiencies, broadening of the product line, and profitable acquisitions. "Most of the increased income," he said, "came from the industrial group and other divisions in the consumer group." He continued:

> We have just completed the most successful year in the past six years of our long corporate history. The improved sales and profits picture reflects the beginning results of planned programs. Effective last March the company acquired the Welby Corporation and the Bradley Time Corporation, two clock companies with fine reputations and proved sales and earnings abilities. With the acquisition of Lohengrin Diamond Ring and its subsidiary, Syndicate Diamonds, last November, Elgin is provided with a prime source of diamonds for our watches as well as lines of diamond rings and related products that can be readily marketed through our present distributing channels.

753

exhibit 1 ELGIN NATIONAL WATCH COMPANY AND SUBSIDIARIES

Consolidated balance sheet

	2/28 1962	2/28 1961	2/28 1960	2/28 1959	2/28 1958	2/28 1957	2/28 1956	2/28 1955	2/28 1954	12/31 1953
Assets										
Cash	$ 1,029	$ 1,197	$ 1,626	$ 2,156	$ 2,490	$ 2,107	$ 2,357	$ 2,018	$ 2,119	$ 2,460
Marketable securities (+ accrued int.)	—	—	1,742	4,492	293	3,801	4,256	5,817	3,106	3,100
Accounts receivable (net)	9,163	8,513	7,948	5,505	6,621	9,114	9,681[b]	6,926	8,036	15,051
Inventories, lower of cost (FIFO) or mkt.	13,132	11,149	10,288	8,475	12,418	14,343	15,471[b]	14,679	18,094	16,380
Income tax refund	—	—	—	—	1,499	—	—	—	—	—
Invest. in govt. defense work (less prog. payments)	399	248	188	161	201	213	221	5,354	6,036	6,345
Prepaid insurance, etc.	—	—	—	—	—	—	—	217	173	220
Total current assets	$23,723	$21,107	$21,792	$20,789	$23,522	$29,578	$31,986	$35,011	$37,564	$43,556
Patents, less accum. amortization	—	—	—	—	10	99	114	106	—	—
Land, plant & equipment (cost)	13,516	12,956	12,577	14,064	16,061	17,526	17,109	16,362	15,293	15,191
Less accum. deprec. & amortization	8,304	7,816[c]	7,613	8,745	9,892	9,340	8,488	8,031	7,444	7,340
Total capital assets	$ 5,212	$ 5,140	$ 4,964	$ 5,319	$ 6,169	$ 8,186	$ 8,621	$ 8,331	$ 7,849	$ 7,851
Total assets	$28,935	$26,247	$26,756	$26,108	$29,701	$37,863	$40,721	$43,448	$45,413	$51,407
Liabilities										
Accounts payable	$ 2,461	$ 1,251	$ 1,365	$ 929	$ 1,427	$ 1,170	$ 1,657	$ 1,946	$ 1,994	$ 1,902
Notes payable	600	600	600	500	500	500	500	300	300	10,250
Accruals (wages, etc.; pension contrib.)	2,279	1,643	1,663	1,437	1,656	2,001	2,247	2,726	3,112	2,174
Fed. inc. tax & other tax reserves	—	—	—	—	302	593	862	1,996	2,086	2,763
Dividends payable	—	—	—	—	—	137	228	502	6	—
Contractual price adjustment provs.	—	—	—	—	1,161	427	1,634	1,890	3,687	—
Provision for reloc. of operations	—	—	—	346	—	—	—	—	—	—
Total current liabilities	$ 5,340	$ 3,494	$ 3,628	$ 3,212	$ 5,046	$ 4,828	$ 7,128	$ 9,360	$11,185	$17,089
Reserve for casualty insurance	5,000[b]	5,600[f]	6,200[f]	6,800	7,300	7,800	8,300	8,800	9,300	9,350
Long term notes payable	—	—	—	—	—	—	—	—	—	—
Capital stock [a]	9,245	9,228	9,227	9,227	9,227	9,227	9,227	9,227	13,840	13,840
Paid-in surplus	4,633	4,615	4,613	4,613	4,613	4,613	4,613	4,613	—	—
Earned surplus	4,717[e]	3,309[e]	3,196[e]	2,370[e]	3,629[e]	11,509	11,567	11,562	11,214	11,257
Less treasury stock at cost	—	—	108	114	114	114	114	114	126	129
Total shareholders' equity	18,595	17,153	16,928	16,096	17,355	25,235	25,293	25,288	24,928	24,968
Total net worth & liability	28,935	26,247	26,756	26,108	29,701	37,863	40,721	43,448	45,413	51,407

a Paid-in capital arising from reduction in par value of capital stock (from $15 to $5).
b Includes Government defense operations.
c Includes provision for abandonment of machinery & equipment $523,505.
e Cash dividends restricted under long-term agreement. No dividends to be paid unless retained earnings exceed $5,153,405 after Dec. 30, 1954 plus $1,000,000 and working capital of at least $18,000,000.
f $600,000 due annually 1960–1964; $3,800,000 due in 1965.

ELGIN NATIONAL WATCH COMPANY AND SUBSIDIARIES
Consolidated Statement of Earnings

	3/1 1962	3/1 1961	3/1 1960	3/1 1959	2/28 1958	2/28 1957	2/28 1956	2/28 1955	2/28 1954	12/31 1953
Net sales	$40,429	$33,352	$30,973	$26,992	$31,123	$42,405	$51,477	$60,085	$ 7,012*	$56,721
Cost of goods sold	29,407	24,188	22,549	21,681	27,314	31,074	37,715	45,222	5,148*	39,958
Depreciation	580	516	487	471	760	828	822	668	115*	660
Advertis., selling & gen admin.	9,118	8,331	6,967	6,601	6,847	8,842	9,966	10,186	1,452*	10,752
Pension fund contribution	—a	—a	—a	—a	—a	—a	542	516	132*	807
Other income	182	202	76	148	127	92	138	185	16*	155
Interest expense & misc. chgs.	1,142	114	221	241	270	307	612	495	89*	720
Inc. before fed. inc. taxes	265^b		826	d1,761	d3,941	1,446	1,958	3,244	94*	3,979
Special charges/credits					4,540^g				—*	
Provision for fed. inco. taxes		114			cr,1,499	775	1,040	1,680		1,930
Net income (loss) after taxes	1,407^c		826	d1,761	d6,982	671	918	1,564	94*	2,049
Special debit				cr,502^f	578^i			508^j		
Earnings retained beginning of year	3,309^e	3,196^e	2,370^e	3,629	11,507	11,567	11,562	11,414^k	11,257*	10,383
Dividends (cash & stock)	—e	—e	—e	—e	319	730	913	909	137*	1,175^l
Treasury stock at cost		108	108	114	114	114	114	114	126*	129
Retained earnings end of year	4,717^e	3,309^e	3,196^e	2,370^e	3,629	11,507	11,567	11,562	11,214*	11,257
Earnings per share	1.52	.12	.90	d1.93	d2.67	.74	1.01	1.71	.10*	1.76^l
Dividends per share					.35	.80	1.00	1.00	.15*	.60^l

* Two months ending 2/28/54—Change in fiscal year ending from 12/31 to 2/28.
a No contribution made to the company's pension fund. Company states fund satisfactory.
b Recovery of costs and expenses charged to prior year's operation through settlement of contract claim.
c Tax-loss carry forward to 1964 amounted to $3,400,000 on 2/28/62; $5,000,000 on 2/28/61; $5,400,000 on 2/28/60.
e Cash dividends restricted under long-term debt agreement. No dividends to be paid unless consolidated retained earnings exceed $5,153,410 after Dec. 30, 1950 plus $1,000,000 and working capital of at least $18,000,000.
f Previous year's tax refund.
g Special charge. For relocation of operations $1,440,000; abandoned machinery & equipment $1,440,000; inventory write-off $1,400,000; liquidation of watch case & microphone operations $500,000.
i Provision for federal income taxes of previous years & for loss of future tax benefits applicable to vacation accruals.
j Provision for vacation pay earned prior to 3/1/54, net of applicable tax credit of $550,000.
k Includes $200,000 reserve for casualty insurance restored to retained earnings.
l Cash at the rate of $.60 per share ($541,000); stock-one share for twenty—42,287 shares at par value of $15 each ($634,000).

He stated further that the watch division historically had been plagued with the problem of high operating costs which stemmed in part from an outmoded plant built at the turn of the century, and in part from foreign competition. He pointed out that in order to meet this problem the board of directors had decided to sell the main Elgin plant contingent on "the appropriateness of the selling price" and to institute a pilot assembly watch plant somewhere in the South so as "to provide Elgin National Watch Company with greater flexibility in the marketplace to meet the severe international competition in the watch industry."

Mr. Margolis also voiced concern over President Kennedy's tariff program and its impact on the watch manufacturing industry. He conceded that "if the administration determined that lowered tariffs were best for the country, Elgin must go along." But he questioned the soundness of the program and urged that Congress and the President "reconsider the importance of watchmaking skills in the national defense."

In his report to the shareholders in 1961, Mr. Margolis stated:

> The American watch industry cannot operate any longer as an isolated force within the domestic market. In addition to the traditional competition of the Swiss, the American watch industry is now faced with intense competition from the French, the Germans, the Japanese and most recently, from the Russians. The rash of cheap products made abroad and domestically has confused the public, downgraded values, downgraded quality and the industry. After evaluating both the nature of the economy and of the competition, management of your company has embarked on a program of . . . aggressive marketing and diversifying into fields geared to the space age.

He emphasized also that the company would continue to adhere to two basic tenets: support of the jeweler, and dominance of quality over price. He closed his remarks by stating that "Elgin will seek to offset inordinately low wage costs of foreign nations through high productivity gained from efficient plant and equipment and cooperation of workers utilizing newer techniques and efficient planning."

Mr. Margolis, Elgin's chief executive officer, took over the day-to-day running of the company in May, 1962, when his appointment, Mr. Robert O. Fickes, resigned as president of the company over ". . . differences of policy as to the future direction the company will take." Mr. Fickes, who had served in various executive capacities with General Electric for more than thirty years, had been president of Elgin National Watch Company for thirteen months. In discussing Mr. Fickes' resignation, Mr. Margolis acknowledged that the latter had accelerated the long-range plans designed to cut costs and improve efficiency—including the automation of certain manufacturing operations at the Elgin, Illinois, watch plant. Mr. Margolis also remarked that at the time that Mr. Fickes had taken over the reins of the company, Elgin had been moving toward a "rather cumbersome decentralization of management" which he and Mr. Fickes felt had led the company to "slow decision-making" and an unnecessary "diffusion of responsibilities." Messrs. Fickes and Margolis reorganized the operations and established long-range objectives calling for the "expansion of industrial products sufficiently so that they would contribute about one-half of the sales volume."

CORPORATE DEVELOPMENT AND BACKGROUND

The company was originally incorporated in 1864 as the National Watch Company, but because the firm became so closely identified with the village of Elgin its name was changed shortly after 1900 to Elgin National Watch Company. Since its founding Elgin had been one of the best known watch manufacturers and had enjoyed the prestige of building the finest watch in America. The company produced its watch movements at a plant in Elgin, Illinois, and also at a plant in Lincoln, Nebraska, until the latter was sold in 1958. Elgin also produced its own fashion components up until 1958; watch cases were produced by its subsidiary, the Wadsworth Watch Case Company, Dayton, Kentucky; and watchbands by another subsidiary, the Hadley Company, Inc., Providence, Rhode Island.

Elgin had also operated an observatory where time was measured from the stars. This practice was discontinued in 1960 with the perfection of electronic timing devices. In addition, the company for many years ran the Elgin Watchmakers' College in order to provide its retail outlets with an assured supply of competent watch repairmen (known as watchmakers), and to train its retailers in jewelry repair, engraving, ordering of materials, and store management. This operation was also discontinued in 1960.

Elgin's market was greatly curtailed during World War II and the Korean War when the company devoted nearly all of its efforts to war production. During this period Swiss watches flooded the American market and gained acceptance. In an effort to alleviate this problem Elgin, along with other watchmakers, attempted during the 1950's to obtain relief from foreign competition by lobbying for protective tariffs on the basis that the watchmaking industry was essential for the national defense.

The company also recognized that another of its major problems stemmed from the fact that its watch sales were sensitive to changes in disposable income. For example, in the years in which personal income declined 10%, Elgin's sales often slipped 20% to 30%. Elgin's management attributed this to the fact that consumer expenditures for watches usually were considered a luxury and therefore postponable.

DIVERSIFICATION

Early in 1953, as the result of an intensive study made by management and aided by outside consultants, Elgin decided to undertake a program of diversification to offset its declining share of the watch market. Its stated objectives were to satisfy these corporate goals:

Expansion. The watch business had become essentially a replacement business. According to the consultants who advised Elgin, the average annual rate of growth for all firms in the watch industry from 1940 to 1951 was 5%. Elgin's rate was 4.38% and its share of the market was declining, due mainly to imports. As Elgin increased its import of watch movements, it created an additional problem of plant utilization. In 1953 watch production was only 75% of capacity; by 1961 it constituted less than 50%.

Improved Return on the Investment of Its Shareholders. The unit cost of watch movements rose from $5.10 in 1941 to $11.05 in 1951, and despite a substantial increase in manufacturing efficiency in the next decade, unit cost remained approximately at that level. The primary cause for the increased unit cost was labor, which rose from $.61 an hour in 1941 to $2.48 an hour in 1962. Elgin's average return (net income to net worth) was 7.7% for the period from 1946 to 1952, whereas the return from all manufacturing came to 15%.

Greater Stability in Long-term Operations. Since Elgin's watch sales were sensitive to changes in disposable income, the consultants advised the company to diversify into products less sensitive to disposable income or which moved in different or contrasting cycles. Following these principles, Elgin initially selected two fields which it believed were well adapted to the company's specialized talents—miniature electronics and precision production instruments. Later diversification brought the company into development of communications systems and equipment.

a. *Miniature Electronics.* This field included small specialized electronic components of a mechanical, electro-mechanical, and electronic nature. It also involved semi-conductors, capacitors, vibrators, resistors, printed circuits, and specialized batteries. Highly competitive radio parts were not included in the field. The consultants reported that electronics sales had risen from $600 million in 1946 to more than $4.3 billion in 1952. The industry had broad product markets in consumer, industrial, and governmental fields. Miniaturization was a basic trend in portable radios, hearing aids, guided missiles, ammunition, and communications equipment.

b. *Precision Product Instruments.* This field included mechanical, electrical, and electro-mechanical measuring and controlling instruments. The instruments measured, indicated, recorded, and controlled such factors as composition, optical properties, thickness and temperature, speed, fluid flow, and pressure. Elgin's interest was in instruments having high precision requirements. Elgin's consultants reported that the industry had enjoyed an annual growth rate of 21% during the 1946–1952 period, compared to an annual growth rate of 8% in gross national product and 6% growth in industrial plant and equipment. This increase had resulted from factors which had forced automatic production methods upon industry thereby increasing wage rates, demand for better quality, and production speeds surpassing human ability to control. The automatic instruments industry was generally considered to be on the threshold of major expansion. Members of Elgin's management believed that the company would make a special contribution in areas too intricate for manufacturers not experienced in highly precise operations which involved microscopic tolerances and the most complex assemblies.

c. *Communications Systems and Equipment.* This area included activities related to the design, development, production and installation of advanced communications equipment, such as advanced telephone and telegraph switching equipment, multiplex digital data handling, and other advanced communication equipment utilizing solid state and magnetic logic techniques.

After examining some 70 companies and 45 products, the first tangible results of Elgin's diversification program occurred with the cash acquisition in October, 1954, of Neomatic, Inc. (renamed Elgin-Neomatic, Inc.), Los Angeles, California, specialists in the design and manufacture of subminiature relays for guided missiles, aircraft, and mobile communications equipment. In March, 1955, Elgin acquired the American Microphone Company, Pasadena, California, manufacturers of microphones, phonograph pickups, cartridges, and related products, and the Advance Electric & Relay Company, Burbank, California, a leading relay producer.

With the purchase of these new companies Elgin's business fell into two main areas: *consumer products* manufactured and sold by the Elgin Watch Division, The Wadsworth-Hadley Division, and the Elgin Watch Company Ltd.; and *industrial products* manufactured by the Abrasives Division (later changed to Precision Products Division), the Electronics Division (later changed to the Controls Division), and the Micronics Division. With the successful bidding on a Navy high-speed teleprinter contract in 1961, a Communications Division was added to the industrial group. In 1961 the company purchased the Bradley Time Corporation, the Welby Corporation, and the Lohengrin Diamond Ring Company, each of which was added as a division to the consumer group, replacing the Wadsworth-Hadley Division. (See Exhibit 2.)

When the company undertook its diversification program in 1953, Mr. Joseph W. LaBine, Elgin's director of public relations, thought that shareholder and financial community relations were matters of first concern. "One of the basic jobs in our diversification program," he stated, "is that of improving the market value of our shares which currently sell for about half of their book value—a situation that presents a real problem should we ever be interested in diversifying through an exchange-of-stock transaction. The market price of our shares has been depressed in part by our record of low dividends and in part by unfavorable publicity incident to the tariff fight, in which we were in the unpleasant position of having to publicize a competitive problem that appeared to indicate financial insecurity." He noted that 62% of the shareholders, who owned 75% of the stock, lived in Elgin and the Chicago area; over 1,000 of these shareholders lived within the city of Elgin proper. The average holder had about 220 shares, and 645 employees owned 103,045 shares.

exhibit 2
ELGIN NATIONAL WATCH COMPANY
Organization Chart

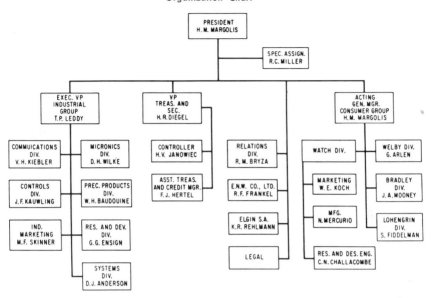

In June, 1954, the company reduced the par value of its shares from $15 to $5 and had received an authorization to issue 300,000 new shares on which shareholders waived their preemptive rights.

THE CHANGING WATCH MARKET

Management recognized the marked shift in the sale of watches over the years. Total watch sales had increased, but since 1932 there had been a shift away from pin-lever [1] watches to jewel watches. However, domestic watch manufacturers did not benefit from this increase. During and after World War II the added jeweled watch sales consisted mainly of large increases in imported Swiss watches. The switchover came as a result of World War II when the domestic watch manufacturers turned their facilities almost entirely to war work. The Swiss, who were neutral, made watches and were permitted by the Germans to export them. Swiss watches flooded the U.S. domestic

---

[1] A pin-lever watch is constructed without the use of jewels as bearings. This is the typical construction in watches retailing for less than $15.

market and acquired wide public approval and acceptance. Swiss watches were generally moderately priced, came in a large variety of case designs, and, with their more rapid turnover, brought larger profits to the retail jeweler. In 1944 total domestic watch sales of all kinds fell to an all-time low of 200,000 units, most of which came from prewar inventory.

SWISS COMPETITION AND TARIFFS

When the war was over the American jeweled manufacturers had no backlog of civilian orders and only three companies still manufactured most of their jeweled movements within the United States—Elgin, Hamilton, and Waltham. Bulova produced some movements domestically, but 70% of the watches sold under the Bulova name were manufactured in a plant owned and operated by the company in Switzerland. The three watch manufacturers formed the American Watch Manufacturers Association in an effort to obtain tariff protection on movements with 17 jewels or less. It was their contention that the human skills necessary for the making of precision instruments were essential for the country's defense.

In 1952 Elgin entered the low-priced watch field by importing Swiss movements, casing them, and selling them under the Wadsworth name, but was unable to capture more than 3% of the "under $30" market in any year. Prior to this time Elgin relied entirely on domestic watch production. But in 1954 it began importing for sale, under the Elgin name, certain Swiss specialty watches—mostly automatic or self-winding—which the management felt would round out the Elgin line but which, in its opinion, promised such low sales volume that it was not practical for the company to manufacture them in its own facilities.

Under the Tariff Act of 1930 the tariff on imported movements with 17 jewels or less ranged from $2.50 to $4.00; above 17 jewels the tariff was $10.75 per watch movement. In 1936 the United States signed a reciprocal trade agreement with Switzerland and lowered its tariffs on imports of watches. The new rates ranged from $1.80 to $2.70 on imported movements with 17 jewels or less, and no change in the rate on watches with movements above 17 jewels. The net effect of the reduced tariffs was that movements with 17 or fewer jewels, representing 99% of all movement imports, could be landed in the

U.S. at a duty-paid cost which was 25% less than the cost of making comparable watch movements in this country. The change in tariffs was followed by a further decline in the American manufacturers' participation in their own market, which had dropped from 52% of all jeweled timepieces sold in the United States in 1930 to approximately 38% of the market at the beginning of World War II, and to less than 20% during World War II. (See Exhibit 3.) Elgin, along with other American watchmakers, sought the protection of the higher tariffs by resorting to production of higher-jeweled and consequently higher-priced watches. Neither Elgin nor any other domestic watchmaker turned out a jeweled watch with fewer than 17 jewels after 1953.

Practically all watch movements imported in 1954 came from Switzerland. Moreover, the Swiss supplied 95% of the world market. Unlike many foreign industries which were inefficient by American standards, Swiss watchmakers were skilled craftsmen using efficient production techniques. Modern Swiss methods and machinery were adaptations of the so-called "American system." Late in the nineteenth century, American watchmaking machinery was freely exported to Switzerland and the Swiss horological industry was almost completely revamped.

The Swiss industry was rigidly regulated by Swiss federal legislation under which prices, the number of workers engaged in the industry, many aspects of trade relations, and even the right to engage in production were government controlled. There were restrictions on the exportation of watchmaking machinery and the furnishing of technical advice to foreign watchmaking enterprises. In addition, the Swiss government levied a tax of one franc against each jeweled watch movement exported. This tax produced a fund of about $15 million annually and was used for institutional advertising of Swiss watches.

The cost of a Swiss movement was about one-half that of an American-made movement, according to an Elgin official. One of the major reasons for this was the fact that the Swiss industry's labor rate was almost 60% lower than U.S. wage rates for comparable jobs, and labor constituted approximately 80% of the cost of making a watch movement. This differential had been increasing through the years. In 1936, when the reciprocal trade agreement with Switzerland had been negotiated, the Swiss advantage had been only 50%.

Until 1951 the trade agreement with Switzerland contained no

exhibit 3 COMPARISON OF SALES OF DOMESTIC AND IMPORTED JEWELED-LEVER
WATCHES IN THE UNITED STATES
5-year moving average 1926–55, annual 1946–1961 (in thousands of units)

Period or Year	Total Domestic Jeweled-lever Watches		Total Imported Jeweled-lever Watches		Total Jeweled-lever Watches	
	Units	%	Units	%	Units	%
Average						
1926–1930	1,787	39.0	2,780	61.0	4,567	100.0
1931–1935	778	51.6	730	48.4	1,508	100.0
1936–1940	1,652	38.5	2,639	61.5	4,291	100.0
1941–1945	1,561	19.6	6,404	80.4	7,965	100.0
1946–1950	2,379	24.6	7,303	75.4	9,682	100.0
1951–1955	2,249	21.9	8,017	78.1	10,266	100.0
Annual						
1946	1,678	16.7	8,347	83.3	10,025	100.0
1947	2,280	24.9	6,873	75.1	9,153	100.0
1948	2,918	28.5	7,332	71.4	10,250	100.0
1949	2,620	29.1	6,367	70.9	8,987	100.0
1950	2,398	24.0	7,594	76.0	9,992	100.0
1951	3,093	26.1	8,759	73.9	11,852	100.0
1952	2,312	21.2	8,607	78.8	10,919	100.0
1953	2,301	19.3	9,613	80.7	11,914	100.0
1954	1,670	19.1	7,045	80.9	8,715	100.0
1955	1,871	23.6	6,062	76.4	7,933	100.0
1956	1,996	22.4	6,904	77.6	8,900	100.0
1957	1,453	17.4	6,910	82.6	8,363	100.0
1958	917	14.1	5,581	85.9	6,498	100.0
1959	1,574	18.2	7,068	81.8	8,642	100.0
1960	NA	—	6,846	—	NA	—
1961	NA	—	6,928	—	NA	—

SOURCE: U.S. Tariff Commission, *Reports on Watch Movements*, 1956 and 1962.

"escape clause" whereby either party nation could raise or lower
tariffs on individual items without affecting the rates on all items in
the trade agreement. The Trade Expansion Act of 1951 included an
escape clause in connection with a year-to-year extension of the trade

agreement to provide relief in the form of increased import duties if articles being imported into the United States seriously affected an industry. As a result of this provision several governmental agencies and investigating committees, including the Tariff Commission, recommended relief for the United States watch industry. President Eisenhower's action in raising tariffs 50% in July, 1954, climaxed a ten-year effort on the part of Elgin to secure protection for the jeweled watch industry. The 1954 increase in tariff ranged from $.09 on 1-jewel watches to $1.15 on 17-jewel watches and averaged about $1 per unit. There was no increase in tariffs on watches containing more than 17 jewels and in no instance did the new tariff schedule exceed the original rates set in the Tariff Act of 1930. (See Exhibit 4.)

The immediate impact of the 1954 increase in tariffs was a reduction in total import units, a decrease in market share of imported watches sold from approximately 59% in 1953 to 53% in 1955, and an increase in the retail price of such units. (See Exhibit 5.) A watch which formerly had been imported for a duty-paid cost of $8 sold to a dealer for

exhibit 4   RATES OF DUTY UNDER THE TARIFF ACTS OF 1930, 1936, AND 1954

	Tariff Rates		
Item	1930	1936	1954
Watch movements less than 1.77 inches wide:			
Having more than 17 jewels	$10.75	$10.75	$10.75
Having 2 to 17 jewels	1.25–2.50	0.90–1.80	1.25–2.50
Having no jewels or only 1 jewel	0.75–1.50	0.75–0.90	0.75–1.35
Additional duties on watches with 17 jewels or less:			
For each jewel in excess of 7	0.15	0.09	0.135
For each adjustment	1.00	0.50	0.50
Self-winding, or designed to operate in excess of 47 hours without rewinding	1.00	0.50	0.50

SOURCE: U.S. Tariff Commission, *Report on Watch Movements*, 1958, p. 21.

exhibit 5   COMPARISON OF SALES OF DOMESTIC AND IMPORTED WATCHES IN THE UNITED STATES

5-year moving average 1926–55, annual 1946–1961 (in thousands of units)

Period or Year	Total Domestic Watches		Total Imported Watches		Total All Watches	
	Units	%	Units	%	Units	%
Average						
1926–1930	9,836	71.4	3,937	28.6	13,773	100.0
1931–1935	7,252	90.4	771	9.6	8,023	100.0
1936–1940	11,100	79.6	2,838	20.4	13,938	100.0
1941–1945	4,888	42.0	6,739	58.0	11,627	100.0
1946–1950	9,978	55.0	8,168	45.0	18,146	100.0
1951–1955	8,741	45.6	10,426	54.4	19,167	100.0
Annual						
1946	6,378	42.1	8,765	57.9	15,143	100.0
1947	11,104	60.8	7,173	39.2	18,277	100.0
1948	13,936	62.3	8,447	37.7	22,383	100.0
1949	8,810	53.9	7,527	46.1	16,337	100.0
1950	9,659	51.9	8,927	48.1	18,586	100.0
1951	11,422	50.9	11,007	49.1	22,429	100.0
1952	8,361	43.5	10,877	56.5	19,238	100.0
1953	8,337	41.2	11,875	58.8	20,212	100.0
1954	7,183	44.3	9,017	55.7	16,200	100.0
1955	8,358	47.2	9,355	52.8	17,713	100.0
1956	9,286	43.1	12,262	56.9	21,548	100.0
1957	7,782	38.9	12,243	61.1	20,025	100.0
1958	9,448	47.6	10,387	52.4	19,835	100.0
1959	11,282	45.6	13,472	54.4	24,754	100.0
1960	9,407	42.1	13,158	57.9	22,565	100.0
1961	9,689	43.4	12,627	56.6	22,316	100.0

SOURCE: U.S. Tariff Commission, *Reports on Watch Movements*, 1956 and 1962.

$12 and retailed for $23.95. A $1 increase in the tariff meant that the import price increased to $9, the dealer price became $13.50, and the watch retailed at $26.95.

In addition to the increased price and reduction in imported movements there was a significant shift in the composition of imports away from the movements containing 16 and 17 jewels toward pin-lever movements containing no jewels, or movements containing but one jewel. (See Exhibit 6.) "The President's action is a boon to national security and to the business prospects of the American jeweled watch industry," said Mr. James G. Shennan, who was president of Elgin at the time. "So far as Elgin is concerned, we believe that the new tariff schedule will permit us to resume profitable operation of our domestic watchmaking facilities and to increase our sales by serving a larger segment of the jeweled watch market. This in turn will provide the broader mobilization base which the government believes to be essential for national security."

In 1957 imported watches regained their share of the U.S. market and constituted more than 61% of the watches sold in the United States. Although in the following year there was an increase in the number of domestic watches sold, the number of imported watches continued to increase and leveled off at approximately 57% of the U.S. market over the next four years.

INDUSTRY BACKGROUND

The American watch industry consisted of three types of firms. One manufactured jeweled-lever watches made wholly, or almost wholly, of domestic materials. These firms specialized in jeweled timepieces of quality. The second manufactured pin-lever or "clock-type" watches, most of which were non-jeweled and made primarily of domestic materials. Pin-lever watchmakers usually made clocks and other types of timing instruments. Firms of the third type were generally called assemblers. They imported movements, jeweled and non-jeweled, cased them in domestically manufactured cases, attached straps, and then packaged the watches for retail sale.

In the jeweled-lever watch field, in 1962, there were over 100 companies preparing finished watches. The major concerns were Elgin, Hamilton, Benrus, Bulova, Gruen, and Longines-Wittnauer. Of these, only two manufactured most of their jeweled movements within the United States—Elgin and Hamilton. Bulova produced some movements in this country but 70% of the watches sold under the Bulova name were manufactured in a plant owned and operated by the company in Switzerland. Elgin, Hamilton, and Bulova, as members of the American Watch Manufacturers' Association, consistently pushed for higher

exhibit 6 COMPARISON OF IMPORTED WATCH
MOVEMENTS, BY JEWEL COUNT
For the years 1946—1961 (in thousands of units)

Year	Movements Containing 0–1 Jewel	Movements Containing 16–17 Jewels
1946	618	6,226
1947	401	5,300
1948	1,215	5,577
1949	1,260	4,959
1950	1,433	5,868
1951	2,448	6,757
1952	2,470	7,060
1953	2,752	8,432
1954	2,532	6,217
1955	3,866	5,599
1956	5,986	6,177
1957	5,805	6,222
1958	5,294	4,692
1959	6,990	6,082
1960	7,085	5,971
1961	6,792	5,790

SOURCE: U.S. Tariff Commission, *Reports on Watch Movements*, 1956 and 1962.

protective tariffs. They consistently reaffirmed their stand that the industry was essential to the national defense. A second organization,
The American Watch Association, was established by Longines-
Wittnauer, Gruen, Benrus, and the other jeweled-lever watch companies who imported Swiss movements. This organization voiced opposition to higher tariffs and took the position that watchmaking
skills were not essential to the national defense.

In the pin-lever watch field, in 1962, there were only four companies
—U.S. Time Corporation, General Time Corporation, E. Ingraham
Company, and The New Haven Clock and Watch Company. The New
Haven Clock and Watch Company, which went into receivership in
December, 1956, had all but eliminated its production of movements.
By far the largest number of firms were engaged in watch assembly,

i.e., in the casing, boxing, timing, and marketing of imported movements, mostly in jeweled counts of 17 or less.

DESIGN

At the time of the first World War, a revolution occurred in watch fashions—watches came out of the pocket and onto the wrist. Shortly thereafter women's wrist watches appeared. In the 1920's Elgin switched its production from 90% pocket to 90% wrist watches and gradually placed emphasis on styling. Watches grew smaller and thinner, and the old unwritten law that watches had to be round passed away. Except for the highly-jeweled pocket watches, the split-second accuracy of the older watch became unimportant, for anyone could learn the exact time by turning on the radio. No real merchandising program was initiated until the 1920's when Elgin began designing and producing its own cases and dials for its new line of wrist watches. Style was featured in national advertising.

"Our company is staking a large part of its future on the eye appeal of its products," stated Mr. William V. Judson, Elgin's director of design in 1947. "Elgin quality is well known. The performance of an Elgin watch is taken for granted. But today a watch must have something more than a fine and trusted movement. If a watch is to move from the jeweler's showcase to the customer's wrist, it must have good appearance. It must be well styled."

To regain and strengthen its market position, Elgin made four market surveys of the retail watch market in 1947 in the form of questionnaires in the *Saturday Evening Post*. From 136,000 responses received, the company was convinced that the American watch industry was failing to keep up with contemporary fashion designs. As it affected its own product, Elgin found that (1) its watches appealed to people over forty, (2) its watches had less allure to the growing younger market than others, (3) its lady's wrist watches were too big, and (4) the better grade Swiss watches with which Elgin competed had greater style acceptance.

Based on these findings, a campaign aimed at capturing more widespread consumer acceptance was launched. Elgin hired fifteen designers from the country's leading art schools and started its own design training school. The company broke with the tradition of following foreign leadership in design, chose six new designs through free-lance competition, and to keep its line fresh, thereafter introduced about 40 new models each year. In 1962 it had about 250 models in its entire line.

New design development and retooling were costly. Retooling costs for each new model ranged from $4,000 to $15,000. In 1950 Elgin spent approximately $350,000 on designing, and continued its expenditure at this rate for the next 12 years in an effort to assure its continued leadership in design. As one official remarked, "The company's aim was to achieve integrated design, which meant that everything having to do with the appearance of the watch had to harmonize. Case, dial, numerals and markers, hands, crystals, strap, cord, and even the package and the price tag had to belong together." He mentioned that price presented a real problem in design, and emphasized that the problem was one of designing a balanced line—a line including watches to be sold at different levels: Elgins, Elgin 19's, Lord and Lady Elgins, and diamond watches.

MARKETING

Prior to World War II the standard pattern of distribution for American jeweled watch manufacturers had been to sell to wholesale jewelers and to have several contact men call on large retailers. Elgin used these channels and had the same scale of markups as other leading jeweled lever producers—20% to 25% to the wholesaler, after which the retailer took 80% to 100%. This had been Elgin's sales pattern for 82 years. In 1946, however, after examining surveys which had shown that 90% of all Elgin watches had been purchased at jewelry stores, the company changed its distribution system by eliminating wholesalers and selling directly to jeweler retailers.

Under the new distribution system the country was divided into six geographical sales regions, each headed by a regional sales manager who reported to the general sales manager at Elgin. Where previously the company had only 72 wholesalers, it now sold to thousands of retailers. In 1946 Elgin had 31 "missionaries" who made goodwill calls. Six years later it had a nation-wide staff of trained salesmen. In 1962 its staff of 66 salesmen sold direct to about 17,000 active accounts. Each salesman had between 250 and 300 accounts. Salesmen called on the typical account four times a year; they called more frequently on the larger accounts, some as often as once a month. In areas where a small account was inconveniently located, a salesman might not call on it more than once a year.

Elgin consistently spent large amounts on its advertising. Initially, advertisements were carried in papers and magazines. When television became a national communication media, Elgin became a heavy user and ranked first or second in terms of dollars spent on TV advertising in the industry annually. In addition, the company consistently advertised in *Life, Look, Time, Sports Illustrated, Fortune,* and *National Geographic.* Lesser amounts were spent in radio advertising, mostly on a local basis. Elgin also had a full scale point of purchase program with displays and direct mail pieces for the jeweler.

Despite the severe foreign competition, Elgin's sales had increased significantly during the early 1950's and reached a peak of $60 million in 1955, with net income over $2 million in 1954. But when sales fell to $26 million in 1959, and when losses of $7 million and $1.8 million were suffered in 1958 and 1959, Elgin officials recognized that the company had lost a major share of the watch market, and instituted an evaluation of its product and distribution policies. It identified the major causes of its difficulties as (1) the general unrest and confusion existing in the watch market as a result of many "off brand" Swiss watches sold in the lower-priced field, and (2) the disruptive influence on conventional distribution channels and retail prices by discount houses which were at their peak in 1957.

Company officials admitted that Elgin had not completely kept abreast of changing trends such as the increased demand for round watches, sweep-second hands, shockproof, waterproof, and self-winding watches. Prior to 1958 the company had not produced a watch which could be retailed below $33.75 with the customary trade margin of 50%. Company policy had been positive and explicit in refusing to produce a watch under the Elgin name to retail for less than this amount. Management stated that selling a low-priced watch with Elgin's name would degrade the tradition of quality and craftsmanship built up by the company over many years. Some executives cited Packard automobile as an example of what would happen if a lower-priced watch were marketed. However, management agreed that the inexpensive "fashion" watches such as the Swiss timepiece in the $20 to $30 bracket, and the cheaper pin-lever watches—primarily American brands such as Timex—were gaining increasing acceptance. Although Elgin's Wadsworth line had been introduced a few years earlier to capture a share of this market, its failure to do so forced management to import certain Swiss specialty watches under the Elgin name—mostly automatic or self-winding watches—to round out its line.

In early 1958 Elgin was dealt a severe blow when the Office of Defense Mobilization ruled that the American watch industry was not essential to national defense. This decision precluded the possibility that higher tariffs might be imposed to restrict imports in the foreseeable future. During the next few months Elgin's management conducted a mail and personal interview survey among its dealers; 917 dealers answered the question, "Would an Elgin watch retailing at about $25 help your sales?" The results were:

	Personal Interviews	*Mail Survey*
Yes	76.5%	66.1%
No	23.5%	33.9%
Number answering	47	870

On the basis of this survey the marketing department in June, 1958, introduced its marketing plans for increasing Elgin's total watch sales with special emphasis on the "under $30" market. Consequently, the company eliminated the production and marketing of the Wadsworth watch, introduced a 19-jewel model in the medium-priced field to sell from $34.95 to $69.50, and began marketing a 17-jewel, low-priced Elgin, retailing from $19.95, which consisted of imported movements assembled in company-designed cases.

By the end of 1958 imports of watches by the company had increased substantially with the result that less than half of Elgin's watch manufacturing capacity was being used. Subsequently the company closed down and disposed of its Lincoln, Nebraska, plant; the Wadsworth Case Company plant at Dayton, Kentucky; and the Hadley Division plant at Providence, Rhode Island. To improve the reliability and reduce the costs of importing watches and watch movements, a subsidiary was established in Switzerland in 1959, and an important portion of the watch line was purchased from France.

Early in 1959 Elgin management instituted what it called "fresh marketing approaches" and made extensive changes in its distribution channels and methods. Although the company had always felt a great loyalty for the established legitimate local jeweler, who had distributed the product so successfully, and recognized that jewelry stores still dominated the retail sale of watches above the $30 price bracket which had been Elgin's strong field, management hesitated to break away from its traditional distribution policy. "Nevertheless," remarked an Elgin official, "because of the dynamic changes which are taking place in the watch market, we are determined to meet our competition, no matter how bizarre." Consequently, the Lord and Lady Elgin line was restricted to franchised jewelry outlets and marked with a suggested retail price that provided the retailer with the conventional 50% margin. The medium-priced line which was also restricted to retail jewelers carried a suggested retail price that provided a margin of 50% to 60%. Other watch lines were extended to selected catalogue and wholesale distributors and to premium houses, with suggested retail prices which provided margins of 40% to 45%.

EMPLOYEE RELATIONS

In November, 1961, Mr. Robert Bryza, formerly director of industrial relations of the Burton Rogers Company and a management consultant with the A. T. Kearney Company, was appointed general manager of the newly created Relations Division with specific responsibility for public relations, labor relations, and wage and salary administration.

Prior to this time these activities were handled by each division on a piece-meal basis. "When I accepted this position," remarked Mr. Bryza, "my major objective was to centralize and coordinate these scattered activities so as to insure uniform application of corporate policies and programs."

Within one year the insurance and benefits program was revamped. "Whereas previously each division developed, negotiated, and administered its own insurance plan," Mr. Bryza explained, "the new program was negotiated with a single insurance company and administered on a company-wide basis." He went on to say that similar arrangements were made in the labor relations area and culminated in a central industrial relations unit. Mr. Bryza also stated that his department planned company-wide labor-strategy six months in advance of negotiations. "However," he pointed out, "even though we develop over-all policy and plans in the home office, we have an employee relations manager at each plant conducting the negotiations on a local basis, subject to our approval. In addition, administration of the contract is handled at the plant level, except that grievances necessitating arbitration are handled in the home office."

In August, 1962, Elgin negotiated a new two-year agreement with the Elgin National Watch Workers' Union (affiliated with the American Watch Workers Union). The new contract provided for no change in wages in the first year and a 3% increase in the second year. Similar arrangements were negotiated with the International Association of Machinists. "Not all of our plants are unionized," remarked Mr. Bryza. "As a consequence we have had several unions attempting to take over our newer plants. Thus, in September, 1962, the I.B.E.W. and the I.A.M.[2] demanded recognition in our Chatsworth, California plant, claiming 30% representation of our employees. The NLRB held an election and fortunately 78% of the votes cast were for 'no union.' But less than 60 days later, as we were starting up operations in our Gadsden, Alabama plant, the I.B.E.W. began circulating membership cards to our employees in their homes. With our centralized policy and planning we were able to cope with this situation immediately and the organization drive fell through." According to Mr. Bryza, the labor relations picture was further complicated by the acquisitions of newer companies whose previous union contract agreements were often at variance with Elgin's labor policies. This was particularly true of the consumer products group.

As Elgin expanded into government contracts, Mr. Bryza established and headed an Industrial Security Division to enforce the security regulation required by the Defense Department.

Mr. Bryza pointed out that the company was confronted with a unique problem of planning for simultaneous contraction and expansion of operations. "Our industrial products are expanding at a rapid rate," he remarked, "while in our consumer products group we have been engaged in a steady retrenchment. Thus, we are faced with the problem of releasing skilled personnel in one area, while seeking skilled personnel in another area. Transfer of personnel between jobs is hampered not only by the differences in skill requirements, but also by the different locations of plants."

[2] International Brotherhood of Electrical Workers; International Association of Machinists.

MANAGEMENT AND ORGANIZATION

In a discussion on American business in general, and National Elgin Watch Company in particular, Mr. Margolis stated, "American industry is the most overmanaged in the world." At the time Mr. Margolis took over operating control of Elgin, the company had a complex decentralized organizational structure with ten committees functioning at the corporate level. When the resignation of Mr. James G. Shennan as president of Elgin in September, 1960, was followed shortly after by the resignations of three other key executives—Mr. George J. Daly, executive vice president and treasurer; Mr. S. D. Moorman, vice president for marketing, Watch Division; and Mr. Leroy A. Mote, secretary and general attorney, Mr. Margolis acted as president, financial vice president, and manager of the Watch Division while he scouted the country for a strong management team. For president he chose Mr. Robert O. Fickes, but when the latter resigned after thirteen months, Mr. Margolis again assumed the presidency of Elgin. For executive vice president and head of the industrial divisions he picked Mr. Thomas P. Leddy, a communications expert and former vice president with the Kellogg Division of International Telephone & Telegraph Corporation; Mr. Melvin Skinner, also of ITT Kellogg, was hired as marketing manager of the industrial group; and Mr. Harold F. Diegel, controller of Chrysler Corporation, was elected financial vice president and treasurer.

In his discussion of the previous organization Mr. Margolis remarked that in his opinion the Shennan management had been "too conservative" to grapple with what he called the "brutal" consumer market. Mr. Margolis also felt that the company had become too decentralized for its size and remarked that there were too many assistants around. An example of the unusual decentralized organization was the industrial group, whose four divisions were completely autonomous. Each division had its own accounting, marketing, advertising, sales personnel, and manufacturing departments. On many occasions salesmen for one division turned down orders for equipment from other divisions.

Streamlining of the organization was effected within a few months according to Mr. Margolis. More than 30 people from all administrative levels, including secretaries, were dropped as the new management consolidated and realigned the operations and put an end to the widespread decentralization. Mr. Margolis insisted that even though the management was being reduced, it was being strengthened. He estimated that his consolidations had reduced annual payroll and other outside fees by $500,000.

During 1961 the Industrial Products Group, under Mr. Leddy's guidance, was completely reorganized as the company stepped up its operations in the design, development, and production of precision miniaturized mechanisms, sophisticated communications devices and systems, electrical controls of high reliability, and special cutting and abrading tools. Three new executives with wide engineering backgrounds in the design and development of electronic requirements for the government's space, missile, and satellite programs, and formerly employed by ITT Kellogg, were added to key positions in the Industrial group. Each of the six industrial divisions maintained responsibility for manufacturing and reported directly to Mr. Leddy. All industrial marketing functions were grouped under a centralized marketing organization headed by Mr. Skinner, who also reported to Mr. Leddy. Financial matters were centralized under Mr. Diegel, who reported directly to Mr. Margolis.

By mid-1962 the Industrial Group had boosted its backlog to an all-time high of nearly $20 million as a result of Elgin's increased role in the nation's military and space programs.

The Consumer Products Group, which consisted entirely of the Elgin watch division, was also reorganized in 1961 into four divisions as a result of the acquisition of two clock companies—Welby and Bradley—and the purchase of Lohengrin Diamond Ring Company. (See Exhibit 2.)

NEW DEVELOPMENTS

In September, 1961, Elgin reentered the United States clock market with an extensive line of newly designed home, decorator, and travel timepieces. Elgin had withdrawn from the clock market in 1954, although it had never offered home and decorator clocks for sale under the Elgin name. All decorator and kitchen clocks contained self-starting, cordless, electric movements capable of operating for two years on one standard 1½-volt flashlight battery.

In 1960 the company introduced 72 new styles, including an electric watch. Two years later the Elgin Electronic, the thinnest, smallest electronic wrist watch manufactured in the world, was introduced on a national scale following three years of market testing.

In the industrial field Elgin was a leading source of safety and arming devices for shells, rockets, and guided missiles. One of Elgin's most important projects in 1961–1962 was the design and development of an electronic communications system for the United States Navy —a high-speed teletypewriter routing set capable of handling 20 different punches simultaneously and sending messages at the rate of 850 words per minute for a peak efficiency processing of 17,000 words per minute. The company also produced components for the Skybolt missile, the F4H-1 Phantom fighter plane, the Bomarc missile, the Pershing missile, the Minuteman missile, the Atlas missile, and the Apollo space vehicle. In addition, Elgiloy, a cobalt-base alloy patented by Elgin, was used in the manual control switch of Colonel John Glenn's Friendship VII space capsule. In 1959 industrial products contributed nearly 35% of the total sales volume. By 1961 the sales volume was split 50–50 between consumer and industrial goods. In mid-1962 an Elgin official estimated that industrial goods would account for nearly 65% of total sales volume for fiscal 1962.

In September, 1962, Mr. Margolis announced that Elgin had selected Blaney, South Carolina, for the establishment of its pilot watch assembly plant as a "first step to provide Elgin National Watch with greater flexibility to meet severe foreign competition" of watch sales.

RAILWAY SUPPLY CORPORATION

Early in 1959 Mr. John Mayer, president of Railway Supply Corporation, reviewed his company's current position with his executive group —George Jensen, Frank Noble, and Wilbert Bailey. He proposed that the next several months be spent in appraising the company's resources, markets, and growth potential. The changes within the organization and in its operation during the past few years had been many and drastic as the company struggled to regain the profitable position it formerly enjoyed. Mr. Mayer thought that the present activities of the company, although in some respects new to its experience, indicated a more promising future.

COMPANY OPERATIONS

Railway Supply conducted its operations under two principal divisions. The Fiber Division processed and fabricated insulation materials, mainly asbestos, operating a weaving plant at Nashville, Tennessee, and a fabricating plant at Aurora, Illinois. The Steel Division consisted of a Draft Gear Department which made hand brakes for railroad cars; the Railroad Car Parts Group which sold accessories to railroad refrigerator car manufacturers; and the Railroad Steel Parts Group which performed the manufacturing functions for the Railroad Car Parts Group. All steel fabricating was done in a single plant located in Harvey, Illinois. The Robust Rack operation, which produced an extensive line of adjustable storage racks, was purchased in March of 1958 and added to the Steel Division's product line.

EXECUTIVE GROUP

John Mayer was elected president of Railway Supply in 1948 when his father, Benjamin Mayer, assumed effective control of the company. The original holdings of the Mayer family were acquired from the estate of Charles Kahn who died in 1943. Mr. Kahn was one of the original founders and major stockholders of Railway Supply. Benjamin Mayer was the president and sole owner of Universal Rolling Mill Products Corporation. In 1959 Universal Rolling Mill owned 34.7% of Railway Supply, and the Mayer family owned an additional 6% of the outstanding stock. John Mayer was authorized to vote both blocks of stock.

All the major decisions of Railway Supply were made by John Mayer; however, he did not concern himself with day-to-day administration. He had many other interests in both business and the community.

Wilbert Bailey, a C.P.A., was the executive vice president and treasurer. He administered all of the accounting and financial matters of the company. He spent all of his time in the central office and made many of the detailed operating decisions. Mr. Kahn, the founder of the company, hired him in 1930 as an auditor; shortly thereafter he was elected treasurer, and in 1947 became executive vice president. Mr. Bailey worked closely with Mr. Mayer and executed the administrative policies set by him.

Frank Noble, vice president and general manager of the Steel Division, joined the company in 1952 at the invitation of Mr. King, who at that time served as chairman of the Board of Directors of Railway Supply. Mr. Noble had worked for ten years with Baldwin Locomotive where he had attained the position of assistant vice president and district sales manager. As a result of experience gained in Washington during the World War II period, he became a special Washington representative for a number of railway supply and equipment manufacturers. Through his work in this position he became acquainted with the management of Railway Supply and subsequently joined the company.

George Jensen, vice president and general manager of the Fiber

Division, was employed by Railway Supply in 1941. His prior experience included positions in financial control, sales, and production with several firms engaged in the manufacture of heavy machinery. Although Mr. Jensen was not formally trained as an engineer, he had acquired through experience a wealth of technical knowledge and manufacturing know-how. He was primarily concerned with the production activities of the Fiber Division and tended to allow his executive staff relatively free rein in other functions, particularly in sales and marketing. Mr. Jensen spent three or four days a week in the Aurora plant and each Monday in the Chicago central office. This day was reserved for conferences with Mr. Mayer, when he was available.

CORPORATE DEVELOPMENT

In 1910 Charles Kahn and Ralph Samuels organized a company to job miscellaneous supplies to railroads. Mr. Samuels had a talent for purchasing at bargain prices and Mr. Kahn, who was a highly competent salesman, marketed their supplies to the railway industry. In the early years of the company sales were confined mainly to asbestos products and rubber hose.

After World War I the partners bought an asbestos textile plant in Nashville, Tennessee, where they wove asbestos yarn, cloth, and tape. In 1936, through a license arrangement with a Dutch firm, Railway Supply became the American distributor for Tempbestos, a high-temperature asbestos. The distinguishing feature of this product was a long-fiber asbestos called Amosite which was found only in mines located in South Africa.

The partnership was dissolved and a corporation formed in 1918. Mr. Kahn acquired the bulk of the Railway Supply stock after the dissolution.

In 1940 the company bought an old factory in Wilmington, Delaware, which it converted to the manufacture of insulation materials for the Navy and for industry. In 1947, in its plant in Sherman, Texas, it began to produce pipe coverings for the oil refineries of the Southwest. In 1951 Railway Supply bought a large plant in Aurora, Illinois, which had once housed the repair shops of a railroad. This was adapted to the production of insulating blankets for the railroads.

In 1954 the company's general asbestos fabricating operations were moved to the Aurora plant.

Through the years Railway Supply had acquired several operations outside of the field of asbestos. In 1931 a small company, which manufactured draft gears marketed by Railway Supply, became insolvent and was acquired at an attractive price. In 1939 the company purchased the business and manufacturing facilities of a producer of railroad refrigerator car components. Railway Supply had served as the sales agent for this organization since 1925. The manufacturing facilities acquired in this transaction included a large plant in Harvey, Illinois. This unit became the central manufacturing facility for the Railroad Car Parts Group and all products fabricated out of steel and other metals.

Products of the Railroad Car Parts Group formed the backbone of the family of products which were consolidated into the Steel Division in 1956. The varied items manufactured and supplied to the railroads had, for the most part, been acquired or developed by Mr. Kahn. They had proven to be consistently profitable through the years. Although their profitability had declined in the post World War II period, they still formed an integral part of the company in 1959.

Prefabricated Housing. In 1950 Railway Supply entered the prefabricated steel building field. John Mayer believed that the market for buildings of this type was rapidly expanding and the company, by virtue of its plant and facilities for forming and stamping light steel, was well suited to compete in this industry. In an effort to take advantage of what was thought to be a lucrative market, Railway Supply rushed into the production of a line of low-cost residential dwelling units. In commenting on this venture Frank Noble, vice president of the Steel Division, remarked, "Apparently the company had difficulty from the start in producing these units. Large competitors in the industry were already pretty firmly entrenched when we entered the field. Their designs were standardized, much simpler, and much more functional than ours. The company moved too hastily in this operation. Too little thought went into the production and marketing problems."

After two years in the prefabricated housing field, Railway Supply's units were selling for less than 4% over the actual cost of producing the units. The selling, administrative, and erection costs produced a substantial loss on each unit which was sold. In 1953, after experiencing a loss of approximately $1.5 million, the company terminated the production and sale of its prefabricated housing units.

Heating and Cooling. In 1953 John Mayer became interested in the expanding market for air conditioning equipment. He decided that the manufacture and sale of air conditioning units would prove to be a profitable supplement to Railway Supply's business. After preliminary investigations of the market, he concluded that it would be necessary to combine the manufacture and sale of heating equipment with air conditioning units to keep pace with the current trend in the industry. A separate Heating and Cooling Division was organized for the administration, selling, and promotion of the new products and two plants were purchased to serve as the manufacturing units—one was located in North Carolina, and the other in South Chicago, Illinois.

The company's engineers designed and put into production a high quality thin-wall baseboard heating unit. At the same time Railway Supply's products were put on the market, competitors in the field introduced units constructed of copper tubing and aluminum fins. These products proved to have advantages of cost, design, and eye-appeal which rendered Railway Supply's steel radiators noncompetitive. John Parry, assistant general manager of the Steel Division, in commenting on the company's heating unit, stated, "We put a lot into our product. I think we would have done all right except for the fact that we were selling a Cadillac product for a Ford price."

After 18 months of losses and little success in penetrating the market, Railway Supply disposed of its assets in the heating and cooling business at a net loss of approximately $2 million.

Organizational Changes. When John Mayer was elected president in 1948, Louis Stern, a close friend of Mr. Kahn, was elected chairman of the board. Mr. Stern, through a long friendship with Mr. Kahn and an active interest in his company, had acquired an extensive knowledge of the railroad supply and asbestos business. As chairman of the board Mr. Stern assumed a very prominent role in policy-making. In an effort to relieve himself of an increasing administrative burden, Mr. Stern hired Norbert King as an administrative assistant. Organizational difficulties soon emerged mainly because of a lack of a clear-cut division between the functions of the chairman of the board and the president. Mr. Stern felt compelled to make an increasing number of significant operating decisions. Many of these decisions were critically questioned by Mr. Mayer. However, Mr. Mayer expressed great confidence in Mr. King, and in 1949 Mr. King replaced Mr. Stern as chairman of the board.

Late in 1949 Mr. King announced that the management was to be reorganized on a functional basis. He brought his friend, Frank Noble, into the company as vice president and general sales manager. George Jensen, who had been superintendent in the company's Aurora plant, was made vice president in charge of all manufacturing, including steel products. Wilbert Bailey, the treasurer, continued to be responsible for financial and accounting matters, and was given a new title of executive vice president and treasurer. (See Exhibit 1.)

Under the new arrangement Mr. Noble, who had little experience in selling asbestos, found himself depending upon Mr. Jensen for the direction of asbestos sales. Mr. Jensen, whose previous manufacturing experience had not included metal fabrication, continued to operate in the same way he had previously, except for reading and checking the weekly reports of the foremen to whom he left the active management of the steel fabricating plants. Neither Mr. Noble nor Mr. Jensen approved of the new management arrangement. After trying it for eighteen months with what he termed unsatisfactory results, John Mayer asked a management consulting firm to make a study of the company's organizational structure. As a result of their study and recommendations a reorganization was undertaken by the company. (See Exhibit 2.)

In the President's letter which accompanied the 1956 Annual Report of Railway Supply, Mr. John Mayer explained the reorganization in the following terms:

> The disposition of the former Heating and Cooling Division and the elimination of the problems attending it have permitted your management to concentrate its attention upon the development and promotion of other products.
>
> Based upon an intensive study made by a firm of management consultants during the past year, your board of directors has made several changes in the organizational structure of your company. Among other things, there was put into effect by your management a decentralization and integration program whereunder each of the two basic activities of the company would be under the guidance of an executive officer located at the division headquarters.

In discussing the results of the reorganization in early 1959 Mr. Bailey, the executive vice president, stated, "After two years we now

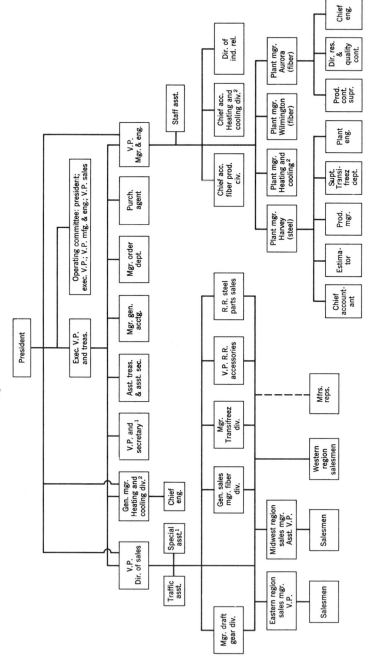

exhibit 1

RAILWAY SUPPLY CORPORATION

Functional Organization Prior to 1956 Decentralization

NOTES: [1] Special Assistant for R.R. Sales. [2] Heating and cooling business sold in mid-year 1956.

feel that our two divisions are completely decentralized. We have reduced our central headquarters staff from about 100 to the present number of 25. Approximately 25 of this number were moved to the division offices in Aurora and Harvey. An additional 25 people were dropped when we eliminated the Heating and Cooling Division, and the remainder were determined to be excess personnel which had just been built up over the years.

"We are now able to operate much more effectively. Prior to the reorganization monthly reports and financial statements were frequently as much as one month late in arriving at the headquarters office. We traced most of this delay to the excess of information which passed between the cost accounting departments of the two plants to the general accounting department in headquarters. We have made many changes in our personnel and control functions. The following functions are now handled by the executive and office personnel of the headquarters organization.

General administration
Policy formulation
Long-range planning
Control over capital expenditures,
   operating expenditures, manpower,
   general wage levels, salaries,
   and product lines
Review and approval of major appro-
   priations, budgets, appointments,
   and salary changes
Appraisal of divisional performance
General accounting
Internal auditing
Credit and collections
Accounts payable

Property ledgers
Insurance
Bank statements
Key punch operations
Consolidation and preparation
   of financial reports
Salaried payroll
Personnel records of headquarters
   personnel
Tax matters
Corporate secretarial duties
Receptionist-switchboard
Office secretarial duties

"In an effort to make our two divisions more self-contained operating units, we are now in the process of transferring the following functions:

General accounting for the divisions
Preparation of division financial statements
   and balance sheets
Accounts receivable
Accounts payable
Property records
Insurance records
Sales and expense reports now prepared at headquarters

exhibit 2
RAILWAY SUPPLY CORPORATION
Organization After 1956 Decentralization

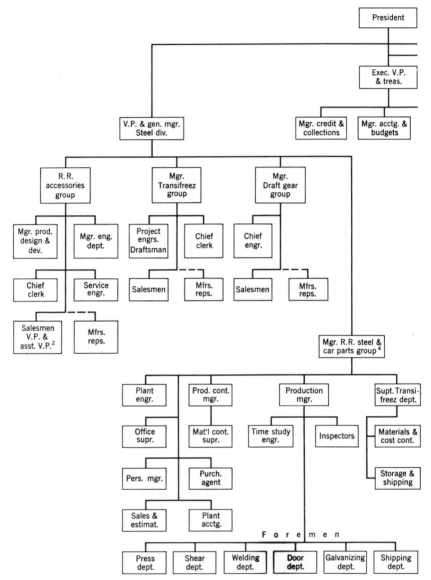

exhibit 2 (continued)

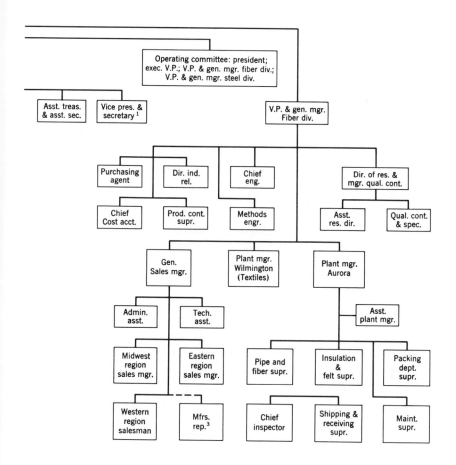

NOTES: [1] Also acted as Mgr. Draft Gear Div. [2] Titles were holdovers from the early and prosperous era of selling R.R. equipment. [3] Served as Mfrs. Reps. for both the Fiber Div. and the Draft Gear Div. [4] Included the newly acquired and added products of the Robust Rack and Rectangular Tubing Groups.

"I would say we operate fairly effectively despite the separation of the headquarters and division offices. Our operating committee is made up of our president, John Mayer, myself, the two division vice presidents, and their general managers. The committee concerns itself mainly with the annual sales forecast, reviewing operating costs, and profit potentials. Of course, both George Jensen and Frank Noble spend at least one day a week at headquarters to review their operations. I take care of the day-to-day policy matters; however, Mr. Mayer is in on all of the major policy decisions—as a matter of fact, I would say he initiates most of them. This certainly has been true about our recent acquisitions. At the present time all members of the executive committee are vitally concerned about our future."

THE STEEL DIVISION

In 1956, when Mr. Frank Noble was placed in charge of the Steel Division, this unit of the business performed all of the fabricating operations except those involving insulating materials. The manufacturing processes consisted of forming, pressing, punching, welding, and hot dip galvanizing. Some machining was done, but foundry work was contracted to others. Most of the products were made from steel sheets, bars, rods, and shapes. (Exhibit 3 illustrates the major products of the Steel Division.) All of the division's manufacturing operations were centralized in the Harvey plant. The division's activities, however, were divided into product groups, each under the direction of a manager reporting to Mr. Noble. (See Exhibit 2.)

Draft Gear Group. The Draft Gear Group manufactured and sold three types of draft gears for railroad cars. A major factor in the manufacture of draft gears was the production of castings. Railway Supply purchased castings from independent foundries but did all of the required machining and processing for the gears in their own shops. The personnel of the group consisted of the manager, a chief engineer, and four salesmen who called on railroads. The group also sold through manufacturers' representatives (agents), in New York, Cleveland, St. Louis, New Orleans, and Louisville. These were the same sales agents who handled the company's fiber products. Sales volume was fairly steady, but profits depended upon the cost of purchased components. In 1958, when the railroads cut their maintenance activities, draft gear sales did not suffer as much as fiber products, but were sharply curtailed. (See Exhibit 6.)

Railroad Accessories Group. Railroad refrigerator car equipment, including steel floors and grates, racks, drain spouts, and hatch closures, made up the Railroad Accessories Group. Almost all of the manufacturing for these products was done in the Harvey plant; only minor components were purchased from outside sources. In addition to a manager, the personnel of the unit included a manager of Product Design and Development, a manager of Engineering, a chief clerk, a service engineer, a staff of nine draftsmen, and two salesmen. The group also used manufacturers' representatives in St. Louis and Toronto. The units were sold to refrigerator car manufacturers which comprised about ten principal accounts. Sales of the units fluctuated widely depending on the construction of refrigerator cars.

Management thought that the long-range future of this product group was clouded by the threat of mechanically refrigerated cars and the possibility that railroads might switch to carrying refrigerated truck trailers piggy-back on flat cars. Some of Railway Supply's customers considered the cost of mechanical refrigeration too high. The cost of a refrigerated car was approximately $25,000, and an iced bunker car about $13,000. However, the trend toward mechanically refrigerated cars was evident and several of the major companies, such as Carrier Corporation and Thermo-King, had installations in service. While the company did not view any significant market expansion for mechanically refrigerated cars in the near future, it entered the field in 1958 through a working arrangement with a noted inventor who held many patents on refrigerated car equipment. The system which the company acquired the right to manufacture and sell was based on circulating cool air around the walls of the car and not directly on the produce or perishable materials being transported. The company maintained that this provided for greater accuracy in temperature control. In October of 1959 the company had three units in service on a test basis with the three largest refrigerated car organizations. In the 1958 railroad maintenance recession, Railroad Accessories sales did not drop as sharply as the company's other products. (See Exhibit 6.)

Railway Steel and Car Parts Group. The Railroad Steel and Car Parts Group performed the manufacturing function for the Railroad Acces-

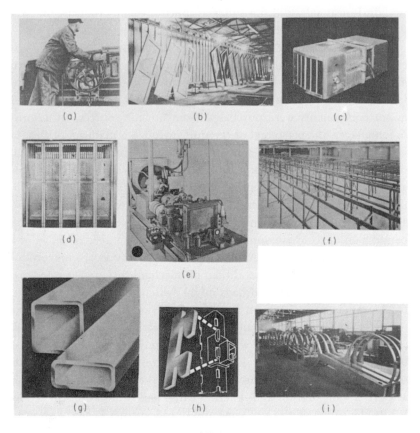

exhibit 3

Products of the Steel Division: (a) Draft Gears (hand brakes), (b) Custom Steel Fabrication, (c) Transifreez Units (truck refrigeration), (d) Refrigerator Car Specialties, (e) Mechanical Refrigeration (for R. R. refrig. cars), (f) Robust Racks Adjustable Storage Racks, (g) Square and Rectangular Tubing, (h) Adjustable "Snap-on" Units, and (i) Forming, Welding, Galvanizing.

sories and the Transifreez groups. It also did a sizable volume of contract steel fabricating and galvanizing for five key accounts:

Railco—Railroad car parts, principally refrigerator car parts. The Great Northern, Burlington, and St. Paul railroads were the principal customers because of a long-standing relationship established by the owner of Railco.

Concorp—A contractor's equipment company for which Railway Supply manufactured steel doors and frames. This operation was profitable for Railway Supply; however, it had expanded to such an extent that the management of Concorp was considering doing its own manufacturing.

Franklin—This company manufactured and sold a line of poles for lighting and advertising, and allied equipment. Railway Supply was able to produce electrically welded steel poles for Franklin because of its 40-foot shearing and forming press brake and the method the company had perfected of making a tight, smooth weld of that length.

Guard Grill—For which Railway Supply fabricated, by pressing and forming operations, steel grill guards for various machine tools such as punch presses, power saws, heavy duty grinders, and power shears.

Excel Door Hardware—A railroad equipment concern for which Railway Supply manufactured railroad car door parts, such as hinges, latches, rollers and glides, and bracings.

In selling to these contract customers, Railway Supply used a pricing formula that consisted of adding to its factory cost $2\frac{1}{2}\%$ for local administration and $6\frac{1}{2}\%$ for corporate expense, plus a markup for profit. In practice this had resulted in a profit of between 5% and 10% of the selling price. This formula had assured that sales would be profitable, but restricted the profit margin. The railroad equipment business from Railco and Excel Door was a significant portion of the Railroad Steel and Car Parts Group sales volume, but it fluctuated widely in keeping with the railroad equipment industry sales. The management of Railway Supply was aware that both of these accounts had frequently considered the possibility of doing their own manufacturing.

Robust Rack. Early in 1956 through Mr. John Mayer, the Steel Division secured a large subcontract from the Manufacturers' Equipment Company to fabricate a line of industrial heavy-duty steel shelves, racks, and bins. This patented line was sold under the trade name Robust Rack. Its distinguishing feature was an ingenious method of clips by which the parts, such as corner posts and shelves, could be hooked together quickly and simply without the use of nuts and bolts. The racks and shelving could be expanded into a wide variety of sizes. Robust Racks by Railway Supply had gained relatively widespread acceptance among manufacturers for storeroom and warehouse purposes.

Production of Robust Racks increased three-fold in the first four months of the contract. In view of the increased sales John Mayer made a proposal to the owners to buy their entire operation and, after six weeks of negotiations, succeeded in doing so. By October, 1958, the Robust Rack operation was the largest user of space in the Harvey plant. In December, 1958, the galvanizing department was sold to provide the Robust operation with more plant capacity.

Welded Steel Tubing. In March of 1958 Railway Supply began the production and sale of square and rectangular steel tubing in shapes up to 40″ in girth and ½″ in wall thickness. The company's entry into the field was preceded by a survey of the market made by a management consulting firm. The report of the consulting firm indicated that a promising market existed for certain sizes and types of tubing. Their survey indicated the following major conclusions:

1. There was a growing market for square and rectangular welded steel tubing, but its exact size could not be calculated from the findings.

2. Present suppliers of 3 x 3 to 4 x 4 inch squares (or comparable rectangular sizes) were fairly well entrenched and were apparently able to satisfy the current market demands for such sizes.

3. For larger sizes, and for wall thicknesses in excess of ¼ inch, the market was smaller but was not satisfactorily supplied, either in quality or quantity, by present manufacturers.

4. Distributors were generally receptive to a new entry into the field, and many of them would consider buying tubing from a new source, particularly in the sizes and wall thicknesses larger than those produced by such suppliers as Republic and Van Huffel.

5. The building construction industry was the most promising single market for square and rectangular welded steel tubing, but this industry was unusually demanding with respect to product quality and would show definite resistance to two-piece construction in some instances, notably where surfaces were exposed.

6. In order to make a successful entry into this field, a manufacturer would be required to produce competitively-priced tubing in 24-foot lengths with true dimensions and uniformly penetrating welds.

7. In addition, a new manufacturer had to be prepared to incur some promotional expense in order to develop its brand acceptance and to create a more general recognition among distributors, architects, and end-users of the product features and practical applications of square and rectangular welded steel tubing.

8. Geographically, a sizable portion of the total market could be reached by a tubing manufacturer located in the Chicago area.

Encouraged by this report, President Mayer requested the Steel Division to attempt to produce a smooth welded tube in excess of $\frac{1}{4}''$ in wall thickness, up to 40'' in girth and 24' in length. After much time and effort the company managed to produce satisfactory models. In commenting on this new venture John Parry, the assistant general manager of the Steel Division, stated, "We didn't have too much trouble producing a smooth welded tube in small sizes but we had great difficulty in producing tubing 24 feet in length. Until we accomplished this, as far as I know, no other company had been able to successfully produce a single-piece tubing unit of this size. This was because a copper follow bar, a holding back-up bar, had not been developed which was long enough and strong enough to perform the weld. We licked the problem in another way which we are now in the process of patenting.

"Our competition in tubing of this length is, outside of two-piece units, Seamless Steel Tubing which sells for as much as 60% more than our price. Although we still have production problems and our tubing needs to be perfected, we have sales of about $50,000 a month for our tubing."

Transifreez. During the 1940's Railway Supply manufactured ice bunkers for refrigerator trucks on a custom basis for the Donaldson Company of Cleveland. When Mr. Donaldson died in 1949, Mr. Mayer bought the assets of the business from the Donaldson estate. At that time iced trucks were already giving way to mechanical refrigeration. Realizing this, Mr. Mayer in February of 1951 purchased the assets of the Transifreez Corporation of Pittsburgh from its sole owner, Mr. Ray Reagan. The Transifreez refrigerating units had been designed by Mr. Reagan who was considered a very capable engineer. The product, however, had not been developed to the commercial stage due to the lack of capital. For this reason Mr. Reagan consented to sell to Railway Supply.

As part of the purchase agreement Mr. Reagan and the principal members of his technical staff were employed by Railway Supply. However, Mr. Reagan and Mr. Mayer became involved in a dispute over the development expenses and marketing plans for the Transifreez units. Aggravated by this and other disagreements, Mr. Reagan, after being in the employ of Railway Supply for six months, left the company. Six of his associates also resigned. Mr. Mayer then brought Mr. William Grimes, a Canadian refrigeration engineer, into the company as general manager of the Transifreez operation.

Mr. Reagan had designed three basic models of units for large truck trailers. These units (called the TR-15, the TR-20, and the TR-30) were expected to sell for $1,800, $2,200, and $2,900, respectively. Power units and compressors were purchased from the Omar Corporation of Akron, Ohio. Railway Supply fabricated the remainder of the unit and assembled it. In his first two years with Railway Supply, Mr. Grimes developed three additional truck trailer models: the TR-10 at $1,700; the TR-40 at $4,000; and the TR-50 at $5,000.

Mr. Grimes was convinced that there was a large potential market for a lighter unit, one capable of refrigerating small trucks which made store deliveries to retailers. This unit had to be light and compact, and capable of maintaining a temperature of 0° Fahrenheit under conditions which assumed the constant opening and closing of the truck doors. Early in 1956 Mr. Mayer consented to the development of such a light unit. By spring of 1957 Mr. Grimes was conducting breakdown tests of several hand-made models in his laboratory hot room. He made 35 models for tryout under field conditions. He was enthusiastic about the project in the testing stage; however, he doubted that a trouble-free unit could be put into production before 1959. The new unit was called the Runabout and was priced to sell for $500.

Sales of the Transifreez units varied from $65,000 in 1951, the first year of operation, to a high of $905,000 attained in 1957. (See Exhibit 6.) Four salesmen operating out of New York, Cleveland, Chicago, and Memphis worked out specifications and gave technical advice to prospective customers. Distribution was made through six manufacturers' representatives located in St. Paul, Detroit, San Antonio, New Orleans, San Diego, and St. Louis. Twenty-five distributors covered the entire country and had outlets in every major city. Mr. Grimes was not satisfied with the quality of these distributors. In his opinion four of them were good, six were fair, nine were worthless, and the remainder were too new to be judged. Within the next two years Mr. Grimes intended to replace six of the ineffective distributors and add sixteen new ones in the Pennsylvania-Ohio region, in the deep South, and the southwestern states. He planned to double the number of manufacturers' representatives and then to add another fifteen distributors to cover the West Coast.

Mr. Grimes eagerly looked forward to the introduction of the Runabout. He estimated that its unit sales for the next five years would be:

1959	500
1960	2,000
1961	3,000
1962	6,000
1963	well over 10,000

Mr. Grimes based his optimism on the trend toward the refrigerated trucking of such items as meat, produce, dairy products, fruits, and vegetables, and the rapidly growing consumption of milk, ice cream, and frozen foods. He pointed out that an increasing number of states and cities were passing laws requiring refrigerated trucks for milk deliveries. Mr. Grimes did not, however, expect his operation to be very profitable for some time. He thought that research and development expenditures should be increased and that an intensive advertising campaign would be necessary to properly promote the product.

When Mr. Reagan left Railway Supply at the end of 1951 the Transifreez operation was transferred from Pittsburgh to the Harvey plant of the company and became a part of the Steel Car Parts Group.

In discussing the Transifreez operation John Parry, the assistant general manager of the Steel Division, stated, "While we have the formal responsibility for the manufacture of the Transifreez units in our division, actually we have little to do with the whole operation. I would say Transifreez is still in the exploratory stages. It has produced about four or five models, none of which has worked well. No two units produced are alike. We still do not have a complete set of drawings for any model which could be considered standard. It seems to me that all models in production are really prototypes. This operation is losing about $3,000 a month currently."

Frank Noble, vice president and manager of the Steel Division, reinforced Parry's comments. "There are still a number of things wrong with the Transifreez units. The basic problem is that of a new unit designed by a new crew which has not had time to work out the bugs. You also have to remember that our shop is a poor place to manufacture a refrigeration unit. This type of operation requires precision work and clean facilities. Transifreez shares floor space with our heavy stamping, forming, and welding operations. Our shop is noisy and, because of the multipurpose, a dirty shop. We are accurate to only $\frac{1}{32}$ of an inch. While this is accurate enough for our basic operations, it does not measure up for refrigeration units.

"In addition to the problem of production facilities, our union relations are not right and we don't have the proper second-line supervision. Basically our Harvey workforce has little skill in precision fabrication. However, the shop union is strong and many employees have long years of service with the company. Many of the Transifreez positions pay higher rates than our other fabricating jobs. As openings occur in the Transifreez operation veteran employees insist their seniority rights entitle them to the higher paid positions which practically all of our workforce are unqualified to fill."

During 1957–1958 72% of the department's man-hours of labor had been spent on units which had special features and were not stocked as regular models. Mr. Grimes acted as chief engineer, but an increasing amount of his time was spent on administrative and promotional matters.

Sales of the Transifreez units were limited by Railway Supply's lack of service facilities. Only those distributors located in large cities operated service stations and carried repair parts. This limited Transifreez sales to homebased haulers who operated regularly scheduled runs. Railway Supply's principal competitor, the Kold King Corporation, had contractual arrangements with 92 service stations across the country for servicing long distance haulers. Transifreez had not organized a program for the service training of distributors. Parts lists, manuals, drawings, and instructions suitable for service were in the preliminary drafting stages.

Early in 1959 Mr. Mayer seriously considered liquidating the Transifreez operation. He said that he would like to sell it as a going business, or sell the assets. While he thought that market opportunities and prospects for the products were promising, he was concerned about the additional time and investment needed to make the Transifreez units competitive. As a result of a survey made by a management consulting organization Mr. Mayer had concluded that it would require an investment of approximately $300,000 to $400,000 and three to four years to rebuild the Transifreez operation to a point where it could take advantage of the market opportunities and prospects for refrigerated truck units.

In discussing the operations of the Steel Division and the future of the company, Frank Noble made the following statements:

"I'd like to emphasize that the character of our Harvey plant is changing rapidly. We acquired the Robust Rack Company in March of 1958. Our company was historically a manufacturer of refrigeration car ice bunkers. We had a reputation for high quality and good service. In recent years there had been a tendency toward mechanical refrigeration. Ice bunker manufacturing requires shearing, welding, and cutting, all of which we do well. We pretty much had a monopoly in the ice bunker field but now we have new competition in mechanical refrigeration and we are being forced into making a new product.

"There will be two major changes at our Harvey plant. The first will be the Robust Rack operation. We are now in the process of removing the galvanizing equipment. We need the space for the Robust Rack operation. It will cost us about $100,000 over the next several months to revamp the plant and to take some losses on conversion.

"The second major change is our entry into the manufacture of square and rectangular tubing. We are the only ones in the country that are now producing this type of tubing and currently we can sell more than we can make. Rand Mills can out-produce us in tubing up to 20 inches in girth and $\frac{1}{4}$-inch wall thickness but above those sizes we have the market pretty much to ourselves; however, we have to have long runs to turn out this seamless tubing efficiently. We make a smooth finish tubing on our press brakes and we have oversold our total production at practically no sales expense. This production operation sounds like a pretty simple thing but to produce a quality product requires quite a bit of know-how, and we're the only ones who have it so far.

"It is a vital necessity that we change our thinking from that of a job shop to that of a semiproduction shop. With the acquisition of the railroad refrigerator car parts operation many years ago we became pretty much a job shop. Making metal bulkheads was a feast or famine sort of business with production on the basis of large contracts from large railroads. In between we've tried to fill the holes with custom production for people like Concorp for whom we make metal doors which are a low-profit item. Our emphasis now will be on more proprietary products. In 1957 our railroad business was about 7 million dollars. We are nowhere close to that today. We probably will never achieve a General Motors type of mass production but we intend to standardize our items more so we can do at least some order filling from stock. There will be more standardization of products and much more standardization of parts. In the metal tubing end of the business small runs will be grouped to make longer runs."

John Parry, the assistant general manager, supported the opinion of Mr. Noble and added, "The railroad business just isn't what it used to be. There were times when our division made a 25 to 35% profit on certain products. But the railroad supply business seems to have gone dead altogether. From January to July of 1958 there was a 95% drop in the industry's purchases. Railway expenditures have declined drastically. (See Exhibit 4.) The outlook for 1959 might be better, but I doubt it."

exhibit **4 CLASS 1 RAILWAYS GROSS CAPITAL EXPENDITURES (IN MILLIONS OF DOLLARS)** *

Year	Equipment	Roadways & Structures
1946	319,017	242,940
1947	565,901	298,788
1948	917,449	356,035
1949	981,320	330,880
1950	779,399	286,443
1951	1,050,849	363,146
1952	935,090	405,822
1953	857,893	401,904
1954	498,726	321,520
1955	568,202	341,319
1956	821,357	406,500
1957	1,007,749	386,956
1958	479,680	258,358

NOTE: When comparisons for outlays for previous years are made, consideration should be given to the increase in the average cost of all railway materials. In most cases, the prices of locomotives, freight and passenger cars, and other materials have more than doubled in the past ten years.

* Moody's *Transportation Manual*, 1959.

FIBER DIVISION

"Since the decline of the steam locomotive," stated George Jensen, vice president of the Fiber Division, "we have had our problems in seeking new markets for our products. Diesels don't need our long-fiber asbestos and they have knocked hell out of our market. We have tried a number of products in an effort to fill in the gap created by the loss of the railroad business."

Until 1950 the largest volume of product lines made by Railway Supply had been railroad insulation applications. After 1950 conversion to diesel locomotives by the major railroads was accelerated and requirements for asbestos were reduced to a relatively insignificant amount. Steam locomotives in service for Class 1 railways declined from 37.5 thousand in 1946 to approximately 2 thousand in 1958. The diesel units in service for this period increased from 4.4 thousand to 27.1 thousand.[1] During these years the railroads found themselves caught between rising operating costs and inflexible tariff rates. Threatened with insolvency, the industry reacted by drastically cutting expenditures for replacement and maintenance. After 1950 the company's railroad business dropped significantly, and by 1958 asbestos production for the railroads was almost at a standstill.

Product Line. Railway Supply processed and fabricated two types of asbestos.[2] It imported short-fiber, weaving-grade asbestos, called Chrysotile, from Canada, whose mines supplied 70% of the world's asbestos requirements. The balance of its material was the long-fiber asbestos called Amosite, obtainable only from South African mines. Railway's products were classified in two broad categories: (See Exhibit 5 for illustration of products.)

1. *Asbestos textiles* were produced by applying a layer of short-fiber asbestos upon cotton cloth or wire mesh. Asbestos textiles were fabricated into tapes and yarns used in construction work and flexible protective coverings. These products were typically used for low temperature applications—below 500–600° F.
2. *Insulation* was made from the long-fiber asbestos, which was pressed into rigid shapes, mostly pipe coverings, for high temperature applications (800 to 1200°F.). The Amosite pipe coverings were used

---

[1] Moody's *Transportation Manual*, 1959.

[2] Asbestos is a mineral which has all of the fibrous qualities of animal or vegetable fibers such as wool, cotton, or silk. It also has an extraordinary resistance to heat and rot. The heat and rot resistance properties are the basis of its industrial and commercial value. The crude asbestos fiber, as it is received from the mines, is processed in a manner similar to wool or cotton. These processes consisted of opening, carding, spinning, plying, weaving, and braiding. Also, by mixing the fiber with cohesive binding materials, it is possible to mold asbestos into hard, dense shapes, such as rigid pipe coverings and hard insulation blocks.

in power plants, in ships, and in various industrial applications. The division further classified its products into the following lines:

a. *Pipe covering*—rigid sectional pipes and block insulation molded from Amosite which could be formed into pipe sections 30″ in diameter and 5″ thick. This covering provided high thermal efficiency and unusual mechanical strength before and after ex-

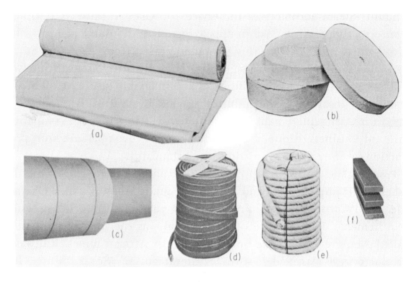

exhibit 5
Products of the Asbestos Division: (a) Asbestos Cloth, (b) Listing Tape, (c) Pipe Coverings, (d) Braided Tubing, (e) Asbestos Rope, (f) Block Insulation

posure to high temperatures. Amosite was also fabricated into a removable flexible blanket insulation, a woven sheathed felt used in marine, utility and refinery work. The pipe covering line made the largest sales and gross profit contribution of any line carried by the Fiber Division. (See Exhibit 7).

b. *Block insulation*—was molded from Amosite, as were pipe coverings, and was also used in high temperature applications. The blocks were rectangular in shape and included sizes from 1″ to 3″ in thickness, and from 6″ x 36″ to 36″ x 36″. The insulation block line had been unprofitable for some time and the management considered dropping the line but hesitated to do so because they thought pipe covering sales might suffer without a complementary line of blocks to sell to distributors.

c. *Flexible Insulation*—included asbestos in soft flexible forms such as blankets and tailored pads; Flexirock, a re-usable flexible pipe covering sheathed in a waterproof jacket which snapped open or shut by patented hooks; Asbesto-wrap, a sheathed flexible tape which was spiraled along steam pipes; Tempotube, a soft, flexible asbestos made in hollow pipe form and jacketed, and designed to slide over lengths of low temperature oil and heater lines. The flexible insulation line was second only to the pipe coverings in sales volume and percentage of gross profit. (See Exhibit 7.)

d. *Felt*—a soft rotproof and waterproof blanket which provided high thermal efficiency. Felt was sold in rolls 5′ long and from ¾″ to 1½″ thick. This product returned the highest percentage of gross profit of any line in the company, but sales, which were principally to the Navy, were difficult to forecast and had shown a decline since 1952.

e. *Open Fiber*—carded asbestos fibers, furnished in 25- or 50-pound cartons were used as filtering mediums for processing liquids such as beers, wines, and acids, and were also used for electrical insulations and for packing the walls of home gas heaters. While this line required very little processing, the company recognized that it was a low-volume gross profit item.

f. *Jobbing Items*—called "trading items" by Railway Supply, were not manufactured by the company but were purchased and re-sold by the division to accommodate customers and round out the line. Volume was erratic, but the operation was usually profit-able. (See Exhibit 7.)

g. *Packings and Gaskets*—included packings for pumps, either air, water, or high pressure steam; throttle, water heater, and stoker packings. Some packings were formed, some sold in coil lengths. Gaskets were stamped from sheet asbestos according to cus-tomers' specifications. Sales and profits of these lines were de-clining.

The first asbestos product Railway Supply manufactured in quantity was the woven tape which it had named Asbesto-wrap. This tape was spiraled around the steam lines of railroad locomotives to act both as an insulator and as a protective covering. Previous coverings used by the railroads had disintegrated when subjected to the abrasive impacts encountered in desert and mountain country. Asbesto-wrap was a new application of asbestos which had been designed and developed by a Mr. Tilley, a small manufacturer. Mr. Kahn purchased his patents and hired him. This new wrapping, a waterproof coated fabric, held together well under heavy usage and was quickly adopted by the railroad industry.

Other asbestos products for the railroads which the company manufactured included weatherproof tubing, pump packings, insulation jackets, and gaskets. Steam locomotives required large quantities of asbestos in a variety of forms and applications.

"We have a relatively broad line of asbestos products," stated Mr. Jensen, "however, we are very dependent upon our main raw material supplier. We have exclusive rights to produce Tempbestos in the United States. This is our trade name for the long-fiber asbestos called Amosite which is found only in South Africa. We are, of course, subject to the usual problems of price negotiations with a single supplier and we find competition from other kinds of asbestos, which use lower cost raw materials, to be very severe. In fact, we are almost ruled out of the lower temperature fields with our Amosite materials. The fine insulating properties of our Tempbestos in high temperature fields, however, has given our company the exclusive contract to supply the insulation requirements for the United States' fleet of atomic submarines.

"We gained our foothold in the Navy during World War II. Our insulation material became specified as standard for most of the United States naval vessels. The knowledge we picked up on our naval contracts aided in gaining an entry into the petroleum refiners and chemical plants. Supplying insulating materials for these industries constitutes a significant part of our business."

Sales. Fiber Division sales were made principally through distributors. Railway Supply was the only company in the industry which gave its distributors exclusive franchise rights within their sales territories. The sales manager of the Fiber Division considered distributor relations to be the key to a successful sales program and he emphasized this.

Fiber Division salesmen received a base salary plus a bonus based on quotas. The salesmen did not take orders. Their function was to supply customers with technical assistance in the determination of engineering specifications. They were also expected to promote the Railway Supply name in their territories. On occasions they worked with contractors directly on large-scale projects, such as the construction of power plants, oil refineries, and chemical plants. All customers sent their orders directly to the Aurora plant and each salesman was credited with sales emanating from his territory.

In 1957 there were sixteen salesmen in the Fiber Division. In November, 1958, eight salesmen were dismissed and two trainees were added to the staff. At the time the force was reduced, the salesmen's compensation was changed to a straight salary basis. The general sales manager explained that this action was necessary because of the many disputes over commissions on sales which overlapped several territories. He stated that in the future salesmen would be given a Christmas bonus whenever their performance and the income of the Division warranted it.

"We have been making a definite effort to sell, but on a smaller scale than we did three or four years ago. Our packing and textiles are perhaps receiving less attention from our salesmen than they should," said Mr. Jensen. "Our salesmen are basically pipe covering salesmen and that's where our primary effort is made. We have only one salesman for textiles in New York and one in Chicago. In comparison to our railroad business we are newcomers in the asbestos textile field. During the good years in the post-World War II period we oversold our production of insulation for railroads by 15% or more. With the decline of the railroad business we are now selling 80% of our production outside of this field.

"We use the Canadian asbestos, Chrysotile, a weaving grade asbestos, in our textile line. While it has definite cost advantages over our Amosite asbestos materials, price competition for asbestos textile materials is far greater. There is overcapacity in the asbestos textile business and we have great difficulty competing on a price basis. As a result we are proceeding cautiously in this field. The big margins we enjoyed in the railroad industry and on the jobs where specifications and know-how were important are definitely lacking in the asbestos textiles."

When the fiber operations became a separate division under Frank Jensen in 1956, the company had consolidated all of its asbestos manufacturing in two plants. The Aurora plant performed the bulk of the manufacturing operations and served as the headquarters for all personnel in the Division. The Nashville plant housed the weaving operation for asbestos textiles.

"The Aurora plant," stated Frank Jensen, "was converted from an old railroad shop into a facility for producing railroad insulating blankets. We acquired the plant in 1950 and by 1956 we had consolidated all of our fabricating operations in this facility. We have over 300,000 sq. ft. of manufacturing space at Aurora and we absorbed the operations of four smaller plants.

"While our Aurora plant is adequate and we made a good deal when we took over the property, it is not as efficient as the plant we lost to the Air Force through condemnation proceedings. We were sorry to lose this installation. It was located in Arkansas close to our markets and we enjoyed cheap gas fuel and a good labor situation. Before we were forced to give up this plant we had seriously considered enlarging it and making this location the center of our asbestos fabricating operations. Because of the necessity of finding a substitute for the Arkansas plant, and the need for consolidation and cost cutting caused by the drop in sales of insulation to the railroads, we decided to use the capacity we had available at Aurora.

"Our Nashville plant is really a weaving plant for our asbestos textile operations. The plant is in good condition and well maintained despite the fact that much of the weaving equipment dates back to the 1920's. However, we purchased four new cloth looms two years ago. We have about 140 employees at Nashville and plenty of room for expansion on our 20-acre site. While we are only in the asbestos business our Nashville plant is really a textile operation. Asbestos cloth and the varied related products are fabricated by overlaying asbestos on a fabric base. Our equipment is essentially the same as a textile plant. We have 14 cloth looms and 12 tape looms in the weaving department. Our yarn department, however, is not balanced with the weaving department and we are generally required to operate three shifts to keep pace with the two shifts of the weaving department. To obtain the needed equipment to assure a continuous production flow we would need to acquire additional equipment requiring an outlay of approximately $75,000.

"Currently one-half of the capacity of the Nashville plant is utilized for cloth and tape production. In order to save set-up time which requires 4 man days to change each loom to a cloth, looms are left with cloth standing so that they are ready for start-up when new orders are received. We would like to operate with a 30-day supply of yarn ahead of the weaving department. The backlog we had was absorbed by a hurry-up Navy order and we have not been able to build up an adequate reserve since that time.

"Our inventory level is affected by the amount of finished cloth and tape carried in stock and, of course, the yarn backlog ahead of the weaving department. Raw material also enters into the picture. It takes about 10 days in transit for a shipment of asbestos to reach Nashville from Canada. Taking all of these factors into account with the proper balance of backlogs, our inventory investment usually runs around $300,000. Because of the lack of proper backlogs, which affects our deliveries from time to time, we are running about ⅓ less than this figure at present.

"Aurora directs and schedules all of Nashville's production. We feel we can get better coordination this way. A good part of the Nashville output, approximately 35% at standard manufacturing costs, is transferred to Aurora for further processing. This is mainly in the packing and insulation lines."

"The asbestos textile products present somewhat of a problem," said Mr. Jensen. "We really can't measure our share of the market very well. I'd guess in terms of all our line we probably have 2 to 3% of the total business. The figures of the American Textile Institute indicated that we acquired about 6% of the total business. Their figures, of course, include only the sales of member firms. Practically all of the firms sell essentially the same product lines. There is, of course, specialization in the industry; as a result we vary in terms of our share of the market for any particular product. The Institute's figures in recent years showed that we ranged from 0.3% of the lap asbestos business to as high as 38% of asbestos cloth sales. Asbestos cloth is the only item we sell in any volume. We definitely need new products and we have some we recently introduced to the market. It is too early to tell, however, what kind of reception they will get. For example, we are now taking orders for ironing-board cloth, Fortisan asbestos yarn for cables, a special insulation for electric cables, and a few other specialty items. I also believe some of the products we have on tap but have not yet marketed, may prove out. We now have an asbestos drapery material ready to market. We can produce it in a variety of colors and have put some style into it. We also have dishcloth material, a new type of overlapping insulating tape, and an absorbent brake lining yarn composed of asbestos and jute."

exhibit 6 RAILWAY SUPPLY CORPORATION

Steel division net sales and operating profits by product division, 1951–1958 (in thousands of dollars)

Year	Draft Gear			Railroad Accessories			Railroad Steel and Car Parts			Prefabricated Housing		
	Net Sales	Operating Profit		Net Sales	Operating Profit		Net Sales	Operating Profit		Net Sales	Operating Profit	
		Amount	% of Sales		Amount	% of Sales		Amount	% of Sales		Amount	% of Sales
1951	$547	$ (13)	(2.3)	$3,852	$520	13.5	$2,026	$468	23.1	$ 300	$(154)	(51.3)
1952	540	11	2.1	3,990	965	24.2	1,806	402	22.3	1,060	(440)	(41.5)
1953	629	35	5.5	2,331	469	20.1	1,661	302	18.1	740	(300)	(40.5)
1954	351	8	2.2	4,973	895	18.0	1,891	285	15.1	—	—	—
1955	573	44	7.7	3,088	422	14.0	3,600	332	9.2	—	—	—
1956	469	30	6.4	3,770	455	12.1	3,741	289	7.7	—	—	—
1957	475	45	9.5	4,371	692	15.8	4,441	600	13.5	—	—	—
1958	433	(22)	(5.1)	2,402	(90)	(3.7)	2,110	(94)	(4.4)	—	—	—

Year	Heating and Cooling			Transifreez			Robust Rack			Total Steel Division		
	Net Sales	Operating Profit		Net Sales	Operating Profit		Net Sales	Operating Profit		Net Sales	Operating Profit	
		Amount	% of Sales		Amount	% of Sales		Amount	% of Sales		Amount	% of Sales
1951	—	—	—	$ 65	$(10)	(15.4)	—	—	—	$ 6,790	$811	11.9
1952	—	—	—	260	(2)	(.8)	—	—	—	7,656	936	12.2
1953	$ 780	$ (150)	(19.2)	455	18	4.0	—	—	—	6,596	374	5.7
1954	4,160	(686)	(16.5)	585	30	5.1	—	—	—	11,960	532	4.4
1955	3,807	(1,349)	(35.4)	796	60	7.5	—	—	—	11,864	(491)	(4.1)
1956	1,747	(300)	(17.2)	910	15	1.6	—	—	—	10,637	489	4.6
1957	—	—	—	785	40	5.1	—	—	—	10,072	1,377	13.7
1958	—	—	—	506	(35)	(6.9)	$1,790	$(54)	(3.0)	7,241	(295)	(4.1)

exhibit 7 **RAILWAY SUPPLY CORPORATION**

Fiber division net sales and operating profits by product lines, 1951–1958 (in thousands of dollars)

Year	Pipe Covering			Asbestos Textiles			Flexible Insulation		
	Net Sales	Operating Profit		Net Sales	Operating Profit		Net Sales	Operating Profit	
		Amount	% of Sales		Amount	% of Sales		Amount	% of Sales
1951	$2,721	$541	19.9	$1,677	$ 33	2.0	$1,745	$285	16.3
1952	3,050	221	7.3	1,727	(34)	(6.9)	1,735	120	6.5
1953	2,920	161	5.5	1,319	(133)	(10.1)	1,751	79	4.5
1954	2,269	209	9.2	554	(50)	(9.0)	1,238	99	8.0
1955	2,113	43	2.0	860	(91)	(10.6)	1,182	8	.7
1956	2,350	188	8.0	872	(49)	(5.6)	1,193	72	6.0
1957	2,402	204	8.5	1,029	(41)	(4.0)	1,263	82	6.5
1958	1,807	27	1.5	723	(83)	(11.5)	918	(9)	1.0

exhibit 7 (continued)

	Felt			Block Insulation			Open Fiber		
1951	$862	$271	31.4	$287	$(23)	(8.0)	$144	$10	6.9
1952	521	114	22.0	373	(37)	(10.0)	137	3	2.2
1953	318	60	18.9	338	(39)	(11.5)	99	2	2.2
1954	290	55	19.0	150	(15)	(10.0)	81	2	2.5
1955	121	7	5.8	140	(27)	(19.3)	66	1	1.5
1956	130	13	10.0	111	(14)	(12.6)	47	1	2.1
1957	124	13	10.5	117	(12)	(10.3)	43	1	2.3
1958	90	4	4.05	68	(11)	(16.2)	32	(1)	(3.1)

	Packing and Gaskets			Jobbing Items			Total Fiber Division		
1951	$915	$ 23	2.5	$619	$95	15.3	$8,970	$1,235	13.8
1952	994	(30)	(3.0)	594	59	10.0	9,131	416	4.5
1953	931	(29)	(3.1)	549	46	8.4	8,225	147	1.8
1954	753	(120)	(16.0)	450	47	10.5	5,785	226	3.9
1955	716	(100)	(14.0)	361	22	6.1	5,559	(137)	(2.5)
1956	744	(60)	(8.1)	403	25	6.2	5,850	176	3.0
1957	788	(26)	(3.3)	394	25	6.4	6,160	246	4.0
1958	588	(61)	(10.4)	294	(1)	(.3)	4,520	(134)	(3.0)

exhibit 8 RAILWAY SUPPLY CORPORATION

Selected financial data 1951–1958

	1958	1957	1956	1955	1954	1953	1952	1951
As a per cent of sales:								
Gross profit	13.2%	22.8%	19.0%	12.7%	19.3%	18.2%	19.8%	24.9%
Selling and administration	16.8	12.8	15.0	16.3	15.0	14.7	11.7	11.9
Operating profit	(3.6)	10.0	4.0	(3.6)	4.3	3.5	8.1	13.0
Net income before nonrecurring items	(1.8)	5.0	3.3	(2.3)	1.8	1.6	3.8	6.2
Current ratio	8.5:1	7.5:1	2.7:1	2.1:1	2.1:1	2.3:1	3.3:1	2.4:1
Working capital (in thousands)	$5,903	$6,117	$4,833	$4,621	$5,038	$4,374	$4,645	$4,878
Book value (in thousands)	8,892	9,199	8,253	8,233	8,585	8,147	8,242	8,057
Market value (in thousands)	3,801	3,326	3,197	4,277	3,801	4,752	7,128	6,653
Earnings before nonrecurring items (in thousands)	(221)	812	547	(394)	318	232	632	984
Earnings including nonrecurring items (in thousands)	(306)	946	20	(352)	438	214	801	996
Dividends (in thousands)	—	—	—	—	—	309	617	617
Total capital employed (in thousands)	$9,482	$9,254	$8,320	$8,314	$8,677	$8,206	$8,242	$8,057
Earnings before nonrecurring items:								
As a per cent of total capital employed	(2.3)%	8.7%	6.6%	(4.7)%	3.7%	2.8%	7.7%	12.2%
As a per cent of book value	(2.5)	8.8	6.6	(4.8)	3.7	2.8	7.7	12.2
As a per cent of market value	(5.8)	24.4	17.1	9.2	8.3	4.9	8.9	14.8
Number of shares common stock outstanding	950,350	950,350	950,350	950,350	950,350	950,350	950,350	950,350
Per share:								
Working capital	$ 6.21	$ 6.43	$ 5.08	$ 4.86	$ 5.30	$ 4.60	$ 4.89	$ 5.13
Book value	9.36	9.68	8.68	8.67	9.04	8.58	8.68	8.48
Market value	4.00	3.50	3.37	4.50	4.00	5.00	7.50	7.00
Earnings before nonrecurring items	(.23)	.86	.57	.41	.33	.24	.67	1.04
Dividends	—	—	—	—	—	.33	.65	.65

exhibit 9 RAILWAY SUPPLY CORPORATION

Consolidated balance sheets 1951–1958, years ending December 31 (in thousands of dollars)

	1958	1957	1956	1955	1954	1953	1952	1951
Assets								
Cash	$ 1,977	$ 1,997	$ 823	$ 454	$ 1,131	$ 780	$ 966	$ 1,104
Accounts and notes receivable	1,803a	1,693b	2,570c	2,759d	1,828	1,695	1,545	2,437
Inventories	3,910	3,368	4,203	5,520	6,782	5,179	4,167	4,948
Total current assets	$ 6,690	$ 7,058	$ 7,596	$ 8,733	$ 9,741	$ 7,654	$ 6,678	$ 8,489
Land, buildings and equipment	$ 5,420	$ 5,187	$ 5,218	$ 5,608	$ 5,309	$ 6,204	$ 5,916	$ 5,286
Less depreciation	2,545	2,330	2,134	2,123	1,876	2,563	2,490	2,295
Net property	$ 2,875	$ 2,857	$ 3,084	$ 3,485	$ 3,433	$ 3,641	$ 3,426	$ 2,991
Notes receivable	125	148	172	—	—			
Deferred charges	579	132	231	276	263	270	252	269
Total assets	$10,269	$10,195	$11,083	$12,494	$13,437	$11,565	$10,356	$11,749

< ># exhibit 9 (continued)

Liabilities

Notes payable	$ 40	$ 13	$ 1,638	$ 3,263	$ 3,263	$ 1,957	$ 325	$ 1,300
Accounts payable	521	716	936	655	876	1,134	1,436	2,044
Accruals	226	198	189	194	390	189	272	267
Federal income tax	—	14	—	—	174	—	—	—
Total current liabilities	$ 787	$ 941	$ 2,763	$ 4,112	$ 4,703	$ 3,280	$ 2,033	$ 3,611
Insurance reserve	26	—	—	68	57	79	81	81
Notes payable	16	33	40	46	52	59	—	—
Mortgage payable		22	27	35	40	—	—	—
Patents	548	—	—	—	—	—	—	—
Stockholders equity:								
Common stock	$ 3,220	$ 3,220	$ 3,220	$ 3,220	$ 3,220	$ 3,220	$ 3,220	$ 3,220
Capital surplus	798	798	798	798	798	798	798	798
Retained earnings	5,211	5,518	4,572	4,552	4,904	4,466	4,561	4,376
Less reacquired stock	337	337	337	337	337	337	337	337
Net common stock & surplus	$ 8,892	$ 9,199	$ 8,253	$ 8,233	$ 8,585	$ 8,147	$ 8,242	$ 8,057
Total	$10,269	$10,195	$11,083	$12,494	$13,437	$11,565	$10,356	$11,749

a Including claims for tax refund $299,000.
b Including notes receivable from heating and cooling division $280,000.
c Including receivable from heating and cooling division $621,000.
d Including advances to supplier $480,000 and tax refund claim $312,000.

exhibit 10 RAILWAY SUPPLY CORPORATION

Statement of income and retained earnings 1951–1958, years ending December 31 (in thousands of dollars)

	1958	1957	1956	1955	1954	1953	1952	1951
Net sales	$11,761	$16,232	$16,487	$17,423	$17,745	$14,821	$16,787	$15,760
Cost of sales	10,210	12,530	13,343	15,207	14,334	12,117	13,471	11,835
Gross profit	$ 1,551	$ 3,702	$ 3,144	$ 2,216	$ 3,411	$ 2,704	$ 3,316	$ 3,925
Selling and administrative expense	1,980	2,079	2,479	2,844	2,653	2,185	1,964	1,879
Operating profit (loss)	$ (429)	$ 1,623	$ 665	$ (628)	$ 758	$ 519	$ 1,352	$ 2,046
Interest expense (net)	—	5	118	116	108	33	33	5
Income before federal taxes and special items	$ (429)	$ 1,618	$ 547	$ (744)	$ 650	$ 486	$ 1,319	$ 2,041
Provision for federal taxes	cr.208	806	—	cr.350	332	254	687	1,057
Net income before special items	$ (221)	$ 812	$ 547	$ (394)	$ 318	$ 232	$ 632	$ 984
Add or deduct special items								
Gain or (loss) on sale, liquidation or abandonment of properties and relocation expense	(85)a	134b	(527)c	42	120d	(18)	169	12
Net income including special items	$ (306)	$ 946	$ 20	$ (352)	$ 438	$ 214	$ 801	$ 996
Earnings retained in business at beginning of year	5,517	4,571	4,551	4,903	4,465	4,560	4,376	3,977
	$ 5,211	$ 5,517	$ 4,571	$ 4,551	$ 4,903	$ 4,774	$ 5,177	$ 4,993
Dividends	—	—	—	—	—	309	617	617
Earnings retained in business at the end of year	$ 5,211	$ 5,517	$ 4,571	$ 4,551	$ 4,903	$ 4,465	$ 4,560	$ 4,376

a Loss on sale of property
b Gain on condemnation sale of property.
c Loss due to liquidation of cooling and heating division.
d $389,000 gain on sale of properties less $269,000 due to moving and other nonrecurring expense.

RAILWAY EQUIPMENT INDUSTRY NOTES[3]

Few companies experience sharper ups and downs than railroad equipment builders, whose fortunes hinge to a great degree on the erratic changes in railroad earning power. With railroad purchases of rolling stock necessarily geared to changes in operating income, the "feast or famine" characteristics of the equipment market have forced most of the major equipment companies to widen sales opportunities through diversification. Some of these moves have been into heavy metal goods lines, which are also subject to considerable fluctuation from time to time.

In recognition of the railroads' major role in defense transportation, a provision of the 1950 tax law allowed five-year amortization of that portion of a purchase certified for wartime or emergency needs. Accordingly, equipment buying expanded sharply, reaching a peak late in 1955, when certifications of new purchases were discontinued. Since then, the decline in amortization tax deferment benefits, coupled with deterioration of railroad earnings and finances, resulted in a significant drop in new orders.

Permission by Federal authorities in 1956 and early in 1957 for several railroads to depreciate equipment over shorter life spans for tax purposes was conditioned on agreement by the carriers to replace rolling stock at the end of its depreciated life. Unfortunately, these agreements—which would provide larger depreciation cash flow for investment purposes—do not embrace a wide portion of the carrier group. The railroad industry presently is seeking broad changes in depreciation policies and initiation of a construction reserve fund. The latter would permit the industry to set aside tax-deductible reserves.

The railroad equipment industry is highly specialized, cumbersome, and inelastic. New techniques tending to check the rise in cost evolve slowly. Markets are limited and of such nature that volume usually cannot be stimulated by lowering prices; indeed, inflation of production costs, and hence selling prices, in postwar years has inhibited the railroads' ability to purchase more units. Necessary facilities involve large investment in plant and equipment. Accordingly, overhead burden is heavy. Labor costs are disproportionately high in dull periods because of the necessity of retaining minimum staffs of skilled workers and engineers.

[3] SOURCE: Standard & Poor's *Industry Surveys*, Standard & Poor's Corporation, Ephrata, Pa.

Reflecting the cyclical nature of orders, a fundamental condition of overcapacity exists except when demand is unusually strong. Overcapacity has been aggravated in some areas by the pressure of new competitors in the railroad equipment field. Thus, Timken Roller Bearing, primarily an automobile accessory maker, is aiming to increase its share of the railroad equipment market. The Budd Company, primarily a producer of automobile components, is a leading fabricator of railroad passenger cars.

To help offset the effects of wide cyclical fluctuations in sales and to attain fuller use of plant facilities, most railroad equipment concerns have pursued diversification programs in recent years, such as the pleasure boat business, dust and fume collecting fields, and electronics. Many diverse items are now manufactured, but most fall into the capital goods classifications. In some instances, sales of industrial goods exceed those of railroad products.

Under a war or armament economy, the industry's picture changes. The large plants and massive machinery are adaptable for production of large castings and various heavy tools of war, particularly aircraft components and tanks. Rising railroad traffic in such a period increases demand for primary products, so that the industry operates close to capacity. However, heavy taxes prevent corresponding gains in net income.

RAILROAD EQUIPMENT INDUSTRY
Employment and average earnings

Year	Production Workers (1,000)	Av. Hourly Earnings	Av. Weekly Earnings
1958	36.1	$2.65	$100.70
1957	54.7	2.52	100.80
1956	48.6	2.37	94.56
1955	41.7	2.25	90.45
1954	41.7	2.12	82.26
1953	62.4	2.03	80.39
1952	61.9	1.90	77.83
1951	59.0	1.87	76.48
1950	46.0	1.68	66.33
1949	59.1	1.62	63.54
1948	68.7	1.56	62.24
1947	66.6	1.41	57.06

SOURCE: U. S. Dept. of Labor.

Chart 1

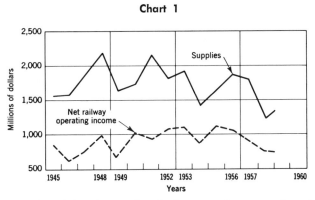

SOURCES: Association of American Railroads, Interstate Commerce Commission

SELECTED COMPANIES FINANCIAL DATA
Stanray Corp.

	Net Sales*	Oper. Inc.*	Net Bef. Taxes*	Net Income*	Net Wkg. Cap.*	Curr. Ratio Assets To Liabs.
1958	14.07	0.59	0.16	0.16	9.90	6.3–1
1957	30.70	6.95	6.24	2.92	11.06	3.3–1
1956	26.93	6.05	5.57	2.75	9.77	3.1–1
1955	19.82	3.43	2.82	1.41	8.67	4.0–1
1954	12.14	0.69	0.27	0.24	8.80	6.8–1
1953	25.14	4.31	3.92	1.92	8.94	3.9–1
1952	22.91	3.38	3.19	2.08	8.03	2.9–1
1951	35.16	7.94	7.84	3.20	9.84	2.6–1
1950	19.45	4.77	4.62	2.61	10.38	4.1–1
1949	17.29	4.26	3.98	2.31	7.49	10.2 1

American Brake Shoe Co.

	Net Sales*	Oper. Inc.*	Net Bef. Taxes*	Net Income*	Net Wkg. Cap.*	Curr. Ratio Assets To Liabs.
1958	138.00	16.41	9.68	4.78	42.8	4.1–1
1957	186.85	26.90	19.92	9.12	44.1	3.3–1
1956	186.14	24.50	19.16	8.96	32.4	2.2–1
1955	147.10	18.37	14.14	6.44	26.4	2.2–1
1954	109.92	12.68	9.20	4.30	19.4	2.3–1
1953	139.78	16.51	12.25	4.85	29.2	2.6–1
1952	135.38	14.77	11.34	4.64	25.8	2.5–1
1951	147.57	20.73	18.02	6.47	24.6	2.2–1
1950	106.58	14.07	12.34	5.94	22.5	2.6–1
1949	91.73	8.71	5.99	3.99	20.2	3.9–1

American Steel Foundries

	Net Sales*	Oper. Inc.*	Net Bef. Taxes*	Net Income*	Net Wkg. Cap.*	Curr. Ratio Assets To Liabs.
1958	94.54	12.02	8.92	4.52	27.95	3.4–1
1957	122.61	19.37	16.11	8.01	34.06	3.0–1
1956	117.13	20.15	17.47	8.37	33.24	2.8–1
1955	80.66	10.48	8.17	3.77	27.60	3.3–1
1954	89.01	9.55	8.01	3.63	30.40	3.8–1
1953	149.69	20.68	18.57	6.34	32.07	2.5–1
1952	139.56	19.32	17.03	6.04	29.76	2.2–1
1951	116.76	21.21	19.29	6.68	28.18	2.2–1
1950	54.40	7.35	6.32	3.72	29.11	4.3–1
1949	74.62	12.02	10.93	6.51	29.47	4.1–1

General Railway Signal Co.

	Net Sales*	Oper. Inc.*	Net Bef. Taxes*	Net Income*	Net Wkg. Cap.*	Curr. Ratio Assets To Liabs.
1958	18.44	3.13	3.22	1.62	11.86	4.8–1
1957	25.73	6.57	6.51	3.17	11.40	3.0–1
1956	25.71	6.62	6.48	3.14	9.21	2.7–1
1955	16.96	3.30	3.22	1.64	9.85	4.0–1
1954	15.99	2.36	2.32	1.21	11.51	5.4–1
1953	19.79	3.59	3.47	1.23	11.07	3.7–1
1952	21.62	5.06	4.91	1.44	10.85	2.9–1
1951	18.56	4.23	4.20	1.43	10.10	3.0–1
1950	13.61	2.98	2.90	1.50	9.38	4.1–1
1949	34.60	4.23	3.47	2.02	11.42	4.8–1

National Castings Co.

	Net Sales*	Oper. Inc.*	Net Bef. Taxes*	Net Income*	Net Wkg. Cap.*	Curr. Ratio Assets To Liabs.
1958	44.77	2.06	0.11	0.09	13.98	3.2–1
1957	64.89	8.03	6.32	3.12	15.80	2.9–1
1956	65.23	10.04	7.93	3.83	14.61	2.3–1
1955	58.96	7.48	5.49	2.38	11.96	2.4–1
1954	37.62	2.14	0.32	0.33	10.42	3.0–1
1953	57.73	7.55	5.25	2.25	12.90	3.2–1
1952	54.30	9.03	7.76	2.46	12.06	2.3–1
1951	63.92	13.54	12.83	4.13	12.27	2.0–1
1950	44.81	8.12	7.52	4.02	13.21	3.0–1
1949	34.60	4.23	3.47	2.02	11.42	4.8–1

Poor & Co.

	Net Sales*	Oper. Inc.*	Net Bef. Taxes*	Net Income*	Net Wkg. Cap.*	Curr. Ratio Assets To Liabs.
1958	26.6	1.47	1.48	0.87	10.13	6.0–1
1957	38.5	3.63	3.32	1.60	10.19	4.9–1
1956	42.3	4.53	4.33	2.05	9.97	3.4–1
1955	34.5	3.39	3.36	1.55	6.64	2.3–1
1954	28.1	2.29	2.29	1.07	7.13	3.6–1
1953	38.5	4.11	3.93	1.54	7.17	2.8–1
1952	34.4	3.77	3.56	1.27	6.99	2.6–1
1951	38.3	5.21	4.93	1.73	6.88	2.3–1
1950	26.0	2.87	2.70	1.44	6.60	2.9–1
1949	19.3	1.79	1.69	1.03	4.77	5.5–1

Youngstown Steel Door Co.

	Net Sales*	Oper. Inc.*	Net Bef. Taxes*	Net Income*	Net Wkg. Cap.*	Curr. Ratio Assets To Liabs.
1958	12.96	1.41	1.30	0.66	10.58	6.4–1
1957	31.05	5.82	5.63	2.70	10.56	5.1–1
1956	28.42	5.88	5.85	2.81	9.59	3.0–1
1955	20.19	3.36	3.32	1.51	8.83	3.5–1
1954	10.95	1.10	1.04	0.55	8.16	5.9–1
1953	17.36	3.08	3.04	1.17	8.18	3.8–1
1952	17.54	2.66	2.55	1.15	7.83	4.0–1
1951	24.56	4.99	4.83	1.67	7.66	2.9–1
1950	14.97	2.77	2.68	1.46	6.88	3.8–1
1949	9.64	1.36	1.16	0.70	6.25	7.4–1

Symington-Wayne Corp.

	Net Sales*	Oper. Inc.*	Net Bef. Taxes*	Net Income*	Net Wkg. Cap.*	Curr. Ratio Assets To Liabs.
1958	39.98	4.41	3.65	1.64	15.84	3.9–1
1957	43.64	3.61	3.08	1.68	15.00	3.3–1
1956	20.66	2.05	2.08	1.21	5.86	3.1–1
1955	15.37	1.66	1.64	0.92	5.69	3.3–1
1954	9.62	0.38	0.21	0.19	5.75	5.9–1
1953	19.24	2.67	2.43	0.85	6.53	3.0–1
1952	20.64	2.62	2.45	0.87	6.52	3.0–1
1951	18.59	2.40	2.36	0.91	4.73	2.5–1
1950	11.37	2.00	2.20	1.17	4.75	3.3–1
1949	10.07	1.21	1.10	0.67	6.45	8.2–1

SOURCE: Standard & Poor's *Industry Surveys* and Standard's *Listed Stock Reports*, Standard & Poor's Corporation, Ephrata, Pa.

* In millions of dollars.

OZARK OIL COMPANY

For the Ozark Oil Company the year 1963 resulted in a slightly higher total net income than the previous year and a modest increase in net income per share. Prior to this, there had been a reversal of a fairly steady downward trend in earnings that had begun in 1957. During this period Ozark's financial performance had not compared favorably with others in the industry. In 1963 Ozark's sales volume was $586 million; in 1953 it amounted to $358 million. However, income per common share in 1963 was only 98% of that in 1953, despite the higher sales volume (see Exhibits 1 through 4).

HISTORY

Ozark Oil Company had its origin in 1910 in the Kentucky Power Company, which operated electric generating stations in the Louisville area. Kentucky Power owned several coal fields in southern Illinois where natural gas fields were discovered, which led the company into the gas business, with St. Louis as one of its principal markets. Subsequent discovery of oil on its coal lands took the company into the oil business. Between 1910 and 1913 Kentucky Power acquired a number of petroleum operations, including various production leases in the Midwest and refineries in Ohio. A major acquisition of the period was a small, prospering, integrated oil company, the Ozark Oil Company, of Hannibal, Missouri, which had production and refining facilities and a chain of service stations. By 1914 the Kentucky Power Company had liquidated all of its gas and utility interests and had adopted the name Ozark Oil Company.

During the 25-year period which followed, Ozark grew through a series of mergers, acquisitions, and consolidations, from which formed the basic geographic pattern of the company's future operations. After 1939 the company expanded by internal growth, developing an extensive network of production fields, pipelines, transport facilities, refineries, and service stations.

In 1948 the management embarked upon a major expansion program. It decided to allocate resources simultaneously to (1) increasing refining capacity; (2) expanding its marketing facilities; (3) increasing domestic expenditures for oil exploration. All three phases of the program were undertaken at the same time, management assuming that the discovery of new oil fields was almost a mathematical certainty, based upon its past experience and the expenditure of additional funds for exploration. The refining and marketing facilities were successfully enlarged according to plan, but discovery of significant new reserves of crude oil failed to materialize. The enlarged refining-marketing operations were retained without retrenchment from year to year, and increasing allocations were made to a stepped-up program of explorations which consistently failed to discover new sources of crude oil. Ozark Oil, since that period, existed with production facilities which supplied only about 40% of the crude oil necessary to supply its refinery and marketing capacities; it purchased remaining crude oil requirements at high cost from independent producers and from crude-rich integrated companies. "This situation is livable," said an Ozark executive, "when retail gasoline prices are high. When prices are low, we agonize."

Throughout its history the Ozark management had not attempted to expand marketing to a nationwide operation. Neither had it made any concentrated effort to align production, refining and marketing activities in the same geographic area.

THE MILLER ACQUISITION

Believing that its facilities would complement those which Ozark already owned, the Ozark management acquired the Miller Oil Company of Cleveland on August 1, 1959, for 955,100 shares of Ozark stock. Miller assets included crude oil and gas reserves, largely in Texas and British Columbia; undeveloped acreage in the United States and

Canada; an interest in a refinery near Cleveland; and an interest in oil pipelines in Ohio and Ontario. The acquisition added 3 million barrels annually to Ozark's crude production and about 75 million barrels of reserves.

THE COMPANY

In 1963 the Ozark Oil Company was considered a medium-sized integrated oil company engaged in exploration, production, transportation, refining, and marketing. It owned 3,492 oil and gas wells in the United States, Canada, Alaska, Latin America, and Africa. It was basically a domestic company; only in recent years had management ventured abroad.

Ozark had crude oil and condensate reserves estimated at 490 million barrels, of which 450 million were in the United States, 20 million in Canada, and 16 million in Venezuela. In addition, it had reserves of over two trillion cubic feet of gas in the United States. It held lease or option rights on the following acreage:

Locality	Undeveloped Acreage (Net)	Developed Acreage (Net)
United States and Canada	3,680,800	314,000
South and Central America	9,056,000	5,450
Other foreign	12,025,600	
Totals	24,762,400	319,450

Ozark had crude oil production in 21 states. Over 50% of its production was in the state of Texas, where production was restricted by Texas conservation regulations. It also produced in Illinois, Colorado, and Oklahoma.

Ozark owned an interest in 5,132 miles of crude oil pipelines; 2,700 miles of gathering lines; and 9,400 miles of product lines. It operated forty-five terminals for finished products, three tankers, four towboats, and nine barges. It had five refineries with a total daily capacity of 155,000 barrels. It sold its products in 15 North Central states through 13,046 retail gas stations (10,151 dealer-owned) (see Exhibit 5), 222 truck stops, and 825 bulk plants. It employed 240 scientists and technicians in its new research facility. It had over 8,000 employees. Since

1958 all activities were administered from a large new headquarters building it had erected at Ferguson, a suburb of St. Louis.

INDUSTRY TRENDS

From the end of World War II until 1958 domestic demand for oil increased steadily at a rate of about 6% annually. Overseas demand rose about 12% during the first postwar decade and continued to rise during the 1960's. After 1958 the United States rate of growth began to decline. In 1961 demand increased only 2.2%, the record postwar low. In the years which followed, the growth rate revived moderately, but forecasters agreed that the growth rate for the next several years would be only about 3%. Investment analysts no longer rated oil as a vigorous-growth industry.

During the 1950's additions to refinery capacity created a condition of excess capacity in the world petroleum industry. For the United States alone the excess was estimated to be over 20%. Refiners strove to keep their refining costs low by operating at as high a volume as possible. This brought pressure upon retail prices, and the result was intense price competition in every state. During 1963 15 out of 20 leading oil companies had profit margins which were lower than they had been during the declining-demand period from 1958 to 1961. "The oil industry," said an industry leader, "has achieved the singular distinction of being able to convert a sharply higher product demand into lower profits."

MANAGEMENT (SEE EXHIBIT 6)

Mr. Michael Randall, the president of Ozark, had joined the company in 1928 as an assistant treasurer. Thirty-one years old at the time, Mr. Randall had been an investment analyst with one of the largest banks in Houston, Texas. Mr. Randall progressed gradually through the financial departments of Ozark, became treasurer in 1950, and was elected president in 1954 to succeed Mr. Courtenay King, who had been elected chairman of the board.

Mr. King had spent his entire career with Ozark, having joined its predecessor, the Kentucky Power Company, on his graduation from college in 1910. Mr. King was a nephew of Mr. Myron Bullock, a distinguished Texas attorney and a major stockholder in Ozark, whose law firm had been legal counsel for the Ozark Oil Company almost from the inception of the business. Throughout his career Mr. King had been considered a protégé of "Judge" Bullock, consulting closely with him on any major move. Judge Bullock was a man of substantial means and was a director and major stockholder of the Houston bank where Randall had been employed. It was the Judge who had suggested to Courtenay King, then treasurer of Ozark, that he should invite young Randall to leave the bank and come to Ozark.

Judge Bullock's first introduction to Ozark had come from a family which dated back to prominence in the colonial period. This family had moved to Kentucky where it developed extensive business interests. Members of the family were large stockholders in Kentucky Power, and later, when the Ozark Oil Company's affairs came to center around its Texas oil fields and Galveston refining plant, the family looked to their Texas attorney, Judge Bullock, to represent their interests. As Ozark became a major oil company, Judge Bullock, on behalf of the family and later as a substantial stockholder himself, worked closely with Courtenay King and Michael Randall in directing the company's affairs. The Judge had never been an executive of the company. He had been a director for only a few years, and he had been an intermittent member of the executive committee. In 1964 Judge Bullock, then 91 years old, was still a major stockholder, as was the "colonial" family, and the Judge was still taking an active interest in Ozark affairs.

It was widely observed that, after his elevation to chairman of the board, Mr. King spent much of his time in Mr. Randall's office. Judge Bullock, then in retirement, never appeared at the Ozark headquarters office, but periodically Mr. King and Mr. Randall together visited him in his Galveston home. Announcements of major company events were made by Mr. King and Mr. Randall jointly. The board usually approved Mr. King's proposals. Mr. Randall had seldom disagreed with him in earlier years, but lately there had been rumors that Mr. Randall was no longer in agreement with Mr. King and the Judge because of their ultraconservatism.

Mr. Randall was a man of unquestionable good will who was zealous and eager to vitalize Ozark but was also indecisive, reluctant to take a determined stand against opposition, and a willing compromiser. As early as 1949 Mr. Randall had proposed that Ozark undertake a heavy exploration program, but Mr. King had not supported his proposals before the board. It was Mr. Randall who had sponsored such innovations as the Ozark Inns, truck stops, and Super Service Centers, projects which had been coolly received by Mr. King and certain veteran members of the Ozark board.

There were 17 members of the board in 1964, and they averaged 72 years in age. Board meetings had been tranquil and harmonious until 1959. In this year, as part of the Miller Oil merger, Mr. Barton Severe, former owner of Miller, came into a large block of Ozark stock, and the merger terms entitled him to two seats on the Ozark board. Mr. Severe declined a seat himself but nominated Wilbur Force, who had been president of Miller. Mr. Severe, then only 43, was known as a self-made man of great wealth and great force of personality. Mr. Force was equally aggressive. There was a growing awareness that at board meetings Mr. Force was found to be asking penetrating questions of Mr. King, who was no longer receiving the support of Mr. Randall.

In 1964 Mr. Severe asked that Mr. Force be made a member of the executive committee, which was composed of the chairman, the president, and the heads of each of the operating divisions. In making the request Mr. Severe pointed out that most major oil company executive committees met weekly; that Jersey Standard's met daily. Ozark's had been meeting once every two months.

EXPLORATION

In 1964 Ozark had still been unable to eliminate its poor "crude-sufficiency" ratio. The accelerated exploration program launched in 1949 had cost $412 million, an amount which was considerably above the industry average for a company of Ozark's size. During the first 10 years of the program, Ozark's discovery ratio, measured in terms of the value of reserves found per dollar expended in exploration, was 30% below the industry average. In 1952 Ozark produced 59,972 barrels of crude oil a day; in 1963 it was producing 58,881 barrels a day.

Although technicians in the oil industry claimed that the development of scientific equipment for locating new oil fields had taken most of the gamble out of exploration, it was generally conceded that Ozark had experienced incredibly bad luck in its explorations. In 1964 there was a joke circulating among oil men that Ozark had the dubious distinction of being the only company in the oil industry which could guarantee that every well it sank would result in a dry hole. That year Ozark outbid every major oil company to pay $19 million for an interest in several coveted offshore leases. After drilling eight dry holes, Ozark wrote off the tract as a total loss. An adjacent block, geographically less desirable, was leased by another major oil company, which brought in a heavily producing well on its first drilling.

In the period from 1955 to 1964 the cost of discovering additional oil reserves in the United States had increased significantly. During the five years ending with 1964 it had cost Ozark an average of $2.13 per barrel to discover new oil. Added to that were development, lifting, and administrative costs of $1.48 per barrel. This was a period when crude oil was generally selling for about $3 per barrel. However, a significant portion of the crude oil being produced by Ozark was from wells which the company had drilled over 20 years ago at a discovery cost of about 25¢ per barrel.

In the United States Ozark estimated that it cost $250,000 to drill an inland well and $1 million to $1.5 million to drill offshore. In both cases its recent experiences had resulted in less than one success in four attempts.

Over the years the Ozark management had consistently refrained from any foreign exploration and production because it feared the political instability abroad. In 1959 it decided to break with tradition and to venture abroad. By that time almost every major American oil company had extensive operations in various parts of the world, and generally prime land locations for exploration in the United States had been preempted. Therefore, in 1959 Ozark resorted to extensive explorations in the areas of the Gulf of Mexico offshore Louisiana and Texas, and in such areas as Alaska, Guatemala, Peru, Venezuela, and the Sahara Desert.

Ozark's search in Alaska, Peru, and the Sahara had been extremely disappointing. The Peruvian venture had produced no results and had been abandoned. The Sahara search was showing so little promise that the management was considering abandoning the project. Ozark's only activity in other areas of the Middle East consisted of a contribution toward the drilling of five wells in Arabia and some geologic seismatical studies.

Domestic wells had to be drilled deeper to tap new reserves; the flow from the deeper wells was diminishing; the cost of retrieving oil from the deeper wells was steadily increasing. Speaking of these costs, Mr. Randall said, "A barrel of domestic crude might cost somewhat more to produce than a barrel of foreign crude, but it costs twice as much

per barrel to find foreign crude. Maybe we waited too long. If we
don't find what we are looking for, we have only ourselves to blame."

In the years 1960 through 1963 Ozark spent $14 million in Alaskan
explorations, $26 million in Guatemala, Peru, and the Sahara desert,
and $9 million in the Arabian desert. During the period it spent a
total of $238 million for exploration and discovered 68 million barrels
of oil reserves. These 68 million barrels had cost Ozark $3.66 each to
find at a time when crude could be purchased in the open market at
about $3 above ground.

REFINING

The processes by which crude oil was converted into finished products
were fairly uniform throughout the industry. Catalytic cracking was
the same at most refineries, and most technical innovations were available to all refiners either free or by license. The size of refineries had
been growing, while the number of refineries in the country had been
diminishing. In 1934 600 United States refineries processed 3 million
barrels of oil a day; in 1964 290 refineries processed 9 million barrels of
oil a day.

In 1964 Ozark operated the following five refineries, none of which
was considered large by industry standards:

	Capacity in Barrels per Day
East St. Louis, Illinois	20,000
Whiting, Indiana	40,000
Galveston, Texas	40,000
Houston, Texas	30,000
Cleveland, Ohio	25,000

In 1955 Ozark's refining capacity had been expanded abruptly by over
40% when it bought the Whiting refinery. This installation was purchased at what Ozark officials thought was a bargain price. The Cleveland refinery, which added another 12% to Ozark's capacity was obtained as a result of a corporate acquisition.

Technicians in the industry were of the opinion that Ozark had
lagged in refinery modernization to such an extent that in terms of
modern technology its refineries were obsolete. The Houston refinery
had been built by Ozark in 1931. The East St. Louis refinery was 40
years old, and the management periodically considered dismantling or

selling it. It was estimated that Ozark would need to spend $75 million to bring its refineries up to the efficiency level of modern plants. It cost Ozark 1¢ per gallon more to refine gasoline than it did other major oil companies, which resulted in about 9% higher cost per gallon.

"Using our own crude," said Mr. Randall, "we are able to net about $1 a barrel. But when we charge our refineries the $3 or so a barrel for the crude we have to buy on the open market, we lose money. There is no question about it. Our rate of profitability is riding on the amount of crude oil we can find."

TRANSPORTATION

The major portion of the crude oil which Ozark produced, purchased, and refined was transported through the company's own pipelines or ones in which Ozark owned an interest. Throughout the oil industry the over-all crude oil movements via pipeline were declining because of shrinking oil production in the older fields served by the pipelines and because of the increasing use of imported crude oil. Ozark's transportation operations, however, continued to be a profitable segment of the company's business. Especially profitable were the operations of certain segments of the network which continued to be fortunately located and which had been acquired decades ago at a fraction of their current value.

The management of Ozark felt that its transportation network was one of its strengths. Every year Ozark made additions to and improvements on the system. In 1963 it added a 73-mile wholly owned crude line in Wyoming and a 67-mile extension of an existing line in Texas to connect it with an existing line running to the company's Houston refinery. In addition, Ozark was one of seven owners of the 2,900-mile South States Pipeline being constructed between Houston, Texas, and Bayonne, New Jersey. The line would pass through the southern end of some of Ozark's marketing area, and spur lines were being added to reach some of the larger cities in the North Central states.

SERVICE STATIONS

"It is difficult to understand," said Mr. Randall, "why the industry continues to build stations on all four corners of an intersection with a market potential that can adequately support only one station. When a representation becomes more important than profitability as a means of determining a station-building program, we are bound to suffer the consequences in price fights between dealers, high rates of dealer turn-over, and inadequate return on service station investment.

"Although there are fewer service stations today than for some years, there are still obviously more stations than the needed in most markets. Our company has been undertaking an extensive program of eliminating marginal stations. If the industry generally would adopt such a program, the results would be very beneficial to all of us. The economic health of every service station is directly affected by the health of every service station which is its neighbor."

Mr. Randall suggested certain guidelines which would direct Ozark's marketing efforts. There was to be restraint exercised in building more new service stations, and the locations of the new ones were to be determined by exhaustive traffic studies. Service station operations were to be profit-oriented rather than volume-producing. Ozark would make every effort to fully exploit the retail potential within its limited marketing area rather than to expand its market territory to additional states. This full exploitation was to be accomplished by eliminating marginal stations; by a program aimed at a smaller number of stations, each of which would be larger and more profitable; by introducing better merchandising practices; by intensive advertising; and by dealer training.

Ozark had already implemented this thinking as early as 1953, when it launched a determined drive to eliminate those stations which were hardly surviving. In the 10 years which followed, well over 1,000 marginal and uneconomical stations were liquidated, and over 500 unprofitable leases on service stations were terminated. The proceeds were used to build successful ones. In disposing of fee-owned stations, a studied effort was made to sell them to buyers who would convert them to non–service-station use. Many of them were remodeled to become gift shops, grills, realty offices, and even barber shops.

Studies indicated that a customer would trade, first of all, at whatever station was most convenient to him, provided that the brand was not unacceptable. In keeping with this, Ozark was highly selective in choosing new station sites. Preference was given to outlying sites in larger cities, to suburban locations, and to strategic locations on new highways.

A major feature in the program, introduced in 1959, was Ozark's Super Service Centers. These mammoth stations were positioned in central locations in certain fairly large cities, and wherever possible, they were located in new shopping centers. Two of these stations were opened in 1959; four in 1960; ten in 1961; twelve in 1962; eight in 1963; and nine in 1964. In each instance the opening of a new Super Service Center was introduced with a concentration of local advertising, and in some instances Ozark station attendants, clad in new Ozark uniforms, canvassed the entire local residential area in a doorbell-ringing campaign to solicit customers by telling them of the many services which would be offered at the new Super Service Center. Ozark's experience with the new super stations during the first few years indicated that they returned an exceptionally high volume of business, Furthermore, as a result of the Super Service advertising and merchandising programs, the business done by most of the old-line, smaller Ozark stations increased significantly.

In 1954 Ozark had 11,785 service stations. In 1964 it had 13,046 (see Exhibit 5). Statistics indicated that for the year 1964 the national average for gallons of gasoline pumped per station was 188,000. Most of Ozark's stations were selling over 300,000. The Ozark management felt that the appearance of its stations, as a result of its dealer-indoctrination program, was superior to that of any other major oil company.

A major phase of Ozark's marketing strategy was its development of a chain of commercial service stations. These large service stations were located along heavily traveled cross-country highway truck routes. Besides offering gasoline and diesel fuel at trucker discount prices, the commercial stations also furnished repair services, food, and lodging for the night. The grill-type restaurants offered hearty meals; lodging consisted of simple but clean and comfortable small rooms. These outlets were spaced out along the length of routes in such a way that a trucker could make a long trip through Ozark's territory and never be out of reach of an Ozark commercial station along the way.

In 1964 Ozark had 258 truck stops, one of the largest chains in the industry. The commercial outlet business had grown to such an extent that it accounted for 21% of Ozark's retail gasoline and diesel fuel sales. Every outlet had diesel fuel sales of over 100,000 gallons a month, and a number of them went over 500,000. Ozark planned to expand the system until it covered all of Ozark's market territory.

THE OZARK INNS

In 1963 Ozark's marketing executives conceived a new idea in travel units which would combine at a single convenient location a complete service station, a motel, and a restaurant. These units were to be located at strategic points along superhighways where there was likely to be a high incidence of travelers stopping for a night's rest. The units were intended to satisfy the three principal needs of most highway travelers: car service, meals, and lodging.

As a result of an extensive search, Ozark invited two nationally known companies to join it in the venture. Pierre's Pancake House, a well-known national restaurant chain, contracted to operate the restaurants on a concession basis. Their simple menu offered popular entrees, service was prompt and in good taste, prices were moderate, and the units, known as Ozark Inns, remained open around the clock. The motel units were leased out under franchise to the Homestead Hotel Corporation, an international hotel chain. Ozark leased the service stations to operators of proven performance and stipulated the extensive services which they were required to offer. At evening the traveler could leave his car at the service station while he stayed at the Inn. His car would be completely serviced, ready and waiting for him in the morning.

In 1963 Ozark opened its first three Ozark Inns on the Wisconsin freeway system. Initial acceptance of the Inns was good; management believed that they had far outdrawn any other service stations on the freeway. As far as the Ozark management knew, its Inns were unique in the industry, and no other major oil company was planning to duplicate them. Ozark opened six more in Illinois and Minnesota in 1964 and had plans to open fourteen more in other states in 1965.

PRICING

Gasoline price wars had been frequent throughout the industry during the postwar period, but Ozark had been especially plagued by competitive price-cutting in the 15 states which were its limited marketing area. Addressing stockholders in mid-1964, Mr. Randall said:

> Individual companies, and sometimes individual dealers, often trigger explosive price wars in their attempt to capture for themselves a larger share of the existing market. In the end such price competition is self-defeating; it inflicts damage upon everyone concerned, including the one who triggered the price war. These sporadic wars are entirely unconstructive; they do nothing to stimulate any over-all increase in the consumption of gasoline. Everyone in the oil industry would be better off if the energies and efforts dissipated in price wars would be applied to generating an enhanced public demand for more of our products—

in the form of increased motor travel and transport—and in the form of greater usage of heat and energy derived from petroleum sources.

Price wars come and go. There seems to be no relationship between them and the over-all condition of the industry. They vary in locale and in degree, are entirely erratic and unpredictable. It seems that there has always been an incidence of price-cutters in every market, some of whom believe that they have an inalienable right to indulge in cut-throat competition. There is no doubt that these marketing tactics have had a demoralizing effect upon the oil industry in recent years.

Price wars cannot achieve an enduring gain for anyone. Costs and expenses continue unabated during the period of the lower prices, and the only result is a struggle for higher volume on a lower profit basis. These axiomatic truths apply especially to the oil companies who use price as a sales tactic, for in recent years the cost of producing crude oil has grown progressively and wage rates have risen well over 25%.

Oversupply is generally blamed for our price troubles. This is by no means generally the case. Recently we have seen major oil companies extend the range of their products to lower-quality grades, which they introduce at lower prices. Several large oil companies also attempted to expand their retail distribution to a nationwide basis, using temporary price-cuts as a means of gaining a foothold in markets which had already been pre-empted. Furthermore, company suppliers who grant price protection to jobbers and dealers are often to blame for prolonging price wars.

We in the industry are the cause of our own price problems, and it is within our power to put our house in order. We believe that the petroleum industry can restore order in its own economy by (1) a reasonable regulation of supply and demand; (2) refraining from adding to the already excessive production capacity of the industry; (3) refraining from unreasonable additions to the existing marketing facilities by aiming for profitable operation rather than high volume and by taking a more statesmanlike attitude toward marketing policies to curb the existing malpractices. Oil companies expenses do not drop automatically with any drop in prices. During the price decline of recent years the cost of finding and producing crude oil has grown progressively. Also, industry wage rates rose about one third.

There is more to the price situation than oversupply. A factor in triggering many of the recent price wars was the introduction by some major oil companies of additional grades of lower-quality gasolines at lower prices. The recent moves of several large companies to expand their service station operations to nationwide coverage also caused product price-declines in a number of areas. Futhermore, price wars were prolonged as a result of price protection granted by supplier companies to jobbers and dealers.

Mr. Randall believed that an important factor in Ozark's declining profit level had been the abuse of the practice of providing marginal price protection on sales to unbranded marketers, allowances to dealers, and guaranteed margins to jobbers. He said:

> There might be some justification for help to dealers and other marketers when prices deteriorate. But when the profit margin guarantee is used to *beat* popular prices, rather than just matching them, then this does violence to the principle of the guarantee itself.
>
> Today we are witnessing the black-marketing of gasoline and the artful manipulation of inventories to enrich the unscrupulous at the expense of the supplier. In the interest of economy, ever-larger storage tanks are being placed in new service stations. In the hands of unscrupulous dealers, these large storage capacities can be used to juggle inventories by buying low and selling high. I know of one city where retail prices have been drastically below normal, where some dealers have been working on margins averaging up to 9¢ a gallon, and the dealer fills up just before the price restoration sets in. He will be selling his inventory of gasoline at the new price with a margin of 13½¢.

Mr. Randall also pointed out that 2.6 billion gallons of product sold by Ozark in 1964 brought the company about $36 million less than they would have brought at 1957 prices.

RESEARCH AND DEVELOPMENT

In 1955 Ozark had built a new research center at Florissant, Missouri, which the Ozark management considered to be the most modern in the industry. The Ozark management paid premium salaries to attract accomplished scientists and technicians of superior skill. The research center was about 25 miles from Ozark's administrative headquarters at Ferguson. One reason this location had been chosen was that, as the research director put it, it was far enough removed from headquarters and from any operating facilities to discourage production and refining managers from foisting upon the laboratory their technical operating problems. Others in the industry commented that the considerable expense of Ozark's extensive new research facility could not be justified by the support which it gave to the company's sales promotion efforts and that pressure from headquarters caused the research center to give priority to the study of production and research problems. In 1964 its major projects were:

1. The development of a novel system for automatic processing of many types of exploration and oil field data

2. A simulation system, using scale models of terrain, to speed the analysis of exploration data developed on the actual search site

3. Improved methods for recovering additional crude oil from proven fields

4. An improved Ozark tire, which was undergoing extensive road tests

5. The development of electrochemical fluids for chucking industrial devices

6. A rustproofing compound which permitted Ozark dealers to under-coat heretofore inaccessible places on auto and truck bodies

7. The design of two new plant additions for the expansion of the petrochemical production facilities at Whiting

PETROCHEMICALS

The term *petrochemicals* was used to define any chemical which was made wholly or substantially from the hydrocarbon contents of petro-leum or natural gas. Petrochemicals were finding acceptance in a wide variety of industrial usages, where they were replacing chemicals which had formerly been produced from more expensive animal and vegetable fats and oils. Almost every major oil company was engaging in the pro-duction of petrochemicals, which, as a class, were high-margin products. Many major oil company research programs were also being concen-trated on the development of new petrochemicals.

Except for the manufacture of an extensive line of solvents and naphthas in conjunction with refinery operations, Ozark, until 1960, had not made any major investments in the petrochemical field. Between 1960 and 1964 Ozark made a series of petrochemical production addi-tions to its Galveston and Whiting plants. The petrochemicals produced were used in the manufacture of decylic alcohol, plasticizers, and nylon and as lube additives. The marketing of petrochemicals was handled by the company's Midwest Mineral Oils division, which had advan-tageous marketing outlets. The Ozark management intended to continue to explore the possibility of expanding into other petrochemical proj-ects. Management stated that manufacturing petrochemicals upgraded its simple oils into more refined products which yielded higher margins and were sold in less competitive markets. The expansion of the com-pany's petrochemical activities was not, however, given priority in the company's over-all planning. Prior preference in the allocation of re-sources went to the exploration for new sources of crude oil.

FINANCIAL ACCOUNTING

"Oil industry accounting," said Mr. Randall, "is just about as comprehensible as the logic in Alice in Wonderland. Even C.P.A.'s are at times confounded by the intricacies of oil accounting. Some of the counterplays might look like a shell game, but the amazing thing about them is that they are perfectly legal." Mr. Randall was himself reputed to be as astute in matters of petroleum finance as anyone in the industry.

In 1961 Ozark began to include in its sales figures consumer taxes collected at the pump. This was a direct departure from previous practices and increased Ozark's already sharply rising sales volume figures.

Because of special tax regulations on depletion allowances, intangible developmental costs such as geologic surveys, and other considerations, oil companies were permitted to accumulate sizable revenues not subject to taxation. In spite of this, Ozark had by 1964 accumulated several years of tax credits, indicating that it had suffered operating losses. Ozark's 1964 report to stockholders had shown a profit of $31 million, while the report of the company made to the Internal Revenue Service showed a loss of $21 million after allowing $21 million for depletion.

Ozark used "carved-out production payments," which involved the sale of oil still in the ground on terms which entitled Ozark to repurchase rights. One effect of this was to enable Ozark to show its tax credit on its balance sheet as an account receivable. "What Ozark is actually doing," said a competitor, "is selling off corners of the farm to keep alive."

In 1961 Ozark switched its policy on exploration costs. Instead of charging off 100% of exploratory costs every year, it charged off 70% and capitalized 30%, reasoning that this was about in keeping with its current ratio of successful explorations. The result was a $2.6 million increase in income which was not explained by any note on the balance sheet.

In 1963 the management wrote off $24 million worth of nonproductive foreign properties. These write-offs were offset by reallocating a series of unused reserves which had been accumulated for refinery modernization. The end result was a $3 million addition to net income for that year. Mr. Randall became aware of the danger of loss years in 1962 when a Wall Street securities firm quietly bought over a million shares of Ozark during that year at prices ranging from $28 to $35, which were considerably lower than the book value. By 1963 adverse publicity had aroused in other financial interests an awareness of the plight of

Ozark. Several combines began to accumulate Ozark stock, and by mid-1964 Ozark stock was listed at $61 bid, $64 asked. By this time Mr. Randall was highly concerned at the imminent threat of a proxy fight, and he was fending off demands from several stockholder interests that they be given representation on the board.

PROSPECTS

Addressing a press conference in December, 1964, Mr. Randall read the following prepared statement to the assembled reporters:

> The Ozark Oil Company will observe its 50th birthday on May 24, 1965. During these 50 years the company earned over $600 million; it paid out over $300 million in dividends. We processed 1.2 billion barrels of crude oil into 60 billion gallons of products. Vehicles using our fuels drove half a trillion miles. Our other products heated countless homes, offices, and plants, powered jet planes, trains and vessels, and performed a myriad of other useful services.
>
> We at Ozark feel a justifiable pride in looking back over this creditable record of service to the nation. It is especially comforting to us at this time when prophets of doom have been indulging in dire predictions.
>
> We hear a lot of comments these days to the effect that the continuing weakness in product prices has taken all of the rose color out of the oil industry's outlook. I must admit that I have never seen such a fierce struggle for new markets and for added volume. I feel that this is a period of crucial trial, not only for the Ozark Oil Company, but for the industry as a whole.
>
> We are moving into an era of expanding demand caused by the population explosion of the sixties, the completion of our network of expressways, and by continuing record-breaking sales of new cars. But we are frustrated by many problems, both real and psychological. We need to thoroughly analyze these problems and to distinguish between policies and practices which have a real and lasting effect upon profits and those which pay in the short run but have detrimental long-run effects.
>
> I am convinced that our company is sound and that our industry is sound, and that we are a useful part of society. It would behoove us, therefore, as members of the oil industry, to make our company and the industry profitable and sound in every way. Furthermore, we have an obligation to the nation to keep the oil industry in such condition that it will stand ready to supply all forms of petroleum to the armed services in times of national emergency.
>
> We at Ozark feel that we are aware of our strengths and weaknesses. Our objectives are clearly defined and are aimed at capitalizing upon our strengths and correcting our deficiencies. We face the future with a sober degree of confidence. We have a feeling of urgency, and we are working to achieve our goals as soon as possible.

exhibit 1 FINANCIAL REVIEW

	Total Income*	Net Income	Net Income Per Common Share‡	Dividends Per Common Share†	Book Value Per Common Share†	Net Working Capital	Long-term Debt	Capital Expenditures	Depreciation, Depletion, and Amortization	Motor Fuel and Oil Taxes Paid	Salaries, Wages, and Employee Benefits	Number of Employees
1963	$586,533,086	$23,813,880	$2.42	$1.28	$38.65	$ 83,844,800	$72,259,200	$49,111,200	$30,483,100	$102,136,800	$59,016,000	7,738
1962	557,345,700	23,160,000	2.34	1.28	37.50	85,775,200	75,360,000	67,667,200	28,082,100	98,264,800	57,608,000	7,831
1961	541,069,600	24,081,600	2.41	1.28	36.71	92,096,000	63,141,600	56,975,200	25,851,200	97,291,400	59,586,400	8,128
1960	523,560,000	26,044,000	2.63	1.28	35.35	103,446,400	64,620,000	48,020,800	26,496,000	99,452,800	58,706,400	8,686
1959	497,149,600	23,124,000	2.66	1.28	36.67	103,664,800	65,618,400	35,561,600	25,127,200	93,237,600	59,951,200	8,592
1958	468,146,400	23,057,600	2.68	1.28	35.29	95,461,600	69,106,400	37,501,600	23,967,200	85,509,600	58,451,200	8,785
1957	496,374,400	28,419,200	3.30	1.28	33.89	94,650,400	72,338,000	45,925,600	22,497,600	85,680,800	59,405,600	9,364
1956	474,238,400	29,248,000	3.42	1.28	31.86	84,788,800	68,892,800	46,504,800	22,325,600	82,331,200	58,920,800	9,682
1955	467,257,600	28,131,200	3.26	1.16	29.75	76,815,200	63,665,600	50,964,000	21,621,600	74,948,800	56,070,400	10,295
1954	376,852,800	24,930,400	2.85	1.20	27.96	71,263,200	24,962,400	41,792,800	19,086,400	63,409,600	50,536,000	9,738
1953	358,001,600	21,684,000	2.47	1.00	26.31	66,873,600	20,504,800	34,003,200	17,806,400	61,824,800	47,584,800	9,330

* Motor fuel and oil taxes paid are included in total income.

† For comparative purposes, data for years prior to 1955 have been restated to reflect the two-for-one stock split made in April, 1955.

‡ Based on the average number of shares outstanding during the year.

exhibit 2 OPERATING REVIEW

	Net Crude Oil Production, Barrels		Net Natural Gas Production MCF*	Natural Gasoline and LPG Produced, Gallons	Net Wells Completed—United States and Canada		
	United States and Canada	South America			Oil Wells	Gas Wells	Dry Holes
1963	21,090,400	1,419,200	82,545,600	62,868,800	65	7	38
1962	20,288,800	1,733,600	88,156,800	59,768,800	62	8	30
1961	20,266,400	2,012,000	89,698,400	57,080,000	77	14	61
1960	20,078,400	2,170,400	91,691,200	58,271,200	72	12	46
1959	17,300,000	1,865,600	85,544,800	58,396,000	112	15	43
1958	17,148,800	235,200	83,027,200	52,309,600	54	8	36
1957	19,220,800	....	75,098,400	57,386,400	85	14	46
1956	19,643,200	....	80,241,600	60,374,400	103	14	56
1955	19,747,200	....	78,587,200	56,302,400	158	13	46
1954	19,178,400	....	64,476,000	55,188,800	175	10	38
1953	20,618,400	....	51,339,200	59,230,000	78	6	26

* Thousands of cubic feet.

exhibit 2 (continued)

	Undeveloped Acreage (Net)			Crude Oil Processed, Barrels			Sales of Gasoline, Gallons	Sales of Other Products, Gallons	Retail Outlets
				In Ozark Refineries		By Others			
	United States and Canada	South and Central America	Other Foreign	For Ozark	For Others	For Ozark			
1963	3,680,800	9,056,000	12,025,600	49,392,000	3,745,600	3,746,400	1,215,384,000	1,476,131,200	13,046
1962	4,560,800	8,980,800	12,008,800	48,196,800	3,606,400	3,878,400	1,164,181,600	1,417,413,600	12,552
1961	5,848,000	9,103,200	275,200	44,884,800	3,504,000	4,032,800	1,171,540,800	1,246,259,400	12,798
1960	3,919,200	606,400	275,200	45,245,600	3,513,600	4,025,600	1,203,073,600	1,142,421,600	12,532
1959	3,670,400	1,428,000	....	45,072,000	3,504,000	3,338,400	1,127,877,600	1,079,032,000	12,832
1958	3,473,600	4,862,400	....	44,393,600	3,679,200	820,000	1,113,818,400	944,607,200	12,763
1957	3,896,800	4,348,800	....	43,200,000	2,879,200	....	1,125,167,200	969,153,600	12,441
1956	3,924,000	....	....	44,405,600	3,450,400	....	1,105,824,800	985,025,600	12,790
1955	3,341,600	....	....	44,744,000	3,650,400	579,200	1,125,478,400	1,002,756,000	12,265
1954	2,679,200	....	....	36,212,000	1,530,400	3,631,200	925,834,400	860,529,600	11,650
1953	2,667,200	....	....	32,896,000	....	4,285,600	858,667,200	865,801,600	11,785

exhibit 3 CONSOLIDATED BALANCE SHEET
December 31, 1963 and 1962

Assets

	1963	1962
Current assets:		
Cash	$ 22,073,162	$ 25,401,435
United States government and other securities at cost, which approximates market	36,129,940	11,901,542
Accounts and notes receivable, less reserves of $1,081,659 in 1963 and $1,161,542 in 1962	53,497,716	52,390,566
Inventories		
Crude oil, refined oils, and merchandise	55,277,898	49,018,939
Materials and supplies, at latest cost, less allowance for condition	6,684,854	7,856,426
Total current assets	$173,663,570	$146,568,908
Investments, advances, etc.:		
Investments in and advances to subsidiaries not consolidated, at cost	$ 321,514	$ 425,517
Investments in securities of other companies, at cost	8,227,396	8,379,654
Receivables, etc., less reserves of $122,851 in 1963 and $360,002 in 1962	4,424,869	9,122,571
	$ 12,973,759	$ 17,927,742

Property, plant, and, equipment, at cost:

Classification	*Gross*	*Reserve*		
Producing	$413,749,958	$175,798,365		
Refining	109,925,544	80,533,486		
Marketing	135,660,456	74,897,867		
Transportation	34,624,301	14,393,947		
Other	10,086,435	4,393,319		
	$704,046,694	$350,016,984	$354,029,710	$346,197,933

	1963	1962
Prepaid and deferred charges	2,401,734	3,326,626
Contracts, rights, patents, trade-marks, etc.	1	1
	$543,068,774	$514,021,210

Liabilities

	1963	1962
Current liabilities:		
Current portion of long-term debt	$ 9,174,143	$ 8,933,245
Accounts payable	39,184,455	38,740,761
Dividend payable March 1, 1964 and 1963	3,158,646	3,156,181
Accrued liabilities	9,501,633	9,963,576
Federal income taxes ($1,322,781 in 1963, less U.S. government securities in same amount; none in 1962)		
Total current liabilities	$ 61,018,877	$ 60,793,763
Long-term debt, excluding current portion:		
Promissory notes, 3¾%, due semiannually, 1981 to 1990	$ 40,000,000	$ 40,000,000
Bank loan, 3¾%, due annually to 1966	9,600,000	14,400,000
Pipeline mortgage sinking fund bonds, average interest 4·34%, due semiannually to 1976	8,448,800	9,154,400
Bank loan, 4½% to July 1, 1967, variable 4 to 5% thereafter; $960,000 due annually July 1, 1967 to July 1, 1969, $1,920,000 due July 1, 1970	4,800,000	
Notes payable, 5¼%, due quarterly to July 1, 1967	1,980,000	2,700,000
Serial notes, 2·95%, due semiannually to 1965	1,580,000	3,149,000
Purchase obligations, etc.	5,850,339	5,965,917
	$ 72,259,139	$ 75,369,317
Reserves and deferred credit:		
Reserve for replacement of inventories	$ 376,800	$ 601,600
Reserve for contingencies	3,195,931	3,171,228
Deferred income	24,369,417	3,873,511
	$ 27,942,148	$ 7,646,339
Minority interest in capital stock and surplus of subsidiaries	$ 342,361	$ 266,615

exhibit 3   (continued)

	1963	1962
Liabilities		
Capital stock and surplus:		
Common stock authorized, 20,000,000 shares, par value $4 per share; 10,072,280 shares outstanding in 1963, and 10,064,593 shares outstanding in 1962, including treasury shares	$ 40,289,120	$ 40,258,372
Surplus (per accompanying statements)		
Paid-in surplus	39,820,503	39,635,239
Earned surplus	307,085,740	295,749,679
	$387,195,363	$375,643,290
Less treasury stock at cost, 200,000 shares	5,689,114	5,689,114
	$381,506,249	$369,954,176
	$543,068,774	$514,021,210

exhibit 4 CONSOLIDATED STATEMENTS OF INCOME AND SURPLUS
For the years ended December 31, 1963 and 1962

Statement of Income	*1963*	*1962*
Income:		
Gross operating income	$580,316,188	$552,717,522
Dividends, interest, etc.	6,216,898	4,628,170
	$586,533,086	$557,345,692
Costs and expenses:		
Costs, operating, selling, and general expenses	$356,063,211	$335,480,933
Taxes paid (including Federal income tax credit of $1,029,800 in 1963, and $2,080,000 in 1962)	112,558,571	108,665,113
Salaries, wages, and employee benefits	59,015,701	57,608,042
Provision for depreciation, depletion, and amortization	30,483,135	28,082,106
Interest expense	3,301,907	3,126,780
Cash discounts allowed	1,256,740	1,187,062
Income applicable to minority interests	39,941	36,050
	$562,719,206	$634,186,086
Net income for the year	$ 23,813,880	$ 23,159,606

Statement of Earned Surplus		
Balance at beginning of year	$295,749,679	$288,383,136
Undistributed earnings of subsidiary not previously consolidated	152,052	
	$295,901,731	$283,383,136
Add net income for the year	23,813,880	23,159,606
	$319,715,611	$311,542,742
Deduct cash dividends on common shares:		
Declared and paid during the year	$ 9,471,225	$ 12,636,882
Declared in 1963, payable March 1, 1964	3,158,646	
Declared in 1962, payable March 1, 1963	. . . .	3,156,181
	$ 12,629,871	$ 15,793,063
Balance at end of year	$307,085,740	$295,749,679

Statement of Paid-in Surplus		
Balance at beginning of year	$ 39,635,239	$ 39,635,239
Add excess of the option price received ($34.70 per share) in 1963 over par value ($4 per share) of common shares sold under the terms of the incentive stock ownership plan	176,251	
Excess of the amount received ($46.88 per share) in 1963 over par value ($4 per share) of common shares sold to the trustees of the employees' savings and stock bonus plan	9,013	
Balance at end of year	$ 39,820,503	$ 39,635,239

exhibit 5   OZARK SERVICE STATIONS

	Number of Stations	Estimated % of Local Market
Kentucky	1,520	8.0
Ohio	1,040	6.1
Illinois	1,040	6.7
Michigan	760	4.3
Minnesota	730	5.5
Nebraska	560	5.3
Iowa	1,520	5.7
Wiscosin	1,120	6.6
South Dakota	720	5.1
Montana	690	4.5
Wyoming	690	3.8
North Dakota	330	7.6
Tennessee	410	4.6
Total	13,046	

exhibit 6

OZARK OIL COMPANY ORGANIZATION

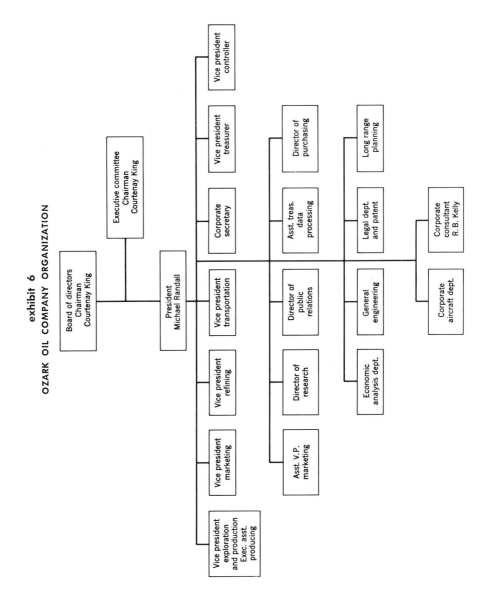